OF PERMANENT VALUE

THE STORY OF WARREN BUFFETT

Revised Expanded Edition
1996

By Andrew Kilpatrick

Printed in the United States of America

Published by AKPE
Financial Center 1030
505 20th Street North
Birmingham, Alabama 35203
Fax/Phone: 205-251-2828

Revised Edition

Cover design: Nancy Line Jacobs

Book Design: Lori Leath Smith and Cherie C. Kosak

10 9 8 7 6 5 4 3 2 1

Library of Congress Catalog Card Number: 96-94403

Kilpatrick, Andrew. 1943-
Of Permanent Value: The Story of Warren Buffett /Revised/Andrew Kilpatrick

ISBN 0-9641905-1-6

In memory of my father,
Carroll Kilpatrick
who loved newspapers

and to

Don Pippen
who loves books

Table of Contents

AKPE Expands By 50%

Thanks for the help, "book widows."

Last year Andy Kilpatrick Publishing Empire (AKPE), publisher of this book, expanded by 50%, adding more than 100 square feet to allow for a storage room. There were no changes at the actual World Headquarters office and there are certainly no plans to buy a corporate jet this year.

AKPE still has only one so-so employee.

Although this is a modest enterprise, many people have offered it a helping hand.

Writing a book is an odyssey and I needed help. My thanks first to my mother, Frances Kilpatrick, and my wife, Patricia Ann Burgess Terrell Kilpatrick, who says she's become a "book widow." Some say the B in her name is for Burgess; I say it's for Borsheim's where we bought a wedding ring.

Thanks to Don Keough, former president of Coca-Cola; Miami Dolphins' Coach Don Shula; J. Richard Munro, former co-chairman of Time Warner; Ann Landers; New Mexico state legislator George Buffett; Howard Buffett; trader Arthur Rowsell and others for interviews.

Most of all, I would like to thank Harvey Terrell, Birmingham's Mr. Birmingham who gave almost everyone in town a first loan, and who was all along most reassuring, convinced that I had a worthwhile project.

The person who was the most helpful with editing was Michael Assael of New York City, a door-to-door floor wax salesman at age 14 and later a Columbia Business School graduate who is now a lawyer, accountant, author, linguist, and investor who has Warren Buffett's autograph on a 1934 edition of *Security Analysis.* Michael is my idea of a Renaissance man. He was the spiritual guide for this book. Thanks to his wife, Eiko.

John C. Bird, and his son, John T. Bird, and Loretta Cobb, all of Birmingham, helped with editing. Thanks to Chris Stavrou of New York, Arthur Clarke of Boston, Bruce Wilhelm of Daly City, California, Phil McCaull, of Greenwich, Connecticut, and Allan Maxwell of Omaha, Nebraska. Computer buffs Lonnie Drew and Sabrina Ward of Birmingham did the index.

LaVerne Ramsey, of Birmingham, George Morgan of Omaha, commander-in-chief of Buffett Wannabes and with me every step of the journey, Nancy Line Jacobs of Omaha and Jane Liss, Columbus, Nebraska were all real friends of the book. Many thanks to the folks at the Omaha Public Library, the *Omaha World-Herald* and Southern Publishers Group of Birmingham.

Don Pippen, who started out to sell some books and wound up helping with every facet of publishing from editing to sales, Jim Lunsford, Anita Smith, Carolyn Joseph, Steve Parker, Lori Leath Smith, Cherie C. Kosak, Tommy and Jane Johnson, Earl Bloom, Bobby Vann, Bobby Luckie and Andy Campbell, all of Birmingham; Russ Fletcher, of Bermuda, Chris Robinson of Cullman and Giri Bogavelli and James McCluskey of San Francisco all helped.

George Eyraud, Birmingham, put things in Alabama terms with our state's top salute: "Buffett is the Bear Bryant of investing."

Special thanks to Judith Goodnow Prus, Grosse Pointe Farms, Michigan; talk about class.

Dr. Frank Kilpatrick and Robert, John and Sarah Kilpatrick, Madison, Wisconsin, were helpful.

My children, Jack and Anna, who I hope one day will write their own books, and to Pat's children, that happy band of musicians: Tommy, Michael and Mark (on the drums).

Floyd Jones of Seattle, Steve Wallman of Madison, Wisconsin, Peter Bradford, Nassau, New York, my old tennis partner; and Chris Reid of New York.

And, Gladys Kaiser, retired as Berkshire Hathaway's administrative assistant, who patiently endured fact-checking missions. And to Debbie Bosanek, whose duties can range from momentarily running Berkshire to being an usherette at Omaha Royals games. She is "db" on Buffett's typed correspondence.

Thanks also to Rose Printing Company in Tallahassee, Florida.

Finally, because the book is self-published I want to encourage other writers to take up self-publishing, a go-it-alone style that long has been downplayed, but now is coming more into vogue.

I took as my heroes James Joyce, Mark Twain and Sigmund Freud who self-published and Carl Sandburg who set type, rolled presses, hand-pulled galleys and did the binding himself.

Well, Buffett says have fun.

Preface

"I wish you well, but not too well."

This book is about legendary investor Warren Buffett, his spectacular investment vehicle, Berkshire Hathaway Inc. and the range of businesses he and Berkshire own.

The work is a look at Buffett's transcendent career as well as his wit and wisdom. This is a revised edition published because so much has happened at Berkshire.

Mr. Buffett has neither approved nor disapproved of the book, which is an attempt to portray him as he really is—a remarkable man by almost everyone's account.

Buffett told me in 1990 that he contemplates a book of his own, which will probably be in the style of his annual reports, and therefore doesn't plan to help others with works about him.

Later I wrote Berkshire shareholder Ann Landers asking for an interview. She forwarded my letter to Buffett, who sent me a copy of his reply to her and added a note to me.

In his letter to Ann Landers, Buffett said:

> Andy Kilpatrick is a decent and well-intentioned fellow, but I am not personally cooperating on the book. On the other hand, whatever my friends decide to do is up to them.
>
> My reason for not helping Andy personally is that someday I'll write my own book—if I can get Carol Loomis to do about 90% of the work—and I don't see any sense in giving away any of the punch lines.
>
> I hope you're coming out for the Annual Meeting next year, but it would be better if you would come by much sooner for dinner. Best wishes, Warren E. Buffett.

Buffett's note at the bottom said: "Andy, As you can see, I wish you well, but not too well. Actually everything I do is public, so I am trying to save a few things for a fresh look at some time. Warren"

He later got me back for writing a book about him with a note, "Wait till I write a book on you!" My heart stopped. So I know how he felt. My reply was, "I wish you well, but not too well."

I make no claim to have access to him, although I have lunched with him and have watched him, mainly at Berkshire annual meetings and related functions for more than a decade. In all, I have been around him about 70 hours while he was operating at full throttle.

You'll want to read his book some day. But in the meantime, there will be deservedly many books about Buffett and his remarkable life. This one is offered as a look at how things stand now for Buffett and Berkshire.

This is not a book about investment advice. Bear in mind that any position reported here as held by Berkshire could now be sold.

It should be read in the following light: I am a Berkshire shareholder. Ultimately I became interested in Buffett as a result of his investment in The Washington Post, where my father, Carroll Kilpatrick, was White House correspondent during the Kennedy through Ford administrations (1961 to 1975).

My father and I were always amazed that one person could own such a huge piece of the Post, which seemed to us such a mighty enterprise.

Personally, I regard Buffett, as do many people, as an extraordinary human being combining, in a single package, financial genius, impeccable ethics and a wonderful sense of humor. Pound for pound, Buffett is one of the funniest people around.

My relationship to Buffett is reporter to public figure, but we have had a few conversations and laughs along the way. Once we talked about the grand, but imperfect world of publishing and he mentioned that typos drive him nuts. I had the feeling if he found a typo in the Berkshire annual report he'd jump off Kiewit Plaza.

So he, and you, may enjoy this one. When I took bids to print this book, I proudly gave the full title and got back a bid for *Permanent Valve.* Editor Michael Assael often wishes me the best of luck for the book, which he has nicknamed *Permanent Wave.*

The book–*Of Permanent Value: The Story of Warren Buffett*– is generally chronological, although the fast-paced chronology sometimes is broken to group together Berkshire's major, "permanent" investments, its "Sainted" businesses and the company's preferred stock holdings. Some of the early chapters fall into the "breaking news" category. Like the man himself, some chapters stand alone. All the chapters are a humble effort to track ("stalk" my wife says) Buffett's fast-paced odyssey.

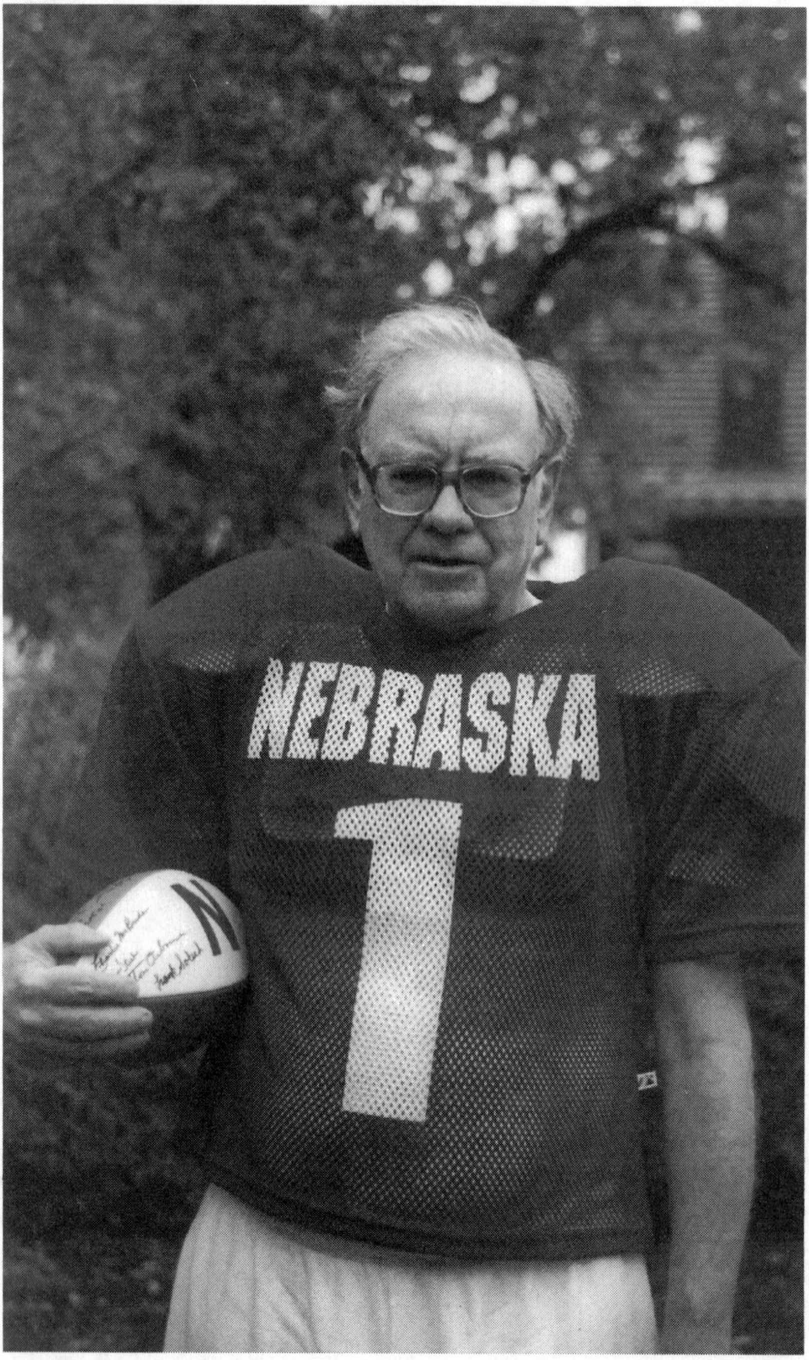

(Photo courtesy of Warren Buffett)

Warren Buffett revealed! Berkshire Hathaway's quarterback likes the Nebraska football team and Berkshire's finances to be No. 1.

1

Midnight at McDonald's

Warren Buffett ordered a Big Mac, fries and a Coke at a McDonald's in Hong Kong just about midnight between October 1 and 2, 1995.

"He was walking back from the counter when I saw him. I had seen him before," said Mark Langdon of Omaha. "I jumped up and basically used the Omaha connection to introduce myself. He stopped and chatted and then set his tray down at my table. He looked around and said, 'I have some friends here and I don't want to miss them.'"

"My brother and I had heard that Buffett had been in China with [Microsoft Chairman] Bill Gates," Langdon said. "Then Bill Gates walked up and Warren introduced Gates to me and my brother. I had to scrape my jaw off the floor."

"Buffett said to Fred and me, 'This is Bill Gates,' like you have to do that," Langdon said of the introduction.

Then Gates's wife, Melinda, and Gates's father, Bill Gates, Sr., came over to the table. "It was crazy," said Langdon, a 33-year-old application analyst with Applied Communications Inc., in Omaha, a company which writes software for the transfer of electronic funds.

Buffett explained to Gates that it was companies like Applied Communications that kept Omaha's jobless rate so low.

"The six of us sat at the table for about 20 minutes," Langdon said.

Langdon was returning from a trip to Jakarta. His brother, Fred, 35, was on his way from Omaha back to his job as an engineer with Procter & Gamble in Kobe, Japan. The brothers decided to meet and tour Hong Kong.

(Photo by LaVerne Ramsey)

Mark Langdon of Omaha had a late night dinner at McDonald's with Buffett and Gates.

"We had been sightseeing all day and came back to the hotel. We watched TV and fell asleep and woke up hungry so we went to McDonald's," Langdon said.

Buffett's party was preparing to leave for home the next day after their trip through China together and Buffett explained they had come to McDonald's "to get some familiar food."

As the six ate, Buffett made a point of the familiarity and consistency of McDonald's servings worldwide. Langdon felt that Buffett was, to some extent, analyzing the meal, as well as eating it.

"He picked up the bun a little and looked at the bun and the meat and said, 'the bun is the same [whether in the U.S. or Asia], the meat is the same and the fries are the same. And the price is about the same,'" Buffett told the group.

Buffett said his group also had eaten at McDonald's in Beijing during their trip to China.

"I knew he was a Coke junkie so I asked him, 'What do you think of the Coke?'" Buffett joked: "It might be a slightly richer mixture for my taste, but it'll do."

"I was talking to him like any other person. It was hard to believe these were the two richest people in the world," Langdon said.

Buffett, he said, was dressed in a white polo shirt bearing a small insignia: "Nebraska 1994 National Champions." Gates was in a button-down shirt. Both wore casual pants. "I knew Buffett was this way [casual], but I didn't know Gates was. He was kind of the same way."

Langdon was struck that apparently there were no bodyguards around, that Buffett and Gates were out at midnight and that nobody recognized them.

"I saw just one gentleman turn and look a couple of times." said Langdon, adding that most people in McDonald's that night were Asian.

The Buffett group was staying at the famous old Peninsula Hotel, but never said how it traveled from the hotel to McDonald's. "I saw no evidence of a driver," Langdon said.

There was some talk between Gates and Fred Langdon about the Internet, but the main thing Mark Langdon recalled about Gates was that he ate two Big Macs. He devoured his and one that his wife brought over. "He inhaled them," Langdon said.

Buffett paid for the meals with McDonald's gift certificates and gave the Langdon brothers what certificates were left over. Buffett said, "They gave us these," without saying exactly who gave them to him, according to Langdon. After Buffett handed over the gift certificates, he cracked, "You don't have any frequent flier coupons, do you?"

Langdon said he had heard the rumors that Buffett was buying McDonald's stock, but had no proof from the late night meal with Buffett.

"My brother and I did come away with the impression, just vibes, that Buffett and Gates both were interested in McDonald's. The two of them were talking about McDonald's," Langdon said.

2

Warren McBuffett's Big Mac Attack

"Two all-beef patties special sauce lettuce cheese pickles onions on a sesame seed bun."

Rumors were rampant in 1995 that Warren McBuffett was taking a big stake in McDonald's, and this time the rumors were true as confirmation first came March 6, 1996, that an SEC filing showed Berkshire owned 4.9 million shares of McDonald's at the end of 1994.

Buffett was at it again, taking a stake in a universally recognized brand name, a company with exploding overseas growth, even as growth in the U.S. seemed mature.

It all began with the McDonald brothers, Dick and Mac, in 1937 in California where drive-in restaurants were becoming a craze for Californians on the go in their automobiles.

The first restaurant was opened near Pasadena and then a grander one was opened in San Bernadino in 1940. It was a huge success.

Ray Kroc, a high school dropout who was an excellent salesman, met the McDonald brothers in 1954. The brothers were a good account for Kroc who sold them Multimixers to make milk shakes.

John F. Love's book, *McDonald's: Behind the Arches* best describes how history was made.

"He (Kroc) had parked his rental car in the McDonald's lot a full hour before noon, but already lines were forming at the two front windows, where the main orders were filled, and the side window, where orders for french fries were handled separately…It was not the shape of things that caught his eye, but the speed of them."

What Kroc was so excited about on that first visit was that one in three orders included milk shakes made with his Multimixers.

"The McDonalds were making milk shakes so fast that they…cut a couple of inches off the spindles on Kroc's Multimixer so that they could mix shakes right in the twelve-ounce paper cup, not in the sixteen-ounce stainless steel mixers the soda fountains used…

"He was bubbling over with enthusiasm as he walked inside to introduce himself… 'My God, I've been standing out there looking at it all but I can't believe it,' he told the brothers. Dick and Mac assured him that his reaction was normal—and as typical as that day's business. 'When will this die down?' Kroc asked. 'Sometime late tonight,' Dick replied. 'Some way,' Kroc declared, 'I've got to get involved in this.'"

Later Kroc, well into his middle age, bought out the McDonald brothers and led the company to enormous success. Kroc, who had dropped out of high school after his sophomore year, had come a long way.

When World War I had started, he went overseas, joining the Red Cross at age 15 and working in the same company as Walt Disney. Each liked one another but they were opposites. Love's book quotes Kroc as saying, "He was always drawing pictures while the rest of us were chasing girls. Therein lies a lesson, because his drawings have gone on forever - and most of those girls are dead now."

Late in life Kroc opened his first McDonald's in Des Plaines, Illinois, and Kroc perfectly caught the fast-food craze in the country. He insisted on low prices for his hamburgers and on quality, service, cleanliness and training.

The rest is now history. As Love's book points out:

- Fully 96% of American consumers have eaten at one of its restaurants in the past year.
- Slightly more than half of the U.S. population lives within a three-minute drive to a McDonald's.
- McDonald's has served far more than 100 billion hamburgers.
- McDonald's captures 14% of all restaurant visits in the United States—one out of every six—and has a 6.6% share of all dollars spent on eating out.
- McDonald's sells 34% of all hamburgers sold by commercial restaurants and 26% of all french fries.
- Control of such a market share has given McDonald's a big impact on the food processing business in the U.S.
- McDonald's is the country's largest purchaser of beef and sells so many french fries it buys 5% of the entire U.S. potato crop harvested for food.
- McDonald's stores account for 5% of all Coca-Cola sold in the U.S.
- Key item: McDonald's is the world's largest owner of retail real estate.
- McDonald's has enjoyed an average return on equity of 25% and a 24% earnings growth annually since becoming a public company in 1965.
- An initial investment of $2,250 for 100 shares of stock has grown through 11 stock splits and one stock dividend to 27,180 shares worth more than $1 million in mid-1994.

Also McDonald's provides one in 15 Americans with his or her first job.

When McDonald's opened a store in Moscow on a cold day on January 31, 1990, more than 30,000 people showed up, the most customers a restaurant had ever served in a single day. The Moscow restaurant served 15 million customers in its first year of operation—a number the average U.S. restaurant takes 30 years to achieve. McDonald's opening in Beijing on April 23, 1991, shattered the opening day record that had been set in Moscow, attracting 40,000 customers.

McDonald's in 1995 had two restaurants in China. It plans 500 by the turn of the century in that country of 1.2. billion people.

The company, headed by Michael Quinlan, who started his McDonald's career as a mailboy, now has more than 18,000 restaurants in 89 countries worldwide and the pace of growth is continuing with an emphasis on lower startup costs and smaller restaurants. These satellite units, located in retail stores, hospitals, schools and travel points draw on resources from existing restaurants thereby lowering operating costs.

McDonald's, which is opening a restaurant every three hours, plans to have 20,000 restaurants by the end of 1996.

About 15% of the stock ownership of the company belongs to employees, franchisees and suppliers.

McDonald's is widely known for its Ronald McDonald House which has dozens of houses throughout the world, providing a home-away-from home for families of seriously ill children receiving treatment at nearby hospitals.

Buffett's close friend, Donald Keough, the former Coca-Cola president, serves on McDonald's board.

Where Keough goes, Buffett seems to go. And where McDonald's goes, Coke goes. Who's to say there's no synergy at Berkshire?

3

The Walt Disney Company Sing along: M-I-C, K-E-Y M-O-N-E-Y

"The Mouse doesn't have an agent."

"Walt Disney, Capital Cities agree to merger." - Dow Jones news wire, 7:56 a.m., July 31, 1995.

The jokes started flying immediately. "I knew Cap Cities was a Mickey Mouse operation...My new boss is Mickey Mouse." Headlines read: "The Mouse that Roared" or "The Mouse that Scored." But underneath the jokes, the largest merger of entertainment and media companies in history was being launched.

It was a big day for everyone. Disney Chairman Michael Eisner, Cap Cities/ABC Chairman Tom Murphy and Buffett held a press conference

(Photo by Maria Melin-ABC)

Warren Buffett and his wife, Susie Buffett, celebrating as Mickey and Minnie Mouse with Disney CEO Michael Eisner and President Michael Oritz at a Cap Cities management meeting in Phoenix, Arizona, about the time of the Disney-Cap Cities merger.

to talk about the $19 billion merger being paid for in Disney stock and cash.

The deal got its real start at investment banker Allen & Co's annual summer getaway for media executives held in Sun Valley, Idaho, in the middle of July, 1995. Eisner and Murphy had talked before about a possible deal, but Murphy wanted Disney stock and Eisner wanted to offer cash. Soil for such deals had been watered by expectations that Congress would remove some restrictions on TV ownership. It sounds Goofy, but here's how the mega-deal occurred.

Eisner, bumping into Buffett on Wildflower Lane, who was on his way to a golf game with Murphy, asked Buffett if Cap Cities were for sale. Buffett said, "I think so, let's ask Murphy."

Eisner later told Murphy that both companies were running on all cylinders. The two men came to terms in a few weeks after Murphy consulted with Buffett and Eisner consulted with Sid Bass, a big Disney investor. A contract was drawn up over a three day period.

Investment bankers had only a slight hand in the merger. The deal was presented to the Cap Cities board on Sunday afternoon, July 30. It was approved the next morning and the merger was announced.

The deal was for Disney to buy Cap Cities for about $127 a share. Cap Cities shareholders would get a share of Disney and $65 in cash. Cap Cities shareholders could choose to get a different mix of cash or stock than provided for, which Disney would pro-rate if the stock or cash portions were oversubscribed.

A stock swap seemed advantageous for many investors who were long term Cap Cities investors because a stock swap is tax free.

Murphy joined the Disney board and Buffett was back in an investment he had touched upon in the 1960s, buying 5% of Disney in 1966 at a time when Disney was "selling at five times rides," as Buffett described it. He sold the stake in 1967 for $6 million, scoring a nice gain. Huge mistake. That Disney stock today is worth about a billion dollars.

The day of the announcement Cap Cities stock soared about $20 from $96. Even the stock of Disney, the acquiring company rose. It's unusual for the stock of an acquiring company to go up, but Buffett won a $100 bet with a Disney official that Disney's stock would rise.

And Berkshire's stock spiked up $550 to $24,750.

It was a good day for Buffett. Since Berkshire owned 20 million shares of Cap Cities which was up about $20 on the day, about $400 million rolled in for Berkshire that day.

The Dow Jones wire service pointed out that it would take 16,000 Americans making the U.S. average of $25,000 a year to earn that.

There had been no flurry of options trading, no news report or any hint the deal was coming. The announcement shocked Wall Street, unlike the long rumored and widely reported takeover of CBS by Westinghouse which came the next day.

Eisner, Murphy and Buffett—those three Mouseketeers—were suddenly telling the world about the blockbuster combination.

"Exportation of U.S. intellectual product has been going on forever, but now it can be more organized," said Eisner, who once worked for ABC. "This is the real beginning of U.S. companies being global."

Murphy said: "On a personal basis...this is the high point of my career: seeing these two great companies go forward together."

Buffett explained the deal was a boon for the shareholders of the companies involved: "It's a wonderful marriage of the No. 1 content company and the No. 1 distribution company."

The merger, the second largest ever after the takeover of RJR Nabisco, created the largest entertainment and media company in the world, far larger than even Time Warner. Two weeks after the merger announcement, Michael Ovitz of Creative Artists Agency, was named Disney's president.

Disney, home of Mickey Mouse and Donald Duck, has sales of more than $10 billion a year that it reaps from its theme parks, movies such as *The Lion King*, music, books, stores, sports and other properties. Cap Cities brings in more than $6 billion a year from its ABC television network, 225 affiliate stations and a range of other media properties such as the globe-spanning ESPN sports channel.

How did it come to pass that one of the great business mergers in all history ran through a fellow from Omaha, a man fabulously famous in some circles, yet still widely unknown?

Why would Michael Eisner ask Buffett about whether such a deal was possible and why did he probably figure the deal was done when Buffett again replied: "Sure, but you should go find Tom."

Michael found Tom who got with Warren and the triumvirate marched off into the "Wonderful World of Disney."

Later at a party held in Phoenix, Arizona, to celebrate the merger Buffett brought hundreds of Cap Cities and Disney executives to their feet when he and his wife appeared on stage in full costume—as Mickey and Minnie Mouse.

Buffett said : "I thought I would prepare a little by checking out the Academy Awards to see how they did it. I would at this time like to thank my hairstylist, my wardrobe consultant and, of course, my personal trainer."

Still donning his mouse ears and while Wall Street waited to hear whether Buffett would take Disney stock or cash as a result of the merger, he sang:

"Shall we go for stock or cash?
Paper money turns to trash.
Stocks, however, sometimes crash.
Shall we go for stock or cash?"

His magical decision was made known on March 7, 1996.

Here's how it happened: On March 5, 1996, Buffett walked into Harris Trust in New York and handed a trust officer two envelopes.

"Envelope No. 1 was stock worth, gulp, $2.5 billion: Berkshire's 20 million shares of Capital Cities/ABC., being delivered to that company's purchaser, Walt Disney Co.

"In envelope No. 2, sealed and marked, 'Do not open until 4:30 p.m. on March 7,' were Buffett's wishes—kept secret from even the management of Disney and Cap Cities..." (*Fortune*, Carol Loomis, April 1, 1996) received and with some additional purchases in the open market, Buffett wound up with about 3½% of Disney's shares. Suddenly he was another large shareholder in one of the great brand name companies on earth.

When Buffett gave a talk to Harvard Business School on March 21, 1996, he was asked why he liked Disney stock.

His reply: "The Mouse doesn't have an agent."

4

Harvard-rejectee returns in triumph

Harvard flunks spelling test

Buffett, who as a teenager was rejected at Harvard Business School, spoke to Harvard in early 1996 before a standing room only crowd.

Predictably, *The Harbus*, Harvard Business School's student newspaper, wrote an intelligent, sophisticated article, although it left out a "t" in Buffett's name.

Comparing the merits of a Harvard Business degree or just investing the tuition money with Buffett early on, the story began:

"$45,000,000. This is the fortune a 1956 Harvard Business School graduate would have amassed today had he traded in his tuition money and degree back then and given it instead to Warren E. Buffett of Omaha,

Nebraska."

Buffett gave a short talk about honesty and integrity, mentioning the personal qualities of Tom Murphy, the former chairman of Cap Cities/ABC and a graduate of Harvard Business School's Class of 1949.

"In the 20 years I've known him, he has never done anything he couldn't put on the front page of the newspaper," Buffett said.

Then he threw it open for questions. *The Harbus* said:

> Students questioned Buffett on topics ranging from technical issues of valuation and finance to personal philosophies of success and fulfillment...Buffett stood steadfast by his well-known policy of never discussing current or future investment targets. He also shunned discussion of business school finance topics such as the Black-Scholes model and the efficient market hypothesis in favor of strike zones and fast pitches.
>
> He stressed common sense, discipline, and patience, as opposed to IQ, as the keys to good investing. When asked what is the key to picking good stocks, Buffett responded, 'understanding and picking good businesses...'
>
> At the conclusion of the talk, fans rushed the stage with cameras flashing, while Buffett autographed dollar bills, T-shirts, annual reports and assorted unauthorized biographies...
>
> After a 15 minute post-speech melee, Buffett excused himself and was hurried off to his private jet, *The Indefensible*, which was waiting to whisk him home in time for work the next day.

5

Of Permanent Value

$10,000 into $140 million—AFTER TAX.

If you had handed Warren Edward Buffett $10,000 in 1956, today it would be worth about $140 million.

AFTER TAX!

So if your grandparents didn't give you $10,000 back then and tell you to invest with Buffett, you should make a note.

That figure is after all taxes, fees and expenses. Had you invested in his Buffett Partnership—disbanded in 1969—you could have chosen to reinvest in an ongoing business called Berkshire Hathaway, which Buffett also ran.

That's a 14,000-fold return on your money in an era when the Dow Jones Industrial Average rose about tenfold. And the Dow Jones number is a pre-tax figure.

That's right. The original $10.000 investment is now worth about

$140 million after all taxes, fees and expenses, if Berkshire were trading at $36,000 a share.

Before fees, a few of which existed back in the original partnership, but still after all taxes, the $10,000 would have mushroomed to way beyond $140 million!

One problem with the Buffett/Berkshire "Buy Low, Don't Sell" story is that it seems unbelievable. People are skeptical because most investors have trouble just treading water. Therefore, it's hard to relate to making millions upon millions of dollars. Billions of dollars.

It's a little like Mark Twain's saying, "Of course truth is stranger than fiction. Fiction has to make sense."

Had you arrived late at the party and not invested in Berkshire until 1965 when Buffett took it over, a $10,000 investment then would be worth about $30 million now.

Since 1965 Berkshire is up more than 3,000-fold; during a time the Dow Jones Industrial Average, emanating from the Street of Dreams, is up about fivefold, from roughly 1,000 to about 5,000.

During that time, Berkshire's return on book value beat the Standard & Poor's 500 Stock Index returns in 28 of 31 years, failing to do so only in 1967, 1975 and 1980. And that's with Berkshire's numbers calculated after its tax liability. The S&P pays no tax so its numbers are pre-tax.

Even so, since 1965, on an annual basis, Berkshire has clobbered the S&P Index with a 23% annual return compared with a 10% annual return by the S&P.

Through his partnership and later through Berkshire, a now defunct New England textile mill, Buffett built a financial empire beyond anyone's wildest dreams. Buffett and Berkshire now own pieces of some of the world's most prominent businesses, including an 8% stake in The Coca-Cola Company worth about $9 billion.

If your investment made you a millionaire, you may wonder what it did for Buffett. Answer: It made him a billionaire many times over.

Buffett, who didn't inherit any money, owns about 41% of the stock of Berkshire, an investment holding company which has vast stock, bond and cash holdings and a number of operating businesses.

Because of Buffett's huge stake in Berkshire, in many ways Buffett is Berkshire and Berkshire is certainly the creation of Buffett. He calls Berkshire his canvas. "I feel very good about my work. When I go to my office every morning I feel like I'm going to the Sistine Chapel to paint," Buffett told *Women's Wear Daily*, October 10, 1985.

Of his canvas, Buffett has said, "I hope it's an example in some ways of corporate action that people might emulate over time." (WOWT-TV in Omaha, October 14, 1993) On his canvas, Buffett draws sweeping, nearly priceless investment pictures.

Buffett is the Michelangelo of business.

Berkshire's record vies with almost anything in American business. Yet Buffett—ultra-famous in financial circles—was still largely unknown until he stepped in to save the Wall Street firm of Salomon Inc in 1991. He manages one of America's largest corporations from a small office in a nondescript building in midtown Omaha, Nebraska.

Over the years, as Buffett has sat in the office reading and thinking, he has spawned billions of dollars in shareholder value making multimillionaires of dozens of early investors and ordinary millionaires of hundreds more.

Berkshire's stock has traded higher than $30,000 a share, higher than any other stock on the New York Stock Exchange and sky-high above its give-away 1965 price of $12.

By comparison General Motors stock trades for not a lot more than it did in 1965, with just one 2-for-1 split along the way in 1989. You can say that General Motors during that time has roughly quadrupled and paid a handsome dividend, hardly keeping up with inflation.

So how did Buffett multiply his money 14,000 times over the past 40 years?

"We like simple businesses," Buffett says.

A persistent corporate acquisitor who loves to buy and hates to sell, he usually stays away from businesses saddled with large plants, lots of technology, constant product changes and those requiring high retiree health costs and big pension funds.

Simply put, he compounded the invested money at a shooting star pace. But just how he achieved his remarkable results—through his trademark value-oriented, marathon distance investing—is even more remarkable.

The Buffett Partnership, in 13 years, never had a down year despite some nasty bear markets. Instead, it forged a 29.5% compound annual rate of return. And Berkshire's own annual increase in stock price, more than 25% a year (the best was a 59% return on book value in 1976), has exceeded its annual return on book value of better than 23%.

Although for several years Berkshire's stock price has ended lower than it began, Buffett has NEVER EVER had a down year for return on stockholders' equity. In other words, Berkshire has never had a year in which it lost money.

Berkshire's worst years were 1973 and 1974 when it made 4.7% and 5.5% return on book value, respectively. Although that sounds mediocre, the S&P was down 14.8% and 26.4% respectively so that Berkshire's results relative to the market were plus 19.5% in 1973 and plus 31.9% in 1974—a sensational performance because most money managers cannot beat the market. The average performance is average and with frictional costs like commissions, the average performance becomes below average. Therefore, most money managers bring no new value to the table, Buffett says.

Buffett rang up a 29%-to-30% return in the partnership days. It was about 29% for the partnership and about 24% for his limited partners after Buffett's slice.

Along the way he created an enterprise of permanent value, enormous permanent value.

His Berkshire was created by making a few large, staggeringly successful decisions. More than half his net worth is attributable to fewer than a dozen investment actions. Buffett almost always buys at distressed times and bargain prices, then holds for the long term. Long term in some investment quarters means settlement date or posting of the next quarter's earnings. Buffett instead has held on to many of his present investments for years, decades, through good times and bad, for a far sunnier day. When it comes to investing, Buffett is a marathon man still out to capture a greater piece of the world's business pie.

Beyond the dollars Buffett has accumulated, beyond the worth of the businesses, stocks, bonds and cash Berkshire owns, there is an even greater value.

The permanent value he has created is a statement—a statement about how to do things right, how to do them ethically, sensibly, simply and inexpensively.

There is, for example, no waste.

Buffett, who would get no objection from Berkshire shareholders were he to pay himself $10 million a year, has kept his annual salary at $100,000 for the past 15 years making him one of the lowest-paid chief executives of a major firm and also making him easily the best price-to-performance money manager on the planet. Buffett is working for shareholders for less than 10 cents a share.

Buffett builds no monuments to himself at shareholder expense.

There is no Buffett Tower, no Buffett Plaza, Airport or Boulevard.

There is no touting of Berkshire shares. If anything, Buffett downplays the historic compounding of their worth and tells shareholders next year's return probably won't be as good as last year's.

Cosmetics are not applied by splitting the stock. To Buffett that's a meaningless exercise of prizing ten $1 dollar bills over one $10 bill. And Buffett doesn't want shareholders who don't understand that.

However, in 1996, a "do-it-yourself stock split" was declared with the creation of a Class B, or "Baby Berkshire" share which trades at about 1/30th of the big Class A share. (See Chapter 124)

There is no company logo for Berkshire, now one of the largest and most financially powerful firms in the world.

Despite Berkshire's extraordinary success and even Buffett's fame, Wall Street still largely ignores Berkshire. Almost no analyst follows it and stockbrokers almost never mention it to investors. It is rarely written up as a stock to buy. In many major Blue Chip corporate lists, it is not even mentioned.

Berkshire itself makes no effort to be known. You have to discover it for yourself.

There are no photos—color or black and white—no bar charts, no graphs in the company's plain looking annual report—which is famous among its fans, but unknown to others. The annual report is the company's only real communication to the public. What it lacks in gloss, it makes up for in value.

Once you have read a Berkshire Annual Report, nothing else in the business world matches it. There is little argument that the report, the bible of finance that includes Buffett's famous letter to shareholders, is a brilliant accounting of business.

There is humor, common sense, insight into the business world and human nature, and high praise for the managers of the disparate group of businesses Berkshire owns.

Buffett's literary pyrotechnics in the report offer commentary on Berkshire's major properties, huge interests—far north of $1 billion in many cases—in some of the country's major apple pie businesses. The holdings include Coca-Cola, Gillette, American Express, Disney, McDonald's and Wells Fargo, an extravaganza of brand names.

The reports offer a unique literary style, spiced with wit and wisdom about the human condition.

The Berkshire annual meeting also is unique. Thousands of shareholders from all over the world make the pilgrimage to investment mecca in Omaha each spring. After Buffett dispenses with company business in five to ten minutes, he answers questions for hours.

"The meeting of Berkshire Hathaway is adjourned," he announces almost as soon as it has begun. "Any questions?" There are—usually about three hours' worth.

Buffett, who is normally self-effacing and leans to an unflamboyant, low-key lifestyle most of the time, describes his principles as "simple, old and few."

Called "Fireball" by his father, Buffett started early from scratch but was buoyed by a family of substance. In addition to starting early, he plans to stay late at his career. After all, it's the compounding of money in the later years that really counts if you want to amass wealth. If Buffett continues compounding at only half his historic rate, he could end up controlling dozens of the world's greatest companies before he stops collecting businesses.

In his early days young, crewcut Buffett operated an investment partnership from his upstairs bedroom and sunporch in his $32,000 home in his native Omaha. He bought the three-story Dutch colonial home in 1958 and has never moved. Homes in his neighborhood today go for about $150,000 to $200,000. That's a lousy return, percentage-wise, compared to Berkshire, but still better than GM.

His house is in the Dundee section of Omaha, appropriately near Happy Hollow Boulevard.

In the early days, he sometimes kept track of intricate financial matters literally on the backs of envelopes. His was a "one-room" operation.

Buffett always has lived beneath his means.

He has always insisted on rock-bottom operating costs, plenty of cash on hand and "little or no debt."

For example, it was not until he was in his late 20s and well on his way to being a millionaire, that he splurged on a $295 IBM typewriter for the partnership.

"He was always saying he didn't need it," recalls William O'Connor, a vice president of Mutual of Omaha who had been an IBM salesman for 30 years. In his early days, O'Connor made the strenuous sale to Buffett. "It was an IBM Standard Model electric typewriter. He bought the standard model rather than the more costly executive model."

Always tight-fisted, Buffett occasionally has dipped into his now $17 billion net worth for such endeavors as adding rooms to his house, including a handball court.

In his garage and home entranceway, he stores cases of Cherry Coke, which he is so well known for drinking. He buys the Cokes himself—fifty 12-packs at a time, getting a good discount. Fewer trips to the store that way.

His habit helps the bottom line at Berkshire, about a penny for every Coke he drinks.

Operating from his spartan office, Buffett is the nerve center—along with business partner Charles Munger, who operates from Los Angeles—of a financial empire whose reach and influence sprawl all across the land and beyond.

Usually Buffett invests when there is some temporary stigma or fear or misunderstanding surrounding a superb business. Such was the case when GEICO, came dangerously near bankruptcy in the mid-1970s. He bought big, made about 40 times on his money and now owns all of GEICO.

A key tenet at Berkshire is to bet big and bet seldom. You work in what Buffett calls your "circle of competence." You find your edge in life and investing. When on rare occasions you're certain of that edge, you swing for the fences.

Buffett is a beacon of simplicity and sanity—and probably a genius. Rationality and common sense, actually uncommon sense, are his guiding lights. For example, there are many reasons he bought Coca-Cola stock, but a main one is that human beings, worldwide, get thirsty, and history shows that once exposed to Coke, people continue to drink it.

His three-word job description: "I allocate capital." His wordy explanation: "My job is to figure out which businesses to invest in, with whom, and at what price."

Holed up in the heartland of America—a locale for steaks and cornstalks, and peace and quiet—Buffett spends most of his time thinking and reading.

"We read. That's about it," says Buffett, who also says: "We like to buy wonderful businesses at reasonable prices."

Mainly Buffett buys whole privately owned businesses outright or stock representing pieces of publicly owned businesses.

What Buffett does not do is as important as what he does. He does no program trading (although Berkshire investee Salomon does). He makes no fast bets on a company's upcoming quarterly earnings. He mouths no threats and will not participate in hostile takeovers. And he does not try to force things with debt, loud talk or wild shots.

The secret to making money, in his view, is not to take risks, but to avoid risks. "We've done better by avoiding dragons rather than by slaying them," Buffett says.

The investment shots he talks about making are layups. He puts money in places he's sure about and then holds on through good times and bad. "Our favorite holding period is forever," he says. That's a different attitude from such trader talk as, "I wouldn't go home long tonight."

On the question of ethics and integrity, there is no question.

Operating far from the maddening crowd of Wall Street, Buffett is the world's richest person. The *Forbes* 400 issue of October 18, 1993, listed Buffett as the richest person in the U.S. with $8.3 billion. In 1994 Buffett came in second in *Forbes's* calculation, with $9.2 billion, behind Bill Gates's $9.35 billion.

"The only reason Gates was ahead is that they counted his house," Buffett said during a talk at the University of Nebraska in Lincoln October 10, 1994. In 1995 *Forbes* found Gates to be No. 1 again with $14.8 billion and Buffett No. 2 with $11.8 billion. But then Berkshire soared and Mircrosoft dropped so that it was about a dead heat.

A *USA Today* story February 28, 1996 calculated Buffett's net worth at $16.6 billion to Gates's $14.1 billion. The paper used Buffett's 479,202 shares and Berkshire's price then of $34,700 dollars and multiplied Gates's 141.2 million shares of Microsoft times a share price of about $100 dollars. The paper declared Buffett the richest business person in the world. Buffett's fans—known as Buffett's Buffs— were cheering him on.

If we take a $17 billion net worth figure now (and we'll find it's too conservative), let's still consider Buffett's debts. To get the numbers in perspective, he has at least $17 billion in assets and his only debt is $70,000 on a mortgage for a three-bedroom, two-bath second home he bought in 1971 in Laguna Beach, California, in Emerald Bay, overlooking the Pacific Ocean where he goes at Christmas. He bought the home for $150,000 when the assessed value was $185,000.

The $70,000 debt, which he has kept because of a low interest note, means he has more than two billion dollars in assets for every $10,000 of debt. Buffett's assets to debt ratio clearly qualifies for a term he looks for when he makes investments: "Margin of Safety."

Speaking to Salomon's clients on September 13, 1991, about his distaste for debt, Buffett said, "You're looking at a fellow who owes $70,000 on a second home in Laguna and I've got that because of the low rate...and that's all I've owed for I don't know how many years."

"If you're smart, you don't need debt. If you're dumb, it's poisonous," he said.

Samuel Butler once wrote, "All progress is based upon a universal innate desire on the part of every organism to live beyond its income."

Buffett is the exception to the rule.

In the late 1980s the Ivan Boeskys and Michael Milkens of the world, using inside information, lots of debt, threats and fraudulent schemes, ultimately ran afoul of securities laws. Buffett's friend, Michael Yanney, chairman of America First Capital Associates in Omaha, refers to that era as a time when "Greed on Wall Street exceeded its intellect."

What was Buffett doing in that era of frenzy? He was running businesses such as World Book encyclopedias, See's Candies and the Buffalo News, and buying Coca-Cola stock.

Beyond his wealth, Buffett is the most influential investment mind and voice in the land.

He has two concrete rules for all who seek riches:

Rule No. 1. Never lose money.

Rule No. 2. Never forget Rule No. 1.

With an appearance and manner slightly reminiscent of Jack Benny, he remains modest and dryly witty. Once a Berkshire shareholder, knowing of Buffett's love for bridge, sent him an Omar Sharif bridge tape. Buffett thanked the shareholder in a note saying, "If I listen to it long enough, will I be as handsome as Omar Sharif?"

Another time before he was to talk to University of Nebraska students he was asked "Do you want extra security here?" His reply: "We don't need any security; just ask the attendees to check any soft fruit at the door."

In describing Berkshire's acquisition policy, he once told shareholders, "It's very scientific. We just sit around and wait for the phone to ring. Sometimes it's a wrong number."

He lives an extraordinarily independent, stirringly original life. More than 99% of the monetary proceeds and 100% of the human proceeds of his life are to be "returned to society."

There may be a stunning denouement. It's not yet spelled out, but expect a rousing finale when it comes to the eventual use of his fortune.

Buffett's Triple A reputation, built block by block and stock by stock from a methodology of value investing, has risen to mythological levels as he now resides as the richest person on earth.

When he shuffles off this earth to investors' heaven, he has promised to keep in touch with us. He once told author Adam Smith, "I see myself running Berkshire as long as I live and working on seances afterward."

The mystique of Warren Buffett is so out of this world he just may do that.

6

"Who's Warren Buffett?"

"He's the guy who'll paint any car for $99.95."

At 6:45 a.m., August 16, 1991, the phone rang at Buffett's home, waking him up. It was some of Salomon's top officers telling him they planned to resign.

That afternoon news wires were crackling with word of a scandal at Salomon.

"S&P puts Salomon ratings on creditwatch: Negative," flashed one.

A few minutes later came another: "Salomon stock, bonds plunge on spreading scandal news."

"Salomon says Gutfreund, Strauss prepare to resign," flashed another.

At the same minute as the previous bulletin—at 2:27 p.m., as Salomon's world was crashing—yet another bulletin flashed: "Salomon says Buffett to become interim chairman."

Buffett is Warren Buffett—the multi-billionaire from Omaha, the world's greatest investor.

Throughout his life, people have asked, "Who's Warren Buffett?" A follow-up question sometimes is, "Where's Omaha?" Omaha, shareholders know, is in the state of Berkshire.

With time, Buffett has become better known, but the story is still not out fully. Here's a recent inquiry from a reporter in late 1995: "Is he American?"

When Buffett was inducted into the Nebraska Business Hall of Fame February 8, 1996, the program featured an irreverent 7-minute video about Buffett narrated by celebrity interviewer Robin Leach.

Leach: "Excuse me, sir, do you know who Warren Buffett is?" Unidentified man: "Yeah, he's that guy who'll paint any car for $99.95."

Despite his private ways, Buffett became vastly famous to an ever growing cadre of investors. He remained largely unrecognized by the rest of the world because of his down-home lifestyle and avoidance of interviews.

It was the bond trading scandal at Salomon—the giant securities firm in which Buffett was holding a $700 million investment—that finally forced him into the limelight.

In short order authorities wanted 12 sets of fingerprints from Buffett to meet a variety of securities business rules.

"There was also a rule that because I was an officer of a securities firm I had to take the Series 7 exam [for stockbrokers]. I kept delaying it until I left because I wasn't sure I could pass it," Buffett once said.

The scandal at Salomon, caused by illegal trading activities and failure to report them, forced the firm to turn to Buffett. It had no other choice. Buffett was the one person the firm, its clients, the U.S. Government, regulators, investigators and investors all around the world could trust to set Salomon straight. And Buffett already was sitting on the Salomon board.

Who is Warren Buffett, this modest, mild-mannered, tough-minded Midwesterner chosen to save Salomon?

Brilliant graduates of Harvard, Columbia and Stanford, in unsolicited remarks, have used the word "genius" to describe this semi-eccentric, financial wizard.

Buffett's longtime counterpart, Berkshire Vice Chairman Charles Munger—no dim bulb himself—indeed a magna cum laude graduate of Harvard Law School, has said, "There were a thousand people in my Harvard law class. I knew all the top students. There was no one as able as Warren."

Salomon spokesman Robert Baker, who spoke with Buffett often during the Salomon bond scandal crisis said, "He's everything as advertised and more. Everytime I told him something he was waiting at the end of the sentence for me...and his moral compass is due North."

Rich. Smart. Honest? The people who know Buffett best, his children, say he's the most honest person they've ever known.

Within hours of being called upon to serve as Salomon's chairman, Buffett saddled up his corporate jet. It's one of the few expensive worldly trappings the multi-billionaire allows himself.

The airplane he's dubbed *The Indefensible* flew from Omaha to Teterboro, New Jersey, and the billionaire made his way to Seven World Trade Center, Salomon's one million square foot headquarters in New York.

As the crisis unfolded, Salomon's own stock plummeted with revelations the firm's traders bought up more than the legal limit of bonds at Treasury auctions. Salomon's problems were compounded because top management knew about the bond trading violations for months but had failed to report them. This coverup turned the matter into a full-blown scandal, one so intense some thought it capable of bringing down mighty Salomon.

This was the second time, not the first, that Buffett rescued Salomon.

In 1987 when corporate raider Revlon Chairman Ronald Perelman—backed with financing from junk bond king Michael Milken—was threatening a takeover of Salomon, Buffett quickly stepped in with $700 million in cash to halt the Perelman-Milken takeover.

Buffett made his Salomon investment for Berkshire three weeks before the October 19, 1987, stock market crash. The crash itself created deadly air pockets for Salomon and its Wall Street counterparts. Buffett faced no less rocky turbulence in his second effort to save Salomon, this time from a seemingly incomprehensible trading mess that seemed likely to cause the failure of a big engine of Wall Street.

As he prepared to take Salomon's top position, amidst client defections, Buffett met immediately with the managing directors and told them point-blank that Salomon's reputation was on the line. Staying just within the bounds of the rules, Buffett warned, would NOT be acceptable—Salomon's very future depended upon the firm's reputation. No reputation. No Salomon. Indeed no jobs.

Buffett told Salomon's managers that the firm faced a huge management job in facing fines and litigation, that he would name a new chief operating officer and that—following an emergency board meeting Sunday, August 18, 1991, he would hold a press conference. That was newsworthy because Buffett rarely holds press conferences or grants interviews.

The Salomon executives were so impressed with Buffett's straightforward approach, they burst into applause.

Buffett began preparations for Sunday's dramatic board meeting where he accepted the resignations of Salomon's top executives: John Gutfreund, the chairman once described as "King of Wall Street"; Robert Strauss, president; and John Meriwether, Salomon Brothers's vice chairman—key men who admitted knowing of the violations but who failed to report them.

It would be only hours before the names of the top managers implicated in the scandal were removed from the glass-cased directory on the main floor of the headquarters building. One new name was inserted: Warren E. Buffett.

In combating the scandal, Buffett also fired two men in the bond trading department and later would fire Salomon's law firm, name a new chief operating officer and put into place tighter internal controls.

In the midst of this chaos, Buffett convinced U.S. Treasury Secretary Nicholas Brady to reverse a major portion of a potentially crippling, five-hour-old ban on Salomon's highly profitable government securities trading.

This allowed Salomon to continue bidding at government bond auctions for its own account, even though it was still banned from placing orders for customers. In the process of handling the crisis, Buffett drew Brady's warm praise.

Buffett, already ensconced in Gutfreund's 43rd floor office with a new phone line, next went out to meet the press. He won them over in a split second by saying, "I will attempt to answer questions in the manner of a fellow who has never met a lawyer. We'll stay as long as you wish."

In the next three hours he took a tell-all approach, saying, "It looks to me, like in the case of the two people we fired, there were things done you and I would characterize as a coverup."

In his inimitable homespun style, Buffett described the Salomon atmosphere as "what some people might call macho and others cavalier."

"I don't think the same things would have happened in a monastery," he added.

He was asked if he had read *Liar's Poker*, the book about Salomon's rough-and-tumble corporate culture. Buffett said he had. Well?

"I just don't want there to be a second edition," he replied.

The next day Buffett went to Washington to meet with regulators and to continue his fast-paced mission to save Salomon.

About a week later he was giving the Salomon sales force a 15-minute pep talk beamed to Salomon offices around the world. "I don't want anyone playing close to the lines...," he counseled. "You can do very well hitting down the middle of the court."

Later he added, "If you lose money for the firm by bad decisions, I will be very understanding. If you lose reputation for the firm, I will be ruthless."

Buffett had to make fast judgments about how best to keep clients, how to keep employee defections down, how to reassure Salomon's creditors and the government. He decided to sell some $40 billion of Salomon's securities to finance the firm's operations, keeping it competitive at a very dangerous time.

The government seemed reassured by Buffett's leadership at the firm. Investors and clients breathed a sigh of relief and Salomon's stock, which had lost about one-third of its value during the ordeal, steadied, then rallied.

For Buffett, who far prefers his quiet existence in Omaha, it was an action-packed time of racing from Omaha to New York and Washington and living out of a suitcase.

Asked if such a hectic pace were a problem, Buffett quipped, "My mother's sewn my name in the underwear, so it's all okay."

(Ad ran in *The Dundee News*, June 16, 1950; photo courtesy of Allan Maxwell)

The folks at Buffett & Son grocery store: Sidney Buffett, Ernest Buffett and Fred Buffett. "81 years of selling foods in Omaha."

7

Roots

Politics, commerce and media

Warren Buffett was born August 30, 1930, on a hot humid day in Omaha, just blocks from where he now runs Berkshire. He arrived at the old Doctors Hospital in downtown Omaha into a family prominent for six generations in the city's political and business endeavors.

The first Buffett to reach Nebraska, Sidney H. Buffett from Dix Hills on Long Island, New York, opened a grocery store on Omaha's Fourteenth Street on August 20, 1869. In the store's early days, the delivery wagon was mule drawn and the mules were kept in a stable behind the store.

Ernest Buffett, Sidney Buffett's son, joined his father in working at the store February 1, 1894. The store was moved to Omaha's Dundee section in 1915. Ernest Buffett's son, Fred, joined his father in the business at 5015 Underwood on June 1, 1929.

The Dundee News ran an ad for the Buffett & Son grocery store on June 16, 1950, with photos of Sidney, Ernest and Fred Buffett under the headline, "81 years of selling foods in Omaha." All the Buffetts were known as upright citizens.

Warren's father edited the *Daily Nebraskan* at the University of Nebraska, where he met Warren's mother in 1924 when she came calling for a job to earn money for college.

She had set type in her family's printshop and was a reporter for her father's weekly newspaper, the *Cuming County Democrat*, in West Point, Nebraska.

Buffett's grandfather had bought the newspaper in 1905 and his family lived on a top level of the newspaper building.

Warren Buffett is the grandson of Ernest Buffett and the son of Howard Homan Buffett, who was a rock-ribbed Republican U.S. Congressman. In addition to Howard and Fred, Ernest Buffett had an older son Clarence, who was killed in an auto wreck in Texas in 1937, and a daughter, Alice Buffett, who never married and was a revered schoolteacher for years at both Benson High School and Central High School in Omaha. Warren Buffett, through his Buffett Foundation, gives an award of $10,000 each to 15 teachers every year in her honor.

The money has no strings attached. As Buffett told NBC's Tom Brokaw for a segment about education aired April 12, 1994, the teacher can blow it all in Las Vegas.

Warren's father, Howard H. Buffett, was a stockbroker who founded Buffett-Falk & Company in 1931. He also sold diamonds to clients who wanted an inflation hedge.

Howard Buffett served in Congress from 1942 to 1948 and from 1950 to 1952. He was known as a forceful writer and astute observer of politics and commerce who called things as he saw them. Howard Buffett died April 29, 1964, of cancer at age 60.

In a May 6, 1948, article in the *Commercial and Financial Chronicle*, when gold was illegal to own, Howard Buffett wrote:

> I warn you that politicians of both parties will oppose the restoration of gold, although they may outwardly seem to favor it. Also, those elements here and abroad who are getting rich from the continued American inflation will oppose a return to sound money. You must be prepared to meet their opposition intelligently and vigorously.
>
> But unless you are willing to surrender your

> children and your country to galloping inflation, war and slavery, then this cause demands your support. For if human liberty is to survive in America, we must win the battle to restore a return to sound money. There is no more important challenge facing us than this issue—the restoration of your freedom to secure gold in exchange for the fruits of your labor.

Warren Buffett's sister, Mrs. Doris Byrant, says of her father, "Mainly he had a fear of creeping socialism. And he worried about inflation. He was ahead of his time about inflation and wrote about it and was advising clients to hedge against it in 1932. He encouraged people to buy art and jewelry."

Buffett's father, widely regarded for his staunch integrity and conservative views—was an early member of the John Birch Society in Nebraska, attracted to the controversial organization because of its fierce opposition to Communism.

Howard Buffett gave an interview to the *Dundee and West Omaha Sun* about why he was a member of the John Birch Society. The article, which ran as the paper's lead story on April 6, 1961, carried the headline, "Why I Joined Birch Society."

The story began, "The John Birch Society, which apparently has had just one member in Nebraska for the past 2½ years, is likely to grow as a result of recent publicity.

"So says the lone acknowledged member, Howard H. Buffett, 2501 N. 53rd, a member of a pioneer family and a former Congressman.

" 'I've had half a dozen people ask me in the past day or so how they could join the society,' Buffett told *The Sun*. 'If my health permits, I plan to seek some new members.' "

Warren Buffett's mother is Leila (Stahl) Buffett, 90, a lively woman with an easy, humorous manner who walked into the Berkshire annual meeting in 1992 and said, "I'm still here." And she was there in later years, too, giving interviews.

Leila Buffett, twice widowed, took back the Buffett name after the death of her second husband, Roy Ralph, because she was married to Congressman Buffett for more than three decades.

She still attends Dundee Presbyterian Church and lives at the Skyline Manor and Villa retirement home in Omaha.

Buffett's parents also had two daughters, Mrs. Doris Bryant, of Morehead City, North Carolina, and Mrs. Roberta Bialek, of Carmel, California.

(Photo by Allan Maxwell)

This is the home where Buffett grew up in Omaha at 2501 North 53rd Street. He and his family once sang "America the Beautiful" in the living room for one of his father's congressional campaigns.

The three children, who all skipped grades in school, grew up in a respectable red brick home in the popular Country Club area of Omaha at 2501 North 53rd Street at the corner of 53rd and Lake Street, after living first at 4224 Barker.

Warren Buffett's roots and heredity gave him a lifelong love of the newspaper industry in which he has moved from delivery boy to Pulitzer Prize winner to mass media owner.

8

"Warren couldn't put a nut on a bolt...

but he could add 20 two-digit numbers in his head."
—Don Danly

Buffett attended Woodrow Wilson High School in Washington D.C. after his father was elected to Congress.

When Buffett was 16, he and a friend, Don Danly, 17, who also was attending Wilson, bought a 1928 Rolls Royce for $350 and rented it out for $35 a day.

Danly, a retired Monsanto director of technology who lives in Pensacola, Florida, recalls that in 1947 he and Buffett went to Baltimore to buy the car.

"We drove it back, but it didn't have a tag. When we got to D.C., we were stopped by the police because we didn't have a tag. Warren pulled rank and said his father was a congressman and we were let go.

"We put the car in Warren's garage. I'd work on it. I was the technical fellow and he was the finance guy. Some have said we worked on the car together, but Warren couldn't put a nut on a bolt or do anything technical. He sat there and read business books to me. He read 100 business books before he left high school. He read other books, too. One was called *How to Lose Friends and Alienate People*.

"Sometimes he'd have me give him about 20 two-digit numbers to add in his head," said Danly, who went on to Cornell. Danly would add the figures with the aid of paper with pencil. "He'd be right," Danly marveled.

Danly was one of 11 students to tie for first in the 1947 class at Woodrow Wilson. He said Buffett was 16th in the class of about 350. "He did that without even trying. I hit the books hard."

Buffett's bio in the 1947 Woodrow Wilson yearbook is a little thin compared with his classmates: "W. Club, Debate Team, Golf Team. A sportsman...basketball and golf: the favorites...likes math...a future stock broker."

The two youngsters rented out the Rolls a few times. Danly still has a photo of the two entrepreneurs standing by the Rolls. Between them in the photo is Danly's girl friend of the time, Norma Jean Thurston (Perma), bearing a resemblance to another Norma Jean. In the photo, Buffett is wearing a coat and tie, the tie stopping about four inches above his belt. "It was rare for Warren to be in a coat and tie," Danly said.

In addition to the Rolls rent-a-car business, the two had other enterprises. "We had a peanut vending machine and a pinball machine business."

Later on Buffett sent Danly a series of letters starting in 1951 telling Danly how he was investing his money for him—about $6,000 Danly inherited after his parents died early. Danly saved Buffett's letters because he thought Buffett was special. "But I didn't know it was going to come to this," he said.

The two have stayed in touch over the years.

"In 1993, on his way to a Coke board meeting, he stopped in for dinner. I reminded him that we had agreed (in our early business ventures) we'd split everything 50/50."

Danly has struggled along very well with a $25,000 investment he made in the Buffett Partnership in 1961.

When Buffett visited them in Pensacola, Danly and his wife, Vera, picked him up and brought him to their home overlooking Mackey Cove. Then they took him to dinner and came back home, all the while talking about the old days and business.

"Then he excused himself and went to the bedroom and made telephone calls for two or three hours. He was on the phone long after we went to bed," Danly said. "He works very hard."

The next day Buffett and the Danlys boarded Buffett's plane, *The Indefensible,* and flew to Atlanta where Buffett arranged a tour of the Coca-Cola Museum for them while he went off to a Coca-Cola board meeting.

Danly said the two have kept up an interest in antique cars and that in the 1980s Buffett made an offer for Harrah's antique car museum in Reno, Nevada, but a price was not agreed upon.

Buffett told Danly that he had seen Norma Jean Perma in 1993. Asked if she still looked good, Buffett told Danly she did: "She looked like her daughter; actually her granddaughter."

Mrs. Perma, of Potomac, Maryland, said Buffett's humor was always there. "He hasn't changed at all since I knew him.

"I was never in the businesses they started, but I was interested in them," she said. "We were like the three musketeers. I'd go with them to pick up the money from the pinball machines. Warren was always picking up the money and Don was always repairing the machines."

"I remember when Warren got going on golf balls. He got them from a golf course. Sometimes, he'd even dive in places to get them. He'd clean them and sell them.

"He told me he'd be a millionaire by the time he was 30 and I believed him."

9

Youth

"I was conceived during the stock market crash."

"I was conceived during the stock market crash" in the fall of 1929, Buffett has said, noting that his father was a stock salesman at the time.

Had his father had enough business to be out making his regular calls at the time, Buffett says there's "no telling what might have happened." (WOWT-TV in Omaha, October 14, 1993)

One of young Warren's first and favorite toys was a metal money changer he strapped around his waist. "He loved it," recalls his older sister, Mrs. Doris Bryant, who describes young Warren as a "typical younger brother."

Like a Good Humor ice cream man, Buffett went around making change. He was fascinated by the process of making change and keeping track of the money. Making math calculations, particularly when it concerned money, was a pastime that absorbed him from his earliest days.

"As a child he was so cautious he walked with his knees bent so he wouldn't have too far to fall, but as an adult he was capable of grand gestures...It was a broad stroke," Mrs. Bryant said, referring to Buffett's purchase of $1 billion of Coke stock.

Young Buffett's first real business venture was in soft drinks, fitting for a fellow who would one day own billions of dollars of Coca-Cola stock. His mother recalls that her son's first appreciation of free enterprise occurred when Buffett was six years old. The escapade involved peddling, yes, Coca-Colas.

"We were at Lake Okoboji in Iowa. Warren paid twenty-five cents for a six-pack of Coke and sold it for five cents a bottle. Warren always had a fascination for numbers in connection with earning money," Mrs. Buffett recalls.

Buffett also bought Coca-Cola from his grandfather's grocery store in Omaha and sold it to neighbors.

By the time he was 10, Buffett's favorite soft drink to sell was Pepsi. As he later explained to Berkshire shareholder Paul Cassidy of North Andover, Massachusetts, "I originally started on the Pepsi because at the time (1940) Pepsi came in 12-ounce bottles and Coke came in 6-ounce bottles, and the price was the same. That was a pretty powerful argument."

Buffett's recall for numbers, an important facility for any businessman, may have come from both parents—his father was a stockbroker and his mother calculates numbers well, too, according to Ed Conine, who lived near Buffett.

Conine, president of J Bragg women's apparel department store chain in Omaha and Lincoln, before his death in 1993, recalled that Mrs. Buffett once told him that when she was in her late 70s, Buffett gave her both an exercise bike and a Cadillac. "I have 34,000 miles on the bike and 5,600 miles on the Cadillac," Mrs. Buffett quipped.

"While most youngsters were content to get sodas out of machines and never give things a further thought, Buffett was retrieving the discarded bottle caps from soda pop machines, sorting and counting them to find out which soda brand was really selling," says Berkshire shareholder Irving Fenster of Tulsa, Oklahoma, one of Buffett's early investors.

Buffett's auditor's instinct—the ability to get at the real numbers, not the supposed numbers passed along by others—remains one of his trademarks.

And he hasn't relied on traditional wisdom. After all, he says, "Traditional wisdom can be long on tradition and short on wisdom."

The precocious youngster was popular, witty, and industrious. But even at Rosehill Elementary School, a kindergarten through eighth grade school in Omaha where Buffett skipped a grade, young Buffett was known more as an "egghead" than as an athlete. In class photos, his hair is unkempt.

"What I had forgotten, but he remembered is that he was out for three weeks with appendicitis. He was very ill and the other students wrote him," recalls Marie Madsen, his second grade teacher.

"He was never a problem or I would have remembered that. He was a good boy. . . He was a good student and kept his nose to the grindstone. I don't remember how good he was in math, but I'm sure he was good. I know he was good in English because he corrected me once. It had to do with a contraction of a word and he was right.

"I remember him standing up in the back of the room looking around. If he was funny, I don't remember it. He may have been with his classmates."

She said her overall impression of him during his years at Rosehill was as a young fellow "who wanted to go off and do something himself."

(Photo by Allan Maxwell)

At Rosehill Elementary School, Buffett daydreamed about stocks. When he was 12 years old, he left— not very willingly— for Washington, D.C., after his father was elected to Congress in 1942.

At Rosehill he picked up the nickname, "Bathless Buffett." It didn't stick long. The name was taken from a "Li'l Abner" character of the time.

That's not to say he didn't get along well with his peers. He did. He mixes so well these days that he sits on the board of directors of Coca-Cola, Salomon and Gillette. But Buffett always has had a private, independent streak.

That streak appeared once when Buffett's father encouraged Warren and his sister, Doris, to spend part of a summer at the Elmer Benne farm near West Point, Nebraska.

(Photo courtesy of Doris Buffett)

Roberta (Bertie), Doris and Warren Buffett in front of a neighbor's home in Washington, D.C.'s Spring Valley area. Photo was taken when Warren was a skinny 13-year-old; Doris was 16 and Bertie 10.

The idea, recalls Mrs. Bryant, was that farm values would be instilled in the children. Buffett knows the lessons of hard work and independence, but apparently he didn't learn them by working behind a plow from dawn to drop; others say hot and heavy labor never interested Buffett.

"I never saw him behind a plow. He was reading a lot of the time," said Mrs. Bryant.

Kathryn Haskell Smith, recalling a story her deceased sister Carolyn Haskell Hallquist told her, said, "He wanted to be around the guys and he would play basketball with them and then while the others were still playing, he'd be over reading the *Wall Street Journal*. The others would just say, 'That's Warren.' He'd play a little basketball with the guys, then go off and read the *Journal* and come back and play with them again.' "

It was Carolyn Haskell whom Buffett often dropped over to see when the Buffett and Haskell families lived a few blocks from one another in the Country Club section of Omaha, an area that had a golf course until about 1926 when the Omaha Country Club moved to a new site in northwest Omaha.

Some evenings the young pair struck up a duet with Buffett on the ukulele and Carolyn on the piano.

One hot summer evening, as young Buffett was strumming along, he remarked, "All we need now is some mint juleps," recalls Kathryn Smith.

Mrs. Smith, wife of Omaha's Homer Smith, a football coach who for some years oversaw the offense at the University of Alabama, and now is at the University of Arizona, knew the Buffett family as a result of a friendship that her father, John Haskell, and Buffett's father formed back in their days at the University of Nebraska. For years Haskell's stockbroker was Howard Buffett.

"He (Warren Buffett) would come over to our house sometimes and talk finances with my father...My father agreed with Warren's father that you should buy good stocks and keep them for a very long time," she said.

"He was always so quick and witty...He was a great guy, lots of fun but it was obvious he was way ahead of us in brains," she said.

Buffett, Mrs. Smith, and other students all walked to school together. Many of Buffett's friends went on to Benson High School where students were known as Benson High School Bunnies.

Even the school sign says: "Benson High School. Home of the Bunnies."

"Benson High School's mascot is the bunny. Hence, we were known

(Photo courtesy of Howard Buffett)

Four generations of Buffetts: Warren Buffett and his mother, Leila Stahl Buffett; his son, Howard Graham Buffett; and his grandson, Howard Warren Buffett, a Coke stock accumulator.

as 'the bunnies.' At the time we didn't think it was funny, but it has been the brunt of many jokes since," said Mrs. Smith.

Buffett himself didn't go to Benson because he moved to Washington, but he still attends the 1947 and 1948 high school class reunions because he has friends in those classes.

Buffett always could keep classmates in stitches with his joke-telling.

"I was aware he wanted to make money. He was very industrious and was always trying to get money to buy stocks, but no one ever dreamed it would come to this," Mrs. Smith said.

Even though young Warren was a math prodigy, his fascination with finance came as a surprise to Buffett's frugal father, who had little interest in amassing money for its own sake. He found his son, whom he hoped would one day join the clergy, spellbound by the power of the dollar.

The Buffetts came from a long line of staunch Republicans, but all the Buffetts have an independent streak. Warren Buffett, largely persuaded that Democrats had a better approach to civil rights matters, shocked his family when he and his wife, Susan, became Democrats. Susan Buffett told *Forbes* (October 21, 1991), "It caused great commotion" [in the family].

Buffett told *Forbes,* October 18, 1993, "I became a Democrat basically because I felt the Democrats were closer by a considerable margin to what I felt in the early 1960s about civil rights. I don't vote the party line. But I probably vote for more Democrats than Republicans."

Congressman Buffett was such a straight arrow and fiscal conservative he once turned a $2,500 annual pay raise (from $10,000 to $12,500) back to the United States Treasury.

Buffett adored his father, who referred to Warren as "Fireball" because of his energy and precociousness.

"Yes, he called him Fireball and Warren called him Pop. They were the best of friends. When he died, Warren cried for days," Mrs. Leila Buffett recalls. Buffett was 33 years old when his father died.

Buffett remains close to his mother and once at the height of the Salomon crisis flew home from New York just in time to be with her when she was honored as Woman of the Year by the Nebraska Chapter of the Arthritis Foundation. Quipped Buffett, "She's been woman of the year for the last 87 years."

While Buffett was still a Rosehill student, he briefly published a racetrack tip sheet, called *Stable-Boy Selections*, about handicapping and betting on horses. He printed the sheets in his parents' basement and sold them for a quarter.

When Buffett was eight years old, he began reading books about the stock market, that his father left around the house.

He continued to be enraptured by the stock market, charting the rise and fall of stock prices. "I was fascinated with anything to do with numbers and money," he has said. (*Los Angeles Times*, Linda Grant, April 7, 1991)

In April, 1942—when Buffett was 11—he began buying stocks in a small way: three shares of Cities Service Preferred, which he bought for $38 a share. That was his net worth at the time.

And he talked his sister, Doris, into doing the same thing.

He recalls that on walks to Rosehill with his sister, "she would remind me I wasn't setting any records." So he sold at $40 a share, making $5 after commissions. A few years later the stock went to $200 a share.

Buffett already had been following the stock market, computing averages, and had begun to realize his views about the markets were more astute than those of others.

He once told *Forbes*, (November 1, 1969), "I'd been interested in the stock market from the time I was 11, when I marked the board here at Harris Upham where my father was a broker. I ran the gamut, stock tips, the Magee charting stuff, everything. Then I picked up Graham's *Security Analysis*. Reading it was like seeing the light."

Buffett, ever the student, took in the early stock investment lessons well; that is, do not be guided by what people say and don't tell fellow investors what you are doing at the time you do it.

The lesson was later reinforced by Ben Graham, his teacher at Columbia Business School, who taught that whether someone else agrees or disagrees with you does not make you right or wrong. That hallmark idea never left Buffett, who in 1965 was writing members of the Buffett Partnership, "We derive no comfort because important people, vocal people, or great numbers of people agree with us. Nor do we derive comfort if they don't. A public opinion poll is no substitute for thought."

Buffett added that when you find a situation you understand, where the facts are ascertainable and clear, then act, whether the action is conventional or unconventional and whether others agree or disagree.

When you are dead sure of something and are armed with all the facts, then everyone else's advice is only confusing and time-consuming. When almost everyone was dismissing the newspaper business as unappealing in the 1970s, Buffett spotted its monopoly-like franchises and bought one media stock after another.

(AP/Wide World Photos)

Ben Graham, the father of value investing and Buffett's teacher at Columbia University. "He was my god," Buffett says.

From his early days Buffett rarely showed his hand until he had to. The practice would take on far greater significance later when Wall Street would try to guess what he was doing. Only rarely did his moves in the market leak out. To this day Buffett tries to keep his investments secret until publication of Berkshire's annual report every March.

Buffett has said it's not easy to keep secrets, especially when talking to attractive members of the opposite sex.

When he was 12, at a time his father was elected to Congress, Buffett lived with his grandfather, Ernest Buffett, for about four months. President of the Rotary Club in Omaha in 1934 and a grocer by trade, Ernest Buffett was working on a book. Each night he dictated a few pages to his grandson.

The title of the book was *How to Run a Grocery Store and a Few Things I Have Learned About Fishing.* Buffett has joked that he was overexposed at an impressionable age to his grandfather's long-winded literary style.

In 1942 Buffett's father was elected to the first of four terms as a congressman on the Republican ticket, and Buffett's days in Omaha were interrupted.

His family moved to Fredericksburg, Virginia, in January, 1943, and although his two sisters were happy, 12-year-old Warren felt uprooted and unhappy. "I didn't like the change at all, so I made a real pain of myself over this move. My grandfather was quite keen on me, and he was back in Omaha. I'd write him and tell him how terrible things were. He finally said, 'You'd better send the boy back here.' " *(Regardie's,* February, 1986)

The next month Buffett returned to Omaha to live with his grandfather and his unmarried aunt, Alice Buffett. He continued to attend Rosehill.

He often had lunch with the Carl Falk family. Carl Falk and Howard Buffett had run the Buffett-Falk brokerage firm. In June, 1943, young Buffett rejoined his family in Fredericksburg, but went back to Omaha for much of the summer, staying at a Presbyterian manse while its minister was away. The Buffett family, including Warren, moved to Washington, D.C., in July, 1943, to 4211 49th Street N.W. near Massachusetts Avenue, not far from the Apex Theater.

Young Buffett, a crewcut lad in those days, went back and forth from Omaha to Washington so much that one retired executive in Omaha recalls that back then Buffett "was like a phantom."

Buffett told L.J. Davis (*New York Times Magazine,* April, 1990) about his days in Fredericksburg, "I was miserably homesick. I told my parents I couldn't breathe. I told them not to worry about it, to get themselves a good night's sleep, and I'd just stand up all night."

When he was 13, Buffett ran away briefly from his Washington, D.C., home. "He ran away with a friend, Roger Bell. I think they were picked up by the police," his sister Doris Bryant recalls.

Buffett's escape had to be a little different and of course business related. He ran away to Hershey, Pennsylvania, enchanted with the idea of touring the Hershey chocolate plant and getting a free candy bar. But he didn't tour the plant and apparently didn't consider buying the company.

Buffett told this story to *Atlanta Constitution* business writer Melissa Turner who asked him if he might sample Hershey stock some day. His reply: "I've driven a car all my life, but I haven't bought any car companies."

Still, Buffett often mentions the attributes of Hershey when he gets going about the concept of consumer "franchises." He explains that consumer franchises or "name brands," as people call them, such as Coca-Cola, Gillette and Wrigley, have extra value. A valuable consumer franchise exists, he says, when people prefer a certain brand name so much they would pay extra, even walk across the street for it because they want it. Even if another chocolate bar is five cents cheaper, one is still likely to choose the Hershey name.

In Washington, Buffett attended Alice Deal Junior High School, where his grades were poor. They improved only when his father threatened to take away his cherished paper routes. (While still 13, Buffett began paying taxes on an income of $1,000 he earned from newspaper routes.)

Still rebellious and looking for his place in the world, Buffett hit once again on his main passion—business.

He undertook a series of financial ventures, including retrieving lost golf balls at a country club in Washington, but his main pursuit was being a newspaper boy.

According to Robert Dorr of the *Omaha World-Herald*, Buffett at one point delivered 500 newspapers on five paper routes, mainly to apartment complexes.

Buffett combined two *Washington Post* routes in the Spring Valley area with two *Times-Herald* routes and later added the Westchester apartments to his routes.

"Thinking he could better use the time to collect from his customers, he developed an effective scheme for selling magazine subscriptions. He would tear the stickers with the expiration date from discarded magazines, file them, and at the right time ask the customer for a renewal," Dorr wrote in a May 29, 1966, story.

Eugene Meyer would later merge the *Post* and *Times-Herald* into a large, successful newspaper. Buffett would one day make an investment in the *Post,* an enormously successful move that vaulted him to the top ranks of investors.

Buffett always remained fascinated by the stock market, recalls Mrs. Bryant. "I never had any doubt. I never knew it would amount to this, but even back then everyone recognized he knew about the stock market."

Even when Buffett was starting his partnership in his bedroom, it did not create a stir in the family. "We took it for granted he knew what he was doing," Mrs. Bryant said.

According to stories by his longtime friend, Carol Loomis, a journalist with *Fortune* magazine since 1954, Buffett as a youngster virtually memorized a book called *A Thousand Ways to Make $1,000,* fantasizing in particular about penny-weighing machines. He pictured himself starting with a single machine, pyramiding his take into thousands more.

The Loomis connection began in the mid-1960s when Carol Loomis's husband, John, a Wall Street money manager with First Manhattan Corp., in New York, went to Omaha to discuss business with Buffett and reported back to his wife, "I think I just met the smartest man in the country."

Buffett was constantly running calculations in his head. In church he calculated the life span of the composers of hymns, checking to see if their religious calling rewarded them with extra longevity. His conclusion: no.

Perhaps that was the reason Buffett settled on being an agnostic.

In Washington, Buffett attended Woodrow Wilson High School, where he was known for always wearing sneakers.

Buffett and his friend Danly began a pinball machine business when they bought a $25 pinball machine they fixed up. They installed it in a barbershop on busy Wisconsin Avenue.

After the first day of operation, the young entrepreneurs returned to find $4. Buffett has said, "I figured I had discovered the wheel."

As other barbers asked for the machines, the youngsters said they would check with their hardnosed boss—"Mr. Wilson," (themselves actually) and wound up installing other machines.

In time, the Wilson Coin-Operated Machine Company expanded to seven machines and was hauling in $50 a week. "I hadn't dreamed life could be so good," Buffett said. (*The Midas Touch*, John Train, p. 5)

He also was pulling in about $175 a month from paper routes. *(Supermoney,* Adam Smith, p. 184)

While Buffett was still in high school in 1945, he was able to save enough money to buy a $1,200 unimproved 40-acre farm in northwestern Nebraska. His father had bought the farm years earlier. Buffett paid his father in cash.

This extraordinary force—a Nebraska special—was on his way. Buffett became so extraordinary he has been called "a five-sigma event," a statistical aberration so rare it practically never occurs. (*Fortune*, Carol Loomis, April 11, 1988)

I once wrote Buffett that my mother, Frances Kilpatrick, taught at Woodrow Wilson High School, the school he attended. Buffett replied:

> ...I went to Woodrow Wilson in 1945-1947. I don't remember a Mrs. Kilpatrick, so she must have been teaching one of the harder courses at the time. My high school career was not particularly illustrious—I was more interested in the pinball machines than in the classroom. Best regards, Sincerely, Warren E. Buffett

(Actually, my mother taught there after he left.)

In school Buffett was neither cool nor a nerd, just a maverick. "I would not have been the most popular guy in the class, but I wouldn't have been the most unpopular either. I was just sort of nothing." *Regardie's,* February, 1986)

During his high school days, he pursued Carolyn Falk of Omaha, but so too did Walter Scott, now head of the Kiewit conglomerate, who married her. "Unfortunately, the best man won," Buffett says. (*Forbes*, October 24, 1994)

If Buffett was still trying to establish himself in high school, he was already something in the business world.

By the time Buffett graduated from high school at 16, in a "chartist" phase in his study of the stock market, he had amassed the extraordinary sum of about $6,000, largely from his paper routes.

Although he could have, he did not pay for college. His parents did, letting Buffett keep his money for investing.

By the end of 1950, he had $9,800. And that's about all the money Buffett has saved in his life. He's made money, yes, but he has not saved money since he was a teenager.

At the urging of his father—and it took some doing to convince Buffett to go to college instead of going on with his business pursuits—he headed for the Wharton School of Business at the University of Pennsylvania. There he was president of the Young Republican's Club and found time to make arrangements to rent an elephant to ride in a Republican victory parade, but Truman upset Dewey and the plans were canceled. He was at Penn from 1947 to 1949 and then transferred in his junior year to the University of Nebraska—Lincoln College of Business Administration, where he earned a B.S. degree in 1950. He breezed through both schools, earning his degree in just three years.

"I didn't feel I was learning that much," he has said of his experience at the University of Pennsylvania.

During college, at Penn and later at the University of Nebraska, where he was regional circulation manager for the *Lincoln Journal*, he found time to work for J.C. Penney. At Penn, he worked at Penney's one summer and during a Christmas vacation. Minimum wage was no way to get rich. The upside, however, was that Buffett saw firsthand how the business worked.

In the summer of 1950, after graduating from the University of Nebraska at age 19, Buffett applied to Harvard Business School.

He took a train to Chicago where a Harvard alumnus interviewed him. Years later Buffett told Carol Loomis all the Harvard representative saw was, "a scrawny 19-year-old who looked 16 and had the social poise of a 12-year-old."

When the interview was over, so were Buffett's prospects at Harvard, and so too was the infallibility of the Harvard admissions office.

"The interview in Chicago took about 10 minutes and they threw me back in the water," Buffett said.

The rejection stung, but it turned out to be for the best because he soon realized that the greatest business professor was teaching at Columbia. Buffett applied to Columbia Business School, was immediately accepted, and graduated in June, 1951.

As a senior at the University of Nebraska in 1950, Buffett had read Benjamin Graham's newly published book, *The Intelligent Investor*, which preached "value investing"—finding companies that are undervalued in the stock market, that is, companies whose intrinsic values are substantially greater than the value the stock market assigns to the enterprise. A value investor tries to buy stocks for substantially less than what the underlying business is worth in the real business world. He wants to buy stocks selling at a discount to the "transactional value" of the business.

Graham thought investors should buy a stock only if it traded at less than two-thirds of its net assets.

It is *The Intelligent Investor* that offers one of Buffett's key business beliefs: "Investment is most intelligent when it is most businesslike." That means investments should not be swayed by emotions—hopes and fears—and fads.

Graham, born in London in 1894 to a Jewish family in the bric-a-brac trade, encouraged investors to pay attention to intrinsic business value—what a reasonable businessman would pay.

Also, an investor should keep in mind a "Margin of Safety," being sure the business you're buying is worth significantly more than you pay for it in the stock market. Only price and value count.

Buffett would become the world's greatest practitioner of value investing.

For Buffett, reading the book was an epiphany. "It was like Paul on the road to Damascus," Buffett told *Omaha World-Herald* reporter Robert Dorr (March 24, 1985).

Buffett has said, "I read the first edition of this book early in 1950, when I was nineteen. I thought then that it was by far the best book about investing ever written. I still think it is."

Graham's *Intelligent Investor* is a popular version of *Security Analysis*, the classic study written by Graham and Columbia Professor David L. Dodd.

"I don't want to sound like a religious fanatic or anything, but it really did get me," Buffett told L.J. Davis. (*New York Times Magazine*, April 2, 1990)

Buffett always has recommended the book as required reading for any successful investor. He has said Chapter 8 about investor attitudes toward an erratic, unpredictable stock market and Chapter 20 on "Margin of Safety" about buying at bargain prices are among the most important pieces of investment advice ever written—that the true investor takes advantage of stock prices when they become silly in either direction and he buys at a good price compared to real business value.

Chapter 8 says when approaching the stock market, you should imagine you're in business with "Mr. Market" but you have to watch him because he lets his enthusiasms and fears run away with him. The chapter says, "Basically price fluctuations have only one significant meaning for the true investor. They provide him with an opportunity to buy wisely when prices fall sharply and to sell wisely when they advance a great deal. At other times he will do better if he forgets about the stock market and pays attention to his dividend returns and to the operating results of his companies."

Chapter 20 talks about "a favorable difference in price on the one hand and indicated or appraised value on the other. That difference is the margin of safety." Therefore, the margin of safety depends on the price paid.

Buffett also recommends the early books by investment guru Philip Fisher as well as *The Money Masters* by John Train.

Buffett's academic record was one of the best ever at Columbia Business School where he earned a masters in economics in June, 1951.

It is said at the time Graham was teaching him, he believed young Buffett would become the greatest financial mind of his time.

Buffett made an A+ under Graham, according to Jim Rogers, who teaches finance at Columbia, and John Burton, former dean of the Columbia Business School. Indeed, it is said that Buffett made the *only* A+ under Ben Graham, but that feat is not documented.

Rogers, born in Demopolis, Alabama, educated at Yale and Oxford, hit Wall Street in the 1970s, hooking up with famed investor George Soros. Their Quantum Fund, which often shorted stocks, assuming prices would fall, did so well Rogers retired at age 37 with a reported $14 million.

Rogers still has a letter of March 5, 1987, from Buffett to Columbia University Graduate School of Business Dean John Burton which reads:

> I appreciate the invitation to the Annual Dinner but will have to decline. My extended trip to New York always occurs in May—and even then I like to skip formal dinners as I find I can do a lot more catching up with friends in four- and six-people lunches and dinners. In fact, I'm not sure I can quite remember the last formal dinner I've attended. I enjoyed the Columbia Business School Annual Report. From everything I hear, Jim Rogers continues to be regarded as the best finance teacher in the country.

Dean Burton said, "He [Buffett] was gifted in math, but his ability to perceive economic value is his genius."

Graham himself had enrolled at Columbia on a scholarship and graduated second in his class in 1914. Graham was the sort of genius who masters a wide variety of intellectual disciplines, and Buffett was his greatest student.

Bill Ruane, a Harvard Business School graduate who became interested in the teachings of Columbia's Ben Graham and David Dodd, took one of Graham's courses and thus became a classmate of Buffett's in 1951. Today Ruane heads the Ruane, Cunniff & Co. investment management firm, runs the Sequoia Fund (which has large investments in Berkshire, Freddie Mac and Salomon stock), and is also a director of The Washington Post Co. and was a director of GEICO until Berkshire bought the rest of GEICO it didn't already own.

Ruane, who has joked that the only difference between himself and Buffett is billions of dollars and 100 points of IQ, says a kind of intellectual electricity coursed between Graham and Buffett and that the rest of the class was a rapt audience.

"Sparks were flying," recalls Ruane. "You could tell then he (Buffett) was someone who was very unusual."

At Columbia, Buffett ran into a friend from Nebraska, Bill Christensen, and discovered the two were dating the same girl. Buffett told Christensen he'd back out of the situation.

(Photo by Laverne Ramsey)

Buffett's friend Bill Christensen.

Christensen, a history professor retired from Midland College in Fremont, Nebraska, laughed, "That girl told me he'd be a millionaire someday." Christensen said the woman married someone else, lives in Colorado and he has kidded her over the years about not marrying Buffett.

After Columbia, Buffett offered to work for Graham's investment company, Graham-Newman & Co. for free "but Ben," Buffett jokes, "made his customary calculation of price to value and said no."

Rejected, Buffett, armed with a Columbia masters degree at age 20, returned to Omaha to work in his father's brokerage firm, Buffett-Falk & Co., as an investment salesman from 1951 to 1954.

He felt his public speaking was inadequate, so he took Dale Carnegie courses when he was 21.

During that time, he also taught a course in investing in the University of Omaha's adult education program. One time he arrived for a course and found only four students; he dismissed the class, saying he was sorry there wasn't enough interest to hold the course. Eventually his class got off the ground. *Omaha World-Herald's* Robert Dorr has written that a student in that course has recalled that class members, whose average age was in the 40s, snickered slightly when they first saw young Buffett. Buffett told Dorr, "I was skinnier then and looked like I could get into a basketball game as a high school student."

The moment Buffett began speaking, the snickering stopped. "After two minutes he had the class in his hands," said the former student.

As always Buffett was investing, but not every venture worked out.

"I guess my worst decision was that I went into a service station when I was 20 or 21. And I lost 20% of my net worth. So that service station's cost me about $800 million now, I guess. It's very satisfying when Berkshire goes down because the cost of that service station mistake declines," he said at the Berkshire annual meeting in 1992.

In those days he devoured financial books. While he worked for his father's brokerage firm, he would go to Nebraska's capital, Lincoln, and read statistical histories of insurance companies. He told *Forbes*, October 18, 1993, "I read from page to page. I didn't read brokers' reports or anything. I just looked at raw data. And I would get all excited about these things. I'd find Kansas City Life at 3 times earnings, Western Insurance Securities at 1 times earnings. I never had enough money and I didn't like to borrow money. So I sold something too soon to buy something else. I was over-stimulated in the early days and I'm under-stimulated now. I bought into an anthracite company. I bought into a windmill company. I bought into a street railway company, or more than one." Buffett bought cheap and found the stocks were cheap for good reasons.

Buffett now calls his efforts at statistically cheap buys his "used cigar butt" approach.

"When you're buying cigar butts, you've got to get rid of them. There aren't lots of puffs in it," Buffett said in a talk to Columbia business students October 27, 1993, as reported in the *Omaha World-Herald*, January 2, 1994. In the same talk, Buffett added:

> When I got out of Columbia the first place I went to work was a five-person brokerage firm with operations in Omaha (Buffett-Falk & Co., which his father founded). It subscribed to *Moody's* industrial manual, banks and finance manual and public utility manual. I went through all those page by page.
>
> I found a little company called Genesee Valley Gas near Rochester [New York]. It had 22,000 shares out. It was a public utility that was earning about $5 per share, and the nice thing about it was, you could buy it at $5 per share.
>
> I found Western Insurance in Fort Scott,

> Kansas. The price range in *Moody's* financial manual...was $12-$20. Earnings $16 a share. I ran an ad in the Fort Scott paper to buy that stock.
>
> I found the Union Street Railway, in New Bedford [Massachusetts], a bus company. At that time it was selling at about $45 and, as I remember, had $120 a share in cash and no liabilities.
>
> Nobody's going to tell you about the Union Street Railway Co...or Genesee Valley Gas. Sometimes the management's buying it themselves. You can't do this for big money, but it's somewhat the same principle. You find something that shouts at you.

Those early days for Buffett were also courting days. On April 19, 1952, he married Susan Thompson of Omaha, a petite brunette with a winning smile and manner, the popular daughter of Dr. William Thompson. "We used to call him 'Wild Bill'," says Buffett's son, Howard. Thompson was a psychology professor as well as dean of the School of Arts and Sciences at the University of Omaha, which later became part of the University of Nebraska. Susan Thompson had been attending Northwestern University where she roomed with Buffett's sister, Bertie.

Mrs. Buffett, always interested in music, pursued her passion in earnest in the mid-1970s after her children were grown, singing blues and jazz. For a time she sang at Omaha's French Cafe and has been quoted by Associated Press writer Kiley Armstrong as saying, "I sing to keep my soul alive."

Music had long been a small part of Buffett's life. At age 11, he sang "America the Beautiful" with his sisters as part of a radio campaign for his father's first successful race for Congress.

The singing took place in the living room of the Buffett home at the corner of 53rd and Lake Streets.

And music may have helped Buffett in winning his wife's hand.

During their college days, Buffett won Susie's attention by playing the ukulele with her father, a mandolin player.

"It was obvious I was not number 1 with her. But he [Susan's father] became very pro-me. It was two against one," Buffett is quoted in the Armstrong story.

"That's true. My father really did court her through her father," says Howard Buffett.

Warren and Susan Buffett, who grew up blocks away from one another, have three children. After the children were grown, Buffett and his wife followed their own paths and have lived apart since 1977. Mrs. Buffett moved to San Francisco and still lives there. She and her husband remain on very close terms. In 1991 she was named to Berkshire's board, replacing Ken Chace of Maine, who retired.

Astrid Menks, a vivacious woman and once a hostess in the same cafe where Buffett's wife sang, has lived with Buffett since 1978, the year after Mrs. Buffett left for San Francisco. Buffett and Astrid Menks live together in the standard sense of the term living together.

"Astrid was not around until after my mother left for San Francisco," said Buffett's daughter, Susan Buffett.

Buffett and his wife see each other about once a month and at Christmas with the family at Laguna Beach. She travels with him on many non-business trips.

"My dad was so involved with his work which is his fun. My mother had a very different life...We have such great parents. They are very affectionate. They still have strong relations. Once the kids were raised, my mother didn't want to sit home," Buffett's daughter said.

Buffett's wife was interested in her musical career and in travel.

Buffett, his wife and Ms. Menks all showed up at a party held for shareholders at Borsheim's, the jewelry store Berkshire owns, the day before the annual meeting in 1990. They were all cordial to one another as usual and have attended the same annual meeting events every year.

Astrid Menks and Buffett are clearly very close. Buffett has given her bejeweled mementos, including a gold piece in the form of a Berkshire stock certificate, and other gifts, some bought at Borsheim's. Astrid Menks has been a Berkshire shareholder for many years.

Buffett has said his arrangement with his wife and Astrid Menks is unusual. "But if you knew everybody well, you'd understand it quite well." *(Regardie's,* February, 1986)

Buffett finally succeeded in getting a job with Graham at Graham-Newman on Wall Street in 1954.

"Between 1951 and 1954, when I was pestering Ben Graham for a job (he turned me down when I got out of school, even though I offered to work for him for nothing), he mentioned me to Bill Rosenwald (son of Julius Rosenwald who developed Sears, Roebuck into a mass merchandiser) with the result that I received an exploratory letter about going to work for the family. I couldn't follow through at the time because National Guard obligations kept me in Omaha. I will never know if Ben was trying to do Bill Rosenwald a favor, or whether he was just trying to get me off his own doorstep." (from letter Buffett wrote July 24, 1985, to Maria

Anagnos, author of "Financial Theory and the Formation of an Investment Empire", a thesis for an MBA degree at New York University Graduate School of Business Administration in 1986.)

Today Buffett gets many requests to work for him, some even offering to pay him their salary. Buffett says, "O.K., fine. I'll even double your salary." (Anagnos thesis)

"When Warren Buffett became a junior employee at Graham-Newman in the 1950s, he made a detailed study of arbitrage earnings from 1926 to 1956—the entire life span of the company. He discovered that

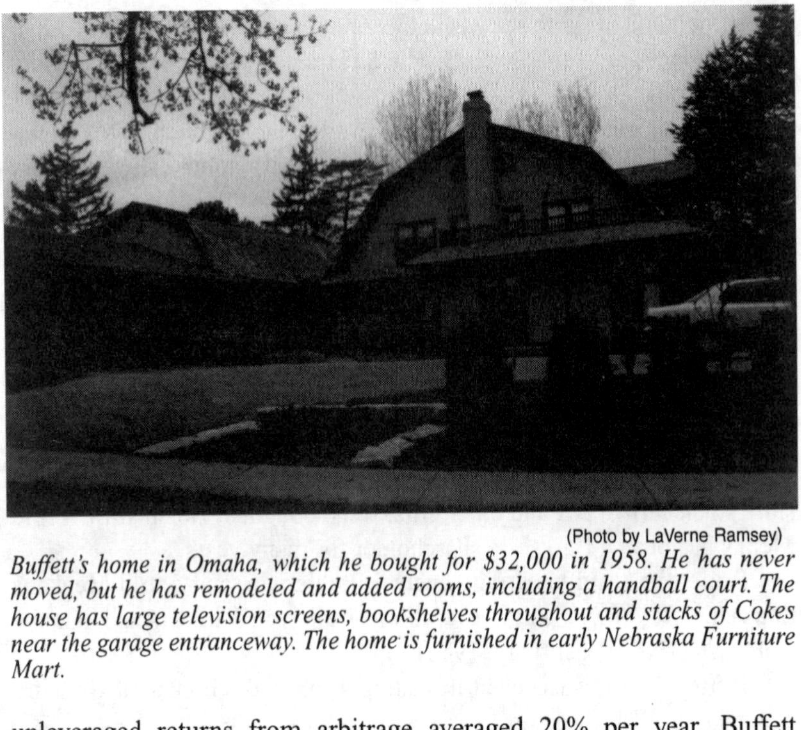

(Photo by LaVerne Ramsey)

Buffett's home in Omaha, which he bought for $32,000 in 1958. He has never moved, but he has remodeled and added rooms, including a handball court. The house has large television screens, bookshelves throughout and stacks of Cokes near the garage entranceway. The home is furnished in early Nebraska Furniture Mart.

unleveraged returns from arbitrage averaged 20% per year. Buffett soaked up the tricks of arbitrage used at Graham-Newman and has used and improved on them ever since." (*Benjamin Graham on Value Investing*, Janet Lowe, p. 75)

Buffett stayed there two years until Graham closed the business in 1956 and retired. During his stay in New York, Buffett taught an education course on the stock market at Scarsdale adult school in 1955. Buffett and his wife, who was pregnant with their second child, rented an apartment in White Plains, New York. Both Graham and his partner, Jerome Newman, died wealthy. Ben Graham died in 1976.

(Photo by Allan Maxwell)
There goes the neighborhood...But with Buffett's investment in a visit from Roto-Rooter, the neighborhood should rebound. This photo, taken by a neighbor of Buffett's, is evidence that even billionaires have problems.

The Graham-Newman firm was small. "It operated with $6 million in capital," Buffett said at Berkshire's annual meeting in 1992.

In addition to Buffett, the Graham-Newman firm hired Walter Schloss, Tom Knapp and Bill Ruane, all of whom became famous value investors.

Irving Kahn, head of Kahn Brothers & Company, Inc. in New York, who worked for Graham for 27 years as an assistant at Columbia and at Graham-Newman, recalls young Buffett at Graham-Newman as Graham's prized protégé.

"He was much the same as he is now but he was a brash, cocky young guy...He was always busy on his own. He has tremendous energy. He could wear you out talking to you. He was very ambitious about making money," said Kahn, adding that Buffett had an extraordinary understanding about how business worked.

Kahn said Buffett's father knew Ben Graham and that both men, seared by the Depression, sought ways to restore old values and to find ways that would ensure price stability.

"Warren's father was at the forefront of the Depression in Omaha, and for farmers he had a deep feeling that the system had broken down...It was a widespread farmbelt feeling. He was also in the securities business. Coming out of the Depression he met Ben Graham in Wash-

(Courtesy of Walter Schloss; photo taken in 1968 at Del Coronado in San Diego)

Ben Graham and his disciples—From left: Warren Buffett, Bob Brustein, deceased friend of Ben Graham's; (Brustein's widow, Hannah, married Alan Pakula, the movie producer) Ben Graham, David "Sandy" Gottesman, Tom Knapp, Charles Munger, Jack Alexander, Henry Brandt, Walter Schloss, Marshall Weinberg, Ed Anderson, Buddy Fox and Bill Ruane.

ington who was a sort of Renaissance man. They talked a lot about tying price stability to commodities and what could be done for lesser developed countries."

In addition to having an eye for business and value investing, Graham also had an eye for willowy blondes. As Buffett said in a *Fortune's* 1988 Investor's Guide interview: "It was all open and everything, but Ben liked women. And women liked him. He wasn't physically attractive—he looked like Edward G. Robinson, but he had style."

During his time with Graham-Newman, young family man Buffett commuted by train from his Westchester County apartment.

"It didn't seem like much of a life," he told Linda Grant. "People kept coming up to me all the time, whispering into my ear about some wonderful business. I was getting excited all the time. I was a wonderful customer for the brokerages. Trouble was, everyone else was, too."

He decided to strike out on his own, never again to have a boss. Along the way, Buffett discovered that he and Graham had somewhat differing views of practical investing.

"Ben was not that interested in going deeply into corporate analysis as I might have been," Buffett told Davis. Buffett, at Berkshire's annual meeting in 1992, said Graham—seeking simple ways for safety for investors—focused on measures of cheapness in selecting stocks. Graham was after such benchmarks as buying stocks for two-thirds of the net working capital of a company.

Buffett began to look beyond only measures of cheapness. "I tried hard to get business insights," he said, adding that he began looking at stocks as businesses and that while he looked for value, as do all investors, he also looked at growth as another part of value.

Berkshire shareholder Michael Assael says, "It's the classic case of Buffett getting two for the price of one. Buffett teaches us that growth is always a component in the calculation of value, constituting a variable whose importance can range from negligible to enormous and whose impact can be negative as well as positive. Just take a look at Coke!"

Buffett ultimately became interested in not only strict value investing, emphasizing a company's balance sheet, but also in the fundamentals of a company, as well as its growth prospects, taking into account its competitive position.

At age 25, Buffett returned to Omaha where he expects to live the rest of his days in the midwestern city 1,100 miles from Wall Street.

Buffett got little encouragement about going into the investment business in 1951 after his days at Columbia. "The two people I respected the most were my dad and Ben Graham and they both said it was a bad time to go into it," Buffett said at the Berkshire annual meeting in 1992.

To begin working at home in his bedroom took courage. Not many young men would make much of an impression if they announced they were going to their bedroom to start a business.

"I first met him when he came home after working for Ben Graham," recalls William O'Connor, the former Mutual of Omaha executive. O'Connor got to know Buffett in investment club circles in Omaha. "I invited him to our investment club. Like most of us he was about our age of 24, but unlike us he was so profound when it came to business and finance. He was so well received we invited him back the next year and each time he played a little penny-ante poker and he left some small sums. He would say it was against his better judgment, but frequently said, 'I'll call.' "

O'Connor took Buffett's 10-week investment course at the University of Omaha, now the University of Nebraska. During breaks Buffett and the students would drink a Pepsi and students soaked up Buffett's investment insights.

"He rarely gave specific advice, but he gave you a lot to think about. He left his students well grounded in the principles of compounding," O'Connor said.

O'Connor sold Buffett an IBM typewriter for the Buffett Partnership in December, 1958. "I installed it at his home. Over the years I sold him an office replacement typewriter and a dictating machine. Perhaps what he got the most use from was the dictating machine I sold to his wife, Susie, who used it for her correspondence with 60 or 70 minority children she helped with college and moral support."

In late 1958 O'Connor sold about $16,000 of his IBM stock and some other small holdings, and on January 1, 1959, invested $18,600 in the Buffett Partnership.

Over the years he added to his holdings, occasionally selling some holdings for family needs.

"My wife, Jean, questioned my judgment" about putting so much with Buffett, but O'Connor told her that if she knew what he knew about Buffett, she'd understand.

O'Connor's faith paid off and he became one of Buffett's many millionaires in Omaha. Good thing—William and Jean O'Connor have 10 children. "Warren really is a very uncomplicated person. He's a super nice guy who just keeps things simple," O'Connor said.

"He is truly a remarkable person. His technical knowledge and his humor are unique. It's truly entertaining to be associated with him...He has an insatiable thirst for knowledge. He reads from all the sources and he has a photographic memory that helps him recall and reconstruct things in an orderly, logical fashion...

"He plays a little tennis and golf, but I think he'd rather read—and play bridge—than anything."

Over the years Buffett has changed little. He reads. He plays bridge.

But above all, despite a wide range of intellectual pursuits, his most consuming passion is business. He has found little reason to change the way he is.

In 1956, at age 25, he was married with two children. His personal fortune stood at $140,000. "I thought it was enough to retire on...I had no master plan," Buffett told reporter L.J. Davis. Before that, in his first year out of college, the net worth of Buffett's investments had soared 144% when he was dealing with about $10,000. He started fast.

In those days, he was approached by family members who wanted investment advice. As a result he founded the Buffett Partnership in 1956 telling investors, "I'll run it like I run my own money, and I'll take part of the losses and part of the profits. And I won't tell you what I'm doing."

Buffett managed the partnership while the other shareholders were limited partners who made none of the decisions.

He pooled $105,100 from friends and relatives to form his partnership. Other than going around town trying to solicit money mainly from doctors, Buffett rang up only a few expenses. The price of the rent was right. Buffett would hold dear his low-cost operating habits always.

He ran the partnership from the sun porch of his house located just off his upstairs bedroom. If ever someone lived over the store—in the store actually—Buffett did in the early days as he began his unmatched career in money management.

The man who would become known as the Wizard of Omaha, the Oracle of Omaha, the Sage of Omaha was on his way.

One day in the summer of 1956 Homer Dodge, a physics professor from Vermont who heard of the wunderkind as a result of being a friend of Ben Graham's, arrived in Omaha after a canoe trip, sought out Buffett and became the first outside partner.

The canoe trip was apparently incidental. Dodge had driven 1,500 miles alone in hopes of persuading 25-year-old Buffett to manage his family's savings. (*Fortune/1990 Investors Guide*)

Recalls Buffett for the *Fortune* piece, "Homer told me, 'I'd like you to handle my money.' I said, 'The only thing I'm doing is a partnership with my family.' He said, 'Well, I'd like one with you.' So I set up one with Homer, his wife, children and grandchildren."

Dodge invested $100,000 for his family in the Buffett Partnership and when Dodge died in 1983, that sum had multiplied into tens of millions of dollars.

Dodge's son Norton has said, "My father saw immediately that Warren was brilliant at financial analysis. But it was more than that."

The elder Dodge saw a uniquely talented craftsman who loved the process of investing and who had mastered all the tools. The same *Fortune* article quoted Berkshire Vice Chairman Charles Munger, "His [Buffett's] brain is a superbly rational mechanism. And since he's articulate, you can see the damn brain working."

In the early to mid-1960s a fellow named Laurence Tisch, later to become chairman of Loews and CBS, sent Buffett a check for $300,000 and a note saying, "Include me in."

Tisch, no slouch as an investor, would later describe Buffett as "the greatest investor of his generation." Adds Michael Assael, "That's an understatement. I think we'll see why in about 10 years."

In those early days some investors signed on with Buffett, but others didn't. John Train wrote (*The Money Masters*, p. 10): "I made the opposite decision when, looking for a good place to park some capital, I first met Buffett. At that very early stage he had no office at all, and ran things from a tiny sitting-room off his bedroom—no secretary, no calculator. When I found that the holdings could not be revealed, I decided not to sign up."

One day Buffett called on his neighbor, Donald Keough, then a Butternut Coffee executive, later president of The Coca-Cola Company and a Washington Post Co. board member. Keough also declined:

"I had five small kids and left for work each day," Keough recalled for a profile of Buffett by Bernice Kanner in *New York* magazine (April 22, 1985): "Buffett had three and stayed home. He had this marvelous hobby, model trains, and my kids used to troop over there and play with them. One day Warren popped over and asked if I'd thought about how I was going to educate these kids...I told him I planned to work hard and see what happened. Warren said if I gave him $5,000 he'd probably do better (for me). My wife and I talked it over, but we figured we didn't know what this guy even did for a living—how could we give him $5,000? We've been kicking ourselves ever since. I mean, if we had given him the dough, we could have owned a college by now."

By the time Buffett was 31 in 1961, he was a millionaire.

"I had a lot better ideas back then than I do now," he's told *Money World's* Adam Smith, whose real name is George J.W. Goodman. Smith took his *nom de plume* from the 18th-century Scottish economist who outlined the mechanics of capitalism.

In 1965, through his Buffett Partnership, Buffett acquired a controlling interest in Berkshire Hathaway, a New Bedford, Massachusetts, textile mill, for about $14 million.

At the time, Berkshire was suffering from a prolonged slide and Buffett bought its unimpressive operations for the proverbial song.

Despite hard work and a new management, the textile operations never paid off.

It would become one of the few businesses that never really made it under Buffett and in 1985, after years of struggling to keep it afloat, he sold it for scrap.

In 1969, Buffett determined that he could no longer find real values—buying a business or part of a business at wide discount to its intrinsic business value—and he decided to dissolve the highly successful partnership.

The partnership—after 13 years of average annual 30% growth—was worth $100 million and Buffett's stake was worth about $20 million.

Buffett, then 38, wrote his limited partners:

> I am out of step with present conditions. When the game is no longer played your way, it is only human to say the new approach is all wrong, bound to lead to trouble, and so on...On one point, however, I am clear. I will not abandon a previous approach whose logic I understand (although I find it difficult to apply) even though it may mean foregoing large, and apparently easy, profits to embrace an approach which I don't fully understand, have not practiced successfully, and which possibly could lead to substantial permanent loss of capital.

He distributed to his investors their stakes in the partnership and their pro rata shares in Berkshire.

John Train wrote a chapter about Buffett in his book, *The Money Masters*. Of the partnership he wrote, "He never had a down year, even in the severe bear markets of 1957, 1962, 1966 and 1969. That achievement stands alone in modern portfolio management."

Three years after the Buffett Partnership was disbanded, the market suffered one of its worst periods in decades, the collapse of 1973-74.

Guess who was buying in 1973? Buffett picked up media and advertising stocks at rock-bottom prices, including $10.6 million in Washington Post Co. shares in the spring and summer of 1973.

10

"I Make No Further Provision For My Son, Warren."

Congressman Howard H. Buffett signed his last will and testament on August 5, 1963, the year before he died. After his death, an inventory of his estate amounted to $563,292.77, of which $334,739.00 was invested in the Buffett Partnership.

The elder Buffett left his entire estate to his family after bequeathing $20,000 to The Nebraska Methodist Hospital, $10,000 to The Immanuel Deaconess Institute and $5,000 to Harding College of Searcy, Arkansas.

He left the rest of his estate to his "Beloved Wife," Leila. He named her as executrix and his son as trustee.

Howard Buffett's instructions were, "Upon the death of my wife and myself, the Trustee shall divide the trust into as many equal shares as there are then living daughters of mine and deceased daughters of mine who have left issue then surviving."

Warren Buffett was to receive nothing, except a few personal effects.

(Photo courtesy of Matt Seto)

Teenage stock-picker Matt Seto: "What I like about him is that he started from nothing."

Congressman Buffett explained why he was leaving nothing to his son: "I make no further provision for my son, Warren, not out of any lack of love for him but because he has a substantial estate in his own right and for the further reason that he has advised me that he does not desire the same and has requested that I not make any further provision for him."

At his death the elder Buffett, in line with the probity of his life, had checking accounts at local banks with a total of about $7,000, about $30,000 in Treasury bonds, a 1961 Buick automobile worth $1,800 and quite a solid stock portfolio with such holdings as 300 shares of DeBeers Consolidated Mines, the diamond company, 300 shares of Dome Petroleum, 200 shares of Handy and Harmon, 500 shares of Kewanee Oil Co. and 100 shares of Weyerhaeuser—all positions reflecting concern about inflation.

He also had some investments in agriculture such as 185 shares of South Omaha Feed & Supply Co., and 208 shares of Government Employees Insurance Co., one of Warren Buffett's favorite stocks.

The latter position and a few others were sold by Mrs. Buffett after her husband's death to be invested elsewhere, according to court documents. What Congressman Buffett started as a compiling of solid wealth, Warren Buffett finished. None of Warren Buffett's wealth was inherited from his father.

"What I like about him is that he started from nothing," said teenage stock picker Matt Seto, from Troy, Michigan, who later was written up in the *Wall Street Journal* and widely interviewed for his prowess in running the Matt Seto Fund.

"So many of the wealthy people you read about started out wealthy. Buffett didn't," Seto said.

11

Buffett Partnership

A $100 investment and a 49-cent ledger from Woolworth's

Flashback to the Buffett Partnership days, the Fabulous Fifties.

To talk to Buffett face to face during the first years, "You went in the back door of his home, walked through the kitchen, the living room and went up the stairs to the bedroom," the *Omaha World-Herald* quoted one partner in a May 5, 1986, story. "If you were impressed with show and image, Warren was not your man."

During the life of the partnership—from 1956 to 1969—average annual returns were 30%, before fees. $10,000 became $300,000.

At the partnership's inception, Buffett had been married for four years and had two small children. He was fresh off a brilliant academic career and a two-year stint on Wall Street. But Buffett, calling on his pioneer spirit and self-reliance of the agrarian Midwest, shunned Wall Street and would forever operate from his beloved Omaha.

At one peak in his career, when Buffett was testifying before Congress about the Salomon scandal, he was introduced to the House Energy and Finance Subcommittee by U.S. Representative Peter Hoagland (D.-Nebraska) who said it was his pleasure to introduce one of his state's most illustrious and inspiring citizens.

Hoagland attributed Buffett's success "to growing up in Omaha, a beginning that instilled in him the old-fashioned values of integrity, discipline and character."

Above all, Omaha is a town where almost everything is dedicated to economic activity. It is the home of such no-nonsense enterprises as Mutual of Omaha, Union Pacific, ConAgra, Woodmen of the World Insurance, a Campbell's Soup plant, Creighton University, a large health care industry and the nearby SAC headquarters.

Born of a substantial family fully involved in the community, blessed with extraordinary mental gifts and operating in a perfect economic soil of capitalism, Buffett arose one morning and entirely on his own founded the Buffett Partnership.

Organized May 5, 1956, when Buffett was 25, the tiny partnership had seven limited partners—four family members and three close friends—who contributed $105,000 but had no voting power, no say in the running of things.

For the history books, according to a certificate of limited partnership filing at the Douglas County Courthouse in Omaha, the following limited partners were the real lottery winners of 1956:

Charles E. Peterson, Jr.	$ 5,000.	(friend, Omaha)
Elizabeth B. Peterson	$25,000.	(Charles' mother, Omaha)
Doris B. Wood	$ 5,000.	(sister)
Truman S. Wood	$ 5,000.	(brother-in-law)
Daniel J. Monen, Jr.	$ 5,000.	(attorney friend, Omaha)
William H. Thompson	$25,000.	(father-in-law)
Alice R. Buffett	$35,000.	(aunt)

General Partner Warren Buffett, listed as residing at 5202 Underwood Avenue where he rented a home, chipped in $100 and so the partnership actually began with $105,100. "Buffett's initial investment for the partnership (not including the $100) was purchase of a 49-cent ledger from Woolworth's." (Maria Anagnos thesis) He would add more of his own money later to the successful enterprise. As manager young Buffett received 25% of the profits above 6% annually with deficiencies carried forward.

"I got the idea for my partnership form because I had worked for Ben. I was inspired by the example. I changed certain things, but it was not original with me. That has never been recognized," Buffett says. (*Benjamin Graham on Value Investing*, Janet Lowe, p. 170)

Over the life of the partnership, the setup made Buffett rich.

Two additional single-family limited partnerships were formed in 1956. By January 1, 1957, combined assets were $303,726.

To seek new money, Buffett called on investors, sometimes approaching them with his tax return asking, "Don't you wish you could pay this much in taxes?"

Buffett approached one Omaha businessman in the early partnership days and asked for a $10,000 investment. The businessman told his wife he wanted to do it, but his wife told him they didn't have $10,000. "We could borrow it," he said. "Like hell," she replied.

Today that businessman's son bemoans that his parents didn't make the investment and missed out on being millionaires, adding: "We've all been working our asses off ever since."

As time passed, some original partners added money and other partners came on board. Later there were other partnerships, amendments to the original partnership really, and at yearend 1961 Buffett merged 10 of his partnerships and changed the name from Buffett Associates to Buffett Partnership.

In 1957, the partnership had recorded a gain of $31,615.97—a 10.4% increase. That may not sound so hot, but when compared to the Dow Jones Industrial Average that slumped 8.4% that year, it was splendid.

Here are the Dow and partnership results in percentage terms as presented in *The Intelligent Investor* (Fourth Revised Edition, 1973):

	Dow	Buffett Partnership
1957	-8.4	10.4
1958	38.5	40.9
1959	20.0	25.9
1960	-6.2	22.8
1961	22.4	45.9
1962	-7.6	13.9
1963	20.6	38.7
1964	18.7	27.8
1965	14.2	47.2
1966	-15.6	20.4
1967	19.0	35.9
1968	7.7	58.8
1969	-11.6	6.8

Buffett, worth about $100,000 when he started the partnership in 1956, was worth about $400,000 by 1959.

(Buffett's net worth ballooned to about $250 million by 1982 when *Forbes* magazine listed Buffett as one of the 400 wealthiest people in America. By 1984 Buffett was worth about $700 million.)

The partnership never failed to beat the Dow. It never had a down year. On average, from 1957 through 1962, while the Dow grew 8.3% a year, the partnership grew 26% a year.

Net assets of the partnership, compiled by Buffett while still under his own roof at home, were $7,178,500!

In November 1962, the partnership, which along the way had invested in windmill makers and anthracite producers, began buying shares of a textile mill, Berkshire Hathaway.

Buffett bought his first shares of Berkshire at a price of $7.60 and kept on buying between $7 and $8 a share. By 1965 he gained financial control of Berkshire and became a director.

From the beginning, Buffett knew his mission was to compound his cash at a hefty, steady clip.

In 1963 Buffett wrote his partners the following epistle about the "Joys of Compounding:":

> I have it from unreliable sources that the cost of the voyage Isabella originally underwrote for Columbus was approximately $30,000....Without attempting to evaluate the psychic income derived from finding a new hemisphere, it must be pointed out that even had squatter's rights prevailed, the whole deal was not exactly another IBM. Figured very roughly, the $30,000 invested at 4% compounded annually would have amounted to something like $2,000,000,000,000 (that's two trillion for those of you who are not government statisticians) by 1962.

He adds, "Historical apologists for the Indians of Manhattan may find refuge in similar calculations. Such fanciful geometric progressions illustrate the value of either living a long time, or compounding your money at a decent rate."

In the same letter Buffett told partners he had moved from an office off his bedroom "to one a bit (quite a bit) more conventional. Surprising as it may seem, the return to a time clock has not been unpleasant. As a matter of fact, I enjoy not keeping track of everything on the backs of envelopes."

Buffett moved the partnership in 1962 to 810 Kiewit Plaza and by then had splurged by hiring his first employee, Bill Scott, who managed Berkshire's bond portfolio until his retirement in 1993.

In 1965 Buffett was telling partners, "If our record is better than that of these (market averages) we consider it a good year whether we are plus or minus. If we do poorer, we deserve the tomatoes."

By 1969 the partnership's assets had grown to $104,429,431.

From the beginning partnership expenses were worrisome. From 1963 to 1969 rent had gone from $3,947 to $5,823. Dues and subscriptions skyrocketed from $900 to $994. "At least the situation hasn't gotten completely out of control," Buffett wrote in his partnership letter of January 22, 1969.

Along the way—in 1963—a Dun and Bradstreet Report dated November 13, 1963, gave approval of the fledgling enterprise: "Volume steady. Condition sound."

The partnership received this one-sentence description of its creditworthiness: "Due to the nature of this business subject is not a general seeker of mercantile credit however maintains a prompt local pay record."

As for its finances, the report found that at the start of 1963, the partnership had a worth of $9.4 million, "consisting of cash resources, income-producing securities and other investments. A sound condition continues. Cash averages a low to moderate six-figure amount in two local depository [sic] with a high six figure amount owing secured and relations satisfactory...Employs one. Location: Rents office space on eighth floor of multi-story brick office building located [in an] outlying business district. Premises orderly."

At that time there were more than 90 limited partners.

In his January 18, 1964, letter, Buffett reports the partnership began the year with assets of $17,454,900. "Susie and I have an investment of $2,393,900 in the Partnership. For the first time, I had to withdraw funds in addition to monthly payments, but it was a choice of this or disappointing the Internal Revenue Service."

Two years later he wrote, "Susie and I have an investment of $6,849,936, which should keep me from slipping away to the movies in the afternoon."

At this time Buffett kept telling of three main investment categories the partnership was engaged in:

1. **"Generals"**—Undervalued stocks generally to be

held for a long time.

2. **"Workouts"**—Securities with a timetable, arbitrage situations arising from sell-outs, mergers, reorganizations and the like.
3. **"Controls"**—Owning such a sizeable block that the partnership gains control of the business.

In the midst of all this Buffett was saying, "We like good management—we like a decent industry—we like a certain amount of 'ferment' in a previously dormant management or stockholder group. But we demand value."

One undervalued investment that started as a "general" in 1956 was Dempster Mill Manufacturing Co., a farm equipment maker. Buffett reported that the stock was selling at $18 a share with about $72 in book value.

One Berkshire shareholder thinks the overall play at Dempster was along these lines: buy the company at a quarter of book value, liquidate a substantial portion of the book value to generate funds for investment, borrow money on the unlevered company for further investment and then spin off the core business.

Buffett continued buying the stock in small quantities for five years. By mid-1961 the partnership owned more than 70% of the company.

Things didn't go particularly well and that's when Buffett called in Harry Bottle, who later became an investor in Berkshire, to run things. Harry still pops up at times to get some operating doldrums moving for Buffett. Two years later the business, later named First Beatrice Corp., was sold.

Because it was the largest employer in Beatrice, Nebraska, the city helped finance the acquisition of Buffett's stake.

By 1965, the partnership's net assets—through contributions and growth—had grown to $26 million from $105,100 ten years earlier.

Buffett celebrated in the spring, renting an additional 227 square feet of space at headquarters, about the size of an ordinary room.

"Our War on Poverty was successful in 1965. Specifically, we were $12,304,060 less poor at the end of the year," began Buffett in his January 20, 1966, letter to partners.

For the year (1965), when the Dow was up 14.2%, the Buffett Partnership orbited the world. A 47.2% return! That was about the time Buffett started saying, "Democracy is great but not in investment decisions."

Although Buffett had told partners his goal was to beat the Dow by

10 percentage points, in reality he was beating it by nearly 20 points. From 1957 through 1965, the Dow rose 11.4%, on average. The partnership returns were 29.8% a year! Goal achieved and surpassed.

"I now feel that we are much closer to the point where increased size may prove disadvantageous," he said.

He would say it almost every year afterwards. He's been saying it for more than a quarter century. Yet average returns have continued coming in at more than 20% a year.

Of Berkshire, Buffett wrote:

> This price ($7.60 a share) partially reflected large losses incurred by the prior management in closing some of the mills made obsolete by changing conditions within the textile business (which the old management had been quite slow to recognize). In the postwar period the company had slid downhill a considerable distance, having hit a peak in 1948 when about $29½ million was earned before tax and about 11,000 workers were employed. This reflected output from 11 mills.
>
> At the time we acquired control in the spring of 1965, Berkshire was down to two mills and about 2,300 employees. It was a very pleasant surprise to find that the remaining units had excellent management personnel, and we have not had to bring a single man from outside into the operation. In relation to our beginning acquisition cost of $7.60 per share (the average cost, however, was $14.86 per share, reflecting very heavy purchases in early 1965), the company on December 31, 1965, had net working capital alone (before placing any value on the plants and equipment) of about $19 a share.
>
> Berkshire is a delight to own. There is no question that the state of the textile industry is the dominant factor in determining the earning power of the business, but we are most fortunate to have Ken Chace running the business in a first-class manner, and we will have several of the best sales people in the business heading up this end of their respective divisions.
>
> While a Berkshire is hardly going to be as prof-

> itable as a Xerox, Fairchild Camera or National Video in a hypertensed market, it is a very comfortable holding. As my West Coast philosopher [Buffett also has called on an East Coast philosopher] says, 'It is well to have a diet consisting of oatmeal as well as cream puffs.'

In a July 12, 1966, letter, Buffett reported that the partnership, with two 10% partners, had purchased all the stock of Hochschild, Kohn & Co., a privately owned Baltimore-based department store chain, for about $5 million.

Buffett's partnership bought 80% of Diversified Retailing Co., and Diversified purchased Hochschild, Kohn for about $12 million.

The chain, which never did well, was sold on December 1, 1969, to Supermarkets General for about the same price.

The partnership continued its astounding success in 1966. In his January 25, 1967, letter Buffett wrote: "The Partnership had its tenth anniversary during 1966. The celebration was appropriate—an all-time record (both past and future) was established for our performance margin relative to the Dow. Our advantage was 36 points which resulted from a plus 20.4% for the Partnership and a minus 15.6% for the Dow."

His January 24, 1968, letter began: "By most standards, we had a good year in 1967. Our overall performance was plus 35.9% compared to plus 19.0% for the Dow, thus surpassing our previous objective of performance ten points superior to the Dow. Our overall gain was $19,384,250 which, even under accelerating inflation, will buy a lot of Pepsi [which in those days he was spiking with cherry syrup]. And due to the sale of some long-standing large positions in marketable securities, we had realized taxable income of $27,376,667, which has nothing to do with 1967 performance but should give you all a feeling of vigorous participation in The Great Society on April 15."

This was also when he reported that through the partnership's two controlled companies, Diversified Retailing and Berkshire, two other companies were acquired—Associated Cotton Shops, later named Associated Retail Stores, and National Indemnity, along with National Fire & Marine, an affiliated company.

Associated was bought by Diversified Retailing and National Indemnity was purchased by Berkshire Hathaway.

"The office group, spouses and children have over $15 million invested in BPL on January 1, 1968, so we have not had a need for NoDoz during business hours."

In his July 11, 1968, letter, Buffett is clearly worried about a speculative blowoff for the market:

> I make no effort to predict the course of general business or the stock market. Period. However, currently, there are practices snowballing in the security markets and business world which, while devoid of short-term predictive value, bother me as to possible long-term consequences.
>
> ...Spectacular amounts of money are being made by those participating (whether as originators, top employees, professional advisors, investment bankers, stock speculators, etc.) in the chain-letter type stock-promotion vogue.

From 1957 through 1968, the Dow's annual compound growth rate was 9.1%; Buffett Partnership's rate was 31.6%. Buffett wrote, "The investment management business, which I used to severely chastise in this section for excessive lethargy, has now swung in many quarters to acute hypertension. One investment manager, representing an organization (with an old established name you would recognize) handling mutual funds aggregating well over $1 billion, said upon launching a new advisory service in 1968:

> The complexities of national and international economics make money management a full-time job. A good money manager cannot maintain a study of securities on a week-by-week or even a day-by-day basis. Securities must be studied in a minute-by-minute program.

"Wow!" wrote Buffett. "This sort of stuff makes me feel guilty when I go out for a Pepsi."

By May 29, 1969, he wrote, "About 18 months ago I wrote to you regarding changed environmental and personal factors causing me to modify our future performance objectives."

He said the investing environment was becoming more negative and frustrating and, further, "I know I don't want to be totally occupied with out-pacing an investment rabbit all my life. The only way to slow down is to stop."

Of course today, in a slightly different business structure, Buffett remains occupied with outrunning that investment rabbit for the best investment carrots.

From 1957 to the end of 1969, the partnership had rung up a 29.5% annual compound return while the Dow had a 7.4% annual return!

Buffett liquidated the partnership and distributed to the investors their profits and their pro rata interest in Berkshire. He gave them a range of options, maintaining proportional interests in Diversified Retailing or in Berkshire. Or the partners could take cash. Also he offered to help investors make bond investments.

He even recommended another money manager, his old friend from Columbia Business School, Bill Ruane, who established the Sequoia Fund on July 15, 1970, to serve limited partners when Buffett Partnership closed.

The successful Sequoia Fund has long invested in some of the same stocks that Berkshire has, such as Salomon and Freddie Mac. About a quarter of Sequoia's money is in Berkshire.

The Buffett Partnership was terminated at the end of 1969 and the market was well into a long tailspin culminating in the collapse of 1973-74. Perhaps Buffett was familiar with Shakespeare's stage direction in *The Winter's Tale*: "Exit, pursued by a bear."

Buffett's caution about conditions and his withdrawal were perfectly timed.

When the partnership closed, Berkshire had 983,582 shares outstanding. Buffett Partnership owned 691,441 of them.

It had grown to about $105 million and Buffett's own stake was worth about $25 million, much of which he quietly invested in Berkshire Hathaway. His interest, managerial and financial, had increased in Berkshire, which in 1969 had bought the Illinois National Bank and Trust of Rockford, Illinois.

Berkshire started business on the 14th floor of Kiewit Plaza on August 1, 1970.

Berkshire then had three main businesses: the textile operation, the insurance operation conducted by National Indemnity and National Fire & Marine, and the Illinois National Bank and Trust. It also owned Sun Newspapers, Inc., Blacker Printing Company and 70% of Gateway Underwriters, but these operations were not financially significant. Berkshire also bought the *Omaha Sun*, along with a string of weeklies in 1969, and sold them in 1981, two years before the *Sun* folded.

In a final letter to partners on February 18, 1970, Buffett thanked his partners—numbering about ninety by then—for giving him a free hand.

"My activity has not been burdened by second-guessing, discussing non sequiturs, or hand holding. You have let me play the game without telling me what club to use, how to grip it, or how much better the other players were doing.

"I've appreciated this, and the results you have achieved have significantly reflected your attitudes and behavior. If you don't feel this is the case, you underestimate the importance of personal encouragement and empathy in maximizing human effort and achievement."

"Herein lies the motivational and management aspects of Buffett's genius," says Michael Assael.

"But Warren Buffett's business and investment genius goes deeper. It now revolves around three elements, and the interplay among them:

1. **Finance**. Buffett understands the "return on investment" concept is paramount. He knows how to get the most bang for Berkshire's buck.
2. **Economics**. Buffett is sensitive to the economic landscape and uses the changing economic environment to Berkshire's advantage. He knows where the world has been. He senses where it is headed.
3. **Management** and the ability to motivate people. Buffett is touched by the importance of human sensitivity, encouragement and empathy in maximizing human achievement.

"Combining these elements makes Buffett unique," Assael continues. "He views the business world in a multi-dimensional way, much as Einstein viewed the solar system, and Freud the human brain and nervous system. The results of Buffett's genius speak for themselves."

As the partnership closed out, a young man with a bizarrely offbeat manner was planning bigger things.

But first here's a look back at two partnership letters:

Warren E. Buffett
5202 Underwood Ave.
Omaha, Nebraska

SECOND ANNUAL LETTER TO LIMITED PARTNERS

The General Stock Market Picture in 1957

In last year's letter to partners, I said the following:

My view of the general market level is that it is priced above intrinsic value. This view relates to blue-chip securities. This view, if accurate, carries with it the possibility of a substantial decline in all stock prices, both undervalued and otherwise. In any event I think the probability is very slight that current market levels will be thought of as cheap five years from now. Even a full-scale bear market, however, should not hurt the market value of our work-outs substantially.

If the general market were to return to an undervalued status our capital might be employed exclusively in general issues and perhaps some borrowed money would be used in this operation at that time. Conversely, if the market should go considerably higher our policy will be to reduce our general issues as profits present themselves and increase the work-out portfolio.

All of the above is not intended to imply that market analysis is foremost in my mind. Primary attention is given at all times to the detection of substantially undervalued securities.

The past year witnessed a moderate decline in stock prices. I stress the word "moderate" since casual reading of the press or conversing with those who have had only recent experience with stocks would tend to create an impression of a much greater decline. Actually, it appears to me that the decline in stock prices has been considerably less than the decline in corporate earning power under present business conditions. This means that the public is still very bullish on blue chip stocks and the general economic picture. I make no attempt to forecast either business or the stock market; the above is simply intended to dispel any notions that stocks have suffered any drastic decline or that the general market is at a low level. I still consider the general market to be priced on the high side based on long term investment value.

Our Activities in 1957

The market decline has created greater opportunity among undervalued situations so that, generally, our portfolio is heavier in undervalued situations relative to work-outs than it was last year. Perhaps an explanation of the term "work-out" is in order. A work-out is an investment which is dependent on a specific corporate action for its profit rather than a general advance in the price of the stock as in the case of undervalued situations. Work-outs come about through sales, mergers, liquidations, tenders, etc. In each case, the risk is that something will upset the applecart and cause the abandonment of the planned action, not that the economic picture will deteriorate and stocks decline generally. At the end of 1956, we had a ratio of about 70-30 between general issues and work-outs. Now it is about 85-15.

During the past year we have taken positions in two situations which have reached a size where we may expect to take some part in corporate decisions. One of these positions accounts for between 10% and 20% of the portfolio of the various partnerships and the other accounts for about 5%. Both of these will probably take in the neighborhood of three to five years of work but they presently appear to have potential for a high average annual rate of return with a minimum of risk. While not in the classification of work-outs, they have very little dependence on the general action of the stock market. Should the general market have a substantial rise, of course, I would expect this section of our portfolio to lag behind the action of the market.

<u>Results for 1957</u>

In 1957 the three partnerships which were formed in 1956 did substantially better than the general market. At the beginning of the year, the Dow-Jones Industrials stood at 499 and at the end of the year it was at 435 for a loss of 64 points. If one had owned the Averages, he would have received 22 points in dividends reducing the overall loss to 42 points or 8.4% for the year. This loss is roughly equivalent to what would have been achieved by investing in most investment funds and, to my knowledge, no investment fund invested in stocks showed a gain for the year.

All three of the 1956 partnerships showed a gain during the year amounting to about 6.2%, 7.8% and 25% on year end 1956 net worth. Naturally, a question is created as to the vastly superior performance of the last partnership, particularly in the minds of the partners of the first two. This performance emphasizes the importance of luck in the short run, particularly in regard to when funds are received. The third partnership was started the latest in 1956 when the market was at a lower level and when several securities were particularly attractive. Because of the availability of funds, large positions were taken in these issues whereas the two partnerships formed earlier already substantially invested so that they could only take relatively small positions in these issues.

Basically, all partnerships are invested in the same securities and in approximately the same percentages. However, particularly during the initial stages, money becomes available at varying times and varying levels of the market so there is more variation in results than is likely to be the case in later years. Over the years, I will be quite satisfied with a performance that is 10% per year better than the Averages, so in respect to these three partnerships, 1957 was a successful, and probably better than average, year.

Two partnerships were started during the middle of 1957 and their results for the balance of the year were roughly the same as the performance of the Averages which were down about 12% for the period since inception of the 1957 partnerships. Their portfolios are now starting to approximate those of the 1956 partnerships and performance of the entire group should be much more comparable in the future.

Interpretation of Results

To some extent our better than average performance in 1957 was due to the fact that it was a generally poor year for most stocks. Our performance, relatively, is likely to be better in a bear market than in a bull market so that deductions made from the above results should be tempered by the fact that it was the type of year when we should have done relatively well. In a year when the general market had a substantial advance I would be well satisfied to match the advance of the Averages.

I can definitely say that our portfolio represents better value at the end of 1957 than it did at the end of 1956. This is due to both generally lower prices and the fact that we have had more time to acquire the more substantially undervalued securities which can only be acquired with patience. Earlier I mentioned our largest position which comprised 10% to 20% of the assets of the various partnerships. In time I plan to have this represent 20% of the assets of all partnerships but this cannot be hurried.

Obviously, during any acquisition period, our primary interest is to have the stock do nothing or decline rather than advance. Therefore, at any given time, a fair proportion of our portfolio may be in the "sterile" stage. This policy, while requiring patience, should maximize long term profits.

I have tried to cover points which I felt might be of interest and disclose as much of our philosophy as may be imparted without talking of individual issues. If there are any questions concerning any phase of the operation, I would welcome hearing from you.

February 6, 1958

Buffett's letter in 1961 said:

<u>The General Stock Market in 1960:</u>

A year ago, I commented on the somewhat faulty picture presented in 1959 by the Dow-Jones Industrial Average which had advanced from 583 to 679, or 16.4%. Although practically all investment companies showed gains for that year, less than 10% of them were able to match or better the record of the Industrial Average. The Dow-Jones Utility Average had a small decline and the Railroad Average recorded a substantial one.

In 1960, the picture was reversed. The Industrial Average declined from 679 to 616, or 9.3%. Adding back the dividends which would have been received through ownership of the Average still left it with an overall loss of 6.3%. On the other hand, the Utility average showed a good gain and while all the results are not now available, my guess is that about 90% of all investment companies out-performed the Industrial Average. The majority of investment companies appear to have ended the year with overall results in the range of plus or minus 5%. On the New York Stock Exchange, 653 common stocks registered losses for the year while 404 showed gains.

<u>Results in 1960:</u>

My continual objective in managing partnership funds is to achieve a long-term performance record superior to that of the Industrial Average. I believe this Average, over a period of years, will more or less parallel the results of leading investment companies. Unless we do achieve this superior performance there is no reason for existence of the partnerships.

However, I have pointed out that any superior record which we might accomplish should not be expected to be evidenced by a relatively constant advantage in performance compared to the Average. Rather it is likely that if such an advantage is achieved, it will be through better-than-average performance in stable or declining markets and average, or perhaps even poorer-than-average performance in rising markets.

I would consider a year in which we declined 15% and the Average 30% to be much superior to a year when both we and the Average advanced 20%. Over a period of time there are going to be good and bad years; there is nothing to be gained by getting enthused or depressed about the sequence in which they occur. The important thing is to be beating par; a four on a par three hole is not as good as a five on a par five hole and it is unrealistic to assume we are not going to have our share of both par three's and par five's.

The above dose of philosophy is being dispensed since we have a number of new partners this year and I want to make sure they understand my objectives, my measure of attainment of these objectives, and some of my known limitations.

With this background it is not unexpected that 1960 was a better-than-average year for us. As contrasted with an overall loss of 5.3% for the Industrial Average, we had a 22.8% gain for the seven partnerships operating throughout the year. Our results for the four complete years of partnership operation after expenses but before interest to limited partners or allocation to the general partner are:

Year	Partnerships Operating Entire Year	Partnership Gain	Dow-Jones Gain
1957	3	10.4%	-8.4%
1958	5	40.9%	38.5%
1959	6	25.9%	19.9%
1960	7	22.8%	-6.3%

It should be emphasized again that these are the net results to the partnership; the net results to the limited partners would depend on the partnership agreement that they had selected.

The overall gain or loss is computed on a market to market

basis. After allowing for any money added or withdrawn, such a method gives results based upon what would have been realized upon liquidation of the partnership at the beginning of the year and what would have been realized upon liquidation gains and losses and is different, of course, from our tax results which value securities at cost and realize gains or losses only when securities are actually sold.

On a compounded basis, the cumulative results have been:

Year	Partnership Gain	Dow-Jones Gain
1957	10.4%	-8.4%
1958	55.6%	26.9%
1959	95.9%	52.2%
1960	140.6%	42.6%

Although four years is entirely too short a period from which to make deductions, what evidence there is points toward confirming the proposition that our results should be relatively better in moderately declining or static markets. To the extent that this is true, it indicates that our portfolio may be more conservatively, although decidedly less conventionally, invested than if we owned "blue-chip" securities. During a strongly rising market for the latter, we might have real difficulty in matching their performance.

Multiplicity of Partnerships:

A preceding table shows that the family is growing. There has been no partnership which has had a consistently superior or inferior record compared to our group average, but there has been some variance each year despite my efforts to keep all partnerships invested in the same securities and about the same proportions. This variation, of course, could be eliminated by combining the present partnerships into one large partnership. Such a move would also eliminate much detail and a moderate amount of expense.

Frankly, I am hopeful of doing something along this line in the next few years. The problem is that various partners have expressed preferences for varying partnership arrangements. Nothing will be done without unanimous consent of partners.

Advance Payments:

Several partners have inquired about adding money during the year to their partnership. Although an exception has been made, it is too difficult to amend partnership agreements during mid-year where we have more than one family represented among the limited partners. Therefore, in mixed partnerships an additional interest can only be acquired at the end of the year.

We do accept advance payments during the year toward a partnership interest and pay interest at 6% on this payment from the time received until the end of the year. At that time, subject to amendment of the agreement by the partners, the payment plus interest is added to the partnership capital and thereafter participates in profits and losses.

Sanborn Map:

Last year mention was made of an investment which accounted for a very high and unusual proportion (35%) of our net assets along with the comment that I had some hope this investment would be concluded in 1960. This hope materialized. The history of an investment of this magnitude may be of interest to you.

Sanborn Map Co. is engaged in the publication and continuous revision of extremely detailed maps of all cities of the United States. For example, the volumes mapping Omaha would weigh perhaps fifty pounds and provide minute details on each structure. The map would be revised by the paste-over method showing new construction, changed occupancy, new fire protection facilities, changed structural materials, etc. These revisions would be done approximately annually and a new map would be published every twenty or thirty years when further paste-overs became impractical. The cost of keeping the map revised to an Omaha customer would run around $100 per year.

This detailed information showing diameter of water mains underlying streets, location of fire hydrants, composition of roof, etc., was primarily of use to fire insurance companies. Their underwriting departments, located in a central office, could evaluate business by agents nationally. The theory was that "a picture was worth a thousand words" and such evaluation would decide whether the risk was properly rated, the degree of conflagration exposure in an area, advisable reinsurance procedure, etc. The bulk of Sanborn's business was done with about thirty insurance companies although maps were also sold to customers outside the insurance industry such as public utilities, mortgage companies, and taxing authorities.

For seventy-five years the business operated in a more or less monopolistic manner with profits realized in every year accompanied by almost complete immunity to recession and lack of need for any sales effort. In the earlier years of the business, the insurance industry became fearful that Sanborn's profits would become too great and placed a number of prominent insurance men on Sanborn's board of directors to act in a watchdog capacity.

In the early 1950s, a competitive method of underwriting known as "carding' made inroads on Sanborn's business and after-tax profits of the map business fell from an average annual level of over $500,000 in the late 1930s to under $100,000 in 1958 and 1959. Considering the upward bias in the economy during this period, this amounted to an almost complete elimination of what had been sizable, stable earning power.

However, during the early 1930s Sanborn had begun to accumulate an investment portfolio. There were no capital requirements to the business so that any retained earnings could be devoted to this project. Over a period of time about $2.5 million was invested, roughly half in bonds and half in stocks. Thus, in the last decade particularly, the investment portfolio blossomed while the operating map business wilted.

Let me give you some idea of the extreme divergence of these two factors. In 1938 when the Dow-Jones Industrial Average was in the 100-120 range, Sanborn sold at $110 per share. In 1958 with the Average in the 550 area, Sanborn sold at $45 per share. Yet during that same period the value of the Sanborn investment portfolio increased from about $20 per share to $65 per share. This means, in effect, that the buyer of Sanborn stock in 1938 was placing a positive valuation of $90 per share on the map business ($110 less the $20 value of the investments unrelated to the map business) in a year of depressed business and stock market conditions. In the tremendously more vigorous climate of 1958 the same map business was evaluated at a minus $20 with the buyer of the stock unwilling to pay more than 70¢ on the dollar for the investment portfolio with the map business thrown in for nothing.

How could this come about? Sanborn in 1958 as well as 1938 possessed a wealth of information of substantial value to the insurance industry. To reproduce the detailed information they had gathered over the years would have cost tens of millions of dollars. Despite "carding," over $500 million of fire premiums were underwritten by "mapping" companies. However, the means of selling and packaging Sanborn's product, information, had remained unchanged throughout the years and finally this inertia was reflected in the earnings.

The very fact that the investment portfolio had done so well served to minimize in the eyes of most directors the need for rejuvenation of the map business. Sanborn had a sales volume of about $2½ million per year and owned about $7 million worth of marketable securities. The income from the investment portfolio was substantial, the business had no possible financial worries, the insurance companies were satisfied with the price paid for maps, and the stockholders still received dividends. However, these dividends were cut five times in eight years although I could never find any record of suggestions pertaining to cutting salaries or director's and committee fees.

Prior to my entry on the Board, of the fourteen directors, nine were prominent men from the insurance industry who combined held 46 shares of stock out of 105,000 shares outstanding. Despite their top positions with very large companies which would suggest the financial wherewithal to make at least a modest commitment, the largest holding in this group was ten shares. In several cases, the insurance companies these men ran owned small blocks of stock but these were token investments in relation to the portfolios in which they were held. For the past decade the insurance companies had been only sellers in any transactions involving Sanborn stock.

The tenth director was the company attorney, who held ten shares. The eleventh was a banker with ten shares who recognized the problems of the company, actively pointed them out, and later added to his holdings. The next two directors were the top officers of Sanborn who owned about 300 shares combined. The officers were capable, aware of the problems of the business, but kept in a subservient role by the Board of Directors. The final member of our cast was a son of a deceased president of Sanborn. The widow owned about 15,000 shares of stock.

In late 1958, the son, unhappy with the trend of the business, demanded the top position in the company, was turned down and submitted his resignation, which was accepted. Shortly thereafter we made a bid to his mother for her block of stock, which was accepted. At the time there were two other large holdings, one of about 10,000 shares (dispersed among customers of a brokerage firm) and one of about 8,000. These people were quite unhappy with the situation and desired a separation of the investment portfolio from the map business, as did we.

Subsequently our holdings (including associates) were increased through open market purchases to about 24,000 shares and the total represented by the three groups increased to 46,000 shares. We hoped to separate the two businesses, realize the fair value of the investment portfolio and work to re-establish the earning power of the map business. There appeared to be a real opportunity to multiply map profits through utilization of Sanborn's wealth of raw material in conjunction with electronic means of converting this data to the most usable form for the customer.

There was considerable opposition on the Board to change of any type, particularly when initiated by an "outsider," although management was in complete accord with our plan and a similar plan had been recommended by Booz, Allen & Hamilton, Management Experts. To avoid a proxy fight (which very probably would not have been forthcoming and which we would have been certain of winning) and to avoid time delay with a large portion of Sanborn's money tied up in blue-chip stocks which I didn't care for at current prices, a plan was evolved taking out all stockholders at fair value who wanted out. The SEC ruled favorably on the fairness of the plan. About 72% of the Sanborn stock, involving 50% of the 1,600 stockholders, was exchanged for portfolio securities at fair value. The map business was left with over $1¼ million in government and municapal bonds as a reserve fund, and a potential corporate capital gains tax of over $1 million was eliminated. The remaining stockholders were left with a slightly improved asset value, substantially higher earnings per share, and an increased dividend rate.

Necessarily, the above little melodrama is a very abbreviated description of this investment operation. However, it does point up the necessity for secrecy regarding our portfolio operations as well as the futility of measuring our results over a short span of time such as a year. Such "control situations" may occur very infrequently. Our bread-and-butter business is buying undervalued securities and selling when the undervaluation is corrected along with investment in "special situations" where the profit is dependent on corporate rather than market action. To the extent that partnership funds continue to grow, it is possible that more opportunities will be available in "control situations."

The auditors should be mailing your financial statement and tax information within about a week. If you have any questions at all regarding either their report or this letter, be sure to let me know.

Warren E. Buffett
1-30-61

12

Cornering the Market

on 1954 Blue Eagle Four-cent Airmail Stamps

Noted value investor Walter Schloss of New York, who became friends with Buffett during Buffett's Columbia days and worked with him under Ben Graham, recalls a time when Buffett tried to corner the market on a Blue Eagle four-cent airmail stamp.

It was after Buffett had left Graham-Newman. Schloss recalled, "He and Tom Knapp got a tremendous stake in a 1954 Blue Eagle airmail stamp with the idea it was going to be a collectible." The stamp was no longer being issued since being taken off the market in the late 1950s.

"I don't know exactly how they did it, but they went to post offices and bought up the stamps. It was a huge number, probably more than 500,000. The stamps were all over the place, some stuck together, etc....It was after Warren had returned to Omaha and he had stamps in his house."

Knapp, a Princeton chemistry major, kept some of the Blue Eagle stamps at the Tweedy, Browne & Knapp brokerage firm he helped found, but the stamp never became a hot item and a lot of the stamps were used as ordinary postage at the brokerage firm. Schloss said he doesn't know what became of all the stamps Buffett had (after a few years Buffett sold them). But he knows what happened to some of the stamps Knapp had.

"I got out of the Army Signal Corps at the end of 1945...In 1960 I was feeling sentimental about my buddies and I decided to write all of them. It was about 140 people. Knapp saw that I had all these letters and he said he had stamps for them," recalled Schloss.

Schloss put the stamps on all his letters and mailed them. Soon, "I got a call from the postmaster asking if I was the guy using airmail stamps on the letters." Schloss said he was, and the postmaster said he wouldn't send the letters because they were airmail stamps for postcards so he couldn't use them.

Finally, the postmaster said he'd mail the letters if Schloss would come to the post office and write "not an airmail letter" on each letter. "I remember the story as if it was yesterday. A 4-cent postcard is now 19 cents and going up," Schloss said. Schloss said he knew back then that Buffett was an unusual person. "I could tell he was brilliant and would be successful, but I never thought he'd be this successful. He's very focused. He's always thinking of the future...He's been like a shooting star."

"There's never been anything like him...The continued growth will be very hard. Maybe he'll merge it [Berkshire] with Canada."

13

Appearance and Style

"He looks like a dressed up farmer."...Sunny disposition

Warren Buffett is a genial, pleasant-looking, rather muscular man with large horn-rimmed glasses.

At 5 feet 11 inches tall, medium build, 190 pounds, he possesses an ordinary body in which God implanted an extraordinarily fine-tuned mind.

Slightly overweight, with a pale complexion, Buffett easily could pass for a clerk, accountant, banker, or the next guy in line at Wal-Mart. Buffett once made a nonspeaking, cameo appearance in 1988 as a bartender in an ABC-TV soap opera, *Loving.*

In 1991 Buffett and his friend, Cap Cities Chairman Thomas Murphy, made a four-minute appearance on ABC's soap opera *All My Children.* Playing themselves, they were beseeched by *femme fatale* Erica Kane (Martin Brent Cudahy Chandler Montgomery Montgomery), played by actress Susan Lucci. She asked the financiers for advice about her cosmetics company. Buffett's recommendation: "Go public."

For their advice, Ms. Kane gave Buffett and Murphy big hugs and Buffett said, "Murph, Erica Kane gives a whole new meaning to the word 'takeover.'"

Buffett would later say of his brief showbiz appearance, "If we run against the test pattern on the other two networks, I expect to do very well." He followed up with flowers to the show's producer and a note saying he wanted to renegotiate his contract.

In 1993 he made another cameo appearance on *All My Children.* A Cap Cities spokesman said Buffett changed the scripted line when he called his office for messages from "Hi, Marie. Any messages?" to use the real name of his assistant, Debbie Bosanek.

During the segment Buffett is approached by the outrageous Opal Cortlandt (Jil Larson) who wants Buffett to finance her husband's company. Buffett, on the phone from ABC headquarters says, "Debbie, don't go anywhere. I may need your help."

After Cortlandt, vamping in a wild hairdo, leaned over the desk, cooing, "Is this kismet, or what?" Buffett put her off first asking if she left her medication behind and finally told her, "Cap Cities is not a lending institution."

At the Berkshire annual meeting in 1992, Buffett said that because of union rules he was paid $300 for his 1991 appearance and given a $10 wardrobe allowance, adding that the allowance was appropriate.

On the wall across from his desk at Berkshire headquarters, there's a small photo of Buffett, Murphy and Susan Lucci, accompanied by documentation of the fees he received.

Showing a visitor the $10 wardrobe fee, Buffett once said, "My daughter thinks that's about what I spend on my wardrobe."

And Berkshire Vice Chairman Charles Munger has said, "Buffett's tailoring has caused a certain amount of amusement in the business world." (*Los Angeles Times Magazine,* April 7, 1991)

"He looks like an old college professor," says Omaha stockbroker Cliff Hayes, who for years executed some of the stock trades—including The Washington Post Co. and GEICO—that were to make Buffett a famous billionaire. "He's often just in casual clothes." "He looks like a dressed up farmer," says one observer.

Someone once said, "I wouldn't recognize him if he walked in with a group of three people, except for the halo over his head." His manner of dress is rumpled. His tie often comes up short, several inches above the belt. His shoes are sometimes scuffed. Coat and tie rarely match. If he has a suit on, it is off-the-rack conservative—few Continental cuts here, thank you, although his family has given him a few.

His hair is not blow-dried or brushed to the last strand. It looks instead as if he ran his hand through his hair in the morning and got on with his day.

Buffett is the first to kid about his appearance, once telling Salomon clients during a telephone conference call that they were in a "preferred position" because they could hear him but not see him.

Buffett's view of clothes corresponds to his view of most things. "There's nothing material I want very much," he has said. *(Esquire,* June, 1988)

But while his material desires are pedestrian, his personality is ablaze, making Johnny Carson seem catatonic. Various people have described Buffett's offbeat, brilliant personality in different ways: "has an almost photographic memory"..."used to read encyclopedias"..."his mind is encyclopedic, has tremendous concentration"..."fast reader"..."has no peer in security analysis."

There must be some downside. Ask people to cite criticisms of Buffett and this is the sort of reply: "He needs help turning on the radio"..."Can barely start a car"..."Wouldn't know if a new piece of furniture or a rug were put in his home"..."I don't think he understands how to use the fax machine." Buffett admits: "I have a little trouble turning on a light switch."

Buffett can be every inch the absent-minded professor—tousled hair, bushy eyebrows, rumpled clothes, serious talk punctuated by a high Midwestern cackle and laugh.

It is when he opens his mouth that people snap to attention with awe because of the crystal clarity, penetration and facile summary he can bring to a complex problem. He is a master communicator and a wonder as both a businessman and an investor.

Buffett speaks to people as if they were as intelligent as he is; he somehow makes the person believe for a moment he is with Buffett in his reasoning. The feeling is conveyed because Buffett is so articulate that most listeners actually do understand what Buffett is talking about—even if it involves complicated business concepts.

One day in 1986 Buffett showed up at Omaha's Red Lion Inn for an interview with *Channels* magazine (November, 1986). West Coast Editor Patricia Bauer reported Buffett was wearing khakis and a jacket and a tie. "I dressed up for you," he said, smiling sheepishly.

Although the *Wall Street Journal* once reported he wears $1,500 Italian suits, that is true only on rare occasions.

As his daughter, Susan, says, "My mother was in town one day and said, 'Let's get him a new suit.'...We were so sick of looking at those clothes that he's had for 30 years."

"So we bought him a camel-hair blazer and a blue blazer, just to get some new ones. And he had me return them. He said, 'I have a camel-hair blazer and a blue blazer,' and he was serious. I sent them back.

"Finally I went out, unbeknownst to him, and picked out a suit. I didn't even look at the price tag. I looked for something that would be comfortable and conservative looking. He won't wear anything that isn't extremely conservative.

"And he tried it on. It was comfortable. He didn't even look at the price tag. The suit was very boring and conservative, and he bought a few of them.

"Now he's getting criticized, and it makes me furious because I'm the one to blame for that."

Susan added, "He'll wear clothes until they are threadbare."

Of course, virtually no one could care whether Buffett wears a tux or a swimsuit to work.

Occasionally, Buffett buys a suit that's somewhere between off the rack and custom made, requiring some slight alterations.

One Berkshire shareholder, who says he talked with a tailor who has fitted Buffett, once asked why Buffett's suits always looked so ill-fitted. The Omaha tailor replied, "He's the hardest guy in the world to fit. Basically he has no butt."

A cowlick, and an unruly thatch of thinning hair that seem to fly around, stand atop a round, open, owlish face that somehow says, "I am from the Midwest," and that often has an eager, quizzical look. His head is somewhat egg shaped, dotted with hazel eyes that need the help of thick bifocals, hooked around ears reminiscent of Lyndon Johnson.

His gait is loping. In his eagerness to get where he's going, he seems to overstep slightly what would be a normal stride, looking a bit ungainly as if he were trying to step across a room in one less stride than normal.

The forehead is high above rather wild, bushy eyebrows. His mouth is large, the smile wrinkles are deep and an impish grin comes easily. His face is usually animated, but can become positively grim at the bridge table where he concentrates so hard.

He has a fast, dry wit, a sunny disposition and folksy manner; he comes across as a mix between Jack Benny and Will Rogers.

When he speaks, his talk comes in a rapid, fully-edited form in a Midwestern twang delivered in total intellectual honesty.

He has great energy and a zest for life.

In the manner of a wise teacher searching restlessly for the truth, he seems to be trying with all his heart to pass on to others his homespun wisdom about how to cope in an imperfect world that features an imperfect stock market. Buffett teaches that the true investor swings at the misappraised stock price, the one that offers great value, as if it were the perfect pitch. As Buffett has said, you wait as long as it takes for the right pitch and when it's "two inches above the navel," you swing for the fences.

Like all great teachers, he remains an eager student. The reasons for his success are his common sense, his own genius, and his lifelong intense study of his area of greatest interest—business. It's as though Buffett has two brains, one of which is always thinking about business. It never sleeps. The other brain works on public policy questions, talks with friends and plays bridge and golf.

But his immersion in business has done nothing to hamper a great sense of fun and sophisticated sense of humor, whether it be needling himself, Wall Street, or general human conduct.

A large worry line runs straight down his forehead just to the left of center. One would guess it's the result of intense study over the years, of reading the *Wall Street Journal*, *Value Line* and *Moody's,* the mainline business magazines such as *Forbes, Fortune* and *Business Week* as well as trade publications such as *American Banker* and annual reports by the hundreds. Buffett is a subscriber to Henry Emerson's *Outstanding Investor Digest*, joking that reading it is a good way to keep up with what Munger, Berkshire's number two man, is doing.

Buffett is an avid reader of a huge range of annual reports, who wants the reports mailed directly to him and not through the slow bureaucracy of brokerage firm mailings that often take several weeks longer. And he tells shareholders to do the same, to have at least one Berkshire share registered in one's own name.

His aw-shucks attitude is genuine and his manner is open and straightforward. Most often it is described as folksy, corn-fed, homespun.

Once a Peter Kiewit & Sons, Inc. pilot, who flies the Berkshire plane, called Buffett's office to inquire if Buffett needed lunch reservations anywhere. Buffett's administrative assistant at the time, Gladys Kaiser, said not to bother, that Buffett wouldn't need a thing.

"He arrived with his mother and a picnic lunch when he came to the airport," says Omaha stockbroker George Morgan. (It so happens Morgan works for the Omaha brokerage firm of Kirkpatrick, Pettis. Buffett's father, Howard Homan Buffett, was with the Buffett & Falk brokerage firm founded in 1931 that merged into the Kirkpatrick firm in 1957.)

For lunch Buffett often has popcorn, potato chips and Cherry Coke. He munches Cracker Jack at ball games. The menu has not impressed his doctors, but they declare him healthy. Lately Buffett has taken up walking on a treadmill and he is cutting back a little on the junk food.

One Sunday in the mid-1980s, Buffett found himself unable to pay a small bill.

"He was in his grubbies having a malt and chips or something, and I realized there was some problem in paying the bill," recalls Virginia Lee Pratt, a retired schoolteacher in Omaha who is a longtime bridge playing friend of Buffett's mother.

"I said, 'Warren, could I help?' and he said, 'This is pretty embarrassing.' "

The bill at Goodrich Dairy was $3.49 and Buffett was unable to pay, he said, because he had given his children his small bills and had only a $100 bill on him that the little dairy shop couldn't change. Pratt stepped in and paid the bill.

"He sent a check the next day with a letter saying that since he had established credit could he up his line of credit to five dollars," she said.

She said she was so honored to have a check signed by Buffett that she didn't cash it and wrote him that he should check his books because he'd be off by the amount of the bill. (No one would cash Picasso's checks either.)

"At our next bridge game, his mother brought me $3.50 in cash," Pratt said.

Buffett is conscientious about paying his bills, but he also wants full payment when he's on the receiving end, even to the point of taking advantage of coupons.

Once Buffett was having dinner at the French Cafe. Before dinner Buffett had presented a coupon for $3.95 off the dinner to the waiter, Chris Nisi. "I want this to show up on the check," Nisi recalls Buffett telling him. "When the bill came, he checked it over and found it was there. He had kidded about it all along. He was half kidding, but he was half serious, too."

Using coupons is not a one-time event for the Wizard of Omaha. In 1990, at a time when Berkshire's stock price was heading south, Buffett showed up at Bronco's, a hamburger drive-in in central Omaha. He presented a coupon and said, "This [stock dip] isn't going to stop me from buying lunch here, is it?"

A waitress at Ross's steak house (across from the Nebraska Furniture Mart) where Buffett often has dinner with the Blumkin family that runs the mart, recalls serving Buffett in early 1993.

"He was through dinner and the check had come and he wanted a Shirley Temple. He said just run a new tab and I did. It was for $1.50 and he forgot to pay it. The joke around here is that I had to buy Warren Buffett a drink," she laughed.

Taxicab drivers and waiters say Buffett tips adequately, but not generously.

For all his folksy ways, it's the high and mighty who seek his advice. Back in 1984 when the Getty family was embroiled in complex merger talks, Ann Getty flew to Omaha to seek Buffett's counsel.

Buffett's easy manner and down-home ways mask a highly sophisticated man. Occasionally he does put on a black tie as he did to escort The Washington Post Co.'s Katharine Graham to her 70th birthday party. He has had dinner with Ronald and Nancy Reagan and been seated next to both Barbara Bush and Jane Muskie at a dinner party. He has been to small, private dinners with President Bill Clinton at the White House.

But he does not try to make every social occasion and in September, 1993, declined an invitation from Mrs. Graham for dinner with President Clinton on Martha's Vineyard. (*Forbes*, October 18, 1993)

However he showed up at Martha's Vineyard August 27, 1994, for a golf game with Clinton. "I can give you a scoop," he told the (*Omaha World Herald,* August 29, 1994). "The president had a 39 on the front nine with a couple of birdies." Buffett said he played only the front nine with Clinton, who finished the 18 with Microsoft's Bill Gates. "The president finished with an 83," Buffett said. "He played better with me than he did with Gates."

Buffett has popped up at fancy watering holes such as Lyford Cay. He showed up at the 1988 Winter Olympics in Calgary, Alberta, where Agnes Nixon, creator of "All My Children" talked him into his first soap opera appearance.

On March 16, 1993, Buffett showed up at New York's "21" for a celebrity-studded party for the opening of the TV version of *Barbarians at the Gate*, the story of the RJR Nabisco takeover.

James Garner, who played RJR Chairman Ross Johnson in the movie, was there along with Lauren Bacall, Robert and Georgette Mosbacher and Carl Icahn. Oreo cookies and caviar were served.

And a photo of him pops up in the book *Lilly* which is about playwright Lillian Hellman of Martha's Vineyard. There's Buffett, in sneakers, slacks, golf shirt and white hat, standing on a dock, with Lillian Hellman, Barbara Hersey (wife of writer John Hersey), and author William Styron.

In July, 1993, Buffett showed up in Sun Valley, Idaho, for an investment conference hosted by investment banker Herbert Allen. Among the participants were Gerald Levin, chairman of Time Warner, Sumner Redstone and Frank Biondi of Viacom International, H. Wayne Huizenga of Blockbuster Entertainment, Michael Ovitz of Creative Artists Agency and now Disney; Tom Pollock of Universal Pictures, Jeffrey Katzenberg of Disney, Robert Wright of NBC, John Malone of Tele-Communications, Inc., (the nation's largest cable operator), and Barry Diller of QVC. There were also top officers of Coca-Cola, McDonald's, Fidelity Investments and J.P. Morgan as well. (*New York Times*, August 15, 1993) In September, 1995, he took a trip to Ireland, went on a train trip in China with Microsoft Chairman Bill Gates and showed up in Switzerland for a Coca-Cola board meeting.

Buffett, no hayseed, can talk for hours about business, politics, literature or public policy.

In an article for the *Washington Post* September 14, 1993, he wrote that one way to keep the federal deficit under control was to pass an amendment making legislators ineligible for re-election if during any year they served the deficit is more than 3% of GDP.

Despite his kidding about how little he knows about technology, particularly computers, he has spent hours at a time swapping stories with Bill Gates. *Washington Post* editorial page editor Meg Greenfield introduced the fellow billionaires July 5, 1991. The two have attended Nebraska-Washington football games together and they spent a week together in Bermuda with other business leaders in the fall of 1993 in connection with a reunion of "The Buffett Group," a close circle of his friends that meets every two years to discuss world affairs. Buffett, who has visited Microsoft several times, has encouraged Gates to study Ben Graham.

Gates was once asked *(Forbes ASAP*, December, 1992): "Who's your favorite CEO outside Microsoft?"

Gates replied: "Warren Buffett. The guy thinks. I love people who just think. The conventional wisdom, they don't fall into it."

Buffett, who calls Gates and himself "the odd couple," returned a compliment in a *Fortune* story December 29, 1992, about Gates, saying, "I'm not competent to judge his technical ability, but I regard his busi-

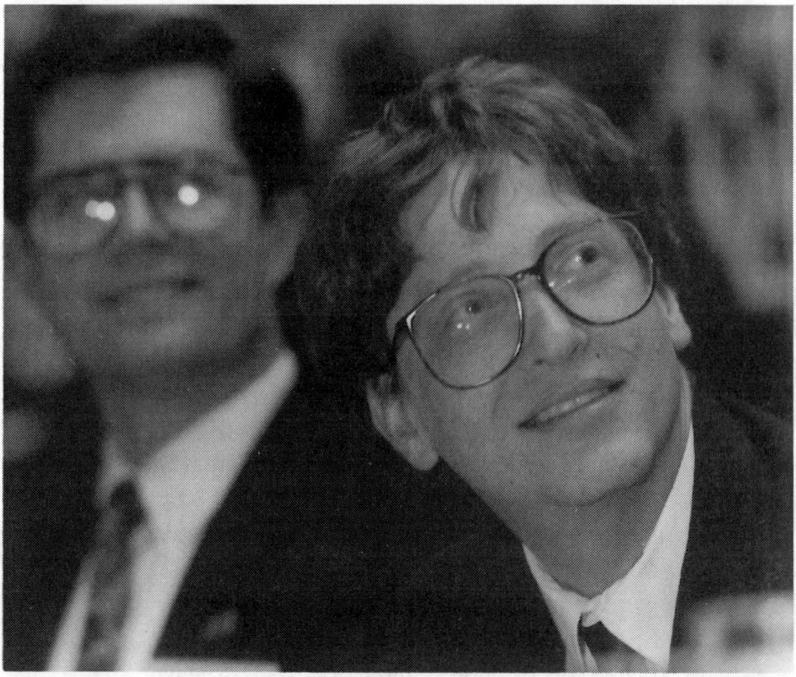

(AP/Wide World Photos)

Microsoft Chairman Bill Gates. Buffett of Gates: "He may be the smartest guy I ever met." Gates of Buffett: "Favorite CEO...he thinks."

ness savvy as extraordinary. If Bill had started a hot dog stand, he would have become the hot dog king of the world. He will win in any game. He would be very good at my business, but I wouldn't be at his."

Buffett told *Forbes* (October 18, 1993), "Bill Gates is a good friend, and I think he may be the smartest guy I've ever met. But I don't know what those little things [computers] do." "I bought 100 shares of Microsoft personally [not for Berkshire] the day I met him to get the reports," Buffett said at Berkshire's annual meeting in 1995. But Buffett said that doesn't mean Berkshire and Microsoft will be doing business with one another. Buffett said he doesn't understand software companies.

Gates has said he wrote his book, *The Road Ahead,* with a bit of the non-technical Buffett in mind as his audience:

> Warren Buffett, who's famous for his investment savvy, is a good friend of mine. For years I kept trying to think of how to induce him to use a personal computer. I even offered to fly out and get him started. He wasn't interested until he found he could play bridge

> with friends all over the country through an online services. For the first six months he would come home and play for hours on end. Despite the fact that he had studiously stayed away from technology and technology investing, once he tried the computer, he was hooked. Now, many weeks, Warren uses online services more than I do. (p. 207-8)

Buffett means it when he says he's no expert in the computer business. Early in his career he passed up an offer from a relative to buy into fledgling Control Data, the large computer firm in Minneapolis. *(Regardie's,* February, 1986)

At a *Fortune* seminar in Palm Springs in the spring of 1995, Carol Loomis surprised a breakfast gathering by introducing Buffett and Gates, saying: "One of these men is the richest man in America and the other is second." (*Fortune*, May 1, 1995)

Gates, in an article he wrote about his friendship with Buffett for *Harvard Business Review*, January-February, 1996, said:

> We recently vacationed in China with our wives. I think his jokes are funny. I think his dietary practices - lots of burgers and Cokes - are excellent. In short, I'm a fan...
>
> When you are with Warren, you can tell how much he loves his work. It comes across in many ways. When he explains stuff, it's never, 'Hey, I'm smart about this and I'm going to impress you.' It's more the 'This is so interesting and it's actually very simple. I'll just explain it to you and you'll realize how dumb it was that it took me a long time to figure it out.
>
> We are quite candid and not at all adversarial. Our business interests don't overlap much, although his printed *World Book Encyclopedia* competes with my Microsoft *Encarta.* Warren stays away from technology companies because he likes investments in which he can predict winners a decade in advance—an almost impossible feat when it comes to technology...

In his early days Buffett served on some civic boards, furthering the cause of organizations like Planned Parenthood or the local Boys Club—but he has so many self-imposed demands on his time that he doesn't do a lot in the way of civic or charity functions, and there is some grumbling about that in Omaha. But he has certainly made substantial contributions to the local United Way, education generally and a little to AIDS education, specifically.

The main focus of his charity efforts is toward reproductive freedom (pro-choice). His efforts for civic and charity causes may be just beginning. After all, he is leaving his fortune to the Buffett Foundation which will give it back to society.

Some have described him as almost reclusive.

"He's not comfortable around people he doesn't know. He's even a little shy. He doesn't like parties...He would be happy in a one-room apartment with his *Wall Street Journal*, his TV and a Pepsi [now Coke]," said his daughter, Susan. *(Register,* February, 1984) One of Buffett's pals who attended a New Year's party with him in the early 1980s has said Buffett spent the bulk of the party off in a corner, killing time until he could leave. Neighbors rarely see him. He is not much of a yardman and doesn't tend his well-tended yard himself. Instead he spends time indoors reading or attending board meetings related to Berkshire's far-flung empire. At his office, very few people drop in—maybe two or three people a week will get a short audience—and they do not include stockbrokers or analysts.

But he has an extraordinarily wide range of friends with whom he stays in contact by phone and letter. He occasionally lectures at colleges such as Columbia, Stanford, Harvard, Notre Dame, Vanderbilt and Creighton University in Omaha. Dartmouth's Amos Tuck School induced him to speak in May, 1993, for the dedication of the business school's Byrne Hall in honor of his longtime friend, Jack Byrne, a top figure in the insurance world who once headed GEICO and now heads Fund American Enterprises.

Buffett almost never goes on television and rarely grants an interview. However, he's gregarious around friends. He hoards a good portion of his time for reading and studying. Although some people have described him as shy, he can talk up a storm and dominate conversations.

And if he is shy, it does not mean he doesn't have confidence in his own abilities. After all, he has said he has known all along, even as a youngster, that he would be rich. Anyone starting an investment partnership in his own bedroom has to have confidence and ignore those pushing him to get a real job.

Buffett is not physically imposing, yet when he starts talking people stop to listen to his every word. His commanding personality is a reflection of his electrifying intellectual powers. In person, Buffett is totally unpretentious, though well aware he is a folk hero and that Wall Street—

and others in the room—watch his every move.

"I watch my every move and I'm not that impressed," he quips.

Even where his fame might be obvious, sometimes it is not. *Who's Who in America* carries just a brief mention of him, describing him as a "corporate executive," the equivalent of saying Barry Bonds plays baseball. The *World Almanac* (1994, p. 317) does list Buffett among "noted personalities" but misspells his name!

In person, Buffett, though he doesn't particularly care for small talk, is open, accessible, forthright and cheerful.

"He's like talking to a neighbor," says Ronald K. Richey, chairman of Torchmark, an insurance and financial services company in Birmingham, in which Berkshire has a small investment—about $10 million. By Berkshire's standards, that's small.

"He called up one day and said he'd like to meet with us," Richey recalls. Richey, who was in Torchmark's New York office at the time, said he'd be glad to meet with Buffett wherever he liked, including Omaha.

Buffett, in New York at the time, said, "Oh, no, I know where you are. I'll just walk over."

Richey said a short time later Buffett walked in, basically told him and Jon Rotenstreich, then Torchmark's president, that he was not a threat to the company, just an investor, and left.

Herbert Sklenar, president of Birmingham's Vulcan Materials, the nation's foremost producer of crushed stone, grew up on a farm near Omaha, attended Benson High School and is among those who see Buffett at class reunions. "He (Buffett) was the second person I ran into at the reunion in 1988," Sklenar recalls.

During the reunion attendees were asked to update their lives and Sklenar said he was with a company "that makes big stones into little stones."

Buffett himself got up before the group and offered a little witty investment advice.

Sklenar, who went to Harvard and has hefty experience on the financial side of corporations, admits he'd want to think twice about any possible business proposition with Buffett. "He's just so darn smart," Sklenar said.

Buffett's style is to tackle problems his intellectual brilliance can solve but to steer clear of problems it cannot. Often he has said he's trying to step over one-foot obstacles, not jump over seven-foot obstacles. He strives to make things as easy as possible by seeking sensible, efficient ways of doing things, making the layups he talks about. There are no high-percentage shots from half court. He works hard at the possible and avoids the impossible. One of his great messages is to avoid trouble. In the stock market, that means staying away from capital losses. Ben Franklin-like, Buffett is generally early to bed and early to rise although his sleep hours do vary.

He watches television about seven hours a week, keeping abreast mainly of news and sports. He is a statistics nut and his recall of baseball batting averages and trivia is nearly encyclopedic. However, his baseball interest was most intense in high school.

Whether watching baseball games or not, you can bet his eyeballs would rather be glued to ABC-TV than to any other channel because of his large stake in Cap Cities.

Whatever he's doing, it's with self-confidence. "I've never had any self-doubt. I have never been discouraged," he says. (*U.S. News & World Report*, June 20, 1994)

An occasional trace of ego slips through. L.J. Davis wrote in a *New York Times Magazine* story (April 2, 1990) that Buffett has no calculators, no Quotrons, and no computers in his office. "I am a computer," Buffett flatly told Davis.

For better or worse, a lot of Berkshire's records are kept in Buffett's head. Once John Hillery, a Canadian investment advisor, wrote Buffett for a breakdown of Berkshire's bond portfolio—what was taxable, tax free, which bonds were convertible and what the maturities were.

Buffett replied in a letter December 15, 1980: "We may be able to put something in the reports, such as you suggest, relating to bond types and maturities. We get very little in the way of formal reports, and most of that sort of information is in my head rather than in any computer printout. But I may try to give some general impressions if I have a section on bond investments again this year."

Buffett's small office is located in Omaha's Kiewit Plaza, a modest building, far less imposing than the nearby headquarters of Mutual of Omaha, whose annual returns are in turn less imposing than Berkshire's. For a haircut, Buffett goes down to the basement to the Kiewit Plaza Barber Shop where he is described as "a regular man." Berkshire's headquarters have been expanded and upgraded so everything's roomier—but still under 4,000 square feet. Headquarters has been described as "linoleum floors and throw rugs." That's a slight exaggeration, but it is far from some deeply white-carpeted corner office with mahogany paneling. On the outside of the door is a sign saying, "No admittance except by appointment."

Russ Fletcher, now with CAT Limited, a reinsurance firm in Bermuda, had an appointment one day in the mid-1980s to see Berkshire's Michael Goldberg. Fletcher arrived for his appointment set for a Saturday morning. "I walked in and he (Buffett) was behind his secretary's desk opening the mail," Fletcher recalls. "He was dressed in blue jeans and a turtleneck...He said 'Hi' and we exchanged pleasantries...He's very unassuming."

Another fellow who got into the inner sanctum once in 1988 was Michael O'Brien of Austin, Texas. "I was there to shoot a picture of him for *Esquire*...I asked him about the crash, if that made him fearful. He said no, that if the market had dropped another 500 points, he'd really have found bargains."

Inside headquarters there is a mini-conference room and places for about a dozen people to operate.

Berkshire does have other locations for its team of accountants responsible for insurance subsidiaries, and a data processing building elsewhere in Omaha to track the insurance operation's complex finances, but Berkshire's operations are lean beyond belief.

Buffett runs Berkshire's empire from a rather small desk near the corner of his office strewn with newspapers such as the *Wall Street Journal* and the *Omaha World-Herald* and magazines. The desk, at times, sports notepads that read, "In case of nuclear war, disregard this message."

He has other notepads as well. Buffett once sent me a photo of Coca-Cola's President Don Keough (now chairman of Allen & Co.). A number of Berkshire shareholders had their picture taken with Keough at the Berkshire annual meeting in 1991. Coke folks sent Buffett the photos and he forwarded them to shareholders. Mine came with a little Post-it note saying he thought I'd enjoy the photo. It was signed in his usual way with a large W, a legible "a" and a sort of loop representing two r's, but definitely signed "Warren."

What was unusual about the note was the inscription at the bottom, which read:

"An absolutely brilliant memo"—*NY Times*

"Clear...concise...to the point"—*Fortune*

"Masterful use of the language"—*Atlantic*

Visitors to his pale emerald-green office in the building owned by privately held construction conglomerate Peter Kiewit Sons', Inc., are greeted by a small porcelain plaque given him by his wife. The inscription, hanging just inside the door of his headquarters, reads, "A fool and his money are soon invited everywhere."

Mementos of the stock market abound, such as the crash of 1929. Scattered about are miniature sculptures of bulls and bears. On the walls are stock quotations from the crash, a portrait of Buffett's father and a photo of Ben Graham. There is a Pulitzer Prize for the exposé of Boys Town by his now defunct *Omaha Sun* newspapers.

His desk is neither clear nor messy. "It's in between," says Dr. Ronald W. Roskens, former president of the University of Nebraska, who has occasionally called on Buffett at his office about civic or charitable missions. "It's what makes sense...He's trying to keep things simple." "There's a sofa here, his desk is over there. It's not a dump but it's not ornate either," he added.

His tiny staff of a dozen people for years included his administrative assistant, Gladys Kaiser, with him from December, 1967, when she walked in as a "temporary" Kelly Girl. She retired in 1993, replaced by Debbie Bosanek. Mrs. Kaiser still has lunch with Buffett every month or so.

Of her he once said, "Things just wouldn't quite work around here without her...I wish her immortality. If Gladys can't have it, I'm not sure I want it either." *(Fortune,* April 11, 1988)

One of the few people working close to Buffett is Michael Goldberg, an intense, hard-driving man who long headed Berkshire's disparate, far-flung nationwide insurance operations, and remains a vice president. "He's so damn smart and quick that people who are around him all the time feel a constant mental pressure trying to keep up. You'd need a strong ego to survive in headquarters," Goldberg has told Buffett's friend and chronicler, Carol Loomis of *Fortune* magazine.

Goldberg, who attended Columbia, Northwestern and Stanford Business School and who came to Berkshire as a young man who was already a top executive with the Pacific Stock Exchange, told Loomis, "I've had a chance to see someone who can't be believed. The negative is: How do you ever think much of your abilities after being around Warren Buffett?"

Goldberg later told Linda Grant (*Los Angeles Times,* April 7, 1991): "Warren Buffett is a person who, the closer he gets, the more extraordinary he gets. If you tell people about him, the way he is, they just think you were bamboozled."

Precisely. A lot of things about Buffett and Berkshire are so unbelievable—such as its five-digit stock price—that at first people are skeptical.

Buffett's one acknowledgement of modern technology is a bank of two telephones that connect him with different brokerage firms when the need arises. Berkshire has gone high tech and has a fax machine.

Buffett roams around the five-room suite of offices at Kiewit Plaza getting his own Cherry Cokes, pulling his own files from the office storeroom. He doesn't mind if someone brings him a hamburger for lunch so he can stay and answer the telephone. Not all calls to Buffett are about billion-dollar deals. "Sometimes it's a wrong number," Buffett has joked.

And sometimes it's a request for an annual report. "I called Berkshire in 1988 because I didn't get my annual report. I cannot prove this in a court of law, but I'm 99% sure I got him...He had a clipped, fast voice. He said 'That's awful' that I didn't get the report," recalls Dr. Wallace Gaye, a Berkshire shareholder who lives in Durham, New Hampshire.

Dr. Gaye, a former medical school teacher, left the medical world, in part, to track the ticker tape and his Berkshire shares.

"I started to ask if he was Warren Buffett, but I just couldn't...He was fast. He said something like he'd fix it. Two days later I got the report," Gaye said.

Gilman Gunn, of Wellesley, Massachusetts, who in the late 1970s sold securities for Mabon Nugent, once called Buffett, got him on the phone and tried to sell him some Doubleday publishing stock, 600 shares of the stock which was trading at $13,000 a share.

"He said send the information and that he'd take a look. I called him a few days later and he said he had reviewed it and decided, 'It wasn't cheap enough for us,' " said Gunn, surprised Buffett took his calls.

Other folks have encountered Buffett's quick responses. As his fame has grown, well-meaning people have besieged Buffett with investment advice. But only rarely does he want it. Once a large Berkshire shareholder, Ernie Williams of Village of Golf, Florida, called him, excited about an investment publication he wanted to share with Buffett. Buffett's reply: "Please don't send it."

Buffett is basically a homebody, preferring to stick close to his own office and home and counsel. But he also has to travel, as he serves on so many corporate boards, and occasionally he manages to get away to his second home in Laguna Beach, California.

There is rarely any pomposity or any moodiness in this multi-billionaire. People who have known him for years say they have never seen him angry. His response to things is not anger, but rationality. His reply to things that are okay with him usually is: "Yeah, sure." If something displeases him, his reply can be, "We don't need any of that."

He responds to the world by examining it thoroughly and in a positive and witty way. He often delivers self-deprecating humor as in "Your chairman has blundered again," or offers stories about how he studied the soft drink industry for more than 50 years and eventually determined that the industry's two main rivals, Coca-Cola and Pepsi-Cola, both have done well.

Those who have worked with him describe him as almost unfailingly upbeat and supportive, practically never testy. He works very hard, long hours. "He's thinking about three things at a time. He's thinking about it [Berkshire] 24 hours a day," says an employee of a Berkshire subsidiary. And yet he says his work is not work, but fun. Fun to Buffett is studying the world of business through voracious reading. His health has always been good although he suffers somewhat from a back problem, the result of playing handball years ago. It has forced him to cut back his tennis.

Buffett, a member of Augusta National, site of The Masters, has played some golf over the years. He has a 22 handicap. Those who have played with him describe his game as so-so, but they say he is very competitive, improving as the round progresses and most likely to come through in the clutch, say, when things are tied up on the 18th.

His style in golf is to save his two mulligans for the last two holes, says a golfing partner.

Bob Hancock, head of Robert Hancock Investments in Omaha, once asked Buffett how he'd play Augusta and Buffett said, "I'd tee it up and hit it directly into the water."

Once a fellow asked Buffett how he had managed to shoot a round of 108. Buffett replied: "I three putted 18."

Buffett seems practically oblivious to temptation—living a modest lifestyle marked by few parties, no cigarettes, and very little drink other than the Cherry Cokes he craves. Buffett carries no moral outrage about smoking or drinking. He just doesn't find much point to either.

He shuns fancy restaurants, settling on Gorat's steakhouse with its "Go Big Red" signs (that's only one notch below a "Go, God, Go" cheer) or Ross's steak house in Omaha for a dinner of steak and potatoes. Linda Grant described his eating habits this way: "He orders Cherry Coke for his aperitif and consumes steaks and thick, juicy hamburgers with no regard for the current cholesterol phobia. Heavily salting his T-bone one recent evening at Gorat's Steakhouse, his favorite Omaha hangout, Buffett said, 'You know how our life span depends on how long your parents live? Well, I watch my mother's exercise and diet very carefully. She has 40,000 miles on her bike.' Chuckling, he dives into sides of hash browns and spaghetti."

One Friday evening in January, 1993, Buffett attended a function for the powers that be of Omaha's Emmy Gifford Children's Theater. Everyone except Buffett had a Greek buffet. He had a cheeseburger, fries and a Coke.

Buffett just says no to all drugs except one: caffeine. The man is fairly wired on the stuff. To satisfy his caffeine habit, bolstered by a desire to give wings to Coke stock, Buffett constantly drinks Cokes and has an occasional piece of See's candy.

Over the years a slight paunch has developed in his middle, but it's one that might be attached to someone 15 years younger. He admits his diet and exercise habits are not all they should be. Once at the height of the Salomon crisis, Buffett called his friend James Burke, the former chairman of Johnson & Johnson. Buffett said he was having trouble sleeping and asked Burke for help. When Burke said he ran three to five miles a day during Johnson & Johnson's Tylenol crisis, Buffett hesitated and then said, "Any other suggestions?" (*Wall Street Journal*, November 14, 1991)

Even so, Buffett is the picture of health and is enormously energetic.

His house is fixed up these days into a perfectly respectable home, with a well-kept yard, surrounding trees and a roomy driveway. Over the years he has furnished the home largely with items from Omaha's Nebraska Furniture Mart, a business he bought in 1983. In short, his nice, rambling home—with a 40 by 20-foot handball court and exercise equipment in the basement—is a pleasant addition to the quiet, tree-lined neighborhood. Ostentatious it is not.

Harvey Lipsman of Omaha recalls that his son, Rocky, used to visit the Buffett home to see Buffett's son, Howard. Their talk was often about girls, not money. Later in life Rocky—realizing Warren Buffett's success—got him to sign a book. Warren Buffett wrote: "Rocky, you should have talked to me instead of Howie."

Once Washington Post Co. Chairman Katharine Graham visited Buffett's modest home and joked, "Warren, is this all you can afford?"

The home is plainly furnished and has only a few luxuries such as 30-inch, 40-inch and 50-inch television screens, according to Nebraska Furniture Mart salesman Doug Clayton, who sold him two of the big screens.

His home is full of books, including a shelf of Bertrand Russell tomes from which Buffett can quote long passages. He admires the writings of British economist (and investor) John Maynard Keynes. Buffett

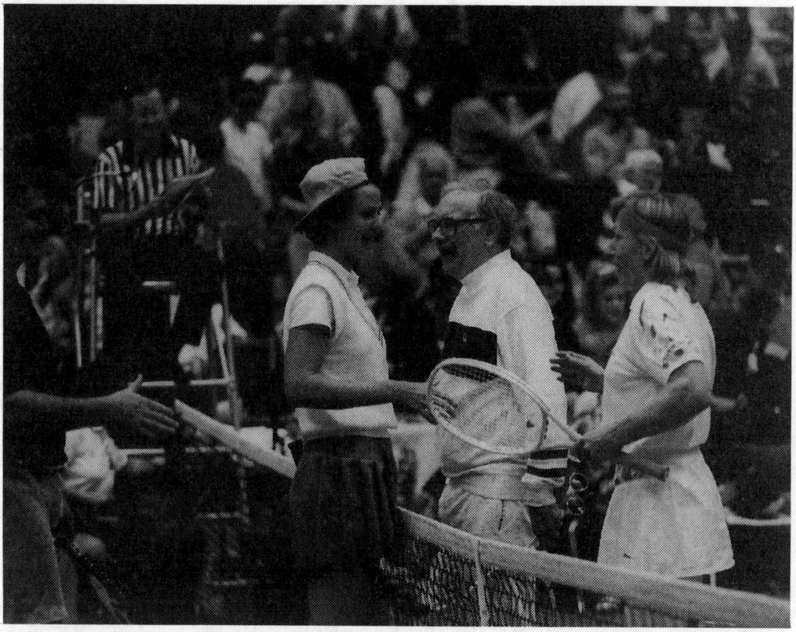

(*Omaha World-Herald*)

Buffett, who invested little in his game for a celebrity tennis match in Omaha in 1992, plays here with tennis champions Pam Shriver and Martina Navratilova and former NFL quarterback Danny White. Buffett said his preparation for the match was to learn to say, "yours" in Czech to Navratilova. Even that didn't work because Miss Shriver and White won the match on a one-point tie-breaker.

particularly likes biographies. He has read such books as *Father, Son and Company, McDonald's, Behind the Arches, The Big Story, Influence, Bonfire of the Vanities, Liar's Poker, Den of Thieves* and *Barbarians at the Gate*. "He's read all the usual books but they are usually financially related," said his daughter, Susan.

(For investors he says required reading includes the chapters about "Margin of Safety" and about investor's attitutes towards the market in *The Intelligent Investor*, the 1934 edition of *Security Analysis*, *The Money Masters* and investor Phil Fisher's first two books. At the Berkshire annual meeting in 1994 he stressed reading John Maynard Keynes.)

From his house, Buffett can nose down Farnam Street in less than five minutes to his spartan office. Another several minutes away is downtown Omaha, should he need to go that far. One of his mantras is that it's much easier to stay out of trouble now than to get out of trouble later. Along with keeping things simple, he wants to keep distractions to a minimum and to be consistent. If you can live close to the office, do. If the

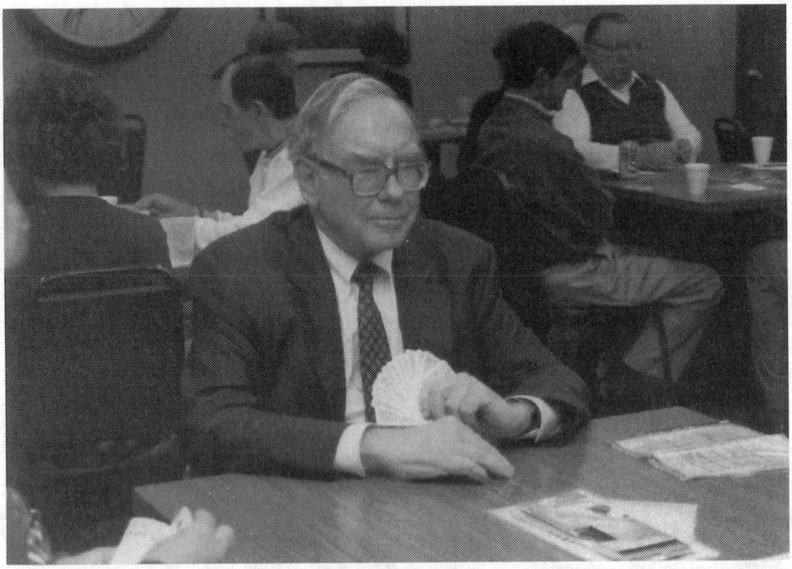

(Photo by Nancy Line Jacobs)

The Oracle of Omaha, whose idea of downtime is an intense game of duplicate bridge, plays here at the Omaha Bridge Studio in November, 1993. A can of Coke, another fraction of a penny to Berkshire's bottom line, is on the floor.

restaurant serves a hamburger or steak you like, why search out a diner across town?

One Wall Streeter, Marshall Weinberg, a stockbroker with Gruntal & Co., recalled going to the old Ruben's restaurant in New York for a meal with Buffett.

"He had an exceptional ham-and-cheese sandwich. A few days later, we were going out again. He said, 'Let's go back to that restaurant.' I said, 'But we were just there.' 'Precisely. Why take the risk with another place? We know exactly what we're going to get.' "

One of Buffett's tenets is don't run all around without a good reason. You can do most of what you need to do right where you are. "I'll be in Omaha as long as I live," Buffett has told Berkshire shareholders.

Another lesson is to do things yourself. He drove himself to the Berkshire annual meeting in 1989, parking his car around back of the Joslyn Art Museum. Just before he got in to drive away after the meeting, a Berkshire shareholder came up to him with a thick pile of papers and asked him if he would look at them. He said he would and she asked if she should mail them to him.

"Oh, no. I'll just take them and read them back at the office." He took the papers, got in his 1983 dark blue Cadillac and no doubt drove back to the office and read the papers.

It was not until 1991 that Buffett actually bought himself a new car, a Lincoln Town Car four-door sedan. "I think he's getting a little mellower," said Omaha stockbroker George Morgan of the purchase. When filling up, Buffett uses the self-serve pump.

(Buffett owns a Lincoln Town Car because it has dual air bags. After GM CEO Jack Smith pointed out a Cadillac has air bags for the passenger, the driver and a person in the middle, Buffett told Smith his next car will be a Cadillac.) *(Fortune,* May 2, 1994)

In earlier years, Buffett, already wealthy, picked up friends in a Volkswagen. One Berkshire shareholder recalls a time in the early days when he visited Buffett in Omaha. "He picked us up in a Volkswagen and was sort of apologetic about it," the visitor said. Buffett later bought the Cadillac, not for prestige reasons, but because he thought it was safer.

In addition to tennis, golf, and handball, Buffett's hobbies include Scrabble, but his particular passion is for bridge—played at times with a deck of cards inscribed, "Make checks payable to Warren Buffett." Bridge, he is fond of saying, is better than a cocktail party.

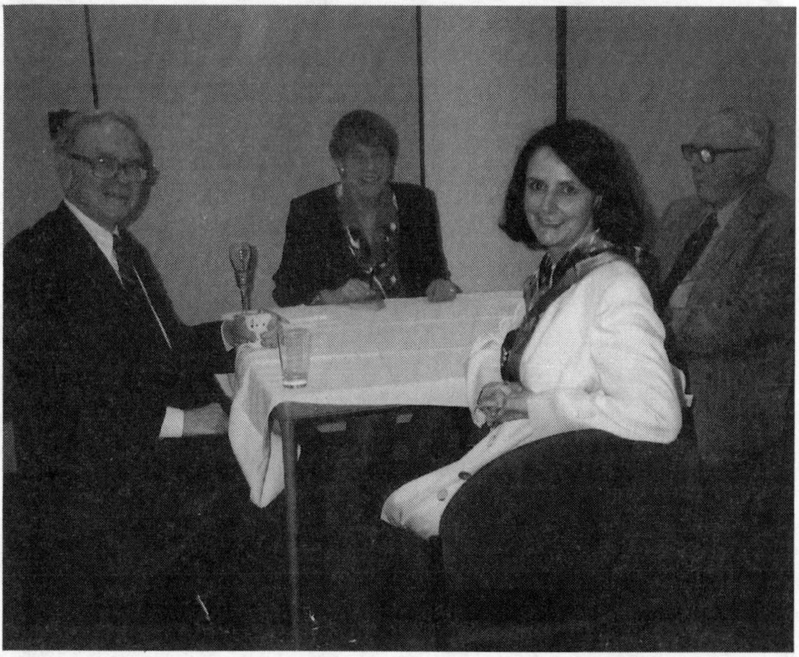

(Photo by Nancy Line Jacobs)

Buffett, Carol Loomis, Sharon Osberg and Charles Munger settle in for a bridge game the day before Berkshire's annual meeting in 1996.

"I always say I wouldn't mind going to jail if I had three cellmates who played bridge," says Buffett, whose bridge partners have ranged from Peter Lynch to George Burns. The ageless Burns played Buffett (and Munger and others) at a table reserved for Burns at the Hillcrest Country Club in Los Angeles under a sign that reads, "No Cigar Smoking if Under 95." Burns, an excellent bridge player, and his team beat Buffett's.

In 1993 Buffett was captain of a corporate team that for three years topped a team from Congress in bridge matches.

Buffett likes to play bridge with Sharon Osberg of San Francisco, twice a member of the world's women's championship team.

Ms. Osberg, a senior vice president at Wells Fargo Bank said, "I met him about three years ago at a celebrity bridge tournament through Carol Loomis." Later Ms. Osberg gently tried to convince Buffett to play computer bridge. Finally Buffett agreed.

"We bought a computer at the Nebraska Furniture Mart, of course, and set it up in his home. We play a couple of times a week in the evenings. He really loves it."

Ms. Osberg, who acts as Buffett's bridge teacher, says his game has improved to the point of being a world class player. "We played in the World Championship recently. We had to drop out because he had a business emergency, but we made it to the finals. He is moving toward holding his own at the world level. He can play with anyone. It's because of his logic, his ability to solve problems and his concentration." Ms. Osberg through her friendship with Buffett has played with Bill Gates, Katharine Graham and U.S. Supreme Court Justice Sandra Day O'Connor.

"The most intense game I've ever played was a six hour game with Bill Gates. We played Buffett and Munger. We lost $28. Warren named the stake of ½ cent a point. I thought Charlie would pass out. [from the ½ cent stake]

At festivities connected with Berkshire's 1996 annual meeting, Osberg and Loomis played Buffett and Munger. "We won," said Osberg proudly.

Buffett's handle for computer games is: "T-Bone."

Buffett has since become so entranced by the computer he's now regularly surfing the Internet, Ms. Osberg said, adding he sends and receives E-mail messages and looks up corporate filings.

Often Buffett plays bridge with his sister, Bertie, or with William H. Gates, Sr., the Seattle attorney and father of Microsoft's founder. And he occasionally plays bridge with his Omaha friends. One is Richard Holland, a retired advertising executive who says, "Warren's an excellent bridge player. If he had time to play enough, he'd be one of the best in the country." (Omaha World-Herald, October 30, 1993)

Perhaps there is a link between the intuitive abilities common to great bridge players and great security analysts as they both try to figure probabilities. They trust their decisions relating to intangible factors. And they always are being dealt new hands.

Buffett concentrates hard when he works or plays bridge. Once Nancy Line Jacobs of Omaha asked if she could take his picture playing bridge, hoping it wouldn't distract him. Buffett replied, "It won't distract me, but I'll pretend it will."

Afterwards Mrs. Jacobs sent him some photos to sign with a note that she had "crashed" the previous annual meeting as a member of the press, though she didn't write an article, but was now a Berkshire shareholder and would be at the next meeting in an honest way. "He even returned my pen," Mrs. Jacobs said.

Buffett signed a photo for her, "To Nancy, Finally, an honest woman." For a photo for Omaha stockbroker George Morgan, who says his net worth is no different from Buffett's except for some zeros, Buffett wrote, "To George, Here's to more 0's." To me he wrote, "To Andy, You have treated me better than I deserve—thank God!"

Instead of drinking and dancing at some big city disco, he takes an interest in his family, gets some exercise and stays in touch with friends.

When he is in New York, he often stays at Katharine Graham's apartment and usually calls on John and Carol Loomis and George Gillespie, III. Gillespie, a close friend, is a partner in the Cravath, Swaine & Moore law firm in New York which does Buffett's estate planning and has advised The Buffett Foundation. Gillespie is a large Washington Post Co. shareholder and a supporter of the fight against Muscular Dystrophy.

The foursome passes the evening playing bridge and eating peanuts, ice cream and deli sandwiches—Buffett's idea of a big night in the Big Apple.

Buffett has no aides, no advance team. When he was already the richest person in the country, he once arrived at National Airport in Washington, D.C., walked up to the corporate jet counter and asked: "How do I get a taxi?"

There are no airs. His shoes are scuffed, the watch is a Timex and the pen is a Bic. Buffett does his own taxes, saying they are really quite simple. He's even kept all his tax returns since 1944. Buffett is anything but simple, though his tastes are. And things at Berkshire seem and are simple. But the reality of what's been built, which Buffett has created with a unique combination of simplicity and genius, is something to behold.

14

Dusty Sundae Recipe

"My ideas about food and diet were irrevocably formed quite early."

Here's Warren Buffett's idea of a good meal, found in a recipe he provided for William D. Orr's First Gentleman's Cookbook (p. 178):

My ideas about food and diet were irrevocably formed quite early—the product of a wildly successful party that celebrated my fifth birthday. On that occasion we had hot dogs, hamburgers, soft drinks, popcorn and ice cream.

I found complete gastronomical fulfillment in this array and have seen no reason subsequently to expand my horizons. In fact, I am thought to be so expert in this specialized area of food preparation that I am often called upon to act as a consultant for pre-puberty dinner parties. The loudest applause at such affairs is invariably rendered when I sculpt my Dusty Sundae.

This sophisticated-sounding delicacy is really quite simple in preparation: First pour generous quantities of Hershey's Chocolate Syrup over vanilla ice cream, and then build a mountain of malted milk powder atop the chocolate.

The caloric consumption produced by this concoction is inconsequential. Assume that your basal metabolism rate is 2,800 calories per day. Simple arithmetic tells us that you can—indeed you must—consume slightly over one million calories per year. In my own case—with a life expectancy of about 25 years—this means that, in order to avoid premature death through starvation, I need to eat some 25 million calories. Why not get on with it?

15

A Golf Outing

Warren's World

Each year Buffett hosts a day-long golf event for the benefit of Omaha charities, including the Rose Blumkin Center for Performing Arts where his daughter Susan heads the foundation.

The event, a mini-Warren's World, in 1993 raised $175,000 and in 1994 $900,000 and in 1995 $350,000 to help pay the center's operating expenses. Buffett personally matched the 1994 and 1995 contributions.

For the outing, Buffett sported not only a Cherry Coke hat, but also a golf shirt displaying a fistful of money inside the Berkshire Hathaway name.

U.S. Senator Sam Nunn of Georgia and about 100 political and business leaders attended the event. Participants were invited by the event co-chairmen, Walter Scott, chairman of Peter Kiewit Sons' and Michael Yanney, chairman of America First Companies.

Those attending the golf and tennis outing, called Omaha Golf Day, at the Omaha Country Club included top officers of Salomon Brothers

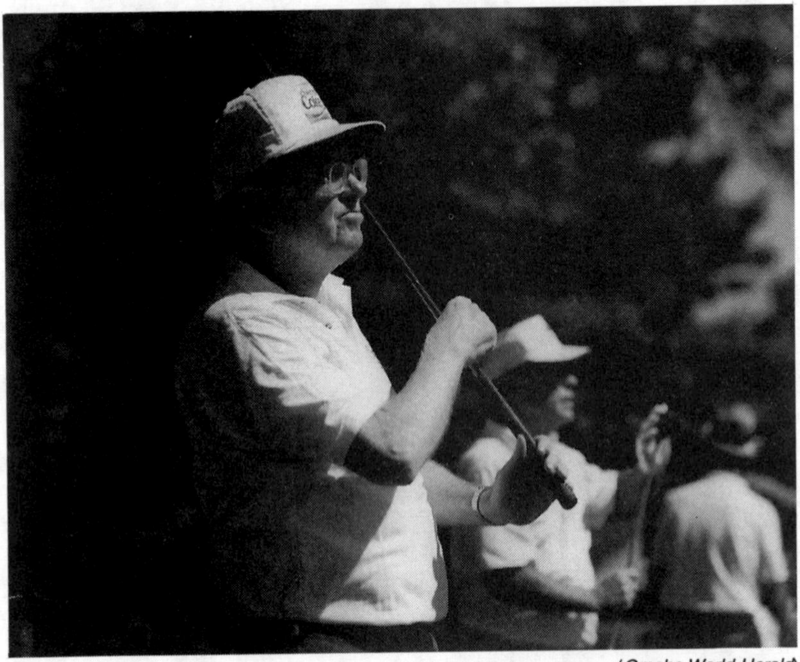

(Omaha World-Herald)

Sporting a Cherry Coke hat, Buffett hosts an annual golf outing, a benefit for the Emmy Gifford Children's Theater in Omaha.

(Deryck Maughan), Merrill Lynch, AT&T, Sprint, The New York Times, Bozell Inc., ConAgra, Coopers & Lybrand, Deloitte & Touche, Caterpillar, Schering Plough, U.S. West, Bank One, the *Omaha World-Herald* and others.

Former Treasury Secretary Nicholas Brady, Jack Byrne of Fund American and Nebraska's U.S. Senators Bob Kerrey and J. James Exon found time for the event, which included dinner with Buffett.

Buffett told Nunn he'd attend a conference of Nunn's to discuss ideas for overhauling the federal tax system. (*Omaha World-Herald*, August 31, 1993)

"Buffett said Nunn's effort to overhaul the tax system could bring a consumption tax 'one notch closer' to reality.

"Buffett said he favors a 'progressive consumption tax' to replace the federal income tax. The schedule would allow people to pay for basic living expenses and to deduct what they save or invest. They would pay taxes on the rest of the money they spend on consumption."

"As the amount spent on consumption increases, the taxed amount would increase," he said.

"I personally would prefer to make it steeply progressive as a matter of social equity," Buffett said.

Shortly thereafter, on November 8, 1993, Buffett, saying Kerrey was, "good for Nebraska, good for business," announced he would serve as honorary chairman of Kerrey's re-election bid for the Senate.

In the summer of 1993 Kerrey turned to Buffett for advice about President Clinton's economic plan. Kerrey was the last and deciding vote in the Senate and he finally voted for the president's package. Buffett's recommendation to Kerrey was: "Hold your nose and vote for it." (*The Agenda*, Bob Woodward, p. 306)

Buffett Event Draws Cash, Corporate Luminaries

BY JOHN TAYLOR
WORLD-HERALD STAFF WRITER

■ The list of participants in the golf tournament. Page 2.

Warren Buffett wore a blue Omaha Royals cap (he owns 25 percent of the team), golf spikes (he is host of his own tennis and golf outing) and a smile (he is, after all, the second-wealthiest individual in the world) as he greeted participants arriving Tuesday for his fourth Omaha Classic.

The classic is a combination golf, tennis and dinner outing he started in 1992 to raise money for four Omaha-area organizations on a rotating basis.

More than $500,000 was expected to be raised from the Tuesday event for this year's recipient, Girls Inc. The others in the rotation are the Omaha Children's Museum, Boys Clubs of Omaha and last year's recipient of $1.9 million in assistance, the Emmy Gifford Children's Theater.

Each golf foursome contributed at least $10,000 and each tennis team $5,000, and Buffett pledged to match the teams' amounts.

As it has in the past, the event attracted presidents, chairmen and chief executives of some of the most powerful corporations in America.

They arrived at the Omaha Country Club in Cadillacs, stretch limos, Lincoln Town Cars and even a tour bus.

However, none of them came from farther away than Fadel Muhammad, president and chief executive officer of Bukaka, a company based in Jakarta, Indonesia.

Muhammad, whose company is a partner with California Energy Co. of Omaha on a power project in Indonesia, said his trip to Omaha took nearly 20 hours.

"I completely rescheduled everything to be here," Muhammad said as he walked to the practice tee in the sweltering heat. "The weather is like we have in Jakarta."

Buffett took note of the distance Muhammad traveled for the event,

Please turn to Page 2, Col. 1

KILEY CHRISTIAN/THE WORLD-HERALD

ABOVE PAR: From left, Paul Smucker, chairman of the executive committee of J.M. Smucker Co., host Warren Buffett and Phil Fletcher, chairman and chief executive officer of ConAgra Inc., at Buffett's fourth Omaha Classic golf and tennis fund-raising event at the Omaha Country Club on Tuesday.

Buffett Event Draws the Elite

Continued from Page 1

using it as evidence that pleasure, not business, is the magnet.

"I think they're here for a good time," Buffett said. "If they didn't have a good time you wouldn't be able to get them here."

From the first year, Buffett has used the event to boost Omaha.

"These people seem to like Omaha when they get here," he said. "People have a notion that it's just all prairie here, and then they get here and play on a course that has hills, and, well

While an event like the Omaha Classic brings business executives together, raising the possibility of future business deals, Buffett said that none of his business transactions has ever had its roots in the gathering.

"But you never can tell," said the man whose company, Berkshire Hathaway Inc., has just proposed paying $2.3 billion for the portion of an insurance company, GEICO, it doesn't already own.

"I wouldn't bet against it if we do this for 10 more years. More things happen when you are moving than when you are sitting still. If you get around, things do happen.

"I found that when I was in my 20s, when I would go to New York. Even if I didn't have anything planned, something would come up when I was there, some idea or something."

Buffett's outing is unique to Omaha, attracting a wide assortment of people from business, sports and the entertainment industry.

At one end of the practice tee area Tuesday was Wayne Huizenga, owner of the Miami Dolphins of the National Football League, the Florida Marlins of major league baseball and the Florida Panthers of the National Hockey League, taking a quick lesson from Gary Wiren, Omaha native and PGA master teacher.

At the other end of the tee area was Jack Valenti, for 27 years the president of the Motion Picture Association of America.

"I don't go to these things for business," said Valenti. "I do business all week. I go to join people I know, and Warren Buffett's a wonderful friend."

Earlier, Huizenga spotted NFL rival owner Alex Spanos of the San Diego Chargers on the tee.

"I arrived before him this morning and wrote, 'Go Dolphins' on his name tag," Huizenga confessed.

Spanos played in the 1960 British Amateur golf championship, but he tried to deflect attention. "Hey, that was 35 years ago," he protested when someone pointed it out.

Among the approximately 130 participants, golfing handicaps range from close to scratch to the high 20s.

Gov. Nelson admitted to having one of the higher handicaps. He wore a pressure bandage on his left elbow to help alleviate pain from tendinitis. "I've even tried acupuncture," he said.

At least one executive, Jack Schneider, managing director of Allen & Co., brought along the latest biography of Buffett for an autograph.

The book is "Buffett: The Making of an American Capitalist," by Roger Lowenstein.

The Buffett Golf Tournament

Participants in Warren Buffett's golf outing, by foursome sponsors, with dinner guests in parentheses:

■ **America First Cos.:** Mike Yanney, chairman and chief executive officer of America First (Gail Yanney); Bob Dedman, chairman and CEO of Club Corp. International (Nancy Dedman); Ben Love, retired chairman and CEO of Texas Commerce Bancshares; Charles Duncan, chairman of Duncan Interests.

■ **America First:** Bill Strauss, retired chairman of InterNorth (Jan Strauss); Dick Callahan, president of U S West International, London; Don Brown, principal of JBG Cos. (Ann Brown); C.R. "Bob" Bell, president of the Greater Omaha Chamber of Commerce (Carol Bell).

■ **American Business Information:** Vin Gupta, chairman and CEO of American Business Information (Crystal Grow); Bert Winemiller, president and chief operating officer of American Business Information (Debby Winemiller); Bill Hambrecht, chairman of Hambrecht & Quist; Jack Valenti, president and CEO of the Motion Picture Association of America.

■ **Blockbuster Entertainment:** Wayne Huizenga, chairman and CEO of Blockbuster Entertainment; Steve Berrard, president of Blockbuster Entertainment; Jack Schneider, managing director of Allen & Co.; Clarke Keough, vice president of Allen & Co.

■ **Burlington Northern Inc.:** Jack Chain, executive vice president of safety and corporate support of Burlington Northern (Judie Chain); Roger Staubach, chairman and CEO of the Staubach Co.; Paul Ray, chairman and CEO of Paul Ray Berndtson Inc. (Sarah Ray); Clark Johnson, chairman and CEO of Pier 1 Imports (Joan Johnson).

■ **Central States Indemnity Co.:** Bill Kizer Sr., chairman of Central States; John Kizer, president of Central States; Dale Browning, founder of Plus System; Scott Marks, executive vice president of First Chicago Corp.

■ **Commercial Federal Corp.:** Bill Fitzgerald, chairman and CEO of Commercial Federal (Barb Fitzgerald); Jim Laphen, president and chief operating officer of Commercial Federal; Herb Lurie, director of Merrill Lynch; Bud Koch, president and CEO of First Federal Savings Bank.

■ **ConAgra Inc.:** Phil Fletcher, chairman and CEO of ConAgra (Sue Fletcher); Paul Smucker, chairman of the executive committee of J. M. Smucker Co.; Mike Wright, chairman, president and CEO of SuperValu Inc. (Judy Pentz); Lee Lochman, president and chief operating officer of ConAgra Refrigerated Foods.

■ **Coopers & Lybrand:** George Behringer, managing partner of Coopers & Lybrand in Omaha; Hal Johnson, managing director of Norman Broadbent International; Pat McDonnell, vice chairman of Coopers & Lybrand; Barry MacLean, president of MacLean Fogg Co.

■ **Deloitte & Touche:** Ron Burgess, Omaha managing partner of Deloitte & Touche (Mary Kaye Burgess); Dennis Chookaszian, chairman and CEO of CNA Insurance Cos.; William Daley, partner in Mayer, Brown and Platte; Tom Flanagan, Midwest regional managing partner of Deloitte & Touche.

■ **Durham Resources:** Charles Durham, chairman of Durham Resources (Margre Durham); Charles Fairbanks, president of Fairbanks Realty; Ron Roskens, president and CEO of Action International (Lois Roskens); Jack MacAllister, chairman emeritus of U S West Inc.; Steve Durham, chairman of S. H. Durham Enterprises (Barb Durham).

■ **Fairmont Group:** Dave Karnes, president and CEO of Fairmont Group (Liz Karnes); Bill Aldinger, president and CEO of Household International; Ron Wilwerding, chairman of Accent Service International (Pauline Wilwerding); Jim Oesterreicher, vice chairman and CEO of J. C. Penney Co. Inc.

■ **FirsTier Financial Inc.:** David Rismiller, chairman, president and CEO of FirsTier Financial (Anne Rismiller); Bill Esrey, chairman and CEO of Sprint Corp.; Don Hall, chairman of Hallmark Inc.; John Grundhofer, chairman, president and CEO of First Bank System Inc.

■ **First National Bank:** Bruce Lauritzen, president of First National Bank (Kim Lauritzen); Rich Roberts, president of PMT Services Inc.; David Wysong, owner of Wysong Cos.; Matt Gogel, professional golfer (Blair Lauritzen).

■ **Guarantee Mutual Life Co.:** Bob Bates, chairman, president and CEO of Guarantee Mutual (Judy Bates); John Turner, chairman and CEO of ReliaStar Financial Corp.; Joe McErlane, president of National Benefit Resources (Fluff McErlane); Herbert Kohler, chairman and president of Kohler Co.

■ **Heider-Weitz Partners:** Charles Heider, general partner of Heider-Weitz Partners (Mary Heider); Frank Salizzoni, president and chief operating officer of USAir Group; Bill Esping, president and CEO of Business Records (Kathy Esping); Dick McCormick, chairman and CEO of U S West Inc. (Mary Pat McCormick).

■ **Dick Holland:** Dick Holland, retired (Mary Holland); Gary Wiren, president of Golf Around the World (Ione Wiren); Henry Bloch, chairman of H & R Block (Marion Bloch); Paul Jessen, senior partner in Koley, Jessen (Mary Jessen).

■ **Inacom Inc.:** Bill Fairfield, president and CEO of Inacom (Deanne Fairfield); Grant Gregory, chairman of Gregory & Honemeyer Inc.; Jeffrey Cunningham, publisher of Forbes Inc.; Ron Burns, president and CEO of Union Pacific Railroad.

■ **Kutak Rock:** Joe Armstrong, partner in Kutak Rock (Darlene Armstrong); Dick Weill, president of MBIA Inc. (Judy Weill); Charles Russ, executive vice president and general counsel of U S West Inc.; Pete Willis, partner in Kutak Rock.

■ **Mutual of Omaha:** Jack Weekly, president and chief operating officer of Mutual of Omaha (Bette Weekly); Nebraska Gov. Ben Nelson (Diane Nelson); Oklahoma Gov. Frank Keating (aide Clinton Key); Carroll Campbell, president and CEO of the American Council of Life Insurance.

■ **Peter Kiewit Sons' Inc.:** Walter Scott, chairman and president of Peter Kiewit Sons' Inc. (Sue Scott); Eric Gleacher, chairman and CEO of Gleacher & Co.; Fadel Muhammad, president and CEO of Bukaka (Astrid Puspakesuma Fadel); Bill Child, chief executive officer of R. C. Willey Home Furnishings.

■ **Kiewit:** Ken Stinson, president of Kiewit Construction Group (Ann Stinson); Sam Skinner, president of Commonwealth Edison Co.; Len Pieroni, chairman and CEO of the Parsons Corp. (Marilyn Pieroni); George Brett, vice president of baseball operations, Kansas City Royals.

■ **U S West Inc.:** Ron James, regional vice president of public policy of U S West Communications; Alberto Santos, president of Empress Santos; Pete Higgins, senior vice president of North America for Microsoft Corp.; Jeff Raikes, senior vice president of desktop applications of Microsoft.

■ **Wells Fargo Bank:** Paul Hazen, president of Wells Fargo Bank; Bob MacDonnell, partner in Kohlberg Kravis Roberts & Co.; George Roberts, partner in Kohlberg Kravis; Charles Schwab, chairman of Charles Schwab & Co.

■ **The Omaha World-Herald:** Bill Donaldson, vice president of The World-Herald (Beverly Donaldson); Alex Spanos, president of A. G. Spanos Cos.; Tim Hoeksema, president of Midwest Express (Jan Hoeksema); Doug McCorkindale, vice chairman and chief financial officer of Gannett Co.

Expected to participate in the tennis competition, whose sponsors are Alan Baer & Associates, Peter Kiewit Sons' Inc., Dick Holland, Omaha Steaks International, HunTel Systems and Bill Strauss:

Jaime Alatorre, chairman of the Mexican Investment Board; Phil Anschutz, chairman of Southern Pacific Railroad (Nancy Anschutz); Dick Berry, chairman of United Seeds Co. (Pam Berry); Jack Blanton, chairman of Houston Endowment Inc. (Laura Lee Blanton); Richard Breeden, co-chairman of Coopers & Lybrand.

Ann Brown, chairman of the Consumer Product Safety Commission (Don Brown); Gen. Michael Carns; Dan Chao, managing director of Bechtel Enterprises; Adm. Hank Chiles, commander of Stratcom; Myrvin Christopherson, president of Dana College (Anne Christopherson); Andy Heyward, president of DIC Entertainment; Hugh Hunt, chairman and president of HunTel Systems (Jane Hunt).

Rich Jaros, executive vice president of Peter Kiewit Sons' Inc. (Lori Jaros); Linda Manaster, president of CompuCook; John Martin, correspondent with ABC News (Kathryn Martin); Deryck Maughan, chairman and CEO of Salomon Brothers; David McCort, chairman and CEO, C-Tec Corp.; Scott Miller, CEO of United Infrastructure; Mike Platt, president of Ideal Water (Barbara Platt); Henry Schimberg, president and chief operating officer of Coca-Cola Enterprises.

Joe Semrod, chairman, president and CEO of UJB Financial; Fred Simon, executive vice president of Omaha Steaks International (Eve Simon); Stephen Simon, vice president of the food service division of Omaha Steaks (Kathy Simon); Todd Simon, vice president of consumer direct of Omaha Steaks (Shirly Loring).

Tom Sloan, president and CEO of Sloan Implement Co.; Col. Bob Smith, general manager of the Officers Club at Offutt Air Force Base (Linda Smith); Tim Smucker, chairman of J. M. Smucker Co.; and Dwight Sutherland, manager partner of Sutherland Lumber (Norma Sutherland).

Listed as attending the dinner:

Warren Buffett, chairman of Berkshire Hathaway (Astrid Menks); Susan Buffett; Howard Buffett, chairman of the executive committee and president of the GSI Group; Alan Baer, president of Alan Baer & Associates (Marcia Baer); Mike Faust, assistant to the chairman of Kiewit; Rajat Gupta, director and CEO of McKinsey & Co.; Diny Landen, past president of the board of Girls Inc.; Carmen Policy, president of San Francisco '49ers; and Jan Roos, assistant to the chairman of America First.

(*Omaha World-Herald*, August 30, 1995)

16

Dinner at Senator Daniel Moynihan's Home

Buffett, along with U.S. Senator Bob Kerrey and some health care CEOs, had dinner at Senator Daniel Moynihan's home in Washington, D.C., on November 24, 1993.

One person at the dinner/health reform workshop was Richard Scrushy, chairman of HealthSouth Rehabilitation Corp. in Birmingham which specializes in treating sports and head injuries.

Scrushy, who came in thinking Buffett could not possibly be as good as advertised came away saying, "I was really taken with him."

The two shared a ride from the airport to the dinner and Buffett told him about his early paper route and pinball machine days in Washington. Scrushy wound up seated next to Buffett for a time as Buffett, Kerrey and Moynihan rotated among the several tables.

"He did not know about my company, but he asked a lot of questions. He was fascinated by the rehabilitation aspect of our company," says

Scrushy.

The dinner conversation centered on health care reform and how to pay for it. Also, there was discussion about how to revamp the entire tax system.

"He wanted the tax code to be more consumption-based instead of income-based...He felt the tax system should be more progressive, that it's actually regressive as it is. He said it's discouraging to entrepreneurs and wealth building, that incentives should be in place to encourage entrepreneurs and wealth building," Scrushy recalls.

The talks covered a number of issues, even the importance of fighting the drug problem, all agreeing it was a huge health care cost. At the end Buffett and Scrushy had photos taken of themselves tugging at Buffett's wallet.

"He's not only brilliant. He's very funny," Scrushy said.

Another person at the dinner, Barry Morton, CEO of Robins & Morton, a health care building firm in Birmingham, said that Buffett, on meeting a politician at dinner, would pull out his wallet and say, "Here, take all my money."

(Photo by Barry Morton)

HealthSouth Rehabilitation CEO Richard Scrushy and Buffett in car after dinner at Senator Moynihan's; Buffett reenacts his trademark of pulling out his wallet and handing it over whenever he meets a politician.

17

Warren Buffett, Jimmy Buffett

That's double f, double t.

Warren Buffett's name—that's double f and double t—is often spelled with one t, as in breakfast buffet. It's spelled "Buffet" in such prominent places as the 1992 Nike Annual Report, major newspapers and by top stock jock commentators.

His name is Buffett—as in pop singer/songwriter Jimmy Buffett who is also the author of *Tales of Margaritaville* and *Where Is Joe Merchant?* Warren and Jimmy are distantly related.

And there is some confusion between the two. The Buffett of business fame can sing a little and the one of singing fame has done some investing.

Don Bohmont of Omaha, a math professor at the University of Nebraska, says as famous as Buffett is, he's still confused with Jimmy Buffett, even by some people who work in the securities business.

Bohmont often calls his daughter Amy Scott, a stockbroker in St.

Petersburg, Florida, sometimes leaving a message to call a famous person.

"I've left messages to call Ted Turner or Larry Tisch in Omaha. This time I left her a message to call Warren Buffett in Omaha. If I say Omaha she knows I'm calling."

When his daughter returned and got the message from "Warren Buffett," an awed co-worker said, "You mean you know him?"

"Of course, he lives in my hometown of Omaha," Bohmont's daughter replied.

It turned out, however, her brokerage house colleague still thought the caller was Jimmy Buffett, not Warren Buffett—double t. Jimmy, with all his flourishing book, movie and retailing interests, occasionally calls Warren for advice.

"He calls from time to time for advice, but I should be calling him," says Warren Buffett. (*Forbes*, January, 16, 1995)

Forbes, reported July 31, 1995, that Warren, Jimmy and Peter Buffett were planning an album. It quoted Peter Buffett saying, "My dad will play the ukulele and sing a bit, too." Oh, God.

This just in...(*Bloomberg News Service*, October 11, 1995):

DETROIT—Chrysler Corp. made a meal [sic] out of billionaire investor Warren Buffet's name when it tried to take a slap at Kirk Kerkorian, its largest shareholder.

Jerome York, vice chairman of Tracinda, Corp., said in a speech in New York that his company, of which Kerkorian is chairman, follows the same tight staffing regimen that Buffett imposes in his investment firm Berkshire Hathaway.

The Detroit auto maker sent out a press release objecting to any comparison between Buffett and Kerkorian, who launched an abortive $21 billion bid for Chrysler in April.

"We know Warren Buffett" the Chrysler release said, 'and believe us, Kirk Kerkorian is no Warren Buffet.'

The line, which mirrored Sen. Lloyd Bentsen's famous put down of that other great speller, Vice President Dan Quayle, was the result of a typographical error, Chrysler spokesman Steve Harris said.

"Ooh, we do have a typo there, don't we?" Harris said.

It's Buffett - double f, double t.

18

"All My Children"

"Thought he checked alarm systems"

The Buffetts have three energetic, grown children: Susan Buffett, born July 30, 1953; Howard Graham Buffett, born December 16, 1954, (named after Buffett's father, Howard Buffett, and Ben Graham) and Peter Buffett, born May 4, 1958.

As with any family raising children, things have at times been like a soap opera. All of Buffett's children attended college, but none finished. All are healthy, intelligent and productive.

Susan worked as an assistant to the CEO of Century 21 in California before she worked for the *New Republic* and later as an administrative assistant to the editor at *U.S. News and World Report* in Washington, D.C. Then she returned to Omaha where she heads the Rose Blumkin Center for Performing Arts foundation.

Susan recalls a time she needed cash to pay for airport parking in Washington D.C. Her father was there. but to get the money, Susan had to write him a $20 check.

"Sometimes it's frustrating, but unfortunately, I basically agree with him," Susan said. (*Omaha World-Herald,* May 26, 1996)

"What makes my dad happy, she added, "is hanging around the house, reading, playing bridge and talking with us. He's about as normal as you can get."

While Susan was in Washington, she and her daughter, Emily, often saw Katharine Graham, longtime chairman of The Washington Post Co. "I remember Mrs. Graham being impressed with Emily because she could eat avocados and caviar. That's unlike my father and me. All we want is hamburgers," Howard Buffett said.

Howard Buffett, a Republican who served most of one term as chairman of the Douglas County Commission, where he was known as an advocate of programs for the disadvantaged, has a 406-acre farm north of Omaha where he raises corn and soybeans.

He long has been outspoken on behalf of the state's ethanol industry. He drives a 1988 Corvette convertible with "Ethanol" printed on the license plate.

And he has been an avid speaker promoting the benefits of using the corn- and sugar-based fuel additive. He served on the Nebraska Gasohol Committee and served as chairman of the Nebraska Ethanol Authority and Development Board until 1991, when he was named to the International Policy Advisory Committee on International Trade which advised the Bush administration on trade issues.

Howard was elected to the board of Archer-Daniels-Midland Co., the food processing company, known as "Supermarket to the World," based in Decatur, Illinois. Howard replaced Robert Strauss after Strauss was named ambassador to the Soviet Union and later to the Commonwealth of Independent States. (Strauss was renamed to the board in 1993.)

It was early 1992 when Howard resigned his county commission post to take a job under ADM's Chairman Dwayne Andreas as corporate vice chairman and assistant to the chairman.

"This is a big decision. It's probably the largest one I've ever made in my life," Howard said.

"For someone like me who is interested in agriculture," said Howard, "the opportunity to work under him would be like someone who is interested in investments getting to work under my father."

Howard asked for his father's advice. Warren called the job, "a once-in-a-lifetime opportunity."

In 1995 Howard resigned from ADM, apparently troubled by a price fixing investigation of the company. He is now the chairman of the executive committee and president of international operations for The GSI Group, a farm equipment firm in Assumption, Illinois.

A lot of people hated to see Howard leave Omaha.

"He's a rare breed of a young politician," says Buffett family friend Michael Yanney. "He has excellent intellect and a high degree of political sensitivity, but more importantly he exhibits his father's integrity."

Howard has recounted a time when as county commissioner he backed a project to bring basketball immortal Michael Jordan to Omaha for two days of events.

Berkshire's corporate jet, *The Indefensible,* was called into action to pick up Jordan in Lawrence, Kansas.

Howard showed Jordan the long list of activities and Jordan said, "I'm not doing all this stuff."

Howard said, "I was about to die."

Then Jordan winked and after two full days of activities told Howard, "Howie, I want you to remember one thing. You really owe me one."

At one of the events, a celebrity basketball game, Jordan ejected Howard for not wearing Nike (a stock tip?) shoes.

"Michael Jordan...did more for Omaha in two days than most people could do in two years," Howard said.

Buffett's daughter, Susan, asked about her father being a Democrat and her brother being a Republican said that both her father and brother are more concerned with principles than politics. "My father and my brother are very principled. Politics does not come between them." In fact, she added, they kid each other about it.

Susan said she would never have any idea what stocks her father was buying. "He might ask a consumer question about what kind of candy I liked, or something, and maybe three years later you could see why." But she said he would never walk around the house and say some stock was a great buy.

Peter Buffett, who studied music at Stanford University, is a successful musician/businessman in Milwaukee. For part of 1994 he lived in Los Angeles recording the sound track for an eight-hour miniseries, "500 Nations," about Indians, directed by Kevin Costner and aired by CBS. Peter writes commercials that he says, "support me and my habit, which is my studio." (*Fortune*, August 24, 1992)

A New Age composer whose creations include a synthesized musical score for the Infiniti 20 television spots, Peter also scored the fire-dance scene for Costner's Oscar-winning movie, *Dances with Wolves.*

Most of Peter's business is recording commercial jingles for companies like DuPont, Infiniti, CNN and Levi Strauss.

Peter told Linda Grant of *The Los Angeles Times*, (April 7, 1991), "My dad says the money is not important to him, but it is. Not because he wants to spend it, but because it makes him a winner. My dad casts a big shadow. I remember sitting at the dinner table with him, and there was nothing you could tell him that he didn't already know. But I always got the impression he would support me in whatever I chose."

Peter has said his father calls and visits frequently and enjoys hearing about the music industry.

"It's neat to be able to talk to him about what's happening in my life. I read about what's happening in his," Peter said. (*Omaha World-Herald*, August 30, 1991)

His childhood was nothing unusual, Peter told *The Lincoln Nebraska Journal* (August 8, 1991). "It was incredibly normal, almost to a fault. He (Warren Buffett) really didn't reach notoriety until the 80s. When I was a kid, I never thought twice about who he was and what he was doing. We didn't live in what would be considered a special neighborhood, we didn't go to a special school, we didn't have special friends. So I never really noticed anything out of the ordinary."

Peter Buffett told *Worth* magazine (April, 1996): "For as long as I can remember, he thought all three of us should do what made us happy. He was great that way. He is, essentially, the same way he was 30 years ago. He'll ask me, 'What do you get paid for something like *The Scarlet Letter*?' 'Well, I got this or that, and he'll be like, 'Wow, that's a lot of money!'"

Peter also told the magazine he long ago had sold his Berkshire stock, an amount that would be about $20 million today.

Warren Buffett, who doesn't plan to leave much money, relatively speaking, to his children, has said his reasoning is this: "As Jesse Owens' child, your development would not be facilitated by letting you start 100-yard dashes at the 50-yard line."

Buffett's daughter, Susan, has told any number of jokes about vague disgruntlement with her father's tight-fisted policy about not leaving his wealth to his children.

Susan says she understands his reasoning, but indicates that now that his children are grown he can lighten up on the heavy lessons.

As Howard says, "I still think there is hope for him yet. He has demonstrated a little more flexibility in the last few years."

She told Linda Grant that because Buffett is her father, everyone assumes she is rich. Not the case, she has told reporters. "They don't understand that when I write my dad a check for $20, he cashes it. If I had $2,000 now, I'd pay off my credit card bill."

Howard says, "I told her I'd loan her the money! Someone in the family has to have deep pockets, even if they have holes in them."

Buffett doesn't believe in leaving it all to his children and has set aside only a few million for each, all told less than .1% of his net worth. The rest will go to The Buffett Foundation.

Susan tells many stories about her father, perhaps the most amusing being the one about what her early classmates thought her father did for a living.

She has told Adam Smith, "For years I didn't even know what he did. They asked me at school what he did, and I said he was a security analyst, and they thought he checked alarm systems."

19

"My Dad Couldn't Run a Lawnmower...

(but) he once told me it takes a lifetime to build a reputation and five minutes to ruin it."

—Howard Buffett

Buffett's son, Howard Graham Buffett, met Ben Graham in Warren Buffett's New York days. Howard was just a toddler then and has but one recollection of him.

"He gave me a stuffed animal...a stuffed dog," recalled Howard Buffett. "Obviously, he had a lot more impact on my father than he did on me."

Howard Buffett's wife, Devon, came into the marriage with four children. The couple added Howie Buffett. Howie Buffett's middle name is Warren and it may be that he has inherited the family's financial genes.

"He owns 10 shares of Coke, it may be more now, and he's always asking his grandfather for advice about Coke stock," said Howard Buf-

(Courtesy of Howard Buffett)

Warren Buffett, Howard Buffett and former Cap Cities Chairman Tom Murphy.

fett. "He called my dad the other day to ask him about it."

"I sometimes talk to him about investments...I do take his advice. We have some Coca-Cola stock," said Howard Buffett.

Howard Buffett, who jokes of his father, "He learned it all from me." He says he never really regarded his father as different in most respects. "I never thought of him as any different, just as my dad, just as anyone else would." But Howard Buffett admits there were a few puzzling things going on even in his youth.

"I really remember him up in his office (at the house) reading *Moody's* or something. He worked really hard. He could work 18 hours a day," he said.

"I do remember once when we were on vacation in California and he was constantly on the phone with Stan Lipsey of *The Buffalo News* for about three days straight. There was a strike at the paper and my father was going through every business calculation," he said. His father was nearing the conclusion it was going to be more economical to close the paper than keep publishing, Howard added.

It never came to that, but those on the other side underestimated how seriously his father was thinking of closing it because reason dictated it, said Howard Buffett. "I've watched him go through the process...He takes all the emotion out of a decision. He just goes through the fundamental reasons when he makes a decision. He doesn't deviate."

Buffett is a caring person, but when it comes to business decisions he just boils it all down to facts and reasons.

"My father couldn't run a lawnmower...I never saw him cut the grass, trim a hedge or wash a car," Howard Buffett said. "I remember that used to be irritating and only when I got older and understood the value of time did I realize why he did things the way he did. His time is so valuable."

Howard Buffett said in his own life he tries to save some time for those things. "I want time to farm and do other things."

The younger Buffett said his father cares nothing for comfort or style. "He had an old Volkswagen for years and only gave it up when he thought it was unsafe. He's had other cars but he doesn't care a thing about them...It could be a car or a horse. All he cares about is getting there."

Once Buffett was returning from an East Coast trip on his private jet when it developed hydraulic problems and landed in Indianapolis, leaving Buffett temporarily stranded. So how did he get back to Omaha?

"He flew coach," his son said. "He was proud he flew coach and I'm not sure he may not have wanted to go first class, but I'm sure he couldn't have stood it if he had been spotted on first class."

Howard Buffett says his father often offered guideposts to live by. "I remember once, we were on Dodge Street near a McDonald's (another stock tip?) that's no longer there, and my father told me, 'It takes a lifetime to build a reputation and five minutes to ruin it.' "

"He's so basic and so very fast paced," he said.

"All the stories about him sticking to basics are true. A lot of CEOs are flamboyant, not all, but many are. He's not. He's not phony. He's totally sincere."

Howard says there's just one real problem being around his father. He's so smart, it's frustrating.

"He's a walking Almanac...When I was a kid it was discouraging. In fact, it was overwhelming," said Buffett, who found it was almost impossible to tell his father anything he didn't already know or achieve some success that ever compared with that of his father.

Howard Buffett told *Fortune* magazine (September 10, 1990) about how he farmed 406 acres and loved the work: "I've been farming nine years. It's a very independent type of activity—everything's up to you. It teaches you a value system and gives you the instrument to achieve that." So far so good.

Except for one thing: "Dad owns the land. I pay him a percentage of the gross income as rent. The rent is based upon my weight. I'm 5 foot 8, and I weigh around 200 pounds. He thinks I weigh too much—that I should weigh 182.5. If I'm over, my rent is 26% of gross income. If I'm under, 22%. It's the Buffett family version of going to Weight Watchers. I don't mind it, really. He's showing he's concerned about my health. Even at 22%, he's getting a bigger payback than almost anybody around..."

Howard Buffett said later that although his father is receiving the high end of a normal return on farm ground rental, that's OK.

After all, said the younger Buffett, "I feel very fortunate that my dad has enough interest in my farming activity that he was willing to purchase a farm. It's my dream, but it's his farm, and it's his privilege to determine how he wants to rent it to me."

As things turned out, when Howard Buffett moved to Decatur, Illinois, he sub-leased the land at a good profit above what he pays his father. But he missed the tractor and the ploughing. There's a story about Howard that occurred after he moved to Decatur. On some snowy days, Howard's neighbors would find their driveways cleared. A man discovered Howard ploughing one day and asked him why he was doing it. Howard said he missed being on his tractor so much that he got one out to be on it and was happy to play snow remover.

Before Howard moved, he had lunch with his father every Tuesday. "We have a great relationship. He has been a great instructor, a great teacher. I never look at my dad as the Warren Buffett that you see in *Forbes* magazine. All I see him as is my dad. But at the same time, I realize he has so much experience and knowledge to offer," he told the *Omaha World-Herald*. (October 31, 1993)

Back in 1985 Buffett once financed a 30-day shopping spree for his daughter as a bribe for her pledge not to gain weight in the coming year, but she won the deal on a technicality because they agreed it would be off if she became pregnant which she did. (*Fortune,* August 24, 1992)

Finally, in the son's eyes, what is it that makes Warren Buffett tick?

"I think it stems from his basic philosophy that you ought to want to give back to society and not just be a consumer of it. That's totally consistent with what he does," he said. "He does want to be a success and he likes to be creative. He's extra creative and intelligent...He has all the tools and all that's combined with a drive and determination...There's an inside drive. He wants to do good things. He wants respect and to be in a position to have a positive influence."

"What he really likes is a challenge. What he's really about is finding a better way to do it," he said in an interview several months before the Salomon scandal occurred.

In June, 1993, Berkshire expanded its board from five to six members and Howard Buffett was named to the board. Howard is a director of Lindsay Manufacturing Co., an irrigation equipment maker in Lindsay, Nebraska, and he's a director of Coke's 43%-owned Coca-Cola Enterprises Inc. board, a modern-day version of Buffett & Son continuity.

20

Berkshire's History

How much of this issue can you take? "Well, all of it."

To find out where Buffett's billions came from, let's start at the beginning.

Back in 1929, several textile operations with common ownership were joined together with Berkshire Cotton Manufacturing Co. (incorporated in 1889) and renamed Berkshire Fine Spinning Associates.

Apparently the earliest of these corporations opened its doors in 1806. The resulting operation was a textile giant that once spun a quarter of the nation's fine cotton.

In the 1930s its many mills used about 1% of the electric output in the New England states. However, the company was not a money maker and therefore preferred dividends were omitted in late 1930 and for the next six years.

World War II and the immediate postwar years, however, brought profits.

She's 6 years old
...and so are the
***Hathaway Nylon** curtains!*

After six years of wear in many homes all over the country, HATHAWAY NYLON curtains are still giving excellent service . . . still looking luxurious and beautiful.

Six years ago, it was HATHAWAY who made the first nylon marquisette available for curtains! In these six years, many millions of yards of HATHAWAY NYLON have been decorating American windows, and not one yard has ever been returned because of damage by sunlight!

HATHAWAY NYLON with its high thread count has *everything* you want (and need) in a curtain fabric. It is easy to wash, quick to dry, beautiful, strong, non-inflammable, heat-resistant. It shrinks less than 1%. Its wonderful properties are "sealed in" by an exclusive HATHAWAY process.

So, look for the label "HATHAWAY 100% NYLON MARQUISETTE" when you shop for curtains. Feel HATHAWAY NYLON curtains, hold them to the light... *see* the difference! *Buy* them, and *know* the difference! Always ask for HATHAWAY NYLON!

HATHAWAY NYLON
MARQUISETTE

FREE! "ALL ABOUT CURTAINS"

HATHAWAY MFG. CO., Dept. D103, New Bedford, Mass.

Send for this free booklet of decorating ideas. Shows how to use standard curtains to achieve beautiful effects.

NAME____________________
ADDRESS____________________

(Ad courtesy of Alan Sears)

In 1955, Hathaway Manufacturing Co., a New Bedford, Massachusetts-based textile firm, founded in 1888 by Horatio Hathaway, was merged into Berkshire Fine Spinning Associates. The name was changed to Berkshire Hathaway Inc.

Although Berkshire has no relation to Hathaway shirts made famous by ads featuring a man with a patch over his eye, Buffett has said when he first bought Berkshire Hathaway, "I must have had seven calls in Omaha asking if I had to wear an eye patch."

Once *Barron's* Editor Alan Abelson described Berkshire this way: "Warren Buffett, for recent émigrés from Minsk and Pinsk, is the investor who runs a funny company called Berkshire Hathaway, which everyone thinks makes shirts but really makes money."

Back in 1948 the combined Berkshire Hathaway companies had profits of $18 million and had 10,000 workers at a dozen large mills throughout New England. That was at a time when IBM's earnings were $28 million.

But by 1964 the business was reduced to near rubble—two mills and a net worth of about $22 million.

The Hathaway Manufacturing firm claimed Hetty Green among its early shareholders.

Henrietta Howland Robinson Green (1834-1916), of Quaker stock, grew up in New Bedford, Massachusetts. In her 20s, she inherited a fortune in trading and shipping interests. Later she became a successful operator in the stock markets causing bull movements when word got out of her investments, most notably in railroads.

She also loaned money and amassed large land interests around Chicago. Reputedly the richest woman of her day, she left an estate of more than $100 million to her children when she died in New York. This financier avoided the outstretched hands of strangers by living a simple and obscure life.

Shades of Warren Buffett? Buffett must have been dreaming of Hetty Green when he bought Berkshire.

Once asked why she had taken out a license to carry a revolver, she replied, "Mostly to protect myself against lawyers. I'm not much afraid of burglars or highwaymen."

Buffett never has been so harsh on lawyers. After all, his right arm is lawyer Charles Munger, but his own preference is to steer clear of legal entanglements and lawyers whenever possible.

In 1955, Berkshire's stockholders' equity was $55,448,000.

During the next nine years, stockholders' equity fell to $22,139,000.

But as late as 1961 its managers were still calling it a strong company with a bright future.

In an address to the Newcomen Society that year, Berkshire President Seabury Stanton said, "Today, Berkshire Hathaway is the largest textile manufacturer of cotton and synthetic fabrics in New England. A total of about a million spindles and approximately 12,000 looms each year produce 225,000,000 yards of fabrics, consisting of fancy colored dress goods, handkerchief fabrics, lawns, voiles, dimities, combed and carded sateens, rayon linings, dacron marquisette curtain fabrics and dacron cotton blends.

"The total employment numbers approximately 5,800 people. All seven plants operate on a three-shift basis and Berkshire Hathaway does an average annual business of better than $60 million," he said.

But business kept sliding in the early 1960s. Buffett began buying shares of Berkshire Hathaway.

Item from the Internet: The Rosetta stone of modern investing

> This amendment No. 49 is being filed solely to report in this schedule 13D the voting agreement among Warren E. Buffett, for himself and The Howard Buffett Family Trust (The "Trust"), Susan T. Buffett, and Berkshire Hathaway Inc. electronic filings.

Item 3. Source and amount of funds or other consideration.

> The 474,998 shares of Common Stock described in Item 5 over which Mr. Buffett has sole voting and investment power were purchased at a cost of $15,415,044. The 4,204 shares of Common Stock described in Item 5 and owned by the Trust, of which Mr. Buffett is sole trustee but in which he has no economic interest, were purchased at a cost of $88,294. The 36,985 shares described in Item 5 and owned by Mrs. Buffett were purchased at a cost of $1,964,491. No borrowed funds were used for such purchases.

"It was in 1962 that Buffett first started acquiring for BPL Berkshire Hathaway stock at seven dollars per share. After a few years, Seabury Stanton, the then president of Berkshire, promised Buffett that he would tender the remaining Berkshire Hathaway shares at 11½. Three weeks later the shares were tendered, but at 11¾. This was one time that Buffett's "handshake and trust" deals did not materialize. Annoyed at Stanton for not keeping his word, Buffett began buying up Berkshire stock from Stanton's brother-in-law, and from Malcolm Chace, the then chairman of the board of Hathaway. Chace, who was also apparently annoyed with Stanton, sold Buffett a large chunk of his Berkshire Hathaway issues. It was at this time in 1965 that Buffett was able to acquire control of Berkshire Hathaway." (Anagnos thesis, quoting Buffett)

Still the business downturn continued and Berkshire's balance sheet on October 3, 1964, showed assets of $27,887,000 and stockholders' equity of $22 million. Berkshire's shares outstanding then were 1,137,778. Today there are 1,193,512.

Buffett kept buying and by 1965 his partnership had a 70% interest in the company, whose textile operations included about 4,700 looms. Buffett's total stake in Berkshire was acquired for about $14 million. *(Forbes,* October 21, 1991)

Buffett became chairman of the board in 1970. He kept the textile business until 1985, although it never prospered. He finally sold the more than 100-year old business for a pittance. It turned out to be one of the few business quagmires into which Buffett ever sank money.

Buffett would explain at the Berkshire annual meeting in 1991 that the textile business was a commodity business and although a large number of men's suits had Hathaway linings in World War II, it all came to mean nothing when a foreign business could make the linings more cheaply. Now he knows to go with the low-cost producer.

"I knew it was a tough business...I was either more arrogant or innocent then. We learned a lot of lessons, but I wish we could have learned them somewhere else," he said.

Today the sites of the Berkshire mills in New Bedford are relics, part of a scene of economic devastation. But the sites actually make more money now than they did when its managers had to come to Buffett for more money to keep the operations going.

The old red buildings are about worthless. But under the management of Bill Betts, who leases parts of them as office space and warehouse storage, they now provide Berkshire a small stream of income which is shipped off to Buffett to invest.

From tiny beginnings, great things followed. Buffett, in 1986, calculated that 52 people in the Omaha area owned enough Berkshire stock to be millionaires. Berkshire stock has soared since then. (*Omaha World-Herald*, August 17, 1991) It's now thought there are about 200 Buffett millionaires in Omaha.

There's even an unwitting beneficiary from New Jersey. Paul Laplante once got a letter from a finder's service saying it had found his deceased father's account—with 66 shares of Berkshire in it. It turns out Laplante's father had once done some legal work for Parker Mills, which paid him in warrants. Parker Mills was acquired by Berkshire Fine Spinning, later Berkshire Hathaway. "Those once nearly worthless warrants had blossomed into 66 shares of what had become Warren Buffett's investment company." *(Forbes,* May 6, 1996)

Although the textile business with headquarters in New Bedford, a west coast office in Los Angeles and an office in New York City didn't last, the Berkshire Hathaway name did.

Omaha stockbroker George Morgan, whose motto is "money doesn't come with instructions," says, "He named the company after his biggest mistake." Buffett bought his first shares of Berkshire Hathaway in 1962. His first order, executed by the Tweedy, Browne firm, was for 2,000 shares at $7.50. That $15,000 investment is today worth about $60 million.

Berkshire Hathaway was once described by its Vice Chairman Charles Munger as "a small, doomed New England textile enterprise."

Even Buffett, in looking back over what he said were the mistakes of the first 25 years, said his first mistake was buying Berkshire. Although he recognized it as an unpromising business, he bought in because of the low price.

Then he deployed Berkshire's cash flow to buy other businesses.

In 1965 Buffett Partnership informed Berkshire it held 500,975 shares, or about 49% of Berkshire's stock. Buffett's partnership had become Berkshire's largest shareholder and it kept right on buying. By January, 1967, it owned 59.5% and as of April, 1968, it owned almost 70% of Berkshire, according to documents filed with the Securities and Exchange Commission.

Meanwhile Berkshire was making acquisitions, venturing into the insurance business with a tender offer for National Indemnity Co. on February 23, 1967.

In early 1969 Berkshire bought 97% of The Illinois National Bank and Trust Co. and about the same time bought Sun Newspapers, Inc. and Blacker Printer, Inc., Berkshire's first entry into the publishing business.

Sun Newspapers published five weekly newspapers in Omaha with a circulation of about 50,000. The related printing businesses were run by

Stanford Lipsey.

In 1970 Buffett Partnership ceased to be a stockholder and parent of Berkshire and distributed, pro rata to its partners, 691,441 Berkshire shares. After the liquidation, Buffett quietly bought Berkshire shares for himself.

An SEC document says:

> Subsequent to the above liquidating distribution, Warren E. Buffett purchased during January, 1970, an additional 87,591 shares of common stock of the registrant from other partners of Buffett Partnership Ltd. who had received these shares on the liquidating distribution. Also, during January, Mr. Buffett purchased in the open market an additional 2,100 shares of common stock of the registrant. Warren Buffett himself on January 31, 1970, owned beneficially a total of 245,129, or approximately 25%, of the registrant's 979,582 shares of presently outstanding common stock. As a result of these transactions, Warren E. Buffett may be regarded as the parent of the registrant (Berkshire).

When Buffett was 40 years old, he controlled Berkshire from his office in Omaha.

Robert Cope, a bond underwriter from Montgomery, Alabama, called Berkshire in New Bedford, Massachusetts in the early 1970s to try to sell some industrial revenue bonds. He was told to call Buffett in Omaha.

"I called and got Bill Scott who told me he wasn't buying anything except industrial revenue bonds and I told him that was the only thing I was selling," Cope said. "He gave me to Buffett and I explained what I had. He understood corporate credits. He didn't have to go look anything up in *Moody's* or *S&P*. He said he was interested in the tax-exempt bonds I had."

When Cope asked how much he could take, Buffett replied, "Well, all of it." "I was used to selling 100 bonds. He took three or four million!" Cope said.

Cope continued to sell bonds to Berkshire. "I'd call and either Scott or Buffett would answer. Frankly, I always was relieved when I got Buffett. Scott was tough and would ask 'Whatcha got?'"

"Buffett was always a prince of a guy. He was cordial. He said, 'Good morning, tell me what you're working on.' Then he'd say he liked the company or that he didn't and would say he'd pass on it or he would take it."

Cope said, "I went out to Kiewit Plaza a few times and I'd go up to his little office. He'd stick his head out and say come in and let's talk a while."

Berkshire's textile business survived until 1985 when he closed the declining business. He got $163,000 for machinery with a book value of $866,000. Looms that were bought a few years earlier for $5,000 were sold as scrap for $26 each, less than the cost of taking them away. (*The Midas Touch*, John Train, p. 67) But long before then Berkshire's other businesses, some of which were partially financed by the meager textile mill income, were flourishing.

Today Berkshire is a far-reaching investment holding company with large stock, bond and cash holdings. It also has a number of operating businesses.

Berkshire fits no category—in corporate listings it variously is lumped with insurance, candy, media, diversified, nonbank financial, investment, miscellaneous or conglomerate firms. Berkshire is a hybrid company: it is all of the above. Although Berkshire's stock market value makes it the 23rd largest public company in the U.S., (*Financial World*, January 30, 1996) practically no analyst follows it.

To find out about the company, you have to make your own effort. Several times a year the company will issue one-sentence announcements of a new investment. About the only way to get a picture of how Berkshire stands is to ask the company for an annual report.

Beyond its plain looks—its largely hidden-from-view chairman, its tiny headquarters in Omaha at Kiewit Plaza at 36th and Farnam Streets, its plain-bound annual report, its largely no-comment policy—lies a world of beautiful businesses.

They're not sexy businesses—uniforms, shoes, vacuum cleaners—that sort of thing. Retraction. They are sexy businesses, if you're talking profitability. Some of the businesses earn a return on capital of 20%. That's outstanding by any measure. And sometimes they earn 30% to 40%.

Buffett's mundane businesses in bad years return an astronomical 50% return on equity on operations alone, and in 1989, reached an astounding 67% return based on historical cost, a figure almost no one in the business world has ever heard about or seen! Most businessmen talk happily in terms of a 10% to 15% return on equity. The number is so far beyond the range of most business numbers that generally it would be deemed a misprint.

Dry-sounding businesses supply these heavenly numbers: *The Buffalo News*, a newspaper firm in upstate New York; Fechheimer, a uniform company based in Cincinnati; Scott Fetzer Manufacturing Group, of Chicago, which has a variety of manufacturing businesses; World Book, also of Chicago, the encyclopedia maker; Kirby, a vacuum cleaner maker based in Cleveland, Ohio; Nebraska Furniture Mart, a large furniture store in Omaha; See's Candies, a San Francisco candy maker with more than 200 stores mainly on the West Coast and H.H. Brown Shoe Company, Inc. of Greenwich, Connecticut, which owns Lowell Shoe of Hudson, New Hampshire. Berkshire also owns Dexter Shoe Co. of Dexter, Maine, Helzberg's Diamond Shops of Kansas City, Misssouri, and R.C. Willey Home Furnishings of Salt Lake City, Utah.

Berkshire owned Borsheim's, a jewelry store in Omaha, might not sound like a big deal until you find it may have more sales than any other single jewelry store in the country with the exception of Tiffany's flagship New York store.

Further, Berkshire's Wesco Financial Corp., of Pasadena, California, in some ways a baby Berkshire, in turn owns a handful of businesses.

In addition to Berkshire's operating businesses, there is a large, separate insurance group of businesses.

It is the property and casualty insurance business—Berkshire's largest operating business—that is the vehicle through which Buffett usually makes his investments.

It's the money from Berkshire's businesses, particularly from the insurance operations as well as the income from Berkshire's stock and bond investments, that gives Buffett the ready cash for new investments to bring in more money.

Berkshire, which is listed on the New York Stock Exchange and trades under the symbol BRKA on financial tapes and as BerkHa in newspaper listings, has about 33,000 employees and roughly another 20,000 (mostly part-time) workers, who sell World Books.

Buffett's 479,202 shares (40.2%) of Berkshire's 1,193,512 shares is by far the largest ownership position. Buffett's wife, Susan, owns 36,985 shares (3.1%) of the stock. Her voting and investment power is shared with her husband.

Most top officers have a substantial portion of their net worth in Berkshire. Buffett's description is apt when he tells people, "We eat our own cooking."

It is a happy, wealthy group that has known the feeling expressed in the Josh Billings quote, "The happiest time in a man's life is when he is in red-hot pursuit of a dollar with a reasonable prospect of overtaking it."

Only about 7% of the stock as of December 31, 1990, was held by institutions owning about 78,000 shares, according to Standand & Poor's. But that has now risen to about 15% according to *Business Week* (March 27, 1995).

The rest of the stock is in the hands of about 25,000 individual shareholders, who don't trade the stock much. With the new Class B stock, there are now many more shareholders. Berkshire has less turnover than any stock on the New York Stock Exchange.

About 90% of Berkshire's shareholders bought in at $100 or less, giving the company an old wealthy family air.

"There are 125 shareholders in my zip code in Omaha, so I can go out and trick-or-treat on Halloween and be assured of good treatment," Buffett said on Adam Smith's *Money World* show October 21, 1993.

Berkshire shareholders almost all come from the United States, the United Kingdom, Germany, India and Canada. Some shareholders own 10 shares or less. Some consider it an honor to own even one share. On the other hand, Buffett, his wife, and Munger own almost 50% of the company.

Berkshire Vice Chairman, Charles Munger, Buffett's friend Sandy Gottesman, who heads the First Manhattan investment firm in New York and Dr. William Angle of Omaha—until his death—have been among the major shareholders. Malcolm Chace, a private investor in his late 80s, who is a former chairman of Berkshire, is a large stockholder whose cost basis on some of his Berkshire shares is said to be 25 cents. Chace and his son, Malcolm G. Chace III, who replaced his father on the Berkshire board in 1992, are among the largest individual Berkshire shareholders after the Buffett family.

Among the largest institutional holders are:

Ruane Cuniff & Co.	39,881 shares	3.34%
T. Rowe Price Associates	25,210 shares	2.11%
Boston Safe Deposit	24,935 shares	2.09%
Old Kent Bank & Trust	11,000 shares	.92%
First Manhattan Company	5,953 shares	.50%
J.P. Morgan & Co.	4,894 shares	.41%
California Public Employees	4,493 shares	.38%
Mercantile Bankshares	2,682 shares	.22%

United States Trust	2,631 shares	.22%
Norwest Bank Nebraska	2,524 shares	.21%
Mellon Bank N A	2,391 shares	.20%
Firstier Bank N A Omaha	2,005 shares	.17%
1st Source Bank	2,000 shares	.17%
Nicholas Company, Inc.	1,900 shares	.16%
ANB Investment Management	1,800 shares	.15%

Source: Bloomberg News Service, July 1, 1995.

Berkshire, operated by Buffett and just a handful of people, operates in such a lean manner it's a parody of other firms. In keeping with its lean structure carefully devised by Buffett, there are only six directors on the board, which has no standing committees and gets little in the way of outside advice.

Munger has said that long ago Berkshire was subpoenaed for its staffing papers in connection with one of its acquisitions. "There were no papers. There was no staff," Munger said at Berkshire's annual meeting in 1991.

Berkshire's board includes Buffett; his wife, Mrs. Susan T. Buffett; Munger; Malcolm G. Chace III, a private investor; Howard G. Buffett, Buffett's son; and Walter Scott, Jr., chairman and chief executive of Peter Kiewit Sons' Inc., a privately held construction conglomerate firm in Omaha whose record is so good that Buffett has said he won't recount it for fear of making Berkshire shareholders restive.

(Photo by Nancy Line Jacobs)

Kiewit's Walter Scott, Jr., and former Cap Cities Chairman Tom Murphy are close friends of Buffett.

The six folks on Berkshire's board are the "WORST" board in corporate America, according to *Chief Executive* magazine. *USA Today* in its May 6, 1994, issue said the magazine had come up with a list of the best and worst boards and that Berkshire's was at the bottom. Apparently the conclusion was reached because Berkshire's board is small, family-oriented and has no real outside directors. Giri Bogavelli, an investor in San Francisco, offers this rebuttal:

> Two of the more important factors in evaluating any board of directors are corporate governance and enhancement of shareholders' value. Berkshire's record on the issue of corporate governance is unblemished. Few philosophers in the arena of corporate governance ever get a chance to translate their well articulated theories into practice. Mr. Buffett has done just that at Berkshire.
>
> As to the enhancement of shareholders' value, Berkshire's record is matched by very few in corporate America. What is more important is that this was achieved with clearly enunciated principles and the highest ethical standards.

Munger is the chairman of Wesco and vice chairman of Berkshire. Buffett is chairman of the board, chief executive officer, and Berkshire's heart and soul.

21

How Far Will Berkshire Go?

"Through chances various, through all vicissitudes, we make our way"...Virgil's *Aeneid*

Just after the Berkshire annual meeting in 1989, Buffett showed up at Borsheim's. There he attracted a small band of shareholders and was going through his often repeated litany about how Berkshire's increasing size was forging its own anchor on growth, and how as Berkshire continues to grow the pace of growth is bound to slow.

Then Buffett said, and there really was a twinkle in his eye, "Well, it will be fun to see how far we can take it."

Soon Berkshire's stock price took one of its biggest leaps ever, moving in a few months from $5,900 a share to more than $8,000 a share. Over the years, Berkshire's 23% average annual return on book value and nearly 30% average annual advance in stock price has put it near the top of the investment charts.

Berkshire, like any other stock, takes its lickings, but it keeps on ticking. It's a case of, "Through chances various, through all vicissitudes, we make our way," as Virgil said in his *Aeneid.*

Can Berkshire keep such a pace? Clearly not. Since the 1960s Buffett has been saying that size is its own drag. Buffett is the first to say Berkshire can't maintain its growth rate.

After all, should Berkshire over the next 35 years keep up its annual 30% pace in stock price rise, the per share price would be about $80 million. Berkshire's stock market worth would be about $90 trillion—many times larger then the gross national product of the U.S. Berkshire would own the planet.

Buffett put it this way at the 1995 annual meeting saying that if Berkshire could grow at 23% of its book value annually, "it could gobble up the GDP. We think about it occasionally, but it won't happen."

And there are parts of the world Buffett doesn't care to own. But he clearly has set out to own some of the best parts and he may see Berkshire having some role in the world. But many investors simply do not believe the stock can go higher.

In my early days as a stockbroker, I tried to sell a share of Berkshire to one fellow. After much back and forth, he wrote, "When I get some mad money, I'd like to buy a share or two. It's hard to justify $12,000 for a share that pays no dividend. How high can it go? We will do some business together." I never heard from him again.

Take this as you wish, but although Berkshire does not have a company logo, it may have a secret symbol found on some Berkshire correspondence paper. A letter dated September 13, 1991, which Buffett wrote to shareholders explaining that year's shareholder designated contribution plan—if held up to the light—reveals a large circle surrounding the letters BH.

I once received the following note from Michael Assael: "Hold this letter up to the light to see Berkshire's secret symbol. Or what's more fun: take this letter, a flashlight, and a mirror into a dark room. There are endless possibilities, holding this letter backwards and forwards."

Berkshire actually has no secret symbol. Still it's curious.

Does it mean Berkshire will give contributions to the world or one day own the world? Does it mean Buffett's son, Howard Buffett, or Buffett's grandson, Howie Buffett, will one day run the company? (Buffett's granddaughter Emily? Bill Gates? GEICO's Lou Simpson? Who knows.) Could it mean that Harry Bottle, whom Buffett used to call in to sort out nasty business problems, will be resurrected? Is it some bonded paper notation that is meaningless?

"I don't think it means anything," says one skeptical Berkshire shareholder. "It'd be unlike him to go to the expense."

Is Buffett having some fun? Is he trying to tell us something about where Berkshire is going? In a circle? From zero to zero in stock price; ashes to ashes? Peace on earth?

Skipping the occult, here are the facts about how far Berkshire has come in terms of its stock price. Phoenix-like, it has risen from $12 in 1965 to more than $30,000 in 1996.

22

The Stock Price

"Honey, you're missing a zero."

A woman once called her broker and said she had $2,500 in her checking account and would like to buy a share of Berkshire.

"Honey, you're missing a zero," the broker replied.

Another time at a party a stockbroker asked a Berkshire shareholder the price of Berkshire. "33" was the reply. The broker leaned over to his wife and exclaimed, "He means 3,300!" Again, a zero was omitted.

One of the most unusual things about Berkshire is its 5-digit stock price. A share of Berkshire would buy a BMW.

"I never bought Berkshire because I always thought it was too high," said the late Ed Conine, who headed J Braggs, the women's clothing chain in Omaha. Conine knew Buffett and was familiar with his record.

Echoes a man who sports a Harvard MBA and has one of the top jobs at one of the largest securities firms on Wall Street, who is well aware of Berkshire and has met Buffett: "I just couldn't buy the stock because of the price...I realize it's what's behind the price but I just can't think in terms other than round lots." The man said he looked at the stock once and it was more than $1,000 a share.

"I couldn't recommend it," a number of stockbrokers have said.

Other reasons investors have offered for not buying Berkshire include:

"It's too rich for my blood."

"That's the one that doesn't pay a dividend."

"That's the one where he doesn't split the stock."

"That's the craziest thing I've ever heard of."

"It doesn't make any sense to me."

"I plan to wait and buy it the day he dies."

You can go down the list on the New York Stock Exchange past many stocks selling for $30 or $40 a share. Then you work through the B's and find Berkshire trading in five figures.

"When Berkshire Hathaway's stock was first to be listed in the *Wall Street Journal*, Buffett received a call and was asked if there were any plans for a stock split in the near future, and if such plans did exist would he please let the *WSJ* know now. Apparently in order to list the stock, the OTC section of the paper had to be reprogrammed to handle the four digit numeric value of the shares. Sufficiently humored, Buffett promised that no stock split would occur and to go ahead and reprogram the columns. Still concerned, the *Journal* programmer told Buffett that his stock was growing too fast and he planned to reprogram the section for five digits, just in case." (Anagnos thesis)

The price itself has left many an investor and stockbroker aghast. "What the hell is that?"..."There's some mistake" are refrains from many brokers over the years after getting the Wall Street inquiry of "How's Berkshire?"

For fun, call your broker and ask for a quote on Berkshire.

"What's that? There's something wrong with my machine," will probably be the reply.

There is no other stock like Berkshire. Many brokers just don't know the stock. Most brokerage firms don't follow the stock, have no opinion about it and thus its brokers can't solicit orders for Berkshire unless they convince their firms they have researched it. Commissions on the stock are unusually low and trying to convince someone to buy a stock trading in five digits isn't worth it for most brokers.

Berkshire is the highest priced and one of the least traded issues on the New York Stock Exchange. Because of its high price, a few shares make a big trade. A quirk in brokerage commission schedules, which usually don't go above $100 a share, involving the combination of the price and number of shares, creates only a tiny commission on trades of Berkshire stock.

At some discount brokerages you can buy 100 shares of Berkshire for a $38.50 commission. Trades of that dollar volume for lower-priced shares of another stock would be in the hundreds of dollars, thousands at a full-service brokerage.

Trades for one to 100 or more shares of Berkshire at full-service firms carry a commission of about $100.

"Berkshire is mutual fund-like, and (because of its low commission structure) it's basically no load," says Tim Callahan, a stockbroker with Prudential Securities in Birmingham. In fact, Berkshire is really a no-load fund with low expenses.

Once investors are in Berkshire, most don't sell. Therefore, a broker is less likely to enjoy a round trip on commissions. Berkshire stock just does not fit into the scheme of things for stockbrokers.

"I began buying Berkshire in the early 1980s. I bought from 1981 until 1987," said Chad Brenner, a lawyer in Cleveland, Ohio, who said Buffett's insistence on quality management and long-term outlook appealed to him. "I'm not a smart seller. I've never sold any shares...My kids will inherit my stock and I'm 37.

Buffett said in 1984 that more than 90% of Berkshire's shares were held by the same people who were shareholders five years before that and that 95% of the shares were held by investors for whom the next largest investment was less than half the size of their Berkshire holdings. Thus, Berkshire has a loyal group of shareholders and ones with a big percentage of their net worth riding on Berkshire's fortunes.

The float is so thin and shares traded so infrequently that one can stand with Jim McGuire, chairman of Henderson Brothers, at his post on the floor of the New York Stock Exchange where Berkshire and more than 80 other companies trade and find there's an hour or two between Berkshire trades. Or a day.

On July 25 and 26, 1991, there were no Berkshire trades. The streak was broken the following day when 10 shares changed hands, giving new meaning to the Wall Street saying "trades by appointment." Buffett likes that.

"Our goal is to attract long-term owners who, at the time of purchase, have no timetable or price target for sale but plan instead to stay with us indefinitely," Buffett wrote in the 1988 Berkshire annual report.

Brokers and journalists often are embarrassed by their lack of knowledge about Berkshire's high stock price.

One day in 1989 when Berkshire was up $100 to $8,550, an office worker at one brokerage firm said, "Something's wrong here. I need to get you a broker...Boy, I was about to blow my mind!"

Frequently, the first digit gets left off and any number purporting to be the actual price can be suspect. For example, Associated Press on November 18, 1989, listed the price-earnings ratio as 11,100. Ouch! On September 2, 1990, the P/E, actually about 17, was still higher at 11,636. But that was nothing compared to the listing March 22, 1991, which carried the P/E at 112,857, hardly in range for value investors.

The high P/E business never seems to get fixed. On July 1, 1991, the P/E was listed as 248,525 and on July 14, 1991, *Barron's* carried the P/E as 258,625! The price of Berkshire shares is so high, many newspapers have trouble squeezing the full price into their listings. In December, 1989, at the Associated Press, a computer program that processes stock prices had to be modified when it was discovered the share price exceeded the program's previous per-share ceiling of $8,192.

For a string of days in late 1989 the Stock Phone stock quote service in Atlanta carried Berkshire at $-83.

In September, 1990, when the early trading volume was 10 shares, Berkshire was listed as trading 6,000 shares. It would be a rare day indeed if Berkshire were to trade 6,000 shares because the stock has a very low turnover rate of about 4% a year. It trades on average about 150 shares a day.

At the same time that a brokerage firm's quote machine indicated 6,000 shares were trading, it correctly listed the high for the year in 1990 as $8,725, but listed the low at $175. 1990 was a bad year, but not that bad.

Another day Berkshire's share price shot up $175 to a new all-time high of $8,300. The next day the Wall Street Journal tables reported the previous day's high was $158, the low $8, and the closing price $108, down $801 for the day. Say what?

A Berkshire stock quote one morning in 1995 on the Bloomberg wire read: 37,000 + 15,000!

All the volatility reminds one of a *Barron's* cartoon (February 5, 1990): "The stock market rocketed up a big four-thousand points today, and then zoomed back down a hefty fifty-six hundred points, before rebounding in the final two minutes to close up one-point-three-two points."

The *Journal* also said Berkshire's 1993 operating earnings were $413,000 a share when they were $413 a share.

One time during a nasty spill in the market, Berkshire shareholder George Eyraud of Birmingham called a broker for a quote and was told that Berkshire was down $700, trading at $200 a share. His bankruptcy was just around the corner.

"I went and got a bowl of soup and tried to pull myself together, but I couldn't eat anything," he said hoping that once again the quotes were awry, which they were.

Another time he called a discount brokerage in Birmingham and asked to transfer $3,000 to his bank account.

"Sir, you only have $2,400 and you owe us $45,000. You'll be getting a big bill from us," the person at the other end of the line said.

"How can that be when I have 32 shares of Berkshire in the account?" he asked.

"Well, your Berkshire stock is selling at $77.50," the broker replied.

"Ma'am, that stock is selling for seven thousand seven hundred and fifty dollars," Eyraud said.

"Well, we'll check into it," a skeptical brokerage firm hand said.

Once Eyraud suggested to a woman stockbroker she buy a share of Berkshire. Her reply was "$8,000! I could get a full-length mink coat for that. You've got to get your priorities straight."

Eyraud also recalls talking to a fellow, suggesting Berkshire was a good investment.

"I would never invest in that," the fellow replied.

"Why not?" Eyraud asked.

"Well, it's just the principle."

"What principle is that?" inquired Eyraud.

"Well, it's just too high," the fellow explained.

Once a young stockbroker, seeing Berkshire's high stock price for the first time said, "Boy, am I going to short that thing!"

He could have shorted it and may have been burned. The short position in Berkshire usually runs about 2,000 shares and as of August 1994, was 3,586 shares. In 1995 it leaped to about 15,000 shares before settling at about 8,000 shares short.

Investors entering the land of Berkshire simply cannot get over the stock price. Once Joanne Englebert of Birmingham, a Berkshire shareholder, suggested to a friend, Dr. Martha Wingfield of Chapel Hill, North Carolina, that she buy a share of Berkshire, then trading at about $7,000. That way, Mrs. Englebert reasoned, she too could go to the Berkshire annual meeting in Omaha.

"I think $7,000 is a little much for a weekend in Omaha, don't you?" Wingfield replied.

One shareholder tells of a time he called a stockbroker who punched up a Berkshire quote. The broker took a hard look at the four-digit figure, then suddenly began apologizing, saying he couldn't read his screen. "I recently had an eye operation," he explained.

The price has thrown off investors, even experienced ones. One lifelong lawyer/investor who took a look at a Berkshire report and kept hearing about the stock price pronounced one day in 1988, "All the gravy's been taken out of that thing." The price then: $4,200.

Years later that person bought a share for $16,000.

Wyomissing, Pennsylvania, money manager Tom Weik recalls that in 1985 a young accountant came to him (back when Weik was a stockbroker in Reading, Pennsylvania), with $2,500 when Berkshire happened to be trading at just about that price. "It took me several days to convince him to invest it all in one share, but we bought the one share," Weik said.

Weik, who has written articles about Berkshire for local publications since the stock was trading at $200 a share back in the 1970s, showed up at the Rotary Club soon after the purchase. He was accosted by a fellow who had read one of his columns about Berkshire and said, "God, I sure wouldn't buy something at that price."

"I looked around and saw the accountant I had sold the share of Berkshire to standing next to him," Weik said.

"I did not blanch because I was that confident about Berkshire, but the accountant looked like he might have difficulty digesting his dinner."

A similar incident occurred in 1988 when Berkshire was trading at about $4,800. "But who would buy it now?" a woman asked Weik.

Weik said, "Well, I just bought it for your retirement plan."

Berkshire has its slow periods and its down periods. Sometimes long-time shareholders who know better wind up selling.

Another selling error was committed by Henry Brandt, Harvard's number one student in 1949 and long a senior vice president with Shearson Lehman Hutton.

In 1982, he sold more than 1,500 of the family's Berkshire shares for millions of dollars less than they are worth today. "I'm very embarrassed about that," he told *Fortune* magazine.

His embarrassment was complete when he learned that the buyer of his shares was a Berkshire subsidiary.

Charles Akre, managing partner of Braddock Capital Partners, L.P., in Arlington, Virginia wrote to his partners September 20, 1995:

> Back in 1977, when I was a young retail broker, I came across Berkshire Hathaway in the course of my research and I bought one share for $120. Over the next four years I accumulated a total of 40 shares, buying them a few at a time. Also during the late 1970s I tried my hand at real estate development. By 1981 I was in the midst of a "condo conversion" project which, owing to the 21% prime rate level, needed to have the construction loan refinanced. The lenders were aware, of course, that I had some liquidity away from the project, and the rest is history; I sold 39 shares for $500 per share. The single original share I still have sells today at an astounding 241 times the purchase price.

Akre made up for his mistake by loading up on Berkshire and International Speedway shares in Braddock Capital Partners.

An investor first taking a look at Berkshire is usually floored by the price and then put off again because it pays no dividend. Of course, the price is high because the underlying value is high and because Buffett has never split the stock, reasoning that such actions are cosmetic, involve paperwork and attract the kind of investor interested in meaningless stock splits rather than those concerned about what the company is really worth. Buffett wants investors, not speculators.

Although it's fun when dividends arrive, dividends are after-tax money from the corporation which then is taxed again when an individual pays taxes. Dividends may look good and they may feel good, but Buffett's not about falsely looking or feeling good. It makes more sense—and that is what Buffett is about—not to have dividends, particularly if Buffett is your money manager.

With Berkshire, the investor is leaving his share of the retained earnings within the company for Buffett to reinvest which he has compounded on the order of 25% a year. Or would you prefer, say a 3% paid-out dividend that would be taxed?

Investor John Slater of New York says he first bought a share of Berkshire at $425. "I had sent away for the annual report and I thought that was a good price for a lifetime subscription to the annual report."

About the same time, he gave a share of Berkshire to Gil Gunn, the newborn son of his friend, Gilman Gunn.

"By the time his second child came along, Berkshire was at $1,000 and I said that it was too much for me, that he ought to buy a share for the second child." Gunn, a widely recognized international investor, never did, although he later became a Berkshire shareholder himself.

Once the following conversation took place between a stockbroker and his sales assistant about Berkshire's stock price:

Stockbroker: "How about calling up a quote on BRK." [now BRKA]

Sales assistant: "It's trading at $15."

Stockbroker: "Are you sure?"

Sales assistant: "Well, there are some extra zeros."

Stockbroker: "Check again. Isn't it $15,000 a share?"

Sales assistant: "No, there's no stock that trades at $15,000."

Early in 1996 Berkshire's stock price hit $36,000 dollars. A customer calling Merrill Lynch for a quote was told: "Could that be right?"

23

American Express

Buffett peeks in the cash register.

One of Buffett's greatest decisions in the early 1960s was to invest in a big way in American Express.

Late in 1963 the Tino de Angelis salad oil scandal occurred when an American Express subsidiary found itself possibly liable for hundreds of millions of dollars worth of claims arising from quantities of salad oil that turned out not to exist.

An American Express subsidiary that issued warehouse receipts mistakenly certified the existence of huge quantities of salad oil that had been fraudulently confirmed to it as being in tanks in Bayonne, New Jersey. It turned out the tanks were mostly full of water. The crisis could have left American Express with a negative net worth.

"A great investment opportunity occurs when a marvelous business encounters a one-time huge, but solvable problem," Buffett says.

The ultimate advocate of a franchise business, Buffett liked the

American Express charge card and travelers check businesses and concluded their strengths were unassailable, and powerful enough to carry the company through troubled times.

Buffett already understood the principle of "Other People's Money." He knew American Express was a good business because of the huge cash "float" generated by American Express's travelers checks.

Buffett knew the float, like a low-cost loan, was valuable. So he went about making sure the underlying business was not hurt by the cloud overhanging American Express. In Ross's steak house in Omaha—one of his favorite haunts—and in other establishments, Buffett stood behind the cashier and peeked into the cash register to see if people were still using American Express cards and checks.

He found that merchants still were accepting the cards. Because the cards were still honored and the American Express empire remained intact, Buffett bought the battered stock. In 1964, investing 40% of the net worth of the Buffett Partnership, or roughly $13 million, Buffett bought 5% of American Express stock, which had collapsed to $35 a share from $65.

In doing so he violated his rule of not investing more than 25% of the partnership money in one investment, but he wrote a new rule of buying great companies when they temporarily stumble. In the next two years American Express stock tripled and the Buffett Partnership reportedly sold out with a $20 million profit. Apparently his partnership made even more because Buffett told the *Omaha World-Herald* (August 2, 1991) he held the stock for four years although published reports indicated he sold out after two years. Over a five year period the stock quintupled from $35 to $189. Buffett's investment lesson: when a great company falters, have a look.

24

Grinnell College

An education in investing

In 1968, not many years after the American Express investment, Buffett became a trustee of Grinnell College in Grinnell, Iowa, when the school's liquid endowment was about $12 million. He soon gave the college some good investment advice. Rule No. 1: Act fast. Rule No. 2: If someone else owns what you want, then buy a piece of their company.

It was at the urging of his friend Joseph F. Rosenfield of Des Moines, a lawyer, investor and retired chairman of Younkers department stores, that Buffett went on the Grinnell board. In 1967, Rosenfield, a member of Grinnell's investment committee, urged the endowment fund to buy 300 shares of Berkshire at $17.50 a share. That $5,250 investment is now worth a few million.

"We bought 300 shares and we sold 100 shares of it at $5,000," says Rosenfield. "We have since bought back more shares but I can't disclose how much. Of course, we bought them back at much higher prices."

In 1976 while attending a conference in New Orleans about the economics of newspapers, Buffett discovered that AVCO Corp. had decided to sell its television stations.

Under FCC rules Buffett couldn't buy the stations for Berkshire because of the number of television holdings already held by The Washington Post Co. So he proposed to Rosenfield that Grinnell College try to buy one of them. Buffett called Rosenfield, told him AVCO was having some financial difficulty and that Grinnell could buy a television station. "It was his idea," Rosenfield said.

Buffett's first choice was to buy a television station in Cincinnati, but the Grinnell board spent so much time discussing the financing that Multimedia, not Grinnell, bought the station for $16 million. Under Buffett's guidance, Grinnell did respond by buying $315,000 of Multimedia stock. The stock soared.

Buffett's second investment deal for the college was AVCO's television station in Dayton. Without waiting for financing, he bid $12.9 million, two and a half times the station's sales. He got it in the late 1970s and in late 1984 Grinnell sold the station to Hearst Corp. for about $50 million. Again, nice work if you can get it.

The transaction about doubled Grinnell's endowment which rose to about $120 million in 1984. "It turned out very well," Rosenfield said. "I got to know him 25 or 30 years ago through some mutual friends in Des Moines and he visited here."

If Buffett has some financial advice for Grinnell's board, he usually just calls Rosenfield.

"I see him every so often. He's still on the Grinnell board. He came to the board meetings for a while, but then stopped," Rosenfield said. "He really doesn't like meetings. Long-winded meetings are not his forte."

Grinnell's trustees have done very well with another Buffett connection, Bill Ruane's Sequoia Fund.

Grinnell, which celebrated 150 years of existence in 1996, is the largest shareholder, with about 13% of Sequoia which has about 25% of its money in Berkshire.

The trustees could consider a name change to Grinnell College and Bank.

Little wonder Buffett is a life trustee of Grinnell College. He is also a life trustee of the Urban Institute; trustee of the Business Enterprise Trust, Stanford, California; trustee of the Wellness Council of the Midlands (Nebraska), and is a member of the American Academy of Arts and Science.

25

Berkshire Hathaway Insurance Group

30 years of free money

"Even Don Wurster, the company president, admitted running a nervous finger down the columns of fine print in the morning newspapers until he found a particular team," wrote Melinda Norris in a May 13, 1990, story for the *Omaha World-Herald*.

"He'd pore over the inning-by-inning scores to make sure the team didn't score four runs or more in a single inning. National Indemnity was betting $1 million that no one on the team would hit a grand slam home run."

National Indemnity, Berkshire's main insurance operation, was underwriting a television contest that offered contestants a chance to win $1 million for predicting the station's secret Grand Slam Inning.

"If the guy hits a grand slam (during that inning), we write a check and some fan is rich," Wurster said. "Fortunately, they never hit a grand slam."

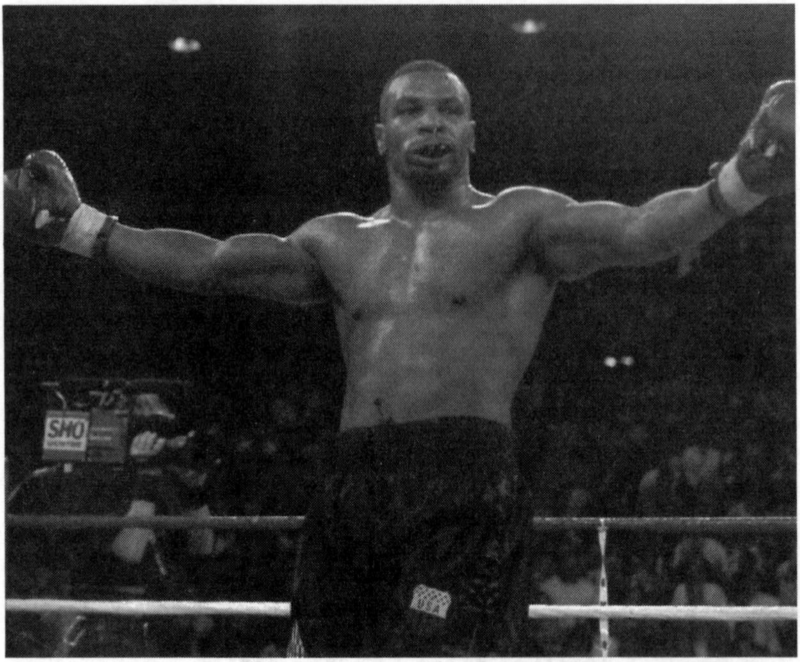

(AP/ Wide World Photo by Jeff Scheid)

Mike Tyson reacts after capturing the WBC heavyweight title when he defeated Frank Bruno March 16, 1996, at the MGM Grand Gardens in Las Vegas.

The same willingness to write unusual business at the right price still exists at Berkshire.

Buffett wrote in the 1995 annual report: "We insured (1) the life of Mike Tyson for a sum that is large initially and that fight-by-fight, gradually declines to zero over the next few years; (2) Lloyd's against more than 225 of its 'names' dying during the year, and (3) the launch, and a year in orbit, of two Chinese satellites. Happily, both satellites are orbiting, the Lloyd's folk avoided abnormal mortality, and if Mike Tyson looked any healthier, no one would get into the ring with him."

Back in 1967 Berkshire paid $8.5 million for two small Omaha insurance companies, National Indemnity and National Fire & Marine. "The two tiny underwriters had $17.3 million in so-called float - or double the companies' acquisition cost." *(Forbes,* January 22, 1996)

Today Berkshire's largest business is insurance—property and casualty insurance—conducted nationwide by a dozen insurance companies that operate with tiny organizational resources, but huge financial strengths. Huge.

Capital expenditures for all the insurance businesses in 1995 was about $1 million. Identifiable assets were $26.5 billion! For all of Berkshire, identifiable assets were $29.9 billion.

Munger at the Wesco annual meeting in 1993 talked about Berkshire's low expenses: "I'm sure we have the lowest ratio of headquarters cost to stockholders' capital of any insurance operation in the country, if not the world.

"In fact, Warren once considered buying a building on a distressed basis for about a quarter of what it would have cost to duplicate it. And tempting as it was, he decided that it would give everybody bad ideas to have surroundings so opulent. So we continue to run our insurance operation from very modest quarters."

Insurance, though risky, has great advantages, not the least of which is that capital gains enjoy a low tax rate. Normally Berkshire writes insurance for commercial vehicles and workers' compensation. But it has insured carnivals, free-throw contests, basketball and hockey games.

Buffett says Berkshire may be the largest writer of super-catastrophe (super-cat) business in the world. It writes such business as $10 million policies against earthquakes and offers coverage other insurance companies buy to protect themselves against a catastrophe.

(Photo by Andrew Kilpatrick)

Nondescript headquarters of National Indemnity Co. in Omaha, Berkshire's leading insurance firm. Many of Berkshire's investments are bought by National Indemnity. Technically, this little building's operations house billions.

In 1993 Berkshire entered the life insurance business, writing annuity policies for injured people who win insurance contract settlements. The firm got its risk-taking philosophy from founder Jack Ringwalt, who died in 1984. Ringwalt founded the company in 1940 for two Omaha cab companies that couldn't get insurance. In 1967 Buffett bought the company, which still had a hefty commercial vehicle business.

Ringwalt's memoirs said Buffett was about 20 years old when the two met. Buffett was trying to raise

$100,000 to start an investment pool. Ringwalt said he offered to invest $10,000. Buffett, however, said he would accept nothing less than $50,000.

"I remarked, 'If you think I am going to let a punk kid like you handle $50,000 of my money, you are even nuttier than I thought,' " Ringwalt wrote. Ringwalt took back his offer of the $10,000. "If I had put in $50,000 at the time he so desired, I could have taken out $2 million after taxes 20 years later. I did pretty well with National Indemnity Co., but not that well."

Although it covers risk, insurance itself can be a risky business as even Buffett's sometimes spotty insurance record can attest. Insurance companies always have a huge potential for liabilities should claims come due. And that potential problem exists for Berkshire, too.

Buffett wrote in Berkshire's 1988 Annual Report, "The property-casualty insurance industry is not only subnormally profitable, it is subnormally popular (As Sam Goldwyn philosophized: 'In life, one must learn to take the bitter with the sour.')" Occasionally, Buffett has misjudged the business known for its boom-and-bust cycles, and is the first to admit it. Overall, his predictions about industry trends have been remarkable, often predicting years ahead how things would turn out.

"It's only when the tide goes out that you learn who's been swimming naked," Buffett said at the annual meeting in 1993.

Berkshire has shown discipline in not writing policies unless it can get good prices. When prices are not attractive, Berkshire simply doesn't write the business. Buffett once said in a talk to Notre Dame students that when prices are unattractive, "We have a lot of people doing crossword puzzles."

Berkshire has more than $10 billion in insurance capital and could write far more business than it does.

At the Wesco annual meeting in 1993, Munger said he's often asked why Berkshire doesn't write more insurance. "People are always saying to Berkshire, 'Gee, why don't you write a lot more volume in relation to capital? Everyone else is doing it. The rating agencies say that you can write twice as much in annual volume as you have capital.' And they look at our $10 billion in insurance capital and say, 'That's $20 billion a year. What are you doing writing only $1 billion?'

"But then...somebody else comes in and asks, 'Why did everybody get killed last year but you?' Maybe the questions are related."

In 1995 Berkshire's net premiums were 5% of the insurance group's year-end statutory surplus, compared to an industry average premiums-to-surplus ratio of about 130% (for 1994).

The appeal of the insurance business is that premiums come up front—cash in the form of other people's money arriving every day at the office for you to run to the bank. You take those premiums and invest the money and the money grows. Essentially, the insurance business provides "float" somewhat akin to deposits in a bank, that can be invested. It brings Berkshire low-cost money. Basically, it's a free margin account.

"Float, per se, is not a blessing," says Buffett. But it is a blessing if you can get it in increasing amounts and above all if you can get it cheap, he adds.

"We have about $1.5 billion at a cost of $20 or $30 million. That's attractive to us," Buffett said at the annual meeting in 1990.

In 1993 Berkshire had an average float of $2.6 billion which cost less than zero. Indeed, Berkshire, because of an underwriting profit, was paid $31 million to hold the money. In 1994, the average float was $3.1 billion and Berkshire was paid $81 million to hold the money. The average float in 1995 was $3.6 billion.

Essentially, the insurance group has provided 30 years of free money.

Float at the end of 1995 was $3.8 billion. And Berkshire got about another $3 billion in float with the purchase of the rest of GEICO it didn't already own in early 1996.

Berkshire usually writes "long tail" insurance policies most likely to be paid off in the distant future. Clearly, it's good to have the policyholder's money for as long as possible, but Buffett also has warned that long tail policies are tricky because by the time it comes to pay policyholders, inflation and regulations may have raised costs so much, profits are elusive.

Court-award judgments far in excess of what was contemplated at the time the policy was written also can hurt insurance profits.

Insurance is an important business, especially in Nebraska where the business has received favorable treatment by state lawmakers. Mutual of Omaha, one well-known business made better known by Marlin Perkins' exploits on *Wild Kingdom*, is based not far from Berkshire's headquarters, its own version of a wild kingdom.

Starting in March, 1967, when Berkshire made a tender offer for National Indemnity and National Fire and Marine Insurance managed by Jack Ringwalt, Buffett bought the more than a dozen insurance businesses Berkshire now owns.

Berkshire entered insurance for diversity and for increased profits. National Indemnity, which even in the late 1980s was still using old IBM card sorters, occupies a six-story, 35,000 square foot building in Omaha and owns an adjoining 9,600 square foot building, not far from Berkshire's headquarters.

In addition to National Indemnity, Berkshire also owns the following insurance companies:

— Columbia Insurance, Omaha, Nebraska
— Cypress Insurance, Pasadena, California
— National Liability and Fire Insurance, Chicago, Illinois
— National Fire and Marine Insurance, Omaha, Nebraska
— Redwood Fire and Casualty Insurance, Omaha, Nebraska
— Continental Divide Insurance, Englewood, Colorado
— Cornhusker Casualty, Omaha, Nebraska
— National Indemnity of the South, St. Petersburg, Florida
— National Indemnity of Mid America, St. Paul, Minnesota
— Wesco-Financial Insurance, Omaha, Nebraska
— Central States Indemnity, Omaha, Nebraska
— Oak River Insurance Company, Omaha, Nebraska
— Gateway Underwriters Agency, St. Louis, Missouri
— Northern States Agency, St. Paul, Minnesota
— Ringwalt and Liesche and Company, Omaha, Nebraska
— Berkshire Hathaway Life Insurance Company of Nebraska

The underwriting activities of these businesses include the handling of almost all forms of property and casualty insurance through agents, in the District of Columbia and in all 50 states except Hawaii.

The main business is the sale of auto insurance, which accounts for about half of all the business. The businesses also sell trucking insurance, workers' compensation, homeowners', fire, and even insurance policies for those who serve as officers and directors of companies. For many years Berkshire wrote insurance for taxicabs in Omaha, but it no longer handles that business.

The insurance group also writes insurance for farm owners, business owners and garage owners. They also write insurance for luxury cars, marine accidents, earthquakes, cargo damage, and burglaries. It also sells personal and commercial package policies.

Berkshire-owned See's Candies buys its workers' compensation insurance at discount rates through Berkshire.

The Berkshire insurance companies also do a hefty reinsurance business, run by Ajit Jain, taking on the insurance risk and reward of insurance written by other companies. The reinsurance operations are run from National Indemnity's offices in Stamford, Connecticut.

"I talk to Ajit Jain about reinsurance deals every night. I do it as much for enjoyment as anything else. He could do it just as a well without me," Buffett says.

(Photo by LaVerne Ramsey)

Ajit Jain, shown here before the Berkshire annual meeting in 1995, and Buffett are friends. They often are on the phone several times a day discussing Berkshire's super-catastrophe reinsurance business which Jain heads.

Reinsurance involves insuring other insurance companies and exists so no one company will get hit with the total cost of something like an earthquake, which might bankrupt a primary insurance company with thousands of dependent, individual policyholders.

Reinsurers repackage and then parcel out the really big risks to someone, spreading the risk around as well as taking some of it themselves. To be in reinsurance means one better be able to take on a big loss. Berkshire is just that sort of company, and its unusual financial strength is a good marketing tool for seeking both insurance and reinsurance business. The Berkshire folks will write the policies and charge a stiff price for them, but if there is a catastrophe Berkshire could take a big hit. "When a major quake occurs in an urban area or a winter storm rages across Europe, light a candle for us," Buffett wrote in Berkshire's 1990 annual report.

At least the super-cat policies have caps on the possible losses although in some cases it has an obligation to renew the policy at once. Buffett has said Berkshire could be exposed to a $600 million loss if a hurricane were to slam the east coast, particularly New York.

Munger has said, "So if we have real disaster—if you had Hurricane Andrew followed one week later by another one just like it—Berkshire would have a very unpleasant year."

Berkshire is choosy about the business it writes, rejecting 98% of what it's offered.

Indeed, in the third quarter of 1992 Berkshire had to pay out $125 million in claims in connection with Hurricane Andrew damage in Florida. Buffett wrote a letter to shareholders reminding them of the volatility of the business:

> At this point, Berkshire may be the largest writer of super-cat policies in the world, an activity that will continue to make our quarterly earnings volatile. But that is of no concern to us: The gold medal in a marathon is awarded to the runner with the best time for the entire race and not to the one who ran the steadiest pace. Whenever the choice is offered, we welcome the chance to forfeit stability of quarterly or annual earnings in exchange for greater long-term profitability.

In 1994 Berkshire underwrote a $400 million reinsurance policy for 20th Century Industries, the California auto insurer.

"We will quote prices for coverage as great as $500 million on the same day that we are asked to bid. No one else in the industry will do the same," Buffett said in the 1994 Annual Report.

Buffett long has wanted to expand the insurance business. In 1985 he joined with American Express's Sanford Weill and some senior Fireman's Fund executives in a plan to buy Fireman's Fund from American Express. But the plan, organized by Weill, was rejected by American Express.

Still more insurance business could be tricky even for Berkshire, which has somewhat hodgepodge, disparate organizations often writing one-time policies as things now stand.

Berkshire's insurance companies own many of the investments Buffett makes, investments that provide such enormous financial strength that it's clear Berkshire can pay policyholders. Carrying far more assets than normally required by the insurance regulators, all the Berkshire insurance companies carry an A+ (superior) grade from A.M. Best & Co., the highest rating offered by that insurance rating firm.

Buffett wrote in the 1992 annual report:

> Currently Berkshire is second in the U.S. property-casualty industry in net worth (the leader being State Farm, which neither buys nor sells reinsurance). Therefore, we have the capacity to assume risk on a scale that interests virtually no other company...Charlie and I continue to like the insurance business, which we expect to be our main source of earnings for decades to come. The industry is huge; in certain sectors we can compete world-wide; and Berkshire possesses an important advantage. We will look for ways to expand our participation in the business...

(Omaha World-Herald)

Buffett, right, and William Kizer, Sr., center, and Kizer's son Richard, of Central States, at a press conference in 1991 when Berkshire bought Central States Health and Life. William Kizer said, "The price he quoted us was that he buys companies for 10 times earnings. I suggested, 'Well, last year we made $10 million, so...that's $100 million,' and I gulped. And he said, 'OK.' And I said, '$125 million?' He said, 'You're too late.' "

In the early days Buffett himself oversaw the insurance business, but he later turned over operations to Berkshire's Mike Goldberg, who is one of the few people who work at Berkshire headquarters with Buffett. His office is next to Buffett's.

In 1993 Goldberg relinquished his responsibilities for the overall management of the insurance group. He remains a key figure in Berkshire's insurance and credit operations.

Because the insurance group is not publicly listed, as are some of Berkshire's other holdings, it's tough to tell exactly what the insurance business is worth. Buffett has never put a figure on it other than to say it's difficult to do because of the nature of the business.

Some Berkshire shareholders say the value of the insurance group is way over $2 billion. On October 20, 1992, Berkshire said it agreed to buy an 82% interest in Central States Indemnity Co. of Omaha for $82 million.

The primary product line of the business, a unit of Central States Health and Life Insurance Co., is credit card insurance distributed through card issuers nationwide. The company pays credit card bills should the policyholder become disabled or lose a job.

Central States, formed in 1977, will continue under the present management led by William M. Kizer, Sr.

"It's a business I like, run by people I like and it's located in a city I like," Buffett said at a press conference announcing the deal.

William Kizer, Sr., said, according to *Omaha World-Herald*, (October 21, 1992), his negotiations with Buffett were straightforward.

"The price he quoted us was that he buys companies for 10 times (annual) earnings. I suggested, 'Well, last year we made $10 million, so if my multiplication is right, that's $100 million', and I gulped. And he said, 'OK.'"

"And I said, '$125 million?' He said, 'You're too late.' "

At a Berkshire annual meeting Buffett was asked about the problems at Lloyd's of London. He said:

> For a century, syndicates of Lloyd's have operated in such a way that its members have unlimited liability. They were a center for certain types of insurance—and a very important center.
>
> The liabilities that have accrued to certain members because of things like asbestos—where they had no idea of the huge scale in which the costs would occur—have caused a number of the people who were willing to be Names to dramatically decrease. And Lloyd's is groping around for some system that handles the problem of the long-tail liability and unlimited liability.
>
> I don't think that they've got any easy answers to that. So I think that they'll still be groping to some extent a year or two hence. Quite clearly, all of that is a benefit to us.
>
> I'll tell you what really benefits us...The hurricane in Florida looks like it will ultimately prove to have caused $16 billion or so of damage....But it's very easy to visualize a hurricane that comes up and hits Long Island that could triple or quadruple that amount.
>
> Well, when you start talking about $50 or $60 billion of losses and very major companies in this business only have a couple of billion of dollars of net worth—Berkshire has a significant advantage to be able to sustain significant losses. We should be able to get the appropriate premium.
>
> I'm not sure what Lloyd's total capital is, but I

> don't think that they have as much capital in aggregate as we do—and most of theirs is psychological, whereas ours is real.

Sequoia Fund's Bill Ruane says: "That insurance company is really a sleeper. Don't expect it to wake up. But if we're ever unfortunate to have true catastrophes that are anything like Andrew, there is one insurance company out there that can write 20 times what it's writing now very capably. Berkshire's got $10 billion or so in capital. Currently he's writing only about $200 million in regular business and about $500 million in reinsurance and catastrophe business. (*Outstanding Investor Digest*, June 23, 1994)

According to a *Financial World* article, November 9, 1993: "While Berkshire Hathaway has long been active in reinsurance, that part of the company's business remained fairly small until 1988. That year, Buffett began to expand both the property and the casualty—or liability—side of his reinsurance business very aggressively. Berkshire's reinsurance premium revenues shot from just $83 million in 1988 to $676 million in 1992. Reinsurance now represents nearly three-quarters of Berkshire's net written premiums."

But even as reinsurance prices have shot up in recent years, many firms still have been hit.

"Since 1988 property insurers have lost 10 cents on every premium dollar, but during the same period, Berkshire Hathaway paid out only $312 million in claims on $379 million in earned premiums. In crude terms that's a five year average return, before expenses, of 17.8%," the *Financial World* story said.

"But Buffett's real genius becomes apparent in casualty reinsurance. Unlike property claims, casualty claims often take years to settle. So here Buffett plays a complicated game that employs both a tax shelter and the float on funds before they're paid to settle claims.

"Berkshire's record in casualty reinsurance may look terrible, but it isn't. Over the past five years it has incurred losses averaging 138% of premiums earned. Add in 5% or so for expenses, and you wonder why anyone in his right mind would be writing casualty reinsurance like this.

"But don't forget the float. Unlike U.S. property reinsurers, U.S. casualty reinsurers get the use of the money for five or more years, compounding it in a tax-free reserve set up in anticipation of future losses. And here is where Buffett's stock market genius comes in. By compounding his cash through common stocks, he can increase the money at prodigious rates: 24% per year for the past 28 years. At that rate, $100 million in premiums becomes $288 million in five years' time, more than enough to pay even large claims with profit to spare."

The article goes on to say the average property and casualty insurer keeps 79% of its capital and reserves in high-grade corporate and government bonds so they can be liquidated without a loss when a catastrophe hits.

"Yet Berkshire Hathaway needs no such cushion, thanks to the rapid rate at which Buffett has been able to build Berkshire's equity portfolio. So Buffett can maintain, as he does, 85% of Berkshire's liquid assets in common stocks. In fact, Berkshire's actuaries may actually be overestimating their losses, in order to create larger reserves to shelter even more of the compounding assets.

"That is why most casualty reinsurers can't hope to keep up with Berkshire."

One of the early Berkshire reinsurance executives was George Young, who met Buffett in 1962 at a financial seminar. In 1969 Buffett asked Young to come to work for him. The two men started Berkshire's reinsurance business. Young, a Ph.D. in political science and regarded as brilliant, viewed Buffett as a mental giant.

"He once told me Buffett was the only fellow who made him feel retarded," says Mrs. Willie Young, Young's widow, a former Eastern Airlines stewardess who lives in Omaha.

Bill Lyons, National Indemnity's retired general counsel, recalls Buffett's wit: "He once asked me to check out a no-fault insurance business in Florida and I reported back that the business was in awful shape and that it would be stupid to invest in it. He said, 'Don't spare me just because it was my idea.' "

26

Kansas Bankers Surety Co.

"He just flat made an offer to us out of the blue."

Berkshire through Wesco acquired Kansas Bankers Surety Co. of Topeka, Kansas, for $75 million, according to a Kansas Bankers announcement April 11, 1996.

Kansas Bankers is an 87-year-old company that insures community banks throughout middle America.

The company's stock, which had been listed on the OTC bulletin board and traded infrequently, was at $19 a share before the announcement. The price Berkshire paid in cash was about $24.50 a share.

"He just flat made an offer to us out of the blue," said Don Towle, CEO of Kansas Bankers, of a letter Buffett wrote to the company in February, 1996. (*Topeka Capital-Journal*, April 12, 1996)

Buffett wrote the letter to Roy Dinsdale, a Kansas Bankers director who is also chairman of Pinnacle Bancorp Inc. of Central City, Nebraska.

Towle said he was initially "shocked," then "flattered" that Buffett would make an offer.

Most of the 600 stockholders of Kansas Bankers—most of whom

were banks or bankers—sold out to Berkshire.

Berkshire's buyout proposal had to be approved by regulators in all 25 states where Kansas Bankers does business.

Kansas Bankers insures bank deposits beyond limits of the federal government and it insures banks against burglaries, robberies and forgeries.

The company insures more than 1,200 banks and about 70% of the banks in Nebraska and is the only bonding firm owned by the banks it serves, according to the *Topeka Capital-Journal.*

Kansas Bankers was founded in 1909 by a group of bankers who shunned government programs designed to insure their banks' deposits. The company started as Bankers Deposit, Guaranty and Surety Co. Its main purpose was to guarantee the deposits of the banks that formed it. By 1922, the company changed its focus, deciding it was no longer profitable to issue deposit insurance. The company's stock, on a pro-rata basis, was placed in more than 700 Kansas banks and the name was changed to Kansas Bankers Surety Co.

By 1979 the company had captured all the market share in Kansas it could and it expanded to other Midwestern states.

Kansas Bankers had a net income of $6 million in 1995 on revenue of $17 million.

27

Boys Town

"I told our editor to get a copy of the Boys Town filing."
—A Pulitzer Prize

Buffett made his first newspaper purchase in 1969 when Berkshire bought the Sun Newspapers, neighborhood weeklies in Omaha. Buffett's role in his many media properties has been almost exclusively devoted to the business side, but in at least one case he had a very definite impact on the editorial end, when he played a key role in helping disclose the scandal at Boys Town in Omaha.

Back in 1917, Father Edward J. Flanagan, a lanky Irish Catholic priest, paid $90 to rent a drafty Victorian house to shelter five homeless Omaha boys. The home expanded greatly; with growth and strong leadership the institution also became a financial powerhouse. It helped children, but it could have helped more with the huge stock portfolio it began accumulating from fundraising.

In 1972 as Buffett described it to then *Wall Street Journal* reporter Jonathan Laing for a March 31, 1977, story, "I knew of an IRS regulation that required charitable foundations to publicly disclose their assets for the first time, so I told our editor to get a copy of the Boys Town filing. I'd heard a lot of rumors during my fund days about Boys Town's large stockholdings, but even I was staggered when we found that the home, which was constantly pleading poverty and caring for less than 700 kids, had accumulated assets of more than $200 million."

The subsequent stories—developed and edited by Stan Lipsey, now publisher of *The Buffalo News*—about Boys Town in the Sun Newspapers won a Pulitzer Prize in May, 1973, for special local reporting. The project was headed by Buffett and much of the research took place in his basement where documents related to the stories were stored.

Buffett sold Sun Newspapers in 1981 and it ceased publication in 1983.

One fellow who recalls working for the weekly as a newspaperboy is Allan Maxwell, now a medical sales representative with Searle Laboratories in Omaha. "I was a carrier for about five years and the pay was great for a 15-cent newspaper. I was able to keep five cents, as I recall," said Maxwell, adding, "I only wish I'd put my profits into Berkshire."

Today the paper no longer exists and Boys Town is a well regarded institution helping thousands of youngsters.

Buffett told Laing why he felt that newspapers are more interesting than most businesses.

"Let's face it. Newspapers are a lot more interesting business than say, making couplers for rail cars. While I don't get involved in the editorial operations of the papers I own, I really enjoy being a part of institutions that help shape society."

(Photo by Pat Kilpatrick)

Boys Town in Omaha

28

Media Connections

Charles Peters, Jay Rockefeller, Kay Graham, et al

Buffett's first tip about the Boys Town scandal was not to his own paper, but to his friend Charles Peters, publisher of *The Washington Monthly* in which Buffett had a small investment.

"I passed it [the tip] on [to his newsmen]...they decided not to pursue the story, largely, on the grounds, I suspect, that an investor's article idea had to be suspect. Warren then gave the story to an Omaha newspaper, which won a Pulitzer for it." (Charles Peters's autobiography, *Tilting at Windmills*, p. 196)

Peters gives an account of how Buffett, Jay Rockefeller and Louis Marx became investors in the magazine and said that Buffett asked him (Peters) for an introduction to Kay Graham:

> Jay Rockefeller and Louis Marx got us to $100,000 with additional pledges. Then Jay introduced me to Warren Buffett...

> In October [1969] he [Buffett] flew into Washington with two friends, Joseph Rosenfield, from Des Moines, and Fred Stanback, a North Carolinian who was heir to a headache remedy fortune. Together, they agreed to put up the remaining $50,000. We took all that money and blew it.
>
> The magazine, praised for its literary efforts, always struggled financially. Jay and Warren Buffett went to New York to ask James Kobak, a prominent magazine consultant, if there was any hope for the *Monthly*....Warren was impressed with Kaplan [Gilbert Kaplan of *Institutional Investor*] and said that he might be willing to put up another $50,000 if Kaplan took over the direction of the *Monthly's* business affairs long enough to get us straightened out.
>
> But in early September came a fifty-minute phone conversation with me in which it was clear that Warren's two sides were still at war. I was grateful for what he had already done for us and could understand his suspicion that the magazine was at best doomed to a life on the fiscal margin. So I wasn't angry when, at times during the conversation, he tried to withdraw from further involvement. But if I wasn't angry, I was desperate, because I knew I had to hold him in if the magazine was to survive. The conversation went back and forth: Warren would come within an inch of pulling out, and I would slowly try to pull him back. Then the dance would be repeated. Warren, who did not get to be a billionaire by being slow-witted, kept finding new escape routes, each of which had enough instant plausibility to put me into a state of near panic. My mind went into its highest gear as I tried to block the exits.
>
> Finally, he agreed to stay in. I have never been more keyed up than at that moment...Warren's sympathetic side had won out over the hard-boiled investor. (pp. 174-5)

Peters said his investors rarely called for favors, and when they did, they were innocent. "Warren, for example, asked me to introduce him to Kay Graham, which I did, and it turned out to be a very good thing for both of them. He became her principal financial advisor and the leading minority holder of Washington Post Co. stock. They have made each other a lot richer than either was before they met. I should have asked for 10%." (pp. 196-7)

29

The Washington Post

Back on board

Buffett bought his shares of The Washington Post Company in the spring and summer of 1973 for $10.6 million, making Berkshire the largest shareholder of The Post Co. outside the Graham family.

"Did it with about 20 orders over a several-month period," he would later say. "Sometimes in life things happen very fast."

He said basically he'd gotten to know Post Chairman Katharine Graham, saw the stock had gone public and wasn't doing well, "and I knew that the *Post* was going to outdo *The Star*, not necessarily make it fold, but outdo it."

It would turn out to be one of Buffett's most remarkable investments, one that he bought early when there was no particular investment interest in media stocks and that he held until the *Post* had a near monopoly in Washington, D.C. The Post Co. went public in 1971. Its Class B common

(AP/Wide World Photos)

Washington Post's Donald Graham, left, Katharine Graham and Ben Bradlee are FOBs—Friends of Buffett. Donald Graham once said of Buffett, "In finance, he's the smartest guy I know. I don't know who is second."

stock was issued at $6.50 a share and over the years has risen to about $300 a share, compounding more than 20% a year. The Class A stock, which controls elections of two-thirds of the board and therefore the company, is held by the Graham family.

Buffett's lifelong interest in media properties—epitomized by his purchase of Post Co. shares—always has gone far beyond cash flows. He is genuinely interested in media businesses, claims top journalists as friends and has said that if business had not been his calling, journalism might have been.

After all, his parents met while they worked at the school newspaper and Buffett was once an industrious *Post* delivery boy.

He has a reporter's instinct for the story, and his search for undervalued businesses combines a sharp business sense and a reporter's detective skills. Had Buffett become a journalist, he would have been a terrific one, but no matter what, he would not have made a tiny fraction of what he has earned as an investor.

In 1973 there were about 14 million shares of Post Co. stock outstanding, of which 2.7 million Class A controlling shares were owned by Mrs. Graham. She is the daughter of the late Eugene Meyer, a wealthy Republican Wall Street industrialist and financier who bought the paper in 1933, for $825,000, when his daughter was 16. Meyer named her husband, Philip Graham, publisher, in 1946.

By 1973, the beginning of the 1973-74 stock market slump, Post Co. stock had dropped from its original $6.50 issue price to $4 a share, adjusted for later stock splits. Buffett struck, buying his $10.6 million of Post stock, a 12% stake of the Class B stock or about 10% of the total stock.

The $4 price implied about $80 million evaluation of the whole company, which was debt free at a time when Buffett figured the enterprise had an intrinsic worth of $400 million. Yet it was not until 1981 that the market capitalization of The Post Co. was $400 million.

Buffett, in a talk to Columbia business students October 27, 1993 said:

> If you had asked anyone in the business what their properties were worth, they'd have said $400 million or something like that. You could have an auction in the middle of the Atlantic Ocean at two in the morning, and you would have people to show up and bid that much for them.
>
> And it was being run by honest and able people who all had a significant part of their net worth in the business.
>
> It was ungodly safe. It wouldn't have bothered me to put my whole net worth in it. Not in the least.

The Post Co.'s revenues in 1973 were about $200 million. Subsidiaries included the *Washington Post* newspaper, *Newsweek* magazine, the Times-Herald Company, four television stations and a paper company that provided most of its newsprint.

Since one rule of thumb is that good newspapers may sell for about two and a half times annual revenues, The Post Co. was worth four times what Buffett paid. Buffett has said the reason he could buy Post stock at a great price was because people just weren't very enthusiastic about the world at the time.

After Buffett's purchase, the stock fell for the next two years, and Buffett's investment sank from $10 million in 1973 to $8 million in late 1974. Post Co. stock did not move solidly ahead of Buffett's purchase price until 1976. But since then the stock has steadily forged ahead and today Buffett's original $10 million stake is worth more than $500 million.

In the beginning Buffett was not a welcome guest. Andre Meyer, a family friend of Mrs. Graham's, (but no relation to her parents, the Meyers) was irate when he found out Buffett had taken a big stake in the Post Co. (*Financier, The Biography of Andre Meyer*, by Cary Reich, 1983, p. 90)

"He was irate when one of the country's most successful private investors, Warren Buffet [sic], took a substantial position in Post Co. shares. As someone who had done that sort of thing himself, Meyer was naturally suspicious of Buffet's [sic] motives...

"Andre kept warning me about Warren Buffett," Mrs. Graham recalled. "He regarded all people who bought into companies uninvited as threats. But I checked Warren out rather carefully and decided that we were quite lucky, in that he was a very hands-off and honorable man."

Although Buffett convinced Mrs. Graham, Meyer kept after her, asking, "How is your boss?"

After his investment, Buffett wrote Mrs. Graham, who still had much concern about this largely unknown man who was buying so much Post Co. stock. Buffett told her he was no threat to her position and he fully understood she controlled the company through her ownership of the company's Class A stock.

"I recognize that the *Post* is Graham-controlled and Graham-managed. And that suits me fine," he wrote her. The letter was later jokingly referred to as the "Dear Mrs. Graham" letter. (*Regardie's*, February, 1986)

Mrs. Graham tried to get a fix on this fellow from Omaha. "I scurried and said 'Who is he and what's he like and is he a threat?' "

One thing that may have broken the ice: Buffett was able to remind her he had worked for the *Post* as a paperboy 25 years earlier. By the way, by delivering the *Post* in the 1940s, Buffett earned about half of his initial investment money as a youngster.

"Buffett had asked Charles Peters, an acquaintance of Kay's, to make the introduction in 1971. Buffett had a specific reason for wanting to meet her: he owned stock in *The New Yorker,* which he believed might be for sale, and he wanted to interest Kay in attempting a takeover, arguing that the *Post* would be the perfect owner for the magazine. Kay dismissed his suggestion." (*Power, Privilege and The Post* by Carol Felsenthal, p. 321)

They had not met again until 1973, at the office of the Los Angeles *Times* after Buffett's Post Co. purchase. Reassured by the encounter, Mrs. Graham asked Buffett to come to dinner in Washington and take a look at the *Post.* A strong friendship and a profitable relationship were born.

In 1974 Buffett was named to the Post Co. board and, appropriately, chaired its finance committee. Soon he suggested the board buy back Post Co. stock. Few companies in the 1970s were doing stock buybacks and very few, if any, in the media business were buying back their own shares.

Here's how what was to become Buffett's hallmark—the stock buyback—worked for the Post Co. Between 1975 and 1992, the Post Co. bought back about 43% of its outstanding shares. Average cost: $60 a share. So it bought back more than 40% of its business at roughly a quarter of its present price.

Also, Buffett suggested that the *Post's* pension fund switch from a large bank to managers with a value orientation. After the move to value managers, returns rose substantially even though The Post told the managers to keep at least 25% of the money in bonds.

Buffett served on The Post Co. board until 1986, when he resigned after Berkshire committed $517 million to help Cap Cities buy ABC. The resulting company became media giant Cap Cities/ABC and Buffett was invited on its board.

Buffett had to leave The Post Co. board because Federal Communications Commission rules prohibit an individual from serving simultaneously as a director both of a company that owns a television network (Cap Cities/ABC) and also one that owns cable television systems.

A similar prohibition applies to overlaps of television signals from stations owned by different companies such as Cap Cities' New York station and The Post Co.'s Hartford, Connecticut station. This overlap also prohibited Buffett from serving on both boards at the same time.

If Mrs. Graham ever had reservations about Buffett or his intentions, they have long since vanished. "Our board was just devastated by his departure. They really miss him," she was quoted in the *Wall Street Journal* (September 30, 1987).

The devastation did not last forever. After Disney bought Cap Cities in 1996, Buffett was re-elected to The Post Co.'s board. Buffett was back on board. Buffett and Mrs. Graham remain close friends and today she sings his praises. "He has wisdom, human sensitivity and above all humor. I think it's a unique combination," Mrs. Graham told Adam Smith, host of *Money World*, in a show about the Berkshire annual meeting of April 30, 1990.

Buffett jokes, not very convincingly, about his lack of influence at The Post Co. since he left the board, citing as an example his lack of a role in The Post Co.'s decision to sell some cellular phone properties.

"My only role with Washington Post Co.'s sale of the cellular phone properties was to recommend against the original purchase of the properties at one fifth of the price they sold it for. And that's the last time they asked. They didn't pay attention to me the first time and they didn't ask the second time," he said at Berkshire's 1987 annual meeting.

But it's apparent Buffett remains a trusted friend of Mrs. Graham's.

Mrs. Graham's son is Donald Graham. In his early days he served in Vietnam and then on the Washington Metropolitan Police Department, becoming a *Post* reporter in 1971.

Donald Graham has said of Buffett, "In finance, he is the smartest guy I know. I don't know who is second."

Buffett thinks Graham is a smart fellow himself and over the years has spent time tutoring him, "sending him annotated balance sheets and teaching him how to judge the value of acquisitions." Graham adopted Buffett's business philosophy of paying for quality and skimping on frills. *(Washingtonian,* August, 1992)

"Once, a group of Post board members was standing around kibitzing, waiting for Donald Graham to show up, and Robert McNamara bet them nobody could name Abraham Lincoln's first vice president. Nobody could. Buffett then bet $5 that Don would know the answer. 'Sure,' Graham said when he arrived. 'It was Hannibal Hamlin.'

"Don is incredibly smart, and his memory is off the charts," says Buffett. 'If I try to remember something from my annual reports, he can quote it back. It's easier to call him than to look it up myself." It was The Post Co. investment—a more than 40-fold return on his money classic—that locked up Buffett's reputation as a master investor. Over the years the *Post* strengthened its dominance of the city's newspaper industry, but the path was not always easy. Coverage of the Watergate scandal, particularly by Bob Woodward and Carl Bernstein, did bring the paper enormous acclaim including a Pulitzer Prize in 1973 for their stories that led to President Nixon's resignation in 1974.

"Deep Throat," the anonymous source of some of the "Woodstein" stories became synonymous for anything smacking of investigative journalism.

Once Woodward asked Buffett a good way to make more money and Buffett suggested investing. Woodward told Buffett, "I don't know anything about investing."

"Yes, you do." Buffett said, "All it is, is investigative reporting."

In 1954, the *Post,* then the third-ranking newspaper in the capital city, bought *The Times-Herald*—buying its 3,500 shares for $1,600 a share or $5.6 million. The paper's rapid growth swept it past the *Washington Star*, which wilted under the competition from the *Post* and folded in 1981.

But before that, The Post Co. faced in rapid order three major problems: the stock market plunge of 1973-74, the Watergate crisis, with all the glory and headaches it brought the *Post,* and a crippling strike in 1975. In 1972 and 1973 The Post Co.'s stock price was sinking because of withering criticism the paper was receiving from the Nixon White House for its Watergate coverage.

At the height of Watergate, according to the Nixon tapes, Nixon encouraged talk of revoking the licenses for The Post Co.'s two Florida television stations, WJXT/TV4 in Jacksonville and WPLG/TV in Miami, the station whose call letters are taken from the initials of Philip L. Graham, the deceased husband of Mrs. Graham.

The license revocations were pushed by a number of people with associations to the Nixon administration, but they were never successful, according to Chalmers Roberts, a long-time *Post* reporter who has written *In the Shadow of Power: The Story of The Washington Post.*

The Watergate scandal was one financial blow; the bitter strike that occurred at the paper in 1975 was worse. Even as the paper prevailed in the Watergate crisis, a new problem was brewing—relations with its unions. In late 1975 the unions went on strike. The strike's ugliest moment came with the trashing of the pressrooms, a blow to both the finances and pride of the mighty newspaper.

Mrs. Graham was uneasy about the risk of holding out, particularly in view of competition from the *Star.*

The strike helped cement the relationship between Buffett and Mrs. Graham. "Characteristically, Buffett—who was 'omnipresent at the *Post,*' according to a former employee—plays down his role. 'I was around,' he says." (*Regardie's*, February, 1986)

Mrs. Graham said, "The strike was terribly hard on me, in the sense of judging how dangerous it was [financially] for us to be on strike with the *Star* publishing. He said, 'Look, if I think it's dangerous, I'll tell you.' He was very supportive." Buffett and Mrs. Graham worked side by side in the *Post's* mailroom more than once, sometimes staying until 2 a.m. to assemble the Sunday papers for distribution.

Buffett kept encouraging Mrs. Graham and guided her business education. "Warren saw how little I knew about business. He would bring about 25 or 30 annual reports and take me through them," Mrs. Graham has said.

During these tumultuous events, Buffett hung steadfast and in the end his investment grew mightily.

In 1984 Buffett wrote Mrs. Graham:

> Berkshire Hathaway bought its shares in *The Washington Post* in the spring and summer of 1973. The cost of these shares was $10.6 million and the present market value is about $140 million....If we had spent this same $10.6 million at the same time in the shares of...other media companies...we would now have either $60 million worth of Dow Jones, $30 million worth of Gannett, $75 million worth of Knight-Ridder, $60 million worth of *The New York Times* or $40 million of *Times Mirror*.
>
> So—instead of thanks a million—make it thanks anywhere from $65 to $110 million. (*The Midas Touch*, John Train, p. 77)

Throughout the 1980s The Post Co. racked up tremendous financial gains and journalistic recognition in the form of Pulitzer Prizes. Today the Post Co. oversees a vast journalistic enterprise with a stock market value of well above $2 billion. The Post Co.'s interests include the *Washington Post*, by far the most influential paper in one of the world's most important cities. Daily circulation of the *Post* is 816,000 and Sunday circulation is 1.14 million.

The Post Co. owns *The Herald*, in Everett, Washington.

In recent years, the *Post* has begun to surpass its bigger archrival, *The New York Times*, in profitability and stock market value. In addition to the *Post* newspaper which accounts for about half of The Post Co.'s profits, the company owns *Newsweek,* the national news weekly with 3.2 million subscribers but which has long run second in circulation to its main competitor, *Time* magazine.

The Post Co. also owns six television stations: WDIV/TV4 in Detroit, WPLG/TV10 in Miami, WFSB/TV3 in Hartford, WJXT/TV4 in Jacksonville. It bought KPRC-TV in Houston and KSAT-TV in San Antonio in 1994 for $253 million. Also, it owns a large cable television franchise it bought from Cap Cities in 1986 for $350 million when the franchise had about 360,000 subscribers. Buffett was a central figure in the transaction. The Post Co.'s cable business, which has grown through acquisitions and new subscribers to more than 600,000 subscribers, is vastly more profitable than when it was acquired.

Further, The Post Co. owns the Stanley H. Kaplan Educational Center, bought in 1984. Its some 150 tutoring centers and 600 satellite locations prepare students for licensing exams and admissions tests, including the revamped Scholastic Aptitute Test. In turn, Kaplan owns Crimson and Brown Associates of Cambridge, Massachusettes, a collegiate recruiting firm that helps employers identify, interview and hire hard-to-find candidates.

The Post Co. owns 28% of Cowles Media Company which publishes the *Minneapolis Star and Tribune* and other properties. The Post Co., which has about 6,000 employees, also owns Legi-Slate Inc. a computerized tracking service covering congressional and regulatory actions. It owns one half, as does *The New York Times*, of the *International Herald Tribune* newspaper published in Paris and printed in eight cities, which circulates both *Post* and *New York Times* stories in 164 countries.

In March 1992, The Post Co. acquired an 80% stake in Gaithersburg Gazette, Inc., the parent firm of Gazette Newspapers which has 11 weekly newspapers in Montgomery, Frederick and Carroll counties in Maryland. The weeklies have a combined circulation of more than 180,000.

Berkshire now owns about a 16% share of all the Post Co.'s wonderful businesses, up from the original 10% of the company Buffett bought in 1973. Over the years, with the Post Co. buying back a portion of its own stock, Buffett's ownership percentage has increased.

The Washington Post was founded at the end of Reconstruction in 1877 by young Stilson Hutchins, a restless man originally from Whitefield, New Hampshire.

"That first edition of *The Washington Post* had four pages, each with seven columns, printed on rag paper," wrote Chalmers Roberts in his book, *In the Shadow of Power*.

As a journalist, Hutchins was on top of the hot story that Thomas Edison was making headway with his invention of an electric lamp. He interviewed Edison on the last day of 1879 and on January 2, 1880, a front-page story by him began:

> New York, January 1, 1880,—I went over to Menlo Park (New Jersey) yesterday afternoon and evening to see Edison and his electric light. The workshop was crowded with people, who arrive and depart by almost every train. They are inquisitive and troublesome, but, notwithstanding the annoyance they frequently cause, they are treated with consideration and politeness. Edison is not only a great inventor, but has as much

> patience as Job.
>
> In all about sixty lights are constantly maintained and others are being added daily. The first lights are still burning, having been in steady operation for twenty-two days. The little carbon horseshoe, as it is called, seems not to have lost an atom of its weight or abated a particle of its illuminating power. If it will last twenty-two days without deterioration or loss there seems no reason why it should not last twenty-two years or an age. So far as the experiment has gone it is literally indestructible. Mr. Edison considers this feature of his invention as perfected, and, as is well known, it was the one over which he has spent the most time and which the world considered unattainable...

Hutchins was so taken with the coming of electricity that he was largely responsible for the electrification of Washington, D.C. Hutchins's was the first of three ownerships before the paper began its modern life in 1933 when Meyer bought it at auction in a bankruptcy sale at the depth of the Depression.

A lawyer, George E. Hamilton, Jr.— representing Meyer, the undisclosed principal, who authorized his representative to bid as high as $2 million— won the paper with a bid of $825,000.

The *Post* on Friday, June 2, 1933, carried the headline: "*Washington Post* sold for $825,000."

Chalmers Roberts wrote: "Rumors of the real buyer's identity floated about the capital but Hamilton would disclose nothing...On June 4 *The* [*Washington*] *Star* carried a Meyer denial to the AP story in New York that he was the buyer. There was a ten-day delay for the necessary court approval...On Tuesday, June 13, *The Post* carried at the top of page 1 a two column box headed: "Eugene Meyer announced as *Washington Post* buyer."

Meyer dedicated his time, energy and considerable fortune to making the *Post* viable. The *Post* rang up a long string of losses. But Meyer's integrity, hands-on management and constant financial support saved the *Post.*

Roberts again: "The *Post's* deficits were massive: $323,588 for the last half of 1933 after Meyer took over: $1,191,597 in 1934; $1,279,262 in 1935; $857,156 in 1936 and $838,937 in 1937. 'One year,' Meyer later remarked to a friend, paying the *Post's* losses 'took more than my entire income.' To another he said, 'No one is rich enough to keep that up.' But not only did Meyer keep on paying the losses, he plunged ahead to improve his paper."

The losses continued through the early World War II years. After nine and a half years of losses under Meyer, it finally rang up profits of $247,451 from 1942-1945.

Enter Philip Graham, who had married Meyer's daughter, Katharine. In 1946 President Truman asked Meyer to be the first president of the World Bank. Meyer was so impressed with the vitality and charm of Graham, who had graduated 10th in a class of 400 at Harvard Law School in 1939 and had been head of the Law Review, that Meyer prepared to hand over the reins of the Post Co. to young Graham.

In 1948 Meyer announced the transfer of voting stock to Philip and Katharine Graham saying that Graham would hold 3,500 shares and his wife 1,500 shares of the 5,000 voting shares.

Meyer explained to Graham: "You never want a man working for his wife." (*In the Shadow of Power*, Chalmers Roberts, p. 258)

The relationship between Meyer and Graham was very close and Graham quickly became a brilliant leader of the Post Co. He set out to make it a journalistic and financial success and succeeded at both.

The real turning point for the *Post* came in 1954 when it bought the *Times-Herald* and became the sole morning paper in the nation's capital. The purchase doubled its circulation and sent ad revenues jumping.

"The purchase capped Eugene Meyer's two-decade gamble with the *Post* and it left no doubt that Philip Graham, now 39, would be a major figure in American journalism," Roberts wrote.

At the time Meyer said: "The real significance of this event is that it makes the paper safe for Donnie (his grandson)."

Philip Graham was a publisher bursting with ideas: pushing The Post Co. into television in a big way, buying *Newsweek* in 1961 and buying an interest in Bowater Mersey Paper Co.—the firm that supplies most of the paper's newsprint. Graham also developed a close friendship with President John Kennedy. Everything was going his way, but then something went terribly wrong.

Graham began suffering periodically from a manic-depressive illness in 1957; on August 3, 1963, he was allowed to leave psychiatric care and with Katharine Graham drove to Glen Welby, their farm near Marshall, Virginia, for a weekend outing.

As the *Post* reported the next day: "Shortly after 1 p.m. while Mrs. Graham was in her room upstairs, Mr. Graham killed himself with a .28-

gauge sportsman's shotgun. He was alone in a first-floor room." Graham was 48.

Responsibility for The Post Co. fell immediately to Mrs. Graham, who had worked as an editor at the paper, but her interest in journalism or business was limited at the time. Her main credentials: her father had owned the paper and her husband had run it.

"When my husband died I had three choices," she has said. "I could sell it. I could find somebody to run it. Or I could go to work. And that was no choice at all. I went to work...It was simply inconceivable to me to dismantle all that my father and my husband had built with so much labor and love."

Once asked if she wasn't terrified, she replied, "congealed." Nevertheless, she built the *Post* into one of the best newspapers in the country, one known for investigative reporting, stylish prose and business success.

Under her leadership, the newspaper and its reporters won 18 Pulitzer Prizes. One Pulitzer had to be returned in 1981 because the winning entry turned out to be a fictitious story by Janet Cooke about a young drug user ("Jimmy's World").

Her first major change at the *Post* was to name self-confident Benjamin Bradlee as managing editor, moving longtime friend and managing editor Al Friendly upstairs to the London bureau. Bradlee, who later occasionally played tennis with Buffett, energized a highly talented and competitive newsroom. Some years later he was one of the heroes of both the 1971 publication of the Pentagon Papers, top-secret documents about Vietnam, and the Watergate scandal from 1972 to 1974.

Publishing the Pentagon Papers in 1971 gave The Post Co. plenty to worry about. The decision to do so came in the midst of plans for the privately held company to make a multi-million-dollar public stock offering. Indeed the day before the public offering, Bradlee asked Kay Graham to publish the Pentagon Papers story.

"The Justice Department had sent her a pre-publication message threatening to prosecute the company, which could have resulted in the forfeiture of its broadcast licenses if convicted," wrote Donald Graham in the company's 1991 annual report in a tribute to his mother.

Bradlee, known for his penchant for "holy shit" stories, argued nonpublication would make the *Post* out a coward and also said the *Post* could start running the story the next day or get a new executive editor. (*Newsweek,* July 1, 1991) Mrs. Graham's response to Bradlee was "Okay, go ahead, go ahead!"

The *Post's* finest hour came with its coverage of Watergate. For the

Post, Watergate began with a call from Joseph A. Califano, Jr., then general counsel of the Democratic National Committee, to Howard Simons, the paper's managing editor, telling him of a break-in at the party headquarters at the Watergate office building.

Simons put the paper to work immediately after the June 17, 1972, break-in.

The *Post* ran a story the next day on the top left side of page 1 of the 306-page Sunday *Post* with the headline: "5 Held in Plot to Bug Democrats' Office Here."

Two of the eight reporters contributing to the lengthy account were Bob Woodward and Carl Bernstein. A new era in investigative journalism was underway. "Deep Throat"—taken from the title of a pornographic movie of the time—epitomized the critical importance of confidential sources.

Later some reporters on a medical story developed a source who came to be known as "Sore Throat." That one didn't stick.

A new age in journalism spawned a new age in counterattack as evidenced by Roberts' account:

> As the Nixon tapes would show, the attack on the *Post* had been planned at least as early as September 15, 1972. On that day, in a conversation between Haldeman and John Dean, the President had said of the *Post,* "It's going to have its problems...The main thing is The Post is going to have damnable, damnable problems out of this one. They have a television station...and they're going to have to get it renewed." When Haldeman added, "They've got a radio station too," Nixon went on, "Does that come up, too? The point is, when does it come up?" Dean replied, "I don't know. But the practice of non-licensees filing on top of licensees has certainly gotten more...active in the, this area." And Nixon: "And it's going to be God damn active here...Well, the game has to be played awfully rough.

In January 1973, challenges were filed before the Federal Communications Commission against the renewal of The Post Co.'s two Florida television stations.

Mrs. Graham noted that all the challenges were filed by Nixon administration supporters, and in an affidavit said she believed the challenges were "a part of a White House-inspired effort to injure the...company in retaliation for its Watergate coverage."

The challengers denied the contention. In any event, The Post Co. kept its stations, but Post Co. stock fell by nearly half. As always, Buffett hung in there.

Woodward and Bernstein went on to write *All The President's Men*. The movie starring Robert Redford (Woodward), Dustin Hoffman (Bernstein) and Jason Robards (Bradlee) made the *Post* more famous.

Buffett, as were most Americans, was absorbed by the Watergate scandal and followed it closely on television and in the newspapers.

In 1991 both Mrs. Graham and Bradlee retired from their main jobs at the *Post* and were contemplating their memoirs. Bradlee's book, a best seller, *Newspapering and Other Adventurers: A Good Life*, came out in 1995.

For years the *Post* was late moving into new technologies because of union-embedded practices of make-work or featherbedding. Things already were uneasy when negotiations deadlocked for a new pressmen's contract in 1975, and the *Post* called for substantive changes. On October 1, at the night pressrun, several pressmen jumped night foreman James Hover, beat him and threatened to kill him.

During the next 20 minutes, a number of others sabotaged the *Post's* nine presses, disabling the newspaper. The *Post* lost just one day's publication before it found six small newspapers within 200 miles of the *Post* willing to print the paper.

As many as 200 employees slept on cots in the building, doing normal jobs during the day and then (in coveralls) handling production jobs at night. Mrs. Graham worked most Saturday nights taking classified ads, according to Roberts's book.

Efforts to mediate were fruitless and the *Post* advertised for "temporary replacements." The strike collapsed on February 16, 1976, after the mailers union voted to accept a new contract. And all through the bear markets, the Watergate scandal, and the strike, Buffett never sold one share of Post Co. stock. For his patience, he was paid.

For decades the *Post* had struggled in its competition with the *Star*, but with the purchase of the *Times-Herald*, it became a much stronger competitor, soon racing by the *Star*. In 1981, the *Star* folded, making the *Post* essentially a monopoly newspaper in one of the world's great cities, the U.S. capital.

For Buffett and Berkshire shareholders, the 1980s were boom times as Buffett rode the tiger of one of his great ideas: that monopoly newspapers are bullet-proof "toll-bridges." Buffett seized on the monopoly, "toll-bridge" concept earlier and with more dramatic results than any other investor.

When customers can satisfy their buying needs by crossing only a particular monopoly toll bridge, there's nowhere else to cross. If you want to advertise, through the printed word at least, there's no other place to get your message across. It's the only game in town, a monopoly bulletin board.

Although the late 1970s and 1980s were boom times for The Post Co., its annual meetings were next to unbearable, marred by unreasonable questions from Accuracy in Media and other advocates, (questions often designed simply to embarrass Mrs. Graham and Donald Graham), and also dominated by harangues from corporate gadfly Evelyn Y. Davis.

One could go to a Post Co. annual meeting and hear several hours of political bickering and learn little about Post Co. businesses. The annual meeting aside, almost everything else at The Post Co. had the mark of great success during the 1980s. But by 1990 newspapers were facing the worst advertising environment in 20 years.

The recession of the early 1990s caught up with even Washington, D.C., and with retailing and real estate in tailspins, the *Post's* ad linage declined, earnings for the year fell, and Mrs. Graham was forced to write in the 1990 annual report that financial results were "very disappointing." Donald Graham later called 1991 a terrible year.

In 1992 The Post Co. acquired 15% of ACTV and helped the company develop entertainment applications for its interactive technology, and in 1993 The Post Co. received the right to buy 51%.

Incidentally, Mrs. Graham attended the Berkshire annual meeting in 1990 as the guest of Buffett's daughter, Susan. Mrs. Graham sat in one of the front rows of the theater where Buffett was holding court. When a question arose after the annual meeting about the future of The Post Co., Buffett said it might have some short-term problems but would be fine in the long run. He turned to Mrs. Graham and asked her opinion and she said, "Ditto."

The short-term air pockets that triggered the well-publicized nationwide recession in advertising were outlasting Buffett's expectations, but The Post Co. has remained a mighty enterprise even though it has become increasingly apparent that newspapers are no longer the only advertising game in town.

Big city newspapers, with advertising nosediving, were underpriced by small newspapers and magazines, by direct mail campaigns, more cable television channels and new technologies such as videotext.

Buffett, after the meeting, kept answering more questions, but could not be heard well because he stood up from the dais and moved away from the mike he used during the meeting.

No one else had the nerve to tell Buffett they couldn't hear him, but Mrs. Graham said, "Warren, get to the mike." He did.

The Post Co. and Buffett have treated one another well. Buffett is often invited to dinners at Mrs. Graham's home. It's an invitation only the high and mighty get for a formal dinner. But when she serves a gourmet meal, Buffett passes it up for a hamburger, fries and a sundae. "He has a limited palate," says Mrs. Graham. (*USA Today*, September 18, 1991)

The Buffett-Graham friendship goes far beyond dinner. Occasionally Buffett has written an article for the paper and when he first testified before Congress in connection with the Salomon scandal, Katharine Graham had a front row seat.

Buffett was surrounded by reporters and photographers throughout his testimony and as he left the hearing room, they pursued him. But he eluded them and slipped into a limousine that took him to the *Washington Post*, where he met with the editorial board.

Buffett and the *Post* know all about scoops.

30

GEICO

Stray brush marks on the canvas transform into Buffett's masterpiece in the making.

Always looking for that edge, Buffett early on took a fancy to GEICO, the auto and homeowners insurance company that sells by mail and telephone. In a seminal event, Berkshire now owns all of GEICO with the purchase in early 1996 of the half of GEICO it didn't already own.

"When I first got interested in GEICO, [Ben] Graham was chairman of Government Employees Insurance [GEICO] at the time. I took his class here at Columbia," Buffett said in a talk to Columbia business students, October 27, 1993.

"I went to the library...and looked it up... and it said it was located in Washington, D.C. So I went down there on a Saturday in January from Columbia. And I got there fairly early, 11 or so o'clock, and the door was locked. And I banged on the door for a while and finally, a janitor came. And I said, is there anybody here I could talk to except you? Well, there was a guy up on the fifth floor, and the janitor said if you like, go up and see him.

"So I went up and met him. He's 90 or 91 years old now. His name's Lorimer Davidson. At the time he was the investment officer there. He later became CEO. He spent about five hours with me that day. He explained the whole insurance business to me, how it worked and how GEICO worked. And I became totally enamored of it.

"And then I came back to New York, back at school, and I went downtown to talk [to]...big insurance specialists. And every one of them told me that [GEICO] was way overpriced compared to these other companies, for all kinds of reasons. And it didn't make any sense to me...

Only 21 at the time, Buffett invested $10,282 in GEICO in 1951. In 1952 he sold out for $15,259, mainly to switch the money into Western Insurance Securities selling at one times earnings.

Buffett told *Forbes*, October 18, 1993, "It was a company selling insurance at prices well below all the standard companies, and making 15% profit margins. It had an underwriting cost then of 13% or so, whereas the standard companies had probably 30% to 35% cost. It was a company with a huge competitive advantage, managed by the guy that was my god."

Eventually Buffett pitched the idea of buying GEICO to stockbrokers and found little interest. He could not convince them of the promise of the business that sold directly to customers, short-circuiting agents and thereby making a 20% profit on its underwriting activities compared to the normal rate of about 5%.

In 1971 Jerome Newman, following Ben Graham into retirement, nominated Buffett to take his place on the board, but because Buffett had sizeable insurance investments, the SEC had reservations and the idea was dropped. (*Benjamin Graham on Value Investing*, Janet Lowe, p. 152)

The entire company, when Buffett bought in, had a market value of $7 million.

In 1976, because of a miscalculation of its claims and underpricing, GEICO was nearing bankruptcy. The stock had dropped from $61 to $2 a share.

GEICO founder Leo Goodwin left his stock to his son, Leo, Jr., who margined his shares and was hit by the stock's slide. Leo Jr., committed suicide.

But Buffett believed that the company's competitive advantages were still intact. Further, he had great confidence in a newly named chief executive, John J. Byrne (now chairman of Home Holdings Inc.).

In 1976 and during the following five years, Buffett invested $45.7 million in GEICO. Buffett's cost basis was $1.31 per share (adjusted for the 5-1 stock split in 1992). Buffett and Byrne, who went off to run Fireman's Fund in 1985, now called The Fund American Companies, became close friends. GEICO became a cornerstone of Berkshire's growth.

Byrne has said, "In a sense, GEICO sort of made Warren's financial career." (*Chicago Tribune*, December 8, 1985)

During its brush with bankruptcy, GEICO needed the help of an investment banker. Salomon Brothers and its partner John Gutfreund, backed the turnaround.

"Charlie and I like, admire, and trust John. We first got to know him in 1976 when he played a key role in GEICO's escape from near bankruptcy," Buffett wrote in Berkshire's 1987 annual report.

Buffett has described his thinking on the GEICO purchase this way (*Investing in Equity Markets*, pp. 11-12):

> It wasn't necessarily bankrupt but it was heading there. It was 1976. It had a great business franchise which had not been destroyed by a lot of errors that had been made in terms of exploiting that franchise. And it had a manager...I felt he had the ability to get through an extraordinarily tough period there and to re-establish the value of that franchise. They still were a low-cost operator. They made all kinds of mistakes. They still didn't know their costs because they didn't know what their loss reserves should be and they got captivated by growth: they did all kinds of things wrong but they still had the franchise.
>
> It was similar to American Express in late 1963 when the salad oil scandal hit it. It did not hurt the franchise of the travelers check or the credit card. It could have ruined the balance sheet of American Express but the answer of course was that American Express with no net worth was worth a tremendous amount of money.
>
> And GEICO with no net worth was worth a tremendous amount of money too except it might get closed up the next day because it had no net worth, but I was satisfied that the net worth would be there. The truth is a lot of insurance companies for the ownership of it would have put up the net worth. We would have put it up. But they were trying to save it for the shareholders,

> which is what they should have done. It had a very valuable franchise. Take away all the net worth. Let's just say that GEICO paid out a $500 million dividend right now which would eliminate the net worth of GEICO, would it still have a lot of value? Of course, it would have a lot of value. You'd have to do something, you'd have to be part of another entity that kept insurance regulators happy, but the franchise value is the big value in something like that...

The nation's seventh largest insurer of private passenger vehicles with 3.7 million cars insured, GEICO relies on direct marketing. And it offers a 24-hour, seven-day-a-week telephone line for customers to call in. "Each week, 10,000 drivers switch their car insurance to GEICO," said a GEICO flier inserted in Berkshire's 1995 annual report.

Since GEICO doesn't have to pay commissions to agents and sells directly to customers, it can undercut its competition because paying agents can cost about 15% of a company's premiums.

Although most property and casualty companies usually lose money in some years on their underwriting, GEICO failed to make an underwriting profit only once in almost two decades. That means that almost every year the company is generating huge amounts of money to invest without having to pay anything for the money. For GEICO, that float is essentially an interest-free loan.

Insurers generally overcome their underwriting losses by making profits from their investments, and here GEICO is well known for savvy investments. It is willing to invest more heavily in the stock markets than most insurance companies, usually outdistancing stock performance averages because of the stock-picking abilities of its co-CEO, Lou Simpson. Buffett has called Simpson the best investment person in the property-casualty industry.

GEICO was founded in 1936 in Texas by Leo Goodwin, an accountant for an insurance company in San Antonio, Texas. (1985 GEICO Annual Report which contained a company history) By studying accident statistics, Goodwin learned that federal, state and municipal employees had fewer accidents than the general population. Of course, GEICO now insures good drivers in many occupations.

And Goodwin also learned that the largest overhead expense for most casualty insurance companies is the cost of advertising and selling. He saw that if you could cut out the middleman and insure better-than-average drivers, you could sell a $30 car insurance policy at a large savings of $6 or $7. Today, GEICO advertises through such media as CNN, but it has traditionally kept advertising costs low.

In 1936, Goodwin chartered Government Employees Insurance Company in Fort Worth to sell car insurance to government workers and military employees, and it eventually grew from that niche into a nationwide writer of coverage for autos and homes.

In the early days, Goodwin sought out Fort Worth banker Cleaves Rhea, who believed in his idea. Rhea agreed to invest $75,000 if Goodwin could put up $25,000 to capitalize the fledgling company, which was chartered September 1, 1936. Goodwin received 25% of the stock and Rhea 75%.

In the difficult early years, Goodwin and his wife, Lillian, worked 12 hours a day, 365 days a year for a combined monthly salary of $250. Goodwin devoted weekends to writing responses to customers' inquiries or complaints.

The Goodwins targeted government employees as safe drivers with steady incomes. There were more of them in Washington, D.C., so the company was moved there and rechartered in 1937.

The company's underwriting losses declined each year until a $5,000 underwriting gain was achieved in 1940, with a $15,000 net income. This was the first of 35 consecutive profitable years.

In the fall of 1941, a hailstorm damaged thousands of cars in the Washington, D.C., area. Goodwin arranged with repair shops to work 24 hours a day exclusively for GEICO policyholders. Anticipating glass shortages, Goodwin had truckloads of glass shipped to Washington, D.C.

Cars of GEICO's policyholders were repaired in days while policyholders with other companies waited weeks.

In 1948 the Rhea family sold its 75% stock holding to Graham-Newman and a small group of private investors. The value of the company was about $3 million. Later that year, Graham-Newman distributed its stock to its shareholders and the company became publicly owned.

In 1949 GEICO passed the $1 million profit mark and began to expand its operations. In 1952 the company broadened its business to include all state, county and municipal employees, thus gaining a larger group of prospects.

GEICO President Leo Goodwin retired in 1958 and became founder chairman. He had seen his novel concept—with its operating principles of selling direct and marketing to preferred-risk customers—grow from $104,000 in written premiums in 1936 to $36.2 million in 1957.

Investors fared well, too. If one had bought $2,000 worth of GEICO shares in 1948, that investment would have grown to $95,000 at Goodwin's retirement ten years later.

But by 1975 GEICO was at the brink of bankruptcy. Enter Buffett. Between 1972-74 the introduction of no-fault insurance and public clamor over skyrocketing insurance rates had resulted in states requiring prior rate approvals.

In May 1976, the board of directors elected John Byrne as chairman, president and chief executive officer. Byrne took three drastic steps to turn the company around:

> **First,** Operation Bootstrap—This included rate increases, vigorous cost controls and a reunderwriting of the entire book of business.
>
> **Second,** Reinsurance—Byrne convinced 27 GEICO competitors that providing reinsurance relief was in their best interest.
>
> **Third,** New Capital—The investment banking firm of Salomon Brothers agreed to underwrite a $76 million stock offering, increasing common stock to an equivalent of 34.3 million shares.

Operating profit returned in 1977.

GEICO created "sister companies" in 1949, and in 1977 it began to buy back stock of those sister companies.

GEICO, long headed by Chairman William B. Snyder (who retired in 1993) is now headed by Tony Nicely, co-CEO of insurance operations and Lou Simpson, co-CEO of capital operations.

The emphasis at GEICO is on stellar driving records; if anything goes wrong with that record, Snyder has said, "We can be fairly unforgiving."

GEICO has kept its underwriting ratios below 100 for all but one year in the past decade, meaning that the company takes in more in premiums than it pays out in claims and expenses.

That sets it apart from most other property-casualty companies, which pay out more in claims and expenses than they collect in premiums, and rely on investments alone for profits. In general, the industry is substantially dependent on investment income for profits.

In the recent insurance industry-wide slump, GEICO has been beefing up advertising and lowering rates in regions where competitors are hurting. The strategy has resulted in slightly increased market share.

GEICO has about 6,000 employees, almost all of whom are on the underwriting side along with just a handful of people under Simpson who

(Courtesy of GEICO)
GEICO's Tony Nicely

make up the investing team.

In 1991 when Berkshire already owned 48% of the stock, the stake was duly noted by Snyder at GEICO's annual meeting held at a regional office in Dallas.

Buffett showed up for the meeting, taking a seat in the back row. More than 90% of the stock was represented in the room. With Buffett in the room, about half the stock was present and accounted for.

Snyder, conducting the meeting and spotting Buffett in the back of the room said, "Warren Buffett is here (applause). Together Warren Buffett and I own 48% of the company."

Actually, Snyder owned well over 1% of GEICO's stock himself.

The prospect of being controlled by Berkshire doesn't seem to bother Snyder who said, "Warren Buffett is such an enlightened owner that we frankly wouldn't be distressed. We thought about this back when he had 35-37% of the stock and we see no problem. Nothing will change." Snyder has said Buffett exercises no control over the company.

Simpson and Nicely said then: "Absolutely nothing changes."

In late 1995 GEICO had a $900 million stock portfolio of such stocks as Freddie Mac, Nike, Reebok and about 1,300 shares of Berkshire. GEICO had more than a $3.7 billion bond portfolio consisting of tax-exempt municipal bonds and Treasury securities. GEICO sold its three million shares of Reebok in late 1995, but kept its 2,350,000 shares of Nike. (*Wall Street Journal*, April 23, 1996)

Unlike many insurance firms, GEICO has no exposure to real estate and little to junk bonds.

The company's earnings have continued to be solid, with really just a few fender-benders along the way. And it has the ability on the investment side to be wise with its money. After all, its investment folks are occasionally in touch with Warren Buffett.

HOLY COW NEWS FLASH ON AUGUST 25, 1995! Berkshire will buy all the rest of GEICO for $2.3 billion. By this time Berkshire owned 51% of the stock and agreed to buy the remaining 49% and to make GEICO a wholly owned unit of Berkshire. GEICO is operated independently of Berkshire's other insurance operations.

Buffett said Berkshire and GEICO officials had been talking earlier about a purchase paid for with securities, but although "it looked like it might work, it was very complicated," and there were tax problems.

"So Thursday of last week management said they would be satisfied if we could do it for $70 [a share]...I gulped and squirmed and said okay," Buffett said. "They got the last penny out of me." (*Washington Post*, August 26, 1995)

Of his investment in GEICO back in 1951, Buffett said, "I felt very comfortable with that commitment, and I feel equally comfortable with the major commitment that Berkshire Hathaway made today."

Here's how Berkshire bought the rest of GEICO, according to a *Washington Post* story which ran in the *Omaha World Herald* on November 7, 1995, quoting proxy information filed with the SEC:

> ...For years, Buffett had mentioned to top GEICO officials that his company, Berkshire Hathaway, should consider acquiring 100% of GEICO. But no discussions took place until August 17, 1994. That was the date on which Buffett met in Washington with Louis A. Simpson, co-chief executive of GEICO and the company's longtime financial whiz, and Samuel C. Butler, chairman of the GEICO board's executive committee.
>
> Buffett suggested that Berkshire acquire GEICO in a tax-free transaction, with GEICO shareholders swapping their shares for Berkshire common stock. Simpson and Butler said they were concerned about the proposal. First, because Berkshire stock did not pay a dividend, as did GEICO. Second because they thought it would be difficult to accomplish the stock swap in a fair way.
>
> Berkshire Hathaway stock, one of the highest - priced stocks on the market, was then selling for $18,700. A GEICO stockholder who had 200 GEICO shares would have received only a fraction of a Berkshire share - and since no fractional shares would be issued, the GEICO stockholder would wind up with taxable cash.
>
> The conversation then turned to the possible use of a new Berkshire convertible preferred stock having a dividend equal to GEICO's dividend. Buffett indicated that he'd be willing to swap one share of the preferred stock - with a stated value of $55 a share - for each share of GEICO. Butler replied that, while he

> would talk it over with GEICO's financial advisors, he would not recommend any such deal to the GEICO board unless the fair market value of the Berkshire preferred was at least above $60...

Meanwhile, Buffett raised questions about tax issues involved in a tax-free stock swap, and the staffs of the two companies started to research those issues.

> On March 1, 1995, Simpson and Butler met in New York with Buffett and his partner, Charles T. Munger. Again they talked about a deal, but each side held firm to its position on price. Butler and Simpson noted that since August, Berkshire stock had climbed to $22,500 a share. And they expressed serious concern about how that lofty price might affect the fair market value of a share of Berkshire preferred stock, especially if something should happen to Buffett...

GEICO officials asked Butler to call Buffett and tell them they would go for a $70-a-share cash transaction or for a convertible preferred stock deal that was worth $70 on the market. Two days later Butler made the call. Buffett asked if the price was negotiable. Butler said no. Buffett then said he really did not want to issue preferred stock at $70 a share. Moreover, he said, he would prefer a cash deal.

Buffett then said he wanted to talk to his partner, Munger, about the deal, which he did. Later in the day, Buffett called Butler and said yes, he would agree to do the deal for $70 in cash.

GEICO is a real Buffett Classic. The purchase of all of GEICO was a huge event for Berkshire.

"To sum up, we entered 1995 with an exceptional insurance operation of moderate size. By adding GEICO, we entered 1996 with a business still better in quality, much improved in its growth prospects, and doubled in size. More than ever, insurance is our core strength," Buffett said in Berkshire's 1995 annual report.

Asked why it took him so long to acquire all of GEICO, Buffett said, "It takes money, you know." (*Omaha World-Herald,* August 26, 1995)

With GEICO now fully owned by Berkshire, little dots and stray brush marks that Buffett made on his canvas years ago now form a complete picture, one big part of the masterpiece in the making.

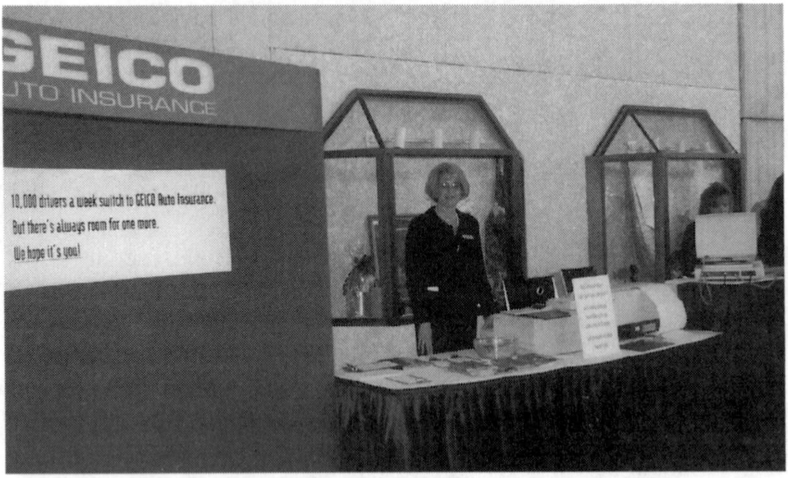

(Photo by LaVerne Ramsey)

The GEICO booth at Berkshire's annual meeting in 1996.

31

A Look at GEICO by a not-your-average 21-year-old

In 1951, when Buffett was 21 years old, he wrote an article about GEICO for the "The Security I Like Best" column of a New York publication. It's a look at GEICO by a not-your-average 21-year-old:

Reprinted from

The COMMERCIAL *and* FINANCIAL CHRONICLE

Thursday, December 6, 1951

The Security I Like Best

WARREN E. BUFFETT

Buffett-Falk & Co., Omaha, Nebr.

Government Employees Insurance Co.

Full employment, boomtime profits and record dividend payments do not set the stage for depressed security prices. Most industries have been riding this wave of prosperity during the past five years with few ripples to disturb the tide.

Warren E. Buffett

The auto insurance business has not shared in the boom. After the staggering losses of the immediate postwar period, the situation began to right itself in 1949. In 1950, stock casualty companies again took it on the chin with underwriting experience the second worst in 15 years. The recent earnings reports of casualty companies, particularly those with the bulk of writings in auto lines, have diverted bull market enthusiasm from their stocks. On the basis of normal earning power and asset factors, many of these stocks appear undervalued.

The nature of the industry is such as to ease cyclical bumps. Auto insurance is regarded as a necessity by the majority of purchasers. Contracts must be renewed yearly at rates based upon experience. The lag of rates behind costs, although detrimental in a period of rising prices as has characterized the 1945-1951 period, should prove beneficial if deflationary forces should be set in action.

Other industry advantages include lack of inventory, collection, labor and raw material problems. The hazard of product obsolescence and related equipment obsolescence is also absent.

Government Employees Insurance Corporation was organized in the mid-30's to provide complete auto insurance on a nationwide basis to an eligible class including: (1) Federal, State and municipal government employees; (2) active and reserve commissioned officers and the first three pay grades of non-commissioned officers of the Armed Forces; (3) veterans who were eligible when on active duty; (4) former policyholders; (5) faculty members of universities, colleges and schools; (6) government contractor employees engaged in defense work exclusively, and (7) stockholders.

The company has no agents or branch offices. As a result, policyholders receive standard auto insurance policies at premium discounts running as high as 30% off manual rates. Claims are handled promptly through approximately 500 representatives throughout the country.

The term "growth company" has been applied with abandon during the past few years to companies whose sales increases represented little more than inflation of prices and general easing of business competition. GEICO qualifies as a legitimate growth company based upon the following record:

Year—	Premiums Written	Policy-holders
1936	$103.696.31	3,754
1940	768,057.86	25,514
1945	1,638.562.09	51,697
1950	8,016,975.79	143,944

Of course the investor of today does not profit from yesterday's growth. In GEICO's case, there is reason to believe the major portion of growth lies ahead. Prior to 1950, the company was only licensed in 15 of 50 jurisdictions including D. C. and Hawaii. At the beginning of the year there were less than 3,000 policyholders in New York State. Yet 25% saved on an insurance bill of $125 in New York should look bigger to the prospect than the 25% saved on the $50 rate in more sparsely settled regions.

As cost competition increases in importance during times of recession, GEICO's rate attraction should become even more effective in diverting business from the brother-in-law. With insurance rates moving higher due to inflation, the 25% spread in rates becomes wider in terms of dollars and cents.

There is no pressure from agents to accept questionable applicants or renew poor risks. In States where the rate structure is inadequate, new promotion may be halted.

Probably the biggest attraction of GEICO is the profit margin advantage it enjoys. The ratio of underwriting profit to premiums earned in 1949 was 27.5% for GEICO as compared to 6.7% for the 135 stock casualty and surety companies summarized by Best's. As experience turned for the worse in 1950, Best's aggregate's profit margin dropped to 3.0% and GEICO's dropped to 18.0%. GEICO does not write all casualty lines; however, bodily injury and property damage, both important lines for GEICO, were among the least profitable lines. GEICO also does a large amount of collision writing, which was a profitable line in 1950.

During the first half of 1951, practically all insurers operated in the red on casualty lines with bodily injury and property damage among the most unprofitable. Whereas GEICO's profit margin was cut to slightly above 9%, Massachusett's Bonding & Insurance showed a 16% loss, New Amsterdam Casualty an 8% loss, Standard Accident Insurance a 9% loss, etc.

Because of the rapid growth of GEICO, cash dividends have had to remain low. Stock dividends and a 25-for-1 split increased the outstanding shares from 3,000 on June 1, 1948, to 250,000 on Nov. 10, 1951. Valuable rights to subscribe to stock of affiliated companies have also been issued.

Benjamin Graham has been Chairman of the Board since his investment trust acquired and distributed a large block of the stock in 1948. Leo Goodwin, who has guided GEICO's growth since inception, is the able President. At the end of 1950, the 10 members of the Board of Directors owned approximately one-third of the outstanding stock.

Earnings in 1950 amounted to $3.92 as contrasted to $4.71 on the

2

smaller amount of business in 1949. These figures include no allowance for the increase in the unearned premium reserve which was substantial in both years. Earnings in 1951 will be lower than 1950, but the wave of rate increases during the past summer should evidence themselves in 1952 earnings. Investment income quadrupled between 1947 and 1950, reflecting the growth of the company's assets.

At the present price of about eight times the earnings of 1950, a poor year for the industry, it appears that no price is being paid for the tremendous growth potential of the company.

This is part of a continuous forum appearing in the "Chronicle," in which each week, a different group of experts in the investment and advisory field from all sections of the country participate and give their reasons for favoring a particular security.

32

Coca-Cola's Don Keough

"Warren, are you buying a share or two of Coca-Cola stock?"

Shortly before Buffett would make stock market history by buying a billion dollars worth of Coca-Cola stock, he took a call from Coca-Coca President Don Keough.

"I asked how things were and I said, 'Warren, are you buying a share or two of Coca-Cola stock?'"

"He said yes and he said it enthusiastically," recalled Keough, chairman of Notre Dame's board of trustees. Keough is known for standing ovations as an after-dinner speaker and is a longtime friend of Johnny Carson, whom he met at an Omaha television station where Keough announced football games.

"It wasn't too long before the announcement that he [Warren] was buying when I called him. We knew somebody was buying the stock. We figured it out by deduction," said Keough, indicating the conclusion was reached by folks at Coke who follow the stock's trading patterns.

"We knew he had an interest in The Coca-Cola Company," said Keough, admitting that one of the tips occurred when "Warren became America's number-one fan of Cherry Coke which we introduced in 1985."

"He really understands the company. He's a terrific board member. He knows the company. He knows the numbers. He's an informed and stimulating director. He has a clear understanding of the inherent value of global trademarks."

And what did Mr. Keough do after Mr. Buffett bought Coke stock? "I became a modest Berkshire shareholder after his purchase of Coca-Cola stock," said Keough, who had an opportunity more than 30 years ago to invest in the Buffett Partnership but passed up Buffett's invitation.

"I wish I had invested back then," Keough said. Had he done so, Buffett would have turned the $5,000 he asked of Keough into something on the order of $15 million. Oh, well.

In 1958 Keough, a native of Iowa and a Creighton University graduate, moved into the house directly across from Buffett on Farnam Street in Omaha. Buffett has said Keough's extraordinary personality is one reason he invested so heavily in Coca-Cola.

The future Mr. Coca-Cola, who drinks his Coke in diet form, was one of many Buffett solicited to join the Buffett Partnership. Although Keough was late investing with Buffett, he was early on another Berkshire investment. "My wife Mickie and I bought furniture from Mrs. Blumkin at the Nebraska Furniture Mart when we were early married in Omaha. We've been married over 40 years," Keough said.

Keough says he can't recall exactly how he met Buffett, just that they were neighbors in Omaha. "I don't remember how we were introduced...He was about 25 and I was about 30.

"He was exactly the same then as he is now...What you see is what you get. He had the same values. His story really is not money. It's values. People should know about his values....What he said at the [Berkshire] annual meeting [in 1991] in his response to a question about choosing careers says it all. He said enjoy your work and work for whom you admire."

Keough, the marketing expert, and Roberto Goizueta, the chemical engineer, began working together in the 1960s and both were on a management fast track. Goizueta joined Coke in 1954 after answering an ad for a bilingual chemist.

On the evening of February 14, 1980, at a birthday party for then Coke Chairman J. Paul Austin at The Four Seasons restaurant in Manhattan, both arrived as rivals to succeed Austin.

Keough told Goizueta: "Nobody knows how this is going to work out. The two of us are quite compatible, and we have different skills. So let's sleep at night. Whoever comes out on top, let's put the other one to work immediately."

Goizueta was picked and he and Keough became one of the top management teams in American business. After Keough retired in 1993, he became chairman of the Allen & Co. investment banking firm.

33

The Coca-Cola Company

"Putting your money where your mouth is"

A brief announcement came over the Dow Jones news wire on March 15, 1989, that Berkshire had bought 6.3% of the stock of The Coca-Cola Company! That stake, because of Coke's own stock repurchases and Buffett's new buying in mid-1994 is now about 8% of the company. Berkshire owns 200 million shares of Coca-Cola with the 2-for-1 stock split in 1996.

With Buffett's Coke purchase, a grandiose era of permanent value was born for both Berkshire and Coke. Buffett, making his largest investment ever, struck during an unusually long period when Berkshire is not required to report—from the quarter ending in September until March when the annual earnings and annual report are issued.

He had spent months in late 1988 and early 1989 secretly putting in buy orders and had just finished guzzling down a $1 billion-plus ocean-size helping of Coca-Cola. "Can't Beat The Feeling."

Buffett's investment, The Real Thing, made him Coke's largest shareholder.

Buffett told *Forbes*, October 18, 1993, "Coca-Cola sells 800 million 8-ounce servings a day. Berkshire Hathaway's share is about 50 million."

"I wish we had bought more," he has said, reminiscent of the view of an anonymous wit: "There are more important things in life than a little money, and one of them is a lot of money."

Perhaps the first tipoff about Buffett's interest in the world's largest soft drink maker came in Berkshire's 1985 Annual Report when he wrote, "After 48 years of allegiance to another soft drink" (Pepsi) he was switching to Cherry Coke. He even declared Cherry Coke "the official drink" of Berkshire's annual meetings. That should have registered with Berkshire shareholders as a wonderful tip.

In Buffett's words, it happened when "Don [Keough] sent me a trial sample of the formula for Cherry Coke very early on—and I loved it. I wrote him back saying he could save all his test-marketing money, send me a portion of what he'd spend otherwise and that it was going to be a great success."

Later Buffett would tell *Forbes* magazine a key reason he bought Coke was that its stock price did not reflect the all-but-guaranteed growth in international sales in a world that is increasingly uniform in its tastes. Throughout the world, for more than a century, fountain clerks have mixed an ounce of Coca-Cola syrup with six and a half ounces of carbonated water. No product is so universal.

Even the Queen of England drinks Coke. Greta Garbo, John F. Kennedy, the Beatles and Fidel Castro have been Coke fans. President Bill Clinton constantly swigs Cokes. British Open champion John Daly, celebrating victory in 1995, turned down champagne for a diet Coke. Bill Gates has starred in an ad, scrounging for change to buy a Coke.

The most widely recognized and esteemed brand names on earth, by far, are Coca-Cola and Coke. And they are the most valuable. In a *Financial World* story (September 1, 1992), it was calculated that Coca-Cola's brand name alone is worth more than $24 billion. Other calculations in 1996 estimated its real value at $39 billion.

Coca-Cola, according to the 1995 Coca-Cola annual report, is the world's second most widely recognized expression after "OK."

John Tilson of Roger Engemann & Associates, says, "The Coca-Cola brand name is worth over twice what it generates in annual sales because its worldwide recognition and established marketing generate both superior operating margins and high market shares." (*Outstanding Investor Digest,* October 7, 1993)

In Coke, Sprite, Tab and Fanta, Coke has four of the five top carbonated drinks in the world. Coke sells more than two billion gallons every year of soft drink syrup and concentrate to bottlers. And Coke's value may rise because it's habit forming, a business trait Buffett likes to see.

Buffett Wannabe George Morgan tells the story of Buffett running into a youngster wearing a Coca-Cola outfit at a mall. Buffett asked him how much he paid for it. The youngster replied $75. "That's a lot to pay to advertise someone else's product," said Buffett, even more convinced of Coke's valuable franchise.

From Australia to Zimbabwe, from Omaha to Osaka, from the Great Wall of China to the Great Barrier Reef, millions of people are drinking those 800 million servings a day.

The company sells 47%—almost half—of the soda pop consumed ON EARTH, about twice as much as its nearest rival, PepsiCo. In the U.S., the Coke and Pepsi empires claim about three-fourths of the roughly $50 billion-a-year soda business. Coke has 41% of that market and Pepsi about 32%.

Coca-Cola USA accounts for 10% of all of America's liquid consumption.

Coke supplies its syrups and concentrates to about 1,000 bottling partners in almost 200 countries. In many of those countries Coke has little competition (except Guinness, but that's a later story).

The sun never sets on the world of Coca-Cola, now Berkshire's shining centerpiece investment. Buffett's stake in Coca-Cola stock is his master stroke. In many nations, "Coca-Cola" is synonymous with "U.S.A."

Says Buffett, "If you run across one good idea for a business in your lifetime, you're lucky, and fundamentally this is the best large business in the world. It has got the most powerful brand in the world. It sells for an extremely moderate price. It's universally liked—the per capita consumption goes up almost every year in almost every country. There is no other product like it." *(Fortune,* May 31, 1993)

As far back as May 15, 1950, Coca-Cola appeared on the cover of Time magazine over the title "World and Friend" with the drawing of a happy-faced, thirsty Earth drinking a Coke.

Coca-Cola sold more than seven billion cases of Coke, or about 180 billion servings of Coke in 1989. Coca-Cola's Chairman, Cuban-born, Yale-educated, Atlanta booster Roberto Goizueta hopes to double that amount by the year 2000.

The way things are going in Atlanta, he might get it all done there where Coke claims an 80% soft drink market share compared to about 42% nationwide.

Goizueta, a big Coke stock owner, knows something about growth. The only property he held onto after the emergence of Cuba's Castro was 100 shares of Coca-Cola he had bought in a custodial account with $8,000 loaned to him by his father. Those shares, which he still owns, are worth about $2 million. (*Business Week,* July 10, 1995) In the years since he became chairman in 1981, he's guided the growth of Coke from a market worth of $4 billion to more than $100 billion. Talk about liquid assets!

(Shortly after the Berkshire annual meeting in 1994 Goizueta said he called Buffett, and Buffett told him there had been only one question about Coca-Cola and kidded Goizueta that it was about management.)

Coca-Cola's return on equity in 1990 was 39%. It has risen each year since to 56.2 % in 1995!

Just what is Coke selling to deliver such remarkable profits? Nothing more than refreshment. Nothing so vital as food or energy. Just refreshment. And although you might say it's just a sugar water company peddling tooth decay, let's stick with the refreshment idea. Over the years Coke has offered so many moments of tasty refreshment it has become entrenched as the world's leading thirst quencher.

(Photo by Phil Skinner
The Atlanta Journal-The Atlanta Constitution)

Coca-Cola President M. Douglas Ivester, left (who succeeded Keough), and Roberto Goizueta, drinking buddies in charge of Coke's future.

Buffett's original investment in mere cans of Coke came to $1,023,920,000. For that money, he bought 23,350,000 shares of Coca-Cola stock, which split 2-for-1 in 1990, giving Berkshire 46,700,000 shares. And with another 2-for-1 in 1992, it has 93,400,000 shares. His mid-1994 refills boosted Berkshire's stock to exactly 100 million shares. Nice round number. As mentioned, the number became 200 million with the 2-for-1 stock split in 1996.

The day after Berkshire's first Coke announcement, Buffett told *Wall Street Journal* reporter Michael J. McCarthy (March 16, 1989) that the purchase of Coke was "the ultimate case of putting your money where your mouth is."

"Coke is exactly the kind of company I like," Buffett told him. "I like products I can understand. I don't know what a transistor is, for example." Further, he said, "More and more in recent years, their superb decision-making and the focus of their strategy have emerged more clearly to me."

The story suggested that analysts saw Buffett's move as protection against recession. "There could be 10 recessions between now and the time we sell our Coke stock. Our favorite holding period is forever," Buffett replied.

Shortly after the Coke purchase was revealed, trading in Coke's stock was halted because of a flood of buy orders. A year and half later the $1 billion stake in Coke was worth $2 billion. Now there's a real return on some mighty large dollars.

Another large Coke shareholder, SunTrust Banks, Inc. holds slightly more than 10% of Coke stock, but that is split between stock it owns—about 2%—and about 8% of Coke stock the bank holds in fiduciary accounts. SunTrust owns more than 48 million Coke shares worth way beyond a billion bucks. So what if it's taken a lifetime to rise from $110,000, or less than half a cent a share, the price the old Trust Company of Georgia took for the stock instead of cash as its fee in 1919 when it helped underwrite Coca-Cola's first stock offering. The Coca-Cola stock is a nice fat percentage of the worth of SunTrust which, by the way, has the only written copy of the Coke formula in its vault.

In 1993 accounting rules changed and SunTrust was allowed to carry the Coke stock at market value, allowing SunTrust to report a roughly billion dollar accounting gain.

Emory University in Atlanta, whose business school is named after Goizueta, owns about 24 million shares of Coke, and its dividends have gone to build the campus and to fund scholarships and professorships.

Remember, Buffett began his business career when he was six years old, buying six-packs of Coke for a quarter at his grandfather's Buffett & Son family grocery store. Selling the Cokes around the neighborhood for five cents a drink was among his earliest business ventures; he found margins to be good.

Despite making pocket money as a Coke salesman, he was drinking

Pepsi-Cola and would not change his taste habits for almost half a century when he, too, joined the ranks of "Cokeaholics." Buffett has said "his eyeballs connected with his brain" in the summer of 1988 and he began buying Coke all the way through March, 1989. Coke itself was buying back shares so there were two huge buyers of Coke stock in the marketplace.

What Buffett saw, and what made him thirst for Coke, was the world's greatest brand name. The Coca-Cola name was being carried for zero on the balance sheet of a company with stunning international possibilities for profit growth and efficient global advertising. Buffett discovered—and it was right there in front of everybody's eyes—a worldwide bulletproof franchise.

Coca-Cola dominates the fountain portion of the U.S. soft drink business and is the primary supplier for many of the major fast food chains, including McDonald's, Wendy's, Burger King, and Pizza Inn restaurants. Where Berkshire investee McDonald's goes, for example, so goes Coke.

Its vending business covers the world. Coke machines are all over Europe and the U.S. There's even a Coke machine at the Berkshire-owned Borsheim's jewelry store and Nebraska Furniture Mart in Omaha.

About 70% of Coke's sales and about 80% of its profits come from its vastly expanding overseas operations.

Pepsico, itself a mighty consumer products company, still bedevils Coke in the United States where Americans drink more pop than water. Somewhat stalemated in its domestic profitability by fierce competition from Pepsico, Coca-Cola is always looking to the rest of the world for growth.

Overseas Coke is way ahead. In Europe, home to 347 million people, 39% more than the U.S. population, Coke's sales are exploding and surpass Pepsi's sales by a wide margin.

The growth prospects for both Coke and Pepsi seem bright. Pepsi Chairman Wayne Calloway has said, "Coke and Pepsi can grow for the next 20 years, and we wouldn't be taking away from each other."

Coke has made huge inroads in Europe and the Pacific Rim. Coke's domination of Europe is being extended into Poland and what was East Germany.

When the Berlin Wall fell in February, 1989, Coke made an immediate foray into East Germany, setting up vending machines by the thousands. By early 1991 it was buying bottling and distribution plants all over Germany. East Germans knew of Coke from television even before the Berlin Wall came down, and Coke is even more popular than soft drink beverages made by the old East German government.

In early 1991, Coke officials were saying East Germans were swallowing an average of 30 servings a year and that the company was aiming to match West Germany's rate of 190 servings within a few years. Coke has quickly expanded operations in East Germany. German unification has been a boon to both Pepsi, with strong operations in a number of Eastern European countries, and to Coke with its strong operations long established in Europe.

Coca-Cola makes more money in Japan than in the United States because of much higher margins. Coke's army of vending machines, which includes more than 760,000 of Japan's two million soft drink machines, helps Coke claim about 30% of the soft drink market there. Coke's Georgia brand of canned coffee is also a huge seller in Japan.

"Our international opportunity is obvious," said Coke's 1989 Annual Report. "As a market develops, as any market develops, people drink more soft drinks. It's only a matter of time. And the time it takes us to develop a market is growing shorter."

Goizueta wrote in the 1993 Annual Report: "When people ask me about the growth prospects of The Coca-Cola Company, I always respond with three simple facts. First, every day, every single one of the world's 5.6 billion people will get thirsty. Second, only in the last few years have world events allowed us true access to more than half of those people. And third, as the world's foremost beverage company, we are in the best position to satisfy their need for refreshment."

The opportunity for Coca-Cola is apparent overseas where foreigners consume only a fraction as much soda pop as do Americans. Although the mature U.S. market consumes 343 servings a person a year, the average person worldwide consumes 54 servings. Think about it. The U.S. per capita consumption is many times the worldwide average. And the gap is now being filled to Coke and Berkshire's advantage.

In Indonesia the yearly per capita consumption is eight servings, in Russia six, in China four and in India two. *Half of the world's population drinks less than two servings per person per year!* Think about the growth prospects!

"If China were to reach the current per capita consumption level of Japan—which is less than half that of the U.S.—that would represent more than half of Coca-Cola's current unit volume of 10 billion cases," said Engemann's Tilson. "The prospects for continued growth become even clearer when you consider emerging markets. These markets comprise roughly 3.5 billion people or close to 65% of the world's population."

The overseas consumption average is growing rapidly. Coca-Cola's aim is to be ubiquitous. Its red and white logo shows up at sports events around the world—at bullfights in Spain, camel races in Australia, sheep-shearing contests in New Zealand, and the Super Bowl in the U.S. It has long been a sponsor of the Olympics.

Along the way, Coca-Cola has been making huge investments in bottlers around the world. In Europe particularly, Coca-Cola is consolidating many of its bottling operations to capitalize on the industry deregulation expected from the economic unity of the European community.

Since bottling is a high fixed-cost business, manufacturing and distributing products from fewer locations will enable Coca-Cola to enjoy significant economies of scale and solidify its position as the low-cost soft drink producer. The financial folks at Coca-Cola seem to have their heads on straight, making careful hedges to international currency exposures and making good use of what little debt they have.

Business Week (November 12, 1990) has described one aspect of Coke's use of debt this way:

> Coca-Cola shows how leverage can be played like a fine instrument. In 1986, the once debt-averse Coke borrowed $2.5 billion to buy up many of its bottlers. Then it sold 51% of the new bottling unit to the public. Coke moved the acquisition debt to the balance sheet of the new unit, which in turn used the proceeds of the offering to help slash its debt. The result: Coke wound up with 49% of a $3.9 billion company—and gained marketing clout by consolidating once-independent bottlers.

Keep this in mind the next time you go to the philharmonic!

You can talk about Coke's splendid balance sheet with lots of cash and little debt and you can even talk about its world empire and how many servings of Coke there are around the world on any given day.

But here may be the most stunning of all the remarkable statistics about Coca-Cola, again noted in its 1989 annual report:

"The Coca-Cola Company began to transform itself into a global enterprise in the early 1920s. For more than 60 years, we have been developing business relationships and investing in a system that today carries an estimated replacement cost of more than $100 billion."

One hundred billion dollars!

Let's say you wanted to enter the soft drink business and match Coke. You can't raise $100 billion. Buffett can't raise $100 billion.

Speaking of $100 billion, here's what Buffett says about competing with Coke if you gave him $100 billion: "If you gave me $100 billion and said take away the soft drink leadership of Coca-Cola in the world, I'd give it back to you and say it can't be done." (*Fortune*, May 31, 1993)

The 1995 Coca-Cola annual report says: "If our Company burned to the ground, we'd have no trouble borrowing the money to rebuild, based on the strength of our trademarks alone."

No brand name is totally immune from competition. GM and IBM weren't. A handful of Japanese tigers took huge bites out of GM and zillions of ants did damage to IBM. But if there's an impregnable business franchise on earth, it's Coca-Cola. It is little wonder that in Berkshire's 1990 annual report, Buffett says he regards Coca-Cola as "the most valuable franchise in the world."

One Berkshire shareholder said of the Coca-Cola investment, "He really doesn't ever have to make another investment."

In other words, Buffett can basically rely on his huge investments in Coke, Cap Cities, GEICO and Gillette and if they do well, they will carry Berkshire for years to come even if Berkshire makes no new investments.

What Buffett saw in Coca-Cola was a bulletproof international brand name growing quickly, with high margins, domiciled in the United States, right there in good old understandable Atlanta, Georgia, home of the 1996 Summer Olympics, a happenstance upon which Coke would capitalize.

Can't one imagine Buffett, Goizueta and Keough—the three marketeers—at the 1996 Olympics sipping Cokes? When Buffett bought Coca-Cola stock, it was trading at only 12 times earnings.

Buffett gave a number of reasons for buying and others supplied other reasons for him, but in the end, it may be more than just a list of reasons.

"It's like when you marry a girl. Is it her eyes? Her personality? It's a whole bunch of things you can't separate," he said.

When Buffett courted Coke, he did so in a quiet and a huge way. For months he had three brokers at the other end of his phones picking off whatever large blocks of Coke stock they could find.

About a week after the March, 1989, announcement, *Atlanta Constitution* business writer Melissa Turner interviewed Buffett at his office in Omaha. She asked him why he hadn't bought sooner and he replied, "You wonder what pushes the needle, don't you? Must have just dawned on me."

He also told her, "Let's say you were going away for 10 years and you wanted to make one investment and you know everything you know now, and you couldn't change it while you're gone. What would you think about?

"If I came up with anything in terms of certainty, where I knew the market was going to continue to grow, where I knew the leader was going to continue to be the leader—I mean worldwide—and where I knew there would be big unit growth, I just don't know anything like Coke.

Pausing for a sip of Cherry Coke, he continued, "I'd be relatively sure that when I came back they'd be doing a hell of a lot more business than they are doing now."

He told her that Hershey Foods would also be here but that humanity wouldn't raise its intake of Hershey bars like it will Coke.

"But people are going to drink eight servings of something every day, and history shows that once they are exposed to it [Coke], and I'm living proof, they like drinking it."

She reported that Buffett's portable office refrigerator is stocked full and that there were three unopened Cherry Coke 12-packs on the counter waiting to be chilled.

"I drink five a day and that's 750 calories, which means really a pound every five days and 70 pounds a year and..." he told Turner. At the Berkshire annual meeting in 1992, he gave things a slightly different spin: "I drink five Cokes a day. That's 750 calories. I would have lost 70 pounds a year if I didn't drink them. Really, it's been a lifesaver."

Five Cokes a day? A fib? A white lie from Mr. Squeaky Clean? Does he drink five Cokes a day? "He drinks eight to 10 a day," says Deep Throat, who sees Buffett almost every day.

Buffett told Turner that the night before their chat, it was so hot in his house that he'd hopped out of bed at 2 a.m. and gone downstairs to the refrigerator. After guzzling a Cherry Coke, he felt a lot better and went back to bed.

Shortly after Buffett completed his huge Coke purchase, he journeyed to Atlanta, Coke's headquarters, and took Goizueta and Keough, the company's top two executives until Keough retired in 1993, to lunch.

So, fellow Coke drinkers, where did Buffett, Goizueta and Keough go for lunch in Atlanta? The Varsity restaurant. The what? The Varsity restaurant.

The Varsity, near Georgia Tech University, is a popular, low-priced, fast food restaurant billed as the world's largest drive-in. The trio came to The Varsity at the request of Buffett, whose culinary interests are largely along the lines of straight Crisco washed down with a Cherry Coke. The

Varsity does not serve Crisco, but there are few non-cholesterol items and the onion rings are sensational.

The restaurant is a crowded, busy place with a number of rooms, some with school desk chairs lined in front of a television set where fans often watch ballgames. Buffett, Goizueta and Keough did not just pop in. "I called," Keough remembers.

Gordon Muir, personnel director of the restaurant, said, "We knew they were coming...Buffett came in and I met him briefly. You could never tell he was rich."

Muir's mother, Nancy Simms, owner of the restaurant that her father founded in 1928, sat with Buffett, Goizueta and Keough at a round table by a window with a perfect view of Coca-Cola's world headquarters several blocks away. The Varsity is the world's biggest non-chain server of Coca-Cola. It's as if Coke were piped from Coke headquarters.

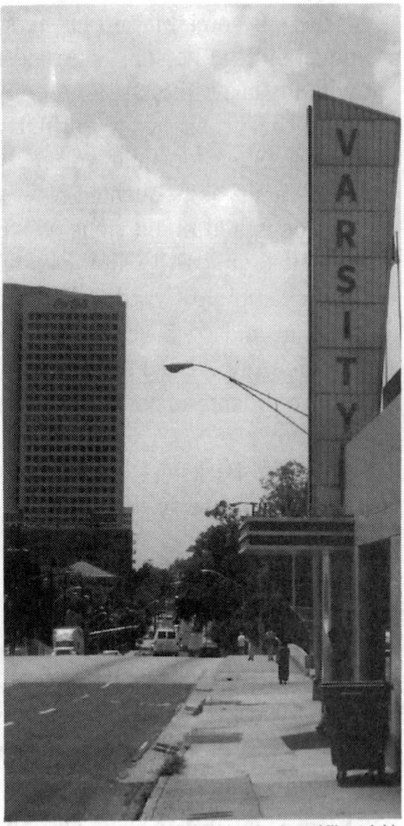

(Photo by Andrew Kilpatrick)

Coca-Cola headquarters in Atlanta supplies sugar water to the world. The nearby Varsity restaurant, where Buffett, Goizueta and Keough have eaten together, offers a big supply of Cokes, onion rings and burgers.

"Our colors are red and white and so I put a checked red and white tablecloth on the table and put some red begonias in a Varsity carry-out box on the table," Mrs. Simms said. "They are all down to earth, people-oriented people...He [Buffett] ordered hot dogs, onion rings and fries. He just loved them...We ate on paper plates...They brought a six-pack of Cherry Cokes with them. That's what he likes," she said.

"They stayed about an hour or an hour and a half. He talked about his businesses, about See's and Nebraska Furniture Mart. He said he likes to buy businesses with good managements and then let them run things as they always have."

"There is something in his personality that comes out that says he's a unique and fun person," she said, adding, "I was hoping he'd buy me out with his last billion."

Sale of The Varsity to Buffett has been kidded about but Buffett's reply was, "She's too smart to sell."

The Varsity is frequented by college students in search of hamburgers, hot dogs and onion rings as well as such people as Jimmy Carter, George Bush and Bill Clinton in search of votes. Former heavyweight boxing champion Evander Holyfield, now a Coke spokesman, has dropped in and so have Burt Reynolds and the late Lucille Ball and Arthur Godfrey. At one time Nipsey Russell worked there. Buffett made his trip to Atlanta about the time he was named to Coke's prestigious board.

After the Berkshire annual meeting in April, 1989, Buffett dropped by Borsheim's jewelry store and was surrounded by a band of shareholders.

Buffett had completed his $1 billion purchase of Coca-Cola stock and was asked if he intended to make it a permanent holding. In the annual report it had not been listed as a permanent holding.

Replied Buffett, "Well, I don't want to move it to that category too fast." But it wasn't very long before he was calling it a permanent holding. There was little doubt it was headed toward being a huge holding of permanent value for Berkshire.

Coca-Cola has been a part of people's lives for 100 years. The world's best-known trademark originated on May 8, 1886, when, legend has it, pharmacist Dr. John Styth Pemberton first made the syrup for Coca-Cola in a three-legged brass pot in his backyard at 107 Marietta Street in Atlanta.

He carried a jug of the new product down the street to Jacobs' Pharmacy, one of Atlanta's leading soda fountains (located not far from today's Underground Atlanta area), where it was sold at the soda fountain for a nickel a glass.

Soon the drink was "Delicious and Refreshing."

Pemberton placed an ad for Coca-Cola in the May 29, 1886, edition of the *Atlanta Journal* claiming the drink was "Delicious, Refreshing, Exhilarating, Invigorating."

On November 15, 1886, legend has it, a man with a hangover asked for something that would ease his headache. Pemberton had touted his drink as a cure for a headache. Whether by design or accident, carbonated water was added with syrup, producing a drink that eased the customer's headache. (*The Real Ones*, p. 6 by Elizabeth Candler Graham, great-great-granddaughter of Asa Candler, and Ralph Roberts.)

Mrs. Graham relates that Asa Candler had sought a cure for headaches all his life since suffering an accident as a child when he fell out of a loaded wagon and a wheel ran over his head.

"One of Pemberton's goals in formulating Coca-Cola was to present a cure for headaches. During almost all of its first decade of life, Coca-Cola was considered a medicine. Candler himself advertised it in the 1890s as 'The Wonderful Nerve and Brain Tonic and Remarkable Therapeutic Agent.'"

In 1887 a patent was filed for a product listed as "Coca-Cola Syrup and Extract."

Thinking that two C's, derived from two of the drink's ingredients—flavoring extracts from the coca leaf and the cola nut—would look nice together in advertising, Pemberton's bookkeeper, Frank M. Robinson, with an ear for alliteration, suggested the name and penned "Coca-Cola" in the flowing Spencerian script now world-famous.

In 1886 sales of Coca-Cola averaged nine drinks a day—an inauspicious beginning for an enterprise whose sales of soft drink syrup now well exceed two billion gallons a year.

Pemberton also started Coca-Cola's push into advertising, making it one of the first American companies to make substantial use of advertising.

His early ad efforts began when he painted squares of oilcloth to hang from drugstore awnings. One oilcloth sign over Jacobs' store said "Drink Coca-Cola."

Pemberton sold 25 gallons that first year, shipped in bright red wooden kegs. Red has been the distinctive color associated with the drink ever since. For his efforts, Pemberton grossed $50—and spent $73.96 on advertising, according to a company publication.

By 1891, Atlanta businessman Asa G. Candler had acquired complete ownership of Coca-Cola for $2,300. Within four years, his merchandising skill helped extend availability of Coca-Cola to every state.

Candler, who like Pemberton developed a number of consumer products, now had the task of mixing the syrup for Coca-Cola. To water he added natural ingredients as well as what came to be known as "Merchandise 7x," the most jealously guarded ingredient in a recipe and trade secret in the world.

Some say the ingredient is cocoa. (*The Real Ones*, Elizabeth Candler Graham and Ralph Roberts, p. 22)

In those days, for a nickel, you got a glass of Coca-Cola and the treat of watching a fellow make it.

A strong believer in advertising, Candler promoted Coke incessantly, distributing souvenir fans, calendars, clocks and other novelties all carrying a Coke trademark.

It was Candler who hammered away at the "refreshing" theme, driving home the message with a line of Coke ads showing Coke-sipping models by the sea.

Along the way, looking for a way to serve beverages at a picnic, candy merchant Joseph A. Biedenharn of Vicksburg, Mississippi, became the first person to bottle Coca-Cola, using syrup shipped from Atlanta. His 1894 innovation was a marketing concept that led to wider distribution of the beverages.

In 1899 large-scale bottling became possible. Joseph B. Whitehead and Benjamin F. Thomas of Chattanooga, Tennessee, landed the exclusive right to bottle and sell Coca-Cola to much of the United States.

The contract launched Coca-Cola's independent bottling system that remains the foundation of the company's soft-drink operations. Today the syrups and concentrates for the company's soft-drink products are sold to bottlers around the world, bottlers who package, market and distribute Coke products in their areas.

Coca-Cola held its first annual meeting in 1892 in Atlanta. There were four shareholders present. Annual sales were $49,676.30; the balance sheet carried $74,898.12 in assets. Cash on hand was $11.42.

In 1919, the company was sold to a group of investors headed by Ernest Woodruff for $25 million. His son, Robert W. Woodruff, became president of the company in 1923. For more than six decades his leadership took the business to new heights.

Buffett, at the Berkshire annual meeting in 1992, pointed out the wisdom of finding great companies and investing in them for the long haul without worrying about temporary setbacks.

"If you're right about the business, that's really the thing," Buffett said. A classic case he said—noting the pun—is that you could have bought a share of Coca-Cola in 1919 for $40 a share. "A year later it was $19.50," Buffett said. "Sugar prices went up and you lost half your money. Today that $40, if you had reinvested all dividends, is worth $1.8 million [$3.5 million in 1996] and that's with depressions and wars. How much more fruitful it is to invest in a wonderful business."

A wonderful business buying back its stock. From 1984 through 1995, Coke repurchased about 483 million shares, about 30% of the com-

McCall's Magazine for July, 1920

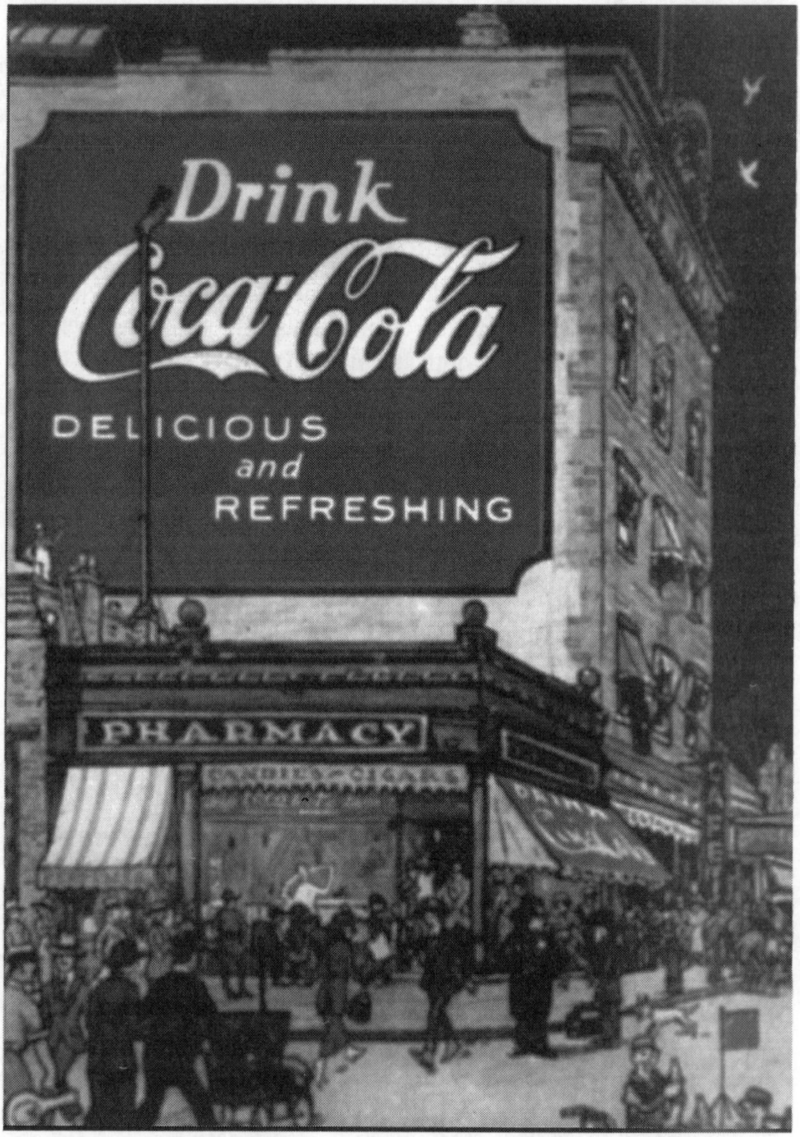

(With permission of The Coca-Cola Company)

pany. In 1992 Coke authorized a plan to buy back up to 100 million shares of stock, a nice round number again, through the year 2000.

Berkshire has done even better. Berkshire's annual increase in stock price since Buffett took over is between 25% and 30%, whereas Coke—from $40 to $3.5 million, is about 20%! It's been about 29% a year during the past decade. But as Buffett says Coke has been through depressions and wars. Berkshire has yet to live through a world war. Coke survived two of them.

Among Woodruff's contributions during many of those years were the six-pack and the open-top cooler, vending and dispensing equipment and displays and promotions. Under him commercially successful Coca-Cola eventually became an institution the world over.

Coca-Cola, which already had gone international in the 1890s by branching out to Canada and Cuba, began its association with the Olympics in 1928, when an American freighter arrived in Amsterdam carrying the United States Olympic team and 1,000 cases of Coca-Cola.

History of One Share of Stock

One Share 1919 (value $40)	
Result of splits/stock dividends 1919-1994	2,304 shares
Price 12/31/94	$51.50
Total value of 1 original share on 12/31/94	$118,656.00
Dividends paid 1919 through 12/31/94	16,942.01
Dividends: Class A	$129.00
Class A redeemed (2 shares @ $52.50)	$105.00
	$135,832.01

Stock Splits

Date	Activity	Cumulative Stock
April 25, 1927		1
	1-for-1 stock dividend	2
November 15, 1935	4-for-1 stock split	8
January 22, 1960	3-for-1 stock split	24
January 22, 1965	2-for-1 stock split	48
May 13, 1968	2-for-1 stock split	96
May 9, 1977	2-for-1 stock split	192
June 16, 1986	3-for-1 stock split	576
May 1, 1990	2-for-1 stock split	1,152
May 1, 1992	2-for-1 stock split	2,304
* [1994	2-for-1 stock split	4.608]
* [1996	2-for-1 stock split	9,216]

Consumer Information Center, The Coca-Cola Company, April 1995

In the 1920s it penetrated Europe and even amid World II, it opened 64 bottling plants abroad with government help.

In 1941, as the United States entered World War II, Woodruff decreed that "every man in uniform gets a bottle of Coca-Cola for five cents, wherever he is and whatever it costs the company."

As Mark Pendergrast, author of *For God, Country and Coca-Cola*, wrote in a *New York Times* article August 15, 1993, successful companies need dedicated consumers, "People like the World War II soldier who wrote home that 'the most important question in amphibious landings is whether the Coke machine goes ashore in the first or second wave.' "

The presence of Coca-Cola not only lifted troop morale, it also gave foreigners their first taste of Coke and paved the way for future bottling operations overseas. Even after the troops left, Coke stayed, establishing its own beachhead as one of the first American products widely available overseas. Naturally this increased the value of its name.

The trademark "Coca-Cola" was registered with the U.S. Patent and Trademark Office in 1893, followed by "Coke" in 1945. The bottle so familar to consumers was designed by Root Glass Co. of Terre Haute, Indiana, in 1916.

In 1982 The Coca-Cola Co. introduced Diet Coke, marking the first extension of the company's trademark to another product. Today, Diet Coke is the nation's top one-calorie soft drink and the third best-selling soft drink of any kind. Cherry Coke, Buffett's particular favorite, was rolled out in 1985, a year most famous for the introduction of New Coke. Diet Cherry Coke came out in 1986.

Later, other drinks were to join a powerful line of Coke products. In addition to Sprite, introduced in 1960 and now the world's number one lemon-lime soft drink, TAB, Fanta, Fresca, Mello Yello, Ramblin' Root Beer and others, Coca-Cola also owns Minute Maid orange juice. Coca-Cola Foods, based in Houston, Texas, is the world's largest marketer and distributor of juice and juice drink products.

Although over the years Coke has expanded to other businesses, more and more it is shedding extra businesses to concentrate on being a worldwide soft drink company. After years of diversification, it is evolving more into a one-product company, unlike Pepsi, which is more of a snackfood and restaurant business company.

Coke sold its minority interest in Columbia Pictures, the movie and television studio it bought in 1982, to Sony Corp. for $5 billion in late 1989, investing much of the money in new bottling systems as well as buying back its own stock, almost always a hallmark of Buffett's investees.

Goizueta spearheaded Coke's buy of Columbia Pictures seven years earlier. But he has since changed his mind and has told *Wall Street Journal's* Michael J. McCarthy, "There's a perception in this country that you're better off if you're in two lousy businesses than if you're in one good one—that you're spreading the risk. It's crazy."

In August, 1990, Coke opened a $15 million museum to itself in Atlanta called The World of Coca-Cola, located next to Underground Atlanta. Its visitors have even included Tibetan monks.

The World of Coca-Cola exhibits include the original patent for Coke, a 1930s soda fountain, Coke's well-known Santa Claus ads, and a gift shop. Among the 1,000 artifacts displayed is the prototype of the famous 6½-ounce curvy bottle. Wider than the one that was actually adopted, the bottle is one of only two in existence and worth about $10,000. Almost 200 flags that line the lobby show the markets where Coke is sold.

As you move through the exhibits, you encounter bathing beauties, sports heroes and movie stars who have popularized Coke's advertising through the years. There are cardboard cutouts featuring such celebrities as Jean Harlow and Cary Grant pitching Coca-Cola.

Besides the displays of print advertising, there is a retrospective look at Coke's television commercials. There is, probably to the delight of Pepsi fans, a 1969 commercial featuring Ray Charles, who later pitched Pepsi's popular ads—"You Got The Right One, Baby. Uh Huh." Perhaps the most delightful item is a 13-minute video where the avuncular Keough gives an introduction and a wrapup to the film, which rightly emphasizes the worldwide reach of the company.

The museum admission fee is $2.50 and yes, every visitor gets a complimentary Coke served from a futuristic soda fountain. The nearby 1930s style soda fountain was the setting for the photo of the board of directors for Coca-Cola's 1990 Annual Report.

In 1991 Coke, making every use of its brand name, opened a store on Manhattan's Fifth Avenue, stocked with more than 500 Coke products, Coca-Cola T-shirts ("Coca-Cola 5th Avenue"), telephones, Christmas cards, radios, coolers and neon signs. And there's now a $3 million Coca-Cola sign at Times Square, too.

Coke does not yet own the world. There's still a Pepsi billboard on the way into Buffett's hometown from the airport in Omaha.

To counter that embarrassment, some surmise Buffett and Coke are planning a CokeWorld on the Moon, a Disney-like concept which,

if successful, could be exported to other orbiting bodies.

Although Coke has only about 10,000 employees in the U.S. and about 23,000 outside the U.S., around the world about one million people have employment in some connection with Coke's products. It has more than 225,000 share-owners.

Coca-Cola, so admired for its marketing skills, committed the ultimate marketing fiasco in 1985 when it changed its famous 7X formula, which has been in an Atlanta bank vault for 99 years. Over the years the formula has been tinkered with at times but only to accommodate better forms of the original ingredients or better ways of processing them. This was a radical change—a whole "new" Coke.

Public outcry over the Black Tuesday announcement was swift and massive. The public relations disaster was immortalized by songwriter George Pickard who recorded, "Coke Was It."

Three months later the company went back to the original formula with Coca-Coca Classic and also kept New Coke. "Coke Are It," said some. The fantastic episode worked in Coke's favor as its overall market share bubbled to 40% from 37.5%. The day Coke announced it was bringing back its original formula, ABC News interrupted "General Hospital" with the news flash, and 18,000 gleeful Coke fans lit up Coke's switchboard in Atlanta.

The museum display explaining this to visitors quotes then Coke President Keough: "Some critics will say Coca-Cola made a marketing mistake. Some cynics will say that we planned the whole thing. The truth is we are not that dumb and we are not that smart."

Speaking of smart and dumb, a Trust Company of Georgia director once said, "Our dumbness in not being smart enough to diversify has been the smartest thing any dumb people ever did." (*Secret Formula*, Frederick Allen, p. 422)

It's not unusual for Coca-Cola to come up with great marketing ideas. In 1923 it introduced a marketing revolution with the carryout six-pack container. But in 1990 its ill-conceived MagiCan promotion was ended after paper money failed to pop out of a few of the special cans.

But all along, Coke has continued to, in Buffett's words, "blanket the world." If all the Coca-Colas ever made were placed in 6½ ounce bottles and laid end to end, they would stretch to the moon and back more than 1,000 times.

Throughout the 20th century, Coke has played a part in national celebrations and global happenings, and Coke has been linked to World's Fairs and national expositions since 1905.

It does not hurt Coke that it has agreements to sell in all Disney theme parks and a joint marketing agreement with Mattel Inc., the toy firm.

And only an alien would not foresee that Coke was planning a massive marketing campaign at the 1996 Olympics in Atlanta. Indeed, Coke's "The World Together—Always" ads started appearing on Atlanta billboards in early 1994. Coca-Cola, the longest-running and largest corporate sponsor of the Olympics, will walk out its own front door for the 1996 Olympics in Atlanta, an event expected to be seen by more people than any in world history.

To assist in that event, Coca-Cola was never unaware that Evander Holyfield, fittingly of Atlanta, could make a knockout ad. Indeed, in November, 1990, Coke and Pepsi were vying for Holyfield's endorsement. In January, 1990, you guessed it, Coke signed Holyfield for a six-year agreement—an agreement billed as "The Real Thing" signing with "The Real Deal." The agreement was probably for a real cost, too, but the real amount was not really disclosed.

It was no accident that Holyfield warmed up for his fight with big George Foreman April 19, 1991, wearing a red Coca-Cola Classic T-shirt, conveniently visible to fans watching the fight on cable television.

The contract calls for Holyfield to appear in advertising for company products as well as to make personal appearances on behalf of the company. Holyfield will work with the company on its Olympic Games activities. Even with Holyfield and whatever ads Coke dreams up in the future, Coke will be hard put to beat the success of some of its previous ads.

Curiously Holyfield pulled a Buffett-like investment, scoring a financial knockout, buying more than a million dollars worth of Coke stock in early 1991. (*Forbes*, December 23, 1991) So Holyfield may have taken Buffett for one round, but there has been no conjecture—even from ABC Sports—about how Buffett would fare, even for a round, in the boxing ring against Holyfield.

Getting back to Coke's sports ads, the early 1980s saw the "Mean" Joe Greene Coke ad. As the lineman from the world champion Pittsburgh Steelers limped out of a stadium he was trailed by a timid young fan carrying a bottle of Coca-Cola.

The boy's offer of a cold Coke was at first refused, then accepted as "Mean" Joe downed the bottle without a pause. Refreshed, he straightened up, flashed a smile and tossed his jersey to the youngster.

Other celebrities who have endorsed Coke or Diet Coke are Sugar

Ray Leonard, Elton John and Ted Turner, whose CNN empire is not far from the Coke headquarters in Atlanta.

But perhaps no ad beats the one aired during Super Bowl XXIV when Coke premiered its "Hilltop Reunion," the new version of one of the most famous television commercials of all time with "I'd Like to Buy the World a Coke." The response to the ad was so overwhelming the company pressed 45 rpm versions of it.

To satisfy an increasing number of requests from disc jockeys, the company put out a second, slightly reworded version, "I'd Like to Teach the World to Sing." Renditions of "I'd Like to Teach the World to Sing" propelled their way to the pop music charts, selling a million copies by the end of the year.

Like the original spot, the contemporary version focused on the simple, but striking imagery of people from around the world joining together on a mountaintop to offer a message of hope.

In 1971, the company's Hilltop commercial brought together young people from around the world to the Italian countryside near Rome for the expression of world unity and, incidentally, to advertise Coke. Many original cast members and their children were located for the new, 60-second spot in 1990.

Finding the young, blond, British woman who opened the 1971 spot with the lyric, "I'd like to buy the world a home and furnish it with love..." is a heartwarming story in itself. Her name was Linda Higson, but old files incorrectly listed her as "Hipson," which temporarily foiled detectives, including Pinkerton's best, scouring Europe for the missing woman.

With production set to begin in Italy, she still had not been found. As a last resort, an advertisement was placed in the classified section of several international and British newspapers. Buffett has long proclaimed the "billboard" benefits of newspapers. The newspaper ad read: "Linda Hipson where are you? If you're the Linda Hipson who was in the Coca-Cola commercial 20 years ago, please call U.S. (212)-984-2611. We'd love to hear you sing again."

In Stockholm, a friend of Ms. Higson's was waiting at the airport and came upon the ad in the *International Herald Tribune* (appropriately owned in part by another Berkshire investee, The Washington Post Co.). The similarity of the names, he figured, was enough. He called Linda in Cheshire, England. Linda, like E.T. phoning home, called McCann-Erickson in New York and Coke's ad agency called the producers in Rome.

As the central character was on her way to Italy, "Hilltop Reunion" was quickly redesigned around her appearance. Linda Higson Neary, now married with four daughters, again opened the 1990s version of the commercial, this time with daughter Kelly, who celebrated her 10th birthday on location. Coke got a great plug out of it.

Buffett has called Coke his favorite stock. He may even increase his position one day. Five months after he announced the Coke investment, Buffett filed a statement with the Securities and Exchange Commission for clearance to more than double his stake to up to 15% of Coke's common stock. J. Verne McKenzie, Berkshire's chief financial officer at the time, said, "This does not say there are plans now to buy," noting that purchase plans would be made based on stock price and market conditions. "This gives us a flexibility to buy to match our flexibility to sell...There are no plans to sell now."

Suggestion: Keep your eye on KO, Coke's stock symbol. Buffett's grandson, Howie, recently saved up and bought, yes, 10 shares of Coca-Cola.

"Things go better with Coke", and "You Can't Beat the Real Thing." Buffett surely believes it. In the year 2000, tune in to see how many billions Buffett's original $1 billion Coke stake is worth. After his first four years of ownership the stake was worth $4 billion. Here's how the Coca-Cola 1991 Annual Report begins:

> The Coca-Cola Company is the world's foremost marketer of soft drinks. Through the world's largest production and distribution system, the Company sells more than twice as many soft drinks as its nearest competitor. Every day in 1991, consumers in more than 185 countries enjoyed an average of more than 668 million servings of Coca-Cola, diet Coke/Coca-Cola light, Sprite, Fanta and other soft drinks. With a market value of more than $53 billion at year-end 1991, the Company was the sixth-largest company in the United States.

And the letter from Goizueta and Keough sent chills of joy through shareholders' bones:

> In 1991 the market value of The Coca-Cola Company increased by more than $22 billion, an amount $6 billion greater than our Company's total market value at January 1, 1989. In other words, last year, in terms of

> market capitalization, we created the equivalent of another company larger than The Coca-Cola Company was less than three years ago.

Coca-Cola is making commercial history.

"Here's an unbelievable statistic," Goizueta said at the 100th annual meeting (read revival) on April 15, 1992. He announced that in the first quarter 54 billion servings of Coke were consumed and that the stock market value of the company was $54 billion.

And where does Goizueta see future growth? China is one place. "The 1.2 billion people in China drink one apiece [annually]. If Coke could boost that to the annual per-person consumption of Australia, which is 217, it would be the equivalent of another Coca-Cola Co., the size it is today." (*USA Today*, August 16, 1993)

In 1993, in *For God, Country and Coca-Cola*, Mark Pendergrast claimed he found a version of the Coke formula—the list of ingredients included such items as citrate, caffeine, extract of vanilla, flavoring oils, lime juice and fluid extract of cocoa. He said he found it in papers belonging to John Pemberton, the Atlanta pharmacist who invented Coca-Cola in 1886.

Coke denied Pendergrast had found the current formula, but even if he had, a Coca-Cola official said it wouldn't make any difference.

"Without our economies of scale and our incredible marketing system, whoever tried to duplicate our product would get nowhere, and they'd charge too much."

As someone once said, "Coca-Cola is more durable, less vulnerable, more self-correcting than the Roman Empire. The product is destined to outlast the USA."

Buffett told Harvard Business School students on March 21, 1996: "Coke has no taste memory. If you drink orange soda, grape or root beer your mouth gets tired of it rather quickly. That's even true of chocolate. But Coke has no taste memory. You can drink all you want. Of Coke's $100 billion value, maybe $80 billion might be from no taste memory. The average human being consumes 64 ounces of fluid a day and Coke is less than two ounces of that. There is nowhere that Coke goes anywhere in the world that people don't drink more every day."

34

Buffett Writes Some Coke Puts

A case of cash and having your Coke, too.

When brand-name stocks, including Coca-Cola, took a hammering after Philip Morris's April 2, 1993, "Marlboro Friday" announcement it was lowering prices by 20% for its Marlboro cigarettes to better compete with generic cigarettes, Buffett did the unusual.

Despite his distaste generally for options, in April 1993, he wrote (sold) out-of-the-money put options, for $1.50 apiece, to buy three million Coca-Cola shares. The options expired December 17, 1993, and were exercisable until then at about $35 a share.

Earlier at the Berkshire annual meeting in April 1993, Buffett confirmed the move and said he had added another two million shares in a similar move.

What all this meant was that Buffett got $7.5 million in cash up front, and consequently, had the stock gone down from the roughly $40 range where it was then trading, to roughly $35 a share, he would have had to buy five million shares of Coke at roughly that $35 price. Since Buffett had already received $1.50 a share, his effective cost would have been about $33.50.

His only risk under this "put" contract, was that if Coke stock dropped below $33.50 in December he would have had to pay $35 for the stock, rather than whatever lower price Coke was selling for in the stock market at the time. But if the stock were lower, he might also have bought more Coke stock anyway, because he was willing to buy Coke stock at $35 a share.

For Buffett, it was pretty much a win-win situation, a case of getting cash and having your Coke stock, too. The options worked and Buffett pocketed the $7.5 million. But don't try this at home, unless you're an experienced investor.

35

Walt Disney and Cap Cities/ABC

Here's a condensed version of the background leading up to Walt Disney's acquisition of Cap Cities, according to a Cap Cities' letter to shareholders:

•In the fall of 1993 Michael Eisner and Sid Bass, whose Bass Management Trust owns 31,125,578 shares, or 5.95% of Disney's stock, met with Cap Cities's Tom Murphy and Daniel Burke and Buffett, a director of Cap Cities, to discuss a potential business combination. Nothing came of the talks.

•In March 1995, Eisner and Murphy met again. Murphy suggested that Cap Cities might consider a stock-for-stock transaction, Eisner said Disney would not be interested in an all stock transaction. Nothing developed.

•While attending an industry conference, Eisner met on July 14, 1995 with Buffett and Murphy. Again, Murphy said Cap Cities would be interested only in Disney stock. But they agreed to talk again.

•On July 21, 1995, Eisner asked if Cap Cities would consider a cash offer. Murphy said no. Eisner suggested the companies consider a strategic alliance involving, among other things, the provision by Disney for the ABC Television Network of Saturday morning programing and certain other programs. Murphy said he'd consider it.

•On July 25, 1995, Murphy called Eisner, and suggested that instead of the strategic alliance, Disney and Cap Cities enter a merger for cash and stock.

•From July 25 through July 31, senior management of Disney, Cap Cities and Buffett hammered out the stock and cash agreement. The boards agreed July 30, 1995, and the $19 billion deal for Disney to buy Cap Cities was announced.

The Walt Disney Company operates Disneyland in California and Walt Disney World in Florida which include Magic Kingdom, Epcot Center, and Disney-MGM Studios. It also earns royalties from Tokyo Disneyland and owns 39% of Euro-Disney in France.

The Burbank, California-based giant supplies entertainment via its Buena Vista, Touchstone, Hollywood Pictures and Miramex outlets to theaters, television and video. It publishes books, records music and sells its consumer products through a chain of 350 Disney stores worldwide. Disney owns Hyperion Press, the California Angels baseball team, the Mighty Ducks of Anaheim hockey team and the stage production of *Beauty and the Beast*. It operates the widely viewed Disney Channel and the KCAL-TV station in Los Angeles.

Disney has been famous throughout its history for its movies which include *Cinderella, Aladdin, The Lion King* and *Pocahontas.* Disney and ABC have long had connections, not to mention Eisner's 10-year stint early in his career at ABC.

Walt Disney's brother, Roy, and ABC's Leonard Goldenson agreed back in the 1950s that Disney would supply a one-hour television series to ABC in return for a $500,000 investment in the Disneyland park.

"In early 1954, Disneyland, Incorporated, which Walt had founded three years before, was reconstituted with Walt Disney Productions and American Broadcasting Company-Paramount Theaters each owning 34.48% with investments of $500,000 a piece." (*Walt Disney*, Bob Thomas, 1994, p. 249)

Later ABC aired *The Mickey Mouse Club* show watched by three-quarters of the nation's television set owners between five and six o'clock each weekday.

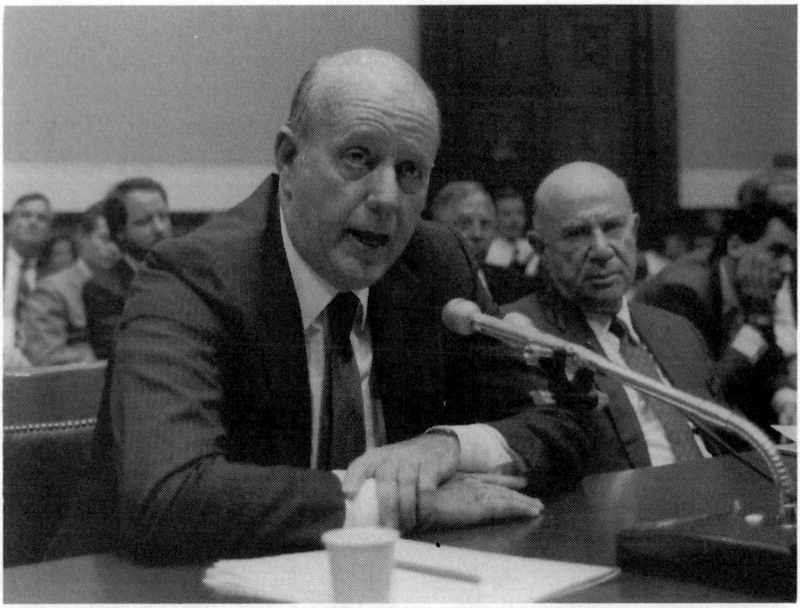

(AP/Wide World Photos)

Former Cap Cities Chairman Tom Murphy, left, and former CBS Chairman Laurence Tisch also are FOBs. "Murph" is what Buffett calls Murphy, and Murphy calls Buffett a "400-pound gorilla."

"Children and adults everywhere were singing the club's anthem — 'M-I-C, K-E-Y, M-O-U-S-E.' The mouse-ear caps worn by the Mouseketeers sold at the rate of 24,000 a day; two hundred other items were merchandised by seventy-five manufacturers. The Mouseketeers became national figures, and millions of children could recite 'Darlene' 'Cubby' 'Karen' and all the other names during the daily roll call. The most popular of the Mouseketeers proved to be Annette Funicello, a gasoline-station operator's daughter who had been discovered at a children's dance recital. She attracted the most fan mail—as many as six thousand letters a month." (p. 275) From those days Disney, which employees 69,000 people, grew into a business with a global brand name and which is buying back its stock.

Capital Cities/ABC

Buffett was in Washington one day in 1985 when an urgent call came from his office to get in touch with his friend, Cap Cities Communications Chairman Tom Murphy. Murphy said he needed advice about financing a $3.5 billion purchase of giant American Broadcasting Companies, Inc. At the time, the Cap Cities acquisition of ABC-TV, announced March 18, 1985, was the largest media purchase in history.

That night, Peter Jennings began *World News Tonight* with, "To paraphrase Pogo, we have seen the news and it is us." (*The House that Roone Built,* Marc Gunther, p. 214)

Neither Murphy nor Buffett at first thought of Buffett being personally involved, but the Wizard of Omaha quickly became a key figure in the acquisition. His role in the huge business combination probably helped Wall Street give its nod to the deal, as the stock prices of both companies went up.

Buffett's great interest in media stocks, evident since the early 1970s, culminated with word that Cap Cities would buy ABC with Berkshire owning almost a fifth of the new media powerhouse.

Without putting pen to paper, Buffett agreed to invest $517.5 million in cash to buy three million shares of Cap Cities at $172.50 a share. (That's before a 10-for-1 stock split in 1994.) That sprung the money that contributed to the merger that spawned Cap Cities/ABC, Inc., in January, 1986.

Buffett's part of the deal was wrapped up one midafternoon of March 1985. "It took about 30 seconds to work. It's all in a page or two," Buffett said of his investment. *(Regardie's,* February, 1986)

Two hours later Buffett was engrossed in a six-hour bridge game with three New York friends, putting the deal out of his mind.

"I don't think about anything else when I play bridge," he told *Omaha-World Herald's* Robert Dorr.

Cap Cities competes for what Buffett calls "viewers' eyeballs" with CBS and NBC, not to mention cable television, particularly CNN.

The call from Murphy had come because he and Buffett had long been friends. Buffett has always had high regard for Murphy, whom he calls "Murph," and of whom he has said, "I think he is the top manager in the U.S." (*Fortune,* April 15, 1985) Murphy has returned the compliment and has said of Buffett, "If I were around him all the time, I'd have a huge inferiority complex...He's one of the greatest friends. He will try and do anything he can to help you. Without him, I wouldn't have been able to buy ABC." (*USA Today*, September 18, 1991)

Buffett once told *Channels* magazine West Coast Editor Patricia Bauer (November 1986), "I love being associated with Murph. I literally do not work with anyone I don't like. I'm fortunate to be able to spend the rest of my life working with people that I like and admire. And here's

Murph up at the top of that list with a terribly interesting business."

But did Buffett plan to shape opinion or tell ABC what programs to air? "No," he told Bauer, "I'm not the right guy to ask about those things." He said it again at the Berkshire annual meeting in 1991: "I'm a director of Cap Cities/ABC, but they don't ask me for my suggestions on shows. That's not my end of the game."

At a Berkshire annual meeting (1987), Buffett was asked if he thought there was too much sex on television. "I don't see anything wrong with sex on television, but there ought to be a few shows where the gal says no."

Buffett met Murphy in the late 1960s when a former Harvard Business School classmate of Murphy's seated them together at a lunch in New York. Murphy was so taken with Buffett that he invited him to be on the board of Cap Cities. Buffett declined but the two remained fast friends.

In 1985, ABC's magisterial Chairman Leonard Goldenson, who founded ABC in 1953 and ran it until 1986 when he was 79, decided that Murphy and Murphy's number two man, Daniel Burke (also a Harvard MBA via the University of Vermont and military service), would be the right men to run his company. (Murphy was a graduate-school roommate of James Burke, Daniel's other brother, who was later chairman of Johnson & Johnson.)

Murphy and Burke have long been known as cost-cutters. There is an oft-repeated story that at the old Cap Cities when an Albany station needed repainting, Murphy had only the sides facing the main road spruced up. (*The House that Roone Built*, Marc Gunther, p. 214)

Goldenson, who was preparing to turn ABC over, is the man who presided over "Charlie's Angels," "The Dating Game," "Monday Night Football," instant replay, and the first miniseries.

In 1991 Goldenson's autobiography, *Beating the Odds*, appeared. Buffett wrote a foreword saying, "Business management can be viewed as a three-act play—the dream, the execution, and the passing of the baton. Leonard Goldenson will be remembered as a master of all three." In Goldenson's book, Buffett told about getting a call from Murphy who said, "Pal, you're not going to believe this. I've just bought ABC. You've got to come and tell me how I'm going to pay for it." Buffett did just that, telling Murphy he needed "a nine-hundred-pound gorilla" investor to keep raiders at bay, and then kicking in $517 million.

But there was still a problem. There was an FCC "cross-ownership" rule banning a company from owning a television station and a newspaper in the same town. Buffett told Murphy he didn't want to sell the *Buffalo News* which meant Cap Cities had to sell a television station in Buffalo. In the Goldenson book, Buffett said he told Murphy he was committed to the *Buffalo News*: "I promised the people there that I would never sell it. I told them, when they wrote my obituary it would say, 'He owns the *Buffalo News*.' "

It's more likely Buffett's obituary will record he was the gorilla investor in Cap Cities, now Disney.

"This deal popped up three weeks ago. Four weeks ago I had no idea it was about to happen," *New York Times* reporter Vartanig G. Vartan wrote March 20, 1985, quoting Buffett. Buffett summarized to *Atlanta Constitution* business writer Melissa Turner (April 2, 1989) the final conversation that clinched Buffett's investment. "I was up there on a Thursday morning. I said, 'How many shares do you want me to buy?' He said, 'What do you say?' I said, 'How's three million?' He said, 'Fine.' I said 'What price should I pay?' He said, 'What do you think?' I said, '$172.50.' He said, 'Done.' "

To shareholders at the time, Buffett inserted just one paragraph in his 1985 annual report—a subsequent event note explaining the agreement had come a week after his annual report had gone to the typographer but shortly before production.

Buffett became a director of Cap Cities. He also agreed to vote with management for 11 years as long as either Tom Murphy or Daniel Burke was in charge. It turned out that the decision to buy Cap Cities reversed a previous one Buffett made in the late 1970s to sell the very same stock.

His explanation: "Of course some of you probably wonder why we are now buying Cap Cities at $172.50 per share given that this author, in a characteristic burst of brilliance, sold Berkshire's holdings in the same company at $43 per share in 1978-80. Anticipating your question, I spent a lot of time working on a snappy answer that would reconcile these acts.

"A little more time please."

Cap Cities was a good investment, despite a long struggle to get the ABC network turned around.

Murphy lured Burke away from the Jell-O division of General Foods in 1961 and, without any instructions, asked him to run a television station in Albany, New York. (*Fortune,* May 6, 1991)

Back in the late 1940s and 1950s, ABC was the third-rated network. Attempts to buy ABC by CBS and 20th Century Fox failed, but in 1953 the struggling network merged with United Paramount Theatres. United Paramount's Leonard Goldenson hired Disney Studios and others to produce programming.

About that time Hudson Valley Broadcasting, owner of a struggling television station, went public, becoming Capital Cities Television Corp.

While Cap Cities founder Frank Smith bought and sold television stations and publications, Murphy ran the company's operations.

Smith died in 1968, and Cap Cities under Murphy's guidance bought Fairchild Publications, publisher of *Women's Wear Daily*,—a real franchise in the fashion industry—and made a steady march of buying other media properties.

Still in third place in the 1960s and known as the Almost Broadcasting Co., lagging behind NBC and CBS, ABC fended off takeover attempts by Norton Simon, General Electric and Howard Hughes. But by the 1970s with hits like "Love Boat" and "Happy Days" (developed by Michael Eisner when he was a Paramount executive and sold it to ABC) ABC became the top network.

As a result of the 1986 merger, Cap Cities owns and operates ABC Television Network, seven ABC Radio Networks serving 2,200 affiliates (radio's largest advertising medium) drawing on ABC News as well as respected radio commentator Paul Harvey, eight television stations and 80% of the highly successful ESPN sports cable channel.

The other 20% of ESPN, owned by RJR Nabisco, was sold in 1990 to Hearst Corp.

ESPN, through its 24-hour-a-day sports cable television programming service reaching 66 million U.S. households and 95 million homes in dozens of foreign countries—more than any other cable network—has been highly successful. In 1995, ESPN bought an 80% interest in Sports Trader, a 24 hour, real-time sports news and information service.

ESPN should be a powerful vehicle for Disney to expand overseas because the Disney Channel can piggyback ESPN's worldwide penetration.

For a time it was more profitable than any of the three networks, according to the Goldenson book. But ESPN was saddled with costly new major league baseball and National Football League television contracts. ESPN had won the right to cover about 175 regular season baseball games in 1990, but losses began to pile up when audience ratings were below expectations in a slow ad environment.

Cap Cities operates ABC Television Network, which has more than 200 primary affiliated stations reaching more than 99% of all U.S. television households.

The company owns 38% of The Arts and Entertainment Network, a cable programming service devoted to cultural and entertainment programming, known for its excellent *Biography* series; one-half of Lifetime, a cable programming service devoted to women's lifestyle and health programming reaching 58 million households; as well as half of Tele-Munchen GmbH. This Munich, Germany-based television and theatrical production/distribution company has interests in cinemas and minority interests in a Munich radio station and a German cable television program service.

Good Morning America and ABC News' *World News Tonight with Peter Jennings* are top-rated shows. Ted Koppel's *Nightline* and *20/20*, with Hugh Downs and Barbara Walters, have also been very successful. Koppel was worried that with the Cap Cities buyout of ABC, the news side of things might be subject to cost-cutting in response to the more free-spending days of Roone Arledge at ABC.

Both Murphy and Buffett went by Koppel's house for lunch to assure him that they cared about the news side and *Nightline*. (*The House That Roone Built*, Marc Gunther, p. 257)

In 1989 ABC News premiered *PrimeTime Live*, hosted by Sam Donaldson and Diane Sawyer and in sports ABC's *Monday Night Football* was the most popular prime-time program among men who were mesmerized in its heyday by the announcing trio of Howard Cosell, Frank Gifford and Dandy Don Meredith. *Wide World of Sports* was the most popular anthology series.

Roseanne, starring Roseanne Barr and *America's Funniest Home Videos* have been hits, the latter known for the woman who got her hair caught in a dishwasher and also for a wedding guest who fell and knocked over a band.

On November 1, 1993, Cap Cities announced it planned to buy back 12% of its stock in a Dutch auction at prices somewhere between $590 and $630 a share. And Berkshire said it would tender a million of its three million shares on condition the entire million shares were bought back.

As it turned out, Buffett sold a million shares back to Cap Cities for $630 a share. Berkshire, with its cash pile bulked up to the $2 billion range, continued to own 2 million shares, or about 13% of the 15.4 million shares of Cap Cities. With the 10-for-1 stock split, Berkshire owned 20 million shares.

A "Mistake Du Jour" is how Buffett later described his sale of Capital Cities shares:

> Late in 1993 I sold 10 million shares of Cap Cities at $63; at year-end 1994, the price was $85¼.

> (The difference is $222.5 million for those of you who wish to avoid the pain of calculating the damage yourself.) When we purchased the stock at $17.25 in 1986, I told you that I had previously sold our Cap Cities holdings at $4.30 per share during 1978-80, and added that I was at a loss to explain my earlier behavior. Now I've become a repeat offender. Maybe it's time to get a guardian appointed. (1994 Annual Report)

At Cap Cities, Burke retired and Murphy became the CEO in 1994. Late that year ABC announced it would create a television studio in partnership with the newly formed "Dream Team" of former Walt Disney studio chief Jeffrey Katzenberg, Hollywood chieftain David Geffen and film director Steven Spielberg. The venture will create TV shows not only for ABC but for other entities as well, directly challenging Hollywood.

Stay tuned. Buffett is.

36

Generics

"Here, Honey, I took the low bid." Business school in an electrifying two minutes.

The Berkshire annual meeting in 1993 occurred just weeks after "Marlboro Friday." Brand managers as well as their ad agencies were shaken badly and many businessmen were wrestling with the question of just how many inroads generic products were making on brand names.

Sitting before a crowd of more than 2,000 people, with no notes, no aides and no idea a question about generics was coming, Buffett stunned the audience with his mastery of the business scene.

Here's how, over a couple of minutes, Buffett answered the question:

"Will developments in the generic brand area hurt Coca-Cola? That's a terribly important question.

"Generic brands have been with us a long time. But lately they've attracted a great deal of attention—partly because they're doing better and in particular because of Philip Morris's actions a few weeks ago—

when, in reaction to the threat and the inroads of generics, they cut the price dramatically on Marlboro.

"I wouldn't say Marlboro is the most valuable brand name in the world. Coca-Cola is more valuable—and I think that's been proven by subsequent events. But Marlboro earned more money than any brand name in the world.

"And all of a sudden, Philip Morris took some actions which dramatically reduced the earnings of that brand and changed the pricing dynamic that had existed in the cigarette business for many decades. And since then, Philip Morris has had $16 billion lopped off its market value and RJR's suffered accordingly.

"It's a terribly interesting case study and it illustrates one of the dangers of generic competition. Philip Morris cigarettes got to where they were selling for $2.00 a pack. The average cigarette consumer uses something close to ten packs a week. Meanwhile, the generic was at about $1 or thereabouts. So you really have a $500 a year differential in cost per year to a ten-pack-a-week smoker. And that is a big annual cost differential. You better have something that people think is dramatically better than the generic for the average consumer to shell out an extra $500 a year. It's happening in other areas, too—whether it's corn flakes or diapers or a lot of things...

"In our case, I think the Gillette brand name, for example, is far better protected against generic competition than the main product of Philip Morris—although there always has been generic competition in blades and there always will be.

"The average male purchases something like 30 blades a year. He pays 70 cents each if he buys the best—which is the Sensor. That's $21 a year. The best he can do if he wants something that leaves him Band-Aids on his face and an uncomfortable experience costs him $10 a year. So you're talking $11 for a 365-day experience...

"I think there's a generic threat of some sort in any industry where the leaders are earning high returns on equity. It just stands to reason that that's going to encourage competition.

"And the threat may be accelerating in many industries. But I think that brand names with the right ingredients are enormously valuable. Sometimes infrastructure is a problem for the generics. The worldwide infrastructure for Coca-Cola, for example, is very impressive and very hard for a generic provider to duplicate.

"But if somebody wants to sell a generic box of chocolates in California against See's Chocolates, that's obviously somewhat of a threat.

And I just hope that they take them home on Valentine's Day and say, "Here, Honey, I took the low bid."

Then Buffett addressed the question of Coca-Cola point blank:

"Wal-Mart's selling Sam's Cola. And Wal-Mart is a very, very potent force. One thing that's helpful is that they were selling it as cheap as $4.00 a case here. And I don't believe that's sustainable. That's 16⅔ cents a can.

"It's been a while since I looked at aluminum—and it's down. But I think the can is close to a six-cent item by itself. The can is far more expensive than the ingredients...Distribution costs, trucking, stocking and all that sort of thing have to be fairly similar. In a 12-ounce can, there's 1.3 ounces of sugar—which at the domestic price, would be around 1¾ cents per can. And that's got to be the same whether it's Sam's Cola or Coca-Cola.

"The Coca-Cola Company sells about 700 million 8-ounce servings—largely of Coca-Cola, but also of other soft drinks—worldwide every day. If you take 700 million and multiply it by 365 days, you come up with 250 billion or so 8-ounce servings of Coke or its products in the world each year.

"The Coca-Cola Company made about $2½ billion pretax last year. That's one penny per serving. One penny per serving does not leave a huge umbrella. The generic is not going to buy the can any cheaper. And they're not going to buy the sugar any cheaper and so on. Their trucks aren't going to be any cheaper."

Buffett, in an electrifying two minutes, just took you through business school.

37

Diversified Retailing Company

A small stream runs into a mighty river and ultimately into an ocean.

Way back in time and space, long before Buffett was making billion dollar investments, he was fishing in far smaller investment streams—bringing those small streams together into a river of income and ultimately into an ocean of assets. Toward the end of 1978, Diversified Retailing was merged into Berkshire.

Buffett, long the largest shareholder of Berkshire, was by this time also the majority stockholder in Diversified, holding 56% of Diversified's stock. Buffett began buying Diversified stock not too long after he started buying Berkshire stock.

Buffett became chief executive officer of Diversified in 1966. All along Buffett gradually was buying up both Berkshire and Diversified stock. By 1976, Buffett, then chairman of both Berkshire and Diversified, owned about 36% of Berkshire and 52% of Diversified.

At the time Berkshire's main executive offices were in New Bedford, Massachusetts, while those of Diversified were in Baltimore, Maryland.

Diversified, incorporated in 1966, was the parent of Associated Retail Stores, Inc.'s more than 80-store chain. Also Diversified owned a large amount of Berkshire stock as well as Blue Chip Stamps stock.

Associated, based in New York, was acquired by Diversified in 1967. Its stores operated in 11 states under such names as York, Amy, Goodwin's Gaytime, Fashion Outlet, Madison's, Yorkster, Lanes and Tops and Bottoms. The Limited, it was not!

In one of its rare business sales, Berkshire sold Associated Retail Stores to Joseph Norban, Inc. of New York in 1987.

Buffett's early retailing efforts never were winners. In the 1970s he owned Munsingwear and the stock was unspectacular.

In the proposed merger of Berkshire and Diversified, Buffett and his wife agreed to vote for the merger only if a majority of the other shareholders did. With the combination Buffett was trying to bring the far-flung elements of his financial empire under one house, Berkshire.

In the negotiations, Berkshire was represented by Malcolm G. Chace, Jr., Berkshire's former chairman. Diversified was represented by David S. (Sandy) Gottesman, a director of Diversified who would become one of Buffett's close friends and a wealthy Berkshire shareholder.

Gottesman, because of his large ownership in Diversified, emerged from the Berkshire-Diversified merger with 17,977 shares of Berkshire.

A number of people at the investment firm he heads, First Manhattan in New York City, also had been Diversified investors and came away collectively owning another 13,158 Berkshire shares.

It's traditional for Gottesman to stand up at the end of Berkshire's annual meeting and eloquently thank Buffett on behalf of shareholders for Buffett's stewardship.

Small wonder Gottesman feels so ebullient and Buffett usually looks bemused or embarrassed when Gottesman gushes forth. Buffett responded to Gottesman's outpourings one year by saying nothing and another year by saying, "Well, thank you, Sandy."

Because Buffett owned big positions in both Berkshire and Diversified, the negotiations took place without him and were conducted by independent directors of each corporation.

The proxy statement relating to the merger explained:

> Berkshire and its subsidiaries are engaged in the underwriting of property and casualty insurance throughout the United States, in the manufacture and sale of woven textiles in the United States and Canada, and, through a subsidiary which Berkshire is required to divest by 1981, in the commercial banking business in Rockford, Illinois. Berkshire and its subsidiaries additionally maintain long-term investments in a number of other businesses...Berkshire owns approximately 18.8% of the outstanding common stock of Blue Chip, whose shares are traded in the over-the-counter market. And Berkshire's insurance subsidiaries hold in their investment portfolios approximately 22.6% of Blue Chip's outstanding common stock.

Blue Chip in turn owned a number of businesses such as See's Candy, the *Buffalo News* and Wesco which in turn once owned 22% of Detroit International Bridge Co., operator of the Ambassador toll bridge between Detroit, Michigan, and Windsor, Ontario. Berkshire no longer has any ownership in the bridge.

Here's what the proxy statement had to say about Diversified:

> Diversified is a holding company which renders financial and operating advice to Associated Retail Stores, Inc., a wholly-owned subsidiary engaged in retailing of popular-price women's and children's apparel, to Associated's wholly-owned subsidiary, Columbia Insurance Company, which is engaged in the fire and casualty insurance business primarily through accepting portions of reinsurance contracts from Berkshire's insurance subsidiaries, and to Southern Casualty Insurance Company, a wholly-owned subsidiary of Columbia engaged in Louisiana in providing workers' compensation insurance, almost exclusively to the forest products industry. In the opinion of Diversified's management, Diversified's most significant asset, other than its Berkshire stock, is its beneficial ownership of approximately 16.3% of the outstanding common stock of Blue Chip...

The merger called for little management change, though Munger, who had become chairman of Blue Chip in 1976 and was a director of Diversified, was to serve as a director of Berkshire.

For years, Buffett had wanted to combine the two companies. He particularly wanted to bring together the two corporations' holdings of Blue Chip, to simplify the corporate structure under Berkshire.

With the merger, Berkshire owned 58% of Blue Chip and Buffett and his family owned another 13% of the stock. It was not until 1983 that Blue Chip was fully merged into Berkshire.

A little stream was merging with other little streams and turning into a mighty river, running toward an ocean. The following chart shows the pre-merger and post-merger ownerships:

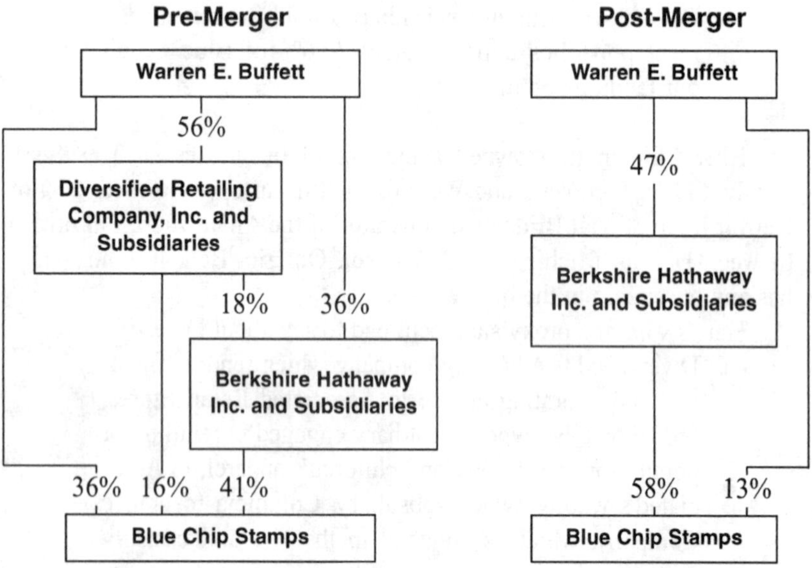

The intricate arrangement meant Buffett was investing on behalf of Berkshire, Diversified and Blue Chip. In 1972 Blue Chip began buying Wesco stock.

To complicate things Wesco entered a merger agreement which was later called off. It all called into question prices Blue Chip was paying for Wesco.

And Buffett and Munger were trying to merge Diversified into Berkshire.

The Securities and Exchange commission launched an investigation into Berksire, Blue Chip and Buffett.

Buffett had to explain the whole puzzle to the SEC. In 1976 the matter was settled without admitting or denying guilt.

Because the SEC found that the Wesco shareholders had been hurt by Blue Chip's trades, they were paid $115,000.

38

Blue Chip Stamps

"Maybe we should buy into another dying business."

Over the years, through the Berkshire subsidiary, Blue Chip Stamps, Buffett bought such businesses as See's Candy Shops, and the *Buffalo News*, still Berkshire cash cows. Blue Chip of Los Angeles, California, started as a trading stamp business and in 1973 bought Wesco Financial Corp. In the late 1960s Berkshire, and separately Charles Munger, began accumulating Blue Chip and by 1983 Berkshire owned about 60% of the company.

When Buffett began buying the stock in 1968, its float was about $60 million in outstanding, unredeemed stamps. In 1972 Buffett took $25 million of the money and bought See's, which had annual sales then of $35 million.

In 1977 Buffett, through Blue Chip, bought the *Buffalo News* for about $33 million from the estate of Mrs. Edward H. Butler, Jr.

When Buffett was 46 years old, he owned about $35 million worth of

(Photo by Andrew Kilpatrick)

Blue Chip Stamps headquarters in Los Angeles. The stamp business was virtually wiped out but its investments in See's Candies and the Buffalo News brought riches.

Berkshire stock and about $10 million worth of Blue Chip stock (according to *Fortune* magazine which in May, 1977, ran an article by Buffett about how inflation swindles the equity investor).

In 1983 Blue Chip, headed by Munger, was entirely merged into Berkshire. Blue Chip offers two main kinds of promotional services: those used by businesses to attract or retain customers, and those used by businesses to motivate their employees.

Blue Chip started its trading stamp business in 1956 and for years that was a successful business. There was a time when a ladies' quartz watch could be purchased for 17 books of stamps. Although the stamp business is still in existence, it has withered. But the company has managed to shrink profitably.

Blue Chip sales hit a peak of more than $124 million in 1970, then dropped to little more than $9 million in 1982, and to about $400,000 a year in the early 1990s.

Munger, at the Berkshire annual meeting in 1994, said of the more than 99% decline: "We're waiting for a bounce."

Most of the decline occurred in the early 1970s, when many supermarkets converted to discount merchandising, and service stations, evaluating the first major gas shortage, decided they didn't need trading stamps for promotion.

The stamp business was dealt an all but fatal blow when a supermarket chain that accounted for 51% of trading stamp revenues discontinued the stamps in 1982. The only benefit the stamp business offered was some continuing float, the cash received in advance of need, which was invested.

Blue Chip Motivation, operated as a separate division, struggled in a competitive environment offering motivation programs for organizations using awards of merchandise and travel to stimulate sales or productivity, promote attendance or safety or otherwise motivate their employees.

Today the stamp operations of Blue Chip are tiny and are conducted from a modest building in Los Angeles that also houses the small K&W Products, which makes products for the automotive aftermarket business. Although K&W is small, it has been expanding through small acquisitions. In the 1983 Blue Chip annual report Munger wrote:

> We began the 1970s with a single business, trading stamps, which was destined to decline to a small fraction of its former size, and a portfolio of securities, offsetting stamp redemption liability, which had been selected by previous owners and would have led to a disastrous result if held through the present time. (The portfolio, for instance, contained a substantial amount of very long-term, low-coupon municipal bonds of issuers with declining credit ratings.)
>
> We began the 1980s with five constituent businesses instead of one. In order of acquisition they are: (1) trading stamps and other promotional services, (2) See's Candy Shops, Incorporated, (3) Mutual Savings, (4) *Buffalo Evening News*, and (5) Precision Steel.

Munger says the businesses have in common both good management and some resistance to inflation.

> The second of these two common characteristics gets more important every year as inflation continues. Many businesses, once good investments when inflation was low, are now, under inflationary conditions, unable to produce much, if any, cash even when physical volume is constant...
>
> Inflation is a very effective form of indirect taxation on capital represented by holdings of common stock. We know of no countermeasure...But, even so, we think a habit of always thinking about and trying to serve

> shareholders' interests in real terms, instead of rationalizing growth of managed assets regardless of real effects on shareholders, is quite useful and may fairly be expected of corporate managements.

Later he signed off, saying:

> This may well be the last annual report our shareholders will ever receive from Blue Chip Stamps as a separate corporation, because work is in progress on a proposal that our corporation be merged with Berkshire Hathaway Inc., long a 59.6%-owner of Blue Chip Stamps.

At the time of the merger, Buffett personally owned more than 10% of the outstanding shares. After Berkshire itself he was the company's second largest shareholder. Munger owned 2.2% of Blue Chip. Berkshire had 986,509 shares outstanding held by about 1,900 shareholders, and Blue Chip had 5,178,770 shares outstanding held by about 1,500 shareholders.

At Wesco's annual meeting in 1993 Munger kidded Bob Bird about his managerial record at Blue Chip. He said Bird had helped take sales of Blue Chip from $120 million a year down to $300,000 a year. "This is a managerial record that not everybody would be proud of.

"Even so, there is some success. If you trace Blue Chip stock, it's way over a billion dollars now."

When Buffett and Munger bought the stock in 1968 and 1969, it was worth about $40 million. (*Outstanding Investor Digest*, June 30, 1993)

Munger said:

> Years ago, before Warren and I bought any stock, Blue Chip Stamps mailed minor amounts of Blue Chip stock out to filling station operators as a class action settlement of some kind. My wife told the guy where she gets her car washed to hold onto it. Well, the other day he dragged her out of the car and kissed her. So maybe we should buy into another dying business.

39

Wesco

"A tourist-class ticket"

Wesco Financial Corp. was written up in the *Wall Street Journal* on April 17, 1990, as a "tourist-class ticket" way to invest in a Berkshire-like way because Wesco, which has many of the same investments as Berkshire, trades in a price range of three digits rather than five. Wesco can be thought of as a poor man's Berkshire.

Wesco, of Pasadena, California, is 80.1% owned by Berkshire through Blue Chip Stamps.

Wesco owns Precision Steel, a steel service center and branded metal specialty products firm bought in 1979 for about $15 million. Precision has locations in Franklin Park , Illinois, and through its subsidiary Precision Brand Products a location in Charlotte, North Carolina. Precision earned about $2.4 million in 1995.

And Wesco long owned Mutual Savings and Loan Association in

Pasadena, California. For years, in the basement of Mutual's nine-story building, Munger held the Wesco annual meeting for a small band of shareholders.

But in the 1992 Wesco annual report, Munger wrote, "We have decided that Mutual Savings will shortly give up its status as a regulated savings and loan association. To achieve this objective, Mutual Savings is negotiating to sell to another financial institution..." (Cenfed Financial)

As a result, about $300 million in capital was transferred to Wes-FIC in Omaha where its place of business is in the headquarters office of National Indemnity. That doubled the capital of Wes-FIC, which writes super-cat insurance policies with Berkshire's insurance group, one of the world's largest insurance organizations in terms of capital, stronger than Lloyd's of London.

"So why shouldn't we do more of what works well for us and what's less complicated?" Munger said. (*Omaha World-Herald*, April 22, 1993)

Munger has noted that the move would result in a cost savings in a less regulated environment. The plan was to transfer Mutual Savings real estate to a newly formed Wesco subsidiary. Afterwards, Mutual Savings retained a majority of former assets such as its Freddie Mac stock and was merged into Wesco's subsidiary, Wesco-Financial Insurance Co., regulated by the Nebraska Department of Insurance. "After all, there are practical advantages in moving hundreds of millions of dollars of assets (at market value) from a high-cost, low-flexibility environment to a low-cost, high-flexibility environment."

"After Wes-FIC's capital and claims-paying capacity have been greatly augmented by the merger into Wes-FIC of Mutual Savings, Wes-FIC plans, through subcontracts with the Berkshire Hathaway Insurance Group, to enter the business of super-catastrophe ("super-cat") reinsurance."

So Wesco left the heavily regulated S&L industry and joined up with Berkshire to boldly enter the more profitable arena of reinsurance.

"It [the S&L] took up time disproportionate to the capital involved," Munger said.

In November, 1993, Wesco said although its Wes-FIC unit had planned to enter the super-cat business, a flood of capital into the reinsurance market had resulted in lower prices and Berkshire might not have enough extra business to give to the unit. Wesco said it would seek other insurance opportunities.

"But what are the predictions of man!" Munger wrote in Wesco's 1993 Annual Report. He said that in February, 1994, Wes-FIC was offered five unusual super-cat reinsurance participations by National Indemnity.

Wesco's headquarters is not far from Cypress Insurance Corp. of Pasadena, one of Berkshire's insurance businesses that does some business with Wes-FIC. Wes-FIC, which carries a rare AAA rating from Standard and Poor's wrote only 1% of its statutory surplus compared to an industry average of about 130% in 1993, Munger wrote in Wesco's 1995 Annual Report.

He added, "On super-cat reinsurance accepted by Wes-FIC to date (March 9, 1995) there has been no loss whatever that we know of. However, no underwriting profit flowed through Wesco's banks in 1994 because none of its super-cat contracts expired in 1994, and our accounting policy requires contract expiration before super-cat underwriting profit is recognized. Needless to say, we would not have similar reticence to report losses before contract expirations. Our super-cat accounting is not intentionally super conservative, although it may amount to 'best-practice' accounting."

Wes-FIC reinsures about half of the book of workers' compensation insurance business of Cypress. Cypress gets some of its insurance business from See's. More synergy at Berkshire?

Berkshire owns about 5.7 million of the 7.1 million Wesco shares outstanding. The stock is thinly traded with about 1,300 shares a day changing hands on the American Stock Exchange. Many of the other shares are held by the Caspers and Peters families, who have family members on Wesco's board.

In many ways Wesco, which has 3,825 shareholders, is indeed something of a baby Berkshire and holds some of the same securities as Berkshire. It owns small portions of the preferred stock positions in Salomon, and USAir and small positions in Coca-Cola, Gillette and Wells Fargo stock. Its main holdings is about 7.2 million shares of Freddie Mac. Wesco's cost for the stock bought in late 1988 was $71.7 million, now worth more than $600 million.

In the 1995 Wesco annual report, Munger wrote of the Freddie Mac position: "For us, at least, our experience in shifting from savings and loan operation to ownership of Freddie Mac shares tends to confirm a long held notion that being prepared, on a few occasions in a lifetime, to act promptly in scale in doing some simple thing will often be enough to make the financial results of that lifetime quite satisfactory."

As a result of a foreclosure in 1966, Wesco also owns about 22 acres of oceanfront property near Santa Barbara, California, carried on the books at $15 million. The land, which is worth much more, is being slowly developed for about 32 houses and recreation facilities to be sold.

Other properties include several buildings in a small shopping center in Upland, California, leased to small businesses.

About the time Mutual Savings was sold to Con Fed, Wesco organized MS Property Company, a real estate subsidiary that is slowly selling some of Mutual's old troubled assets. "Wesco still retains a recently formed real estate subsidiary that, mostly, it does not want," Munger wrote in the 1994 Wesco Annual Report.

Wesco's Chief Financial Officer Jeffrey Jacobson portrays Wesco as a company where nothing fancy happens, where management just tries to keep things in the middle of the road. In short, things are on track.

"We still have the Freddie Mac stock," he said.

As for the long work of trying to make something of the Santa Barbara property, Jacobson said, "We're starting to sell some of the units. A number of the houses have been built."

Apparently Munger and his wife have taken a fancy to the land, paying Mutual Savings $2.1 million in cash for two lots on the Santa Barbara real estate development where Munger has built a palatial home. Buffett has dubbed it, "Munger's Folly."

"He keeps a low profile," Jacobson said of Munger, adding that Munger has lots of irons in the fire. He serves on the board of Good Samaritan Hospital in Los Angeles and he's chairman of The Daily Journal Corp., an over-the-counter firm that publishes the *Los Angeles Daily Journal*, a sort of *Wall Street Journal* for the area's legal profession.

Each year Munger writes to Wesco's small band of shareholders much in the same vein that Buffett does. There's no pulling of punches. Usually there's heavy criticism and sarcasm about the S&L crisis or leveraged buyout operators. Still Wesco has not enjoyed fast growth nor has it found enough of the right acquisitions.

In Wesco's 1989 report Munger mentioned how hard it is for Wesco to find good acquisition candidates, and he likened that search to catching muskies.

To Wesco, as a non-LBO operator, the good-corporate-acquisition game was always tough. And that game in each recent year has become more like fishing for muskies at Leech Lake, in Minnesota, where the writer's earliest business partner, Ed Hoskins, had the following conversation with his Indian guide:

> *"Are any muskies caught in this lake?"*
> *"More muskies are caught in this lake than in*

any other lake in Minnesota. This lake is famous for muskies."
"How long have you been fishing here?"
"19 years."
"And how many muskies have you caught?"
"None."

Munger says: "Wesco continues to try more to profit from always remembering the obvious than from grasping the esoteric. It is remarkable how much long-term advantage people like us have gotten by trying to be consistently not stupid, instead of trying to be very intelligent. There must be some wisdom in the folk saying, 'It's the strong swimmers who drown.' "

In 1989 Wesco, with a stinging letter from Munger, resigned from the United States League of Savings, in protest of the league's reluctance to call for proper reforms in light of the national S&L crisis. Wrote Munger, "It is not unfair to liken the situation now facing Congress to cancer and to liken the League to a significant carcinogenic agent. And, like cancer, our present troubles will recur if Congress lacks the wisdom and courage to excise elements which caused the troubles."

Wesco is a steady, if unglamorous, part of Berkshire, and perhaps can be thought of as having the safety and about the same steady and sure return of a money market account. In fact, once a Berkshire shareholder suggested to Munger he might want to turn Wesco into a money market account one day. Munger did not totally dismiss the idea.

That should not suggest he is about to liquidate things, but then Munger has no problems with cash in the bank earning sure money either.

Munger has always thought that high-quality businesses and stocks will carry the day. Buffett has said that Munger has influenced him greatly towards being concerned about the quality of a business rather than just buying for a cheap price. *The Wall Street Journal* story about Wesco also noted that Wesco's businesses were not considered as good as Berkshire's.

A day after it ran Munger was talking at the Nebraska Furniture Mart to Berkshire shareholder/First Manhattan Chairman Sandy Gottesman about the story. "Well, I hate to see it says our businesses are less good than Berkshire's," Munger lamented, although Munger has said much the same thing himself. He wound up saying, "We'd be fine if we had bought quality stocks in 1968."

Berkshire acquired Wesco in 1973 at about $6 a share. That's on the order of 15% on his money annually, a "money fund" even Buffett could be proud of. After the Mutual Savings sale announcement, Wesco stock rose above $120 a share in 1995, making it a heck of a money fund for Berkshire.

At Wesco's annual meeting in 1993, Munger was asked who really makes the decisions for Wesco; he threw a compliment to Buffett saying, "Well, the most important person is in Omaha."

And in response to another question, Munger said, "I always like to see the nerds win."

Wesco's stock continues to do well though Munger downplays it: "An orangutan could figure out that the stock is selling for miles above the value of the company if it were liquidated. I keep telling people this, but they keep on buying the stock. It may be that a Berkshire groupie sees us as a way to buy into the [Berkshire] complex." (*Washington Post,* November 28, 1993)

In the 1995 Wesco annual report, Munger calculated Wesco's value at $149 a share compared to the stock price of $182 on December 31, 1995.

And he wrote: "Wesco is not an equally-good-but-smaller version of Berkshire Hathaway, better because its small size makes growth easier. Instead, each dollar of book value at Wesco continues plainly to provide much less intrinsic value than a similar dollar of book value at Berkshire Hathaway."

40

Berkshire's "Sainted Seven," Eight, Nine...Businesses

"Last year we dubbed these operations the Sainted Seven: *Buffalo News*, Fechheimer, Kirby, Nebraska Furniture Mart, Scott Fetzer Manufacturing Group, See's and World Book. In 1988 the Saints came marching in."

—*1988 Berkshire Annual Report.*

BERKSHIRE OPERATING COMPANY PROFILES

See's Candies

The Buffalo News

Nebraska Furniture Mart

Kirby

World Book

Scott Fetzer Manufacturing Group

Other

Fechheimer

H.H. Brown, Lowell, and Dexter

Helzberg's Diamond Shops

R.C. Willey Home Furnishings

Commercial & Consumer Finance (which consists of Scott Fetzer Financial Group, Berkshire Hathaway Credit Corporation and Berkshire Hathaway Life Insurance Company of Nebraska)

"If Berkshire's directly owned manufacturing, publishing and retailing businesses alone were separated as an independent company, its financial profits would be impressive. The 'company' would have sales of $2.4 billion, net income of over $200 million, and rank in the Fortune 500. In fact, in terms of profitability defined as return on assets, it would rank in the top 5 of the Fortune 500!" (*Sequoia Fund quarterly report, March 31, 1995*)

41

See's Candies

Nancy Reagan and Sally Field like See's

Candy companies are fun and in the case of See's Candies, both fun and profitable. Buffett is proud of a photo he has of Nancy Reagan boarding Air Force One carrying a large box of See's candy under her arm. And over the years many boxes have been used as gifts on Capitol Hill.

Actress Sally Field is a big See's Candy fan.

The See's Candy Shops, wholly owned by Berkshire, have been making candy for sweet-toothed customers for more than 70 years. Berkshire bought See's on January 3, 1972, for $25 million, buying it through Berkshire's Blue Chip Stamps affiliate. Buffett's decision to buy the company was easy. "It was a no-brainer. I wish I could find 50 more like it.

"Most of the businesses we've bought on the first visit. See's Candy, I went out there one time to see the grandson of Mary See. His name was Harry See...We had a deal. We understood the kind of position they held in consumers' minds and pricing flexibility and so on.

"Did I think they could charge 20 cents a pound more for candy? Sure. And sure enough, they could," he said in a talk to Columbia business students, October 27, 1993.

(Photo by Andrew Kilpatrick)

This See's Candy shop in Pasadena, California, is typical of the more than 200 shops of the West Coast firm for chocoholics. Buffett hopes customers wash things down with Coke, then grab their Gillette Oral-B toothbrushes.

See's, which made 12 cents a pound profit in 1972, now makes 88 cents a pound largely because it has been able to raise prices. Buffett has said that while Blue Chip's sales dropped from about $100 million in 1972 to about $1 million in 1991, See's revenues more than made up for things. They rose from $29 million to $196 million during that time.

When Buffett bought See's for chocoholics everywhere—a company that may be a subtle plug for Gillette's Oral-B toothbrushes—he put Charles Huggins in charge.

Buffett said it took him five minutes to name Huggins and that with the record Huggins has notched, one could wonder what took him so long. Buffett said in the 1991 Annual Report that the compensation agreement was "conceived in about five minutes and never reduced to a written contract—that remains unchanged to this day." Over the years Huggins and Buffett have talked about once every 10 days although Huggins said during the Salomon crisis it was more on the order of once a month. (*Wall Street Journal,* November 8, 1991)

See's was founded in 1921 by a 71-year-old grandmother, Mary See, who went into the business with little more than an apron and a few pans, at a small neighborhood candy shop in California.

See's makes boxed chocolates and other confectionery goodies in two large kitchens, one in Los Angeles and the other in San Francisco. See's distributes candies through its own distinctive white retail stores—more than 200 of them—in many western and midwestern states and Hawaii.

The great majority of them, more than 165 stores, are located in California where the company gets about 80% of its profits. The stores have a variety of chocolate goodies. The mouth-watering names are kept simple: Walnut Cluster, Peanut Cluster, Almond Square, Milk Patties, Molasses Chip and Milk Cherry.

Many sales are made through direct shipments nationwide from a seasonally varying number of order distribution centers. Significant seasonality exists in the business—heavy sales in cold months and light sales in hot months. About half of each year's sales come in the last two months of the year when quantity discounts add to extremely high Christmas and New Year's sales. See's gift-wraps its boxes, the perfect Christmas present. For years, congressmen have sent boxes of See's candies to friends.

In March, 1982, Berkshire received a bid for See's Candy from a British firm for $120 million in cash. Buffett didn't bite. See's net income has grown from about $6 million in 1981 to well over four times that much—$25.5 million in 1992. But it has difficulty expanding.

"We've looked at dozens of ideas of how to expand," Buffett said at the annual meeting in 1988. "And in the end we haven't found how to do it...It's a tough business."

Buffett himself is a big See's eater—probably just taste testing of course. But even when it comes to delicious chocolates, Buffett strives for discipline, limiting himself to one box a month. Still, it's another example of, "We eat our own cooking."

That two-pound box arrives at Berkshire headquarters once a month. Everyone at the office shares it.

In every box of See's Candy, you'll find the following message of See's philosophy:

> For over 65 years we have worked hard to maintain the tradition of quality which literally millions of faithful See's candy eaters have come to expect, year after year.

> Our philosophy is quite simple: Be absolutely persistent in all attitudes regarding quality—buy only the best ingredients obtainable—offer the most delicious and interesting assortments of candies available in the United States—own and operate all See's sparkling white shops, while providing the highest level of customer service.
>
> This may seem old-fashioned, if not unusual, in this day and age—but it works. At the same time we fully believe that we can always do a better job at what we try to do—ultimately making people happy!

Buffett says that in 1991 Americans ate 26 million pounds of See's products. Presumably Buffett's still top-secret plan for synergy at Berkshire calls for all that candy to be washed through everyone's digestive track with Cokes.

And that includes the Tim Moylan family of Omaha. Moylan keeps a stock of See's at his office for visitors, and one day the candy caught the fancy of Moylan's four-year-old son, Dan.

"Remember our friend, Howard Buffett?" asked Moylan. "Well, Howard's father owns the factory that makes the candy." (*Omaha World-Herald*, April 8, 1992)

Replied Dan, "You mean Howard's dad is Willy Wonka?" The writer of the story, Robert McMorris, promptly got a note from Buffett saying he planned to pass out samples of See's candy at the Berkshire annual meeting.

"When business sags," Buffett wrote, "we spread the rumor that our candy acts as an aphrodisiac. Very effective. The rumor, that is; not the candy."

42

The Buffalo News

Some fellow named Stan
(Publisher Stan Lipsey) plays delivery boy.

Buffett bought the *Buffalo News*—sight unseen—in 1977 for $32.5 million from the estate of Mrs. Edward H. Butler, Jr.

Now the newspaper makes more than that in pre-tax income.

Because of his knowledge of newspapers, Buffett could tell how the paper was doing by looking at its financial statements. It wasn't necessary, in his view, to go look at the plant. He already knew what a printing press looked like.

He bought the newspaper, not through Berkshire, but through the other company he controlled, Blue Chip Stamps. The *Washington Post* and the *Chicago Tribune* had turned down purchase of the paper because it was an evening paper.

But Buffett saw that it might be a good business if it could launch a

Sunday edition, so he bought the property. It has been wholly owned by Berkshire since 1983 when Blue Chip was merged into Berkshire.

The *News* quickly decided to launch a Sunday paper and its special introductory offers to subscribers and advertisers brought a reaction—a lawsuit on the grounds the introductory practices were improper—from its competitor, the morning *Buffalo Courier-Express*, a Cowles Media paper that published seven days a week.

The News eventually beat back the lawsuit, but both papers continued to lose money for years. From the time of Buffett's purchase, the *News* lost about $12 million, before taxes, through December 31, 1982. Then in 1982 the *Courier-Express* folded, and what Buffett had was a flourishing monopoly, his favorite kind of business. The *News* began putting out an earlier edition and today the successful paper publishes Sunday and seven editions each weekday.

Munger has told one Berkshire shareholder, "Warren was just plain lucky on that one."

It was a case of "Bridge Over Troubled Waters."

The *Buffalo News*, which has 1,000 employees, serves the large city and surrounding area long regarded as the eastern end of the Rust Belt, an industrial outpost on the Canadian border. Its last decade has seen steady economic dislocation. Still the newspaper has succeeded. It is the only metropolitan paper within its 10-county distribution area and has a high percentage of household penetration in that area.

A monopoly newspaper with great penetration, The *News* has turned into a quintessential Buffett business. It has a return on assets of "an astonishing 91.2%," according to a January, 1991, story in *NewsInc* magazine. "The *Buffalo News* may well be the most profitable newspaper company in the country," it said. The paper has a circulation of more than 300,000 a day.

Buffett is on the masthead, listed as chairman of the *Buffalo News*, and is followed by Stanford Lipsey, publisher and president and Murray Light, editor and senior vice president, who has been with the newspaper since 1949.

Slight of build, the curly-haired Lipsey has been with Buffett since Berkshire bought the now defunct Sun Newspapers in Omaha in 1969. Lipsey was managing that business when Berkshire acquired it, and later took over management of the much larger *Buffalo News*. Lipsey is a close friend of Buffett. They talk on the phone several times a week.

Tim Medley, president of the Medley & Company investment counsel/financial planning company in Jackson, Mississippi, tells this story about meeting "Stan" at a Berkshire shareholder party at Borsheim's the day before the annual meeting in 1990: "While you all were over talking to those bigwigs, I was talking to some regular fellow named Stan who said he was with the *Buffalo News*," he told a small band of fellow shareholders.

Informed that it must be Stan Lipsey, publisher of the paper and a Pulitzer Prize winner, Medley demurred, doubting the fellow was really the publisher since he said he'd be glad to drop off a couple of copies of the newspaper at Medley's hotel room the following morning. Medley had the impression "Stan" might be with the newspaper's circulation department. The end of the story is that Lipsey left two copies of the *Buffalo News* at Medley's hotel doorway the following morning.

Generally a newspaper has great difficulty enjoying better economic times than the area it serves. But someone forgot to tell Lipsey.

"We don't budget at the *News*," he told *NewsInc.* "We maintain a living, everyday awareness of expenses, and thereby we save an enormous amount of time and aggravation that goes into budgeting."

Buffalo lost 23% of its manufacturing jobs in the early 1980s as its industrial base declined, hit by such closings as Bethlehem Steel in 1983. But life began to get better in a hurry for the smokestack, heavily blue-collar city after the U.S.-Canada free trade agreement of late 1988.

The free trade agreement began to change the face of the Buffalo landscape of rusted steel mills, unused auto plants and empty grain elevators, mute symbols of decay. In its place, dozens of Canadian businesses set up offices and branches.

Canadian manufacturers began fleeing their high labor costs and taxes at home. Dozens of Canadian firms crossed the border to set up shop. New businesses came in as Canadians sought services on the cheap south side of the border. The unemployment rate dropped from a high of 13% in the 1980s to a respectable 5% by the early 1990s.

Buffalo, located on the Niagara River separating the United States and Canada, is just a 90-minute drive along Queen Elizabeth Way to Toronto, the highly congested and expensive business hub of Canada. Real estate prices have been improving, and many Canadian businesses have opened offices in Buffalo.

It also hasn't hurt that the Buffalo Bills professional football team improved to the point that they are the first team to appear in four consecutive Super Bowls in the early 1990s.

Businesses still are not enthralled with Buffalo's bitterly cold, snow-belt winters, but local boosters of the city are fond of saying that the city does have four seasons. What businesses do like is that Buffalo's industrial land costs are far below those of Toronto, as are taxes and electricity.

All this has not been lost on the *Buffalo News*, which has been enjoying steadily rising profits even in a sluggish ad environment. Among newspapers published in major markets, the *Buffalo News* claims the highest percentage of its area household coverage, 72% on weekdays and 80% on Sundays.

Buffett has said he believes the "newshole" percentage (percentage of the paper devoted to news as opposed to advertising) of the *Buffalo News* to be greater than any other dominant paper of its size or larger.

During 1989 the newshole percentage was 50.1%, in 1991 it was 53.6%, and in 1992 it was 54%, and in 1993 it was 55%, one of the highest newshole rates in the country.

(Photo by Nancy Line Jacobs)

Buffett near a Buffalo News *display before Berkshire's annual meeting in 1994.*

43

Nebraska Furniture Mart

"I want to buy your store."

"He [Buffett] walked into the store and said, 'Today is my birthday and I want to buy your store. How much do you want for it?' I tell him '$60 million.' He goes, gets a check and comes back right away," Mrs. Rose Blumkin, known as Mrs. B, has said.

Buffett's final purchase price made in 1983 was $55 million for 80% of the store in Omaha, with the other 20% held by management. Berkshire originally had bought 90% of the store, but later management upped its stake to 20%.

Although Buffett just walked in and bought the store, it is not as though he hadn't thought about it for a long time.

More than 10 years before the purchase, he was telling journalist Adam Smith it was a good business.

"We are driving down a street in Omaha and we pass a large furniture store. I have to use letters in the story because I can't remember the

(Photo by Nancy Line Jacobs)

Here's the Nebraska Furniture Mart in Omaha that Buffett bought in 1983 from Rose Blumkin after saying, "I'd like to buy your store." When she said okay, he gave her a check for $60 million. No lawyers, no accountants, no investment bankers. No due diligence. The See's sign is a sign of synergy at Berkshire.

numbers. 'See that store?' Warren says. 'That's really a good business. It has "a" square feet of floor space, does an annual volume of "b," has an inventory of only "c," and it turns over its capital at "d," Smith wrote in *Supermoney*, p. 196.

"Why don't you buy it?" I said.

"It's privately held," Warren said.

"Oh," I said.

"I might buy it anyway," Warren said. "Someday."

The Nebraska Furniture Mart, founded in 1935, is a whopper of a furniture store—the largest under one roof in the United States. It operates a home furnishings retail business from a large—more than 240,000 square feet—outlet and sizeable warehouse facilities of more than 400,000 square feet over a 64-acre area.

The store, which in 1993 expanded by building an electronics and appliance superstore, serves a trade area within a radius of about 300 miles from Omaha. It sells everything from rugs, sofas, lamps, and electronics to cellular telephones.

"Anybody would learn a lot more from watching this business for a few months than from going to business school," Buffett says. (*New York Times*, June 17, 1994)

Buffett and Mrs. B were inducted into the Omaha Chamber of Commerce Business Hall of Fame in 1993. Mrs. B is driving a souped-up motorized cart.

(Omaha World-Herald)

(Photo by Andrew Kilpatrick)

Ross's steak house (across from the Nebraska Furniture Mart) where Buffett and the Blumkins often talk business over steak dinners. Buffett buys his furniture, televisions and carpet at the store.

When Buffett was buying the store, he did not even order an inventory check until the deal was completed; and when Mrs. B, who never spent a day of her life in a school room, asked where were his accountants, lawyers, and investment bankers, he replied, "I trust you more." The contract was one page long and Mrs. B signed by simply making a mark. She never learned to read or write.

It is a well-known story that years ago, Rose Blumkin, born December 3, 1893, talked her way past a border guard in her native Russia, assuring the guard she would be back after buying leather for the army and a bottle of vodka for him. She made her way to this country and forever after did only two things: run her business and raise her family.

Mrs. B, a feisty 4-foot-10, came to the U.S. in 1917 at the age of 23, began selling furniture in her basement in 1936 and started Nebraska Furniture Mart in 1937 with only $500. "Just imagine what she could have done with more," Buffett jokes. And following her own advice of "Sell cheap and tell the truth," she eventually made the Nebraska Furniture Mart the success that drew Buffett's attention.

By controlling costs and offering value to the customer, the business flourished. It's now the dominant furniture store in the region. In fact, when Mrs. Blumkin was sued by a competitor for selling too cheap, the judge not only ruled in her favor, he also decided to buy yards of carpet from her.

For years Buffett brought friends by to see her and he bragged at annual meetings and in the annual reports about how she was picking up speed as she got older. His portrait of Mrs. B was of a business heroine. But in May, 1989, at age 96, following a dispute with her family about the remodeling and running of the Nebraska Furniture Mart's carpet department to which she was so devoted in her later years, she quit.

Further, she demanded and got from Berkshire $96,000 for unused vacation time. Although she received every penny of it, she stormed out and set up shop across the street from the Nebraska Furniture Mart. She called her new store Mrs. B's Warehouse and she still sells carpet. "Their price $104; our price $80," a sign in her store used to read.

"I got mad. I expect too much," she later told *Forbes,* April 26, 1993.

She still moves around Mrs. B's on her famous motorized cart and for a while gave interviews saying Buffett was not her friend and that she was running her store to get revenge. For years her family members preferred not to talk about it.

Buffett was once asked how he was able to inspire such loyalty in such a range of business managers and he joked that he tended to have trouble with them in their 90s.

In his annual report, Buffett told it straight to shareholders and he was more than gracious in his remarks about Mrs. B. Nevertheless, it was a distressing moment in a storybook business relationship.

But the story would have a happy ending when Berkshire bought her out again in 1992.

The Nebraska Furniture Mart is always a must-visit for Berkshire shareholders.

Once I wandered in the Furniture Mart a day prior to the annual meeting and happened to be told that Buffett had been in earlier. I assumed he had left.

But when I turned into the carpet section, I saw a scene that would have warmed the heart of any Berkshire shareholder. There in the middle of the carpet section was Buffett with a man I would learn was his long-time friend Sandy Gottesman, chairman of the First Manhattan investment firm in New York and a large Berkshire shareholder.

The two were talking to Mrs. B as she sat in her cart. One had the feeling that if Buffett and Mrs. B were really on the carpet section floor talking business, you were a shareholder in the right company.

Normally shy, I walked up to Buffett and introduced myself as a Berkshire shareholder. He said, "Good, come to the annual meeting. Ask questions."

We had a very brief chat in which, instead of asking about business, I asked about how his tennis game was and he said he wasn't playing much any more because he had hurt his back.

He and Gottesman wandered around the carpet section inspecting the operations and so I wandered around inspecting them.

One year I asked a Nebraska Furniture Mart employee if Buffett had been in lately. She said yes that he was with a friend. Naturally, I inquired who the person was and she replied, "Some guy named Tisch." I inquired whether it might be Larry or Preston Tisch. She said she had no idea.

Yet another year I found Charles Munger, wearing a well-worn casual travel jacket, blue shirt and dark slacks, wandering around in the lower level of the store, appropriately checking things out.

That same year, standing again in the carpet section, I saw an energetic young man in casual clothes come up to Mrs. B's grandson, Robert Batt, and ask to use the telephone. The man was Buffett's son, Howard Buffett, then county commissioner of Omaha's Douglas County.

He talked politics for a time and then I said hello and asked him a question he's heard a time or two in his life.

"What's your father like?" The younger Buffett replied, "He's great. I've been working on him a long time and he's improving a lot."

Batt, who had just been talking about Buffett said: "I often fly in the plane with Buffett to go to New York to buy rugs.

"Buffett will talk to all of us. Actually he does the talking and we listen. We really don't talk to Buffett. We listen...and then he'll read a lot of the way.

"He knows more about our business than we do. He knows about our business and he knows about competitors. It's not just that he knows about See's. He knows about Russell Stover's. He knows all about Coca-Cola, but then he also knows all about Pepsi, too."

Batt also said Buffett has told him that he should have bought a huge stake in Disney, that he recognizes Michael Eisner's talents.

Both the *Washington Post's* Katharine Graham and the *Buffalo News*' Stanford Lipsey have visited the store.

Of late, Berkshire-style synergy has come to the Nebraska Furniture Mart. There is now a See's Candy shop at the store. As Buffett wrote in the 1990 Annual Report to shareholders, "While there, stop at See's Candy cart and see for yourself the dawn of synergism at Berkshire."

Installed October 21, 1990, the See's Candy cart—the first See's outlet east of Colorado—sold 1,000 pounds of candy in its first week. It didn't hurt sales when Buffett went on an ABC affiliate in Omaha notifying chocoholics of the See's Candy cart's existence.

Now Borsheim's sometimes also offers a small See's candy box with its advertising materials. Expanded synergy. Who knows, maybe one day See's and Coke will be combined into a Berkshire Foods Division based at the Nebraska Furniture Mart.

In October 1991, the Nebraska Furniture Mart opened a new store called Trends just behind the Mart. The store sells mainly ready-to-assemble contemporary furniture, including leather sofas, day beds, children's furniture and cribs.

Buffett was on hand for the ribbon cutting and predicted the store would become the second largest furniture store in sales in the Midwest, second only to the Nebraska Furniture Mart itself.

With synergy apparently still on his mind, Buffett went over to the store's soda fountain and asked Judy Troutman for a Cherry Coke.

On December 1, 1991, just before Mrs. B's 98th birthday, Buffett paid a call and presented her with two dozen pink roses and a 5-pound box of See's candy. (*Omaha World-Herald*, February 2, 1992)

Mrs. B was quoted as saying, "He's quite a gentleman." Rapprochement? Could be. The story said Louie Blumkin had recently asked his mother whether she might be willing to sell her business to Berkshire.

Would she ever sell? "Who knows?" said Mrs. B. "Time will tell...I would sell only one way—if they let me work."

The rapprochement seemed well on its way when Rose Blumkin told the *Omaha World-Herald,* July 14, 1992, that she planned to sell her furniture business to her son, Louie Blumkin.

"I do a very good business there, but it's hard to manage it," she said. "My son offered to buy me out, and I'm going to sell."

She said her son is buying the business for the Nebraska Furniture Mart owned by Berkshire.

Under the agreement, closed on December 31, 1992, did Mrs. B contemplate early retirement?

No way. She plans to keep selling carpet.

Mrs. B was having her headaches at her store because there had been some theft and she was getting cantankerous with employees and customers.

Buffett wound up buying out Mrs. B.

Now the Nebraska Furniture Mart operates from a more-than-200,000 square foot outlet, and it has bought a 360,000 square foot building and ten acres of land located adjacent to its existing retail store and warehouse for $5 million.

"I am delighted that Mrs. B has again linked up with us," Buffett wrote in the 1992 annual report. "Her business story has no parallel and I have always been a fan of hers, whether a partner or a competitor... But, believe me, partner is better.

"This time around Mrs. B graciously offered to sign a non-compete agreement—and I, having been incautious on this point when she was 89, snapped at the deal. Mrs. B belongs in the Guinness Book of World Records on many counts. Signing a non-compete at 99 merely adds one more."

Explaining his oversight a decade earlier in not thinking of the non-compete agreement then, 62-year-old Buffett conceded to *Forbes,* April 26, 1993, "I was young and inexperienced."

"Maybe I was wrong. Maybe I was too hard on them," Mrs. B said in an interview (*Omaha World-Herald*, April 24, 1993) when Buffett and Mrs. B held dedication ceremonies for Mrs. B's after the Nebraska Furniture Mart bought it.

As the start of an era of better feelings, Buffett pulled out a stuffed bee, playfully putting it in Mrs. B's head and mugging for photographers.

Shortly afterwards, she said, "He's an honest person. He's never stuck-up. He's straight."

Riding around in her cart in the carpet section, Mrs. B, who never even attended kindergarten, said, "You can't get good help these days," adding that she had recently threatened some wayward employees by bluffing that she was going to throw acid in their eyes.

Then her tough side gave way and she said, "I live alone now and so that's why I work. I hate to go home. I work to avoid the grave."

At the age of 100, Mrs. B was still working at the store 60 hours a week.

"Rose Blumkin's going to be 100 years old in December. Incidentally, she still works 7 days a week. The nights the store's open until 9 o'clock, you'll find her there at 9 o'clock. She rides around in a little golf cart, and if the salesperson isn't waiting on someone and she gets a little disgusted, she goes up and rams him with her cart and makes her point," Buffett told an audience at Columbia University's Business School on October 27, 1993.

"We'll do $200 million (in sales) in that store this year. A very remarkable woman, remarkable family. She has done it by having a terrific mind, an incredible desire."

The Furniture Mart also owns a flooring business in Lincoln, Nebraska, and a commercial sales office in Des Moines, Iowa.

Nebraska Governor Ben Nelson, Senator Bob Kerrey, Representative Peter Hoagland and Omaha Mayor P.J. Morgan all showed up at Mrs. B's Clearance and Factory Outlet for her 100th birthday celebration.

Kerrey said, "We all have noticed that sometimes we, as a consequence of profession, are held in somewhat low regard. So what we try to do is appear in photographs with people who are held in very high regard."

Buffett couldn't make the party because he was in New York for a Cap Cities board meeting.

But that weekend Buffett gave her a $1 million check for the Rose Blumkin Performing Arts Center in Omaha, the new home of the Emmy Gifford Children's Theater.

The check was written on the Buffett Foundation account at FirsTier Bank. It was folded up, rumpled and had a Coke stain on it.

At the annual meeting in 1994, Buffett offered a display of Berkshire's products, including a See's candy assortment commemorating Mrs. B's 100th birthday, featuring her picture rather than Mrs. See's on the package.

Buffett, at Berkshire's annual meeting in 1995, wondered aloud why students of business don't study Mrs. B. "She started a business with $500 with not a day of school... Look what she accomplished...Who is studying her?" Buffett said business schools are preoccupied with teaching things like "Economic Value Added," and just see Mrs. B. as a curiosity. Buffett said it was probably asking too much for folks to come out to the Nebraska Furniture Mart and "study a woman in a golf cart."

In the fall of 1994, the 64-acre mart opened the Mega Mart, billed as the "Greatest Store on the Planet". The 102,000-square-foot store carries more than 50,000 items, mainly electronics, computer equipment and appliances. The items include built-in refrigerators, microwaves, cam-

(Photos by Pat Kilpatrick)

Tommy Johnson of Birmingham at the Mega Mart. A grown man buys a haul of CDs.

Meanwhile his wife Jane, shopping until she drops, buys a Braun coffee maker, giving the Mega Mart, Gillette and Berkshire a boost.

eras, video games, whirlpool baths, cuisinarts and coffee makers. CDs, normally $14, sell for about $10.

At the opening ceremony Buffett said, "the Nebraska Furniture Mart is never finished."

In 1995 Microsoft opened a "concept shop" at the Megamart to sell Microsoft products.

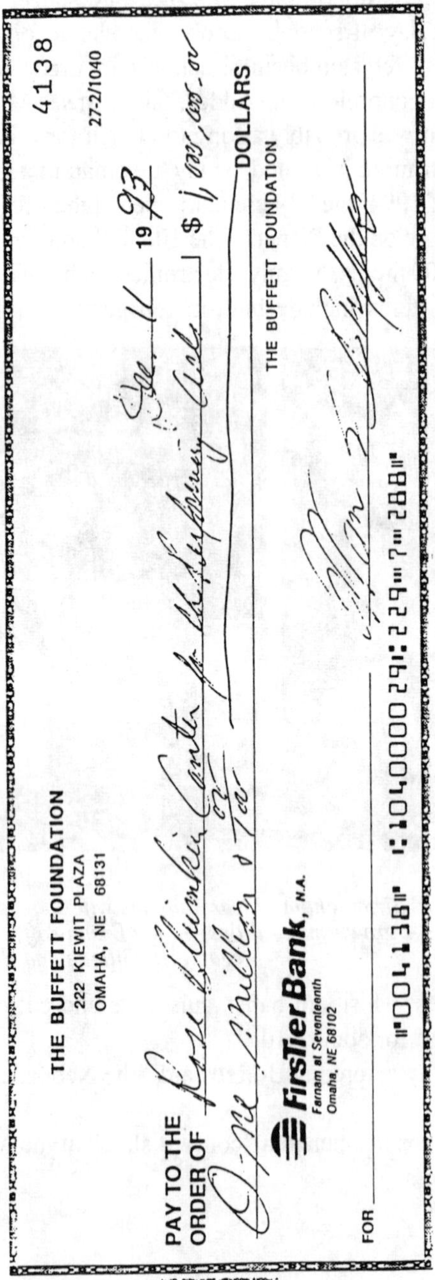
THE BUFFETT FOUNDATION
222 KIEWIT PLAZA
OMAHA, NE 68131
4138
27-2/1040
19
$ 1,000,000.00
PAY TO THE ORDER OF
DOLLARS
THE BUFFETT FOUNDATION
FirsTier Bank, N.A.
Farnam at Seventeenth
Omaha, NE 68102
FOR
⑈004138⑈ ⑆104000029⑆ 229⑈7⑈288⑈

44

The Scott & Fetzer Company

"Scott Fetzer to acquire Berkshire Hathaway"

Berkshire bought The Scott & Fetzer Company of Cleveland, Ohio, in early 1986 for $315 million. Scott Fetzer doubled Berkshire's sales to about $2 billion. Scott Fetzer had been on the auction block since 1984, but nothing had clicked. Finally a plan involving heavy Employee Stock Ownership Plan participation was approved by shareholders. But when difficulty arose in closing, the plan was dropped.

Buffett's ever watchful eye tracked the progress, or lack thereof, in the newspapers. He phoned Chief Executive Ralph Schey and asked for a meeting. Schey is an unusual businessman who has found the time to be actively involved with The Cleveland Clinic, Ohio University, Case Western Reserve and a venture capital firm that has backed a number of Ohio firms.

Buffett and Munger dined with Schey in Chicago on October 22,

(Photo courtesy of World Book)

Ralph Schey heads Berkshire's Scott Fetzer unit which includes World Book, Kirby vacuums and other businesses.

1985. The following week, a contract was signed.

Word of Berkshire's purchase of Scott Fetzer was carried by the Dow Jones news service, which startled Berkshire shareholders: "Scott Fetzer to acquire Berkshire Hathaway." The report was quickly corrected to show that Berkshire was buying Scott Fetzer.

At Berkshire's annual meeting in 1987, Munger and Buffett said they were presented an inch-thick notebook prepared by Scott Fetzer's investment bankers before the purchase. But they handed it back saying they didn't want to get confused. As usual, they just wanted to keep things simple. They saved some time and energy.

With Scott Fetzer, Berkshire acquired such businesses as World Book encyclopedias and the Kirby, Douglas and Cleveland Wood divisions of the Scott Fetzer Company, and various small businesses, many now lumped with Berkshire's other small businesses, collectively referred to as "other businesses."

Talk about dull businesses!

There's nothing very sexy about any of them, but together they're another little stream winding its way into Old Man River. The main business, and clearly Buffett's favorite of the businesses from the Scott Fetzer acquisition, is World Book.

But he likes Kirby, too.

45

Kirby

"It leaves the others in the dust."

With the acquisition of Scott Fetzer, Berkshire became the owner of Kirby vacuum cleaners.

"See, it actually picks up the carpet...it collects sand," says Hank Smith, vice president of Kirby South in Birmingham, demonstrating the vacuum cleaner's prowess.

"If we get in the home, we usually make the sale," Smith explains.

In one consumer survey after another, Kirby ranks at the top. "It leaves the others in the dust," Buffett likes to say.

Kirby tends to cost more, about $1,300 for its Generation 3 model with a power-assisted drive. But users say the strong engine, the space-age materials, the strength and durability are all worth it.

Kirbys are sold all over the world. Indeed almost a fourth of its sales are overseas. Kirbys are so powerful that they are often used for commercial use (not recommended by the company) as well as in homes.

Kirby sells to about 700 factory distributors. They in turn sell the Kirbys to a network of area distributors and dealers. Some of these independent dealers sell the vacuum cleaners door-to-door using in-the-home demonstrations.

Although Berkshire's home cleaning segment is led by Kirby, it also includes Douglas Products, Cleveland Wood, and a host of other profit centers.

Douglas makes specialty hand-held electric and cordless vacuums and distributes through department and hardware stores and catalog showrooms.

Cleveland Wood manufactures vacuum cleaner brushes. They distribute through discount, hardware and department stores and catalog showrooms.

46

World Book

"I bought World Book, too."

After Bob Kerrey was governor of Nebraska and before he was elected to the U.S. Senate from the Cornhusker State, he visited Birmingham, and following an interview, I asked if he knew Buffett. He related this story:

Kerrey, the Navy SEAL Vietnam-veteran Medal of Honor winner who dated actress Debra Winger, said he once told Buffett he had bought a set of *The World Book Encyclopedias* for his two children.

"I bought *World Book,* too," replied Buffett, meaning, of course, he had bought the whole company. Kerrey has said, if ever elected President, he'd turn to Buffett for economic advice. The two men occasionally have dinner at the French Cafe in Omaha, and Kerrey calls Buffett for advice about economic matters, including tax, health reform, finance and trade policy.

Buffett, an avid reader of encyclopedias as a youngster, did not read

World Book then, but in 1962 he bought a set for his children and has used them since.

Bill Gates read *World Book* from beginning to end when he was only seven or eight years old.

World Book is available on a compact disk version, *Infofinder.* It contains 17,000 articles, 1,700 tables, 150,000 index entries, 60,000 cross refrences, 1,600 reading lists and 229,000 entries form *The World Book Dictionary.*

Other products include the 16-volume *Childcraft*, a children's resource, and Early World of Learning, a preschool educational program.

One fact, according to *World Book* brochures, is that the average 16-year-old has spent about 20,000 hours watching television—more hours than it takes to earn a bachelor's degree. Solution: read *World Book.*

Almost 10 million pounds of paper were used to print the 1993 *World Book*, according to the company so fond of compiling facts. The paper would stretch 106 million feet—nearly 20,000 miles—or across the continental United States more than 7 times.

The paper would fill 70 railroad cars, which means every day during the printing of the 1993 *World Book*, a carload of paper moves from Luke, Maryland, where it's loaded, to the Crawfordsville, Indiana, printing plant.

There are about 100 million characters of type in a *World Book* set.

Competing in a $500 million encyclopedia industry, *World Book* is found in four of every 10 homes in the U.S. and Canada that own an encyclopedia. And it's estimated that $1 of every $10 spent for books is spent on encyclopedias.

Almost 300,000 sets of *World Book* are sold every year.

However, *World Book*'s profits took a dive in 1993 to $13.5 million, down from $19.5 million in 1992. They were $17.3 in 1994 and plummeted to $7 million in 1995 in the face of tough competition from CD-ROM and on-line offerings.

A yearbook is published annually to update the set and is marketed by mail to owners of earlier editions. Otherwise products are marketed primarily through demonstrations at homes, schools, and libraries by a commissioned sales force of more than 20,000 throughout the U.S. and Canada, Australia and the British Isles and distribution points in many other countries.

A set of *World Book* includes a 32-page article with color maps and color photographs on many aspects of Russian life; from religion, family life, government to natural resources, the ballet and architecture. More than seventy other major references in various volumes include biographies and photographs of Russian leaders and articles on major Russian cities and physical features.

World Book products have been translated into many languages including Arabic, Chinese, Finnish, French, Indonesian, Japanese, Korean, Malay, Portuguese, Spanish, and Swedish. *World Book* plans to print a Chinese-language edition for distribution by the Chinese government.

Education is *World Book*'s best selling point. And about half of *World Book*'s sales force consists of current or former teachers.

The encyclopedia industry has a number of major players, including *Encyclopaedia Britannica*, *Grolier* and *Collier's*. *World Book* is the market leader, selling more than twice as many sets as any competitor. It sells more sets in the U.S. than its top three competitors combined. A large portion of encyclopedia sales is made on an installment basis. Buyers can finance their purchases through *World Book* Finance, Inc., a Scott Fetzer subsidiary.

In 1988, *World Book* made a major revision of its format. The 70th anniversary edition was three years and $7 million in the making, featuring its most extensive revision in 26 years. Every revised edition of *World Book* involves more than 500 scholars, specialists, editors, artists, researchers, cartographers, contributors, production specialists and illustrators, who check about 5,000 information sources and review 5,000 to 10,000 photographs.

The publication is known for extensive fact checking. At *World Book*'s request, an official of Quebec's Department of Transportation measured the width of the Sous-le-Cap Street (8 ft. 10 in.) in Quebec, Canada, reputedly North America's narrowest street. The 22-volume *World Book* includes 14,000 pages and 7,000 articles by some 3,900 of the world's leading experts in their fields, such as Sir Edmund Hillary, "Mount Everest" contributor and Georgetown University Coach John Thompson, "basketball" contributor. The encyclopedia also includes 28,000 photographs and illustrations and 2,200 maps.

It's estimated that more than 100 million people have grown up with *World Book* since 1917 and that there are 12 million *World Book* sets in use worldwide. *The World Book Encyclopedia* was introduced by J.H. Hanson of the Hanson-Bellows Co. in Chicago in 1917 as *The World Book-Organized Knowledge in Story and Pictures*. He created *World Book* by spending $150,000 to revise his then popular encyclopedia, *The New Practical Reference Library*. In 1918, Hanson's money ran out and he sold *World Book* to one of his former accountants, W.F. Quarrie, also of Chicago, and the company flourished.

Celebrities such as the late FBI Director J. Edgar Hoover, etiquette expert Emily Post and Bishop Fulton J. Sheen became *World Book* contributors.

In 1945, Marshall Field III bought *World Book* to be the flagship of a new company that ultimately became Field Enterprises Educational Corp. Field believed that "education is the keystone of the democratic form of government" and that *World Book* was a key tool for education. In 1978, *World Book* was bought by Scott Fetzer.

There are many stories about the gentle persistence of dedicated *World Book* sales agents, not the least of whom is Joyce Fishman of Marshfield, Massachusetts, a top *World Book* saleswoman who was once bitten by a dog and still managed to make the sale (perhaps because the potential customer was fearful of reprisal).

World Book's part-time and full-time sales consultants make anywhere from $100 to more than $30,000 a year and generally have the luxury of flexible hours. They get a minimum $100 commission for a set of *World Book* which in 1994 ranged in cost from $679 to $849 a set, depending on binding quality. Managers, who get a cut from all the sales force under them, make substantially more, and a top branch manager can make as much as $250,000 a year.

Munger, at the Berkshire annual meeting in 1994, said, "I give away more of that product than any other product that Berkshire Hathaway makes...It's a perfectly fabulous human achievement. To edit something that user-friendly with that much wisdom encapsulated is a fabulous thing."

Ever the advocate of eating one's own cooking, Buffett has gently pushed sets at his children and grandchildren. He keeps a set of *World Book* at both his home and office.

47

"Other"

It's not a bad Berkshire subsidiary if a $24 million profit in 1995 means anything to you.

Berkshire has an interesting "subsidiary" called "Other," which includes about two dozen small businesses.

Just exactly what all this is, Buffett has not let us in on except to say in the 1990 annual report it includes the non-operating assets (primarily marketable securities) held by Berkshire's manufacturing, publishing and retail businesses.

In 1977, "Other" made $48,000. Here's how "Other" has done since in annual profits:

1978—$261,000
1979—$753,000
1980—$1,255,000
1981—$1,513,000
1982—$1,780,000

1983—$8,490,000
1984—$3,476,000
1985—$2,102,000
1986—$8,685,000
1987—$13,696,000
1988—$27,177,000
1989—$12,863,000
1990—$35,782,000
1991—$47,896,000
1992—$36,267,000
1993—$15,364,000
1994—$22,275,000
1995—$24,400,000

That's no lemonade stand.

The other mention of "Other" was made in another annual report: "Amortization of intangibles arising in accounting for purchases of businesses (i.e., See's, Mutual and Buffalo News) is reflected in the category designated Other."

Don't mention it. Buffett barely does. But Other is a nice business.

The group's largest business is Campbell Hausfeld, the country's leading producer of small and medium-sized air compressors, with annual sales of about $100 million.

Berkshire's little businesses:

Adalet-PLM	Explosion proof electrical enclosures, cable couplers and terminations
BHR	Real estate management
Berkshire Hathaway Credit Corporation	Commercial financing
Berkshire Hathaway Life Insurance Co.	Annuities
Blue Chip Stamps	Marketing motivational services
Borsheim's	Retailing fine jewelry
Campbell Hausfeld	Air compressors, air tools, painting systems, pressure washers and generators

Carefree	Sun and shade control products for the home and campground
France	Appliance and HVAC controls, ingition and sigh transformers
Halex	Zinc die cast conduit fillings and other electrical construction materials
Halzeberg's Diamond Shops	Retailing fine jewelry
K&W Products	Automotive compounds
Meriam	Pressure and flow measurement devices
Northland	Fractional horsepower electric motors
Powerwinch	Marine winches and windlasses, general purpose winches and hoists
Precision Steel Products	Steel service center
Quikut	Cutlery for home and sporting goods markets
ScottCare	Cardiopulmonary rehabilitation and monitoring equipment
Scott Fetzer Financial Group	Commercial and consumer finance companies
Scot Labs	Cleaning and maintenance chemicals
Stahl	Custom service bodies, flatbed bodies, cranes and tool boxes for trucks
Wayne	Furnace burners; sump, utility and sewage pumps
Wesco Financial	Real estate management
Western Enterprises	Medical and industrial compressed gas fittings and regulators
Western Plastics	Molded plastic components

48

K&W Products

"Small business, big margins."

K&W Products, a small boring business selling lubricants and chemicals to the automotive and industrial aftermarket, came into the Berkshire fold in the mid-1970s.

"I went to work for Dick Cate in 1977," says investment advisor Page Golsan of Salem, Oregon, picked by Cate to succeed him in running the firm.

As Cate's health worsened, Cate sold the business to Berkshire in 1976, partially as a result of a friendship between Cate and Charles Munger.

"It was an easy, straightforward sale...in the mid-1970s," recalls Golsan, who came into the business with science degrees.

One person Munger and Golsan often called on for advice about the business, which had \$3.5 million in sales in 1982 and \$3.8 million in sales in 1983, was Harry Bottle, once K&W's controller.

Bottle is famed in Berkshire lore for turning things around, and Buffett has often said Bottle is probably not everyone's idea of a corporate executive because his "hair is not blow dried, or something."

"Bottle is a problem-solving, turnaround, accounting guy, a sharp guy and a fun guy and I learned a lot from him," said Golsan. "Working for Berkshire is far better than getting an MBA."

Bottle often performed cleanup and turnaround missions for Berkshire as well as other businesses.

Buffett once called on Bottle to get out of a jam with a windmill business, the last of its kind in Nebraska. Bottle gave extra value to the business by figuring out that its inventory was valuable to other windmill businesses across the country because of its stock of spare parts.

"I would call Bottle in on accounting projects. He was very bright in cost accounting," he added.

Golsan, a Berkshire shareholder whose grandfather knew Ben Graham and whose family business once offered a line of K&W Products, says Buffett left him almost entirely alone to run the business. He practically never saw Buffett.

But one night the two had dinner at Ross's steak house in Omaha.

"Buffett is super bright. He's always asking questions. He's a very pleasant guy, but the conversation moves very fast. You have to stay on the edge of your chair. He asked me how I thought the business would do. We had a couple of flat years and a number of good years. He really does leave the operating heads alone. All they have to do is run the thing.

"He's not in the business of training executives and that tends to make him pick senior people," said Golsan who explained Berkshire's corporate culture is not warm and fuzzy, but is honest and businesslike.

It's not a crowd that goes in for swapping stories, back-slapping or social show, he indicated. It's a culture where you're left alone to run the business and if you have a problem, then give headquarters a call.

And so Golsan ran K&W Products from 1977 to 1986 when he moved on to an oil business in Chicago.

K&W ultimately moved in with the Blue Chip organization in Los Angeles, in typical Berkshire fashion, "to save space."

"K&W is a small business. It's a small business, with big margins," Golsan said.

49

Fechheimer

"He knows the size uniform every prisoner needs."
—Buffett of Bob Heldman

Berkshire bought its 84% ownership in Fechheimer Brothers Co., a uniform company in Cincinnati, Ohio, in June, 1986. This was after Bob Heldman, a longtime Berkshire shareholder, wrote Buffett that he had a business he believed met Buffett's famous acquisition tests.

Buffett frequently has referred to his "ad" for what he is looking for in businesses: large purchases; demonstrated, consistent earning power; businesses earning good returns on equity while employing little or no debt; management in place, ("we can't supply it"); simple businesses ("if there's lots of technology, we won't understand it") and an offering price.

Heldman, a longtime reader of the Berkshire annual report, and well aware of what Buffett was looking for, convinced Buffett his company was a good fit for Berkshire. He wrote Buffett about Fechheimer, a uniform manufacturing and distribution business owned and operated by the

Heldman family—Bob and his brother, George, (now retired) and a subsequent generation of Heldmans.

"We wrote several times and I think convinced him the business fit the tests he lists in his ad. I had a meeting with him in Omaha," recalled Bob Heldman.

"We had the parameters of a deal set and met just one last time. It turned out it was in Middle Fork, Idaho, on the Snake River. There are no roads. You have to fly in. We had planned a board meeting at a lodge there and decided that was a good time to settle it.

"He (Buffett) flew into Boise and I met him and then we got on a little plane and went to Middle Fork. Munger flew in from California and we all met most of the afternoon with our lawyers and we were going to meet the next day but a storm warning came up and we left," said Heldman.

Heldman recalls that Munger asked him, "What are you least proud of?" Heldman said.

"I really couldn't think of anything. We have made a few bad deliveries," Heldman said.

Buffett never went to Cincinnati, either before or after Berkshire's purchase of the Cincinnati concern.

The buyout of Fechheimer closed shortly afterwards with Buffett paying about $46 million for the stake in Fechheimer based on a $55 million valuation for the whole company.

Buffett has said the only problem with Fechheimer is its small size, but it remains a steady contributor to Berkshire's earnings stream and has been expanding. It now has more than 50 stores nationwide.

The uniforms are mainly for police, fire, postal and service industry workers and Fechheimer makes uniforms for schools and bands. It also offers socks, belts and jackets.

Fechheimer, founded in 1842, makes uniforms at plants in Kentucky, Ohio, Tennessee and Texas, for marketing through its stores and by independent dealers who together serve more than 200 of the country's major metropolitan areas.

Fechheimer stores go by different names. For example, the stores in Birmingham and Mobile, Alabama, are called McCain Uniform Co.; in Arizona they are Pima Uniforms; in Tennessee, Kay Uniforms and in Texas, Uniforms of Texas stores.

The Heldmans are hands-on managers known for starting their day sitting around a table and personally opening the company's mail whether it be bills, a complaint, a compliment or a new business idea. A stockbroker showed up once to make a pitch while the Heldmans were opening the mail. He was told to go ahead and make his case as the Heldmans went right on reading the mail. The inscrutable Heldmans, hardly looking up, finally nodded approval to the idea and went right on poring over the mail, which they believe keeps them in close touch with every aspect of the company.

Not much gets by the circumspect, play-it-close-to-the-vest Heldmans.

During the cocktail party at Borsheim's the day before the annual meeting in 1990, Buffett and the Heldmans slipped off to a back office room of Borsheim's for a game of bridge.

Buffett teamed up with his friend, lawyer George Gillespie of the New York law firm of Cravath, Swaine & Moore, and they squared off against the Heldman brothers.

Afterwards, one shareholder had the audacity to ask Buffett if he had won. Grimacing a bit, he said no, adding, "Hard to believe, isn't it?"

The slightly built Heldmans had outslicked their boss at the bridge table, but later would not confirm it even after a casual inquiry made during a ride back to a hotel after the Borsheim's party.

They just grinned ever so slightly and looked out the window to check out the Omaha scenery. Two years later, Bob Heldman said with quiet pride, "Well, we don't like to talk about it, but we did win."

You will not get a lot of fast and loose talk when the Heldmans are around. And you simply cannot tell what their bridge or business hand holds.

With the Heldmans, you get attention to business and the right uniform size.

In 1994 Fechheimer won a 3-year contract to supply uniforms and accessories to the New York Fire Department.

50

Borsheim's

"Sell him the store."

Borsheim's, the jewelry store in Omaha that Buffett bought 80% of in February, 1989, is now the site for the shareholder shopping spree and cocktail party the day before each Berkshire annual meeting.

Each year at Borsheim's the store hosts a special exhibit for Berkshire's stockholders. The one in 1996 featured the world's largest polished diamond. The 545-carat Golden Jubilee Diamond is a gift to the King of Thailand from the people of Thailand. King Bhumibol Adulyadej, who has been on the throne 50 years, is the world's longest reigning monarch.

Buffett himself shows up for the Borsheim's party and so do the likes of Katharine Graham and Ann Landers, Salomon's Robert Denham and Deryck Maughan and a number of Berkshire's luminaries.

A string quartet plays, champagne and salmon are served some

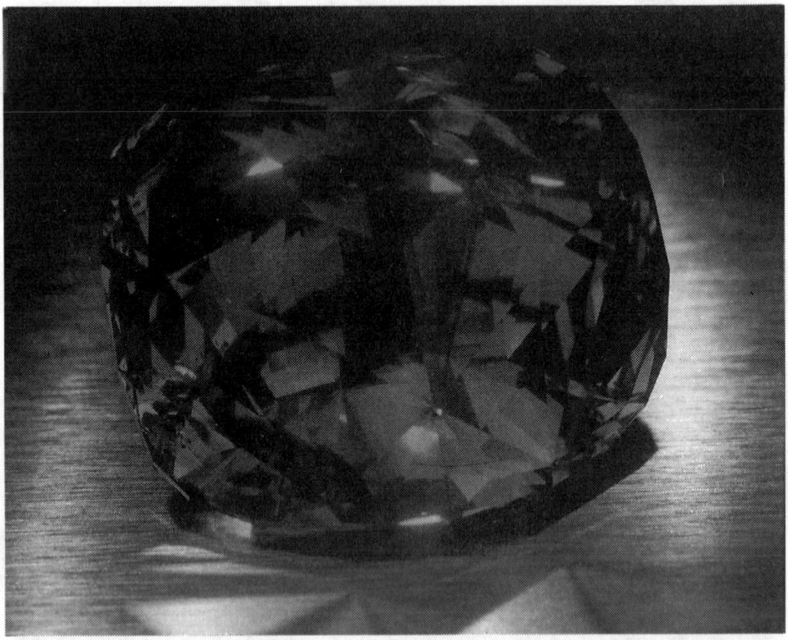

(Courtesy of Borsheim's)

In 1986 this golden yellow diamond weighing 755.50 carats was discovered in the DeBeers Premier Diamond Mine in Transvaal, South Africa. Two years in the cutting, the 545-carat diamond—about the size of a baseball—is the largest polished diamond in the world.

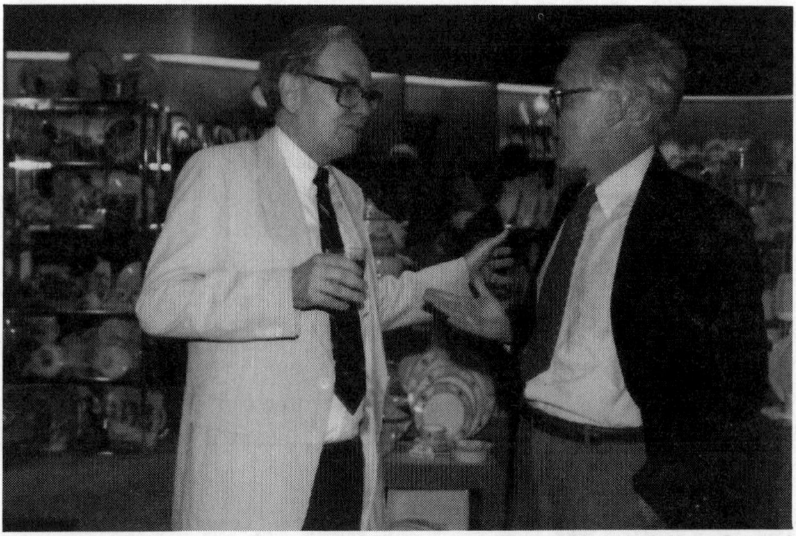

(Photo by LaVerne Ramsey)

Buffett and the author at Borsheim's April 29, 1990. I break news I plan a book about Buffett, who cordially declines interview. Later he said, "I wish you well, but not too well." Years later he kidded me, "Are you up to 1,000 pages yet?"

years. In recent years, the goodies have been cut to wine and Cokes—more cost cutting at Berkshire. Whatever is served, shareholders spend the afternoon swapping Buffett stories. My story is that once I walked up to him, as scores of shareholders do, to shake hands. Thinking he could not possibly know me or where I was from, I told him my name. His instant reply was, "Up from Birmingham, are you?"

His memory is so widely regarded that if it ever fails, people are shocked. One shareholder at the same party, relating that he had a brief chat with Buffett about bridge, came away shaking his head, "Gosh, he didn't remember I sent him a bridge hand (last year)."

The party is great fun. Everyone peers at the merchandise, which ranges from $10 items and inexpensive coffee cups to jewelry priced at hundreds of thousands of dollars. Borsheim's carries pens, rings, watches, bracelets, china, crystal and a myriad of other items. At the store—a Berkshire gem—you can pay as little as $15,000 or as much as $115,000 for a Patek Philippe Swiss watch.

A 35-karat diamond ring has sold for $450,000. Some of the sapphires are almost the size of golf balls.

For Berkshire shareholders, Borsheim's held a special event in April, 1992, an exhibition including a $6 million Patek Philippe watch. Made of gold and 126 jewels, it's the most expensive watch ever made by the company, which produces only 15,000 pieces a year. The collection also included pocket watches owned by Queen Victoria, Albert Einstein and Rudyard Kipling.

The day before the Berkshire annual meeting in 1992, the usual party at Borsheim's was held, but with a twist. Buffett and Patek Philippe President Philippe Stern, held a 1 p.m. Sunday press conference at the store to introduce the watch exhibit. Borsheim's President Donald Yale said "good morning" and introduced Stern, who in a thick Swiss accent proclaimed the watches his company makes as "the finest watches in the world." One watch in the display was a $6 million white gold timepiece the size of an apple. The watch—billed as the most complicated ever made—had 1,800 parts and was equipped with a chime, moon phases, a calendar and a century leap year correction that turns once every four hundred years.

Buffett then addressed the party: "Good afternoon—my watch is keeping more accurate time."

After the press conference, Harvey Knowles, a stockbroker with Merrill Lynch in Cincinnati who is co-author of *The Dividend Factor*, a book touting the importance of high dividends, asked Buffett to sign his book.

Buffett, well known as no fan of dividends because they are taxed at both the corporate and individual level, dutifully signed Knowles's book, then shouted, "Throw him out!"

Also after the press conference, Dr. Michael Prus and his wife, Judith Goodnow Prus, of Grosse Pointe Farms, Michigan, and their daughter, Elizabeth, met Buffett. Elizabeth Prus, then a senior at Princeton University, had received a number of job offers from Wall Street firms, including Salomon and J.P. Morgan; she had accepted the Morgan offer. Buffett said to Elizabeth, "Maybe you could send us some of your extra business." Borsheim's offers it all. If you are interested in—you know, something special for your "significant other"—a Faberge egg, gold chains, Lalique crystal, a Cartier necklace, gemstones or pearls the size of marbles, Borsheim's has them. At the 1993 event at Borsheim's, some items from Joan Crawford's collection were on display.

Maybe you want a Waterman pen. After all, it's made by Gillette. Synergy at Berkshire is coming along. Even a vendor can enter Borsheim's with goods and leave with cash. At the 1991 meeting some jewelry was priced in Berkshire stock. Cute little signs: two shares of Berkshire for this diamond, three shares will get you that necklace. One diamond ensemble went for 15 shares—$120,000 at the time.

Borsheim's was founded in 1870 by Louis Borsheim, and in 1947 it was bought by Louis Friedman and his wife, Rebecca, the younger sister of Rose Blumkin of Nebraska Furniture Mart fame. Their son, Ike Friedman—who once worked at the Nebraska Furniture Mart—took over the business after his father. Ike, his son, daughters, and sons-in-law owned and managed the business when Berkshire bought it.

But later Berkshire redeemed Alan Friedman's (Ike Friedman's son's) share of the business so that Berkshire now owns 85.72% of Borsheim's. The (Donald) Yales and (Marvin) Cohns each own half of the remaining 14.28% of the business.

Between Thanksgiving and Christmas in 1991, 58,500 customers—an average of 2,250 a day—bought 38,500 items. (*Omaha World-Herald*, February 23, 1992)

In 1986, Borsheim's moved from its 6,800 square-foot location with its 35 employees in downtown Omaha to a 37,000 square-foot site in the Regency Fashion Court Mall. In 1996 the store was expanded to 44,000 square feet.

The store—which carries about $60 million to $75 million in merchandise—claims more than half the jewelry market share in Omaha. About 60% of Borsheim's customers are from the Omaha area, and on a normal Saturday more than 2,500 people show up at the store, perusing an inventory of more than 75,000 pieces of finished jewelry, 400 china patterns, 375 flatware patterns and thousands of loose gems.

The other 40% of its sales come from out of state, largely from telephone business.

Borsheim's, the largest jewelry store in the country other than Tiffany's Fifth Avenue flagship, customarily sends trusted customers a custom-made smorgasbord of the store's collection, say $40,000 watches, to look over. You can look them over, buy what you want and send back the rest. Buffett says there's never been a single case of dishonesty in connection with this honor system.

Borsheim's is a single-unit giant jeweler employing 300 people full and part time. Employees do not work for commissions, as management feels that would force them to worry more about making the sale than serving the customer.

The store traditionally has advertised little, but does more now and even offers a special bridal package. Borsheim's first catalog in 1989 was sent to 23,000 people around the U.S., including 11,000 preferred customers, as well as Berkshire shareholders who get a discount at the store. Now the catalog is sent to about 250,000 people.

The store buys in great volume, often directly from the source, and sometimes cuts its own stones. Also, the store is a part-owner of an amethyst mine in Brazil, which explains the large pile of geodes on the floor by an entrance to Borsheim's.

Donald Yale, Friedman's son-in-law who came to Borsheim's management team after a successful accounting practice, played a role in the business going to Buffett.

When Buffett was looking at a ring while Christmas shopping at Borsheim's in 1988, Yale yelled out, "Don't sell Warren the ring, sell him the store!"

After the first of the year, Buffett called and asked if a sale were possible. A short time later Buffett bought the store from Ike Friedman, Borsheim's president, after a brief meeting at Friedman's house with Friedman and Yale.

"The substantive part of the talk was 10 minutes," Yale said. "He asked us five questions and Ike had a price. The three of us later met at Buffett's office and Ike and Warren shook hands on the sale."

"The contract was a short document in which the signatures were longer than the contract. The legal costs for both parties in total was $1,100," Yale said.

Buffett and Friedman agreed not to disclose the price, but it's believed to have been more than $60 million. (*Lear's*, James Traub, October, 1991)

Traub interviewed Friedman about doing business in Omaha and Friedman told him the following story:

"Guy calls from Geneva and says where the hell is Omaha, Nebraska. Guy says, 'Do you think you could use three million dollars worth of diamonds?' "

Replies Friedman, "If you can come up with thirty million dollars worth of diamonds, or three hundred million dollars worth, if it's the right price, we'll buy 'em all." Friedman said the fellow couldn't believe it.

Friedman told Traub, "We buy it right. We sell it right. That's the difference between us and the other stores. I would say that 70% to 80% of our jewelry is cheaper than what a jeweler would pay to buy it. We make money on volume. And compared to other jewelers' expenses, ours are nil."

Of his purchase of Borsheim's, Buffett has said, "I neglected to ask Mrs. B a question that any schoolboy would have asked. That is, 'Are there any more at home like you?' "

Here are the five questions Buffett asked about the business: What are sales? What are gross profits? What are expenses? What's in inventory? Are you willing to stay on?

"He already knew we had no debt," Yale said.

Without referring to books, Friedman answered the questions. Although we now have the questions, we do not have the answers except whether Friedman would stay—yes.

As usual Buffett wrote a check paying cash. Friedman was suddenly a cash-rich man and a happy, fruitful business partnership with Berkshire was born.

Buffett said at the time: "Ike, there are only a handful of people I do business with this way. And none of them is a Fortune 500 company."

Friedman told Buffett, "I'd never have guessed when I was selling newspapers downtown that I would one day sell a business for this kind of money! I'm a lucky man."

Once the agreement was reached, Yale has recalled: "Buffett said, 'Now, forget that it happened, and just keep doing what you were doing.' There was no discussion of future growth and absolutely no discussion of changing our way of making decisions, planning expansion or bringing in additional profits. He made it very clear that he was not in this as a quick-return deal."

In delineating the fundamentals of Borsheim's business, Buffett has listed these attributes:

1. *Huge inventories and enormous selection across all price ranges.*
2. *Daily attention to detail by top management.*
3. *Rapid turnover.*
4. *Shrewd buying.*
5. *Incredibly low expenses.*

"The combination of the last three factors," he says, "lets the store offer everyday prices that no one in the country comes close to matching." (*The Goldsmith*, November, 1989)

"Ike has a big smile on his face today," Buffett announced at the annual meeting in 1990. That was because the previous day's sales figure was $1.5 million. Not bad for an afternoon Berkshire shareholder get-together.

Berkshire's 10-K form explains: "The size of this operation, like several of the Scott Fetzer operations, currently precludes its classification as a 'reportable business segment' of Berkshire. However, it contributes meaningful added diversity to Berkshire's activities."

The day before the 1991 annual meeting, *Buffalo News* Publisher

(Photo by Nancy Line Jacobs)

Borsheim's President Susan Jacques at the center counter of the jewelry store Buffett bought after asking five questions.

Stan Lipsey and his girlfriend spent hours checking out practically everything in Borsheim's. The moment Buffett passed by the couple (giving her a quick kiss on the cheek), they finally settled on an emerald ring.

Once at Borsheim's a shareholder asked Buffett to sign a two-share Berkshire stock certificate. Buffett did so, saying, "I'm not sure they'll cash it if I sign it." The young man said, "Well, I'm never going to sell it."

Buffett replied, "I haven't sold any of mine either."

Those were happy moments.

But on a terribly sad note, Ike Friedman, long a heavy smoker and seriously ill with lung cancer, died September 12, 1991.

Yale was named president and chief executive officer, and Marvin Cohn, also a son-in-law of Friedman's, was named executive vice president. Buffett was named chairman of the board of Borsheim's at a time when he was already chairman of Berkshire and interim chairman of Salomon.

Due to family obligations, Yale left in early 1994. Yale told the *Omaha World-Herald*, "I have family responsibilities and business responsibilities, and it got to the point I couldn't do both. My family responsibilities are my priority...This was my decision solely. Warren was very understanding and supportive of my decision." Yale remained on the board.

Buffett named as president and CEO 34-year-old Susan Jacques, who had joined the firm in 1980 as a gemologist and appraiser. A native of Zimbabwe, she came to the United States in 1980 and once won a prize as the outstanding gemology student worldwide. She joined Borsheim's in 1982 at age 23, making $4 an hour. She is married to Gene Dunn, of Omaha, owner of Mica Mecca, a cabinetry casework firm.

She said, "Becoming a subsidiary of Berkshire Hathaway opened our market to a whole new group of people who previously may not have

(Photo by Nancy Line Jacobs)

The crowd outside Borsheim's the day before Berkshire's annual meeting in 1996. A number of shareholders try to get Buffett's autograph.

been aware of us...We've drawn thousands to shop here and at the Nebraska Furniture Mart, with the added attraction of seeing Warren at the stockholders' meeting." (*Midlands Business Journal*, February 4-10, 1994)

At the Berkshire annual meeting in 1994, Buffett introduced Susan Jacques, saying she had a record day at the Berkshire party the day before. "Keep it up, Susan," Buffett implored.

Once George Morgan introduced his son, Adam, and Adam's fiancée to Buffett and they told him they planned to buy a wedding ring the next day at Borsheim's.

"Good. We'll open the store early and send a cab," Buffett said.

During the 1995 cocktail party at Borsheim's sales popped up 15% over 1994 sales which were up 40% over 1993 sales. "You're a sporty crowd," Buffett said at the annual meeting the next day. Sales during the annual meeting party in 1996 were 60% higher than those in 1995.

A shareholder came up to Munger at the Borsheim's party in 1996 and asked for Munger's autograph on his sales slip from Borsheim's for a $54,000 watch the shareholder had purchased. "That is the kind of autograph we like to give," laughed Munger.

Bill Gates shops for a wedding ring at Borsheim's

Microsoft Chairman Bill Gates shopped for a wedding ring for his fiancée at Borsheim's on Easter Sunday, April 11, 1993. Buffett, stepping in with an assist, met Gates and his fiancée, Melinda French, at the airport and drove them to Borsheim's to get the ring.

The story continued that Gates told his fiancée they were flying to Seattle. When the plane arrived in Omaha, she was very surprised to see Buffett meeting the plane.

During a talk to the University of Nebraska in Lincoln, October 10 1994, Buffett confirmed the story saying that as he drove Gates and Melinda French from the airport to Borsheim's, he said, "It's none of my business—who am I to give you advice?—but when I bought an engagement ring for my wife in 1951, I spent 6% of my net worth on it! We didn't have quite as big a day that Sunday as I had hoped." (talk to University of Nebraska students, October 10, 1994)

Buffett said he was disappointed in Gates' ticket, that it did not come up to 6% of his net worth.

Gates, a Harvard dropout who brought Windows to the world and is known by his E-mail handle "billg," met his wife at Microsoft offices in 1987.

Buffett was one of 130 guests who attended Gates's wedding, New Year's Day 1994, held at a Jack Nicklaus-designed golf course in Hawaii. Gates was the second richest person at his wedding. Other luminaries, such as Microsoft co-founder Paul Allen, whose 154-foot yacht was the site of a champagne brunch before the wedding, Microsoft's Steve Ballmer and singer Willie Nelson were on hand.

Afterwards the couple honeymooned in Fiji.

51

H.H. Brown Shoe

"When a single steer topples, they know."

Lowell Shoe

It was a case of the ultimate in dull businesses, a case of Buffett as a shoe salesman.

Berkshire said it had agreed on June 10, 1991, to buy all of H.H. Brown Shoe Company, a closely held shoe company based in Greenwich, Connecticut, with annual sales of about $200 million.

At yearend 1992, Brown acquired Lowell Shoe Inc., of Hudson, New Hampshire, with yearly sales of about $90 million and a manufacturing facility in Puerto Rico. Lowell makes Nurse Mates, a line of shoes for nurses, and has other shoe lines such as Soft Spots and Day Lights. The Nurse Mates shoes are comfortable, durable and amuse nurses because of the hearts on the shoe boxes and the shoes. Brown operates 15 retail shoe stores.

Berkshire bought Brown from the estate of the owner and board chairman, Ray Heffernan, who had been with the company since 1927 after buying it then for $10,000. His daughter, Frances Heffernan, married Frank Rooney who became the longtime boss of what is now Melville Corp. (formerly Melville Shoe).

Before Heffernan's death, he asked Rooney to run Brown. When the Heffernan family decided to sell the company, Rooney sold to Berkshire after Buffett's friend John Loomis told Rooney (over golf in Florida) that Brown might fit comfortably at Berkshire.

Brown Shoe operates as an independent Berkshire unit run by Rooney, chairman of the board and chief executive officer, and James E. Issler, president and chief operating officer. Employing more than 2,000 people, Brown markets its shoes under the H.H. Brown, Carolina Shoe, Double H Boot and other names. A faded red Double H Boot plant in Womelsdorg, Pennsylvania, gives new meaning to the words nondescript and no frills.

H.H. Brown is the leading U.S. producer of steel-toe safety work shoes. It's the leading North American manufacturer of work shoes and boots, according to Buffett, who says the shoe business in the U.S. is tough since 85% of all shoes sold in America are imported.

Buffett called Brown "exactly the type of business Berkshire strives to acquire: a leader in its industry and already staffed with tested and trusted management."

The company is not related to Brown Group, Inc., a large shoe company in St. Louis that a number of Berkshire shareholders raced to buy a few shares of, thinking it was Buffett's purchase.

Brown makes, imports and markets work, safety, outdoors, western and casual shoes. It carries a variety of men's and women's shoe lines and offers walking, hiking and cowboy shoes. Its stores around the country offer a businessmen's shoe called Comfa.

Many of Brown's work and military boots are sold to the United States and Canadian military PXs, as well as to such retailers as Wal-Mart, Kmart and Payless Shoe Co. The company competes in the middle-price markets where the consumer is often an industrial laborer required by OSHA to wear certain footwear. The company has plants in Morgantown, North Carolina, Womelsdorf and Martinsburg, Pennsylvania, and Canada.

At the Berkshire annual meeting in 1991 Buffett said he was then looking at a business that had some international business because it did business in Canada. Shareholders did some rifling through the usual publicly held stock information guides but couldn't figure out his tip. Since it was privately held, he was hardly giving anything away.

Buffett said at Berkshire's annual meeting in 1992 that Brown management is so good that, "When a single steer topples, they know."

52

Dexter Shoe

"There's no business like shoe business."

Extending his reach in the shoe industry, Buffett bought Dexter Shoe Company in late 1993. Buffett, who rarely gives away stock, did so in this case to the tune of $420 million.

The announcement came on September 30, 1993, and the Dow Jones wire said Berkshire was trading at $6,600 a share. Then Dow Jones ran a correction: Berkshire was trading at $16,600.

Berkshire and Dexter agreed that privately held Dexter, with about $300 million in annual sales and headed by sports philanthropist Harold Alfond, part-owner of the Boston Red Sox since 1983, would merge into Berkshire for 25,203 Berkshire shares.

The purchase increased the number of Berkshire shares by 2.2% to about 1.2 million shares.

Born in Lynn, Massachusetts, Alfond, the son of Polish immigrants, began his career in the shoe industry in Maine in the 1930s for 25 cents an hour, founded Dexter in 1956 with $10,000 and was joined by his nephew, Peter Lunder, in 1958. Their business now makes more than 7.5 million shoes a year, even in a declining domestic shoe industry.

Alfond, 81, says, "Buffett won't let me retire. He's the smartest man in America." (*Forbes,* October 16, 1995)

Alfond has been generous in his gifts of a number of sports facilities in Maine, including the Alfond Arena at the University of Maine campus in Orono.

Early in 1993, at the suggestion of Frank Rooney, head of Berkshire's H.H. Brown Shoe Co., Buffett met with Alfond at an airport in West Palm Beach, Fla. "We went to some little restaurant based on a World War II theme, had a hamburger, and talked about shoes," Buffett said. *(Forbes,* October, 10, 1994)

Buffett made a cash offer on the spot, but Alfond, not wanting to give a third to the government in capital gains, wanted Berkshire stock. Buffett told Alfond he'd think about it.

Several months later Buffett, with Berkshire stock trading near an all-time high, met Alfond and Lunder in Lunder's apartment in Boston. There with no lawyers, accountants or investment bankers, the deal was struck.

Buffett didn't wear Dexter shoes until he bought the company. "Well, I'd never heard of him before, either," Alfond said. *(Forbes,* October, 1994) The Alfond family suddenly owned 2% of Berkshire's stock, becoming the largest shareholders other than the Buffett family.

"Dexter is exactly the type of business Berkshire Hathaway admires," Buffett said. "It has a long profitable history, enduring franchise and superb management."

The Dexter, Maine-based company has about 3,900 employees. About 2,400 work in four factories in Maine and the rest work in a Puerto Rico plant. Dexter makes a variety of men's and women's dress, casual and athletic shoes, golf shoes particularly, at plants in Maine and Puerto Rico. Dexter sells classic "New England casual shoes, including moccasins and boat-type footwear. Nordstrom and J.C. Penney are big buyers of Dexter shoes. Dexter has 77 factory outlet stores from Maine to Alabama.

A pair of Dexter shoes retails for about $70, women's for about $50. The brand appeals to the broad middle range of the shoe industry. "That's where the volume is," Alfond said. (*Forbes,* October 10, 1994)

One observer of the company said, "It's well run. Its margins are good. It has good relations with employees and it makes mid- to lower-quality shoes. It makes $40 loafers that last a year."

With more Berkshire shares on the market as a result of the Dexter purchase, Berkshire shareholders owned a slightly smaller percentage of Berkshire. But then presumably Dexter is worth what Buffett paid or more, since Buffett has often said he will never give away Berkshire shares unless he's getting equal value in return.

The purchase for stock could be read that Buffett saw Berkshire shares as a bit on the high side. And the stock had indeed had a runup in 1993 without intrinsic value going up significantly.

But a Berkshire official said, "We could have done it for either cash or stock, but Dexter shareholders wanted it in stock."

With the acquisitions of Brown, Lowell and Dexter shoe companies, Buffett's shoe size was extra large in the shoe world.

Again Buffett was looking for that everyday, necessary product—and one that has to be replaced from time to time.

Buffett used Dexter as an example of long-term holdings in a talk he gave to Columbia business students October 27, 1993.

"We're just buying something called Dexter Shoe, which is a big shoe company. It's a little like a romance for a while. You spend some time with them, and you know, you have your first date. And then, finally, the big moment comes (laughter). The next day, do you want to start thinking about if somebody offers me "2X" for this or "3X" for this, would I sell it?

"I think that's kind of a crazy way to live. It's a little like marrying for money. It's probably a bad idea under any circumstances but absolutely nuts if you're already rich."

In the 1993 Annual Report Buffett said 1994 sales from Berkshire's shoe operations would top $550 million, with pre-tax earnings of more than $85 million. The prediction was right on the money.

"Five years ago, we had no thought of getting into shoes. Now we have 7,200 employees in that industry, and I sing, *There's No Business Like Shoe Business*, as I drive to work. So much for strategic plans."

In 1994 Berkshire bought a small chain of 11 retail stores in Maryland, Pennsylvania and Virginia which carries H.H. Brown and other shoes. Dexter operates 76 retail outlet stores.

Profits at the shoe companies declined in 1995 amidst fierce industry competition.

Still Berkshire makes more money out of non-athletic shoes than anyone else in the United States.

53

Helzberg's Diamond Shops

Diamonds are forever

The next business to join the Berkshire's Sainted business group was privately held Helzberg's Diamond Shops, of North Kansas City, Missouri. The national retail specialty chain has more than 173 fine jewelry stores located in about 28 states, mainly in malls. The purchase was with Berkshire stock.

Buffett said at the annual meeting in 1995 that the acquisition had come about this way: In the spring of 1994 Buffett was in New York walking near 58th street and Fifth Avenue when a woman stopped him to talk about how she enjoyed the annual meeting. Barnett Helzberg who had a few shares of Berkshire in his IRA, and who had also been to the annual meeting, overheard her talking to Buffett and came up and said he might have a business to sell him.

"I hear this quite a bit so I asked him to write me," Buffett said.

Helzberg said, "I walked over to Buffett, and we had a very detailed 20-second meeting." *(Fortune,* October 16, 1995) Eventually a deal was struck.

Buffett said Helzberg's position in the market is similar to Zales or

Gordon's, but that its sales per store was twice theirs.

Barnett Helzberg, Jr., chairman and owner of Helzberg's, said, that Berkshire's ownership of Helzberg's would allow the jewelry firm continued growth and continuity of its culture. Also it would assure that the headquarters remains in Kansas City and would allow him time to pursue non-profit community interests.

Helzberg added:

> I am extremely pleased with the fact that we have been able to take a three-generation business and allow it to continue its growth and prosperity under the respected umbrella of Berkshire Hathaway. I believe this ownership change is a win for the associates of Helzberg's Diamond Shops, a win for the investors of Berkshire Hathaway, a win for our family, and most importantly, a win for the customers of our fine company.

Buffett said in a Helzberg press release, "I am proud that Berkshire Hathaway is adding Helzberg's Diamond Shops to our family of businesses. I have great confidence in the present management team. The talent pool represented by the Helzberg management and its associates is one of the reasons I place such a high value on this acquisition. It goes without saying that the long term financial stability and very bright outlook for the future of Helzberg Diamonds were also major factors in our decision."

The president of Helzberg Diamonds, Jeffrey W. Comment, formerly president of Wannamaker's, became chairman and chief executive officer of Helzberg's.

Diamonds are forever.

(Photo by Pat Kilpatrick)

A Helzberg's Diamond store at Westroads Mall in Omaha.

54

R.C. Willey Home Furnishings of Utah

Berkshire, widening its reach in the home furnishings business, announced May 24, 1995, it would buy R.C. Willey Home Furnishings of Salt Lake City.

The fast-growing company, with seven stores, including a clearance center and a carpet center in Utah, has about $300 million in annual sales–half of the state's furniture sales. The privately-held firm is the 20th largest furniture firm in the country and has about 1,300 employees.

Buffett said: "Bill Child and his family have built a business that is the envy of merchants throughout the country."

Child and his brother Sheldon and their children, who owned the company, sold to Berkshire, in part, for estate planning reasons.

"Bill Child was talking to a friend [about possibly selling] and the friend [Nebraska Furniture Mart's Irv Blumkin] knew Buffett. Two days later Buffett called and the deal was wrapped up in two months," said

Roger Pusey, business writer for the *Deseret News* in Salt Lake City.

Child and Blumkin had talked while at a fabric industry conference in California. Child said Buffett called and told him, "You've got a jewel of a company. We'd be very interested. I'll have you a price within three days." *(Omaha World-Herald, May 26, 1995)*

Within three days a two-page Federal Express letter came with what Child called "a very fair price."

"I called him and said I was flattered," Child said, inviting Buffett to visit the stores.

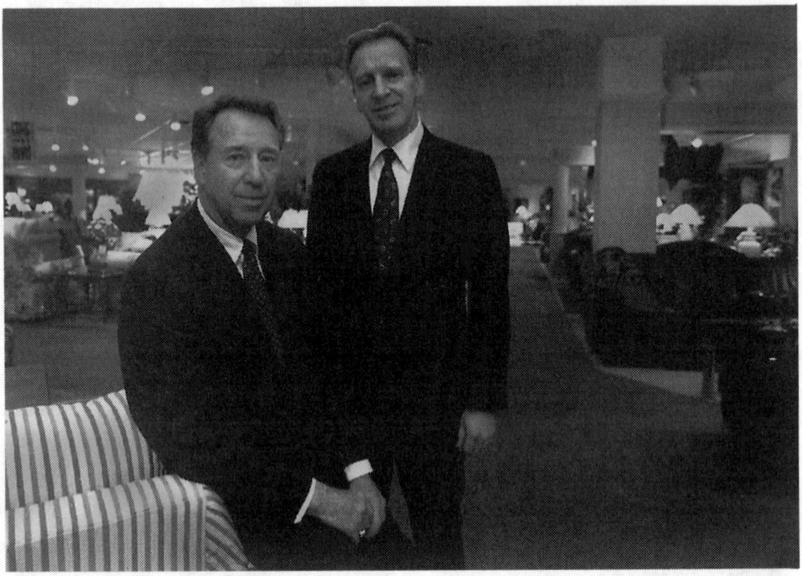

(The Salt Lake Tribune)

R.C. Willey owner William Child and his brother, company President Sheldon Child, sold Utah's largest furniture business to Berkshire.

"I know you, I know your reputation. I know a lot about your company. I really don't need to," Child said Buffett told him. (*Omaha World-Herald,* May 26, 1995)

But Child did talk Buffett into an eight-hour visit and Buffett found all was well. Child asked for some time to work out some tax issues and to think about whether to take the cash or Berkshire stock that Buffett offered.

Child, who said he had always wanted to buy Berkshire stock but delayed because the price kept going up, told Buffett: "We'll go with the stock." *(Omaha World-Herald, May 26, 1995)*

R.C. Willey, Child's father-in-law, had long been known in the community as "someone who started out in the back of his truck," Pusey said. "Then he got a small building, a garage really, and sold appliances to folks."

He was known as someone who could fix anything. He would come over and wire your house and wind up selling you a stove.

In 1932 Rufus Carl Willey started selling appliances door-to-door. The customers had a choice of an electric range or refrigerator. R.C. Willey did this for almost 20 years and made a good living. He let customers buy on an extended finance term program called Farm Plan where customers paid one-third each fall for three years. Customers were delighted because they could keep their food from spoiling and cook their meals without overheating the home in summertime.

In 1950 R.C. Willey built his company's first building which was 600 square feet. The building was located next to his home. A nine-party telephone line ran from his home to the store. He had one employee. In 1954 Willey became ill and his son-in-law, William H. Child, who had just graduated from college was asked to run the business for a short period until Willey recovered. However, he passed away and Bill Child has been running the business since.

"It's a beautiful concern," said Hugh Coltharp, a broker and Berkshire shareholder in Salt Lake City. "They have a big warehouse, and they were smart to get a stop light where you turn into it."

There was no change in name or management and no jobs were affected by the transaction.

So with the Nebraska Furniture Mart having annual sales of more than $250 million a year and with R.C. Willey's $300 million, Berkshire was solidly into the furniture business in America's heartland. R.C. Willey, like the Nebraska Furniture Mart, also sells appliances, electronics, computers and carpets.

A footnote: As part of R.C. Willey's sales promotions, the company offers free hot dogs and soft drinks to customers on many Saturdays.

Child said the soft drink henceforth is Coca-Cola. *(Deseret News, May 25, 1995)*

55

WPPSS Bonds

"Whoops!" for the Bond Gods, but not for Buffett.

Buffett quietly bought $139 million worth of Projects 1, 2, and 3 of Washington Public Power Supply System bonds in 1983 and 1984.

In Berkshire's 1984 Annual Report, Buffett stunned Berkshire shareholders, revealing he had bought bonds issued by the Washington Public Power Supply System (WPPSS), a nuclear power plant construction corporation in Washington state so troubled it was dubbed "Whoops."

The shock deepened when Buffett explained how WPPSS had defaulted on $2.2 billion worth of bonds issued to help finance Projects 4 and 5. That stigma stained other projects and, Buffett was able to buy the bonds at a steep discount.

Steve Wallman, head of Wallman Investment Counsel in Madison, Wisconsin, says: "Our day-to-day lives don't prepare us in the least for going against the crowd. In almost everything we do, success is a function of how well we go along with the crowd, not how well we go against it. As a result, going against the crowd, and ignoring what psychologists call social proof, is contrary to our nature. Little wonder value investing is so tough, and so little used. Most people just don't have the psychological musculature to carry the burden of negative opinion that goes with fifty-cent dollars like WPPSS 1, 2, and 3."

The bonds had a special appeal, however, offering a fixed 16.3%, tax-free current yield, a $22.7 million annual return on the investment.

As usual, the investment worked out profitably for Buffett. The projects went well and the bonds rose to the occasion. The 16% after-tax payoff arrived like clockwork into the Berkshire account. Buffett said he bought the bonds because he probably would have had to pay almost twice his WPPSS purchase price for a business bringing in that much after-tax money.

Some of Berkshire's "Whoops" bonds have been called, but Berkshire still holds some of the bonds.

Although Buffett is not a great fan of bonds, he will buy them under special circumstances. He has a history of buying bonds of troubled companies. In the 1970s he bought the depressed bonds of Chrysler when the firm was near collapsing, and Penn Central bonds for about 50 cents on the dollar after the railroad went bust. Both companies rallied back.

In 1986, he bought an additional $700 million of medium-term, tax-exempt bonds, which he considered the least objectionable alternative to stocks.

Berkshire's bond purchases for decades were handled by J. William Scott, the first employee Buffett ever hired.

56

RJR Nabisco Bonds

"Junk bonds will one day live up to their name."

In 1989 and 1990, Buffett bought junk bond offerings of RJR Nabisco.

The tobacco and food giant known for Winston cigarettes, Life-savers candy, Ritz crackers, Fig Newtons and Oreo cookies was the subject of a leveraged buyout by Kohlberg, Kravis Roberts in 1988.

It was the largest takeover in Wall Street history, with a $25 billion pricetag—a cap to the Decade of Greed.

The first hint that Buffett might be entering the junk bond market came at the annual meeting in 1990 when a shareholder asked if the junk bond market could ever become a fruitful place for a professional investor. "I'll let you know in a year or two," said Buffett, known for saying, "Junk bonds will one day live up to their name."

In late 1989 Buffett started accumulating the RJR bonds issued to help finance the takeover, and in 1990 he added heavily to the holding. No one knew it until the Berkshire Annual Report came out in 1991.

Even then, you could have missed the news because it was not until page 17 of his letter that Buffett made a one-paragraph mention of it.

He wrote, "Our other major portfolio change last year was large additions to our RJR Nabisco bonds, securities that we first bought in late 1989. At yearend 1990 we had $440 million invested in these securities, an amount that approximated market value. [As I write this, their market value has risen by more than $150 million.]"

Had almost any other company made a quick $150 million, it would have been, in newspaper parlance, the "lead" paragraph of the chairman's letter.

Fortune reported the Nabisco purchase and asked Buffett if he wished he had bought more. "There are lots of things I wish I'd done in hindsight. But I don't think much of hindsight generally in terms of investment decisions. You only get paid for what you do," he said.

Many of the RJR Nabisco bonds were paying about 15%, so Buffett was hauling in a splendid return while he waited for management to sell some assets and keep their Oreo cookies stocked at the stores.

As junk bonds tanked, Buffett spotted a gem. But he didn't just wing it and buy large well-known company bonds at random. Only after intensive study of the massacred junk bond market in which he said he found more carnage than he expected, did he pick RJR as offering the best hope of a good return.

Junk bonds, called high-yield bonds for their double-digit interest rates, were popularized in the 1980s by firms trying to find money to finance takeovers.

The bonds were risky because the issuers were saddled with debt. But again Buffett's reading of the overall financial landscape and his precise timing produced another bonanza for Berkshire. Just about the time his RJR investment was made public, financial writers began offering stories about a comeback in the junk bond market.

Not only that, RJR was beginning to get more notice for paring down its debt. Its losses were dropping dramatically; its creditworthiness improved. And RJR was refinancing at lower rates.

RJR seemed on its way back to life under Louis Gerstner, who left a top job at American Express to run things at RJR, then exited to run IBM.

On May 3, 1991, RJR announced it was retiring most of its junk bonds used to finance the buyout, using money it had raised in a stock offering. The company said it planned to redeem the bonds at face value, bonds that Buffett had purchased at a steep discount.

Buffett had made a large and quick profit and now apparently he would have back a lot of cash, which he knows how to deploy. Once again, Buffett was creating permanent value for Berkshire shareholders.

At yearend 1992, Berkshire held more than $1 billion of bonds in such entities as Washington Public Power Supply System and ACF Industries.

The bonds of ACF Industries, the rail-car manufacturing and leasing firm Carl Icahn owns, gave Buffett a handsome profit when they were called in 1993.

57

The Zero-coupon Bond

A lesson in how to structure debt

Berkshire raised $400 million in cash on September 21, 1989, by offering a zero-coupon convertible subordinated note.

The bond-like investment offered investors a kicker—a chance to buy Berkshire stock at $9,815 at a future date. The bonds were priced at a 15% premium to the value of the underlying stock with a closing price of Berkshire at $8,535 a share on September 9, 1989.

With Berkshire already trading above $8,000, Buffett was playing on the popularity of the stock to raise some always-welcome fresh cash.

The underwriter was Berkshire's old buddy, Salomon.

Berkshire offered a $902.6 million redemption amount of the notes. The offering was a huge success, with orders far exceeding supply.

Syndicate officials said the issue was increased from an original $585 million face amount to $902.6 million because of the strong demand.

Institutional investors were eager to buy the notes because purchase would enable them indirectly to buy Berkshire common stock.

The bond offering marked the first time that Berkshire had sold stock, albeit indirectly, since Buffett gained control of Berkshire in 1965, and one of the few periods Berkshire investors would have been about as well off in a money market fund.

The 15-year zero-coupon notes due September 28, 2004, and rated double A-2 by Moody's Investors Service, were offered at a price of 44.314 to yield 5.5%. Each $10,000 face amount note can be converted at any time into Berkshire common at a price of $9,815, a 15% premium over the stock's closing stock price of $8,535 the day before the offering. Since the notes were sold at such a deep discount (at a price of about $4,400 each) and the stock price was high, it would take more than two $10,000 face amount notes to acquire one share of Berkshire.

The issue was non-callable for three years and the notes could have been put back to the company in the fifth and the tenth year.

Stock whiz Mario Gabelli recommended the security in a *Barron's* article January 28, 1991:

> You have a triple-A-equivalent security, with a put on September 24, 1994, selling at 42¾ which is an imputed compound return to the put date—which is a cash put—of close to 9%. In other words, in buying this LYON (Liquid Yield Option Note), you get a three-year bond with a 9% compound return, vs. about 8% now on a "govie." Plus, you get an upside kiss—if, in fact, they come up with a cure for cancer—not that Warren Buffett is working on that—but if he comes up with some magic and the stock goes up substantially, you have full upside. I like that!

When Berkshire was trading at about $6,800, Gabelli was saying the conversion premium of the zero-coupon convert was pretty rich, about 40%, of the conversion price of $9,815.

Berkshire could deduct the 5.5% interest accrual each year, even though it was not actually making any payments to bondholders. Thus the net effect to Berkshire was positive cash flow.

"I've always said that I don't like issuing new stock," Buffett said, but in this case, "We feel we are getting value received. The combination of paying no interest on the (bonds) while selling the stock at a premium" made the prospect more palatable.

Although Berkshire almost never gets a write-up by brokerage firms, there was a write-up from Prudential Securities recommending the bonds.

The last paragraph of the research review said:

> From a practical point of view, Berkshire Hathaway is a 'prestige investment.' Very few investors own BRK shares, and those that do consider it a 'core' holding. The stock trades maybe 100 shares a day, and is not related to computer program trading or fundamental research recommendations. Berkshire Hathaway transcends Wall Street. It represents an investment in one of America's foremost capitalistic institutions, and shareholders perceive themselves as a very special class of sophisticated (and deep-pocketed) investors. The bonds are an extraordinary opportunity to join that group with the added advantage of having a locked-in positive rate of return. I rate these bonds a strong buy only for our firm's top one percent clients: those who can appreciate an extraordinary opportunity.

A number of these "rich" shareholders are struggling to hold one share. And that one share certainly is a core holding for them.

Another point: If Berkshire is so great for 1% of humanity, why isn't it good for everyone? Late in 1992, Berkshire said it planned to redeem the note, through its option to do so. The redemption date was set for January 4, 1993. Each $10,000 principal amount at maturity could be redeemed for $5,291.26. Each note could be converted into .4515 shares of Berkshire stock per $10,000 principal amount at maturity.

Had all bond holders selected cash, Berkshire would have had to pay out $477 million, or a bit less in stock had all bondholders taken stock.

Wall Streeters speculated on both sides of the question as to whether Berkshire management was saying it did not want to issue equity because it thought the stock was going up, or because it wanted to unload the stock because they thought it too high.

A *New York Times* piece (December 17, 1992) by Floyd Norris said, "Perhaps the most likely interpretation is that Mr. Buffett wants to assure that those who convert the bonds to stock will clearly want to own the stock, and not be arbitrageurs who would immediately sell the shares to lock in profits.

"It is clear that issuing the zero-coupon bonds proved a good move for Berkshire, which borrowed at just 5.5%. Under terms of the call, the bondholders will have done much less well than holders of the common stock over the same period, although it is true they had less risk."

In early 1993, Berkshire said the redemption was completed with holders of 15.25% of the principal amount of the note converting into Berkshire stock. As a result, the number of common shares outstanding rose by 6,106 shares, or about 0.5%. The rest of the note with a principal amount at maturity of $764.9 million was redeemed for $404.7 million in cash.

In addition to being an issuer of bonds, Buffett has been a buyer of bonds. Over the years, he has made real money in Chrysler Financial, Texaco, Time Warner, WPPSS and RJR Nabisco bonds. And he's still got a lot of bonds, particularly from the purchase of the rest of GEICO.

There are bonds ranging from U.S. Treasury strips to Birmingham, Alabama, Industrial Water Board bonds and Scottsboro, Alabama, water and gas bonds.

He's got bonds from Los Angeles County to the Suffolk County, New York, sewer district; Cripple Creek, Texas, water and sewer revenue bonds to Utah Housing Authority bonds; Peoria, Illinois, economic development bonds to Massachusetts Turnpike Authority bonds.

And he has bonds ranging from $5,000 to millions of dollars in value. He has bonds ranging from less than a year to more than 20 years in maturity. He has bonds paying from 1% to 15%. But there was virtually no bond buying between 1987 and 1992.

It may have been that Buffett's interest in run-of-the-mill bonds evaporated when convertible preferreds of his own making, such as in Salomon and Gillette, became available, or perhaps he thought interest rates were getting too low to be an attractive alternative to stocks.

But Buffett still has several billion dollars worth of bonds.

58

Salomon Redux

"Deryck, you're the one." —*Warren Buffett*
"I had no idea."—*Deryck Maughan*

Buffett made a $700 million preferred stock investment in Salomon Inc on September 28, 1987, after a lifetime of denouncing Wall Street's demented, short-term mentality.

"It's a huge commitment. We'll know in ten years whether it was a great idea," he said then. He was fortunate to allow himself such an un-Wall-Street-like time frame.

"Without borrowing, it pretty much empties the piggy bank for now," he told the *Wall Street Journal*, September 30, 1987.

Buffett long has been a critic of Wall Street's short-term trading fixation as well as its excesses ranging from corporate jets to swanky dining rooms. So why Salomon? Why did Buffett invest in the heart of Wall Street? And why particularly in a firm widely known for aggressiveness and shrewd, hair-trigger trading?

"Why are we vocal critics of the investment banking business when

(AP/Wide World Photos)

Buffett, left, and Deryck Maughan hold a press conference August 18, 1991, explaining Salomon's bond-trading scandal. Shortly before, Interim Chairman Buffett named Maughan chief operating officer telling him, "Deryck, you're the one."

we have a $700 million investment in Salomon? I guess atonement is probably the answer," he said at the Berkshire annual meeting in 1991.

The real answer may be that he got a sweet deal in a worldwide franchise. Salomon, founded in 1910, is one of the largest and most profitable brokerage firms in the United States.

Before looking at Buffett's transaction with Salomon, let's examine the timing which, in hindsight, simply could not have been worse.

The stock market crash of 1987 was only three weeks away—the day the market would drop 508 points—or almost 23%—its worst single-day loss in modern times.

The crash sent almost all stocks nosediving. Brokerage stocks particularly were hit because of their cyclical nature and partly because overexpansion in the securities industry had knocked down margins. The crash triggered a lasting tailspin for brokerage stocks suctioning Salomon's stock price right down with it.

Salomon's common stock was trading at about $32 a share when Buffett bought the preferred stock. After the crash, the common stock eventually sank to a low of $16 a share. (Called "Shit Brothers" by some at that price).

Some studies suggest Salomon's own huge selling that day was one ingredient in the mounting panic.

Michael Lewis wrote in *The Money Culture*:

> Salomon Brothers found itself censured by the Securities and Exchange Commission for making illegal short sales during the crash of October, 1987. What was interesting about the case wasn't that Salomon in the heat of the moment broke the law, but that management after

> sober reflection tried to hide the evidence. It initially refused to permit the SEC to inspect Salomon's books. (p. 97)

Instead of buying Salomon stock, Buffett and Salomon Chairman John Gutfreund (pronounced Good Friend) agreed that Berkshire would buy a newly issued preferred stock—a Salomon financial instrument that would pay Berkshire a 9% annual dividend.

Preferred stock is a hybrid investment, containing characteristics of both stocks and bonds.

Common stock is a security representing ownership in a company, and although common stockholders can benefit most if business is good, they assume the primary risk if the business goes sour.

Preferred stockholders, on the other hand, get dividends paid before any are paid to common stockholders. If the company goes under, a preferred stockholder also has a claim to the assets before a common stockholder.

Berkshire never lost a cent on its investment in Salomon even though Salomon common stock languished for years after Buffett's purchase. Thus, Berkshire is insulated, short of bankruptcy, through its preferred investment. Buffett has called such investments, "Treasury bonds with lottery tickets attached."

And Salomon's 9% dividend paid to Berkshire is largely exempt from corporate taxes because corporations don't have to pay taxes on 70% of their dividend income on preferred stocks.

Perhaps it was the attractiveness of the deal that triggered Buffett into making a move that could have been a severe miscalculation of upside potential. Berkshire shareholders were surprised. After all, they had listened to him deride Wall Street for years.

In any event, Buffett got into bed with Salomon and it literally caused Buffett some sleepless nights.

Gutfreund had to do some hard selling to the Salomon board to get it to bite on a deal clearly so favorable to Berkshire.

Salomon was under great pressure from a takeover threat from Revlon Chairman Ronald Perelman in 1987. Perelman was trying to buy a 14% stake in Salomon stock held by Minerals Resources, a Bermuda-based company controlled by the South Africa Oppenheimer family who decided to sell its stake. Buffett got his investment and Perelman backed off.

For this and his subsequent preferred stakes in Gillette, USAir and Champion International, where there was a real or a perceived takeover threat, Buffett became known as a "White Knight," stepping in to save the takeover targets.

In Michael Lewis's *Liar's Poker*, an account of his bond trading days at Salomon, he quoted Gutfreund as saying that if Buffett's plan were rejected in favor of Perelman, he, Gutfreund, would resign.

"I never stated it as a threat. I was stating a fact," Lewis quoted Gutfreund telling a companion.

The book's most telling moment of the money madness and loose ways that would ultimately lead to the Salomon scandal in 1991, is Gutfreund, a cigar-smoking, gruff, hard-edged man, challenging his chief trader, John Meriwether, to a hand of liar's poker, a game where a series of players each hold a dollar bill. Bidding begins over what serial numbers are held by the players until a point when all the players challenge a single player's bid.

The particular game—Lewis says it took place in early 1986—started when Gutfreund approached Meriwether for a million-dollar hand, but supposedly Meriwether—realizing a game against his boss was a no-win proposition—outbluffed Gutfreund by saying he'd play only for $10 million, at which point Gutfreund backed off saying, "You're crazy."

At Salomon, the incident was denied. True or not, it's clearly not the sort of thing shareholders care to hear about their firm. Lewis's account of hard-ball bond trading tactics hardly gave potential customers confidence; he painted a disquieting picture that things were fast and loose at Salomon. Salomon has broken the law at times and has a checkered history of oil trading infractions. It has been fined as a result of charges that it cheated customers on both securities and commodities trades.

The high living of Gutfreund and his socialite wife, Susan, was publicized in articles describing an estimated $20 million fix-up of their $6 million duplex on New York's Fifth Avenue. They spent millions more on a home in Paris.

Buffett may have had second thoughts about Gutfreund along the way. A *Los Angeles Times Magazine* piece February 16, 1992, said Buffett "hit the roof" in October, 1990, when Gutfreund came to a Salomon board of director's compensation committee with a plan to boost bonuses by $120 million at a time when Salomon was struggling.

Buffett asked Gutfreund to lower the figure, but Gutfreund countered with a request for $127 million. Buffett voted against the plan, but it passed anyway.

Even operationally, Salomon had a record of overexpansion, exorbitant bonuses, and an overly ambitious plan to invest in and occupy a dramatic new office tower at New York City's Columbus Circle that Mortimer Zuckerman hoped to build. Salomon decided to scrap its plans, causing it to forfeit about $100 million.

In February, 1991, Salomon moved from One New York Plaza, known for the football-sized trading rooms that Gutfreund roamed, to 7 World Trade Center.

A number of Salomon's investments had done poorly. Its forays into merchant banking using its own money for investments in leveraged buyouts of Revco and Southland, which wound up in bankruptcy proceedings, were lackluster. Finally, for all Salomon's worldwide business expertise and range and deep talent apparent from the gilt-edged résumés of its employees, Salomon has done little for its shareholders. Its stock price is not far ahead of where it was a decade ago although its book value has tripled in that time, up from about $11 a share to about $30 a share.

Salomon has three main divisions: Salomon Brothers for securities; Phibro Energy, for energy; and Philipp Brothers, which became the commodity trading division of Salomon in 1983.

Ever since Buffett and Munger came on the Salomon board in 1987, (GEICO's Lou Simpson and Archer Daniels Midland's Dwayne Andreas, both friends of Buffett, serve on the Salomon board) there has been real cost cutting and streamlining of operations. And with an improving securities environment now, the firm is poised for progress.

Buffett has thrown a lot of business Salomon's way just on behalf of Berkshire. Berkshire's zero-coupon bond was underwritten by Salomon, and Salomon and Berkshire have traded huge amounts of securities back and forth.

In 1995 Berkshire bought $3.3 billion dollars in securities from Salomon and sold $3.1 billion, paying fees of $1.9 million. Berkshire and Salomon have done business for a long time. Salomon sold some debt for Berkshire in 1973 and did business with Berkshire even before that.

When Buffett needs a stockbroker, he calls Salomon.

On August 9, 1991, Salomon, a Wall Street powerhouse largely from trading government bonds, disclosed that it had uncovered "irregularities and rule violations" in connection with its bids at Treasury securities auctions, the most important of all financial markets. The Salomon scandal was underway.

Salomon said it had been buying more than its fair and legal share at auctions of Treasury securities, the bonds sold to finance the government's debt.

The reeling firm said bids were submitted in the names of firms which had not authorized Salomon to make them and that the 35% threshold—intended to keep one buyer from dominating the market—was in some instances deliberately breached. Although Salomon itself revealed the infractions and suspended four employees, it was hardly out front with the disclosures, making them known only after the government was six weeks into an investigation of a "squeeze" in the May auction of two-year Treasury notes. A squeeze occurs when one buyer controls a disproportionately large amount of securities and forces other buyers to pay more for securities later, thus undermining fairness in the market. In this case, Salomon had "cornered" the market.

A government probe was launched after competing firms complained that Salomon had corralled too big a piece of the $12.26 billion notes sold in May and then squeezed competitors by driving up prices. (*Wall Street Journal*, August 12, 1991)

But even though Salomon had time to think things over, the Gutfreund management team released information about only part of its maneuvers.

On August 14, the firm said that although top Salomon officials, including Gutfreund, President Thomas Strauss and Salomon Brothers unit's Vice Chairman John Meriwether, knew in April of an earlier illegal bid, they had not reported it to authorities. Salomon had disclosed nothing until faced with a federal investigation. Salomon also said it bought $1.1 billion in government securities from customers under questionable arrangements and further that a bogus bid for $1 billion of bonds was carried out inadvertently as a result of a botched practical joke!

Salomon officials later reported that Paul Mozer put a client up to making a false bid that he would later stop and then have the client call to complain that the order had not been filled. The client was to call and rattle a soon-to-retire saleswoman on whom Mozer was trying to play a joke. But the joke was on Mozer. Although Mozer crossed out the bid, a clerk did not understand that it was canceled and submitted it anyway. Some joke.

Early reaction to the scandal was summarized best by William Simon, former Treasury secretary and former Salomon partner: "Good God. I'll be damned. Good God. That can be my only reaction." (*Wall Street Journal*, August 15, 1991)

Within a few days Salomon's stock fell from $36 to $25 a share, eventually plummeting to a low of $20 a share in September, 1991. Its bonds plunged as credit agencies threatened lower ratings; some big investors ceased to do business with Salomon as many corporations gave their underwriting business to rival firms.

A crisis swept the firm with investigations underway into every facet of its activities while lawsuits in droves were stamped in at the courthouse.

Gutfreund said he would resign, and a frantic call was placed to Buffett, "Mr. Clean," who offered to tackle the top job. He immediately flew to New York.

From that moment of management overhaul forward, Buffett would be unknown no more. But that was hardly the point. Buffett had to face Salomon's life-threatening mess.

Gutfreund told a colleague that reading the *Wall Street Journal* story about top Salomon officials knowing about illegal bidding was like reading his obituary. (*Institutional Investor*, September, 1991) He called Buffett and said that he and Strauss were going to resign. Later that morning, Buffett called Gutfreund back and volunteered to head the firm on an interim basis. In the same interview, Buffett said:

"You won't believe this—because I don't look that dumb—but I volunteered for the job of interim chairman. It's not what I want to be doing, but it will be what I will be doing until it gets done properly."

> Salomon owed more money than any other institution in the United States, with the exception of Citicorp, the big bank...Salomon's total liabilities were just under $150 billion. Now $150 billion was roughly equal to the profits of all of the companies on the New York Stock Exchange that year...The problem about this $150 billion was that basically, it almost all came due within the next couple of weeks...so we were faced with the fact all over the world, because the money was owed all over the world, that people on that Friday and the following Monday were going to want us to pay back $140 odd billion or something close to it, which is not the easiest thing to do," Buffett said. (talk to University of Nebraska students, October 10, 1994)

Buffett faced the complex issues of appeasing investors and clients, dealing with criminal and civil investigators, and worrying about some new bomb exploding on his watch. But Buffett was the logical person to turn to, and got things off on the right foot when he quickly met with Salomon's managing directors at the World Trade Center, telling them that the firm's reputation for staying just within the bounds of the rules would NOT be acceptable. (*New York Times*, August 17, 1991) He told them he would be open, that the firm faced a huge management job in dealing with fines and litigation costs.

The story was covered by everyone including *Barron's* Alan Abelson, who took his usual satirical approach (August 19, 1991), saying, "The caretaker appointed to look after Salomon in the absence of Gutfreund and Strauss is an out-of-towner, from Omaha, Nebraska, to be exact, and he runs a textile company. But he's supposed to be a fast learner, so we've no doubt he'll pick up enough about the securities business while on the job to keep the traders from sneaking off to play paddle ball or catch the 3 p.m. showing of Terminator 2."

Here's what Buffett did on the Sunday afternoon of August 18, 1991: 1) Accepted the resignations of Gutfreund, Strauss and Meriwether; 2) Fired government-bond trading chief Paul Mozer as well as Thomas Murphy; 3) Named Deryck C. Maughan, the formerly Tokyo-based chairman of Salomon Brothers Asia Ltd., chief operating officer, telling Maughan minutes before a press conference, "Deryck, you're the one," 4) Successfully appealed to Treasury Secretary Nicholas Brady to partially lift an hours-old government suspension of Salomon trading in Treasury securities auctions.

"I had no idea," Maughan said at Borsheim's before the Berkshire annual meeting in 1994 when asked if he knew Buffett would pick him. "He called 12 of us in for 10 minutes each and asked each of us who should run the firm. I told him I was not a U.S. national and was not a trader.

"We got in an elevator. He punched a button and he said, 'Deryck, you're the one.' " Two minutes later they met with the press.

Maughan said Buffett immediately had to keep up his constant calls to Nicholas Brady and that he, Maughan, had to be on the trading floor supervising massive selling.

"We were selling out. Our CEO was gone," Maughan said as the firm faced a sudden loss of business and funding. Salomon even had quit trading its own paper.

Buffett said at the Berkshire annual meeting in 1994 that he quickly called Robert Denham, living a peaceful life in California. "I told him I was in a mess." And he called Salomon's treasurer, John MacFarlane, who was competing in a triathlon. "Not a practice Charlie and I follow," Buffett quipped.

Buffett and Maughan met with the press for about three hours August 18, 1991, saying the illegal trading first came to the attention of Salomon in April, when Mozer received a Xerox copy of a letter indicating the Treasury was aware of a problem in one of its auctions. The letter from a federal regulator was sent to a customer whose name Salomon had used without authorization to make a bid.

Mozer approached Meriwether and "showed him a letter which was clearly going to lead to Mr. Mozer being in trouble," Buffett said.

Top management discussed the matter with its lawyers and determined that the government should be told, Buffett said, but it was not done.

"I cannot explain the subsequent failure to report," Buffett said, adding that he had long been an admirer of Gutfreund but that he was distressed by management's actions. "The failure to report is, in my view, inexplicable and inexcusable." Buffett and Gutfreund, on September 3, 1991, agreed not to talk to one another during the investigation.

Buffett pledged to root out the scandal and improve the firm's reputation. The next few days were unusually hectic, with the Soviet Union coup and its collapse in the several days following Buffett's press conference.

The fast-paced events led to a photo mix-up at the Asbury Park (New Jersey) *Press,* which ran a purported photo of Gorbachev's momentary successor, Gennady Yanayev. Actually it was a photo of Buffett.

And Salomon itself was acting under intense pressure during the crisis. Once a reporter called to speak to Salomon's spokesman, Robert Baker, and was told, "I'll have Mr. Buffett call you." The reporter replied, "Gosh, that'd be great."

When Baker called back, he suddenly broke-off saying he'd have to hang up and call back. "Warren's on the line," he blurted. Later Baker said Buffett had set the company on a new path, even while working both from New York and Omaha. During the crisis, Buffett was in New York several days a week and then began to come about one or two days a week. "He's found he can run things from Omaha pretty well," Baker said.

"Warren has given the company its strategic direction...He has kept his focus on the regulators and the capital structure."

Buffett focused most of his attention on matters in Washington. "It's our belief that those who misbehaved are gone. New management dealt with that very swiftly. Warren has cleaned house. I see no reason for the government to shut us down...We are cooperating with the government in an unprecedented way. We are cooperating to a greater degree than in any case in the history of Wall Street," Baker added.

Salomon's business, he said, began rebounding with the return of such clients as the World Bank and the state of Massachusetts.

"Our bond underwriting is returning fast. We still have some trouble on some of the equity underwritings because of the two-, three-, four-month lead time. Some clients don't want to deal with the uncertainty for that long. This has to hurt us in getting some new business," Baker said.

As for a *Wall Street Journal* story that Buffett stayed at the Plaza hotel and wore expensive suits, Baker said Buffett doesn't stay at the Plaza, that he stays at either Katharine Graham's apartment or at the Marriott hotel near the World Trade Center.

"He stays at the Marriott for $190 a night so he can walk to work." Baker said.

Okay, said Baker, he has a couple of expensive suits.

"They're not even tailored and he jokes that when he wears an expensive suit, he makes it look like a $300 suit."

As for staying at the Plaza, Buffett has stayed there in years past on spring trips to New York, largely because Mrs. Buffett liked to stay there, says Buffett's daughter, Susan.

She said he did not stay at the Plaza during the Salomon crisis. "He'd just as soon stay at Motel 6...He's been staying at either the Vista or the Marriott."

In subsequent days of the Salomon scandal, Buffett fired Salomon's top lawyer, Donald Feuerstein, and replaced him with Robert Denham, a 1971 Harvard Law School graduate who was the managing partner of the Los Angeles-based Munger, Tolles & Olson law firm founded by Charles Munger, Berkshire's vice chairman.

Buffett described Denham, who was the top student in his freshman law class, as his first and only choice. For 17 years Denham has worked with Buffett on such Berkshire acquisitions as Scott Fetzer and such investments as American Express, Champion and Salomon itself. (*Business Week*, September 9, 1991)

Soon Buffett told the Salomon sales force, "It's my job to deal with the past. It's your job to maximize the future, and it can be a huge future."

"Everyone must be his own compliance officer. That means that everything you do can be put on the front page of the newspaper, and there will be nothing that cannot stand up to scrutiny," he added.

Buffett even accepted the resignation of Salomon's outside counsel—the Wachtell, Lipton, Rosen & Jurtz law firm—a highly regarded firm that had represented Salomon for years, and had helped Gutfreund bring in Buffett as an investor in 1987. (*Wall Street Journal*, September

3, 1991)

As for the number of lawsuits the firm faced, Buffett later said, "I may be the American Bar Association's Man of the Year before the year is over."

Buffett slashed bonuses, making them payable in stock rather than cash, reduced debt and had every bid cross-checked at least twice.

He told Salomon's Phibro Energy unit to cut all ties with Marc Rich & Co., a major client of Phibro's, saying Salomon wasn't going to do business with Marc Rich, a U.S. fugitive.

Amidst the crisis, what about Berkshire?

"Berkshire works pretty well, some say, without me," Buffett said. "It really is a lot less complicated operation than Salomon. I've always said I could run (Berkshire) working five hours a week. Maybe we'll test that. But I hope not for too long." Added Buffett, "I was practically looking for a job" when the crisis broke. That's because Berkshire's managers run things so well for him.

"The only thing I am is an addressee on the envelope when they send me the check," he added. "...I can spend whatever time is needed...If I quit thinking about this, I'd probably just have a big hole up there."

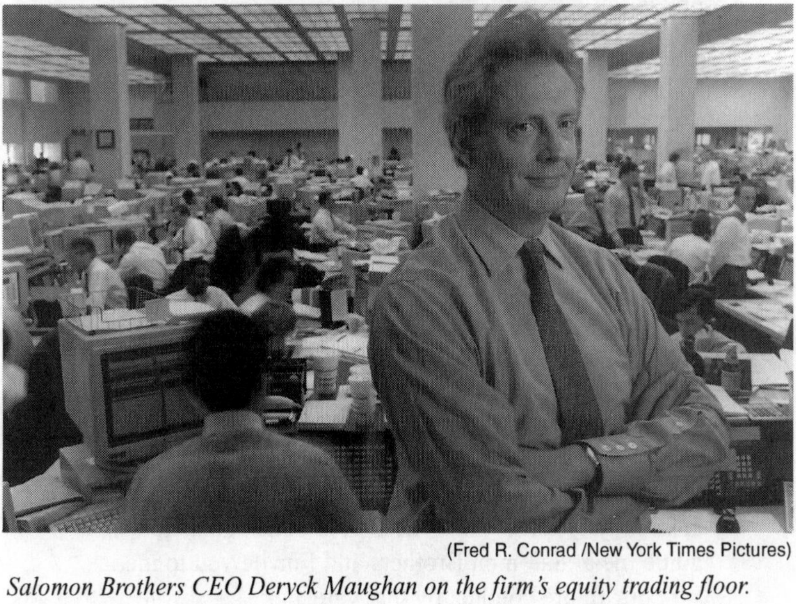

(Fred R. Conrad /New York Times Pictures)

Salomon Brothers CEO Deryck Maughan on the firm's equity trading floor.

Buffett's selection of Maughan quickly took hold as he rose to the occasion, calling for integrity by all at the firm. And Maughan began picking up Buffett's lead on humor.

Maughan pointed out he was not from Salomon's trading culture and there was no way he could be. "You cannot graft the head of an investment banker onto the body of a trader and not get tissue rejection," Maughan said.

Soon Buffett was testifying before Congressional committees. On September 4, 1991, he testified before the House Energy and Commerce finance subcommittee; at the end of the session subcommittee chairman Edward Markey asked him to sum up his recommendations in one minute.

"I'm not sure I can drag it out for one minute," Buffett replied. "Integrity is paramount."

Here's what he told Congress on September 11, 1991:

> A week ago when I testified before the House subcommittee, I began by apologizing for the misdeeds of Salomon employees that have brought us here. Normally I would not wish to be repetitious. But in my opinion this particular message bears repetition many times over. The nation has a right to expect its rules and laws to be obeyed, and Salomon did not live up to this obligation.
>
> Our customers have a right also to expect that their names will not be drawn into some underhanded scheme. So to you and them and the American people I apologize on behalf of more than 8,000 honest and decent Salomon employees as well as myself.
>
> Mr. Chairman, I also want to thank you for holding these hearings in such a timely manner. You and the American people have a right to know exactly what went on at Salomon Brothers and I am here to tell you the full truth as I know it to date. When and if I learn more it will immediately be disclosed to the proper authorities.
>
> Many decades ago J.P. Morgan stated the objective of his firm: 'First-class business run in a first-class way.' I have yet to hear of a better goal. It will guide me at Salomon Brothers and I invite you to measure our future conduct by that yardstick.

When the dreaded results for the third quarter rolled in, they were better than expected. Even with a $200 million charge set aside to cover expected costs and fines, the firm actually registered a profit of $85 million for the quarter. A revamping of Salomon's compensation system lowered Salomon's payroll by about $110 million.

"I believe that we had an extremely serious problem, but not a pervasive one," Buffett said.

Salomon took out an unusual two-page newspaper ad October 29, 1991, in the *Wall Street Journal*, *The New York Times* and *The Washington Post*, at a cost of about $600,000, running Buffett's letter to shareholders as well as the firm's newly shrunken balance sheet.

It was solid good news for Salomon, whose stock price rose 8% that day, and shortly thereafter the World Bank, after a three-month suspension, resumed business ties with Salomon, a major plus for the firm.

But even under Buffett, Salomon still frequently had its snakebit days. On March 25, 1992, a clerk mistook a customer's order to sell $11 million of stock as an order to unload 11 million shares, some $500 million. The huge sale in the closing minutes of the trading day wiped out a 12-point rally on the Dow, which closed instead with a one-point loss.

But remember, Buffett said he'd be forgiving of honest mistakes. The clerk was not fired. Buffett said it was an honest mistake; in fact, Buffett asked that he not be told the clerk's name.

At the three-hour Salomon annual meeting in May, 1992, corporate gadfly Evelyn Y. Davis asked Buffett how he could justify charging Salomon $158,000 for his corporate jet flights from Omaha to New York during the crisis.

Buffett replied that he was working for $1 a year for Salomon. "I work cheap, but I travel expensive," he said.

When she asked him whether the company's $25 million in legal fees to deal with the scandal was too much, Buffett deadpanned, "I would be delighted to have you negotiate with them, Evelyn. And I think the mere mention of that would be enough to induce a little moderation." On May 20, 1992, Salomon reached a $290 million settlement with the government.

Salomon agreed to pay $190 million in fines and forfeitures relating to the cheating in the Treasury auctions, and another $100 million fund was established by Salomon to compensate victims who lost money as a result of the wrongdoing.

As part of the settlement, Salomon was suspended from trading with the Federal Reserve for a two-month period ending August 1, 1992. Also, the Treasury Department said sanctions imposed on Salomon would be lifted, allowing the firm to resume submitting bids for customers. The settlement was the largest ever for wrongdoing in the securities industry, but the good news for Salomon was that it escaped criminal charges.

"We believe," Buffett said, "that the intense regulatory and investigative focus on Salomon has ended. We can now move forward to show that high ethical standards and meaningful profits are not only compatible objectives, but ones that can reinforce each other."

"I believe Salomon would have gone under without Warren Buffett," said Steve Forbes, head of the Forbes publishing empire and Republican presidential candidate in 1996. "There is no question he saved it."

That view is supported by someone in the midst of the crisis, Don Howard, Salomon's chief financial officer who oversaw the sale of $50 billion in assets and a total balance sheet restructuring.

"I never thought, 'We aren't going to make it'...I did wonder how in the hell we were going to get through." *(CFO,* March, 1992)

Howard said if the firm had replaced Gutfreund from within, it might not have survived.

"Warren's reputation gave the market confidence," said Howard, adding, "He's incisive, he knows what he wants, he understands very quickly, he goes to the essence of the problem very quickly."

At Salomon's annual meeting in 1993, Denham addressed Buffett's $1 pay, saying that on a prorated basis Buffett was due 79 cents, but Buffett merited a dollar anyway saying, "given pay for performance, and in light of our belief in pay for performance, I think we should award him the whole dollar."

Buffett replied, "Bob may look at this as pay for performance, but I look at it as interest for late payment. Twenty-one cents for four months is 80% interest, which is a rate I extend only to my best credits."

For years people had asked, "Who's Warren Buffett?"

Now the world knew.

In the end Buffett really did save Salomon.

He ousted the old management and overhauled the firm with a new management—emphasizing ethics, openness and compliance rather than risk-taking and bravado.

Overseeing Robert Denham's legal team in its strenuous negotiations with the government, Buffett managed to guide Salomon, against heavy odds, by avoiding criminal penalties that could have brought the firm to its knees.

Indeed, Salomon—while settling civil matters for $290 million—was able to keep criminal charges at bay in part because it fully cooperated with government investigators.

Late in 1993 Mozer pleaded guilty to two counts of making false statements about two illegal $3 billion bids at a 1991 Treasury auction. Mozer's fine and sentence seemed light to Buffett: "Mozer's paying $300,000 and is sentenced to prison for four months. Salomon's shareholders—including me—paid $290 million, and I got sentenced to ten months as CEO." *(Fortune,* January 10, 1994)

"If he had not repositioned the firm, he would not have been able to get anything in the negotiations with the government," said Omaha stockbroker George Morgan.

Buffett's impeccable reputation helped smooth potentially acrimonious talks with the Treasury Department, the SEC and the Justice Department.

Taking a more conservative fiscal stance, Buffett reduced Salomon's balance sheet by selling about $50 billion in assets, lowering Salomon's exposure to huge borrowings. His message was that ultra-easy access to funding often leads to undisciplined decision-making.

Buffett has pointed out that Salomon's balance sheet is extraordinary and subject to great volatility with market fluctuations. The balance sheet of $170 billion can change dramatically—a one-tenth percentage point change in market conditions is a $170 million change on Salomon's balance sheet.

Slashing bonuses, Buffett set up fairer compensation standards. He restructured Salomon's stock and bond trading units, cutting back on stock trading and moving the firm back to its bond-trading roots, the source of its prominence.

He assuaged clients, employees, shareholders and the government itself, asking all to look for a new Salomon, setting the highest standards in its business dealings. Here he teaches us that good profits and good behavior go hand in hand.

Buffett said Salomon had learned an expensive lesson but was ready to move forward as both an ethical and profitable company, as those elements should complement and reinforce one another.

He kept his pledge about staying on with the firm until the investigations were completed. Better yet, he kept his pledge about turning the firm around and rebuilding its reputation.

"We have managed to preserve a firm with a proud history and promising future," he wrote Salomon shareholders. "You have our pledge that we will conduct our business in the future so as to merit your continued trust."

Along the way, Buffett had setbacks. There were many defections from the firm, and there was some grousing about Buffett's not wanting to play near the edge of the court. There was kidding about his "Jimmy Stewart" ways, his supposed naiveté about Wall Street's quick-buck ways.

But in the end the mild-mannered, straight-arrow, determined Midwesterner had come to town and put a stop to Salomon's brash, cut-corners mentality. The emphasis would be on solid business relationships and understandings—not on rigging Treasury market bids or hiding wrongdoing. Buffett was able to bring about a corporate culture metamorphosis at Salomon by imposing his values of openness and fair-mindedness. As a result, Salomon righted itself and its stock steadily rebounded.

Buffett believes you shouldn't cut corners. You should do things simply, ethically, and without a lot of loud talk. You should do things in a way that would not be embarrassing if you appeared on page one of a newspaper. You should try to be a good guy.

"He demonstrated that an honest person could come in and clean up Wall Street's ways. He showed that honesty, hard work, good relationships, and openness are good—that honesty works," George Morgan said. "That *Liar's Poker* stuff scares me and that's what the world perceived those guys as being...He put in a compensation plan that rewards honest money-making for the firm—not money just because you are there or are generating a lot of activity."

When Buffett stepped down, he named Deryck Maughan to head Salomon Brothers.

There was much speculation about who Buffett would name as chairman of the parent firm, Salomon Inc. But Buffett's "sole recommendation" for the job was Robert Denham, the lawyer who had served Buffett so well during the Salomon crisis. Buffett remains chairman of Salomon's executive committee.

As always, it was all so simple. He kept control of the firm by putting in charge a brilliant lawyer and trusted friend who advised him through the crisis, someone who would ensure that Buffett's reforms remain.

Denham was certainly the person to oversee the remaining lawsuits against the firm, and Buffett said Denham's job—exactly in line with Buffett's philosophy of running things—would include evaluating the performance of the Salomon units, setting compensation for top executives, ensuring legal compliance, allocating capital and avoiding undue risk.

Having imposed boundaries on a wayward firm he had reined in, Buffett returned to Omaha to carry out his duties for Berkshire.

At the Salomon annual meeting in 1993, Denham presented Buffett his salary for saving Salomon, a $1 bill encased in Plexi-glas. Chief Financial Officer Don Howard said, "Don't think you don't have to pay taxes on it, just because it's in Plexi-glas."

Two years to the day after the Salomon scandal broke loose, when Gutfreund called Buffett to say he and other top Salomon executives were resigning—Berkshire announced it planned to raise its stake in Salomon. The plan was to boost it to 15%, up from the 14.3% it holds by way of the preferred stock investment. And Berkshire announced it was seeking clearance from federal regulators to allow it to buy up to 24.99% of Salomon. Permission was granted.

Under the Hart-Scott-Rodino Act, institutional investors must get clearance before buying more than 15% of a company for investment purposes.

Later Salomon announced plans to buy back as many as 10 million of its 110 million shares.

Forbes (October 18, 1993) reported that Buffett waited so long to increase his stake because he felt it wasn't fair to buy more shares when he was involved in Salomon's turnaround.

Buffett later lifted his Salomon's stake to slightly above 20%. Buffett raised his stake to more than 20%, partly, to get a tax break on his Saloman preferred investment. But Salomon stock spent a lot of 1994 declining. "The move was not my most brilliant investment to date," Buffett said. *(Forbes,* December 5, 1994)

Wallman Investment Counsel's Steve Wallman, also a Saloman's shareholder, told Henry Emerson, editor of *Outstanding Investor Digest*, he believed that under Buffett, Salomon's accounting was trustworthy, that its compensation practices had improved and that earnings were expanding at giant Salomon, which trades an astonishing $5 trillion worth of bonds a year.

When Emerson asked how much of a position he had, Wallman said, "Plenty." Pressed, Wallman said: "It's a major swing for the fence kind of thing. And that's as much as I want to say. It's the kind of number you only talk about after it works. Beforehand, you'd sound like the biggest fool on the planet. I'm not sure Buffett went around telling people he had 40% of his partnership in American Express until it worked.

"The moats at Coca-Cola and Salomon really do come down to the same thing: Each has a great moat because each has a huge market share, each makes a lot of money and no one's been able to hurt either's business...I don't think it's the desks, computers, Quotrons and so forth...What's really important in my opinion is the software... I mean the whole culture of the institution—everything known within the institution. That's what makes one institution better than another."

Bruce Berkowitz of Lehman Brothers referred to Salomon, because of its burgeoning worldwide franchise, as the "Coca-Cola of money."

With a worldwide trend in securitization underway, Salomon could be king. At Salomon, Buffett made a hero's journey.

Indeed, Salomon Chairman Robert Denham began the 1994 Annual Report saying: "Your Company's results were awful." Salomon was hit by a world-wide bond market crash.

And 1995 was shaping up as a rocky year as the firm continued to fight trading woes and cost beasts.

With Salomon's strong third quarter results—and the first quarter of 1996 was one of Salomon's best quarters ever—came word Buffett would not convert his preferred stock into common stock. Instead he took $140 million in cash and said:

> I am making a single decision about whether I want to put $140 million into Salomon common stock at $38 today or whether there is something else I would rather have Berkshire do with the money.
>
> Every day the stock market offers Berkshire an option to buy shares of Coca-Cola, Gillette, Salomon or thousands of other companies. So far this year, Berkshire has not exercised this 'market' option to buy shares of any of the three mentioned companies (including Salomon when it was trading below $38).
>
> Obviously, the fact that Berkshire has not exercised its market option to buy more Coca-Cola or Gillette does not mean that I am negative on these companies nor should that interpretation be placed upon the non-exercise of a 'company' option to purchase more Salomon common shares.

59

The Gillette Company

"The Best a Man Can Get"

"He's glad there are more people growing hair on their face," says one Berkshire employee. After all, it has to be shaved off. From a Berkshire view, shaving should be done with a Gillette razor. Twice a day! The stock symbol for The Gillette Company is G, but it once was "GS" for Gillette Safety Razor Company. Some suggest it was for a Good Shave.

"It's pleasant to go to bed every night knowing there are 2.5 billion males in the world who have to shave in the morning. A lot of the world is using the same...Gillette invented almost 100 years ago. These nations are upscaling the blade. So the dollars spent on Gillette products will go up," Buffett told *Forbes,* October 18, 1993.

Berkshire's investment in Gillette, which supplies 60% of all the dollar value of razor blades on the planet, is a direct result of Buffett's voracious reading of annual reports.

Buffett told reporter Sue Baggarly of WOWT-TV in Omaha, October 14, 1993, that he buys 100 shares of many companies. He does it for the purpose of getting the annual reports on time, "not lost at some brokerage house."

Buffett was reading the Gillette Annual Report one night when it occurred to him Gillette could use more capital. He checked the list of directors, called one (Joe Sisco), and asked if he might talk with management about an investment.

Buffett created the investment by proposing to Sisco, "an equity issue that might make sense." (*Business Week*, August 7, 1989)

In July, 1989, when Buffett invested $600 million in a preferred stock stake in Gillette, which was subsequently converted into an 11% common stock stake, Buffett said, "Gillette is synonymous with highly successful, international consumer marketing and is exactly the sort of business in which we like to invest for the long term."

Gillette, with about 70% of its sales and profits from overseas, is a global firm that offers personal care products. It's the dominant producer of razors and blades for men and women worldwide.

As a major force in providing grooming aids, Gillette is also looking sharp. Gillette sells toiletries and offers stationery products, correction fluids (Liquid Paper), Braun electric shavers and Oral-B oral care products. Gillette is the world leader in selling toothbrushes and oral care appliances.

Gillette owns Paper Mate and Waterman pens, and in 1993 it bought privately held Parker Pen Holdings of Britain for $561 million. Parker, which offers mid-priced lines of writing instruments, complements Gillette's low-price Paper Mate and its luxury Waterman lines. The Parker purchase made Gillette the world's largest writing instruments seller. Gillette's products are sold in more than 200 countries and territories.

Gillette thrives on its distribution network. "Think there's little synergy between an Oral-B toothbrush, a stick of Right Guard deodorant and a Paper Mate ballpoint pen? Look closer. They all share distribution channels. That means Gillette can keep costs low by warehousing and shipping products together." (*Financial World*, April 8, 1996)

As with his investment in Coca-Cola, Buffett again picked a U.S.-domiciled company running a huge overseas business, from its Boston headquarters.

It was at Gillette headquarters that Gillette Chairman Colman C. Mockler, Jr., a Harvard Business School graduate who took over management of Gillette in 1975, died of a heart attack on January 25, 1991.

Mockler had fended off takeover attempts and stabilized Gillette after a brief period of negative net worth in the late 1980s; he lived to see the extraordinary success of its magical Sensor razor.

Forbes, in its February 4, 1991, issue that arrived at subscribers' homes the day Mockler died, carried a cover picture of Mockler reaching the top of the mountain against competitors, in a cover story highlighting Gillette's many achievements.

Buffett has referred to Mockler as one of those people we "like, admire and trust." Mockler had planned to retire at the end of 1991 and Alfred Zeien (pronounced Zane) had been named president. Zeien, a graduate of Webb Institute of Naval Architecture, who designed and built his new home on Cape Cod, took over Gillette's top job shortly after Mockler's death.

Clean-shaven Zeien is known for lathering his face and shaving with two razors—one for each side of his face. One side gets shaved with a Gillette razor, one with a competitor's razor. Gillette executives check the competition to be sure of keeping their dominant market share.

Mockler told shareholders in April, 1990, of Gillette's push into the former Soviet Union, "The potential of the Soviet project is encouraging on a number of fronts. First, the large and growing market is estimated at about two billion blades per year. The Soviet Union currently imports about one billion blades, almost half of which this year will be supplied from seven Gillette international plants—in Argentina, Brazil, Colombia, Egypt, India, Mexico and Morocco.

"Secondly, from the outset of the talks, the Soviet negotiating team has been aware of Gillette's position that profit remittance from the operation would have to be paid in hard currency. The ongoing joint team effort between the Soviets and Gillette will verify the means to accomplish this.

"With the dramatic changes in Eastern Europe opening up good long-term growth possibilities, Gillette International also is exploring opportunities to expand its previously limited presence there." For example, Gillette owns an 80% interest in Wizamet, S.A., a leading razor blade maker in Poland.

Gillette has a joint venture in the former Soviet Union for razor blade operations.

It is making inroads into a number of emerging countries as well by following an astute strategy. As was mentioned in *Financial World* (March 2, 1993), Gillette introduces its oldest U.S. technologies and then upgrades the market gradually by rolling out its newer products. The equipment used in producing these products is already depreciated on its books, and hence the setup costs are very low, allowing the new operations to be profitable within a short period of time. And the inroads sliced into these markets by the razors may lead to piggybacks in the company's other businesses.

Gillette was founded in 1901 by King C. Gillette, whose safety razor was a landmark invention. Gillette made business history by inventing the disposable razor and making a fortune on replacements. He was working for Crown Cork & Seal as a salesman and dabbling with investors when his boss, William Painter, advised him: "Why don't you invent something that is thrown away, once used, and customers will have to come for more?"

It is said some men do their best thinking while shaving. Apparently this was true for Gillette because while shaving one morning in 1895, the idea of a razor with disposable blades popped into his head.

Gillette later described how the whole idea of a small, thin piece of steel came to him:

> ... the way the blade could be held in a holder: the idea of sharpening the two opposite edges of the thin piece of steel: the clamping plates for the blade, with a handle halfway between the two edges of the blade. All this came more in pictures than conscious thought, as though the razor were already a finished thing, and held before my eyes. I stood there before that mirror in a trance of joy. My wife was visiting Ohio, and I hurriedly wrote to her. 'I've got it! Our fortune is made! Fool that I was, I knew little about razors and nothing about steel, and I could not foresee the trials and tribulations I was to pass through before the razor was a success. But I believed in it with all my heart. (*The Book of Business Anecdotes*, Peter Hay, p. 269)

In 1903, Gillette's firm began selling the Gillette safety razor and 20 blades for $5.

Unfortunately, for all his success, Gillette died broke in 1932 as a result of poor investments and debts in the 1920s.

By 1960, the firm developed a way to apply a silicone coating to the blade edge, vastly improving shaving quality.

Gillette is riding high on its new Sensor razor—the world's first razor that continuously senses and automatically adjusts to contours of the face. The Sensor features twin blades that are individually mounted and 'float' on tiny springs. The revolutionary Sensor razor was launched in January, 1990, hyped by $3 million worth of ads that claimed Gillette is "The Best A Man Can Get." The ads were first aired during the 1990 Super Bowl.

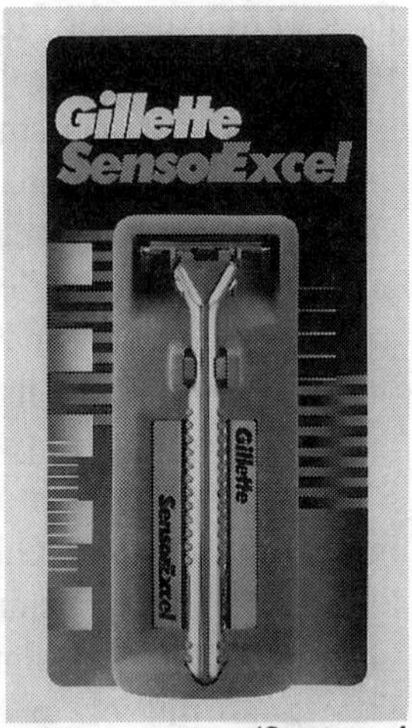

(Courtesy of The Gillette Company)
Gillette SensorExel

By October, 1991, Gillette had made its one billionth Sensor replacement cartridge. In its history, Gillette has made more than 325 billion blades. The first billion were produced between 1901 and 1917. The Sensor captured 9% of the U.S. razors and blades market in 1990 and more than 15% by the end of 1991. Now Sensor and the new SensorExcel shaving system introduced in 1993 together have 25%.

Sensor for Women was introduced in 1992 when for the first time Gillette designed a product solely for women.

The Sensor was 13 years in preparation and cost about $300 million—$200 million in research, engineering and tooling and another $100 million for advertising. Carrying the code name "The Flag," the Sensor was developed at Gillette's south Boston factory behind eight-foot walls.

The project was peaking in 1988 just when Coniston Partners was waging a proxy fight for the company.

To speed things along Gillette executive Donald Chaulk rounded up a nine-person crisis team of product designers, R&D people and engineers. "I put them away and said, 'This is your life. Let us know when you finish it.'" (*Financial World*, January 8, 1991)

Before the Sensor was introduced, top executives were using it for a smooth, clean shave. But they left it at home when they traveled.

The Sensor launch was so successful that Gillette was able to delay some advertising costs while production caught up with demand.

The Sensor has been a big hit, and as the world's economies become more linked, Gillette's value as the leading brand name in razors can only rise.

Gillette's constant barrage of new products includes deodorants, antiperspirants, shave creams, hair sprays, shampoos, conditioners, home permanents, styling aids, ethnic hair care products and bath and skin care products.

The company claims about a fifth of the U.S. deodorant market with its Right Guard, Dry Idea and Soft & Dri brands, second behind giant Procter & Gamble.

Gillette's Braun small household products and electric shaver lines are among international leaders. Braun is the top marketer of electric shavers in Germany and is among the leaders in Europe, North America and Japan. Braun's Flex Control electric razor, was the first pivoting swivel-headed electric razor. The Braun unit, bought by Gillette in 1967 for only $64 million, has sales of about $1 billion a year.

After fending off two major takeover attempts in three years—one by Revlon's chieftain Ron Perelman in 1986 and one by now-defunct Coniston Partners in 1988, Gillette restructured. The workforce was reduced by 8% and under-performing operations were sold. To escape the takeovers, Gillette bought back almost 30% of its common stock, ballooning its debt from $436 million to nearly $2 billion. It has been paying that down quickly.

Although Gillette's balance sheet for a while looked like that of an LBO, Gillette paid down debt because of its superior cash flow and the help of Berkshire's $600 million investment.

Buffett's privately arranged transaction was for $600 million worth of Gillette's 8¾% convertible preferred stock. The stock was convertible after two years into 12 million shares at $50 a share, with the stock trading at about $41 a share at the time. If not converted, the preferred stock would have been required to be redeemed by Gillette within 10 years.

Today, with Buffett literally on board, Gillette is enjoying strong earnings gains, with 45% of sales coming from products introduced in the last five years. Gillette introduced 20 new products in 1994 and 20 more in 1994.

Buffett said that the Gillette preferred investment would be the best of Berkshire's preferred category of investments. He was right.

Newsday columnist Allan Sloan, who has followed Buffett's career off and on since Buffett was buying (and selling) Detroit bank stocks some 20 years ago, argued that Buffett's stake in Gillette was immediately worth about $40 million more than Buffett paid for it, although a Gillette spokesman disagreed.

Sloan said:

> The stock bought by Buffett's Berkshire Hathaway Inc., carries a dividend of 8.75% a year, and he can trade $50 worth of it for one share of Gillette common stock. In other words, he agreed to pay "a conversion premium" of 8⅜ a share over the 41⅝ that regular

> investors were paying for Gillette at the time the deal was negotiated.
>
> But look. Buffett is getting 4⅜ a year in dividend income (the 8.75% interest times $50) for each Gillette share he controls. The holder of a share of Gillette common stock gets a dividend of only 96 cents a year. So, while Buffett has agreed to pay a premium of $8.375 a share for Gillette, he gets an extra $3.415 a year in dividend income ($4.375 minus 96 cents) while he's waiting. Work it out, and in less than 2½ years, the extra dividends that Buffett will receive make up for the premium he has agreed to pay.
>
> You still with me? Now watch. In the arcane world of convertible securities, three and a half years is the norm for breaking even in a security such as this Gillette convertible. Run the numbers through Gillette's black box, which the company graciously did for me, and you'll find that to reach the break-even point in three and a half years, Buffett would have had to pay 53¼ a share, rather than 50. That's a 7% difference. Now, multiply that by $600 million, and Buffett is $42 million ahead...

Sloan reported that Buffett and Gillette agreed with the math, but not the interpretation.

"Gillette claims that certain aspects of the stock—the fact that Gillette can call it in for early redemption, that Gillette has the right of first refusal to buy the stock should Buffett decide to sell, and other arcana—offset the relatively high dividend and relatively low conversion price." He reports that Buffett told him, "We thought we made a good investment or we wouldn't be in it," and noted that Gillette was getting his services. "Charlie and I agree to work on the company for 10 years. We don't charge a fee, we don't even bill for transportation services to come to board meetings." Gillette redeemed Berkshire's preferred stock investment of $600 million, in 1991, and Berkshire converted its stake into 12 million shares of Gillette stock, about 11% of the stock. With a 2-for-1 stock split in 1991, Berkshire had 24 million shares and with a 2-for-1 split in 1995, it had 48 million shares.

Meanwhile Gillette focused on its international blade business, making inroads in China, India, Poland, the former Soviet Union, Turkey and Latin America. In 1995 Gillette bought Thermoscan Inc, a marketer of infared ear thermometers which was merged into Gillette's Braun unit based in Germany.

Gillette employs about 33,000 people, most of whom work outside the U.S.

Gillette, which has a stock buyback program underway to purchase 10 to 15 million shares over the next three or four years, turned out to be a brilliant investment. Buffett was left with a major stake in a fully rebounding franchise, an irreplaceable consumer products company with a wonderfully reinvigorated global brand name.

60

USAir

The Not-So Preferred Way to Fly

Berkshire made its $358 million preferred stock investment in USAir on August 7, 1989. USAir had merged with Piedmont Aviation just two days earlier.

"It is unusual for Berkshire Hathaway to invest in a capital-intensive, labor-intensive industry, such as the airline industry. Our enthusiasm for the investment in USAir Group preferred stock is dramatic evidence of our high regard for Ed Colodny's management," Buffett said. "I like Ed."

Still Buffett saw the USAir stake as a senior security, not a great business. Buffett's strategy may have been spotting an industry which had a few large players and was consolidating. And it may have been it provided some synergy for Berkshire, perhaps with PS Group's travel, leasing, and fuel operations. PS Group's Rick Guerin has said Buffett is a believer in the bright future of the travel industry.

But in this case Buffett's strategy backfired on the runway as many factors hastened USAir's stunning decline amidst turbulence in the airline industry. On May 8, 1996, Berkshire announced it planned to sell its USAir stake, offering first to sell it back to the company.

It was Buffett's idea to buy into the Arlington, Virginia-based airline, which is about 8% owned by Michael Steinhardt's Steinhardt Partners that was increasing its stake in USAir, the fourth largest U.S. airline.

The investment had been a bumpy ride along the wrong flight path. With its jumbo-jet sized problems, the airline lost about $3 billion from 1988-1994. Buffett once told a group of business students at Columbia University not to invest in airlines, saying it's one of the worst businesses in the world, loaded with costs and overcapacity.

Asked by a Columbia student why he invested in the airline, Buffett quipped, "This is my psychiatrist asking this. Actually I have an 800 number now which I call if I ever get an urge to buy an airline stock. I say my name is Warren. I'm an air-aholic and then they talk me down."

USAir started life as Allegheny Airlines in the East, acquired Mohawk Airlines in 1972, established a hub in Pittsburgh in 1978 and became USAir in 1979 before acquiring PSA and Piedmont. The airline now has hubs in Pittsburgh, Philadelphia, Baltimore, Charlotte and Indianapolis.

When Buffett invested, USAir common stock was trading at about $50 a share. Each of the $1,000 face value preferred shares is convertible after two years from the purchase date at a conversion price into 16⅔ common shares when and if the price hits $60 a share. The investment, which represents about a 12% stake, pays Berkshire a 9.25% tax-advantaged dividend a year.

USAir could buy back or call the preferred stock after August 7, 1991, for $100 a share higher than the $1,000 purchase price. Berkshire has until August 7, 1999, to convert its stock, selling any remaining shares of the preferred stock to USAir at the original $1,000 a share price.

What Buffett saw, through his preferred stake, was a way to gamble safely. If he lost, he would earn 9%. If he won, he would control an airline in a consolidating industry. But USAir has been flying at lower and lower altitudes since he climbed aboard.

It's been miserable for USAir and for the entire airline business since Buffett stepped in. "My mistake was I didn't think price competition would get that bad. The cost side, of course, has been abysmal as well, as the result of events in the Middle East," Buffett said at the annual meeting in 1991.

And he added, "When you get six or eight competitors, some of whom are operating in bankruptcy—once an airline goes into bankruptcy, they're in effect debt-free. Eastern picked up hundreds of millions of dollars essentially by selling off gates and other assets to subsidize operating losses at a time when they were effectively debt-free—because they weren't paying anything on their debt. And USAir can't compete with that. To compete with someone who's bleeding copiously, you need a blood bank."

Even before that, it did not help when two passengers were killed as USAir Flight 5050 skidded off a rain-slicked runway at New York's LaGuardia Airport, bellyflopping into the water on an abortive takeoff for Charlotte on September 20, 1989. And on February 1, 1991, a USAir flight and a commuter plane collided on the runway at Los Angeles International Airport leaving 34 passengers dead. That was also the effective date of the airline's decision to cut back on its insurance coverage for its fleet.

When it rains, it pours...On March 22, 1992, a USAir flight during inclement weather crashed at LaGuardia, killing 26 of the 51 people aboard.

After the merger with Piedmont, things were slow to mesh and USAir racked up an unimpressive on-time record. Planes were late. Bags were lost. Useless Air and U.S.-scare became monikers. But gradually during 1990 its on-time performance improved from No. 6 of the major airlines in January, 1990, to No. 1 by June, 1990, and it maintained a number-two rating through 1991. Competition was fierce, and when Iraq invaded Kuwait August 2, 1990, jet fuel prices soared and moneymaking USAir turned in a string of quarterly losses.

Layoffs and discontinued service dominated headlines about USAir. The industry was in disarray as airlines such as Midway retreated and Eastern and others crashed and burned. Chairman Colodny said in the 1989 USAir Annual Report conditions were deteriorating because of industry fundamentals and merger-related problems. Eventually 7,000 furloughs were announced: 14% of the work force. Orders for planes were deferred, the number of flights reduced.

USAir's problems had been building as the airline struggled in a no man's land of being too big to be a regional airline and still too small to be in the league of major domestic carriers.

With many monopoly routes and a fortress hub in Pittsburgh, USAir had it made in the early 1980s.

But it didn't do much marketing. It didn't buy jumbo jets nor offer first-class service. It wouldn't even give customers an extra bag of peanuts.

In 1987 it undertook one of the biggest airline combinations in history, buying both Pacific Southwest Airlines and Piedmont Aviation, Inc.

But because USAir's flights are short, it's a high-cost airline.

The U.S. airline industry has many competitors. The fewer the competitors, the higher the price that can be charged. The higher the price, the more profit.

The airline industry has been described as an industry where perhaps only four or five carriers will survive. All airlines have faced severe pressures that remind one of a cartoon that ran in *Barron's*. It read: "Arrivals, Departures, Bankruptcies."

Indeed, in the year prior to mid-1991, six of the top dozen airlines in the nation filed for bankruptcy protection.

USAir's mergers also forced it into the rough-and-tumble arena of national competition.

On the West Coast USAir got clobbered in a five-way battle with American, United, Delta and low-cost Southwest Airlines, making many of its Western routes unprofitable.

Moreover, in absorbing two successful carriers into its system, USAir adopted what it called a "Mirror Image" strategy of making them do everything exactly its way.

For years, Piedmont served a whole can of Coke rather than handing out a plastic cupful at a time. When USAir dropped the Piedmont practice of serving passengers whole cans of soda, Piedmont frequent flyers put their foot down. Cost-cutting was one thing, but this was stingy. Cost-cutting and large layoffs were the order of the day in the early 1990s.

But Buffett hung in there, telling Martha H. Hamilton of the *Washington Post* early on, "There are no plans—just to be an investor for 10 years or longer. We think when you've got an able management, they should have time to play out their hand."

Buffett's pal from journalism, Adam Smith, serves on the USAir board.

Colodny retired in June, 1991, after 34 years with the company. Seth E. Schofield succeeded Colodny as president and in early 1996 Stephen Wolf, who formerly ran UAL Corp. was named chairman and CEO. In 1991 Buffett was calling the USAir investment "an unforced error" and Colodny was starting his annual report letter to stockholders with, "The year 1990 was the most difficult in the Company's history. The soft domestic traffic and weak economy, skyrocketing fuel prices, fear of travel due to the Persian Gulf crisis, and widespread, sharply discounted fares all contributed to the $454 million net loss for the year."

The letter talked about employee layoffs, aircraft phaseouts and order cutbacks. Things were in bad shape, with no sunlight at the end of the runway for Berkshire shareholders and others.

Not all of Buffett's preferred stock investments were working well because in some cases the underlying common stock was languishing. USAir, Salomon and Champion were all faltering at one point. Still, shareholders were substantially better off with Buffett buying the preferred stakes than were ordinary investors who bought the common stocks.

"Buffett still walks on water. He just splashes a little bit," said Marshall Lewis, senior vice president of the Blunt, Ellis & Loewi investment firm. (*Omaha World-Herald*, October 20, 1991)

Losses continued to stack up. At year-end 1991 Buffett wrote down his estimation of the $358 million investment to $232.7 million. Meanwhile USAir employees, officers and board members walked or took pay cuts.

At the Berkshire annual meeting in 1991, Colodny said, "We give away full cans of Coke. Last year, we bought $6.5 million of Coke—sold none of it, gave it all away. That's over a million cases. We've now begun to give away See's Candies for dessert in our first-class section for flights out of California. And that's been very popular.

"However, we have not yet figured out a way to tie in with *World Book*," Colodny said.

In 1992, British Airways agreed to buy a 44% stake in USAir for $750 million, creating a formidable competitor in the increasingly global airline industry. Although that deal fell through, British Airways eventually invested $300 million in USAir.

In January 1993, Buffett and Munger, taking on a huge new challenge in a weak link of their empire, went on the board of USAir. Buffett wrote that the British Airways investment would help in "assuring survival—and eventual prosperity."

Buffett apparently never has said, as one wag has warned: "Don't invest in anything with wheels on it."

USAir did not turn out to be Buffett's finest hour.

At the Wesco annual meeting in 1993, Munger said of the USAir stake, "We cut that a little fine, but it's not over."

With continued losses, USAir began drumming up new business with a frequent flier program aimed at funeral directors.

"The USAir TLC Award Program is part of the carrier's recent marketing effort to inspire the roughly 45,000 licensed funeral directors nationwide to select the airline for shipping the dearly departed to their final destinations," wrote Jennifer Lawrence in a story for *Advertising Age*, January 4, 1994.

Her story, headlined "TLC for DOA takes USAir to higher plane" quoted sources saying, "USAir's program almost makes dying worthwhile," and noted that Delta, apparently the leading airline in the human remains niche market, wouldn't try to match USAir's "frequent dier awards program."

In March 1994, British Airways said it was suspending plans to invest further in USAir. By then British Airways had invested $400 million with plans to invest another $450 million. The decision sent USAir stock crashing and burning to a single digit share price.

On July 2, 1994, a USAir jet crashed near Charlotte, killing 57 people. In a seeming last straw for the company, a USAir jetliner crashed near Pittsburgh September 8, 1994, killing all 132 people aboard. It was the fifth fatal crash in five years for the beleagered airline. A short time later USAir deferred its preferred stock dividend to Berkshire due September 30, 1994.

In early 1995 Buffett and Munger stepped down as directors of USAir after they had said they would do so if the airline couldn't reach a timely agreement with its labor groups about cost-savings.

For the fourth quarter of 1994 Berkshire wrote down its investment in USAir, taking a $268.5 pre-tax charge. The write-down was to $89 million, about 25 cents on the dollar.

The investment was written up to $214.8 million at the end of 1995. Buffet said in Berkshire's 1995 annual report: "Though we have not been paid dividends since June, 1994, the amounts owed us are compounding at 5% over the prime rate. On the minus side is the fact that we are dealing with a weak credit."

Lesson: do not invest in airline stocks.

At the Berkshire annual meeting in 1995, a stockholder asked if an investment in another airline would be considered. The stockholder, because of the crowd, had not been able to get into the main room and was watching the meeting on a screen.

"Thanks for the question. We're putting everyone who asks us questions about USAir in the other room," Buffett replied.

The first ray of skylight for USAir came with a profit in 1995, its first profit in seven years.

61

A Profit from Champion International

"Trees don't grow to the sky."

The announcement of Berkshire's $300 million preferred stock stake in Champion, the giant forest products company based in Stamford, Connecticut, came December 6, 1989. It was at a time of a hostile bid for Great Northern Nekoosa by Champion's competitor, Georgia-Pacific.

Andrew C. Sigler, Champion's Chief Executive Officer since 1974, long has been a vocal critic of takeovers in general and of his company in particular.

With Berkshire's large stake, which pays Berkshire an 8% dividend, Champion lessened its chances of being swallowed.

Champion, which has about $5 billion in annual sales, bought St. Regis in 1984, playing the role of a so-called White Knight after raiders threatened a takeover of St. Regis.

Sigler praised Berkshire's investment in Champion:

> We wanted to raise capital to help support our cost-cutting, quality improvement, and capacity enhancement programs. Berkshire's CEO Warren Buffett is a remarkably astute investor, and his commitment to the long-term performance of the companies in which he invests is well matched to Champion's needs and goals...

Champion is mainly a producer of pulp and paper with a particular emphasis on white paper. The annual reports are printed on recycled paper made by its mills.

With operations in the U.S., Canada and Brazil, Champion produces publications papers, newsprint, kraft, pulp and forest products. Its worldwide facilities make bleached paperboard, newsprint and packaging products including plywood, newsprint, lumber and studs.

Long a laggard in the forest products industry, Champion's stock price—well under book value—trades not far from where it did a decade ago. Buffett bought the preferred stake when the common stock was about $30 a share.

Champion has cited a litany of reasons for its sluggish earnings in recent years: severely depressed conditions in the wood products business, weakening world pulp markets, lower prices for some of its paper grades, startup difficulties in connection with several major rebuilds and higher tax rates largely attributable to the firm's Brazilian operations as a result of economic reforms in Brazil. Champion has been trying to find a way out of the woods for years.

In 1989 Champion produced about 1.4 million tons of coated and uncoated paper at four mills: Canton, North Carolina; Hamilton, Ohio; Pensacola, Florida; and Courtland, Alabama, where a new uncoated white paper machine went on line in 1993. One of every three paperboard milk containers in the United States is made from Champion paperboard. The company has a large building-product business.

In addition to the stake by Buffett, Laurence Tisch of Loews Corp. has an 18% stake in the common stock which Loews may sell. Over the years Champion has earned a reputation for making large capital investments that have not paid a good return. What intrigues investors is the vast amount of timberlands the company controls—6.4 million acres in the U.S. and 2.5 million in Canada where Champion owns about 85% of Weldwood, a pulp and paper products firm. That's a lot of land and a lot of trees.

In recent years the 30,000-employee firm has spent more than $2 billion on capital projects, completing major portions of its large modernization program.

In early 1991, Champion dropped a poison-pill defense it had maintained since 1986 to ward off potential takeover bids. With little money available for takeover efforts, the threat seemed past.

Financial World magazine, in its February 19, 1991, issue, ran a story about Champion, noting that its big investors were Buffett, Tisch, John Templeton and others. And it listed another interesting investor, Sandy Gottesman, chairman of First Manhattan, who happened to be Tisch's neighbor. Of course, Gottesman is a close friend of Buffett's. Heavyweights are circling around Champion.

Value Line, in its April 26, 1991, issue said flatly, "Champion's three-to five-year prospects are poor...Perhaps they see something Wall Street's missing." Of course Buffett thinks in longer than three-to five-year time frames.

Value Line's July 26, 1991, issue kept to the same theme: "Champion shares are untimely...The stock is no more compelling as a long-term investment."

After years of struggle Champion's modernization program began to kick in and demand for paper products rose. The trees are growing, and the stock price is rising.

In June, 1995, Berkshire converted its preferred stocks into Champion common shares. Champion then exercised its right of first refusal to buy the shares, getting the shares back for $49.125. Berkshire had turned its $300 million into almost $400 million and received a good dividend while it waited.

62

First Empire State

"Convert and Keep"

In 1991 with the banking industry in shambles and Buffett sensing consolidation, he returned to Buffalo for an investment.

First Empire State, then a $7.7 billion in assets bank holding company based in Buffalo, New York, agreed March 14 that year to issue 40,000 shares of 9% preferred stock to Berkshire's National Indemnity Co. for $40 million.

For the second time, Buffett made an investment in Buffalo. His first investment was in the *Buffalo News*. First Empire stock was trading at about $67 a share when the deal was struck and began climbing steadily thereafter. The preferred stock is convertible at any time into shares of First Empire's common stock at an initial conversion price of $78.91 per share.

Based on the 6,637,138 shares of common stock outstanding as of the close of business on March 13, 1991, complete exercise of the conversion privilege would be equal to 506,930 shares, or about 7% of the common stock outstanding following conversion, First Empire said.

First Empire had the right to redeem the preferred stock without premium on or after March 31, 1996. In other words, Buffett had five years, a long time to make his investment work—that is, for First Empire's price to reach about $79 a share, which it did in short order. In the meantime the perfectly satisfactory 9% return kept arriving at Berkshire's doorstep.

In Berkshire's 1995 annual report, Buffett said that on March 31, 1996, Berkshire would "convert and keep" its First Empire common shares. Therefore Berkshire owns far more than $100 million of First Empire's common stock.

First Empire historically has carried low debt levels and has an excellent long-term record. In the past decade its stock is up many times from the $7 to $10 a share level where it traded in 1981, according to Standard and Poor's.

First Empire's subsidiaries are Manufactures and Traders Trust Co., The East New York Savings Bank and M&T Bank, National Association.

The bank, with assets of $12 billion at the end of 1995, has a clean balance sheet and a solid long-term record. It is heavily owned by its officers and directors and institutional investors.

The message to shareholders in First Empire's 1990 annual report is one of the more articulate looks at the U.S. banking scene. It's in English.

For example, in describing Berkshire's complex investment in First Empire, not easy for the layman to understand, the report said: "The issuance and sale of 40,000 shares of preferred stock, mentioned earlier, made a significant addition to First Empire's capital. The preferred...is currently convertible to First Empire common stock at the rate of $78.91 of original purchase price ($1,000 per preferred share) for one share of common. The conversion price was set at 125% of the market price of First Empire common ($63.125) at the time the transaction was agreed on."

In 1991 the FDIC closed Goldome, a Buffalo-based savings and loan, dividing its assets between competitors KeyCorp and First Empire State. Wall Street apparently liked the deal. First Empire stock jumped right through the conversion point so that Buffett, in addition to getting the 9%, is way in the money on the stock side.

First Empire, headed by Robert Wilmers, was a steady performer in the early 1990s and in early 1996, with the company buying back its own shares, the stock was well above $200 a share.

63

American Express Redux

"He has not offered to let me pay for this transaction on my credit card."

American Express announced on August 1, 1991, that it would accept a cash infusion of $300 million from Berkshire.

To the *Omaha World-Herald*, Buffett landed this punchline: "He [American Express Chairman Jim Robinson] has not offered to let me pay for this transaction on my credit card."

Buffett had returned to American Express, the scene of one of his early investment victories. With his newly acquired stake, Buffett became a major shareholder in the giant company known for its credit cards, travelers checks and struggling Shearson Lehman Brothers brokerage firm into which American Express had recently pumped more than $1 billion to restructure. The hard-hit subsidiary had lost $900 million the year Buffett invested.

American Express was founded in 1850 by Henry Wells and William Fargo, who also founded Wells Fargo, another Berkshire investee.

American Express credit cards are accepted as far away as the Mongolian People's Republic, and are honored in 180 countries. Travel and tourism may be the largest industry in the world and American Express is the world's largest travel company with a related network of more than 1,700 offices around the globe.

The company is also a leader in financial planning, securities brokerage, asset management, international banking, investment banking and information services.

Buffett has investments in banks, an airline, and once had a travel agency through PS Group; he almost has his own American Express already. He might as well call it Wells Fargo/USAir Travel Express.

This time Buffett had a much larger amount invested in American Express. Recall that years ago, during the American Express salad oil scandal, Buffett invested only about $13 million. Now it was $300 million. And American Express was pledged to pay him an 8.85% dividend, a return made even better because of the 70% corporate-tax exemption on the dividend income: Berkshire was earning more than 11% on a taxable equivalent basis.

This investment, called a "Perc," is somewhat different from Buffett's earlier convertible preferred stakes in Salomon, Gillette, USAir and Champion; in the end it offered Buffett less potential upside and gave American Express more control over its outcome. Although the arrangement gave Buffett a much heftier dividend on its American Express shares than common shareholders receive, the deal limited Buffett's capital gains.

The preferred shares were exchangeable into common shares at the option of American Express, not Buffett, making them different from convertible shares.

"There's not much upside potential with this one. I'm not sure why he did it," said *Newsday* columnist Allan Sloan.

"Convertible preferred shares have unlimited upside," Buffett told the *Wall Street Journal* (August 2, 1991). "With this, we get less of an investment opportunity."

The Berkshire-American Express agreement called for Buffett's non-transferable preferred shares to be exchanged for common stock within three or four years under terms of the investment, a private placement.

American Express would redeem the securities issued to Berkshire no later than maturity by exchanging common shares for the preferred stock. The number of common shares to be issued were to be determined by the American Express share price at the time of the redemption. If

American Express didn't redeem before maturity, (three years, with the possibility of a year extension if American Express stock was below $24.50 at the time) it would exchange about 12 million common shares for the preferred stake, about a 2.5% stake in American Express. Amex stock was trading at about $25 a share when Buffett bought his preferred stake.

"When I heard they needed some equity funds, I told Jim [Robinson, then chairman of American Express] that Berkshire would be interested in investing $500 million. I was willing to buy more, but Jim didn't want to sell more than $300 million," Buffett told the *Journal.*

In this case, Buffett did not join the board, as he often does when he invests. Robinson told *USA Today* (August 2, 1991), "I don't think he needs to be on the board to provide that [counsel]. We would have welcomed him on our board, but he's on a number of boards. He has a pretty full plate. Also, he's on the Salomon board and we own [rival] Shearson."

As for Buffett, he told the Associated Press he won't play a role in running American Express, but that he would "speak when spoken to." He'll be spoken to.

Taking on numerous interviews in connection with the announcement, Buffett told the *Omaha World-Herald* (August 2, 1991) that the then-recent losses at Shearson were temporary.

"It really doesn't take any of the luster off the really great franchises—the cards, the travelers checks and the information systems," Buffett said, shortly before the company's setbacks in its Optima card operations.

As usual, when Buffett made his investment, things did not look good at American Express.

In addition to its problems at Shearson, subsequently sold off to Smith Barney, American Express had earlier taken a $30 million loss when it had to restate earnings for another unit, The Boston Company unit, also sold off (it specialized in lending money to wealthy individuals).

Moreover, American Express loans to Prime Computer and Balcor Co. were worrisome.

To make matters worse for American Express, but to create the perfect buying opportunity for Buffett, a wave of merchants (initially a group of restaurants in Boston that were subsequently dubbed the "Boston Fee Party") was complaining that American Express cards had been taking too large a commission from sales billed to its cards, as the entire credit card industry was becoming more competitive than ever, with a number of other credit cards, including AT&T's, being introduced.

Visa and Mastercard all along were gaining market share.

Value Line at the time said, "These shares seem unexciting...not confident that the stock will show any special strength for the year ahead. And prospects for 1994-96 aren't well defined." Enter Warren Buffett.

Omaha World-Herald columnist Robert McMorris ran this item August 2, 1991:

> Lunch-table conversation overheard at a west Omaha restaurant: I understand Warren Buffett is investing $300 million in American Express.
>
> That so? You know, American Express owns Shearson Brokerage, and Warren already has Salomon.
>
> Yeah, pretty soon he'll own all of Wall Street. Think he'll move there so he can be close to his money?
>
> I doubt it. Warren would probably say Wall Street is a nice property to own, but he wouldn't want to live there.

Buffett converted his American Express investment into 14 million common shares in the summer of 1994 and began buying more American Express stock, and more and more and more and more. By the end of 1994 he was up to 27.76 million shares and added another 20.7 million in the first month and a half of 1995.

On Valentine's Day, 1995, just over 30 years after his first investment in American Express, Berkshire announced that it owned 9.8% of American Express. The announcement came across the wire as a one liner:

02/15 WSJ Buffett Boosts American Express Stake to 9.8%

That amounted to 48.5 million shares of American Express, or about $1.6 billion. Also he said he wanted clearance to buy above 10% of the company.

Berkshire agreed with American Express that if it acquires more than 10% of American Express, as long as Harvey Golub, known as a hard-nosed businessman, is CEO, Berkshire will vote its shares in accordance with the wishes of the American Express board.

Also, Buffett agreed to limit his stake and influence at American Express as part of an agreement with the Federal Reserve Board that allowed him to buy more than 10% of the stock of American Express.

Because American Express owns a bank, the Fed could decide Berkshire had a controlling interest in American Express and thus was subject to regulations for bank holding companies.

Buffett would have to get out of everything banks aren't allowed to do, such as owning newspaper and candy companies.

With the agreement to be a passive investor, Berkshire can continue its other operations. Under the agreement Berkshire said it will keep its stake under 15% if it receives board representation and below 17% if it doesn't. (*Bloomberg News Service*, November 16, 1995) Berkshire has the right to buy up to 17% of American Express.

In the 1994 Annual Report, Buffett wrote:

> My American Express history includes a couple of episodes: In the mid-1960s, just after the stock was battered by the company's infamous salad-oil scandal, we put about 40% of Buffett Partnership Ltd.'s capital into the stock — the largest investment the partnership had ever made. I should add that this commitment gave us over 5% ownership of Amex at a cost of $13 million. As I write this, we own just under 10% which has cost us $1.36 billion. (Amex earned $12.5 million in 1964 and $1.4 billion in 1994.)
>
> My history with Amex's IDS unit, which today contributes about a third of the earnings of the company goes back even further. I first purchased stock in IDS in 1953 when it was growing rapidly and selling at a price-earnings ratio of only 3. (There was a lot of low-hanging fruit in those days.) I even produced a long report—do I ever write a short one?—on the company that I sold for $1 through an ad in the *Wall Street Journal.*
>
> Obviously American Express and IDS (recently renamed American Express Financial Advisors) are far different operations from what they were then. Nevertheless, I find that a long-term familiarity with a company and its products is often helpful in evaluating it.

"The key will be in how the credit card does over time," Buffett said of American Express at the Berkshire annual meeting in 1995.

Berkshire raised its American Express stake to 49,456,900 shares, about 10.1% of the company, according to an announcement September 8, 1995.

64

Freddie Mac

In late 1988 Berkshire's Wesco unit beefed up its minor stake to 7.2 million shares of the stock of Freddie Mac, formerly known as Federal Home Loan Mortgage.

Buffett and Munger decided to make the investment after conferring for about three hours. *(Forbes,* January 22, 1996)

It was the maximum amount, at the time, that any single shareholder could own under federal rules. The cost of the purchase was $71.7 million.

Explaining the investment to *Fortune* in its December 19, 1988, issue The Sage of Omaha said, "Freddie Mac is a triple dip. You've got a low price/earnings ratio on a company with a terrific record. You've got growing earnings. And you have a stock that is bound to become much better known to equity investors."

When Buffett made the investment, some investors were asking themselves, "Who is Freddie Mac?" Freddie Mac is chartered by the federal government as a private company to provide liquidity to the mortgage market. It buys mortgages, then pools and packages them into securities that it sells to investors. It insures mortgages on about five million homes for a fee of ¼ of 1%.

Freddie Mac helps make the American dream, (or nightmare, depending on your mortgage rate) of owning a home come true. Over the years, Freddie Mac has helped finance one in six American homes, including more than 700,000 apartment units. Freddie Mac buys a home loan every three seconds of every business day—2.4 million loans in 1993.

About 97% of Freddie Mac's business is with single-family mortgages. Since 1970 it has financed the homes of about 12 million Americans.

Chartered by Congress in 1970, the stockholder-owned company buys home mortgages from lenders, guarantees the mortgages against default, packages them as securities and sells them to investors such as S&Ls. It creates a continuous flow of money to mortgage lenders in support of home ownership and rental housing. The company has been profitable every year of its existence.

In 1984, it issued about 15 million shares of participating preferred stock to Federal Home Loan Board-member S&Ls, with trading generally restricted to board members.

In 1988, Freddie Mac stock began trading on the New York Stock Exchange. The company had been owned by thrifts that owned the stock through the country's Federal Home Loan Bank System and were allowed to resell the stock starting in January, 1989. The lifting of trading restrictions on Freddie Mac preferred stock allowed public investors to come in.

So what is Freddie Mac with its 3,000 employees and how does it work to link the nation's mortgage markets with its financial markets?

Freddie Mac provides stability in the secondary market for home mortgages. The moment you drop your monthly mortgage payment in the mail is the start of a long journey for your money.

If your lender has kept the loan on its books, your payment will be processed, your check deposited and the money used to pay interest on deposits and make more loans to new borrowers in your area.

But let's say you take out a 7.5% fixed-rate home loan of $150,000 from your bank and the bank doesn't want to carry it on its books for the next 30 years. One reason it might not want to carry the loan: the bank may wind up losing money if rates skyrocket in the future. To eliminate the risk, the bank sells your loan to an entity like Freddie Mac. Freddie buys your promise to pay, and your local bank gets immediate cash.

Freddie Mac's only real competition is Fannie Mae, making them duopoly businesses, both of which benefited from the decline of the S&L industry nationwide. If Buffett can't locate a true monopoly business, he's usually glad to settle for a duopoly.

The secondary market accomplishes several things. Lending institutions can make long-term mortgage loans knowing they can sell them to someone like Freddie Mac, and at the same time mortgage-backed securities make it easier and safer for more investors to participate in the mortgage market.

After Buffett made the investment in the stock at a cost per share of about $30, it rose in 1990, but then began to plummet along with anything smacking of the suddenly suspect world of real estate.

At its low in 1990, the stock had lost two-thirds of its value from the 1989 peak and was trading at a price/earnings ratio of about five.

The Freddie Mac plunge rocked the stock of Wesco, which owns the Freddie Mac stock directly, and didn't help Berkshire in the tempestuous stock market of 1990.

In late 1990, Freddie Mac was reporting problems in its apartment-backed mortgage business, particularly in New York and Atlanta, but even so profits from the company's single-family mortgage business remained strong and the stock began to rebound.

In its 1990 yearend report, Freddie Mac Chairman Leland Brendsel said, "We estimate that property values underlying our single-family mortgage portfolio stood at approximately $600 billion at year-end, reflecting a decade of home price appreciation. This means, on average, there is almost two dollars of property value underlying every mortgage dollar represented in our single-family portfolio."

In 1991, Freddie Mac stock rebounded strongly as fears about real estate eased and interest rates dipped dramatically. Despite the 1990 scare, Steady Freddie has been profitable in every quarter since 1971. Again Buffett's strategy of patience paid off. At year-end 1991, Berkshire had upped its Freddie Mac stake to about 7.5 million shares. In 1992 Freddie Mac declared a 3-for-1 stock split and a 14% dividend increase. With the split, Berkshire owned about 7.5 million shares of Freddie Mac.

Then the stake was raised to more than 16 million shares, but reduced to 13,654,000 shares at the end of 1993, to 12,761,200 at the end of 1994 and lowered to 12,502,500 at the end of 1995.

Bill Ruane, who heads Sequoia Fund which also has a large Freddie Mac stake, and has said, "Here's a company that has been growing—and they predict will continue to grow—at a mid-teens growth rate selling at about 12 times earnings with a very high return on capital...

"If you were to take Freddie Mac and look at the simple numbers—it's selling at 12 times earnings versus 18 to 20 times earnings for the S&P. It probably has a double-digit earnings growth rate versus an average growth rate over nine years of 7% or even less for the S&P. Its return on equity is 20% or better against an average return of 12½% to 13% for the S&P. So by any simple statistical measure, it's a very attractive stock."

65

The Body of His Work

"Common sense is genius dressed in its working clothes." —*Ralph Waldo Emerson*

From the beginning, common sense is the trait that has most characterized Buffett's body of work.

"We don't buy and sell stocks based on what other people think the stock market is going to do. The course of the stock market will determine, to a great degree, *when* we will be right, but the accuracy of our analysis of the company will largely determine *whether* we are right. In other words, we tend to concentrate on what should happen, not when it should happen," he wrote in a Buffett Partnership letter, July 22, 1966.

Common sense may be the most important factor helping Buffett to make more money in the stock market than anyone; he is the only person on the *Forbes* 400 richest Americans list who got there entirely by investing.

"One piece of advice that I got at Columbia from Ben Graham that

I've never forgotten: You're neither right nor wrong because other people agree with you. You're right because your facts are right and your reasoning is right. That's the only thing that makes you right," Buffett said at the annual meeting in 1991.

Buffett's corporate strategy often is, "hoping the phone rings." He wants bad news out quickly; good news will take care of itself. He wants red tape and meetings cut out in favor of by-the-seat-of-your-pants judgements. He wants action, not paperwork. He likes people who want to manage a business, not one another.

In the words of Ralph Waldo Emerson, "Common sense is genius dressed in its working clothes."

Buffett's emphasis on common sense could remind one of Mark Twain's approach to common sense: "I would rather go to bed with Lillian Russell stark naked than with Ulysses S. Grant in full military regalia."

MENTAL DISCIPLINE

You need mental discipline to stick to what you're about and not go down some dead-end path nor take chances where things aren't your game. Buffett's friend, Jack Byrne, once recalled a story about Buffett's attitude toward betting:

> The bet was the kind that rich golfing buddies like. Investment wizard Warren Buffett's $10 against $20,000 that he wouldn't score a hole-in-one over the three-day outing.
>
> Eight of us had gotten together to play Pebble Beach, and in a loose moment, after dinner and a couple bottles of wine, I offered the bet. It was meant as a fun thing, and the other six took me up on it. Everyone except Warren.
>
> Well, we heaped abuse on him and tried to cajole him—after all, it was only $10. But he said he had thought it over and decided it wasn't a good bet for him. He said if you let yourself be undisciplined on the small things, you'd probably be undisciplined on the large things, too. (*Chicago Tribune*, December 8, 1985)

It doesn't hurt to be gifted either. The same story quoted Byrne:

> He works at his trade awfully hard. And he has the most amazing memory I've ever encountered. Someone can bring up some obscure company, and

> what Warren knows about it will leave you slackjawed. He'll tell you the number of shares outstanding, the square footage of retailing space they have in Minneapolis.
>
> Let me tell you. I follow the insurance industry pretty closely and Warren still will bring up important facts from some annual report that I've missed completely.

Although a stratospheric IQ probably accounts largely for Buffett's success, so too does plain old hard work. Those who work with him in his office say he has a great ability to focus hard, to concentrate completely on the task at hand. "He focuses very hard on the task at hand and then he focuses very hard on the next task," says a Berkshire employee.

BE YOUR OWN REPORTER

Buffett's unique ability is to separate what's true from what merely seems true. The practical manifestation of Buffett's ability in the stock market is to buy a good out-of-favor business. Buffett wants to buy a great business—or, in his words, a "wonderful business," at a time when its price is temporarily depressed due to some unwarranted stigma, fear or misunderstanding about the company.

His purchases of American Express, GEICO, and Wells Fargo are examples. He bought American Express the first time when scandal surrounded that high-quality business and he bought Wells Fargo when it seemed its real estate loans might cripple the bank.

Being your own reporter means keeping up not only with the business you own, but also with competitors.

At the Berkshire Annual Meeting in 1993, talking about the number of annual reports he reads, Buffett said, "And we'd be interested not only in any business that we own or are thinking of owning, but we'll be interested in reading their competitors'. I get the Bic annual report. I get the Warner-Lambert annual report to read about Schick. I get the Pepsico annual report. I get the Cott Beverage report. Cott Beverage makes more of the generic colas than anybody—at least in this hemisphere. I want to know what competitors are doing and talking about, what results they are getting and what strategies seem logical to them."

EFFICIENT-MARKET THEORY

One notion that Buffett has shot holes through is the so-called "efficient-market" theory, which holds that every stock price is fairly priced because it already incorporates all known information about a company. The theory argues there's nothing to be gained by digging for new information.

Since market prices at any given moment reflect all knowledge, the prices in the stock tables are the right prices. There are no bargains. The efficient-market theory says it's useless to try to outperform the market. Further, all future prices are subject to new, random information.

Many times Buffett has said, "It has been helpful to me to have tens of thousands turned out of business schools taught that it didn't do any good to think."

Buffett often has joked that he wished more people would subscribe to the efficient-market theory so there would be fewer investors trying to figure out where the market has gone astray, where it does not reflect intrinsic value. It is in this murky arena that Buffett thrives, doing his lab work, capitalizing on fear and uncertainty while other investors are panicked into selling. That's how Buffett has become the richest person in the world. Buffett thinks the theory is absurd, that it's better to turn the theory on its head, believing that the market can be inefficient, subject to fear and greed, fads and herd behavior—in short—subject to temporary insanity.

Buffett does not maintain the market is always wrong. Indeed, it is often correct, he says. The trick is figuring when, on occasion, it's wildly off base.

"The man is a living refutation of the random walk theory," says *Newsday's* Allan Sloan.

Buffett wrote an article in *Barron's* February 23, 1985, outlining the investment results of a number of value investors who have consistently beaten the market. What one has to wonder about the efficient-market theory is how anything can be efficient when the emotions of fear and greed are dominant forces. Although that is not a mathematical refutation of the theory, there is still a sure way to refute it—just present the record of Buffett, who has consistently beaten the market over a lifetime.

And consider that the market dropped 23% on October 19, 1987. That was the day they were throwing rocks at the stock market. But did the underlying economic world change 23% that day?

PRICE VS. VALUE

Early on, Buffett's common sense led him to the simple premise that there is a difference between price and value.

"Price does not imply that you got a thing equal in value to what you paid," Buffett Wannabe George Morgan wrote in *Buffett and I Have Zero in Common: He Just Has More of Them Than I Do.* Morgan also recalls a story told by Joe Garagiola:

"Yogi Berra once told his friend Whitey Ford that he had just purchased a valuable house. Ford replied that he was familiar with the house and didn't think it was very valuable. Yogi responded with, 'You may not think it's valuable now but you will after I tell you the price.'"

In a different way, Buffett seeks to buy a valuable house for a bargain price.

People who have talked with those who have traded with Buffett describe him as very tough on pricing. "You know people who want to argue about a 32nd on a trade, well, he'll try to get the last 100th out of it," is one description of Buffett's focus on price.

However, Buffett does not like to haggle. Buying or selling, he has one price, then it's take it or leave it.

INFLATION

Another piece of Buffett's approach is to keep in mind what havoc inflation can wreak. An investment that can't beat inflation is useless. Only gains in purchasing power count.

Buffett says, "If you forego the purchase of ten hamburgers and place those dollars in the bank for two years, you will receive interest which after tax will buy two hamburgers. Then at the end of the two years, you will receive back an amount equal to the number of dollars in the original deposit but which will only purchase eight hamburgers. You will feel richer but you won't eat richer."

The hamburger parable is an example of Buffett's genius. You do not have to read a textbook or some economist's bloated explanation about inflation. It's all there, simply put, in one paragraph.

And, said Buffett at the Berkshire annual meeting in 1986, about valuations: "I always crank through something for inflation."

Something else Buffett understands is the beauty of compounding. Buffett says, "$1,000 invested at 10% for 45 years grows to $72,800. At 20% the same $1,000 becomes $3,657,262. This difference strikes me as a significant difference that might conceivably arouse one's curiosity."

George Morgan's example of compounding is this: "You start a company by issuing 100 shares at $10/share. The company is now worth $1,000 (equity). During your first year, you make a $200 profit, which is equal to 20% of your company (equity). You put your profit back into the company and it is now worth $1,200 (in equity). Next year, you experience an additional 20% return on equity which is now $240. This increases your total equity to $1,420. Do this for 79 years and the original investment (equity of the shareholders) of $1,000 is now worth (equity) $1,800,000,000."

Berkshire, since 1965, has averaged a 23.6% annual return on equity. That is how Buffett has pulled off his monumental achievements.

GOOD VS. BAD BUSINESSES: COMPANY A VS. COMPANY E

In addition to a few nuggets of wisdom, Buffett really does know almost all the people, the numbers, the facts, and even the minutiae involved in an investment decision. He makes a dogged, detailed study of things. But the art of investing centers on the search for value—not gimmicks, not hunches. For all his intellectual powers, Buffett long has been boiling things down to investing in good businesses at reasonable prices, rather than bad or so-so businesses even at a bargain-basement price.

No smokestack industries please. There's too much chance for high costs and obsolescence.

On occasion, Buffett has talked about good and bad businesses and has described their characteristics, often talking about a hypothetical "Company A and Company E."

Companies A&E? "That's Agony and Ecstasy," Buffett once told Kiewit Construction's Mike Faust, the assistant to Walter Scott, head of the huge privately held conglomerate. Buffett has owned companies in both categories.

But Buffett has had a lot more company E's than Company A's and now runs one of the greatest Company E's on Earth.

In some ways Buffett adds value to a business when he buys it because then it's not just a business. It's a Berkshire business. Says Kahn Brothers' Irving Kahn, "His skill is finding private companies that are revalued when public."

So many times Buffett has bought an unrecognized business and given it a halo with just a one-paragraph mention in the Berkshire annual report.

If great achievement comes from both natural talent and the environment of one's upbringing, then Buffett has it all. No one disputes Buffett's natural mental gifts, his recall for facts and numbers, his energy.

But he also had advantages: growing up in a family engaged in the commercial and political affairs of its community, and growing up in a place best known for its economic pursuits—mainly meat packing and grain handling in the early decades of this century and now a telemarketing and hotel reservations center among other things such as an insurance center. It all provided the right locale for a passionate businessman like Buffett.

Omaha folks are straightforward, open, friendly and businesslike, just as Buffett himself is open and very quick to respond to matters as they arise. He takes his calls. He responds as quickly as possible to mail. He does not leave people hanging for answers. There is no show, pretense or dissembling. Old-fashioned values prevail. Honesty and decency are assumed.

With Berkshire's financial clout, Buffett could easily pull a lot of tricks—threaten takeovers, corner markets or create market turmoil to his advantage. But there's none of that. Buffett does not go where he's not wanted.

He once took a relatively small stake in a company and expressed interest about a larger stake to the company. A top executive told Buffett the company wanted to buy back its stock and asked him not to buy any more shares. Buffett stopped on the spot and did not buy another share.

Had Buffett wanted he could have bought the whole company; instead he honored the wishes of management.

LOOK AROUND YOU; WORK ON WHAT'S ON YOUR DESK

Omaha provides a stable, comfortable home for Buffett where he can operate without a lot of distractions. "Successful analysis, like successful investment, requires a fairly rational atmosphere to work in and at least some stability of values to work with," Ben Graham wrote in *Security Analysis*.

Buffett took on the qualities of his community—hard work, honesty, a pioneer's independent streak and most of all common sense—and mixed them thoroughly with his natural gifts to become both an original personality and the world's best investor.

Buffett appreciates Omaha, which has produced down-home folks, and famous folks (such as Ted Sorensen, Dick Cavett, Dorothy McGuire, Fred Astaire, Montgomery Clift, Henry Fonda, Malcolm X, Gerald Ford, Bob Gibson, Gale Sayers, Paula Zahn, Nick Nolte and Marlon Brando).

Buffett understands that Omaha has contributed to his success: "I can be anywhere in three hours—New York or Los Angeles...This is a good place to bring up children and a good place to live. You can think here. You can think better about the market; you don't hear so many stories, and you can just sit and look at the stock on the desk in front of you. You can think about a lot of things." *(Supermoney,* Adam Smith, p. 182)

Not everyone is clear that Buffett is from Omaha. Here's a quote from a wire service story: "Buffett's office in Kansas City said he could not be reached to elaborate."

GOOD MANAGEMENT

Buffett has earned success through a love of what he's doing, an ability to keep on learning as well as through extraordinary day-to-day persistence. But for all his ability, he knows what he cannot do. "I don't run the businesses. Can you imagine me doing what [Borsheim's former president] Ike Friedman does?" he has said.

Buffett takes a common sense approach about letting others run the businesses, but he does assert himself in some ways. "I set the price on See's Candy every year. I set the circulation prices at the *Buffalo News*. There are certain things, with certain managers who want me to do it, in which it's better to have it centralized.

"Because a person who is too close to a business probably would not tend to price as aggressively as they can," he told Columbia business students, October 27, 1993.

VALUE INVESTOR, PART CONTRARIAN, DEAL-MAKER

Buffett is part value investor, part contrarian and part deal-maker.

He's shown it's better to buy a great business when the fickle Mr. Market values it unreasonably low.

It is Buffett's genius that leads him to simple solutions. In *The Money Masters*, pp. 40-41, John Train relates the following story: "Buffett once met a leading executive of a capital-intensive business giant at a time when the company was selling in the market for one-quarter of its replacement value.

Buffett asked the executive, "Why don't you buy back your own stock? If you like to build new facilities at one cent on the dollar, why not buy the ones you know best and were responsible for creating at twenty-five cents on the dollar?"

Executive: "We should."

Buffett: "Well?"

Executive: "That's not what we're here to do."

It is through rationality that Buffett, sometimes at the expense of less rational people, has made investing his art form. There is common sense, even genius, but there is an overriding ingredient: a love of what you're doing.

"Buffett loves the investing process in the same way an artist loves his creation," says Omaha stockbroker George Morgan.

Buffett is intensely passionate about what he does. One version of his supposed employment application form other than "What's your IQ?" is "Are you a fanatic?"

Genius, love of what you do, and common sense. Stir well and the result can be huge success.

KISS—"Keep It Simple, Stupid" is another Buffett tenet. His passion is for analysis and problem-solving. His aim is to simplify.

NO STOCK SPLITS

It makes no sense to pay dividends automatically or split a stock. Berkshire did have a back-door split in 1996 (See Chapter 124). Buffett has said there's no sense splitting because transactional costs would be greater and it would draw more speculation to the stock. Besides, he says, splitting the stock is like asking for a pizza to be sliced into five pieces because you can't possibly eat seven.

"I disagree with him about not splitting the stock," says Dr. Wallace Gaye of Durham, New Hampshire. "One, I don't think the transactional costs are less. And I don't think there would be speculation if he split it 10 to 1... but that would make it easier to deal with. My dad left $5,000 for each kid and with that I can't buy a share of Berkshire for them," Dr. Gaye said.

Michael Assael thinks transactional costs are indeed less because you can buy up to 100 shares of Berkshire at a discount brokerage firm for under $50, but Assael thinks there may come a point when the stock becomes too unwieldy.

"Hopefully, if Berkshire's price passes Pluto and the shares look as though they are becoming irretrievably illiquid, Buffett will reconsider. But not to worry—there are always mutual funds that could buy shares at $100,000 apiece," Assael said.

"And perhaps someone will start a fund to invest solely in Berkshire for a pure play on Buffett. Just think of it. You could then invest in Buffett for as little as say, five hundred bucks." Indeed there are new investment vehicles with Berkshire and Berkshire related stocks in them.

For now and perhaps for always, splitting a stock is another thing that to Buffett makes no particular sense, at least for Berkshire. To him splitting a stock is only a cosmetic exercise. It involves paperwork and creates unnecessary stimulation and a false sense of progress.

What is the difference whether you have one share of Berkshire at price x or 100 shares at 100th of x? Stock splits are something stockbrokers often want to increase trading, or speculative investors want so they can feel richer.

Each year Buffett is asked about the possibility of splitting Berkshire's stock. At the annual meeting in 1990, one shareholder asked if he could see splitting the stock in the foreseeable future.

"I don't see a stock split in the unforeseeable future," Buffett replied.

"I have a stockholder friend of mine who is 60. I just sent him a telegram on his birthday that said, "May you live until Berkshire Hathaway splits," Buffett remarked at the Berkshire annual meeting in 1987.

With the issue of the Class B shares in 1996, Buffett may have to revise his salutation to: "May you live until Berkshire's Class Z is issued."

NO DIVIDENDS

Buffett doesn't believe in paying dividends. His misgivings about them arise because they are taxed, doubly taxed. Corporations are taxed on the money they earn and investors pay taxes on dividends corporations pay. So there is a savings if you can avoid that double taxation.

Berkshire did pay a 10-cent dividend in 1967. Buffett said later, "I must have been in the bathroom at the time." *(Forbes,* October 21, 1991) Berkshire has not paid a dividend since.

ARBITRAGE

Perhaps one of the least understood areas of Buffett's success is his use of arbitrage—again an area that calls for common sense, judgment, sizing up the odds on discrepancies in the marketplace.

Arbitrage, a French term for profiting risklessly, involves trading on the differences in prices in different markets. Arbitrage applies to a range of pursuits, but these days often to stock traders' betting on the outcome of a merger deal or reorganization plan. Buffett enters the field of arbitrage only after a deal has been announced. He does not place bets on rumors.

After the takeover announcement when the stock of the target firm often soars to just below the takeover price, Buffett might step in, buy the stock and hold it until it reaches its full takeover price achieved when the deal finally goes through. This technique enables him to make a tidy percentage in a relatively short time.

The deal must go through or the investor/arbitrageur can be axed, if he isn't nimble.

Since Buffett is a good judge of the probabilities of these deals occurring, he has constantly brought Berkshire a little extra return. He describes one of his earliest arbitrage moves, which was not a takeover arbitrage, in the 1988 Annual Report.

> I participated in one of these when I was 24 and working in New York at Graham-Newman Corp. Rockwood & Co., a Brooklyn-based chocolate products company of limited profitability, had adopted a LIFO inventory valuation in 1941 when cocoa was selling for five cents per pound. In 1954 a temporary shortage of cocoa caused the price to soar to over 60 cents. Consequently Rockwood wished to unload its valuable inventory—quickly, before the price dropped. But if the cocoa had simply been sold off, the company would have owed close to a 50% tax on the proceeds.
>
> The 1954 Tax Code came to the rescue. It contained an arcane provision that eliminated the tax otherwise due on LIFO profits if inventory was distributed to shareholders as part of a plan reducing the scope of a corporation's business. Rockwood decided to terminate one of its businesses, the sale of cocoa butter, and said 13 million pounds of its cocoa bean inventory was attributable to the activity. Accordingly, the company offered to purchase its stock in exchange for the cocoa beans it no longer needed, paying 80 pounds of beans for each share.
>
> For several weeks I busily bought shares, sold beans, and made periodic stops at Schroeder Trust to exchange stock certificates for warehouse receipts. The profits were good and my only expense was subway tokens.

Moral: *Know the tax code.*

In 1981 Berkshire bought the stock of Arcata, a forest products and printing firm, at about $33.50 a share. Arcata was the subject of a buyout by KKR. In 1978 the U.S. Government had seized more than 10,000 acres of redwood timber to expand the Redwood National Park. The government was to pay Arcata for the trees, but the question was how much.

Buffett, who has said he "couldn't tell an elm from an oak tree coolly evaluated the claim at somewhere between zero and a whole lot." The deal with KKR fell apart, but Arcata sold out in a later offer. Berkshire made about 15% on its investment, selling at about $37.50 a share, but in 1988 received an additional $19.3 million, or $29.48 a share, when the government agreed to pay a total of $519 million for the timberland. *(The Warren Buffett Way*, Robert Hagstrom, pp. 166-167)

At the end of 1993 Berkshire held $146 million worth of Paramount Communications stock. If Berkshire held through the Viacom takeover of Paramount, Berkshire apparently made money through arbitrage. Buffett is at ease with whatever makes money, be it arbitrage, dealmaking, value investing or understanding the importance of brand names.

After money manager George Michaelis joined Source Capital in 1971, Buffett and Munger through Berkshire bought 20% of the closed-end investment fund. (*Forbes*, August 21, 1989)

Michaelis, much influenced by Buffett and Munger, told *Forbes*, "I think of myself as an investor in really great businesses, whereas Ben Graham was really a purchaser of cheap assets. In that sense Buffett has really evolved away from pure Ben Graham."

Forbes said, "The Buffett-Michaelis version goes beyond tangible assets to count such intangibles as brand names or the kind of "franchise" that makes a newspaper or television station valuable. Such businesses tend to have a high return on book equity. Why? Because they are earning not only on their tangible assets but on the intangible ones as well." Michaelis died in a biking accident in 1996.

Buffett is always looking for value, and value may come in many forms; the Coca-Cola and McDonald's brand names, for example.

And Buffett admits that growth is not separate from value, but is instead an important component of value investing.

Buffett focuses not only on price but value, the mission of any investor. Business folks in Omaha talk about business and value, not price and certainly not about wild bets, program trading and options.

NO DERIVATIVES, PLEASE

Buffett has let his horse sense tell him some other things; one result is he doesn't care much for program trading.

He has often told the story that if a group of people were stranded on an island you might well set a certain number to farming, a certain number to building shelter, even some to figuring out how to get off the island, but you would not select several of the people to trade options based on the output of the other workers. Whenever he tells that story, if Munger is around, Munger will say of program traders, "I like them less than you do."

There are no securities on Gilligan's Island either, but at least no options trading is available on Berkshire's stock.

Buffett deplores options, program and derivations trading and anything else that brings a casino-like atmosphere to the marketplace, especially where a little leverage can control a lot of assets.

In a March 1982, letter to John Dingell, chairman of the House subcommittee on Oversight and Investigations that was considering whether to allow the Chicago Mercantile Exchange to trade futures, Buffett wrote:

> We do not need more people gambling on the nonessential instruments identified with the stock market in the country, nor brokers who encourage them to do so. What we need are investors and advisers who look at the long-term prospects for an enterprise and invest accordingly. We need the intelligent commitment of investment capital, not leveraged market wagers. The propensity to operate in the intelligent, pro-social sector of capital markets is deterred, not enhanced, by an active and exciting casino operating in somewhat the same arena, utilizing somewhat similar language and serviced by the same work force.

Buffett's investments are straightforward—no hot tips, no betting on the next quarter's earnings report. Using his meticulous research and common sense, he comes to decisions to buy common stocks themselves, be they 20th Century Industries, the insurer in California, or National Service Industries, the lighting equipment company in Georgia, or negotiated purchases of pieces of businesses, such as Bowery Savings of New York, which Berkshire had some ownership in from 1985 to 1987.

A TIME TO HOLD, A TIME TO FOLD

Back when Buffett decided to buy shares of The Washington Post Co., he got in touch with Omaha broker Cliff Hayes, now with Wallace Weitz & Co. in Omaha.

"He asked me to buy Post shares," recalls Hayes. Hayes said when he raised a question of what price to try to buy them for and how much to buy, Buffett told him, "You don't understand, I just want to buy."

"It was just totally expected for me to use my best professional judgment in making the purchases. We'd buy a third or a half of the day's volume, then step back."

Hayes said it was understood that the buyer should not rile the market with big orders or alert the market to a big purchaser in the wings.

Offering his version of a verse from *Ecclesiastes*, Buffett told Hayes, "There is a time to bid for them and there is a time to take them."

Does common sense in the stock market always pan out right away? No. "We started buying The Post at $20 (at 1973 prices) and we were buying it at $12 when we were done," Hayes said.

Even though Buffett was a big purchaser, Post's share price steadily declined. All the better for Buffett in the long run.

"He does a lot of his trading now at Salomon—but he often asked me to accumulate small positions sometimes over a two- or three-year period," Hayes said.

"I did the GEICO buying...We bought baskets of it when it was an almost busted company," Hayes said. Again, Hayes bought a healthy percentage of the day's volume but not so much that the market could detect a big buyer.

As for the question of secrecy of the trades, it was understood things were to be kept quiet, says Hayes.

"He didn't say keep it a secret. It was just implied," Hayes said, adding it was also understood everything was to be on the up and up. "We never traded ahead of him."

Hayes said if there was something amiss, it was best to tell Buffett immediately and not let any problem fester. Once, Hayes said, word leaked about what Buffett was buying, and Hayes said he told Buffett about it right away. He wound up trading for Buffett for years.

But other brokers who did not report problems quickly to Buffett were not used again.

"He's dropped brokers," Hayes said.

Hayes emphasized that it would be very rare for a broker to leak a trade, but leaks in the brokerage community often can happen in the back office, through the stock transfer agent—or anyone else along the way who may have access to the trade or stock delivery process.

Buffett has a rule against trading while he's in the frenetic city of New York. He makes his trades in the peace and calm of Omaha. *(Fortune,* November 27, 1995)

BUSINESS FRANCHISE

Buffett discovered early the importance of a business franchise.

A franchise is a business that for one reason or another has a dominance in the marketplace—a leading business such as Pinkerton's in a difficult-to-breach market. It can be a monopoly newspaper such as the *Washington Post* dominating its market, or a strong brand name such as General Foods—a stock Buffett held for years before selling for a big profit when Philip Morris bought it in the mid-1980s—or the ultimate brand name, Coca-Cola—it is always a business with a superior competitive edge. Such a business is so formidable that it is difficult for those wishing to compete with it even to get into the business.

Something Buffett has tried to do, especially in recent years, is to seek out businesses with extremely strong franchises, impregnable but unrecognized franchises.

Buffett saw an archetype of this idea in the monopoly newspaper. He explains:

> The test of a franchise is what a smart guy with a lot of money could do to it if he tried. If you gave me a billion dollars, and you gave me first draft pick of fifty business managers throughout the United States, I could absolutely cream both the business world and the journalistic world. If you said, "Go take *The Wall Street Journal* apart," I would hand you back the billion dollars. Reluctantly, but I would hand it back to you.
>
> Now, incidentally, if you gave me a similar amount of money and you told me to make a dent in the profitability or change the market position of the Omaha National Bank [forerunner of FirsTier Bank] or the leading department store in Omaha, I could give them a hard time. I might not do much for you in the process, but I could cause them a lot of trouble. The real test of a business is how much damage a competitor can do, even if he is stupid about returns.
>
> There are some businesses that have very large moats around them and they have crocodiles and sharks and piranhas swimming around in them. Those are the kind of businesses you want. You want some business that, going back to my day, Johnny Weissmuller in a suit of armor could not make it across the moat. There are businesses like that. Sometimes they're regulated. If I had the only water company in Omaha, I'd do fine if I didn't have a regulator. What you're looking for is an unregulated water company. The trick is to find the ones that haven't been identified by someone else. What you want is a disguised television station or newspaper." (*Investing in Equity Markets*, Summer, 1985)

The reason one would like a monopoly television station or newspaper: most other businesses have to go through that business to advertise.

That amounts to what Buffett calls a royalty on the other guy's gross sales—a payment that almost every business in town must pay. If you have the only newspaper, television or radio station in town, you have to get a good percentage of the advertising business.

This was a major reason, one not recognized by many in the 1970s, that Buffett was buying such stocks as The Washington Post Co., Time Inc., Knight-Ridder Newspapers, Media General, Multimedia, and Affiliated Publications, which owns the *Boston Globe*.

Other huge business franchises Buffett recognized are the large advertising firms. It is the large ad agencies with global interests that the giant global firms wanting to advertise must come to.

An IBM, Coca-Cola or General Motors is going to insist on a worldwide ad campaign, and it doesn't want to fool around with 100 different ad agencies in 100 different countries. Instead it picks an Ogilvy & Mather or an Interpublic Group, two firms Buffett made large profits in before selling in 1985, when he thought their merits were fully recognized.

Another conclusion Buffett reached: there are a number of poor businesses and it's best to steer clear of them.

Buffett has stayed away from big, heavy industries requiring constant new investments, businesses with rising competition, rising labor costs and rising need for more capital. [except USAir]

Also, Buffett tries to examine the opposite of a proposition—there are some good businesses with little need for new capital, businesses that have little competition and hence ultimately throw off new cash.

BUYING PART OF A BUSINESS

Overall, what Buffett sees in the stock market is a way to pick up assets that produce a steady stream of cash. Buffett buys at a good price because he buys only a part—not the whole company, for which he would have to pay a premium.

When a whole company is put on the block, everyone looks at the deal in the open, and it usually sells at full value to the highest bidder.

It is different in the stock market: you can buy shares, portions of the business, often quietly with little competition.

Better yet, you can operate at the time of your picking.

You do not have to join what Buffett terms the "Swing, you bum," syndrome. You can wait for the perfect pitch two inches above the navel, as Buffett says.

"Investing is the greatest business in the world because you never have to swing. You stand at the plate; the pitcher throws you General

Motors at 47! U.S. Steel at 39! And nobody calls a strike at you. There's no penalty except opportunity. All day you wait for the pitch you like; then when the fielders are asleep, you step up and hit it." ("Look at All Those Beautiful Scantily Clad Girls Out There," *Forbes*, November 1, 1974)

That's the appeal of the stock market to Buffett.

Explains Buffett, "When I buy a stock, I think of it in terms of buying a whole company, just as if I were buying the store down the street. If I were buying the store, I'd want to know all about it. I mean I look at what Walt Disney was worth on the stock market in the first half of 1966. The price per share was $53 and this didn't look especially cheap, but on that basis you could buy the whole company for $80 million when *Snow White, Swiss Family Robinson*, and some other cartoons, which had been written off the books, were worth that much. And then you had Disneyland and Walt Disney, a genius, as a partner."

Buffett's huge network of knowledgeable and influential friends also has been a help along the way. Buffett has been an original thinker, but it cannot have hurt to discuss prospects for a television station with Tom Murphy, chat about a common investment with Laurence Tisch, or talk with Jack Byrne about insurance.

"His network of friends has been very important," says broker Hayes.

ABILITY TO READ PEOPLE

For all Buffett's understanding of the interworkings of business, his greater understanding may be of human nature. He reads people quickly and accurately and his judgment of their abilities, motives and ambitions is almost always on the money. He can see the first class person in a flash, and the fraudulent person just as fast.

Exhibit A: He was one of the few people to detect that Larry King of Omaha was not all the community thought he was.

King, once manager-treasurer of the Franklin Community Federal Credit Union, ultimately pleaded guilty and is serving a 15-year prison sentence for crimes connected with Franklin's 1988 collapse and the disappearance of $39 million in deposits.

GQ magazine looked at King in its December 1991 issue: "Very few people in Omaha closed their doors to Larry King. One who did was Warren Buffett...In 1978, King asked Susan Buffett if she would be willing to host his and Alice's (King's wife's) tenth anniversary party at her house, an act of chutzpah even by King's standards. Susan Buffett said yes, but her husband said no. 'I knew that King was a phony,' says Buffett, 'and I think that he knew I knew. I'm probably the only person in Omaha he never asked for money.' How did Buffett know? 'It was like he had a big sign on his head that said 'PHONY, PHONY, PHONY.'"

STICK TO YOUR "CIRCLE OF COMPETENCE"

In the world of business, Buffett sticks to what he can do. He does not try to do what he cannot. He knows he understands media, financial and consumer product companies and has concentrated his assets with them over the years.

AVOID TECHNOLOGY AND DRUG STOCKS

Once a shareholder asked Buffett what he thought of pharmaceutical stocks; he said that was not the sort of thing Berkshire had expertise in. (Of course that was before he bought some Bristol-Myers Squibb stock in 1993.)

Buffett added, "That does not mean there are not good ones."

What Buffett was driving at is that while pharmaceutical firms were beyond Berkshire's expertise, no doubt Merck is a superb firm. But Buffett cannot predict what drug is going to be a winner and which one will wind up drawing lawsuits.

In a way they are like his forbidden category of technology stocks, a group whose performance Buffett says he has no way of predicting, because he knows little about present technology and even less about future competitors' technologies.

Buffett would say there are others who can make those determinations better than he about technology or pharmacology—but then he is not sure their determinations are so hot either. It's too tricky an area for a sensible investor trying to cut risks and guesswork.

DEBT IS POISONOUS, CASH IS GOOD

Buffett's sparing use of debt has been a hallmark of his from the start. When much of the rest of the investing world, burdened by debt, encounters some new crisis forcing a panic, Buffett is usually calmly standing there with little debt and a loaded gun of cash ready to "bag rare and fast-moving elephants."

Little debt and lots of cash give him an ability to respond quickly when the right investment comes in his sights. He does not have to call bankers to get a loan. After dogged investigation in the 1950s, Buffett bought Western Insurance at $16 when it was earning $16 a share, and National American Insurance at one times earnings. (*Forbes*, November 1, 1969)

> Then in 1962 he found Gurdon Wattles American Manufacturing selling at a 40% discount from net worth. 'If you went to Wattles of American Manufacturing or Howard Ahmason of National American Insurance and asked them to be partners, you could never get in at 1 times earnings,' Buffett told *Forbes*.
>
> When the reading puts him on to something, he'll do some informal field research. In one case in 1965 Buffett says he spent the better part of a month counting tank cars in a Kansas City railroad yard. He was not, however, considering buying railroad stocks. He was interested in the old Studebaker Corp., because of STP, a highly successful gasoline additive. The company wouldn't tell him how the product was doing. But he knew that the basic ingredient came from Union Carbide, and he knew how much it took to produce one can of STP. Hence the tank-car counting. When shipments rose, he bought Studebaker stock, which subsequently went from 18 to 30.

On occasion Buffett has asked Omaha cab drivers how their business is doing. He's always asking, reading, looking for investment possibilities.

DON'T OVER-DIVERSIFY

For all his conservative, sure-footed ways, Buffett is also capable of remarkable boldness when he sees an opening. It's not that he's throwing caution to the wind—his intensive research has ferreted out an investment with excellent prospects.

No investment is a sure thing—including Berkshire—and in the early days when he committed so heavy a percentage of his worth to American Express and The Washington Post Co., he had to be right.

BE BOLD AND BE ORIGINAL

Later in life, no matter how wealthy he was, it was a bold move to take $1 billion and buy stock, even if it was Coca-Cola at a down time.

In addition to being bold, he is original. What else is it when, at a time the industry is spooked about writing officers' and directors' liability insurance due to the lack of any statistical history and the unpredictability of court awards, Buffett takes out an ad in an industry publication saying that Berkshire will write the insurance?

"To those paying or who are willing to pay over one million dollars for this O&D coverage—you tell us the amount of liability coverage you want and what premium you are willing to pay—and we will tell you if we wish to write the coverage."

Perhaps because he's in the business, Buffett often comes up with ideas on how to sell insurance. In the fall of 1990 when the S&L crisis and banking problems were front-page news, he came up with a suggestion to help the federal government with depositor's insurance—have private insurers write a piece of the action.

"What is needed is a system that combines the ability of private insurers to evaluate risk with the ability of government to bear it. Co-insurance arrangements, varying by size of bank, would appear to be the way to go," he wrote in a piece that ran in the *Washington Post*.

Later Buffett said Berkshire would be happy to write that kind of insurance.

Over the years he has made investments in scores of companies ranging from insurance firms to R.J. Reynolds and Philip Morris to National Presto, the pressure cooker and appliances firm, to National Service Industries.

Handy and Harman has been one and so has 20th Century Industries, as have General Foods, Affiliated Publications, Interpublic Group, Time Inc., City National Corp., the bank holding company in Beverly Hills, Melville Corp., and the retailer and pet food maker Ralston Purina.

Has Buffett made a few mistakes? Yes. There was too much devotion to buying really cheap companies in the early days. Remember Berkshire's textile operation failed.

And he told *Forbes*, October 18, 1993, he left $2 billion on the table by selling Fannie Mae too early. He bought too little and sold too early. "It was easy to analyze. It was within my circle of competence. And for one reason or another, I quit. I wish I could give you a good answer."

Also, he said he sold Affiliated Publications stock because he didn't fully understand the value of Affiliated's big position in McCaw Cellular. "I missed the play in cellular because cellular is outside of my circle of competence."

Still, Buffett has great trust in his thinking. People often write him with their investment ideas and he has replied, "With my idea and your money, we'll do OK."

For all Buffett's monumental achievements, he still was not known to the ordinary citizen and not universally known even in the business world until he stepped in to resolve the scandal at Salomon.

On October 12, 1986, Alan Gersten, an *Omaha World-Herald* reporter, called a Burroughs executive to inform him that Buffett owned

9.9% of the company's stock, an arbitrage position Buffett soon sold. The spokesman asked, "Who's Warren Buffett?" People were still asking that question when Buffett became interim chairman of Salomon.

Because of Buffett's wisdom, his counsel (and money) are often sought. When Salomon was considering taking part in the bidding for RJR Nabisco, Salomon Chairman Gutfreund called Buffett for advice.

"I'll tell you why I like the economies of the cigarette business," he said. "It costs a penny to make. Sell it for a dollar. It's habit-forming. And there's fantastic brand loyalty."

Gutfreund asked if Buffett wanted to invest in the deal with Salomon. Not this time, Buffett said, because of all the Death Merchant aspects of cigarettes. "I'm wealthy enough that I don't need to own a tobacco company."

Says one Berkshire shareholder who is a doctor, "I appreciate that." Hence, Coke.

Salomon made its own bid, but the Kohlberg, Kravis & Roberts firm eventually won the tobacco giant.

Buffett has many views on raising children and the lessons they should learn. Probably his most famous view, regarded as eccentric by many parents, is that children should not inherit wealth. He believes children should be left enough to cope with necessities, but not really large amounts.

Buffett has said he refuses to leave his children "a lifetime of food stamps just because they came out of the right womb." (Richard J. Kirkland, "Should You Leave It All to the Children?" *Fortune*, September 29, 1986.) Susan recalls a time when she had a car wreck and had to tell her father.

"He was reading *Moody's*. I told him I had had a wreck and he said, 'Anybody hurt?' I told him no. He later came in and said the other guy's always the jerk. What he meant was drive defensively."

Buffett taught her other lessons along the way. One day when young Susan approached her father for a loan, he suggested she go to the bank.

And Howard Buffett has said his father is fixated on finances: "If he drives out to my place (when Howard had a farm) and sees I have $30,000 invested in a tractor, it drives him nuts, especially when it's financed at 15%. But I'd have a hard time getting through life without a John Deere tractor sitting in the garage." *(Register,* February 1984)

Buffett can concentrate so hard on something that he can also be absent-minded on occasion, forgetting momentarily to take a baseball cap off during the National Anthem.

Susan recalls a time when her mother was sick and she asked Buffett to go to the kitchen and bring her a pan. He did and returned with a colander. His mechanical inabilities and his children's stories about his tightfisted ways are representative of the height of criticism of Buffett before Salomon.

Occasionally, behind his back, people refer to him as Mr. Rogers or Jimmy Stewart, a jealous knock at his childlike, country-simple honesty. Although occasionally absent-minded in his personal life, in business he is super alert, concentrating with all his powers.

Buffett does not buy the idea held by many corporations that the chief executive should make the decisions about philanthropy. So in 1981 Buffett announced that each Berkshire shareholder could designate $2—raised as the years went by to $13 a share in 1995—of corporate donations for each share owned to the charity of the shareholder's choice. Back in 1981, Buffett estimated that if every stockholder contributed, the roughly $2 million in contributions would reduce Berkshire's net by about $1 million and its percentage gain in annual net worth by about one-fourth of 1%. (*Forbes*, November 20, 1981)

Charitable contributions in 1995 amounted to $13 million, which went to 3,600 charities.

Here's Berkshire's unusual charity policy: "Each Berkshire shareholder—on a basis proportional to the number of shares of Berkshire that he owns—will be able to designate recipients of charitable contributions by our company. You'll name the charity: Berkshire will write the check."

Buffett has given most of his donations to the Buffett Foundation.

Buffett, the capital allocator, has said that in examining potential purchases, the area he has probably done most of his thinking about, he has three criteria. First, the business should have good economic characteristics; second it must have an able, trustworthy management and finally it must be a business that is interesting to him.

Sounds simple, easy, sensible, right? Well, that's the whole point.

BUY BACK STOCK

Buffett has often been asked about the possibility of Berkshire buying back its stock. Buffett says he has no problem with buying it back.

But rather than just willy-nilly buying back stock, he takes the commonsense approach. Clearly, the stock would have to be at a good price, and if Berkshire were selling at a cheap price, it's quite likely that would be at a time when something else is selling even more cheaply.

"We'd go wherever we'd get the most for our money," he said at the annual meeting in 1991.

ABOVE ALL, AVOID DRAGONS

Buffett often has said he prefers avoiding dragons to fighting them, and he once repeated that theme, praising his friend, Jim Burke, the former Johnson & Johnson chairman.

"I would say Jim Burke is a national asset...There are all kinds of people who have 500 horsepower motors who only get 100 horsepower of output. But Jim has a motor with horsepower equal to anyone else's, and the efficiency is 100%...

"He likes to work on problems; I try to avoid problems." (*USA Today*, February 16, 1993)

Once Buffett was asked just what he does, how he spends his day.

"Well, first of all, I tap dance into work. And then I sit down and I read. Then I talk on the phone for seven or eight hours. And then I take home more to read. Then I talk on the phone in the evening...We read a lot. We have a general sense of what we're after. We're looking for 7-footers. That's about all there is to it," says Buffett of his search for business superstars.

Buffett's looking for 7-footers to make slam-dunks.

BE DEAD RIGHT ABOUT THE BIG DECISIONS

Buffett has said many times that every investor ought to have a lifetime decision card with just "20 punches." Buffett says his success is due to being right on a few big decisions.

Buffett has made a number of small mistakes and might have just an above average record were it not for the monumental decisions to buy big stock stakes at the right time in American Express, The Washington Post Co., GEICO and Coca-Cola.

He looks for haystacks and not needles in a haystack, as he said at the annual meeting in 1994.

"What I try to do is come up with a big idea every year or so."

FINAL NOTE: WHEN YOUR SHIP COMES IN, DON'T BE AT THE AIRPORT

66

The Press Clippings "investment genius... fallen angel... science fiction... God... international icon"

Overall the press coverage of Buffett has been laudatory and generally—but not always—accurate.

Lately a few writers enamored with spotting some flaw in Buffett's character speculate that he hobnobs with celebrities, owns a few expensive suits, and has stayed in an expensive hotel.

For the first couple of decades of his career there was little press coverage of Buffett. People who knew him were aware of his brilliance, but he operated in such a publicity-shy style, or at least a style of choosing his publicity, that the press was late with the story.

Buffett rarely gives interviews, and when he buys or sells his stocks or suits he doesn't yell it out from Kiewit Plaza.

In the 1960s and 1970s, the *Omaha World-Herald* and the *Wall Street Journal* ran stories about Buffett as an investment wunderkind. The first major story was by Robert Dorr in the *Omaha World-Herald*, May 29, 1966.

"I was the business reporter...I had heard stories about how well he was doing. There were rumors in Omaha. I decided to do a story and approached him and he said he didn't want it done...He was reluctant," recalled Dorr. "He said he didn't know how to deal with the press and that it was going to be hard to write an accurate story about what he was doing."

When Dorr said he was going ahead with the story, with or without Buffett's help, Buffett read the story and helped with facts. Dorr got in to see Buffett about the story, several years after Buffett had moved his partnership operations to Kiewit Plaza. "He made a few corrections," said Dorr, still a newsman at the *Omaha World-Herald*. "I believe I was the first person to write a story about him."

Adam Smith in *Supermoney* (1972) wrote a highly favorable chapter about Buffett's investment abilities. And Jonathan Laing wrote a long piece for the *Wall Street Journal*, March 31, 1977.

Buffett's reputation surged in the 1980s as authors Adam Smith and John Train described his endeavors.

More recently some reporters have taken the tack that Buffett is overly famous. A number of press accounts have begun to pick at him—okay, he's an investment genius, but there are some flaws.

One of the first critical pieces (of Berkshire's worth, not Buffett) was a *Barron's* story that suggested Berkshire's stock price was way overvalued. Berkshire shareholders naturally thought the story was off base. (See "Worth" chapter.)

Then with the Salomon scandal, the press became aware of Buffett and everyone wrote stories, with some taking the view that Buffett had little experience in running businesses. An odd thing to say about a fellow who founded his own business, runs Berkshire, ran Berkshire's insurance business for years and has tinkered for years with businesses such as The Washington Post Co. and *Buffalo News*. Further, he speaks constantly with Berkshire's managers.

Most press coverage was accurate. *Institutional Investor* (owned by Cap Cities) had a balanced and detailed article on Salomon (September 1991), as did Bernice Kanner in a cover story about Salomon for *New York* magazine. (December 9, 1991)

Other articles (e.g., *Business Week*, February 17, 1992) said that Buffett did well in stepping in to save Salomon; but in running the firm he had not set a clear strategy, employee defections were rampant, policy was inconsistent on bonuses, and Buffett was wrongly trying to run New York-based Salomon from Omaha.

As for Buffett spending only a day or so a week at Salomon, Berkshire's then Chief Financial Officer J. Verne McKenzie said, "We have telephones in Omaha."

But the story that really got under the skin of Buffett fans was Michael Lewis's cover piece in the February 17, 1992, issue of the *New Republic* entitled "The Temptation of Saint Warren," depicting Buffett as a "fallen angel."

Lewis, author of *Liar's Poker* detailing Salomon's excesses, seemed to favor the theme that because Buffett is not a saint, therefore he's a sinner.

"Suddenly there was a delicious gap between what the moralist said and what he did," wrote Lewis, saying Buffett—a critic of Wall Street—had suddenly accepted all its excessive ways because Salomon dealt in leveraged buyouts, junk bonds, and all the rest. Lewis set Buffett up as on a moral crusade about saving Salomon when what Buffett had said is that he hoped to put the stigma on the dishonest Paul Mozers and get it off the good employees of Salomon.

He had talked about changing the corporate culture at Salomon but he had not talked about becoming a saint himself, and there seems little un-American in Buffett's efforts to save Salomon and help Berkshire. Lewis cast Buffett's efforts as merely trying to save Berkshire's money there.

Lewis maintained that Buffett, as proof of his new fast-buck Wall Street ways, had recently become an arbitrageur speculating on pending takeovers.

Munger, interviewed by the *Omaha World-Herald* (February 12, 1992), said that Berkshire has no rule restricting its activities solely to long-term investing, and that Buffett has practiced arbitrage on publicly announced takeovers every year for the past 40 years and has said so many times. Buffett long has explained in annual reports that Berkshire, from time to time, practices arbitrage.

Further, Lewis portrayed Buffett's financial success as pure luck in the same way that someone could win 40 coin tosses in a row.

Newsday's Allan Sloan says Buffett naturally isn't a saint. "He hasn't ever said he didn't want to make money." And at times, particularly with Gutfreund (rightly so, in Sloan's opinion), Buffett can be very tough on people. He will drop accountants and brokers in an instant if they don't see things his way. "But he is an honorable businessman," Sloan said.

Munger also told the *Omaha World-Herald* (February 12, 1992) that Buffett is not some changed fellow who is a fallen angel.

"I've known a lot of people for a long time," Munger said. "I would say that Warren has changed less in many decades than almost anybody else I know."

Munger was asked at the Berkshire annual meeting in 1995 how much Buffett had changed over the years. Munger said, "about one stone...it takes one to know one."

"What he (Lewis) says is that Buffett has lost his soul. He thinks there's some huge change in the way Warren's mind works, and of course there isn't any big change in the way Warren's mind works."

Munger went on to cite a number of errors in the Lewis story. Lewis, for example, said Buffett considered backing the Ross Johnson bid for RJR Nabisco. Munger said Berkshire turned down a chance to participate in the RJR takeover.

Buffett says emphatically:

> I neither offered nor gave financial backing to Ross Johnson or anyone else involved in the RJR buy-out. Berkshire was invited to participate in an early attempt by Hanson Industries to enter the bidding and declined. Salomon elected to support Johnson and I, as a director, said I believed the transaction would work well at $90 a share. Neither I nor other outside directors were consulted about future escalations in price...
>
> On a Sunday in 1988, I was called in Omaha by Salomon and was asked if Berkshire Hathaway would participate in a small way in a purchase offer that Salomon and Hanson Industries might make for RJR. The reason they needed us (or somebody) in the deal was that each partner wished, for some reason, to keep its interest just below 50%. I said I had previously concluded that I did not want Berkshire to own a direct interest in the tobacco business (a decision I made when we were offered a chance to buy Conwood Co., a maker of smokeless tobacco products). But I said I had no problem if Salomon itself wished to proceed and indeed thought it a good economic decision at the price being

> talked about.
>
> In the process of this discussion about economics of tobacco, I related a story told years before by Father Reinert, then president of Creighton University, as he introduced me to a Creighton class as someone who was going to tell them a lot about investments. But, he said, the real secret of investing was to buy into a business that had a product that "cost a penny, sold for a dollar, and was habit-forming." I have told that story many times in speeches to business schools, and also at the Berkshire annual meeting, to make the point about the economic characteristics of certain companies, among them tobacco companies.

As to Lewis's suggestion that Buffett's success is a coin-flipping matter, Munger fired this cannon: "He's got the idea that Warren's success for 40 years is because he flipped coins for 40 years and it has come up heads 40 times. All I can say is, if he believes that, I've got a bridge I'd like to sell him."

After Buffett saved Salomon, *Business Week* (June 1, 1992) said, "By coming clean with both investigators and customers, Buffett kept the firm alive."

Probably no CEO in the country has been more a subject of the press or understands the press better. He certainly knows how reporters work. Buffett's view is that reporters, like people in almost all professions, range from superb to unethical.

"Some people are very talented; some are not talented at all; and you get a lot in the middle," he said in a talk to the Omaha Press Club. (*Omaha World-Herald*, September 3, 1992). "You get some people who are super-ethical. You get a great majority who are reasonably ethical, but if the story's big enough, they might forget to mention they are a reporter for just a few minutes into the interview.

"And you get a few who are patently unethical...The tough part about it is, essentially, there is no one, virtually with the exception of an assassin, that can do you as much damage as somebody can in the press if they do something the wrong way."

In the same talk, Buffett also said that over the years a number of reporters have interviewed him about Berkshire and written glowing accounts about the merits of Berkshire.

He said the same reporters who wrote the stories have called back asking him to name a good company to invest in.

"Somehow, their brains aren't quite connected to their eyeballs sometimes," Buffett said.

After *Forbes* proclaimed Buffett the richest person in the U.S. in 1993, Buffett made the *National Enquirer*. (October 26, 1993) But there were no aliens, no scandals in the story. The article portrayed the richest man in the country as a regular Joe.

In 1994 Robert Hagstrom, a principal with the Lloyd, Leith & Sawin money management firm in Philadelphia, wrote *The Warren Buffett Way*, a book which looked particularly at Buffett as a value investor influenced by Phil Fisher and Ben Graham. It made the best-seller lists.

In 1995 Roger Lowenstein, a *Wall Street Journal* reporter, came out with *Buffett: The Making of an American Capitalist.* It also made the best-seller lists.

A Creighton University administrator, Richard Blankenau, once spotted Hagstrom's book at the Denver airport. He was taken aback at the way the store categorized the book.

It was in the "Science Fiction" section.

Close to it was a book called *History of God (Omaha World-Herald*, March 22, 1995)

In its April 1995 issue, *Money* magazine said Berkshire was overvalued and quoted the "*Overpriced Stock Servic*e" newsletter as saying Berkshire's stock price "makes sense only if the company is run by God."

In its December 1995 issue, *Money* remained unrepentant:

> In April we told you not to buy Berkshire Hathaway, the firm run by Warren Buffett. The stock was trading in the nose bleed zone of $22,500 per share, a price that made sense, we said, only if your portfolio were run by God. Well, in late October, the stock was up 31% to a staggering $29,5000. We're a little red-faced, that's for sure; but we're still not about to run out and start the First United Church of Warren.

The day the issue arrived at homes, Berkshire jumped $1,100 and then another $1,500 the next day to close at $31,600.

At Berkshire there is some confusion between Buffett, Science Fiction and God.

As Buffett's reputation ballooned ever larger, phrases like these popped up in the press: "living saint of value investing, "near-mythical stock-picking success" and "international icon."

67

Phil Carret

"The grandfather of value investing."

Phil Carret, 100 years old on November 29, 1996, is the grandfather of value investing. He has lived through more than 30 bull markets, more than 30 bear markets, 20 recessions and the Depression.

He got to know Buffett a number of decades ago when Carret found that Buffett owned some stock of retailer Vornado.

Carret (rhymes with hurray) also owned the stock and called Buffett to tell him he knew Vornado's chairman and to ask if Buffett would like to meet him the next time he was in New York. Buffett said he'd like that.

The three men had lunch and afterwards Buffett told Carret he wasn't all that taken with the chairman's discussion of the business scene. "I guess I didn't understand retailing as well as I thought," Buffett told Carret.

"He sold the stock," Carret laughed.

Carret who still puts in a 40 hour week, but draws no salary, said

Buffett is one of the two great investors he's seen. The other was Fred Abbe, three years ahead of Carret at Harvard where Carret graduated in 1917.

"Abbe was a registered representative who never made more than $10,000 a year as a broker. His strategy was to buy and hold. He'd buy for himself some of the stocks he bought for his customers. He would hold on. He was worth millions later... Among his greatest coups was buying $1,400 worth of stock when he was 25 or thereabouts. Sixty years later he still had it and it was worth $2 million," Carret said.

Carret, of course, has been a great investor himself. He has owned Grief Brothers, which makes fiberboard containers, for more than 50 years. It has been a steady winner. It so happens Carret bought the stock in 1946 on the recommendation of Buffett's father. Carret met Warren Buffett when Buffett was a teenager.

Carret said Abbe was often needled for holding so long and was told he should keep a closer eye on his stocks rather than just let them sit. Abbe's reply: "If you buy them cheap enough, they watch themselves," Carret said.

Later Abbe asked Carret if he'd be the executor of his will and Carret said he'd be honored. Abbe picked five people to back up Carret, but when one of them about the age of Abbe died, Abbe tossed out the whole first team, fearing they might predecease him, for a younger team. "So I never did handle his estate," laughed Carret.

In later years, Carret tried to get Buffett to make a contribution to Harvard taking the approach that Buffett likes to invest in businesses that are No.1 in their field run by a management he "likes, trusts and admires." "I told him Harvard was No.1 and that I could introduce him to folks at Harvard that I knew he would like, trust and admire." Nice try. No luck.

Carret, full of anecdotes, sitting in his unpretentious office in New York City, said he had a plaque that reads: "A cluttered desk is a mark of genius." When Carret looked through his cluttered desk, he quipped, "Well, I can't find it. My desk is too cluttered."

In curmudgeonly fashion, Carret has told reporters, in talking about government securities, "I don't like to invest in the operations of insolvent organizations," or "trading in and out of the market is the pinnacle of stupidity." (*New York Times*, November 19, 1995)

Carret, like Buffett, works without a computer. Asked why, Carret replied, "It's up here," he said, pointing to his head. "It works fairly well."

In long hand on yellow sheets, Carret is well into writing his fourth book to be called *The Patient Investor.* His three earlier books include *The Art of Speculation*, a business classic published in 1930.

Except for a stint as an Air Force pilot in World War I in France and one as a reporter in Boston for Clarence Barron, founder of *Barron's,* Carret has been "seduced by Wall Street."

In 1928 he started the successful Pioneer Fund with $25,000 in assets and for years ran Carret & Company, now run by David Olderman and a group of associates including Carret's son, Donald Carret.

As for planning his 100th birthday, Carret said he hoped to have about 150 friends over for dinner. "Of course, I've already celebrated it a few times in case I don't make it," said Carret, who likes parties.

Frank Betz, managing director of Carret & Company explained that Carret started celebrating his centennial when he was 93. A mock newspaper headline in Carret's office reads: "Phil Carret celebrates his 100th birthday again!"

As Carret, Betz and a visitor headed out for a lunch, Carret, instead of waiting for a revolving door, skipped quickly to beat it through, leaving Betz and the visitor in stitches.

In talking about Carret's age, Betz says: "Phil remembers when T-shirts didn't say anything and bicycles had one speed."

Carret, who used to take the subway to work, now has a driver who brings him from his home in Scarsdale. Although he accepts that luxury in his old age, he still refuses to fly first class, mentioning it in connection with an upcoming trip to England and France.

Carret often crosses the street from his office at quarter past noon for lunch, and makes his way to the Waldorf-Astoria Hotel where he enters the Marco Polo Club, a club started by Carret's friend Lowell Thomas, the explorer. This day Carret was relating stories about an early investment in H&R Block. He said someone told him not to buy the stock because taxpayers could have the returns done by the IRS instead. Carret countered that argument with: "Are taxpayers going to get their worst enemy to fill out their returns?" Carret made a killing in the stock.

He talked about the Detroit International Bridge Co. in which Berkshire once had a stake. "It was for the toll-bridge concept...Of course it had auxiliary businesses such as a liquor store on the American side and some souvenir shops."

Carret became a Berkshire shareholder because he had been a Blue Chip shareholder since 1968 and converted that stock into Berkshire at about $400 a share. Carret has had huge winners with Merck, reinsurer Exel and municipal bond insurer MBIA.

Carret talked about his book, saying there would be a chapter about arrogance—a fatal flaw among many executives.

"IBM was a classic example," he said. Carret noted that former IBM Chairman John Akers demonstrated arrogance in 1991 when he told shareholders the $4.20 dividend was "very safe." It was cut to $1.00. Akers also said earnings were in good shape. IBM had losses the next year. "When Lou Gerstner took over IBM, he talked about the prospects of a comeback at IBM: " I *think* that we can do it." That's the reverse of arrogance and Carret was so impressed by that statement that he bought the stock at under $50 a share.

He said Buffett has self-confidence, but is not arrogant. "That there's no arrogance is the remarkable thing about him," Carret said.

In the spring of 1995, Carret, during an appearance on Louis Rukeyser's *Wall Street Week* said that his favorite stock was Berkshire Hathaway.

After lunch a visitor said, "Just one more question. What's your secret for longevity?" Carret's answer: "Pick your parents well, don't smoke and never worry." Carret said the only time he had worried was during the Depression.

Buffett once wrote Carret:

> Dear Phil, Although I know you are still investing for long-term growth, here is the annual dividend on Berkshire Hathaway. [a box of See's Candies]
>
> It was good to have you at the annual meeting last year and I hope you can make it next April. The group

(Courtesy of Frank Betz and Maryland Public Television/Curtis Martin)

Phil Carret loves the markets and parties celebrating his 100th birthday.

is upgraded by your presence.

Happy Holidays and all the best in 1992.

Warren

For decades Carret has been interested in solar eclipses and has traveled worldwide to view many of them.

Buffett also wrote Carret:

Dear Phil, You are the Lou Gehrig of investing and, like him, your record will never be forgotten.

Come out to the annual meeting: I'll try to arrange an eclipse. Happy Holidays.

Warren

68

1974

"He said he felt like a sex-starved man in a harem."

—Steve Forbes

Steve Forbes, who inherited the *Forbes* magazine publishing empire after his father's death February 24, 1990, says his father and Buffett were good friends. Indeed, they played bridge together the night before globe-trotter (by balloon, motorcycle or yacht) Malcolm Forbes's heart attack.

"They were playing in Britain against British Parliament members," recalled the younger Forbes, a 1996 presidential candidate, of the Corporate America vs. British Parliament game.

It took place at a 17th century riverside mansion, Old Battersea House, the London home of Malcolm Forbes, a Victorian art-filled home said to have been built by Sir Christopher Wren.

The Corporate America team was headed by CBS's Laurence Tisch. Buffett, Malcolm Forbes, Bear Stearns's Chairman Alan "Ace" Greenberg, James Cayne, president of Bear Stearns, George Gillespie III, part-

(AP/Wide World Photos)

Forbes magazine's Steve Forbes on Buffett: "I think he's a market timer...We interviewed him in 1969...and he said the market was too high...We interviewed him again in 1974... He said it was a time to buy."

ner of the Cravath, Swaine and Moore law firm and Milton Petrie, chairman of the Petrie Stores, played against the Dukes, Sirs and Lords of England on February 23, 1990. The British team was headed by Sir Peter Emery.

Corporate America played 16 hands against the House of Commons in the morning and 16 hands against the House of Lords in the afternoon. The House of Lords team soundly beat the Americans and the Americans squeaked by the House of Commons team.

In those matches, Tisch was Forbes's partner and Buffett and Gillespie played together.

Buffett came up with the idea for the game after a similar one between Corporate America and Congress. (U.S. Senator Bob Kerrey was on the congressional team.)

Buffett arrived in London with his wife. The Buffetts and Gillespies went to dinner and theater the night before the bridge game.

After the bridge games, Malcolm Forbes hosted a dinner for the bridge teams, friends and press members. "My father came home (Far Hills, New Jersey) the next day and died there," said Forbes. "Warren Buffett wrote me a nice letter about how much my father had enjoyed the bridge game and how he seemed to be in such a festive mood."

"My father was not all that great a bridge player but he felt he had played well that night. He (Buffett) is an excellent bridge player. If he had taken up bridge as a career he would have done very well. It's math, a card sense and he just sees some extra dimension...He has a superb mind."

"Warren Buffett is one of the few people to make their fortunes through investing," Forbes said in an interview in Birmingham, Alabama. Forbes sported a money green tie that said, "Capitalist Tool."

"We know Buffett as a value investor but I think he's a market timer, too...We interviewed him (for *Forbes*) in 1969 when he was a virtual unknown and he said the market was too high and that he was selling everything. We said, gosh, he sure called that one right. We interviewed him again in 1974 when the market had declined two-thirds in value in real terms, after inflation. He said it was a time to buy and that he felt like a sex-starved man in a harem."

69

A Who's Who Shareholder List

"His message is simplicity."—Coach Don Shula

Few things give Buffett more pride than knowing the names of the shareholders he has drawn to his unusual enterprise.

The shareholders are a wide-ranging lot, everyone from yuppies all over the country, investment bankers and money managers of all stripes, to corporate executives, and a number of shareholders who have known Buffett for years.

The Berkshire shareholder list also includes some of the outright rich and famous.

To name drop: U.S. Senator Bob Kerrey, (D.-Neb.), Washington Post's Katharine Graham, Coca-Cola's former president Don Keough, former Cap Cities' executives Tom Murphy and Daniel Burke, GEICO's William Snyder, Tony Nicely and Lou Simpson, CBS's Laurence Tisch, USAir's Ed Colodny, Sequoia Fund's Bill Ruane, First Manhattan's Sandy Gottesman, Wells Fargo Chairman Paul Hazen, PS Group's Rick

(AP/Wide World Photos)

Former Miami Dolphins' Coach Don Shula. "You can take what Buffett says and apply it to your own profession."

Guerin, noted investor Phil Carret. Wall Street's Mario Gabelli and Archie MacAllaster, children's author Martha Tolles, Ann Landers, investment banker John Loomis and his wife, *Fortune*'s Carol Loomis. Bill and the late Mary Gates, parents of Microsoft's Bill Gates are among the shareholders. Former General Dynamics Chairman William Anders, *Outstanding Investor Digest* publisher Henry Emerson and James McGuire, the Berkshire specialist whose Henderson Brothers firm has held a seat on the New York Stock Exchange since the 1860s when it paid $500 for the seat, are shareholders.

Benjamin Graham's sons, Benjamin and Buzz Graham, are also shareholders.

Bruce Wilhelm, a silver medalist weightlifter in the 1976 Olympics known for "Wide World of Sports" appearances, now in the exercise equipment business in San Francisco, has been a shareholder since 1992. In his competitive days, Wilhelm weighed 357 pounds. Maybe he's really Berkshire's largest shareholder.

"I believe Buffett is a genius. The only thing about him that bothers me is I think he drinks too many Cokes and he needs to start lifting weights and hitting the treadmill more," says Wilhelm.

Former Federal Communications Commission Chairman Newton "television is a vast wasteland" Minow and Voice of America's Geoffrey Cowan, author of *The People v. Clarence Darrow*, are shareholders. Chicago billionaire Lester Crown is another shareholder.

Noted investment expert and writer Charles D. Ellis, managing director of Greenwich Associates, Paul Samuelson, an M.I.T. professor and author are significant shareholders, and Richard Russell, author of *Dow Theory Letters,* has been a shareholder since the 1960s. Louis Lowenstein, a professor of law at Columbia University who wrote *What's Wrong With Wall Street* is a shareholder as is his son, Roger Lowenstein, the *Wall Street Journal* reporter who wrote *Buffett: the Making of an American*

Capitalist. Morgan Stanley's Byron Wien is another shareholder.

Also, Agnes Nixon, creator of *All My Children*, the Cap Cities/ABC soap opera where Buffett appeared, is a shareholder.

William Orr, husband of Kay Orr (former governor of Nebraska) and author of *First Gentleman's Cookbook* for which Buffett supplied his Dusty Sundae recipe, is a Berkshire shareholder. And so is Ruth Owades, head of Calyx & Corolla, which sells fresh flowers by catalog. Its biggest investor is Cap Cities, making it indirectly a Berkshire business.

Another is Miami Dolphins' former Head Coach Don Shula.

"Yes, I'm a shareholder," says Shula.

"I had heard about Warren Buffett and a couple of years ago John Loomis of First Manhattan, who handles my finances, arranged for me to meet him. I was on my way to a league meeting in Dallas and I stopped off in Omaha," recalls Shula.

"We were supposed to have dinner, but my plane was late so we had breakfast the next morning," he said. "It was at the Red Lion." Shula, another friend of Loomis's, and Buffett shared eggs and issues that morning. Shula recalls that Buffett interspersed much of his conversation with sports references.

"I mostly enjoyed his anecdotes. He knows a lot about football. He knew even more about baseball," Shula said. "He was interested in our accomplishments."

"Of course, he's a big University of Nebraska fan," the coach said.

"After breakfast he took us over and showed us his office (Shula agreed that the description of throw rugs and linoleum is not far off the mark) and to the Nebraska Furniture Mart.

"I enjoyed it. I came away from meeting him thinking that his message is simplicity. What he says helps you in your own profession, in your own life. You can take what he says and

(Photo courtesy of Bruce Wilhelm)

Berkshire shareholder Bruce Wilhelm, Olympic silver medalist in weightlifting in 1976, kids about Buffett: "I believe he's a genius. The only thing that bothers me is he drinks too many Cokes and he needs to start lifting weights and hitting the treadmill." Recently Buffett has been hitting the treadmill.

apply it to your own profession," he said, agreeing that blocking and tackling—the kind of message Buffett delivers—even at the Miami Dolphins' level should always be kept in mind.

"I think Berkshire is as solid as ever. It's been down lately but I remain a shareholder...I'm pleased with the investment."

And Shula, a savvy stock market investor, admits to keeping a pretty close eye on the stock market.

"I don't live or die over it," he said with the tone of voice of a man who might say the same thing about the outcome of a Super Bowl involving the Miami Dolphins.

70

George Buffett and a Beauty Pageant

George Buffett, of Albuquerque, New Mexico—Warren Buffett's first cousin—is the son of Clarence Buffett. Clarence Buffett, the eldest son of Ernest Buffett, was in the oil business in different states, died in a car wreck in Alvin, Texas, in 1937.

But George Buffett's fortunes would later pick up. He was encouraged to start his own business by his mother, Irma, who died at 95 in 1993.

"I had always wanted to be in the candy business," he said. But he wanted to start at the bottom, learn the business and work with his hands. "I went to California (after graduating from college in 1951) and told them when I applied I had finished the 11th grade which was true."

It turned out the company was See's, long before Warren Buffett bought the company.

"In 1952 I went into a concession business with $250. My partner

(Photo courtesy of Warren Buffett)

Cousins George Buffett and Warren Buffett at an Omaha Royals game in 1995. Buffett quipped: "Mirror, mirror, on the wall, who's the fairest of them all?" This beauty pageant is..."No contest!"

had $200 and four years later I bought him out for $4,000 because he thought we'd never get anywhere," he recalls.

In 1956 George Buffett opened a candy store, Buffett's Candies ("Our Candy is Made to Eat—Not to Keep!") in Albuquerque, a one-store business he has run while also serving in the state legislature since the late 1970s.

Over the years Buffett's candy and other businesses flourished, but of course there were some problems at the store.

"I had a 58-year-old chocolate dipper who liked to party, but I often had to go get her out of jail for partying too much. It would be $40 a pop. And then once I had to get her out three times in one week before one Easter, but I needed her so bad, I did it.

"Then I heard about a machine chocolate dipper in Kansas City and drove there a month after Easter," he said.

After seeing the dipper, George Buffett decided on the spot to drive to Omaha to see his uncle, Howard Buffett.

"Howard Buffett always had me on his mailing list when he was in Congress. He couldn't let me be a liberal so he sent me all his stuff. And he would advise me to save money also."

"I drove to Omaha and went to his office and told him how I was putting a third of my money in stocks, a third in property and a third in the business. He said that was great. Then he said 'why not let Warren take care of your money in stocks. He's honest and he's as good as anybody else.' "

George Buffett said, "That was the understatement of the century."

"So I invested $3,000 in the partnership in 1958 and $5,000 in 1960 and I later bought some more in Berkshire. I put some cash in Sequoia when he closed the partnership.

"I guess you could say I got in because of a partying chocolate dipper," he said.

George Buffett demurred when asked what his investment in Berkshire is worth, saying, "Well, you can say it's more than a half million." That's another understatement.

Asked if he ever sold any Berkshire, he confessed to selling on two occasions. "My wife wanted a condo and I sold some to buy it and I once sold some to buy her a ring from Borsheim's. I figured that was much cheaper than a divorce."

George Buffett had no idea in the early days that Warren Buffett's investing would amount to what it has. "I knew he was honest and I knew he was good, but I didn't know he'd turn out to be the best." He says it dawned on him about ten years ago that he was the best.

"Some people have said we look alike. He's smarter than I am, but my wife says I'm the better looking and I feel like I'm the lucky one."

After the annual meeting in 1995 George wrote Warren:

"Do you remember the night at the ballgame when they were taking our picture? I think you said that you would have our pictures in the next annual report to show that you're better looking. I take it that this means that if there are no pictures you've conceded?"

After the picture was developed Warren Buffett said, "No contest!"

Pressing his point home, George sent Warren a different photo saying, "I wouldn't want you to think the outcome was the fault of your photographers...I know it's tough coming in second twice in one year (Gates), but keep trying. Considering my investment, I'll be rooting for you in the Gates contest."

Buffett asked his cousin George how he prices his candy. "I told him I price it 10 to 20 cents below See's. I let them do all the figuring and then underprice them because I can make it cheaper.

"There's a See's store in Albuquerque, but I know too many people to go in," he laughed.

George Buffett sent me two boxes of candy for Christmas in 1994 with a note: "Here's one for home and one for the office with the name 'Buffett' on it. From: The Good Looking Buffett."

During the weekend of Berkshire's annual meeting in 1995, George Buffett told this story on himself. He writes a conservative newsletter called "Buffett's Bullets." Because of its popularity, folks began sending in donations to support the letter. Buffett wanted to thank those who did and settled on sending a key chain with a bullet. He located a distributor of the items in Montana who asked George Buffett if he were related to Warren. The distributor said he had bought Berkshire at $17 a share and sold at $35. George Buffett said he had bought at about $18, but had not sold.

"Why the hell are you working?" the distributor asked.

71

Ann Landers has a Date with Warren Buffett...

"Behaves shamelessly"

From her Sioux City, Iowa, home, Ann Landers (Eppie Lederer) used to visit her sister, Helen Brodkey, in Omaha to date the Nebraska boys.

"No. I didn't date Warren Buffett," she laughed during a telephone interview, but in the mid-1980s when the advice columnist went to Omaha she did indeed have a date with him.

Landers—who has answered thousands of letters from such people as Anxious in Akron, Fed Up in Fresno and Lonely in Laredo—was invited to a function that involved skits at the Omaha Press Club Gridiron. "I was asked to perform and wrote a little skit which had me doing the shimmy in a fringed evening gown. I think Warren was struck by the incongruity of it all—an advice columnist doing the shimmy.

"He came up afterwards and asked if he could take me to lunch the next day. When I told him I already had a luncheon date, he asked, 'Do

(Photo by Nancy Line Jacobs)

Buffett's daughter, Susan and Ann Landers at Borsheim's in 1994. Ann Landers: "I suggested that perhaps he ought to give some of his money away while he's alive, but I don't think I made a dent."

you think you can get me included'?"

"I told him I was sure that I could since I was having lunch with people from the *Omaha World-Herald*."

The host was Harold Andersen, the publisher, an old friend of Buffett's. "Of course they were thrilled to include Warren Buffett."

"We went to the lunch and sat next to each other and behaved shamelessly. We hardly spoke to anyone else. Warren is a fascinating man and has a marvelous sense of humor. He said 'let's stay in touch' and we have. One of the fringe benefits is See's Candies, which is not available in Chicago. He owns the company, you know."

"I bought Berkshire Hathaway stock immediately after I met Warren. I'm not a plunger in the market, but I do buy when I know the management. I thought if Warren is running a company, then I want to be in on it. When I saw the price, I almost flipped.

"I've been in his home and met Astrid Menks who is a very warm and winning person. I also know his delightful daughter Susie and the grandchildren. I attended a formal party in Lincoln given by Kay Orr who was then the governor and we all went in our formal attire on a bus. I sat with Warren's wife, who is totally captivating and a real stunner. He wanted me to get to know her. He's very proud of Susie and well he might be. Not only is she a knockout, she has all the right values. They have a remarkably warm and pleasant relationship for a married couple who lives apart.

"I've talked to Warren about his immense wealth and asked the logical question: "What are you going to do with all that money?" He told me it's going into The Buffett Foundation and when he dies he's going to leave the largest foundation in the world. I suggested that perhaps he ought to give some of it away while he's alive, but I don't think I made a dent."

72

"I asked if he knew of my father, Hank Greenberg, and he said, '1938—hit 58 home runs, had 183 RBI's in 1937.'"

—Glenn H. Greenberg

"I met him at a Columbia Business School Forum in 1986 in a hotel in New York. There were a bunch of...[financial speakers] and I went along because he's my hero," said Glenn Hank Greenberg, managing director of Chieftain Capital Management in New York, who earned an MBA degree from Columbia in 1973.

"He was surrounded by people and I felt toward him the way some people felt toward my father. There's some human instinct to reach out and make some connection with someone you admire and often it doesn't amount to much," Greenberg said.

"I knew he liked baseball and I asked him if he knew of my father, Hank Greenberg, and he said, '1938—hit 58 home runs, had 183 RBIs in

1937'...heck, I didn't even know them and he repeated three or four statistics. I thought he was trying to show off his memory. As far as I knew they were correct. He has a photographic memory. He was reeling off the statistics...He wasn't telling me [the statistics] because he thought he was coming close."

"My father [Detroit Tigers slugger Hank Greenberg] did hit 58 homers in 1938, eleven years after Babe Ruth hit 60. It was not as big a deal as when Roger Maris hit 61, years later...and my father was always humble about it and [to fans] would say how much he appreciated that they remembered or that the pitchers were hoping he'd break Ruth's record anyway.

"Meeting him [Buffett] was somewhat disappointing from a personal standpoint. There was a crowd around him...but he is without a doubt the best in the investment world. He's done it with no leverage, no cheating...He is my hero."

73

"From Margin Clerk to Millionaire"

The difference in Bill Scargle's life

Bill Scargle, a PaineWebber executive in San Francisco, California, started out life as a margin clerk and wound up a millionaire.

How? By discovering Warren Buffett. "It started with a $2,000 investment in Blue Chip in 1969 because it looked like a growth company."

(Photo by LaVerne Ramsey)

Early investor Bill Scargle

Later as Berkshire bought up Blue Chip and Scargle heard more about Buffett, it was off to the races. "In 1974 and 1975 I poured another $10,000 into Blue Chip which was all the money I had at the time," said Scargle, who was making about $12,000 a year in those days. Scargle said:

Then in 1978 and 1979 I purchased about $4,000 worth of Berkshire at $165 to $175 a share. At that point, my entire life savings was invested in Buffett companies. (Blue Chip merged into Berkshire in 1983.)

As any investor with all his eggs in one basket, I wanted to meet in person the man who held the basket. I attended the Blue Chip annual meetings during the 1970s because Buffett was a director, but he was never there. In the late 1970s...I went to the Berkshire annual meeting. It was held in the cafeteria of the National Indemnity Building. It was attended by a half a dozen shareholders, several employees and a couple of Buffett's relatives.

It lasted a few minutes. Buffett said he had about an hour if anyone would like to stick around to talk about investing. That hour changed my life. I knew at once this guy was one very smart investor. Nothing has ever changed my mind since.

After the meeting, I introduced myself to Buffett and he said, 'You came all the way from San Francisco for this?

I also fly to the Wesco annual meeting to hear Charlie Munger talk.

I always knew they [Buffett and Munger] knew what they were doing. I've thought about it [Berkshire] every day. I've collected almost everything written about it.

I never sold a share until Berkshire was about $7,000 or $8,000. I sold some then because I decided I should pay off my mortgage and all my debts and invest in some 10% Treasuries for my retirement. Sure, I made a mistake. As it turns out, I'd have done better holding on to the stock.

I've given to charities. I even asked Buffett if I could give to The Buffett Foundation and he said not to, that the foundation has plenty of money.

I guess you could say I was a margin clerk who became a millionaire. It's been a fantastic ride and I don't think it's over yet.

74

High school dropout, male model, construction worker, firefighter: "I'm a millionaire thanks to Warren." —Neil McMahon

"I first learned about Berkshire in 1973 from Adam Smith's *Supermoney,*" says Neil McMahon of New York. "I owned 100 shares of Berkshire by 1979 at an average cost of $220. I sold the 100 shares at a profit in the early 1980s and regret it."

"I bought Berkshire back in 1982. Then in 1986 and 1987 I bought 18 more shares. I own 35 shares now, or just over a $1 million of Berkshire and about 4,000 shares of Sequoia Fund so I have more Berkshire indirectly. I got into the Sequoia Fund just before it closed in 1982," he added. "I'm a millionaire thanks to Warren."

McMahon, a high school dropout who later earned a high school equivalency degree, has had long careers as a construction worker, firefigher and as a male model.

In 1962 New York City fireman McMahon saved a two-month old baby from a burning building in Queens after he climbed a ladder with a filter-mask on and found the baby squirming. The baby's mother was out shopping at the time of the fire.

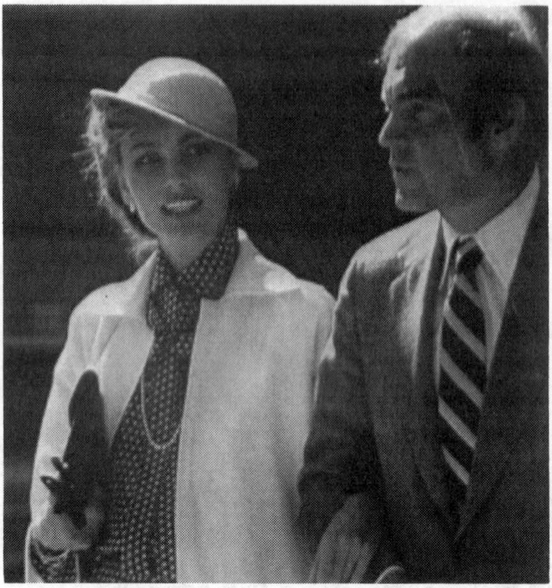

(Courtesy of Neil McMahon)

Photo of models Evelyn Kuhn and Berkshire shareholder Neil McMahon.

Handsome and solidly built, McMahon has posed for hundreds of modeling jobs over the years including a six-page spread for an executive style living ad in *Forbes* in 1982.

McMahon, now 62, is a lifelong bachelor who once was engaged to the 1963 Orange Bowl Queen. "But I always stayed a bachelor and live a simple life," he said.

McMahon, who never inherited a penny, was able to save money because for years he worked as both a fireman and a construction worker and did the modeling jobs on the side.

"I'm like Warren in that I'm very frugal with my money. I buy straw hats in the winter or eight pairs of shoes at one time at discount. I have a home in Connecticut that I rent, but I live in a rent controlled apartment in Queens."

75

Recollections of a Joy Ride from Ed Prendeville, a Train Collector

"I first learned of Warren Buffett in Adam Smith's book, *Supermoney* in the late 1970s," said Berkshire shareholder Ed Prendeville of New Vernon, New Jersey.

(Photo by LaVerne Ramsey)

Train collector Ed Prendeville

"Unfortunately, I did not invest in Berkshire at that time because I had a young business buying and selling old toy trains and all my money was invested there," added Prendeville, owner of Train Collectors Warehouse, Inc., in Parsippany, New Jersey.

"Because Warren's approach to business and investing was rational and most others were not, it made a lasting impression on me. Then in December

1981, I bought a toy train collection in Salt Lake City, Utah, for $280,000, virtually my entire life's savings plus a lot more.

"The collection was all packed in a U-Haul truck and I was driving home through Omaha. It was 3 a.m. and I remembered that Warren Buffett, the man I had read about, lived there. I remember thinking then I had better look into buying some shares of Berkshire when the train business produced some profits.

"A couple of years later when I had some money, I bought some shares of Berkshire and have held them and added more ever since. It has been a hell of a nice ride.

"The longer I own Berkshire, the more I realize what terrific businesses it owns and invests in. Of course, you have probably the best business and security analyst and capital allocator in a generation, possibly of all time as your partner. You would have to be a fool not to go into business with Warren and can do so any day the New York Stock Exchange is open.

"Fortunately, the most important investment decision I will ever have to make is when to sell Berkshire and I may never have to make that decision."

76

Arthur Rowsell: A trader for Buffett, Munger and Guerin.

"Does Warren Buffett have an account at the bank?"... "Well, he owns the bank."

"I started trading for Warren Buffett in about 1963. I got to know him through Rick Guerin," says Arthur Rowsell of Encinitas, California.

> I really didn't know who he was and he was putting in big orders saying he'd pay for them with bonds at First National Bank of Omaha.
>
> He called one day and said he was going to Europe but that he wanted to keep buying Blue Chip at

under $16 a share," Rowsell recalled.

At that point my boss asked me who the hell Warren Buffett was and told me to check him out. I called First National to ask if he had an account there and the fellow said, 'Well, you're putting me in an embarrassing position. He owns the bank.'

Most people buy stocks as they are going up. As they go down, people get fearful. Buffett, Munger and Guerin come alive in a bad market when they are the only bid in the world," Rowsell said.

Warren is so different from anyone else. Some people, if they want to buy 100,000 shares, just put in an order and they get the right amount. They buy it going up. Buffett wants the market to come to him. He's very patient...He's always buying a stock that's going down.

Buffett wants to participate in the market, not move the market. Buffett puts in orders a bit below the market, and doesn't say how much he wants, meaning he wants all he can get at that price or better.

I once asked Rick Guerin how much of a stock he wanted and he said, 'Look, Art, I want to get enough to get on the board and make a whole lot of money.'

That's the last time I asked that question of any of those guys.

Rowsell said Buffett is the same way. You buy all you can and you are not finished buying until the last share has been bought. "If you told Buffett he could buy all the stock of a company at his price, he'd say send it in. If he could buy all of a Salomon or Wells Fargo at his price, he'd take it." Continuing, Roswell, added:

He's highly ethical. Buffett never buys near a news announcement or on either side of a quarterly earnings report.

I ran trading departments. Mind you I was a market maker in these stocks and the lead market maker in Berkshire. The way Buffett buys goes something like this: I'd say something was trading 30 to 30¼ He would say do the best you can but that did not mean paying 30¼ or supporting the stock. If it wanted to go lower, then I was to buy it cheaper.

Over the years as Rowsell worked at Hayden Stone, Doyle O'Connor and Cantor Fitzgerald before becoming a private investor, he bought for Buffett such investments as American Express, California Water, Source Capital, Blue Chip, Doyle Dane, Interpublic Group, General Foods, Affiliated Publications and many others.

> Affiliated was interesting. First Boston did an IPO of 500,000 shares in the depths of the down market in the early 1970s, I believe at $13 per share. The selling shareholders were the founding families of the *Boston Globe*. By the time they listed the stock on the American Stock Exchange a couple of months later Warren had bought 350,000 to 400,000 of the 500,000 share issue. You will recall that some years later he sold the stock near $100 after a 2-for-1 split. The stock subsequently sold down to $8 after his sale.
>
> One of the founders of Intel, Robert Noyce, was a graduate of Grinnell College. Buffett was running the Grinnell endowment fund—for gratis, by the way. Noyce came to Grinnell and asked if they could invest $100,000 in Intel's original venture deal. Buffett told Noyce that if he could get his classmates to contribute $100,000 to their college, the fund would match the $100,000 thereby getting a $200,000 participation. This was accomplished and Buffett some years later sold the stock for about $18 million.

Rowsell executed a lot of over-the-counter and arbitrage trading for Buffett. "He does a lot of trading," Rowsell said.

Over the years it was Rowsell's practice to call Gladys Kaiser at the end of the day with a record of the day's trades.

"I've talked with Buffett thousands of times over the years. When he was really buying something, we'd talk five to eight times a day," Rowsell said.

Rowsell was playing tennis with Buffett at the compound near Buffett's Laguna Beach home one day when he realized Buffett was the greatest investor ever.

> Four of us were sitting around afterwards having a Pepsi and someone mentioned Dunkin' Donuts. I thought I knew Dunkin' Donuts. I mean I worked hard at these things...He said, 'You know, I've looked at that a few times.' And he started talking about how the com-

> pany would be more valuable if it split off its real estate into a REIT, that it was only making 80 cents a share. I mean he had all the facts and figures. He knew Dunkin' Donuts up one side and down the other. That was when I sold my Dunkin' Donuts and bought Berkshire at $300 and $500 a share.
>
> Warren's intellectual capacity and his memory are better than anyone I've ever known. He has the ability to absorb a large number of facts and come out with simple but very effective decisions.

The only person Rowsell's ever met in Buffett's league intellectually was Teledyne's Henry Singleton.

"The difference between the two is interesting. Singleton is just raw daunting brain power but Buffett is just as comfortable as an old shoe. Buffett is equally intelligent but his just presents itself so smoothly."

Rowsell got to know Singleton when they were pitching Teledyne stock to brokers.

"Because I was a market maker in Berkshire, Buffett was kind enough to steer business my way including the liquidation of Ben Graham's estate," Rowsell said.

Rowsell said Buffett, on occasion, read the entire S&P sheets and the 2,500-page *Walker's Manual*. [which was a sort of *Moody's* of West Coast securities] *Walker's Manual*, of Lafayette. California. in a reformed way. still exists.

"He once told me he reads the *Walker's Manual* by starting at the back. He knows about stocks you've never heard of...You could think the earnings of a company were $1.85 and he could tell you they were $1.82. Believe me, they'd be $1.82.

77

"Hey, Jerry, Drive Slow..."

I wanted to interview him as long as possible..."What's your net worth besides Berkshire?"..."It was as if he said, 'Nice try, Jim.' "

—Omaha World-Herald's Jim Rasmussen

Omaha World-Herald newsman Jim Rasmussen requested an interview with Buffett shortly before a *Forbes* article in October, 1993, proclaimed Berkshire's chairman the richest person in the country.

Buffett told Rasmussen he was amenable to it, but first said, "Let's see what *Forbes* has to say."

After the story ran, Rasmussen got back in touch with Buffett who demurred a bit: "I don't see what else there is to write." But Buffett said okay and that a way to do it was to get together before he gave a talk to Columbia University business students on October 27.

"I met him outside Salomon's headquarters [Buffett was there for a board meeting] at the World Trade Center. I was to meet him at 5 p.m. and I was outside 10 minutes early because I didn't want to miss my shot at the interview," Rasmussen said.

"He walked out the door at 5 p.m. and we had to be at Columbia before 6. We got into a Lincoln Town Car. I think it was a Salomon car, and he introduced me to the driver, Jerry. I said, 'Hey, Jerry, drive slow,' because I wanted to interview him as long as possible."

"I asked him how he felt about the Forbes ranking and he said he was glad about it for Berkshire, that if he'd gotten it and Berkshire had done only so-so, it wouldn't have meant as much."

As a result of the story, Berkshire was getting a lot more mail, Buffett said, much of it asking for money.

"One guy wrote this long letter asking for $10,000. And then at the end he said, 'Well, why don't you make it a million?'" Buffett told Rasmussen.

"I asked him about the polar bears on his tie in the *Forbes* piece—if that was any subliminal message and he said no that the folks at Coca-Cola gave him the tie as a memento of its ad campaign.

"But he seemed nervous about the question. I don't think he likes questions about his views of the market," Rasmussen said.

Buffett said he needed to be at Columbia 17 minutes before his 6 o'clock appointment. "He had it down to the minute. We got there a little early and he had the car pull around and park and we continued to talk," Rasmussen said.

"I asked him about his personal worth [besides Berkshire] and he said rankings aren't perfect and don't go into other worth, or debt."

Rasmussen pressed, trying to put a figure—$1 billion perhaps?—as an estimate of Buffett's net worth beyond his Berkshire holdings.

Rasmussen said he didn't get the slightest hint about whether the figure was high or low.

"He didn't even touch the question...It was as if he said, 'Nice try, Jim.' "

Then Buffett got out and met Carol Loomis of *Fortune*, and talked to the students for two and a half hours, devoting his first remarks to the subject of integrity.

"I mean, I can go hear a speech and I know whether I'm entertained or not, but I probably won't change anything I do," Buffett said.

"He was swamped by the students and signed annual reports," Rasmussen added.

The 80 students gave Buffett a 40-second ovation.

Afterwards, Buffett left with Carol Loomis, but asked Rasmussen if he needed a ride and Rasmussen said he'd get a cab back to his hotel to write his story.

"I was pretty pumped up the whole time," Rasmussen said.

78

Arthur Clarke: 2+2=4

Arthur Clarke first became interested in Buffett because he wanted money from him, not for himself but for the University of Chicago where he was director of corporate giving in the 1970s.

Clarke, whose track record for the past 11 years running his eponymous investment firm of Arthur D. Clarke & Co., in Boston, Massachusetts, has been 21.5%, said Buffett once asked him what he liked about fundraising. Clarke replied it was easy enough to figure out who has money; the challenge is to figure out how to approach that person. "Warren's eyes brightened and he said, 'I can see how that could be fun.' I should add also, however, that he realized one had to be deeply committed to the cause for it to be lasting fun."

One day Clarke was doing his detective work and spotted an item while leafing through the latest issue of *Official Summary of Security Transactions*, the SEC's monthly publication of insider transactions. "At the time we were probably the only development office subscribing to it," Clarke said. Lights flashed when he saw that Berkshire had made an investment in The Washington Post Co.

Ed Anderson, a Chicago alumnus who at the time, was managing partner of Tweedy, Browne & Knapp, had put Clarke onto Buffett's trail. "Ed recommended I read the chapter on Warren in Adam Smith's book. I did straight away and was hooked. Here was a man who had his life put together in a remarkable way. It may sound strange, but I put Warren, Milton Friedman and Socrates in the same class: each lets reason be his guide. Emotion leads to false expectations, and therefore, disappointment and mean spiritedness."

Buffett became Clarke's role model, which only intensified his drive to find a way to interest Buffett in the University of Chicago. "The Berkshire purchase of Washington Post stock was the key I was looking for. Most people would have passed right by this item, but I knew that Warren was behind Berkshire and Katharine Graham was behind the Washington Post."

"Katharine Graham is an alumna and was, at the time, a trustee of the University of Chicago. This connection gave Clarke the lead he was looking for. "The next day I called Ed to ask him what was going on between Warren and Kay. 'How did you find out about that?' was his surprised response."

The story continued from there, but before long Clarke left the university to raise money for the Urban Institute, a think tank in Washington, D.C. "I had never heard of the place, but Warren (as well as Kay Graham) was a director and that piqued my interest. That's how I finally met him."

When Clarke did meet Buffett, he told him the University of Chicago story. "I told him the experience brought home to me his oft made comment that arithmetic is not the hard part in life. We learn 2+2=4 early. The hard part is that the 2's rarely come together in the real world. Unless you are paying attention, you miss those few times when you have four.

"Of course, everybody's looking for 5," continued Clarke, "and that's why they end up disappointed. Like Socrates, Warren is very wise because he is rational. Therein lies his happiness."

79

Notes from the Desk of Chris Stavrou

Chris Stavrou of New York—a large Berkshire shareholder since the mid 1980s—has had brief conversations with Buffett over the years and shares these thoughts:

BACKGROUND: "I went to Wharton and from there straight to Wall Street to work as a brokerage house security analyst servicing the more aggressive institutional money managers, such as Fidelity, the Acorn Fund, Robert Wilson, and George Soros…Later I founded a Buffett-style partnership, Stavrou Partners, in 1983, and among other things built up a massive position in Berkshire Hathaway. I have to pinch myself when I think how well it has all worked out. A great turning point for me as an analyst was studying Warren's methodology; and I was so impressed with his character, honesty, and intellect, that I christened my son Alexander Warren, although I named him after Leonard Warren, the opera singer, as well."

HOW I FIRST HEARD ABOUT WARREN: "One day in the early

(Courtesy of Chris Stavrou)

Berkshire shareholder Chris Stavrou and his son, Alexander Warren Stavrou

1970s Lou Vincenti, president of Wesco Financial, started talking about Warren and became very enthusiastic. I'll never forget what he said: 'Warren Buffett is the greatest financial genius I've ever met. A new book has just come out called *Supermoney* by Adam Smith. Chris, don't walk, run to the bookstore and get it. There's a chapter in it on Warren. It will be the greatest lesson on investing that you can get.'"

CONVERSATIONS WITH WARREN: "Finally I met Warren in the mid-1980s...Warren has this way of lightheartedly answering questions, almost seeming to deflect the questioner at times, but really getting to the heart of the question and its relevance to investing. I had heard he had a photographic memory and that he never used a computer or even a calculator, so I asked him whether it was true he never used a calculator, and he said: 'I never owned one and wouldn't know how to use one if I did.'"

"Really? Well, then, say, could you give me an example of how you do division?"

"Ten percent is real easy."

"Seriously, how do you do more complicated calculations? Are you gifted?"

"No, no. It's just that I've been working with numbers for a long time. It's numbers sense."

"Is there a trick? The great mental calculators like von Neumann and Feynman used to do some math operations like addition from left to right instead of right to left. Is there some way like that that you make the math easier?"

"Yeah. You don't have to go four places beyond the decimal point."

"No, seriously give me an example. Like what's 99 times 99?"

"9,801."

"How do you know that?"

"I read it in Feynman's autobiography."

(Sure enough, if you read *Surely You're Joking, Mr. Feynman*, you will see the exact same question asked and answered in the middle of the book.)

"If you have the price of a painting go from $250 to $50 million in 100 years, what's the annual rate of return?"

"13.0%"

"How did you do that?"

"The Union Carbide compound interest tables. They only go out 50 years. You'll do somewhat better in stocks, and a lot better if you live long enough." Needless to say, those tables were nowhere in sight.

"I'm astounded you remember that. (The Union Carbide tables were the first computer generated compounding tables and haven't been published since the mid 1960s.) If they only go out 50 years, how do you do a 100-year calculation? (Here he went through a calculation that I couldn't quite follow. But the point is he didn't just splice two tables together mathematically as you normally would using square roots. He used other simple algorithms I'd never heard of before or since.) But let's say you don't know the compound interest tables or algorithms for using them."

"Then you just go by the number of times it doubles." ($250 doubles about 17.6 times to get $50 million, a double every 5.7 years, or about 13% a year.)"

"Do you use any of this stuff when calculating present values of cash flows?"

"No, no. Forget all the complicated formulas. Just go through *Value Line* and when you find a company you really like and understand and selling for half what it's worth, buy it. And if you can't find it wait. You'll get your chance."

"You were a supporter of the Pugwash group. (It was an anti-nuclear war association founded by Bertrand Russell. Its efforts led to the first nuclear nonproliferation treaty between the superpowers and the ban on atmospheric testing in 1963.)

"Did you know Bertrand Russell?"

"No, I never actually met him. I saw him on TV and read a number of his books."

"Like *Principia Mathematica*?"

"No, no. Not that sort of thing. The philosophical ones. Like *Has Man a Future?*

"Why?"

"Because he thought like Graham."

"I had an occasion to visit Warren's office once when he wasn't there. Sure enough, there were no quotrons or computers. What stood out for me was the file room. There were 188 file drawers. When I subsequently saw him, I said, 'What's in all those files?'"

"Annual reports."

"How about 13Ds?"

"No. It's mostly annual reports and quarterly reports (filed by industry)."

"Do you have them going back, say, 15 years?"

"No. We cull them regularly, although I have some, like Coca-Cola, going back more than 15 years. But you don't have to read 15 years of Coca-Cola annual reports to conclude it's a wonderful company."

"How do you wind up with so many?"

"If I'm interested in a company, I'll buy 100 shares of all its competitors to get their annual reports."

"How do you find time to read them all?"

"I skim a lot. But if I'm really interested, I'll read every single word cover to cover."

INTRINSIC VALUE: "Intrinsic value is the discounted value today, of all future distributable cash generated by an entity less the additional capital, including retained earnings, that the owners must put in to generate that cash. A simple way to get at how much a company is worth is to ask how much you would get for it if you sold it today...

But in the case of Berkshire, we'd get a much better result if we actually made estimates of intrinsic value for both the 80% to 100% owned parts of each business group within the company, as well as for the lesser percentages owned of the investee companies...Berkshire's intrinsic value is not only composed of See's intrinsic value; it's also composed of Coca-Cola's intrinsic value. A very interesting characteristic of these companies is that they can grow without the addition of much owners' capital, which, remember, includes retained earnings.

This, by the way, means that Coke can take its excess cash and repurchase its shares, such that Berkshire's original 6% stake is now 8%. A nice little plus.

If your discount rate is 10%, you are saying you have the low-risk alternative of putting $10 in, say, government bonds that pay you a $1 of interest, which *never* grows. But if you have a company that has $1 in distributable cash that will grow 5% per annum *forever*, you would be happy to own that company and pay up to $20 for it. If that $1 in cash flow grew 8% a year forever, you could pay up to $50 for it. If it grew 9% a year forever, you might even pay up to $100 for it. What you are paying as a multiple of cash flow is equal to 1 divided by (the discount rate less the growth rate). Multiple = 1 divided by (k-g).

"In other words when you are paying $10 for that bond that pays $1 of interest you are paying 1÷(.10-.0) or 10 times interest income; when you pay $20 for the 5% grower, you are paying 1÷(.10-.05) or 20 times. And when you pay up to $50 for $1 in cash flow growing 8% a year forever, you are paying 1÷(.10- .08). Now you can see why you would theoretically pay 100 times cash flow for a 9% grower, and perhaps some phenomenal multiple for a company that grew 11% forever. The only problem is that there are no companies that grow their distributable cash flows at these high rates forever. But of all companies what company or companies come closest to the ideal in terms of high, real, long-term growth of cash flow without massive infusions of new capital? The master found many of them before us. And they are concentrated in the Berkshire portfolio. Of course there are all sorts of caveats. But clearly these companies are worth some big number. We don't really know what it is. High growth rates, above a certain point, become too vulnerable to vicissitudes. More realistically, Berkshire's intrinsic value is within a wide, albeit high, range.

"The other important matter is the issue of float. Warren bought National Indemnity in 1967 for $7.8 million when it had $17 million in float. It is conceivable that he could have turned around in the heated late 1960s and sold it to some insurance company for the price of its float, and made a killing. But clearly, that would have been shortsighted. Today, Berkshire has $7 billion in float, half of which was internally grown at 20% a year at Berkshire. The other half was essentially internally grown at GEICO...

"Think of it this way. What would you pay for a $7 billion mutual fund, where not only could you keep all of the say 10% profits you could make each year with the money of the fund, but each year, the mutual fund shareholders would contribute 20% more money to the fund?...

"I once said on the Adam Smith TV show that Warren Buffett is certainly the greatest investor in the post World War Two period and probably the greatest investor in history. I still think this is true, although I'd now say 'allocator of capital' instead of just 'investor.' And as a human being he is more. He's an original. He's philosophically stimulating, skeptically superwise and witty as hell. He's part Aristotle, part Ben Franklin and part George Burns."

80

"Who was going to go into a foxhole with me?"

Buffett told Columbia business students about the first moments of the Salomon crisis and how he picked Deryck Maughan because of Maughan's integrity.

"I faced the immediate problem of deciding who was going to run Salomon Brothers, the institution, while essentially, I had to deal with regulators and the public and the politicians, etc.

"On Friday night and again on Saturday morning, I met with about 12 people. These 12 people were top-level managers at Salomon. And essentially, I had to pick from that group of 12 someone to run a $150 billion institution that was going to be under great stress and who could lead 8,000 people under very trying conditions.

"It may be of interest to you what went through my mind because you're going to be hired. And how would you develop yourself in some way that you be the one?

"This was the most important hire of my life.

"I interviewed those people Saturday morning over a couple-hour period, knowing that I was going to pick one when I got all through. I didn't have time to do a lot of psychological tests or anything. The good news is I did not ask them what their grades were in business school (laughter).

"They all had the IQ, just like everybody in this room. It doesn't make any difference whether your IQ is 140 or 160 if you're running Salomon or doing most things in this world. They all had the energy level and the desire.

"The question was: Who would be the best leader? Who was going to go into a foxhole with me? Because whoever went into the foxhole with me could stick a gun to my head.

"If they wanted to come around and say they got an offer from Goldman Sachs or something, twice as much money as they were making, or wanted special personal indemnification because of lawsuits—a million things could happen and would happen with some people.

"In the end I picked someone and fortunately, it was not only the most important decision of my life, but probably as good a business decision or hiring decision as I could make.

"I devised this little system in getting you to think about how you might attack that problem yourself, or how you might be the person that would be chosen under those circumstances.

"Imagine that you have just won a lottery I conducted. And by winning it, you had a very unusual prize. The prize you get is the right to pick within the next hour one of your classmates. And you get 10% of the earnings of that individual for the rest of your life.

"What starts going through your mind? Are you going to give an IQ test, or look up their grades and take the person with the highest grades? Are you going to try to measure desire or energy or something? I think you'll decide that those factors tend largely to cancel. They could be important up to some threshold limit, but once you hit those levels, you're OK.

"I think you'll probably start looking for the person that you can always depend on; the person whose ego does not get in his way; the person who's perfectly willing to let someone else take credit for an idea as long as it worked; the person who essentially wouldn't let you down; who thought straight as opposed to brilliantly.

"And then, let's say there's a catch attached. For the right to buy this 10% interest, you had to go short 10% of somebody else in the room. So in effect, you get the 10% of the first person's earnings, but you have to pay out 10% of the second person's.

"Now again, do you look around for the person that's a little slippery, the one that everything has to be his or her idea, the one that never quite does what's expected of them, or pretends to do things that they don't. You really get back to things that interestingly enough...are things that you can control.

"You have these—what I would call—voluntary items of character, behavior. Essentially, you can pick out those qualities of behavior, and if you want them, you can have them yourself.

"Take that one person where you would go short, and if you find a few of those qualities creeping into your own behavior, they are things you can get rid of.

"If you're taking all the credit for things when other people do it, you can do something about that. You can make yourself into the person that you would buy the 10% of, and you can make very sure that you're not the one that you would sell short 10% of.

"And I would say that most of it's habit.

"It's just as easy to have good ones as bad ones, and it makes an enormous difference.

"Deryck Maughan simply behaves well and he behaves in a high-grade manner. He doesn't give up his independence or his ability to think independently or any of those qualities whatsoever.

"I'll give you an example. Deryck, two or three months after he took the job, had never asked me how much he got paid, let alone had a lawyer around negotiating for him or anything of that sort.

"Deryck, when he came in, had one thought in mind and that was keeping the place initially together, and then building a business that fit his image of what he wanted it to be.

"He never asked me for a dime of indemnification, and he could have been targeted. He could have gone broke. There were dozens of suits. He was working 18-hour days. He could have been making more money someplace else.

"Somebody once said that in looking for people to hire, you look for three qualities: integrity, intelligence and energy. And if they don't have the first, the other two will kill you.

"You think about it, it's true. If you hire somebody, without the first, you really want them dumb and lazy (laughter).

"Pick the kind of person to work for you that you want to marry your son or daughter. You won't go wrong." *(Omaha World-Herald,* January 2, 1994*)*

81

The Berkshire Hathaway Annual Meeting

Like a rock concert

Doors opened at 8:00 a.m. for the 9:30 a.m. Berkshire annual meeting in 1995. Crowds were there long before 8:00 a.m. When the auditorium opened, grown men and women ran inside to get the best seats. It was like a rock concert. Before the meeting huge video screens re-ran the come-from-behind victory of Nebraska over Miami in the Orange Bowl. Buffett, in a Husker Red coat, walked on stage shortly after victorious Nebraska football coach Tom Osborne was carried off the field by the National Champion Cornhuskers.

In 1996, even larger crowds gathered. Fifty people showed up at the doors at 3:30 a.m. Before the annual meeting started at 9:30 a.m. shareholders were treated to videos featuring Buffett in some soap opera and Omaha Press Club appearances. One video was a take-off of "The Graduate" where Dustin Hoffman is told the future is in "plastics." In this case the word plastics was substituted: GEICO.

*Left - The Berkshire annual meeting is held the first Monday in May. Here in 1992 Adam Smith of **Money World** was preparing to air a show about the meeting.*

Below - Always a two-fisted Cherry Coke drinker, Buffett gets fortified for his more-than-three-hour annual meeting in 1992.

(Photos by LaVerne Ramsey)

Above - Buffett, decked out in a Coca-Cola apron, signs annual reports before Berkshire's annual meeting in 1992. The next year he wore a See's Candies cap during the annual meeting.

(Photo by Nancy Line Jacobs)

Above - Buffett at 1994 annual meeting in front of a portrait of the cover of the Berkshire Annual Report.

Below - Don Keough, former president of Coca-Cola, in Coke apron, chats with Sequoia Fund's Bill Ruane; both are longtime FOBs. Ruane, a Harvard alumnus, has joked there's little difference between him and Buffett except billions of dollars and 100 IQ points.

(Photo by LaVerne Ramsey)

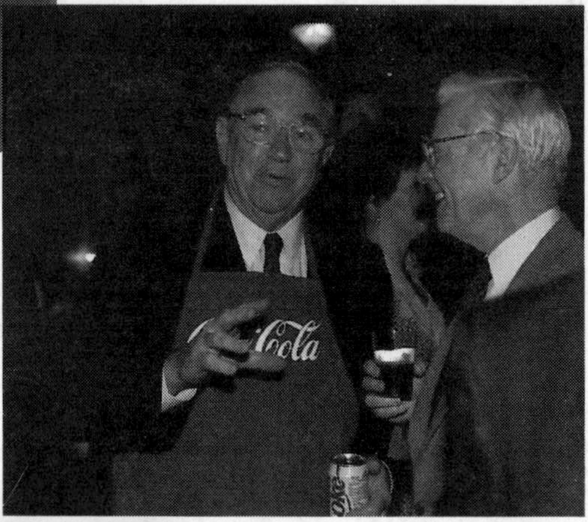

Left - Sandy Gottesman, chairman of First Manhattan and a large Berkshire shareholder, and Buffett chat at Borsheim's in 1992 - possibly about merging with Canada.

(Photo by LaVerne Ramsey)

The highlight of the year for a Berkshire shareholder is the annual meeting held the first Monday in May in Omaha. At the annual meeting in 1991, Buffett and then Coca-Cola President Don Keough donned bright red Coca-Cola aprons to serve shareholders Cokes as they arrived for the meeting. From their perch in front of a display of Coke cases, Buffett and Keough provided a small sip of Coke from the Fountain of Wealth. Buffett sipped on a Cherry Coke, chatted and signed annual reports. Keough sipped a diet Coke and bear-hugged and lavished good humor on any shareholder within reach. A number of surprised shareholders got a handshake or a word with the men and in some cases a quick photo opportunity.

"The [Berkshire] annual meeting is the best thing I've ever seen in all of commerce," says Keough.

In 1992 Buffett and Huggins donned caps with a See's logo and passed out small boxes of See's candy to shareholders.

More than 5,000 happy Berkshire pilgrims now journey to the event featuring Buffett and Munger at the dais, sharing Cokes and See's candies and guiding an adoring shareholder group through a quick course in the wisdom of the financial ages.

Not that many people came in the early days. As few as seven to a dozen people showed up for the annual meetings in the 1960s when they were held in New Bedford, Massachusetts, home of the Berkshire textile business. Later they were held in a fourth floor cafeteria at Berkshire's National Indemnity office in Omaha.

Soon the meetings were held in the cafeteria of Kiewit Plaza with 10 to 30 shareholders showing up, and then at the Red Lion Inn where about 250 shareholders gathered in 1985. A number of Berkshire shareholders still stay at the Red Lion on their annual pilgrimage.

There were about 1,000 Berkshire shareholders at the time Diversified was merged into Berkshire at the end of 1979. There were about 1,900 shareholders in 1982 and 2,900 in 1983, many of those coming in with the Blue Chip merger.

Over the years, with Berkshire's mighty growth and the spread of Buffett's reputation for wit and wisdom, more shareholders came, creating the need for ever larger meeting places.

Eventually, the annual meetings were held at the Joslyn Art Museum ("Temple of Culture," as Buffett calls it) in Omaha where 580 shareholders met in 1988. The meetings for several years were held at the Orpheum Theatre, and now are held at the Holiday Inn Convention Center.

When Adam Smith, who covered the Berkshire annual meeting in

1990 for his *Adam Smith's Money World* television program, asked shareholder Charles Dennison of Princeton, New Jersey, why he attended the meeting, Dennison said: "I hear it's a great show."

Robert Baker, a retired lawyer from Chagrin Falls, Ohio, (who died

(Photo by LaVerne Ramsey)

Buffett and Bob Sullivan near Borsheim's the day before Berkshire's annual meeting in 1995. Buffett asked Sullivan if he brought his dog, "Buffett." Sullivan said instead he brought a friend, a stockbroker. Buffett joked, "That's a bad trade."

in 1992) was among the Berkshire shareholders who regularly made the annual trek to Omaha.

Baker had read about Buffett in the early 1980s. "I read enough to know he was terrific and then on April 8, 1983, the "Heard on the Street" column in the *Wall Street Journal* quoted from his annual report. On April 11th I went and bought five shares. I asked to get them at $920. The broker called back and said I had bought them for $910."

A year later Baker started going to the annual meetings.

"They are fully worth it for the wisdom...It's worth every penny," Baker said. "He always expresses the great truths so simply. We're always too busy making things so complex. He reminds us not to play games or make things complex...I think he looks at the bottom line and looks to see if the managers are having fun, if they love what they do."

There is great camaraderie among shareholders. Shareholders spend the annual meeting swapping Buffett stories. For example, Bob Sullivan of Long Meadow, Massachusetts, once told of writing Buffett that he had named his dog after him. Buffett wrote back that if Sullivan ever got another pet, he should name it Munger. Sullivan got another dog and named it Munger, but Munger died and Sullivan wrote Buffett: "Buffett's still alive, Munger's six feet under."

The annual meeting is a communion for kindred spirits who have found investment heaven. "It's the Club Med for investors," says Berkshire shareholder Pat Mojonnet of San Francisco. "And when you come

(Photo by Celia Sullivan)

From left: Jamie, Ceily Mae holding Buffett the dog, Michael holding Munger the turtle, and Charles. The Sullivan children are a combination of Berkshire, Wesco and Coca-Cola shareholders.

home and tell people about it, nobody believes you."

Usually, the only real status check comes from the query, "How long have you been a Berkshire shareholder?" The longer you've been, the wiser you are.

For the uninitiated, seeing Buffett in action can be a jolt.

It's not the usual annual meeting where the chairman drones on, overstating progress with a studied rosiness. And Berkshire's meetings don't have public relations folks who dread questions from disgruntled shareholders. Even more embarrassing for some chief executives is no questions at all. While most ordinary meetings are forgotten within seconds, Berkshire shareholders still delight in what Buffett said years ago.

At Berkshire, shareholders get no excuse of how the sluggish economy led to disappointing results, or some pie-in-the-sky story about how fabulous the following fiscal year will be. You get no gadfly—no Evelyn Y. Davis—questioning the chairman's motives or pay package.

With Buffett and sidekick Munger you get what you see: the precise opposite to what you get at most ordinary annual meetings. First Buffett and Munger walk on stage. Buffett carries up his Coke supply. Berkshire's duo sits at a plain table adorned by See's candy.

Buffett normally starts off with a joke or two, sometimes ostensibly testing the microphone: "Testing...testing...one million...two million...three million."

Buffett distrusts complicated technology, and his instincts were confirmed at the annual meeting in 1990 when Berkshire's Chief Financial Officer, Verne McKenzie tried to fix the faulty microphone system. "Verne McKenzie is our resident technology expert. Can you hear me? Can you hear me?...This is why we don't buy technology stocks."

In 1993, with so many people, a giant screen was set up so people could see Buffett and Munger better, and when at first there was noise and flickering, Buffett teased, "We're masters of technology here."

Buffett's sister, Mrs. Doris Bryant, recalls sitting with her mother at the meeting in 1992 when Buffett started on one of his Bartles and Jaymes routines with Munger. "There was a heavy man sitting in front of us who thought it was so funny his whole body was shaking. My mother loved it."

In 1992, in anticipation of a question about how long he intends to be at Berkshire, Buffett said, "We plan to be here until we're both sitting here wondering, 'Who's that guy sitting next to me?'"

One year he welcomed his audience to the new meeting site, the Orpheum Theatre in Omaha, explaining, "Most of you know we held our annual meetings at the Joslyn Art Museum the past several years until we outgrew it. Since the Orpheum Theatre where we're meeting today is an old vaudeville theatre, I suppose we've slid down the cultural chain. Don't ask me where we'd go next."

In 1994, with the theater full, Buffett said the next meeting might have to be elsewhere and that sliding down the cultural pole would continue. He thought it might be held at Ak-Sar-Ben (Nebraska spelled backwards) where there is keno and horse-racing.

Buffett usually introduces Munger, sometimes saying, "It's no breach of etiquette to walk out during his answers." And he'll make witty introductions of the Berkshire managers.

He will jokingly warn the audience to be careful not to say anything off-color about him because he has relatives strategically placed throughout the audience.

In 1993, Buffett explained that the meeting would go until noon or until Munger said something optimistic. However, Munger, known for dour, laconic answers, never did say anything cheery, and after each sobering Munger answer, Buffett kept saying, "We'll be here until noon."

After Buffett's initial jokes and introduction, he takes up housekeeping matters such as electing his wife to the board of directors. Straight-faced, he may note that attendants "hired from a local modeling agency" are on hand to give you a proxy card should you wish to change your vote.

In 1992, Buffett made his usual introductions of the managers and the board, and when he introduced his wife, Susan Buffett, Buffett said, "It's a name we got out of the phone book." He then introduced his niece, Cynthia Zak, saying she has a son named Berkshire. "That's a not-too-subtle method of trying to get into my will," Buffett added.

And he'll make his pitch about how shareholders can go to visit Borsheim's or the Nebraska Furniture Mart. In 1991, it went like this: "At noon we'll break. And there'll be buses to take you to Borsheim's, Nebraska Furniture Mart...or anything else that we have an economic interest in."

Voting at the meeting is a moot point since Buffett's block of stock, and the holdings of his wife, insiders, and a couple of friends quickly make up well over 50% of the stock.

Shareholders go along with Buffett's litany of business matters, and after everyone has said aye to some unarguable point, such as dispensing with reading minutes of the prior year's annual meeting, Buffett will utter, "You're doing fine."

He notes that Berkshire meetings are not meant to be democratic and take their "Stalinist manner" and autocratic origins from somewhere deep in the old Soviet Union. He says these things almost every year and they always elicit a little chuckle, about a 3 or 4 on the laugh meter.

At the 1994 meeting, Buffett said, "Let's get the business of the meeting out of the way so we can get on to more interesting things."

He then moved the meeting be adjourned, adding, "Democracy in Middle America."

The whole routine takes just 5 or 10 minutes and if you have not been to a Berkshire meeting before, you are surprised at the move to adjourn the meeting. You have come across the country and suddenly it's over. Over?

Well, not really. The fun is just beginning as Buffett leans back from the table a bit and says, "Any questions?"

Then Buffett offers responses stunning in speed, depth and originality.

Once longtime shareholder Irving Fenster, of Tulsa, Oklahoma, got up with a question and started by saying he was from Oklahoma—Nebraska's biggest football rival; Buffett yelled, "Who let you in?"

When he was asked for advice to young investors, he explained, "Look at stocks as businesses, look for businesses you understand, run by people you trust and are comfortable with, and leave them alone for a long time."

The questions roll on for almost three hours, often with shareholders from the Northeast addressing him as "Warren" and shareholders from the South using "Mr. Buffett."

After the meeting, hard-core fans who want more of Buffett stick around for even more questions, with Buffett fielding everything shareholders can throw his way.

Munger plays the straight man to Buffett. Sometimes Buffett will describe how some business is deteriorating and Munger will interrupt: "He means it went to hell."

Munger sits stone-faced, arms folded across his chest, usually offering comments like "Yes" or "No" or "No comment" or "I have nothing to add." After one "That's exactly right," from Munger in 1991, Buffett said, "He's learning. Susie take notes," referring to his wife, Susan Buffett, just elected to Berkshire's board. Frequently, Munger will invoke the word "Civilization," comprising America's social and economic fabric, as in "the Civilization needs program trading like it needs more AIDS."

In the midst of the annual meeting in 1992, Floyd Jones of Seattle praised Buffett's handling of the Salomon scandal. Jones explained that he had worked for the collapsed Drexel Burnham Lambert firm, adding that he felt Buffett had averted what could have been an international financial crisis had Salomon collapsed. "I think you are a hero in world corporate society."

Early in the meeting, for the sake of rotating the questions around the large crowd, Buffett had divided the audience into various zones, and it so happens Jones's question came from zone four. After Jones's eloquent remarks, Buffett said, "Let's stay in zone four for a while."

After the meeting most shareholders make a run for the Nebraska Furniture Mart or Borsheim's before catching a flight out of Omaha.

And Buffett will help you with the transportation to either store—in a rented school bus with no air conditioning. For the meeting in 1989, Buffett hired two old school buses for $100.

After all, Buffett wants those selling, general, and administrative expenses kept below rock bottom.

"It's great to hear Warren and Charlie answer every question openly.

Mrs. Susan Buffett and Astrid Menks at Borsheim's before the annual meeting in 1992.

(Photo by LaVerne Ramsey)

And it feels good to know your money is in their hands," says Don Keough.

There is plenty of free-wheeling give and take.

One Berkshire shareholder, LaVerne Ramsey of Birmingham, Alabama, asked at the annual meeting in 1991 what would be revealed if Kitty Kelley wrote an unauthorized biography of him and Munger. Buffett, as fast as a Magic Johnson pass, slyly shunted the question off to Munger.

"I'm afraid not very much," Munger said, "But that wouldn't stop Kitty Kelley." Buffett answered the question, "What you see is what you get with the two of us." Mrs. Ramsey, a Buffett admirer, explained later she really asked her question as a test of Buffett's wit. "He passed," she said. A small sequel to that story is that later Mrs. Ramsey sent a note and some photos to Buffett explaining the question was just in fun, as Buffett well knew, and he wrote her back, "LaVerne, Thanks for the pictures. I always enjoy them. Charlie should have some Kitty Kelley material for next year; don't let him off the hook."

Later at the meeting, a shareholder asked him how he spent his day and Buffett started out with "More of the Kitty Kelley bit, eh?" Then he said he spends most of the day and night reading and talking on the phone.

After he gave his explanation of how he spent his day, he said, "That's what I do. Charlie, what do you do?"

Munger was not caught off guard: "That reminds me very much of a friend of mine in World War II in a group which had nothing to do. A general once went up to my friend's boss, we'll call him Captain Glotz. He said, 'Captain Glotz, what do you do?' His boss said, 'Not a damn thing.'"

"The General got madder and madder and turned to my friend and said, 'What do you do'?"

"And my friend said, 'I help Captain Glotz.' That's the best way to describe what I do at Berkshire."

One shareholder in 1992 asked Buffett what books he read, and he said that before the Salomon scandal he had read a lot of books. Then he tossed the question to Munger who said one book he'd enjoyed was *The Third Chimpanzee*. "Are we going to add him up here?" Buffett quipped.

When a shareholder asked about billionaire Ross Perot's entry in the presidential race and whether that gave Buffett any ideas, Buffett said it gave him no ideas whatsoever and added, "We'll see if he's a billionaire when it's over."

Buffett's Investor Club Med is all great fun, which includes talking to other Berkshire shareholders on the bus ride to the Berkshire-owned stores. Again, most conversations start with, "How long have you been a Berkshire shareholder?" or some tiny bit of information you may have about Buffett or Berkshire's latest investment.

Sometimes there are sober reminders from Buffett of the dangers of the marketplace. "You shouldn't own common stocks if a 50% decrease in their value in a short period of time would cause you acute distress," he said at the annual meeting in 1988.

Walking out of the annual meeting in 1992, Berkshire shareholder Paul Cassidy said of Buffett, "He's a great education. I bought a couple of shares early on. He gave me the financial security to open my restaurant (The Loft in North Andover, Massachusetts). I try to carry on in my business the ways he talks about. And I tell my children to be long-term investors. They've been buying Coca-Cola stock. I believe that will help send them to college. Our family gets great laughter and enjoyment from Buffett."

A short time later Tom Weik, president of Weik Investment Services, Inc., in Wyomissing, Pennsylvania, was talking in the afterglow of the annual meeting and another year as a Berkshire shareholder.

Weik, an avid bridge player, has kept up an occasional correspondence with Buffett about bridge, and Weik said Buffett once wrote to him about Ben Graham's relationship with bridge. Buffett said Ben Graham played, but wasn't hard core about it. "This was his only failing."

Reflecting on what Berkshire had done for him, Weik said, "It enabled me to have the comfort to start a business from scratch."

Buffett got a ten on the laugh meter at the meeting in 1994 when Allan Maxwell, a Searle Laboratories salesman in Omaha asked: "Now

*Left—**Fortune's** Carol Loomis and Astrid Menks at Borsheim's in 1992. Mrs. Loomis is sporting a bracelet of mementos Buffett gave her for editing the Berkshire annual reports. Astrid Menks is showing a Berkshire stock certificate replica sold by Borsheim's.*

Right—Susan Buffett, Buffett's daughter, at Borsheim's in 1992. She said her friends in school thought her security analyst father "checked alarm systems."

(Photos by LaVerne Ramsey)

Berkshire Vice Chairman Charles Munger, second from left, with Berkshire shareholders, from left, Irving Fenster, Tulsa; Yves Mojonnet, San Francisco; and Bill Ramsey, Birmingham; at Borsheim's in 1992.

(Photo by Nancy Line Jacobs)

Susan Buffett, striking a Nebraska national championship theme near Borsheim's the day before Berkshire's annual meeting in 1995, with ***Washington Post's*** *Katharine Graham and* ***Fortune's*** *Carol Loomis.*

Left—Former USAir Chairman Ed Colodny and wife, Nancy, at Borsheim's, 1992. Buffett described his USAir investment as an "unforced error." Later he said, "I have an 800 number now, which I call if I ever get an urge to buy an airline stock. I say, 'My name is Warren. I'm an air-aholic' and then they talk me down."

(Photo by LaVerne Ramsey)

*Right—Berkshire shareholder/stockbroker/photographer LaVerne Ramsey and **Fortune's** Carol Loomis at Borsheim's in 1993.*

(Photo by Andrew Kilpatrick)

Buffett and Always Coke at Borsheim's in 1993.

(Photo by LaVerne Ramsey)

Left - Donald Yale, former president of Borsheim's and Berkshire Vice Chairman Charles Munger at the jewelry store in 1993.

Below - The autograph that counts (and keeps on counting). Buffett signing items at Borsheim's in 1993.

(Photos by LaVerne Ramsey)

Above - Berkshire's Michael Goldberg, a key figure in Berkshire's insurance and credit operations. Goldberg: "The negative is: How do you ever think much of your abilities after being around Warren Buffett?"

Left-Buffett, his mother, Mrs. Leila Buffett, and at left, his daughter, Susan Buffett, before the Berkshire annual meeting in 1993

(Photo by LaVerne Ramsey)

Below - Berkshire shareholders Michael and Eiko Assael of New York. Michael is holding Buffett-signed "investment guides," including a 1934 edition of Ben Graham's ***Security Analysis****. Such first editions are worth more than $1,000. Eiko sports her personalized "100 BRK" license plate with a message from Buffett. It's a little Buffettabilia for a Berkshire Museum in their kitchen.*

(Omaha World-Herald)

Judy Prus and her husband, Dr. Michael Prus of Grosse Pointe, Michigan, are regulars at Berkshire annual mettings.

(Photos by LaVerne Ramsey)

Chad and Carol Brenner of Cincinnati, Ohio, are irregulars, depending upon whether Carol is pregnant that year. The Brenners have three children.

that you're the richest person the country, what's your next goal?"

Buffett: "That's easy, to be the oldest person in the country."

Later at the meeting Buffett said he was in pretty good health, then waved at his 2-liter bottle of Coke and said, "This stuff does wonders for you."

Every year he is asked about splitting the stock and every year he says there are no plans to do so. In 1994 a shareholder asked if he planned a reverse split which leaves fewer shares outstanding. "Now you're talking," Buffett said.

At the 1995 meeting, Buffett announced that shareholders had come from 49 of 50 states with only Vermont not represented. And they had come from Australia, France, Israel, Canada, Sweden and Zimbabwe. Because people had come from such distances, Buffett said he would extend the meeting, which lasts until noon or so, until 2:45 p.m.

He began by explaining a proposal to get authorization to issue preferred stock should the board see fit. "There is no downside to the proposal...if we do something dumb we can do it in any form [such as cash]...this gives more forms of currency to make acquisitions."

Buffett said if the acquisitions were huge, like $5 billion, Berkshire would have to come back to the shareholders for another and he said if that unlikely event happened, it would come back to the shareholders, "with the votes already in hand."

As the questions rolled on, one shareholder asked about having his wife and son on Berkshire's board. Quipped Buffett: "It's terrific for family harmony."

Soon a typical answer of "No" came from laconic Munger and Buffett joked: "I was hoping Charlie would have a near-life experience this morning." Munger shot back with, "No comment."

Later when Munger said Berkshire could be successful even if shareholders didn't get as much as fast as in the past, some shareholders groaned. "It's a tie vote," Buffett said.

During the meeting Buffett asked Katharine Graham, Don Keough and Tom Murphy, who were sitting together, to stand. When they stood, Buffett said they were responsible for $6½ billion in profits "so far." (The audience applauded)

The day before the annual meeting in 1996 Buffett and Bank of Granite Chairman John Forlines met for the first time near the Omaha Marriott. They had only traded several letters before. When they did meet, Buffett said, "I just read your report." Then Buffett began citing figures from the North Carolina bank's first quarter report. "He was right. I was surprised. I was overwhelmed, to say the least," Forlines said.

Then Buffett made a mention of the bank at the annual meeting saying the bank was one of the most profitable in the U.S.

"We had 150 requests as far away as Hong Kong for annual reports." Forlines beamed.

(Photo by LaVerne Ramsey)

Bank of Granite Chairman John Forlines

(Photo by Gail Wyman)

Buffett signing autographs at Borsheim's before Berkshire's annual meeting in 1996

82

Poetry Section: "Well, Hell, he must be making some money." Computer Mama Warren's Song: "Her cart is rolling on."

Floyd Jones, principal of First Washington in Seattle, Washington, which serves many clients who have Berkshire stock, bought his first shares of Berkshire in 1985.

"I kept adding to it over the years and was able to start the Jones Foundation, a dream of mine. Berkshire is 80% of the holdings...The best income stock I know of is a growth stock," Jones said.

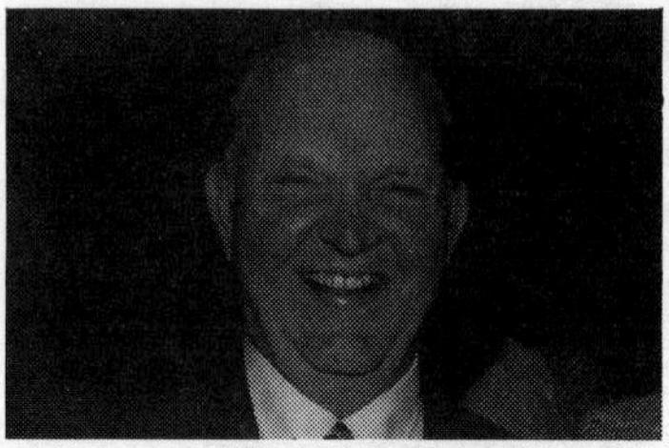

(Photo by LaVerne Ramsey)

Floyd Jones of Seattle

Jones was so moved by his experience with Berkshire that he wrote a poem in the middle of the night before the annual meeting in 1993. Jones left his room to write the poem, but did not awaken his wife, Delores.

"She was reaching for the phone in a panic when I went back to the room [at 4:30 a.m.]...At least I know now that she misses me," Jones said.

That morning, after Buffett called on him for a question, Jones read his poem to Berkshire shareholders:

MECCA FOR WALL STREET

They come! They come!
They come to Omaha-O-m-a-h-a
Out on the Western plains,
no hub since wagon trains
They come to see and hear oracles
of Midas fame, Warren and Charlie!
They come for the journey,
to have the feeling,
to be welcome, to say hello
to touch in handshake, to ask the question
to "help."
They come to know fellow travelers, to boast,
debate, to EVALUATE.

Skeptical but, analytical minds voice a
challenge to method and even the plan.
The Chairman takes no prisoners
but disposes out of hand.

They come from Alabama and to see Mrs. B.
They love the party at Borsheim's 'cause
there's none in Tuskegee.

There's Fortune 500's among you.
Warren's their guru too,
Katharine Graham and Senator Kerrey
may say hello to you.
We'll all be at the Orpheum
To the rafters I hear,
it's investors' Mecca and convenes each year.
There'll be lots of See's Candy
and tons of Cherry Coke,
Then it's on to the shareholders
meeting that's uniquely for
the folks.

Another great year has ended,
Another has begun
Warren and Charlie, our warmest
regards... We'll let our
profits run!

An obviously touched Buffett said, "Thanks, Floyd," then asked for the "next question."

In early 1995 Berkshire's stock vaulted up to about $25,000 and then with a pounding of stories from *Barron's, The New York Times* and *Money* saying Berkshire was overvalued, the stock sank to about $22,000.

Meanwhile Buffett was adding more than $1 billion to his American Express stake, buying about half a billion dollars of PNC bank stock as well as snapping up the Helzberg's Diamond Shops chain.

Jones took exception to the overvalued charges with, "Well, hell, he must be making some money."

Computer Mama

Berkshire Shareholder Judy Goodnow Prus of Grosse Pointe, Michigan, was so moved by Berkshire's stock rise in early 1996, she E-mailed her son Michael:

Hark, what is this I hear?
Thirty-seven thousand three!
Our dear old friend Berkshire
Has astounded even me!

Oh, I could truly wax poetic,
Now 'twil be even more renowned!
All other stocks still look pathetic;
We should see that Warren's crowned!

Love, COMPUTER MAMA

Warren's Song
Her cart is rolling on.

Buffett wrote a poem and gave this recital at the Omaha Press Club in 1987:

WARREN'S SONG
(to the tune of "The Battle Hymn of the Republic")

Oh, we thought we'd make a bundle
When we purchased ABC
But we found it's not so easy
When your network's number 3
So now the load at Berkshire
Must be carried by Mrs. B
Her cart is rolling on.
Chorus:
Glory, Glory, Hallelujah
Keep those buyers coming to ya
If we get rich it must be through ya
Her cart is rolling on.
Ideas flop and stocks may drop
But never do I pale
For no matter what my screwups
It's impossible to fail
Mrs. B will save me.
She'll just throw another sale
Her cart is rolling on.
Chorus:
Forbes may think I'm brilliant
When they make their annual log.
But the secret is I'm not the wheel
But merely just a cog.
Without the kiss of Mrs. B
I'd always be a frog
Her cart is rolling on.

Even with these poetic flights of fancy by Berkshire shareholders, the stature of William Butler Yeats seems assured.

83

The Berkshire Annual Report

"We bought a corporate jet last year."

Buffett gained financial control of Berkshire in 1965, assumed policy control that May and became chairman of the board and chief executive officer in 1970—the year for which he first wrote an annual letter to shareholders.

Nothing has brought Buffett more acclaim than his chairman's letter to shareholders in the annual report, sublime reading for Berkshire aficionados.

Berkshire's owner-related business principles are set out in the first two pages of the report starting: "Although our form is corporate, our attitude is partnership. Charlie Munger and I think of our shareholders as owner-partners, and of ourselves as managing partners. (Because of the size of shareholdings we also are, for better or worse, controlling partners.) We do not view the company itself as the ultimate owner of our business assets but, instead, view the company as a conduit through which our shareholders own the assets.

"In line with this owner-orientation, our directors are major shareholders of Berkshire Hathaway. In the case of at least four, over 50% of family net worth is represented by holdings of Berkshire. We eat our own cooking..."

"About the time I got to 'We eat our own cooking,' I was hooked," says Berkshire shareholder Michael O'Brien of Austin, Texas. Berkshire reports are not easy to come by. If you want more than two copies, Berkshire charges $3 for each additional report. Berkshire reports have a tendency to start this way: "Our gain in net worth during 1991 was $2.1 billion, or 39.6%. Over the last 27 years (that is, since present management took over) our per-share book value has grown from $19 to $6,437, or at the rate of 23.7% compounded annually."

The 1995 report began: "Our gain in net worth during 1995 was $5.3 billion, or 45%. Per-share book value grew by a little less, 43.1%, because we paid stock for two acquisitions, increasing our shares outstanding by 1.3%. Over the last 31 years (that is, since present management took over) per-share book value has grown form $19 to $14,426, or a rate of 23.6% compounded annually.

In these summaries Buffett delivers such jewels as this one from the 1985 Annual Report: "A horse that can count to ten is a remarkable horse—not a remarkable mathematician," quoting Samuel Johnson, and adding, "A textile company that allocates capital brilliantly within its industry is a remarkable textile company—not a remarkable business." Then he repeats one of his most famous statements. "With few exceptions when a manager with a reputation for brilliance tackles a business with a reputation for poor economics, it is the reputation of the business which remains intact." Also, "Gin rummy management behavior (discard your least promising business at each turn) is not our investment style. We would rather have overall results penalized a bit than engage in it."

Through the years, the letters have blossomed in style, substance and originality. The letters are full of humor, uncommon common sense, candor and clarity. Buffett is fond of quoting John Maynard Keynes, "I'd rather be vaguely right than precisely wrong."

Buffett loves to quote Mae West, saying in the 1987 annual report, "Currently liking neither stocks nor bonds, I find myself the polar opposite of Mae West as she declared: I like only two kinds of men—foreign and domestic." He repeatedly has drawn on "the prophet" Mae West for her quote, "Too much of a good thing can be wonderful."

Shareholders receive the annual report every year in late March. The plain-looking, bound publication's cover simply says Berkshire Hathaway Inc. Annual Report—no photo of headquarters, board members, or outstanding employees. Not even a photo of the Ben Franklin of Omaha.

Only Wesco's Munger rivals Buffett in cheaply produced annual reports, often filling in numbers from portions of a previous year's report. For decades Munger ran one black and white photo of Wesco's headquarters, using a photo so old it had cars from the 1960s. (*The Warren Buffett Way*, Robert Hagstrom, p. 21)

The only mystery about the report's appearance is what color Berkshire has selected for its cover each year. Silver was the pick for the 1989 report, teal for 1990, uninviting dark blue for 1991, a burgundy red for 1992; in 1993 it arrived in paperbag brown. It was described as looking like a gravy-colored school exercise-book cover by the *London Independent* (February 19, 1995).

The 1994 report came in Husker red as in, "We're national champs! Go. Big Red. Go."

Each winter Buffett begins writing his letter in his scrawl. He turns it over for editing to his longtime friend, Carol Loomis, and Berkshire's Debbie Bosanek for typing.

Says Loomis, "Warren writes it by hand on yellow pads. I weigh in as editor. He's smart enough to know that everyone needs an editor, though sometimes I could kill him for ignoring my suggestions. Anyway, what I do on the report a lot of people who know something about both business and writing could do, as long as they had Warren's trust. What he does nobody else could come close to doing." (*Fortune,* Carol Loomis, April 11, 1988)

Buffett's first letter of March 15, 1971, in the 1970 annual report is a simple summary, less than two pages, of the year's operations. It's a straightforward report that offers little of the brilliance in writing, the wit, or the quotes from such figures as Goethe, Samuel Goldwyn, Yogi Berra and Ted Williams that would come later, along with possibly the most bizarre line ever to appear in an annual report.

In the 1986 report he wrote, "We bought a corporate jet last year," setting it off in diminutive type. Long a critic of aircraft as an example of corporate waste, Buffett backed and filled with a quote from Ben Franklin: "So convenient a thing it is to be a reasonable creature, since it enables one to find or make a reason for everything one has a mind to do."

The 1970 report began: "The past year witnessed dramatically diverse earnings results among our various operating units. The Illinois

National Bank & Trust reported record earnings and continued to rank right at the top, nationally, among banks in terms of earnings as a percentage of average resources. Our insurance operations had some deterioration in underwriting results, but increased investment income produced a continued excellent return. The textile business became progressively more difficult throughout the year and the final break-even result is understandable, considering the industry environment."

The following year the letter was three pages. It began:

"It is a pleasure to report that operating earnings in 1971, excluding capital gains, amounted to more than 14% of beginning shareholders' equity. This result—considerably above the average of American industry—was achieved in the face of inadequate earnings in our textile operation, making clear the benefits of redeployment of capital inaugurated five years ago. It will continue to be the objective of management to improve return on total capitalization (long term debt plus equity), as well as the return on equity capital. However, it should be realized that merely maintaining the present relatively high rate of return may well prove more difficult than was improvement from the very low levels of return which prevailed throughout most of the 1960s."

From the early days Buffett was constantly hammering away at getting a good return on capital.

"Buffett's business and investment success hinges on his obsession with return on capital rather than on bigness. This, in a nutshell, is what makes Warren Buffett, Warren Buffett. This is what makes Buffett a capitalist classic," said Michael Assael.

The 1972 letter begins, "Operating earnings of Berkshire Hathaway during 1972 amounted to a highly satisfactory 19.9% of beginning shareholders' equity. Significant improvement was recorded in all of our major lines of businesses, but the most dramatic gains were in insurance underwriting profit. Due to an unusual convergence of favorable factors—diminishing auto accident frequency, moderating accident severity, and an absence of major catastrophes—underwriting profit margins achieved a level far above averages of the past or expectations of the future."

In the 1973 Berkshire report, Buffett notes that Berkshire earned almost $12 million and that the company's directors have approved a merger of Diversified Retailing into Berkshire Hathaway. Diversified operated a chain of retail stores and owned 16% of Blue Chip Stamps at the time.

"Diversified Retailing Company Inc., through subsidiaries, operates a chain of popular-priced women's apparel stores and also conducts a reinsurance business. In the opinion of your management, its most important asset is 16% of Blue Chip Stamps," Buffett wrote.

In addition, Buffett proudly reported that a minor holding, the since-defunct Sun Newspapers Inc., a group of weekly newspapers published in the Omaha area, won the Pulitzer Prize for local investigative reporting, the first time that a weekly had won in that category.

It won for its March 30, 1972, report about Boys Town, delineating the contrast between decreasing services and mounting wealth that had taken place at the home since Father Flanagan's death in 1948.

"Our congratulations go to Paul Williams, Editor, and Stan Lipsey, Publisher, as well as the entire editorial staff of Sun Newspapers for their achievement, which vividly illustrated that size need not be equated with significance in publishing."

In the horrible off year of 1974, the stock market languished in excruciating torpor, and Buffett was forced to report what every shareholder dreads to hear. Inside that year's royal blue cover, he broke the news:

"Operating results for 1974 overall were unsatisfactory...The outlook for 1975 is not encouraging." From the beginning of 1973 to the end of 1974, Berkshire's stock price took its worst beating ever, falling from $93 a share in the first quarter of 1973 to $40 in the fourth quarter of 1974.

It would touch $38 a share in the first quarter of 1975 before getting back on track.

Things were unsatisfactory, and Buffett explained that the insurance and textile businesses had subpar years; nevertheless the operating business year, comparatively speaking, was fine. Buffett reported that shareholders' equity was up 10.3%, the lowest return on equity realized by the company since 1970. It was actually a stunning performance in a year in which few companies reported any progress at all.

For 1974, his performance was comparatively splendid. Buffett kept a string of increases in stockholders' equity alive, going back to his start in 1956. Through 1995, the record was intact.

Later in the 1974 report what would become vintage Buffett came through.

"Our stock portfolio declined again in 1974—along with most equity portfolios—to the point that at yearend it was worth approximately $17 million less than its carrying value. Again, we are under no pressure to sell such securities except at times that we deem advantageous and it is our belief that over a period of years the overall portfolio will prove to be worth more than its cost. A net capital loss was realized in 1974, and very likely will again occur in 1975. However, we consider several of our major holdings to have great potential for significantly increased values in future years, and therefore feel quite comfortable with our stock portfolio. At this writing, market depreciation of the portfolio has been reduced by half from yearend figures, reflecting higher general stock market levels."

Although his holding in The Washington Post Co. sank from about $10 million to about $8 million in the first few years after the 1973 purchase, The Post Co. has grown 50-fold since. For the 1975 year, Buffett reported that the property and casualty, and textile businesses were God-awful.

> The property and casualty insurance had its worst year in history during 1975. We did our share—unfortunately, even somewhat more. Really disastrous results were concentrated in auto and long-tail (contracts where settlement of loss usually occurs long after the loss event) lines.
>
> Economic inflation, with the increase of cost of repairing humans and property far outstripping the general rate of inflation, produced ultimate loss costs which soared beyond premium levels established in a different cost environment. 'Social' inflation caused the liability concept to be expanded continuously, far beyond limits contemplated when rates were established—in effect, adding coverage beyond what was paid for. Such social inflation increased significantly both the propensity to sue and the possibility of collecting mammoth jury awards for events not previously considered statistically significant in the establishment of rates.

Of Berkshire's textile interests, Buffett wrote, "During the first half of 1975 sales of textile products were extremely depressed, resulting in major production curtailments. Operations ran at a significant loss, with employment down as much as 53% from a year earlier." There was a rebound in textiles in the second half of the year.

During the year Buffett bought more textile operations, Waumbec Mills Inc. and Waumbec Dyeing and Finishing Co. Inc., of Manchester, New Hampshire, only to report the following year that they had not performed well.

"Our textile division was a significant disappointment during 1976," he wrote. Inside the 1976 report, in a five-page letter, he listed main stockholdings of Berkshire at yearend 1976:

141,987 shares of California Water Service Co.	Cost $3,608,711
1,986,953 shares of Government Employees Insurance Company Convertible Preferred	Cost $19,416,635
1,294,308 Government Employees Insurance Company Common Stock	Cost $4,115,670
395,100 shares of Interpublic Group of Companies	Cost $4,530,615
562,900 shares of Kaiser Industries, Inc.	Cost $8,270,871
188,900 shares of Munsingwear, Inc.	Cost $3,398,404
83,400 shares of National Presto Industries, Inc.	Cost $1,689,896
170,800 shares of Ogilvy & Mather International	Cost $2,762,433
934,300 shares of The Washington Post Co. Class B	Cost $10,627,604

Total: $58,420,839
All other holdings $16,974.375

Total equities: $75,395,214

He praised Eugene Abegg, chief executive of Illinois National Bank Trust Co., who in 1931 opened the doors of the bank Berkshire later bought.

Buffett wrote: "Recently, National City Corp. of Cleveland, truly an outstandingly well-managed bank, ran an ad stating 'the ratio of earnings to average assets was 1.34% in 1976 which we believe to be the best percentage of any major banking company.' Among the really large banks this was the best earnings achievement, but at the Illinois National Bank earnings were close to 50% better than those of National City, or approximately 2% of assets."

By statute, the bank was divested in 1980, the same year Abegg died. Buffett described him as a man who during Buffett's purchase of the bank put all the negative factors face up on the table, but said as years went by undiscussed items of value popped up. That's quite different from business transactions where the good points are touted up front and negatives surface only after the check crosses over.

Toward the end of the 1976 letter, Buffett said Berkshire had boosted its stake in Blue Chip Stamps to 33% of the company's stock.

Also, he devoted two sentences to K&W Products, an automotive products company. In its first year with Berkshire, Buffett said K&W had performed well with sales and earnings up moderately.

In 1976 there were 2,000 Berkshire annual reports printed. By 1985 there were 15,500 with a second printing of 2,500 more. Now more than 40,000 a year are printed by Omaha Printing Companies.

By 1977, Buffett was copyrighting the annual reports and eventually, in response to an increasing demand for back Berkshire reports, the company compiled Buffett letters into bound volumes.

In the 1977 report, a small position in Cap Cities Communications, Inc. popped up.

The following year that position was gone, but there was a holding of American Broadcasting Companies, Inc.; GEICO and Washington Post Co. were mainstays, as they always would be.

Buffett continued to educate his shareholders about Berkshire's holdings, and about the intricacies of accounting or insurance. But it was not until the middle of the 1979 report that he delivered his first real effort at humor: "Overall, we opt for Polonius (slightly restated): 'Neither a short-term borrower nor a long-term lender be.' "

He never looked back. In subsequent years he got funnier and funnier (as he got richer and richer) quoting pithy, applicable remarks, always with the purpose of helping shareholders better understand their investment.

In later years, the letters accompanying the annual reports have turned into 20-page documents with profound observations and witty asides about everything from the intricacies of accounting to insurance, from the stock market to the fear and greed infesting human nature itself. The reports have become a kind of *Prairie Home Companion* in which Wall Street is a Lake Wobegon and Buffett sets out to tell what awful truths are there.

The 1987 report was in full bloom with a description of "Mr. Market" he picked up from Ben Graham. Buffett says anyone in the stock market should imagine the daily stock quotations coming from a remarkably accommodating fellow named Mr. Market who is your partner in business. Mr. Market flashes you stock quotes for businesses constantly, but there is one thing you need to know about this character: Mr. Market has emotional disorders.

At times Mr. Market feels good and offers high buy-sell prices in the stock market. At other times he is depressed and offers only low buy-sell prices.

You are free to (and often should) ignore Mr. Market and his prices, analogous to the specialist on the market floor and the buyers and sellers, in aggregate, who dictate a stock's price.

Mr. Market will be back tomorrow with another price that may interest you. The trick is to know the difference in Mr. Market's emotional offerings—to buy when he is sad and sell when he is happy—and operate on your own and not under the influence of Mr. Market's manic-depressive personality.

Buffett counsels that Mr. Market is there to serve you, not guide you. It is Mr. Market's pocketbook, his money—not his wisdom—that the true investor is interested in.

People have said, including Adam Smith, that reading the Berkshire annual reports is a better education than business school itself.

"An investor who reads the letters Buffett has written over the last 16 years will have taken in perhaps the single best 'textbook' that's available on the stock market, corporate finance and investing," said Frederick Rowe in a piece in *Forbes*, July 19, 1993.

Says former Younkers department store chairman Joseph Rosenfield: "He [Buffett] sends me some annual reports every year and I give them to my friends. Everything's in there."

84

NHP

A small idea when big ones are needed

Berkshire bought a 50% stake in NHP, Inc. in 1986 for $23.7 million. NHP of Washington, D.C., mainly owns and operates multi-family rental apartments and is a large apartment landlord.

Buffett came up with the idea; Munger was always a bit skeptical of it.

In 1990, Buffett, apparently feeling that he was serving on too many boards, sold Berkshire's stake. Then on October 31, 1990, NHP, headed by J. Roderick Heller, III, announced that Berkshire had sold most of its stake to Harvard University. Institutional investors agreed to buy 62% of the privately held company's shares.

Harvard University, through its $5 billion investment management company, bought 50% of NHP shares from Berkshire and Weyerhaeuser. Before the transaction, Berkshire owned 50% and Weyerhaeuser owned

25%. Afterwards Harvard owned 50% and Weyerhaeuser and another institutional purchaser owned 12.5% each.

Management and certain shareholders, who invested at the time NHP subsidiaries were organized in 1970, owned the remaining shares.

Said Heller at the time, "We are very pleased that Harvard, with which we have had business relationships for over three years, has become our major shareholder, and we are looking forward to a long and fruitful association. At the same time, we regret that Berkshire Hathaway will no longer be an owner of NHP. Warren Buffett has been an outstanding shareholder, and his advice has been invaluable during our successful turnaround of recent years."

Terms of the sale were not released, but NHP, whose portfolio of apartments includes about 81,000 units, did say the sale price was more than half the $72 million book value of the company, which would have given Berkshire a 50% profit on its investment.

This particular investment was small by Berkshire standards and the payoff was most certainly affected by 1990's worst phase: real estate. A five-year period which took a lot of Buffett and Munger's time and energy, and some money, brought only fairly small potatoes. For Berkshire the investment was so-so—one that went from a worth of $24 million to about $35 million in five years. It received no mention in the 1990 annual report. Then maybe it shouldn't have. Buffett could have done better in government bonds.

Buffett has said that given Berkshire's size, small ideas will not help much—only big, successful ones will maintain Berkshire's growth.

Because Berkshire had its NHP investment less than five years, it amounted to a day trade.

85

Torchmark

"I'll look at Torchmark."

In late 1986 I wrote Buffett boldly suggesting he look at the stock of Torchmark, an insurance and financial services company in Birmingham, Alabama.

Several days later I received a note dated December 1, 1986:

> "Thanks for the nice comments—and I'll look at Torchmark.
> "I'm glad you are a shareholder, but you are right—I'm not keen on margin buying. However, we'll try to keep you out of trouble. Sincerely, Warren E. Buffett"

His reply about margin buying came in response to my noting that I liked Berkshire so much I had margined things for more of its shares. He was right about being cautious about margin, and although he tried to keep me out of trouble, even he could not swim against the tide. During the crash of 1987, Berkshire stock fell from about $4,000 to under $3,000 a share over a several-day period, about in line with the rest of the market.

But before that disaster, I was the most surprised person in the world when Dan Dorfman reported in August 1987, that Berkshire had amassed a small stake—by Berkshire standards—in Torchmark, a stake not even announced publicly by Berkshire other than through the briefest sort of filings.

Torchmark officials have confirmed such a stake and Berkshire has filed forms with the SEC acknowledging ownership. There's no proof my letter had anything to do with Buffett's purchase, but it was fun to learn he was in the stock.

Let's put it this way. When I later had lunch with the Oracle of Omaha himself, he did NOT ask me for my best investment idea.

Berkshire owned 863,550 shares of Torchmark at one point, but in 1995 Berkshire owned 331,281 Torchmark shares.

Torchmark is the parent firm of a battery of insurance companies, the largest of which is Liberty National Life Insurance Co., employing agents who in some cases still go home to home, selling insurance policies, seeking a niche market of customers at the modest end of the income scale.

The company also owns Waddell & Reed, a financial services company that manages a group of mutual funds. Waddell and Reed representatives sell life and health insurance policies from another Torchmark subsidiary, United Investors Life, and oil and natural gas partnerships managed by another subsidiary, Torch Energy.

Torchmark's other main subsidiaries are United American Insurance, which sells Medicare supplemental insurance and Globe Life and Accident Insurance, which sells health insurance.

During rocky times in the past few decades for financial services firms, Torchmark has set a record as a model of consistent profitability. For the past 40 years it has compiled both per-share earnings and dividend increases every year, a record unmatched by any other company listed on the New York Stock Exchange.

The company has a reputation for tight control over expenses, and its investments appear solid.

Less than 3% of the company's fixed-maturity investments are in securities of less than investment grade, and three-fourths of the investments are in short-term investments or government securities.

Only slightly more than 2% of total invested assets were in mortgages or real estate.

Since 1986, Torchmark has bought back more than a third of its outstanding stock. Alabama's most profitable company is headed by Ronald

K. Richey.

Torchmark's bid to buy much larger American General Corp. for $6.3 billion in 1990 did not come off.

Berkshire's stake in Torchmark has made nice, steady progress as Torchmark's businesses have made nice, steady progress. In the mid 1990s, the stock price suffered in connection with litigation over cancer policy replacements.

"It appears that Mr. Buffett sold approximately a third of his holdings in the fourth quarter of 1993. Nevertheless, Torchmark continues to have many of the characteristics that he looks for in a business: a high return on equity, a low cost structure and cost-conscious management, highly predictable earnings, and a company that repurchases its own stock," said Giri Bogavelli, an investor in San Francisco.

86

Time Warner

"If he had become a major shareholder, we probably would not have gone through what we did." —J. Richard Munro

Buffett, still so much taken with media franchises, bought shares of Time, Inc., in 1982 at a cost of $45 million. By the end of the year the investment was worth $79 million.

Over the next several years, he lowered, then raised, then lowered his investment and in 1986 he sold out completely. That was the year he also sold a stake in Affiliated Publications, the parent of the *The Boston Globe*, for a $51 million profit.

J. Richard Munro, the former chairman of Time, who spearheaded its merger in 1989 with Warner Communications into Time Warner, says he believes Buffett sold out to help finance his stake in the Cap Cities purchase of American Broadcasting Cos. in early 1986.

"I can tell you I have respect for him far beyond the business aspect. It's as a human being. He's one of the more interesting people of our time. It's his no-nonsense, Midwestern thing. There are just no affectations. He

(AP/Wide World Photos)

Former Time Warner Chairman J. Richard Munro. "If he had become a major shareholder, we probably would not have gone through what we did."

is a legendary figure...What you see is what you get," Munro said.

"When he became a shareholder of Time, the company did not know it...His timing of buying and selling the stock was perfect," he said.

Buffett would drop by Munro's office at the Time-Life Building in New York about once a year for a chat.

"We'd talk about everything. He wanted to know what we knew and of course we wanted to know what he knew. We'd talk about the world and exchange views. He was an admirer of Time," Munro said.

A couple of years after Buffett sold his Time shares, he approached the board for permission to make a major investment in the company, according to Munro.

"He came to us wanting to become a big investor on the order of five to 10%," he added.

Buffett's overture was rejected. Munro said he and Nick Nicholas were for it, "but the board rejected it."

"As I recall it was big shareholders who just didn't want it," said Munro, adding that it was something that was considered very quickly and dismissed as something Time didn't need.

Laments Munro, "If he had become a major shareholder, we probably would not have gone through what we did." What Time soon went through was a $200 a share unsolicited offer for Time from Paramount Communications.

The bid was finally beaten back as Time and Warner agreed to a high debt merger that made the combined Time Warner, the largest media and entertainment company in the world, with huge stakes in magazine publishing such as *Time* magazine and *Sports Illustrated* and in books, cable television (including HBO) and films such as *Batman*.

But the combined company wound up with a debt of more than $10 billion, and Buffett didn't think much of that.

"I do not think he (Buffett) approved of the merger, but I will be convinced until I go to my grave that it was right. We would have been acquired or become a second-rate company," Munro said.

87

"Excuse me. Aren't you Warren Buffett?"

One day in 1986, Peter Kenner, who heads Kenner Printing Co. in New York City, saw a man who looked like Warren Buffett at the intersection of Madison Avenue and 55th Street.

"Excuse me. Aren't you Warren Buffett?" asked Kenner. "Yes, how did you know?" replied Buffett.

When Kenner said his father, Morton Kenner, had been an investor since the days of the Buffett Partnership and that he himself was a long-time Berkshire shareholder, Buffett insisted he come to the annual meeting next time around. Kenner had never been, but started going.

Morton Kenner, who attended Berkshire's annual meeting in 1992 with his son and grandson, said four generations of his family have invested with Buffett. "I put $80,000 into the partnership at a time you needed to have $100,000 and I got my father (Marcus Kenner) to invest the other $20,000," said Kenner, whose wife was a friend of Ben Graham's.

"I met Buffett in 1964 through Henry Brandt," said Morton Kenner of the Shearson Lehman executive.

One time Buffett invited Kenner to accompany him on the plane to the annual meeting. Kenner joined Buffett and his wife for the trip to Omaha. "It was that first plane and it had E.T. on it from the movie," Kenner recalled.

By 1990, Kenner's nine-year-old son, Nicholas, a third-generation Berkshire shareholder, was pleading to go. "He had been asking me about going to the meeting," says Kenner, who thought it a bit odd.

But he said his son, who inherited 10 shares of Berkshire, explained that if this was his investment for a college education he wanted to go.

Kenner told his son he could go, but that it was a grown-up affair and he'd have to be quiet and not ask questions. But young Kenner said he wanted to ask why the Berkshire stock price had dropped from $8,900 to $6,700 a share. His father finally gave in.

The Kenners ran into Buffett just before the meeting, and Buffett encouraged young Kenner to ask whatever question he wanted. So young Kenner, posing the first question at the Berkshire annual meeting in 1990, asked the ultimate question of Buffett: "Why did Berkshire's stock go down?"

Buffett, feigning anger, replied, "You're underage! Throw him out!"

The greatest financial mind of our time finally replied that he really did not know, that there was no good answer to that question. Young Kenner had stumped the master.

After an explanation about Berkshire usually trading near its intrinsic value, Buffett ended by saying, "Hold it for your old age."

As it happened, after the meeting Buffett and the Kenners again ran into one another, and Buffett asked Nicholas Kenner if he could pose for a picture with him, a picture that ran with the *Omaha World-Herald*'s story about the annual meeting.

Posing for the picture, Buffett said, "Let's do this right" and handed the youngster his wallet. "Can I keep it?" said Kenner.

"I was just making a wisecrack," the lad explained later.

A short time later Buffett sent Kenner a copy of the photo with a letter saying to come to future annual meetings and ask more questions.

"He's a nice guy. He's very funny," Kenner said of Buffett.

"I just wanted to ask him why the stock price was down. You know, if it's fallen from over $8,000 you want to know why. I definitely want to hold it unless something absolutely amazing happens and it goes down thousands of dollars," he added.

Kenner, such a hit at the annual meeting in 1990, was allowed the first question at the annual meeting in 1991. Buffett had written in the annual report that he would let young Kenner have first crack at him.

Kenner was ready with two questions: His first was, why did Buffett pick Coke instead of Pepsi as an investment? His second was, why, if Buffett listed Kenner's age as 11 in the Berkshire annual report when he was actually 9, should he trust Berkshire's financial numbers in the back of the annual report? That question sent Berkshire shareholders into convulsions of laughter.

Buffett later said he planned "a written response." (*Fortune*, June 3, 1991)

Kenner had started out his questioning of Buffett by saying he owned 10 shares of Berkshire; Buffett interjected, "I'd like you to meet my granddaughter."

Buffett, calling on the help of then Coca-Cola President Don Keough, took on Kenner's first question explaining that Coke is a superb business serving soft drinks in 170 (now almost 200) countries where consumption is increasing. Keough said that consumption internationally was 59 servings per capita a year compared with 300 in the U.S., suggesting Coke's enormous growth potential.

Buffett said he drank five Cokes a day and noted that Munger drinks diet Coke "for obvious reasons."

As for young Kenner's second question about the age discrepancy, Buffett started out with "Charlie wrote that section" and then ducked it with, "That is a very good question. I look forward to seeing you again next year."

Drawing a big laugh, Kenner said, "I'll be back!"

"I know!" Buffett replied.

The repartee was becoming part of Berkshire lore and Buffett wrote at the end of his letter in the 1991 Annual Report: "Nicholas will be at this year's meeting—he spurned my offer of a trip to Disney World on that day—so join us to watch a continuation of this lopsided battle of wits."

(Omaha World-Herald)

Buffett and Nicholas Kenner have engaged in a battle of wits at annual meetings and here they playfully battle over Buffett's wallet.

88

Low-income Housing

Warren Edward Buffett talks with President George Herbert Walker Bush

In 1990, Berkshire invested $25 million in the non-profit National Equity Fund to help finance low-income housing. And in 1991, it invested $20 million in low-income housing efforts, split evenly between the National Equity Fund and the Enterprise Fund. By 1994, Berkshire had invested more than $80 million in low-income housing efforts, including small amounts in the Equity Fund of Nebraska. The money went toward creating low-income housing in several cities, including Houston, Los Angeles, Detroit, Chicago and Buffett's hometown of Omaha.

"I look at it as an investment with pro-social aspects," he said at a press conference in 1991. "I don't view it in a philanthropic context."

The investment that Buffett termed "financially and socially responsible" should earn 15% to 20% a year for over a decade in the form of tax credits created through the federal Low-Income Housing Tax Credit Program, part of the 1986 tax law revision.

In its first four years the fund raised $620 million to build more than 14,000 affordable housing units in 62 cities. Buffett's investment is believed to be the largest made in the fund.

He made the investment in part to encourage other firms to make such investments. Salomon also has pledged a similar $10 million investment in the program and American Express has made a small investment.

Berkshire's investment was made through its *World Book* subsidiary, whose encyclopedias, Buffett said, are "in the homes of millions of Americans" in all income groups. Of the law providing for the investment credit, Buffett said, "It seems to me to be a fine marriage between the corporate community and the local community development organizations. The marriage should provide affordable housing for low-income groups." The tax credit was assured when President Bush signed the new housing bill into law at the White House on November 28, 1990.

Before the signing Bush and Buffett had a private chat. The details were not disclosed.

We may never get them, but the discussion was about business, not politics. The President of the United States, George Herbert Walker Bush, peppered Buffett with questions about the economy.

Let's hope the President's secretary didn't erase the White House tapes.

89

What do you think the markets will do?

"Well, the President (Clinton) didn't tell us anything about what the markets will do."

On June 16, 1993, Buffett and eight other CEOs met with President Clinton at a private lunch. Buffett advised Clinton to raise taxes and cut spending as the only practical way to reduce the deficit.

Interviewed by reporters on the White House lawn afterwards, Buffett said reducing the deficit was important for the economy and the stock and bond markets.

He said he backed Clinton's plan to reduce the deficit and had voted for him.

Clinton and the corporate executives had a two-hour lunch, and afterwards Buffett said the discussion was "quite uninhibited" and that the president was a "good listener."

"The president is articulate and he listens very well. He gets very engaged in the conversation and he is a very engaging person to be with."

Buffett said he endorsed Clinton's proposal to reduce the deficit by $500 billion over five years through a combination of new taxes and spending cuts. The $500 billion figure was significant, although he added he would like to see an even greater reduction via a significant energy tax.

Buffett said he could not speak for the other CEOs, but he thought hiking taxes and cutting spending was the way to battle the deficit.

Asked if he were disappointed in the way the White House was functioning under Clinton, Buffett said, "I've been a little disappointed in the way Congress has functioned. I think that maybe it has lost sight of the ultimate goal, which is major deficit reduction."

The markets would evaluate the deficit-reduction package, he said. "Wall Street will evaluate the whole package. In the end, it will look at how business will do five to ten years out, what interest rates are going to do, the credibility of the administration, the ability of Congress to act. There's a whole host of variables it'll be looking at."

Buffett was asked what he thought the markets would do, and replied, "Well, the President didn't tell us anything about what the markets will do."

Asked if the markets were overvalued, Buffett said, "I've never been a good judge of the markets. I try to evaluate specific businesses. If I could evaluate a few specific businesses every year half-way correctly, I'd look at it as a successful year. I've never made any money guessing which way the market's going."

Questioned about whether it was harder now to find undervalued investments, he said it is harder now but, "It always seems hard at the present time."

To a question about a rumor he was buying Time Warner stock, he said, "I never comment on rumors, particularly my own."

"Let me ask you outright if you are buying Time Warner stock," a reporter asked. Buffett replied, "I never comment about whether we're buying or selling anything. The only thing I will comment about is that I own Berkshire Hathaway."

To a final question about the possibility of a stock split, Buffett said people shouldn't hold their breath.

90

PS Group

Is a significant slice or a sweet and sour stock price worth mentioning? Shoot no.

By the end of 1990, Berkshire owned about 20% of PS Group, a San Diego-based enigma long headed by J. P. "Rick" Guerin. For more than 25 years, Guerin has been a disciple and friend of both Buffett and Munger.

Their friendship is both financial and emotional. Once Munger took Guerin and Buffett fishing in a small ski boat on a large Minnesota lake. Munger accidentally threw the throttle in reverse, causing water to pour in and sink the craft.

Tall and lean Guerin, by far the most athletic (swimmer, football and basketball player, pilot, model, skier, auto racer, bicyclist and marathoner) of the trio, dove down and freed some life vests from the sunken boat, allowing all three to paddle ashore, fully clothed. That's why Guerin calls Munger, "Admiral Munger."

Berkshire accumulated about 11% of PS Group in 1990, paying about $32 a share for many of its shares. Afterwards PS Group's board approved Buffett's request to own up to 22.5% of the company, and later in the year granted Buffett permission to buy up to 45% of the stock, which he could do depending on market conditions, price, and the attractiveness of other investments.

Buffett gradually raised his stake in PS Group to about 22% largely by buying a big block of stock from the Tweedy Brown investment firm. During some of the time Buffett was buying PS Group stock, it carried a PE ratio above 50, so there must be something more to stock selection than just searching for low PE ratios.

What is it that Buffett is intrigued by in what appears to be a hard-to-understand firm with a strange mix of businesses?

PS Group traces its roots to Pacific Southwest Airlines, sold to USAir in 1987. After the sale, PS Group was left with an aircraft leasing operation, a fuel distribution unit, and oil and gas operations. Many of the oil and gas operations were sold in 1989. The company's largest investment is in aircraft leasing. It leases aircraft to USAir (synergy with a question mark). PS Group also has leased aircraft to a number of airlines that landed in bankruptcy court.

In 1987 PS Group, pouring $84 million into the travel agency business (another $49 million would be added in 1989), bought 81% of USTravel Systems, Inc., a large travel management system.

Founder Peter Sontag, a Columbia Business School graduate, and PS Group first came in contact when PS Group was a client of Sontag's firm.

Guerin says Buffett is a believer in the future of the multi-billion-dollar travel industry. At PS Group's annual meeting in 1990, Guerin said that Buffett "really believes strongly that the travel business is going to grow." (*San Diego Daily Transcript*, May 29, 1990)

But PS Group first tried to sell its travel unit agency to the Pritzker family which already owned 15% of the company, but talks fell through. Later the unit was sold to Dallas investor Murray Holland in 1994.

Guerin has said there were no advance conversations with Buffett before he invested.

At the annual meeting in 1991, Chairman Charles Rickershauser, also a friend of Buffett's, and CEO George Shortley (Guerin had stepped down to vice chairman of the firm) said Buffett remains a friend of the company, is available for counsel at any time, but in no way tells them how to run their business.

PS Group now is a combination holding and leasing firm, powerfully strange in its business mix. It is also a major investment for Guerin, who holds his stake in PS Group through Pacific Partners, a limited partnership investment firm he heads in Los Angeles.

Here's an indication of Guerin's investment record:

"The period 1965-1983, for example, beheld a compound gain of 316% for the S&P and 22,200% for Pacific Partners." (*The Midas Touch,* John Train, p. 92)

And during a 22-year stretch, while the Standard & Poor's 500 was up 510%, Guerin's Pacific Partners Ltd., grew 65,500%, or 34.1% annually.

If Buffett's investing results had an influence on Guerin so too did Buffett's operating style. The influence of Buffett on Guerin is apparent from the annual report: "PSG's full-time officers total four and the overall corporate staff totals thirteen...the policy of not discussing PSG operations except by communications sent simultaneously to all shareholders, and by information through public filings or by questions at the annual meeting remains in effect." Sound familiar?

The company later changed the policy and said it would answer questions in forums other than the annual meeting.

The firm came into a big chunk of 5,750 shares of Berkshire in 1986 as a result of a pension plan reversion. The Berkshire shares were acquired at a cost of $27.6 million, but were sold in 1991 for $47.8 million when PS Group, too leveraged, ran into trouble with its banks, a result of losses it was ringing up in its airplane leasing business of the early 90s. The airlines were losing billions, cutting back on flights, filing for bankruptcy, going out of business and just couldn't afford to lease planes.

The Berkshire shares were sold to the Sequoia Fund, headed by Buffett's friend, Bill Ruane, according toWall Street's Bruce Berkowitz.

At the time of the PS Group annual meeting in 1991, when PS Group still held the Berkshire stock, making for cross-ownership of Berkshire and PS Group, Rickershauser, a former head of the Pacific Stock Exchange and the Munger, Tolles law firm, said, "I wish we owned 22% of Berkshire."

But the mystery at PS Group, the one that once sent PS Group's stock on a roller-coaster ride, was the story of a fledgling hazardous waste and metals recycling business called Recontek, Inc.

Recontek? Again, hardly sounds like something of interest to Buffett, who is so insistent on here-and-now earnings, on fresh cash that can be invested right away.

Buffett and those around him say he has little interest in speculative projections, little interest in startup businesses that may be profitable in the by and by. But PS Group may be the exception. Early in 1989, PS Group agreed to invest in Recontek, also of San Diego.

Recontek developed a proprietary recycling process that takes liquid and solid hazardous waste—generated primarily from the plating, metal finishing, and circuit board industries—and recycles the waste into salable metals and industrial chemicals. It extracts salable commodities such as copper, nickel and zinc from metallic sludge by mixing chemicals with waste.

The process is important because it could provide industry a cheaper disposal method than hazardous waste landfills, deep wells or incinerators. It also reduces the liability for potential cleanup costs for underground and soil contamination.

After operating a pilot facility in San Diego, Recontek built its first recycling plant in Newman, Illinois. The company reached agreements with other communities to build recycling plants.

But in 1994 PS Group sold Recontek.

Munger says, "PS Group is another one where we got a little egg on our face. About nine things went wrong at once—including an indirect, huge exposure to USAir. A huge percentage of PS Group's assets depend on USAir's credit. And the shareholders' equity of USAir touched zero at its low point."

PS Group's performance was inspiring some people to yell "bankruptcy" in a crowded theater.

Bankruptcy would be a certainty for PS Group by the end of 1992, Gilford Securities President Robert Holmes told *USA Today* columnist Dan Dorfman. (April 3, 1992) Holmes was shorting the stock.

At the annual meeting in 1991, Buffett was asked about Berkshire's stake in PS Group. Buffett confirmed a position of just over 20% (1.2 million shares, or 19.9% at the end of 1993) but beyond that had no comment. Will we learn more one day? Most likely.

In 1992, when asked about its troubles, Buffett pointed out the company had denied it would file bankruptcy. Pressed about if it were in real trouble and could go bankrupt, Buffett tried to be positive.

"We'll see," he said.

By 1996 PS Group was still struggling and Berkshire still owned 19.9% of the company.

91

Wells Fargo

"A Dead Duck" soars like an eagle

Wells Fargo, the California bank that once owned the Pony Express, announced on October 24, 1990, that Buffett had bought five million shares or almost 10% of its common stock, becoming its largest stockholder.

The company's trademark, the Concord stagecoach, is an enduring symbol of reliability, of "coming through." For example, Wells Fargo has been profitable every year of its existence.

Wells Fargo came through in a big way for Buffett. Since its first stake, which Berkshire bought through Salomon, it has raised its position in the bank to 6.8 million shares or about 14%. Berkshire also holds about 28,000 shares of Wells Fargo in defined-benefit plans for some Berkshire employees, assuring them a better than anticipated retirement.

Once again Buffett struck when there was a stigma surrounding the purchase, because 1990 was a terrible time for banks. The very idea of buying a bank stock seemed outrageous at the time he did it. What the word "bank," meant on that day was layoffs, real estate loan writeoffs, slashed dividends—and some smear by association with the S&L crisis. Some pundits were suggesting that rapidly declining real estate prices could bring down the banking system.

The price-to-earnings ratio of Wells Fargo the day of the news of Berkshire's original investment was a minuscule 3.7!

Now, that's an out-of-favor company. Buffett bought his shares of the San Francisco-based bank holding company at about book value, which was just under 60 at the time.

Wells Fargo long has enjoyed a good reputation. Its management was so well thought of that other bankers trained under it. Henry Wells and William Fargo founded the company as an express delivery service and banking operation in 1852, just two years after American Express was founded.

Dating from the Gold Rush, the company has long provided banking services and an express line, transporting passengers, mail, gold, silver and currency throughout the western United States, Canada and Mexico—by stagecoach and rail.

In those days, a stagecoach traveled only about five miles an hour. Holdups were frequent. The company earned an important spot in the commercial development of the west.

Wells Fargo separated its banking business from its express business in 1905, and the bank established a history of buying other banks. The bank is making a big push toward electronic banking transactions and has made an effort to enter California's supermarkets, opening small branches staffed with a few tellers and an ATM. And through the use of laptop computers, Wells Fargo has streamlined the loan application process for small businesses.

The bank bought Crocker National in 1986, Barclays Bank of California in 1988, the California branch network of Great American Bank in 1990 and others along the way.

Wells Fargo stock had traded as high as $86 a share and as low as $41.25 in 1990. Buffett's initial average cost was about $58 a share. Berkshire soon began enjoying Wells Fargo's hefty $4 dividend.

Throughout his career Buffett has stood by the cash register counting that ever rising, fresh cash pouring in. He probably would concur with the model who once purred, "The nicest thing about money is that it never clashes with anything I wear."

At the time Buffett was buying Wells Fargo stock—he had started with a tiny stake back in 1989—any number of bright investors, including the Feshback Brothers, well-known short sellers, were shorting the stock, that is, betting it would drop. In recent years the stock has been fought over by both short sellers and value investors.

"Wells Fargo's a dead duck," Tom Barton, a money manager for the Feshback Brothers said.

"I don't think it's right to call them a bankruptcy candidate, but I think it's a teenager," he said, meaning the stock price could fall to the teens. "It has one of the highest exposures to real estate of any bank." (*Wall Street Journal*, November 1, 1990)

In one small way the short sellers were right. Soon the dividend was slashed and reserves for bad real estate loans increased dramatically.

Barron's John Liscio weighed in, saying Buffett "won't have to worry about who spends his fortune much longer, not if he keeps trying to pick a bottom in bank stocks." *(Barron's,* October, 29, 1990)

George Salem, an analyst with Prudential Securities Inc., was quoted in the same piece: "He picked the management that underwrites real estate the best. But one thing he didn't realize is that even Mark Spitz (the former Olympic star) can't swim in a hurricane in the middle of the ocean."

So how were Wells Fargo's earnings at the time? Doing quite nicely, really. The bank would wind up earning $712 million or $13.39 per share. However, as commercial real estate prices continued to decline in 1991, Wells Fargo's loan loss provisions rose.

"Despite this extremely difficult environment Wells Fargo remained profitable, as it has in every year this century even during the depths of the Great Depression," said Jim McCluskey, an investor in San Francisco.

The bank, which has never lost money on an annual basis, earned $19.17 in 1929, $14.71 in 1930 and $13.29 in 1931. "That's what Buffett was looking for," McCluskey said.

Buffett's trick is to swim with the tide when it looks to others as though he's swimming against it.

Just what tide did Buffett see? Buffett often kids about how little he thinks about macroeconomics, but Berkshire shareholder Yves Mojonnet thinks in the case of Wells Fargo, Buffett made macroeconomic decisions.

"I think he sees California as one of the largest industrial powers in the world and I think he saw bank consolidation," Mojonnet said. The California-oriented bank is, as is any bank, heavily dependent on the local economy. California's $750 billion economy accounts for about 13% of the nation's Gross National Product and employs almost 14 million people, about 12% of the nation's workforce. California, the world's sixth largest economy, is a vast economy.

Some also see Buffett's Wells Fargo stake as a Pacific Rim economic boom play.

And Mojonnet thinks Buffett saw good management, which Buffett has acknowledged. "Wells Fargo was the first to recognize bad loans to the Third World in 1986-87. Management was on top of it then and is on top of it now, cutting the dividend and increasing loan loss reserves," Mojonnet said several years ago. Now the dividend is being increased.

Buffett had once again taken an important stake in a major American enterprise, a strong franchise with about 20,000 employees, headed then by bank chairman Carl Reichardt, Buffett's friend, and now by Reichardt's successor, Paul Hazen and president Bill Zuendt, known as a hi-tech whiz.

Somehow, during the worst of times, as in the recession of 1990, Buffett always manages to generate the cash to become a major shareholder in the country's best businesses. But the Wells Fargo investment did carry with it plenty of risk, plenty of exposure to commercial and real estate loans, as well as HLTs, highly leveraged transactions, during a virtual California depression in real estate.

On the other hand, Wells Fargo traditionally has been ranked one of the most profitable and efficient banks in the country. Its return on assets in 1990 was 1.4% and its return on equity was 25%. It had the lowest exposure to foreign loans of any major bank in the country.

And the Wells Fargo earnings stagecoach had always driven through plenty of badlands to avoid robberies.

In 1991, Wells Fargo stock recovered, flying in the face of the shorts, burned in part because of Buffett's heavy buying. It was little wonder that in certain short seller circles, T-shirts proclaimed, "(Expletive deleted) Warren Buffett."

One more time, while almost everyone else was panicking, Buffett struck gold, this time out on the West Coast.

Forbes, in its April 15, 1991, issue quoted Munger about the Wells Fargo purchase: "It's all a bet on management. We think they will fix problems faster and better than other people."

When cost-conscious Reichardt found out one of his executives wanted to buy a Christmas tree for the office, Reichardt told him to buy it with his own money, not the bank's.

"When we heard that, we bought more stock," Munger said at the Berkshire annual meeting in 1991. The interest in Wells Fargo continued.

In 1991, Wells Fargo announced that Buffett was seeking permission from the Federal Reserve Board to more than double his stake to as much as 22%. In early August, Buffett got the approval.

Federal change-of-control laws require the Federal Reserve Board to review purchase requests if a buyer intends to acquire more than 10% of a bank holding company stock. One reason Buffett wanted more Wells Fargo was that he knew he could buy some at bargain prices.

In fact, Wells Fargo's gravity-defying ability to stay away from bad loan problems ended in 1991 with a second quarter announcement that the company would post a large loan loss jump and that earnings would be paltry, far below analysts' expectations. The loan loss figure late in 1991 was a stunning $700 million, creating a perfect second buying opportunity.

The stock sank back into Buffett's original buying range, then slowly recovered as a bank consolidation move swept the country.

Buffett's second purchase was made from August 4 to August 10, 1992, at prices ranging from $66 to $68. Buffett's friend, Walter Annenberg, also disclosed he owned 5.3% of Wells Fargo stock. Annenberg, a wealthy friend of Ronald Reagan's and businessman who has given more than $1 billion to educational projects, owned 4.53 million shares or about 8.6% of Wells Fargo by late 1994.

Late in 1992, Buffett said he had invested another $37 million—at prices ranging from $66 to $69 a share.

And Prudential's Salem kept up his sell pitch in late 1992, saying what a terrible stock Wells Fargo was: "When Warren Buffett runs out of money, the stock will plummet," adding that Buffett might just as well make "donations to a good cause."

"He's supporting the stock; otherwise it would be much lower," Salem said.

He said the stock would make a good short, that only Buffett was holding the shorts back from a real onslaught. On January 7, 1993, Wells Fargo reported that Buffett had bought another 66,800 shares in late December, 1992, between $74.46 and $75.43 a share, bringing his total to 6,358,418 shares.

Prudential's Salem came back that month with, "We reiterate our sell rating on the shares of Wells Fargo & Co...Eventual downside risk appears considerable—perhaps to $60 or below...The price more than reflects a nearly complete recovery which we don't see."

While some short sellers were predicting a 50% decline in the stock because of predicted writeoffs, Wells Fargo stock solidly crossed $100 a share.

Then the following item appeared in the *The Atlanta Journal/The Atlanta Constitution* on April 30, 1993:

> Calling it the "strangest stock I have ever covered," Prudential's Salem dropped coverage of Wells Fargo. A vociferous critic of the San Francisco-based bank, Mr. Salem has been bedeviled for years by Wells Fargo.
>
> The analyst has carried a sell recommendation on the stock since December, 1989, when it was trading at about $60. The stock closed Thursday at $105.37½.
>
> Mr. Salem, an often-quoted 25-year industry veteran, insists he isn't giving up on a bad call. 'This is not a surrender of any kind, ... It was a business decision based on where I thought I could spend my time more profitably. Wells Fargo is overpriced, volatile and unpredictable and not many people from investment-land care about it.'

Buffett told *Forbes,* October 18, 1993, "I don't want to start touting Wells Fargo stock or anything. I just think it is a very good business, with the best management, at a reasonable price. And usually when that is the case, there is more money to be made."

The stock kept climbing and Buffett bought more in November 1993, hiking his stake to 6.8 million shares.

A couple of weeks later it was noted that with reserves for bad loans of $2.1 billion, Wells Fargo might be $1 billion over-reserved, money that could go toward profits later on. ("Heard on the Street" column, *Wall Street Journal*, November 17, 1993)

To make a long story short, the stock shot up even higher, past $150, giving Buffett a double in less than four years. In the spring of 1995 Wells Fargo said it planned to buy back 10% of its stock over time. The stock shot well past $200 in 1995.

For Buffett, Wells Fargo delivered. And kept delivering.

ANOTHER NEWS FLASH. On October 18, 1995, Wells Fargo launched a hostile takeover with Buffett's approval, of rival First Interstate Bancorp of Los Angeles.

Why with Buffett's approval when he normally doesn't care for hostile takeovers? It's probably because Buffett doesn't control Berkshire's investees. Buffett, short of a moral turpitude, backs management which has an overriding reponsibility to its owners.

Berkshire's structure allowed Buffett to "avoid the dragons."

The unsolicited bid was for about $10 billion in Wells Fargo stock, the biggest in banking history. That day First Interstate stock was up 35¾ to $141¾ and Wells Fargo was up 15⅜ to $229.

Buffett was in on the failed negotiations between leaders of Wells and First Interstate. "Mr. Buffett stated that he had studied both companies in some detail. He also stated that one could come up with positives and negatives of one company compared to the other, but in the the end. when evaluating each company, one would conclude that they were about equal and that accordingly the exchange ratio of .625 [of a Wells share for each First Interstate share] made sense to him." (First Interstate letter to shareholders announcing on November 6, 1995, that it had entered into an agreement to merge with First Bank System)

The banking combination of Wells and First Interstate would create the nation's eighth-largest bank, with more than $100 billion in assets. Wells Fargo is the No. 3 bank in California and First Interstate is No. 2, after Bank of America.

Wells Fargo said it could eliminate duplicate California operations and save $700 million in expenses.

First Interstate Chairman William Siart said: "I am deeply disappointed that Wells Fargo would take this uninvited action."

First Interstate rejected the Wells Fargo offer and agreed to merge with smaller First Bank System of Minneapolis.

But that was not to be the end of the saga. Gradually as Wells Fargo stock rose faster than First Bank's, the Wells offer became more attractive. And suddenly an SEC ruling ordered First Bank to halt repurchases of its stock for two years after a merger made the deal less attractive to First Bank's shareholders.

Soon thereafter the First Interstate board told Siart to begin merger talks with Hazen.

On January 24, 1996, Wells won the hostile fight for First Interstate. Wells planned to cut 7,000 jobs at First Interstate, including Siart's. And it planned to cut 350 branches.

In the end Wells paid two-thirds of a share of its stock for every First Interstate share, amounting to the biggest U.S. bank takeover ever.

Wells Fargo suddenly was a western powerhouse of a bank, the eighth largest bank in the country. And California's economy was showing signs of recovery.

92

Guinness

Waiting for the world recovery

In 1991 Buffett quietly struck again, buying about $265 million, or 31.2 million shares of London-based Guinness, one of the world's largest purveyors of liquor.

It was Buffett's first significant overseas investment and his first major brand-name purchase since Coke and Gillette. Guinness became another cash cow in the Berkshire pasture.

Buffett compares Guinness to Coca-Cola as a strong franchise, but in the 1991 annual report he wrote: "You'll never get the drinks confused—and your Chairman remains unmovably in the Cherry Coke camp."

Acquisition-minded Guinness is known for its beer, particularly Guinness Stout, a global beer brand, served in some 130 countries—shades of Coca-Cola. Guinness brews Guinness and Harp beers world-wide, and Budweiser and Carlsberg beers in Ireland.

It's well known for its Scotch whiskey brands such as its Johnnie

Walker, Bell's, Dewar's and White Horse lines. Guinness also is known for its Gordon's vodka and gin and Tanqueray gin. Indeed, the company is the world leader in Scotch and gin.

Guinness got its start when Arthur Guinness leased a small brewery in Dublin, Ireland, in 1759 making ales sold in Dublin. And Guinness is famed for publishing the *Guinness Book of Records*, which contains such records as who's won the most Tony Awards as well as facts about First Ladies, the world's largest octopus, paper clip and watermelon (262 pounds). And we learn that the most cinematic costume changes were made by Elizabeth Taylor when she changed dresses 65 times for the filming of *Cleopatra*. Then there's the *Guinness Book of Olympic Records*, an offshoot of the original, begun by a Guinness executive in the 1950s.

In the mid-1980s, scandal hit Guinness when its chairman was jailed for manipulating stock prices during its takeover of United Distillers. Remember one of Buffett's major rules: buy a great company when it stumbles.

First reported in the *Independent Newspaper* of London, the Guinness stake story was picked up by the Bloomberg News Service and the *Omaha World-Herald* but not by any other major U.S. financial publication until a week and a half later, when Berkshire confirmed that it owned about 1.6% of Guinness.

Under British law, stockholders must identify themselves when they own 3% of a company.

Guinness's largest stockholders are the Prudential of London and LVMH (Louis Vuitton Moet Hennessey), a French maker of beverages, luggage lines, perfumes, beauty and fashion products, including Dom Perignon, Moet & Chandon, Hennessey, Christian Dior and Givenchy. So not only does Buffett buy into brand names, but with Guinness he bought into name-brand partners, because Guinness bought 24% of Moet Hennessey in the late 1980s while that French firm bought a similar stake in Guinness in 1990. The firms share sales operations in the United States and Japan.

Guinness's ties with LVMH date back to 1987 when the firms formed distribution agreements. Guinness invested in LVMH to keep it from splitting apart and to protect its joint ventures when a battle for control broke out for LVMH.

The company is a partner in the New Era Beverage in the United States. Its U.S. headquarters is Schenley Industries in Dallas.

Guinness will celebrate its 250th birthday in Buffett's lifetime, if

Buffett's new fitness program continues to serve him well.

The stock did poorly the year following Buffett's purchase and the Bloomberg news service carried a report on January 29, 1993, that Buffett was rumored to be selling his Guinness stake, but there was no confirmation.

Although Guinness had a tough year, Buffett was buying more, not selling. Berkshire's 1992 Annual Report, reflecting business as of the end of 1992 said the Guinness stake had increased to 2%, not decreased. It listed the stake as having a cost basis of $333 million and a worth of $299 million.

Bill Ruane, head of Sequoia Fund, which also has a stake in Guinness, has said, "Guinness...is a wonderful company. It has a phenomenal Scotch business throughout the world. But it's been affected by the worldwide recession—and it's not just in Japan...It has outstanding management and fine brands. Guinness Stout is almost regarded as food in Ireland. I understand it's even approved for medicinal purposes by the government's Group Health Plan there."

However, two years after buying his first shares of Guinness, Buffett remains underwater on this one. Has he gotten too high on Guinness? Or is Guinness about ready to get high itself? As Buffett would say, "We'll know in a few years."

Guinness and LVMH restructured their cross-ownership in early 1994.

The change disengaged the British brewer and distiller from LVMH's perfume and luggage businesses while linking it closer to the French company's champagne-and-cognac unit. Also, it will make it easier for LVMH to diversify further into businesses that don't interest Guinness.

Under the agreement, Guinness sold its 24% indirect stake in LVHM for $1.84 billion and bought 34% of LVMH's Moet Hennessey SA wine and spirits unit. LVMH planned to reduce its stake in Guinness to 20% from 24% by the middle of 1995.

"This is the first good news for Guinness in two years," said Graeme Eadie, an analyst at NatWest Securities, noting that the company has been hurt by the recession and declining consumption of Scotch whiskey. (*Wall Street Journal*, January 21, 1994)

In all Guinness turned flat, and there were unconfirmed reports the Guinness stock has been sold, possibly at a loss. But there has been no word from Berkshire of a sale.

Stay tuned for the world recovery.

93

General Dynamics

So much for: "We-don't-understand-technology."

General Dynamics announced July 23, 1992, that Berkshire had bought 8.7 million shares, counting a 2-for-1 split in 1994, of its outstanding stock for $312 million. Buffett had bought 15% of the nation's second largest defense contractor.

So much for: "We-don't-understand-technology." Maybe his friendship with Bill Gates had an effect.

But was this any way to invest in the post-Cold War era at a time when everyone knew the defense industry was contracting? Since 1989 more than 1.5 million jobs in the defense industry were terminated.

GD spokesman Ray Lewis explained that Buffett bought the stock in the open market just as the Falls Church, Virginia-based defense giant completed a $957 million repurchase of its own shares. Superb timing for a self-proclaimed non-timer. GD itself bought 30% of its own stock back through a "Dutch auction," a process whereby investors (including the

Crown family) tendered their shares, selling them back to the company at a price between about \$33 and \$38 a share. The company repurchased 26.4 million of its 80 million shares at about \$36 a share.

The Crown and Goodman families had reduced their stake to 14.4% of the company, while Berkshire surprised the investment community by becoming GD's largest shareholder.

Under new management headed by William Anders, a former astronaut who took over the joystick in early 1991, GD had been slimming down and selling off non-core businesses.

The company's military contracts have included the F-16 fighter jet, Atlas and Centaur launch vehicles, M-IA tanks (used extensively in Operation Desert Storm) and M-60 tanks, plus the Trident and Seawolf submarines.

GD had sold its Cessna aircraft division for \$600 million in the first quarter and subsequently disposed of other units. Then it announced it would sell its missile business to GM Hughes for a minimum of \$450 million. And management has been selling other non-core businesses to raise more cash.

GD's Electric Boat unit was vulnerable to cancellation of the Seawolf submarine, but Congress voted to build a second Seawolf, at an estimated cost of \$2 billion.

Buffett saw a well-managed company doing a good job of restructuring in a consolidating industry, and buying back stock. The company had little debt, and planned sales were bringing mounds of cash. However, analysts were seemingly blind to the prudence of Buffett's move, saying the industry had little prospects for growth.

One analyst, the day of Buffett's purchase, said he doubted the stock could reach \$40 in 12 months. Hmm. The stock practically reached it a few trading days later, did in mid-September, and shot past \$50 a share in the fall of 1992.

Along the way Berkshire granted GD its voting rights, and GD officials talked of being open to selling even core businesses. In December 1992, Lockheed agreed to buy fast-shrinking GD's fighter plane unit for about \$1.5 billion.

All the while GD held to a strategy of beefing up the core units and selling off others. By January, 1993, the stock was trading at \$56 a share, pretty good post-Cold War work. Large cash dividends—a total of \$25 a share in 1993—resulted in a lower stock price, but still trading not far below \$50.

Buffett explained in the 1992 Annual Report:

> We were lucky in our General Dynamics pur-

> chase. I had paid little attention to the company until last summer, when it was announced it would repurchase about 30% of its shares by way of a Dutch tender. Seeing an arbitrage opportunity, I began buying the stock for Berkshire, expecting to tender our holdings for a small profit. We've made the same sort of commitment perhaps a half-dozen times in the past few years, reaping decent rates of return for the short periods our money has been tied up.
>
> But then I began studying the company and the accomplishments of Bill Anders in the brief time he'd been CEO. And what I saw made my eyes pop: Bill had a clearly articulated and rational strategy; he had been focused and imbued with a sense of urgency in carrying it out; and the results were truly remarkable.
>
> In short order, I dumped my arbitrage thoughts and decided that Berkshire should become a long-term investor with Bill. We were helped in gaining a large position by the fact that a tender greatly swells the volume of trading in a stock. In a one-month period, we were able to purchase 14% of the General Dynamics shares that remained outstanding after the tender was completed.

The investment worked very well. In mid-1993 GD was writing shareholders:

> On January 1, 1991, when your new management team first took office, total debt exceeded $1 billion and debt ratings were falling. We reported a cash account of just $115 million and expected cash flow to be negative over the next year. By the end of 1993, we expect your company to be virtually debt free. Similarly, at the end of May your company will have a cash and marketable securities balance of approximately $1.6 billion and an unused $700 million line of credit. This ample liquidity is especially impressive considering that it comes after your new management team—through debt reduction, dividends, share repurchases and special distributions—has already returned $2.2 billion to General Dynamics' lenders and shareholders for them to reinvest in America for competitive strength and new jobs.

In the first two years of Berkshire's stake, as GD raised dividends and bought back stock, Buffett had more than doubled his money. In April 1994, Buffett sold 20% of the GD stake and by the end of August the stake was 5.7 million shares. By early 1995 the stake had dropped a bit more to 8.4% and according to GD's proxy as of February 14, 1996, Berkshire held 4,963,703 shares, or 7.7% of the company.

By 1996, with its core businesses in nuclear submarines and armored vehicles and even with the 1995 purchase of Bath Iron Works, which builds ships for the U.S. Navy, GD had more than a $1 billion in cash and virtually no debt.

GD was a big winner.

94

UST. Money in the Weeds

Just slide a pinch between your cheek and gum.

Philip Morris stunned the market April 2, 1993, saying it would cut prices on its Marlboro cigarettes—the best selling U.S. brand—in an effort to keep customers from buying discount brands.

The "Call For Philip Morris" giant said it expected its domestic cigarette unit's profits to drop as much as 40%. On that word, Philip Morris stock which had traded as high as $86⅝ in late 1992, fell from $63 to $49, tree chopping about $13 billion off its market capitalization. The stocks of all tobacco companies dived.

Send in Buffett, although it may be controversial that he invests in defense, alcohol and tobacco companies.

On April 13, 1993, *USA Today's* Dan Dorfman reported Buffett had taken almost a 5% stake in UST, formerly U.S. Tobacco, a leading maker of smokeless tobacco.

Not until June 1994, was there confirmation of Buffett's stake in UST when an SEC filing showed Berkshire owned 5.6 million shares, or 2.5% of the firm. Buffett had asked that the stake be kept confidential for a year. In 1996 the 1995 position was revealed to be 5.2 million shares.

UST is known for its Copenhagen and Skoal products. Copenhagen is the world's best selling brand of snuff. And Skoal is America's favorite winter-green-flavored moist smokeless tobacco. Just slide a pinch between your cheek and gum.

UST is one of the nation's most profitable companies with 87% of the chewing tobacco market. It also sells wines, including Chateau Ste. Michelle, Columbia Crest, Conn Creek and Villa Mt. Eden and has a sparkling wine made with the Domaine Ste. Michelle label. UST also owns a video distribution firm, Cabin Fever Entertainment, Inc.

Brand loyalty is strong, with discount brands penetrating only 3% of the smokeless tobacco market compared with 27% of the cigarette market. And chewing tobacco costs about a third of what cigarettes do.

UST has a consistently high return on equity, is debt free, and has paid a dividend since 1912, increasing it for more than the past 20 years.

Buffett had struck again under this scenario: when there's a stigma in the industry, locate a brand name cash cow.

UST has the kind of growth that Buffett likes, reflected by a stock market value of $111 million in 1973 and about $7 billion in the early 1990s. Almost makes you wanna chew.

Moist snuff originated in the Scandinavian countries. Due to societal attitudes and restrictions on "spitting", the product was used in the upper lip where there are no salivary glands.

The product was introduced to America when Scandinavian immigrants brought it along with them. Most of the first wave of immigrants worked in underground mines. Given the prevailing working conditions, they needed to get the dirt out of their mouths constantly so they needed to salivate to spit out the dirt. Thus the product migrated from the upper lip to the lower lip, an area of the mouth which has many salivary glands.

The moist snuff business, which serves only about four million users, has different and stronger fundamentals than the domestic cigarette business. UST operates in an industry with a near monopolistic share of the market, high barriers to entry and few substitute products.

The top two players, UST and Conwood, have a 95% share of the market for smokeless tobacco. The production process is proprietary and secretive—so proprietary that UST designs and makes its own machinery—and not easily duplicated, with the entire process taking about six years.

Also, most of UST's required capital expenses are covered by depreciation and amortization charges. Therefore, a major portion of the cash flow generated is essentially free cash flow available for shareholders.

A controversial issue that remains is pricing flexibility. The fact is Conwood almost always follows a UST-led price increase.

Still in 1995 UST's sales flattened. Its president resigned, and a public health controversy over UST's moist-smokeless-tobacco products showed signs of going up in smoke as all tobacco products drew heavy criticism.

95

Bristol-Myers Squibb

For market headaches, take two Bufferin.

Buffett, after years of saying drug stocks were not up his alley, bought into Bristol-Myers Squibb, a New York company formed by a merger between Bristol-Myers and Squibb Corp. in 1989.

USA Today reported June 9, 1994, that Berkshire owned 957,200 shares that were bought in 1993, according to an SEC filing. The filing wasn't made public for a year so Buffett could have confidentiality.

It was reported that Bristol-Myers officials had no idea about Buffett's investment, which is 0.2% of the stock, until the SEC filing was released.

Like all drug stocks, Bristol-Myers was sluggish during the uncertainty of how health reform would play out, but has since recovered strongly from that battering.

But Bristol-Myers has a worldwide presence, an excellent balance sheet and cash flow. It also pays a good dividend and buys back its stock.

With annual sales of more than $13 billion, Bristol-Myers is the world's third largest drug firm behind Merck and Glaxco and is a major force in offering anti-cancer and cardiovascular drugs. Flagship drugs are Toxol for some cancers, Pravachol, a cholesterol reducer and Capoten for hypertension.

Bristol-Myers distributes consumer products such as Ban deodorant, Bufferin, Excedrin and Clairol hair products. It is also America's second-largest infant-formula maker.

Bristol-Myers, in recent years has cut costs by lowering employee ranks and introducing a line of new products.

Buffett had a toehold in another of America's great corporations whose stock has been a big winner in the last couple of years.

96

Gannett
Extra! Extra!
Read All About It!

On December 15, 1994, Gannett the nation's largest newspaper publisher, announced that Berkshire owned 4.9% of its stock.

Buffett had returned to a large media concern as the stock traded near a low after years of sluggishness in the newspaper industry.

His $335 million investment gave him an additional stake in media companies which now includes the *Buffalo News*, *Washington Post* and Disney.

Arlington, Virginia-based Gannett publishes *USA Today*, the second largest newspaper in the country with a circulation of about two million. It also publishes 91 other daily newspapers, including *The Detroit News* with a circulation of about 370,000 and operates 15 television stations as well as 13 radio stations. Gannett's cable division serves 458,000 subscribers. Additionally, Gannett is the nation's largest outdoor advertising company. It owns the Louis Harris opinion polls, wire service bureaus and a large outdoor advertising business also.

The company, headed by Jack Curley, has 36,000 employees and 14,000 stockholders. Berkshire is the biggest stockholder.

Again, another toe-hold in a major media business which is buying back its own stock.

So what's the strategy here? Maybe, it's to buy all companies beginning with G. Maybe the next annual report will be in Green.

In 1995 Gannett bought Multimedia of Greenville, South Carolina.

97

PNC
An East Coast Regional Bank

On February 14, 1995, the same day Buffett announced Berkshire held 9.8% of American Express, there was a second little noticed news item: "Warren Buffett has 8.3% stake in PNC Bank Corp."

Berkshire had bought 19,453,300 shares of the big Pittsburgh-based bank holding company– the 12th largest bank in the country– at a cost of $503 million.

In the fall of 1994, PNC had announced that rising interest rates had so battered its securities portfolio that 1995 earnings would be 15% below analysts expectations, always a no-no in investment land. The bank also took restructuring charges when it lost six employees in the crash of USAir Flight 427 which went down just outside Pittsburgh September 8, 1994. The stock sank from about $30 to about $20 a share and Buffett bought in the mid-range of those figures.

PNC Bank, with $64 billion in assets, owns Pittsburgh National

Bank, Provident National Bank, Marine Bancorp, Northeastern Bancorp, Hershey Bank, Citizens Fidelity Bank, Central Bancorp and Bank of Delaware. It has more than 600 banking offices in Pennsylvania, Delaware, Ohio, Kentucky, Indiana and New Jersey. In 1995 PNC bought New Jersey's Midlantic Corp. for $2.8 billion and Chemical Bank New Jersey.

In 1995 Buffett reduced his PNC position to below 5%.

Buffett had again bought a large stake in a bank with presumably temporary setbacks.

Remember Wells Fargo?

98

Stakes In Financial Services Companies

A short time later, on March 28, 1994, Dorfman reported that Berkshire held relatively small stakes in three financial services companies: First Interstate Bancorp, a Los Angeles-based bank holding company, SunTrust Banks, Inc., an Atlanta-based banking firm and Federal National Mortgage Association (Fannie Mae).

Dorfman, saying he was quoting 13F filings with the SEC, said Berkshire held 955,000 shares of First Interstate, 567,000 shares of Fannie Mae and 1.55 million shares of SunTrust. It was later revealed that Berkshire had upped its stake in SunTrust in 1994 to 3.1 million shares.

Big First Interstate has the largest multistate branch network, operating almost 1,200 branches. It has a large presence in the West and in Texas. The bank had about 26,000 employees before being bought out by

Wells Fargo.

SunTrust Banks, created from the 1985 merger of Trust Company of Georgia and SunBanks in Florida, headed by James B. Williams who is a Coca-Cola director, is known for owning about $2 billion of Coke stock.

So there Buffett has a Coke and a banking industry consolidation play.

Buffett had extended his banking reach into the South and beefed it up on the West Coast. Perhaps one day he'll merge Wells Fargo, PNC, First Interstate, SunTrust, First Empire and Firstier into Berkshire Bank.

Buffett's tiptoe into the stock of Fannie Mae, a company like Freddie Mac which provides residential mortgage funds, is another move into financial services. Maybe Buffett plans to merge American Express, Salomon and Freddie and Fannie into a Berkshire Financial Services unit.

In 1995 word came that Berkshire held 1.41 million shares of Key-Corp, the big bank holding company in Cleveland, Ohio.

Later in 1995 Minneapolis-based First Bank System acquired First Tier of Omaha for about $700 million in stock. Because Berkshire owned about 5% of FirstTier, Berkshire wound up with 858,178 shares of First Bank System stock.

Also, with Berkshire's acquisition of GEICO, Berkshire received about 1.9 million shares that GEICO had in its stock portfolio. Thus Berkshire wound up with about a 2% stake in First Bank System known particularly for its credit card and trust services.

Also in 1994 Buffett bought 262,000 shares of Merrill Lynch & Co. according to a 1995 SEC filing. (*USA Today*, September 28, 1995)

The Wall Street Journal reported on June 14, 1996, that Berkshire acquired a 2.2 million share stake in Sears, Roebuck & Co. in the first quarter of 1995, according to an SEC filing.

Also Berkshire raised its stake in Dean Witter Discover & Co. to 2.8 million shares in the first quarter of 1995.

The story also said Berkshire cut its holdings in PNC Bank by 3.7 million shares to 16 million shares.

Further, it said Berkshire trimmed its year-ago position in Merrill Lynch by 739,600 shares to 205,400 shares and lowered its holdings of Viacom Class B shares by 495,000 to 512,253 shares.

Buffett was making a large play on bank consolidation and in the financial services industry. He was beginning not only to dominate companies, but industries.

99

The Small Office

"World Headquarters"—3,775 square feet *(leased)*
Putting Buffett on hold

Buffett has dubbed Berkshire's tiny headquarters in mid-town Omaha, "World Headquarters." Mission control has 3,775 square feet of *leased* space.

The office, also called "The Pleasure Palace," "The Temple," and "The Monolith in 2001," is part of a small set of library-quiet offices on the southeast corner of the 14th floor, taking up a section of one floor at modest-sized Kiewit Plaza.

"The whole operation could fit inside less than half a tennis court," says Peter Lynch. (foreword of *The Warren Buffett Way* by Robert Hagstrom)

Michael Assael rebuttal: "But Peter, half a tennis court is 39 x 36 = 1,404 square feet. How could 3,775 square feet fit inside 1,404 square feet?"

Buffett once pointed out the "boardroom" to a visitor, saying of the

Kiewit Plaza in midtown Omaha. Berkshire's offices are on the 14th floor. Buffett variously calls it "World Headquarters," "The Temple" and "The Pleasure Palace."

(Photo by Pat Kilpatrick)

7 foot by 10 foot room, "We could change it to a closet if we had to."

For another visitor when the subject of bridge came up, Buffett instantly pulled from his files a 1929 newspaper article reporting the acquittal of a woman who killed her husband over a bridge game argument.

Here at headquarters, exactly 20 blocks from Buffett's house, 12 people run Berkshire. Buffett, in Berkshire's 1995 annual report said through acquisitions in 1995 Berkshire inherited 11,000 new employees. "Our headquarters staff grew only from 11 to 12. (No sense going crazy.)"

The people at headquarters are Buffett; Michael A. Goldberg, who oversees the insurance and credit units; Marc Hamburg, chief financial officer; Daniel J. Jaksich, controller; Jerry W. Hufton, director of taxes; Mark D. Millard, director of financial assets; Debbie Bosanek, Buffett's administrative assistant; Debbie Ray, receptionist; Kelly Muchemore and K.C. Nussrallah, who are secretaries; and Kerby Ham and Angie Wells, who are in accounting.

Mrs. Bosanek, known for her efficiency, once slowed Berkshire's operations for a moment by causing Buffett to be put on hold.

She had called a fellow who happened to be speaking to Buffett. The man put Buffett on hold and told his secretary he'd take Mrs. Bosanek's call since he wanted to thank her for help on a business matter.

(Photo by Nancy Line Jacobs)

Debbie Bosanek, Berkshire's administrative assistant, fields many of the calls, ranging from important to peculiar.

Buffett and a mortified Mrs. Bosanek figured out quickly that she had caused him to be put on hold. "It was probably the first time he's ever been put on hold," she moaned.

Mrs. Bosanek gets many requests to be put through to Buffett, but she puts through only a few. Once an insistent caller said he had to get in touch with Buffett. When Mrs. Bosanek refused, the caller said he'd see to it her next job was at Burger King.

Another man called once saying he was a good friend of Buffett's and demanded to speak to Buffett. Again, Mrs. Bosanek declined. The caller then said he knew Buffett so well he'd "call him on his car phone." Buffett has no car phone.

Once a caller wanted to speak to Mrs. Bosanek to ask if she ever actually saw Buffett. Buffett happened to be standing at her desk. She looked up at him and replied to the caller, "Yes, sometimes I *do* see him!"

At headquraters, the carpet is industrial; the wallpaper is cypress green, plastic-weave.

Near an area where Buffett stashes his Cherry Coke supply is a sign: "Coca-Cola Sold Here Ice Cold."

Buffett buys his own and brings them from his home to the office when he runs low.

There are no signs, no logos, nothing really to indicate anything about Berkshire. Even Berkshire's insurance business in Omaha is in a nondescript building not far from Kiewit Plaza, which modestly carries a small sign saying National Indemnity Co. It is through "NICO" that Buffett makes a great number of his investments.

But the heart of Berkshire lies in Buffett's 325-square-foot office at Kiewit Plaza. It is here that Buffett reads and works the phone, staying in touch with his managers, friends and brokers and responding, usually with short, witty notes, to wave after wave of mail. To his innumerable requests to speak, he replies with a polite note to the effect: "Too many invitations, too little time." He says, "I spend an inordinate amount of time on the mail."

There are no hovering assistants, no computers; there is no typing pool. There are tan metal filing drawers, almost two hundred of them which contain everything from correspondence with Ben Graham to copies of Buffett's own letters and of course annual reports.

Rare photos of Buffett's office and Berkshire's headquarters show little more than a few remarkably plain chairs, desks, couches, framed documents on the walls. There is an original Thomas Edison stock ticker tape given to him by a friend many years ago. A bookshelf contains financial volumes, including several editions of Graham and Dodd's *Security Analysis*, including a worn copy of the 1934 first edition.

(Photo by Gail Wyman)

Marc Hamburg is Berkshire's chief financial officer and producer of the Hollywood hit: Berkshire's pre-annual meeting videos.

Along the walls are displays of Wall Street memorabilia such as a copy of the *New York Times* from October 31, 1929 bearing the headline, "Stocks Mount in All-day Rally: Rockefeller buying heartens market; Two-day closing ordered to ease strain." And there are headlines about the crash and other Wall Street events.

When Adam Smith interviewed Buffett for a *Money World* show aired after the annual meeting in 1990, the two men simply sat in small, nondescript chairs just a few feet apart facing one another at Berkshire's headquarters.

But very few people ever get access to Buffett's office. Many of the top managers of Berkshire operating units have never even been to headquarters in Omaha. Buffett sees a limited number of people a week, and only very rarely does he give interviews.

Buffett's aversion to interviews was documented in a four-page story in *Money* magazine by Gary Belsky, who told of not being able to get an interview with Buffett after Mrs. Kaiser turned down his request.

Even after Belsky flew to Omaha, he got the same answer when he called Mrs. Kaiser from the lobby of Kiewit Plaza.

He reported that the guard who heard the phone conversation said: "You took that better than most."

Belsky: "Most? Do people drop by like this a lot?"

Guard: "About once a day."

Belsky: "Does she ever let them up?"

Guard: "Sometimes."

Belsky: "Do you think she'll let me up?"

Guard: "No." *(Money,* August, 1991)

The story was reported in the *Omaha World-Herald* under the headline "Buffett Ignores Money."

With few visitors, Buffett hunkers down over his work, often snacking at his desk. The storeroom is filled with staples of Buffett's phoneside lunches—Hawaiian potato chips, Cherry Cokes and See's candy.

Buffett sticks largely to his favorite diet of hamburgers, chips, and Cokes for lunch and rare steaks and a double order of hash browns for dinner. He likes to snack on Planters peanuts and Haagen-Dazs strawberry ice cream.

Then it's back to his reading and phoning.

It is all as simple as simple can be.

100

The Indefensible

"It's shameful how much I love it."

Buffett bought Berkshire's first corporate jet in 1986, and it has been the butt of jokes, mostly from Buffett himself, ever since. "It's shameful how much I love it...I can't explain it. It's a total blank in my mind. I've given speeches against them for years," he says.

"Occasionally a man must rise above principle," he adds.

And Buffett has written, "I find the thought of retiring the plane more revolting than the thought of retiring the chairman.

"In this matter I've demonstrated uncharacteristic flexibility. For years I argued passionately against corporate jets. But finally my dogma was run over by my karma."

The first airplane was a 20-year-old Falcon jet that Buffett picked up for only $850,000. It cost about $200,000 a year to operate. In 1989 he turned it in for a really first-class jet, though again a used one, bought for $6.7 million.

"The old plane had lots of problems," said a worker at Omaha's Eppley Airport. The new one—a Canadair Challenger—is a sleek white jet, seating about 10 people. It's housed at the Sky Harbor facilities at Eppley. It has no insignia—nothing to suggest it belongs to Berkshire.

The pilots for the plane are from the Peter Kiewit firm in Omaha.

Buffett uses the plane often because he travels about 60 days a year, mainly tending to the boards on which he sits. (*Business Week*, August 19, 1991) He's glad to share it with people who have Berkshire business.

If passengers are aboard, Buffett will chat briefly and then read, sometimes going through a large pile of mail. "He'll let us piggyback in the plane," says a Borsheim's employee. "He usually reads." Sometimes Buffett talks to a passenger or two about buying their business.

The plane is the one toy of the rich that Buffett accepts for the convenience it provides.

But Munger has never traveled in the jet, refusing to get in it, kidding Buffett that the thing is a monstrosity against shareholder interests and so he refuses to condone its existence.

Munger, who refers to the plane as *The Aberration*, travels on commercial coach flights and carries his own bags. He showed up at Borsheim's once carrying his own luggage, one suitcase in each hand.

Privately Munger has said that if any CEO deserves a jet it is Buffett and that for his needs it makes sense. Berkshire shareholder Ed Prendeville recalls overhearing Munger coming out of an annual meeting in the mid-1980s telling someone, "It's the most deserved jet in corporate America."

But Munger's public stance is that the purchase of the airplane is total extravagance and something with which he is not familiar.

With that much needling from Munger, Buffett threatened to name the aircraft, *The Charles T. Munger*, but instead dubbed it *The Indefensible*.

In a *Fortune* story November 5, 1990, when Berkshire's stock price had fallen to $5,550 a share from a beginning-of-the-year price of about $8,675, Buffett was asked about *The Indefensible* and quipped, "That'll be the last thing to go."

When the Salomon crisis was at its height and Buffett was constantly using the plane to take him from New York to Omaha and back, he re-christened the aircraft *Somewhat Indefensible*. Could it become *The Indispensible*?

Nothing could beat the punchline in the 1990 Annual Report: Buffett wrote that if he left the scene, Munger immediately would sell the corporate jet, "ignoring my wish that it be buried with me."

If you've ever wondered what would happen to the companies Berkshire owns, such as Coca-Cola, after Buffett dies, consider this: of Coca-Cola Buffett said—Pharoah-like—"There actually will be a short-term bulge (in Coke sales) as I plan to have a large supply buried with me aboard the plane."

In 1995, in his role as pitchman for Nebraska economic development, Buffett posed for photos in front of *The Indefensible* which said "Until Midwest Express came to Omaha this was the only way I could buy a nonstop."

The ad, promoting Midwest's role in Omaha's economic development, quoted Buffett: "Last month I flew Midwest Express to Washington and arrived just as quickly and comfortably as if I had been in Berkshire's corporate jet. (And believe me, it cost a whole lot less!)"

Although Buffett endorsed Midwest Express service, he indicated he wouldn't give up the corporate jet. "Once spoiled, always spoiled," he said. (*Omaha World-Herald*, June 26, 1995)

101

The Importance of Charles Munger

Curmudgeon, sidekick and interchangeable partner "In bad years, he's my senior partner."

Berkshire's Vice Chairman Charles Munger is Buffett's friend, soulmate, sidekick and interchangeable partner. Buffett likes to joke that Munger is his "junior partner in good years and senior partner in bad years."

Unlike Buffett, Munger has sold some Berkshire stock along the way, a few hundred shares which he has given to such entities as Los Angeles' Good Samaritan Hospital, Planned Parenthood, Stanford University Law School and the Harvard-Westlake School, a private day school in Los Angeles. (*Forbes*, January 22, 1996)

"I've tried to imitate, in a poor way, the life of Benjamin Franklin. When he was 42, Franklin quit business to focus more on being a writer,

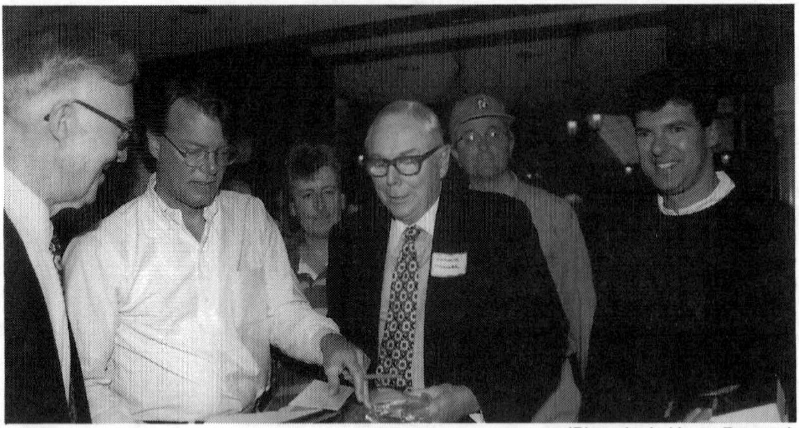

(Photo by LaVerne Ramsey)

Munger is mobbed by Berkshire shareholders the weekend of the annual meeting in 1995.

statesman, philanthropist, inventor and scientist. That's why I have diverted my interest away from business." (*Forbes*, January 22, 1996)

One marvels at Buffett and kindred spirit Munger, a curmudgeon of high standards and temperate habits like Buffett: two oldtimers sitting on the porch taking a shrewd, realistic look at an imperfect world and having a ball trying to figure out how to make the most of it. Buffett and Munger have talked with one another almost daily over the years, although less in recent years as both men's schedules are full.

Still, says Buffett, "I probably haven't talked to anyone on Wall Street one hundredth of the times I speak to Charlie." (*Forbes*, January 22, 1996)

In many ways Munger is a great foil for Buffett, especially when the two are at the dais conducting the annual meeting. Once Buffett was talking about trying to keep Berkshire's investments quiet. Buffett: "Unfortunately, we have to file certain reports. And it has lately been our policy to list our year-end holdings which total $100 million [now 600 million] or more in our annual reports. But in between, we don't say much. Charlie?"

Munger: "No comment."

Quick with a quip, Munger once said of the less rosy prospects for media companies, "We used to think they had a first lien on the advance of time."

When reporters can't get Buffett, which is most of the time, they'll sometimes call Munger for an observation of Buffett and he'll say something such as, "He takes his work seriously, but he doesn't take himself seriously."

Munger has vision problems. In fact he lost an eye in the early 1980s and wears uncommonly thick and sturdy black frame glasses.

He concedes that Buffett is somewhat more talented than he is. But that does not leave Munger in the dummy department.

In addition to saying "no comment", Munger also says things like, "just out of our respective graduate schools, my friend Warren Buffett and I entered the business world to find huge, predictable patterns of extreme irrationality. These irrationalities were obviously important to what we wanted to do, but our professors had never mentioned them. This was not an obvious or easy path...I came to the psychology of human misjudgement almost against my will; I rejected it until I realized that my attitude was costing me a lot of money, and reduced my ability to help everything I loved."

Munger's lecture about worldly wisdom as it relates to investments given to the University of Southern California in 1994 is one of the top investment treatises ever. An example:

> It's not given to to human beings to have such talent that they can just know everything all the time. But it is given to human beings who work hard at it—who look and sift the world for a mispriced bet—that they can occasionally find one.
>
> And the wise ones bet keenly when the world offers them that opportunity. They bet big when they have the odds. And the rest of the time, they don't. It's just that simple. (*Outstanding Investor Digest,* May 5, 1995)

Another Mungerism: "Understanding both the power of compound return and the difficulty getting it is the heart and soul of understanding a lot of things." (*Forbes*, January 22, 1996)

Munger noted at the Berkshire annual meeting in 1995 how little corporate America has studied Berkshire, despite its success. "How much of Berkshire has been copied?...People don't want to do it."

At the annual meeting in 1996 munger summed up things: "Berkshire's assets have been lovingly put together so as not to require continuing intelligence at headquarters."

Munger was educated at the University of Michigan (1941-42) and California Institute of Technology (1943) while he was in the Air Force, serving as a meteorological officer in World War II. He received his law education at Harvard, graduating with an LLB degree (magna cum laude) in 1948.

Apparently Munger was the first person admitted to Harvard Law School without an undergraduate degree. He was admitted to the California Bar in 1949.

He was associated with the law firm of Wright & Garrett; it became Wusick, Peeler & Garrett, when a group of lawyers left to found Munger, Tolles, Hills & Rickershauser, which engaged in corporate matters.

The founders of the firm included Munger, LeRoy Tolles, Roderick Hills, for a time chairman of the SEC, and his wife, Carla Hills, who became U.S. Trade Representative.

The Munger, Tolles firm has been described by *The American Lawyer* as Los Angeles's most elite law firm—13 of its 103 lawyers are former U.S. Supreme Court clerks.

The publication ran an article in April, 1992, headed, "No leverage. No marketing. Consensus compensation. Disdain for management. How Munger, Tolles is breezing through the recession."

The firm's compensation system was described as:

> Every January each partner—there are now 52—gets a ballot listing the names of all the partners with a blank after each name. The firm's net income for the previous year is printed at the bottom. Then each partner fills in the amount of money he or she thinks every partner should make, with no rules other than the numbers must add up to the net. No points, no shares. No seniority, no nothing.

Since the early 1970s, the firm has served as Berkshire's chief counsel. Firm partner Robert Denham has done work for Berkshire since 1974 and now is Salomon's chairman.

Munger has distinguished himself as a lawyer, businessman and investor. His investment record suffers in comparison only to Buffett's.

Munger, the grandson of a federal judge, was born on January 1, 1924, in Omaha and grew up in a house about 200 yards from Buffett's current home. Munger has said that his family and Buffett's knew of each other, but that he and Buffett did not actually meet until 1959, introduced by mutual friends, Dr. and Mrs. Edwin Davis.

Dr. Davis, now deceased, set up the meeting. After Buffett made a call on Davis one night, as he did to many doctors in Omaha in the early days, seeking money for his partnership, Buffett asked Davis why he so quickly decided to invest with him; Davis told him it was because Buffett reminded him so much of Munger.

"I knew everyone in the family except Warren," Munger has said of meeting Buffett. Munger once worked Saturdays in the Buffett & Son grocery store belonging to Buffett's grandfather. The store did not survive the arrival of supermarkets.

Munger had heard about Buffett, but was not prepared to be particularly impressed. Buffett and Munger spent dinner—at Johnny's Cafe in Omaha—talking about the securities markets. But Munger has said that on meeting Buffett he was instantly impressed, recognizing Buffett's sensational abilities on the spot.

"I wasn't just slightly impressed. I was very impressed," Munger has said. (*The Los Angeles Times*, Linda Grant, April 7, 1991)

The two became fast friends and Buffett kept telling him that investing was a quicker way to riches than the law. Munger became convinced and established a long, successful investment record himself even while keeping one foot in his law practice. In 1959, Buffett and Munger became "mental partners."

Independent of Buffett, from 1962 to 1975 Munger managed Wheeler Munger & Co., an investment counseling office from a no-frills office in the Pacific Coast Stock Exchange building. "He earned a highly respectable compound return of 19.8% a year before fees and after expenses." (*Forbes*, January 22, 1996)

They invested together in the mid-1960s, particularly in Blue Chip. Munger became a Berkshire officer in 1976 and has been vice chairman since 1978 with the Berkshire-Diversified Retailing merger of that year.

Munger became a large Berkshire shareholder in the late 1970s when two of his investments, Diversified Retailing and later Blue Chip Stamps, were merged into Berkshire. (*Forbes*, January 22, 1996)

Munger continues to live in Los Angeles, where he is also chairman of the Los Angeles Daily Journal, publisher of the *Los Angeles Daily Journal* for lawyers and eleven small newspapers in California, among a few others.

The Daily Journal, which has about 320 employees, had revenues of $35 million and profits of $2 million in 1995.

In his annual letter to *Daily Journal* shareholders, Munger puts things in his usual succinct way in describing a pre-tax loss of $300,000 at the company's *California Lawyer*, a monthly magazine published in cooperation with the State Bar of California.

"The venture plainly (1) is a contribution to the social order, (2) creates the best style of communications between the State Bar and its members and (3) works well for its advertisers. But its economic effects continue to be unsatisfactory to our company as owner."

Munger has 34.5% of the shares of the over-the-counter company, which he holds through his 16.7% ownership of Munger, Marshall & Co., a California limited partnership, according to the 1991 Daily Journal Corp.'s notice of annual meeting.

It also says that Munger's close friend J.P. Guerin owns 22% of the shares, through Guerin's 80% owned Pacific Partners.

Neither Munger nor Guerin takes any compensation for work on company matters and Munger admits they underpay company president Gerald Salzman.

From the early 1970s to the late 1980s Munger and Rick Guerin ran the New America Fund, which had a terrific record before it was liquidated.

Munger became a director of Berkshire on December 30, 1978, with the merger of Diversified Retailing into Berkshire and he has served as vice chairman of Berkshire. He has long been Buffett's "interchangeable partner."

He is quick with quips and often comes up with important commonsense lessons of his own: "The first chance you have to avoid a loss from a foolish loan is by refusing to make it. There is no second chance." Munger is a staunch Republican, Buffett is a Democrat. Munger likes to fish in lakes and stalk big salmon in Alaskan rivers, while Buffett cares little about fishing. Otherwise, the men agree on almost everything else; Buffett has said that if something got by one of them, it might get by both since their filters are similar.

The two see eye-to-eye on investing, particularly on the subject of doing things as conservatively as possible and keeping the balance sheet all but clear of debt. In the early days, Buffett was obsessed with buying assets as cheaply as possible. He has said it was Munger who stressed to him over the years the importance of buying high-quality businesses for the long run, even if you have to pay a little more.

Munger has addressed the question of strict value investing versus paying up a little for a high-quality business.

At the Wesco annual meeting in 1991, Munger said, "The basic concept of value to a private owner and being motivated when you're buying and selling securities by reference to intrinsic value instead of price momentum—I don't think that will ever be outdated. But Ben Graham had blind spots. He had too low an appreciation of the fact that some businesses were worth paying big premiums for.

In a creditable footnote to one edition of *The*

> *Intelligent Investor*, he [Graham] sheepishly said that he'd practiced this one value system for a long time and achieved a very respectable record doing it, but he got rich in a hurry by buying one growth stock investment. It amused him that half or more of his fortune came to him from one investment. [GEICO]
>
> Graham was insufficiently aware of the possibility that a company could prove a great holding for a long time—even when it sold at a large multiple of book value. Look at Coca-Cola stock. It has a very minor book value compared to its current price.
>
> You will notice that we're not following classic Graham and Dodd to the last detail as it was in Ben Graham's mind. (*Outstanding Investor Digest*, May 24, 1991) Added Munger: Both Warren and I sometimes wonder what would have happened if we'd started out in better businesses instead of trading stamps, aluminum, textile companies—we even had a windmill company at one time. It took us a long time to wise up.

Munger and Buffett work quickly and efficiently and have worked together so long, each knows how the other will view something.

Buffett has said, "Charlie Munger and I can handle a four-page memo over the phone with three grunts." (*The Midas Touch*, John Train, p. 70)

"Charlie and I are interchangeable on business decisions. Distance impedes us not at all; we've always found a telephone to be more productive than a half-day meeting," Buffett has told Train.

Buffett also has said "My idea of a group decision is to look in the mirror."

But if Buffett gets beyond making the decision himself, Munger is the first person Buffett consults.

Buffett told *Forbes* (October 18, 1993) that the three people who most influenced him were his father, Ben Graham and Munger. He said his father, "taught me to do nothing that could not be put on the front page of a newspaper. I have never known a better human than my dad."

Buffett said Graham gave him

> an intellectual framework for investing and a temperamental model, the ability to stand back and not be influenced by a crowd, not be fearful if stocks go down.

> Charlie made me focus on the merits of a great business with tremendously growing earning power, but only when you can be sure of it—not like Texas Instruments or Polaroid, where the earning power was hypothetical. Charlie doesn't have his ego wrapped up in the business the way I do, but he understands it perfectly. Essentially we have never had an argument, though occasional disagreements.

Munger returned a compliment to Buffett in the same *Forbes* story: "One of the reasons Warren is so cheerful is that he doesn't have to remember his lines." Public and private Buffett are the same.

Munger also told *Forbes,* which rated his net worth at $365 million, that he was surprised to be on the 400 richest list in 1993. "I've been associated with Warren so long, I thought I'd be just a footnote," adding that his life's goal had been to stay below the cutoff for the list.

One wag says: *"Warren, Warren. He's our man.*
If he can't do it, Munger can."

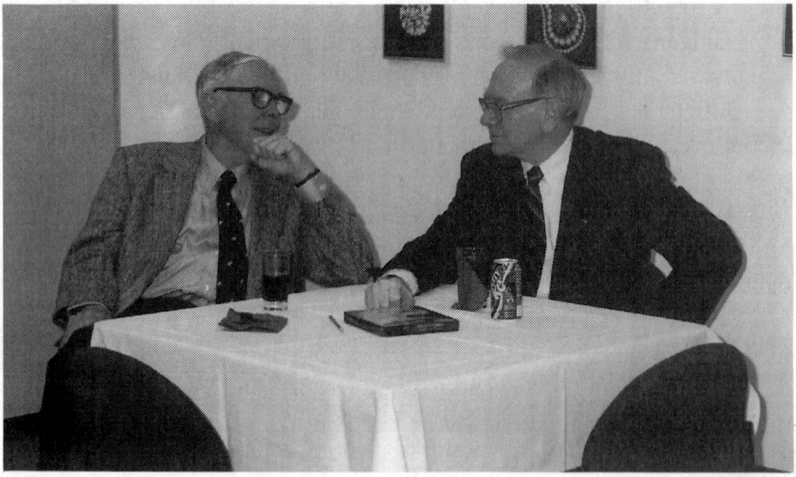

(Photo by Nancy Line Jacobs)

Munger, left, and Buffett—Berkshire's dynamic duo—share a moment in a room above Borsheim's the day before the annual meeting in 1996.

102

Lou Simpson Heir apparent

Buffett, in Berkshire's 1995 annual report, indicated that GEICO'S Lou Simpson is the heir apparent at Berkshire.

"His presence on the scene assures us that Berkshire would have an extraordinary professional immediately available to handle its investments if something were to happen to Charlie and me," he wrote.

Simpson, 59, who in the past has represented Berkshire's interests on the boards of National Housing Authority and Bowery Savings Bank and who is on Salomon's board, clearly has long had Buffett's confidence.

Simpson, co-CEO of GEICO and responsible for its investments, graduated with a master's degree from Princeton. After teaching for a short time at Princeton, he joined the investment firm of Stein Roe Farnham. In 1969, he joined Western Asset Management, where he became president and CEO before leaving to join GEICO in 1979.

A director of Potomoc Electric Power Company and Pacific Ameri-

(Courtesy of GEICO)

Berkshire's heir apparent is GEICO's Lou Simpson.

can Income shares, Inc., Simpson is also a director of the compensation committees of Thompson PBE, Inc. and COHR Inc.

From 1980 to 1995, stocks Simpson managed for GEICO had an annual return of 22.8%, well ahead of the S&P 500 Index during that time which returned 15.7% a year.

Simpson gets to know managements of the companies he invests in and, like Buffett, makes long term stock picks.

Some of Simpson's picks have been Freddie Mac, Nike and Manpower.

Simpson lives in Rancho Santa Fe, California, near San Diego. He earlier had moved from GEICO's base in Washington D.C. to Los Angeles.

Simpson "has the ideal temperament for investing," Buffett told *Institutional Investor* magazine in 1986. "He derives no particular pleasure from operating with or against the crowd. He is comfortable following his own reason."

103

Keep Costs Low

"Fees specified for exhibits are $5.00."
Verne McKenzie

Buffett's talk about keeping costs low, paying bills and collecting for bills promptly is not just talk. At Berkshire, it's a reality.

Buffett has always said good managers know their costs down to how much goes for postage. And better than knowing the cost of a stamp is finding a way around using one in the first place.

Even a sheet of paper is saved. Write Berkshire a letter and you'll generally get a prompt, business-like response. But you may not get it on a new sheet of paper. You may get your answer in a note at the bottom of your own letter to Berkshire!

Once I wrote Berkshire requesting all the back annual reports and received a reply saying Berkshire didn't have back annual reports beyond a certain year. The odd thing about the response: it was typed at the bottom of my own letter! Berkshire had saved a sheet of paper. Perhaps more importantly, it had saved a bit of time, time being more important than money at Berkshire.

On another occasion, I wrote J. Verne McKenzie, Berkshire's former chief financial officer, requesting a Form 10-K Report with related exhibits. Berkshire's annual report had noted these documents were available for a fee.

McKenzie's response, typed at the bottom of my letter—again Berkshire had saved a sheet of letter paper—follows:

> 4/23/91
>
> Mr. Kilpatrick:
>
> Enclosed is Berkshire's Form 10-K for 1990 as you requested including exhibits other than Exhibit 13 which was the Annual Report of which you have already received a copy. Fees specified for exhibits are $5.00. Verne McKenzie.

A multi-billion-dollar firm wanted $5 from me. I wrote a check and it was duly signed by McKenzie who typed on the back, "For deposit to the order of Berkshire Hathaway Inc." and deposited it in the Berkshire account at Norwest Bank in Omaha. It would appear that Berkshire officials subscribe to this old saw: "The two most beautiful words in the English language are 'Check Enclosed.' "

Paul Wolsfeld has his own version of Berkshire's terse communications/save-that-piece-of-paper mentality. Wolsfeld, of La Jolla, California, who cycled across America in search of corporate trivia for a book, hit Omaha in 1987 and made his way to the 14th floor of Kiewit Plaza.

"I got up to the door of Berkshire and there was a camera over the door and a speaker came on asking what I wanted. I asked if Mr. Buffett was in and the speaker said he was out of the country," recalled Wolsfeld.

"Then I asked if I could have an annual report and a hand reached out. That's all I ever saw was half a hand that handed me an annual report. I never even got to say hello," said Wolsfeld.

Wolsfeld later wrote Buffett, asking if he would sponsor his bicycle trip around the country.

"He wrote me back a note saying he was not interested in sponsoring me. He wrote the note at the bottom of the letter I sent him. He saved a piece of paper. So cheap."

104

Ad to Buy Businesses

November 17, 1986

Looking for a $3–5 billion acquisition

In the late 1980s, Buffett circulated the following ad:

We want to buy businesses worth $100 million or more before December 31, 1986.

If you own such a business, there's a vital reason why you should consider selling.

In 44 days the tax you must pay on the sale of your business may soar to 52½%.

All of us know about the change in the Federal capital gains tax rate from 20% to 28%. In most cases, effective state tax rates on capital gains will also materially increase.

A second tax consideration is less well known, but in many cases looms far more important. Effective January 1, the General Utilities doctrine is repealed. This change can produce the equivalent of a 52½% federal capital gains tax on the sale of a business. Ask your lawyer, accountant or investment banker how it will affect your situation.

The change in the General Utilities doctrine will not apply to transactions completed by December 31. Other things being equal, you will net dramatically more money if you close a sale by that date than if you delay. Berkshire Hathaway will have no problem in completing a transaction by the December 31 deadline. We have the money, and we can act with extraordinary speed. Most of the purchases we have made have been agreed to after one meeting with the owners. If you phone us with a general description of your business and tell us the sort of transaction you are seeking, we can immediately tell you whether we have an interest. And if we do, we will proceed instantly.

Here's what we are looking for:

1. Large purchases (at least $10 million of after-tax earnings, and preferably much more). [Now it's $25 million pre-tax]
2. Demonstrated consistent earning power (future projections are of little interest to us, nor are "turn-around" situations).
3. Businesses earning good returns on equity while employing little or no debt.
4. Management in place (we can't supply it).
5. Simple businesses (if there's lots of technology, we won't understand it).
6. An offering price (we don't want to waste our time or that of the seller by talking, even preliminarily, about a transaction when price is unknown).

These criteria are firm so we would appreciate hearing only from owners whose businesses fully meet them.

We invite potential sellers to check us out by contacting anyone with whom we have done business in the past. You'll find we are unusual: we buy to keep (no periodic "restructuring" convulsions); we leave subsidiary managements alone to operate in the future as they have in the past; and our own ownership and management structure is predictable for decades to come.

If you are interested, call me at 402-346-1400. Or, if you like, first call Mrs. Kaiser at the same number to request express delivery of Berkshire

Hathaway's current annual report. Your inquiry will be totally confidential; we use no staff, and we don't need to discuss your company with consultants, investment bankers, commercial bankers, etc. You will deal only with Charles Munger, Vice Chairman of Berkshire, and with me. If you have any possible interest, call promptly. Otherwise a 20% tax will become 28% to 52½%.

Warren E. Buffett

Although nothing came of the $47,000 ad, Buffett personally took at least 100 telephone calls.

One caller who wanted to see if Buffett was interested was a native of Pakistan who wished to sell him a newsstand in New York for $185,000. That one didn't meet Buffett's test on size.

Another caller, from Jackson, Mississippi, wanted to sell her antebellum mansion. Buffett turned that one down politely, but quickly. (*Omaha World-Herald*, December 3, 1986)

Other callers offered farms or small-town businesses. Buffett later told his hometown newspaper that the last strong prospect came in on December 20, 1986, from a potential seller in the eastern United States.

Buffett said the business met all the requirements, such as earning $10 million a year after tax and possessing in-place management. And the price was right. "But it was a business we didn't want to be in," he said, declining to say what kind of business it was. "If you run an ad for a chihuahua, you get a lot of collie replies," and "We're looking for 747s, not model airplanes," he has said.

The ad worked in the sense that the next time people would be more aware of what Berkshire wanted and would be more likely to think of Berkshire.

Also in 1986, Berkshire ran a different ad, published three times in *Business Insurance* magazine, titled, "Berkshire Hathaway wants to see property/casualty risks where the premium is $1 million or more."

As a result of the ads, which cost a total of $20,000, Berkshire's insurance subsidiaries generated new business that produced more than $100 million a year in premiums.

At the Berkshire annual meeting in 1993, Buffett granted a brief interview to Linda O'Bryon of *Nightly Business Report*.

One of her questions had to do with whether he was still trying to buy businesses and he said, yes, he was always looking for new businesses to buy.

Then he sneaked in an ad saying if anyone out in television land had a $2 billion to $3 billion business to sell him, to call him collect.

Here's Buffett's new ad. He's looking for an acquisition in the $3-5 billion range.

105

Buffett's letter telling shareholders that Berkshire may become listed on the New York Stock Exchange

Berkshire Hathaway Inc.
1440 Kiewit Plaza
Omaha, Nebraska 68131
Telephone (402) 346-1400

Warren E. Buffett, Chairman

August 5, 1988

To the Shareholders of Berkshire Hathaway Inc.:

It is likely that in a few months Berkshire shares will be traded on the New York Stock Exchange. Our move there would be made possible by a new listing rule that the Exchange's Board of Governors has passed and asked the SEC to approve. If that approval is forthcoming, we expect to apply for a listing, which we believe will be granted.

Up to now, the Exchange has required newly listed companies to have a minimum of 2,000 shareholders who each own 100 shares or more. The purpose of this rule is to ensure that NYSE-listed companies enjoy the broad investor interest that facilitates an orderly market. The 100-share standard corresponds to the trading unit ("round lot") for all common shares now listed on the Exchange.

Because Berkshire has relatively few shares outstanding (1,146,642), it does not have the number of 100-share-or-more holders that the Exchange has required. A ten-share (ten underlined) holding of Berkshire, however, represents a significant investment commitment. In fact, ten Berkshire shares have a value greater than that of 100 shares of any NYSE-listed stock. The Exchange, therefore, is willing to have Berkshire shares trade in ten-share "round lots."

The Exchange's proposal rule simply means changes in the 2,000 minimum from one measured by holders of 100 shares or more to one measured by holders of a round lot or more. Berkshire can easily meet this amended test.

Charlie Munger, Berkshire's Vice Chairman, and I are delighted at the prospect of listing, since we believe this move will benefit our shareholders. We have two criteria by which we judge what marketplace would be best for Berkshire stock. First, we hope for the stock to consistently trade at a price rationally related to its intrinsic value. If it does, the investment result achieved by each shareholder will approximate Berkshire's business result during his period of ownership.

Such an outcome is far from automatic. Many stocks swing between levels of severe undervaluation and overvaluation. When this happens, owners are rewarded or penalized in a manner wildly at variance with how the business has performed during their period of ownership. We want to avoid such capricious results. Our goal is to have our shareholders-partners profit from the achievements of the business rather than from the foolish behavior of their co-owners.

Consistently rational prices are produced by rational owners, both current and prospective. All our policies and communications are designed to attract the business oriented long-term and to filter out possible buyers whose focus is short-term and market-oriented. To date we have been successful in this attempt, and Berkshire shares have consistently sold in an unusually narrow range around intrinsic value. We do not believe that a NYSE listing will improve or diminish Berkshire's prospects for consistently selling at an appropriate price; the quality of our shareholders will produce a good result whatever the marketplace.

But we do believe that the listing will reduce transaction costs for Berkshire's shareholders—and that is important. Though we want to attract shareholders who will stay around for a long time, we also want to minimize the costs incurred by shareholders when they enter or exit. In the long run, the aggregate pre-tax rewards to our owners will equal the business gains achieved by the company less the transaction costs imposed by the marketplace—that is, commissions charged by brokers plus the net realized spreads of market-makers. Overall, we believe these transaction costs will be reduced materially by a NYSE listing.

As we pointed out in the 1984 Annual Report, transaction costs are very heavy for active stocks, often amounting to 10 % or more of the earnings of a public company. In effect, these costs act as a hefty tax on owners, albeit one based on individual decisions to "change chairs" and one that is paid to the financial community rather than to Washington. Our policies and your investment attitude have reduced this "tax" on Berkshire owners to what we believe is the lowest level among large public companies. A NYSE listing should further reduce this cost for Berkshire's owners by narrowing the market-maker's spread.

Under NYSE rules we must have at least two independent directors. Among the Board of Directors you elect in May, only Malcolm Chace, Jr., meets their test of independence.

But from this deficiency comes a good result. Charlie and I are pleased to inform you that Walter Scott, Jr., CEO of Peter Kiewit Sons', Inc. has joined the Berkshire board. PKS is one of the remarkable business stories of our time. The company, which is employee-owned, has a long-term financial record so good that I'm not going to recite it for fear of stirring unrest among our shareholders. Throughout his lifetime, Pete Kiewit ran the company as a strict meritocracy and it was in this tradition that he picked Walter to succeed him upon his death. Walter instinctively thinks like an owner and he will feel at home on the Berkshire board.

One final comment: You should clearly understand that we are not seeking a NYSE listing for the purpose of achieving a higher valuation on Berkshire shares. Berkshire should sell, and we hope will sell, on the NYSE at prices similar to those it would have commanded in the over-the-counter market, given similar economic circumstances. The NYSE listing should not induce you to buy or sell; it simply should cut your costs somewhat should you decide to do either.

Warren E. Buffett
Chairman of the Board

106

His Personal Portfolio

Buffett is richer than you think.

In addition to his more than 40% ownership in Berkshire, Buffett also has some smaller but substantial holdings in his personal portfolio.

The Lord only knows what the best investor of our time has tucked away in his personal portfolio over the years. Information is skimpy.

In his Buffett Partnership letter of January 25, 1967, Buffett said his investment in the partnership represented more than 90% of his family's worth, so clearly his major personal investment all along has been his stake in the partnership and later in Berkshire stock.

In 1967, Buffett said that most of his money was in the partnership, excluding an investment in Data Documents stock. Buffett told reporter Jonathan Laing for a March 31, 1977, story in the *Wall Street Journal* that his personal portfolio of stockholdings was worth $30 million.

If those holdings have increased 25 times since then—substantially less than the rate of Berkshire's growth—today they would be worth a big figure. And that's if Buffett has made no new investments.

In late 1986, Buffett invested about $38 million in the stock of Illinois's Servicemaster for his personal portfolio. Servicemaster cleans hospitals and provides laundry, food preparation and maid services for hospitals, office buildings, colleges and factories.

Servicemaster runs a variety of cleaning businesses, and the company operates on Christian principles. The name means Service to the Master. There were subsequent reports that Buffett was selling the stake, and Servicemaster officials have said he is out of the stock.

That investment came to light because Buffett bought slightly more than 5% of Servicemaster stock, making it a public transaction; when confusion arose as to whether Berkshire bought the stock, Buffett told shareholders the purchase had been made for his personal portfolio, not for Berkshire.

When some shareholders said they wished he had bought Servicemaster for Berkshire, he explained that the investment, because of tax reasons, was better suited for personal accounts.

Over the years reports of small personal investments, one in FirsTier Bank in Omaha, an early one in Nebraska's sole minority-owned bank—the small Community Bank of Nebraska, and a little investment in the Omaha Royals, have come to light. It's safe to say Buffett is not standing idly by as his own investor, although by all accounts the huge majority of his investment thinking is devoted to Berkshire.

On April 15, 1996, Property Capital Trust, a real estate investment trust in Boston, Massachusettes, said Buffett had bought a 6.7% stake in the company, or 610,800 shares which were trading at about $9 a share. Property Capital Trust plans to sell its real estate investments over the next three to five years.

The fate of Buffett's personal portfolio, which could be worth a billion dollars, is an intriguing question. Something good will come of it. Asked about the fate of his personal portfolio at the annual meeting in 1991, Buffett gave it little recognition, saying his real stake is in Berkshire and that in any case almost all his money will ultimately be returned to society.

"My personal portfolio is Berkshire," he said.

In 1996 he said almost all of his money is in just one stock: Berkshire.

In an "Owner's Manual" to all shareholders in June 1996, he said more than 99% of his net worth is in Berkshire.

107

Mrs. Susan Buffett

Wife, board member and heiress

Buffett and Susan Thompson married in 1952. Their parents had been friends and she roomed with Warren's sister Bertie at Northwestern University.

When Buffett dropped in, courting her, she dropped out of college to marry him. Mrs. Buffett grew up a block and a half from Buffett's present home.

After their marriage, Mrs. Buffett was a cabaret singer at the French Cafe, a fancy restaurant in downtown Omaha with a décor of mirrors reflecting nude paintings.

Mrs. Buffett radiates a calm, understanding demeanor. Once in the late 1970s during the Christmas season, she came into a Little Professor bookstore in Omaha, dressed in full-length mink and blue jeans, and bought about $70 worth of books, recalls Martha Line, who waited on her.

"I knew who she was, but the store manager explained to her he would have to run a credit card check because the amount was more than $50. She was not indignant or insulted, quite calm about it. She handled it a lot better than I would have," Mrs. Line said.

Mrs. Buffett, an open, friendly and dignified woman, lives apart from her husband, although she has described him as the most interesting person she's ever met. "He's like a color TV instead of black and white. Most people come in black and white," she has said. (*Register*, February, 1984)

She has indicated that a factor in her move from Omaha was getting "hit from all sides" by community groups in Omaha looking for help. *(Regardie's,* February, 1986)

For a long time she has lived in San Francisco, although she has said she really lives everywhere because she travels so much, often for a variety of civic causes, especially civil rights. She has worked with minority youths, keeping in touch with them by letters over the years and encouraging their studies.

She and Buffett remain close. They are separated but by no means estranged. They travel and socialize together, seeing each other about once a month.

Of the separation Buffett has said, "It works well this way. She sort of roams; she's a free spirit." (*Forbes*, October 21, 1991)

Howard Buffett says, "If the comment 'behind every good man there is a good woman' has any truth to it, then you absolutely must give my mother credit for a good share of my dad's success. She is the most understanding and kind person I have ever known, and her support throughout his career has been very important to him."

Her daughter, Susan, says her mother was long active in race relations and women's causes in Omaha, but in recent years has had less time to work for causes.

She devoted much time to helping Susan through a difficult pregnancy with Susan's son, Michael. She helped her own son, Howard, campaign for the county commission, and she has helped her sister face a lengthy battle with cancer.

Mrs. Buffett is a major Berkshire shareholder, owning 36,988 shares—about 3% of the company. It's a shared investment with her husband. The block of stock is worth more than a billion dollars.

In 1991, Mrs. Buffett was named to Berkshire's board, and Buffett has said that she shares his views about maintaining the character of Berkshire.

Should Mrs. Buffett outlive her husband, she would inherit his stake and with 44% of the company would effectively control Berkshire, probably making her by far the richest person in the world. After her death, her Berkshire stock is slated to go to charity, to The Buffett Foundation, (where Mrs. Buffett is president), and eventually back to society.

Buffett has no written contract with his wife that the shares will go to the foundation, but there is an understanding between the two that it will. *(Forbes,* October 18, 1993) "The deal is whoever dies last will leave the Berkshire Hathaway shares with no strings attached. I've got this fund that's growing at a rate of 25 to 30%.

"When I'm dead, I assume there'll still be serious problems of a social nature as there are now. Society will get a greater benefit from my money later than if I do it now."

Buffett has said leaving his Berkshire stock to his wife first, before it goes to the foundation, preserves the most flexibility in terms of reacting to changes in the laws. Wives are not taxed on inheritance from their husbands, no matter how large the amount.

(Photo by Nancy Line Jacobs)

Mrs. Susan Buffett talks with Borsheim's Donald Yale at the party at Borsheim's before Berkshire's Annual Meeting in 1995.

108

The Omaha Royals

Right-hander Buffett: "Humiliating performance... I barely missed my foot." A strike

In July, 1991, Buffett and Walter Scott, Peter Kiewit Sons' chairman and Berkshire board member, stepped in to buy a stake in the Omaha Royals minor league baseball team when a deal with the previous buyer fell through.

The switch occurred when Philadelphia real estate developer Craig Stein backed out of an ownership plan because he couldn't live with a requirement that gave Union Pacific veto power over any plan to move the franchise from Omaha.

Union Pacific railroad had announced that it would buy 49% of the Omaha Royal AAA franchise with Stein, but when he backed out, Buffett and Scott came to the rescue with $1.25 million each. Union Pacific contributed $2.5 million and the deal was done.

Buffett, a longtime baseball fan, told the *Omaha World-Herald* that he and Scott would sell $100,000 shares of their ownership to interested

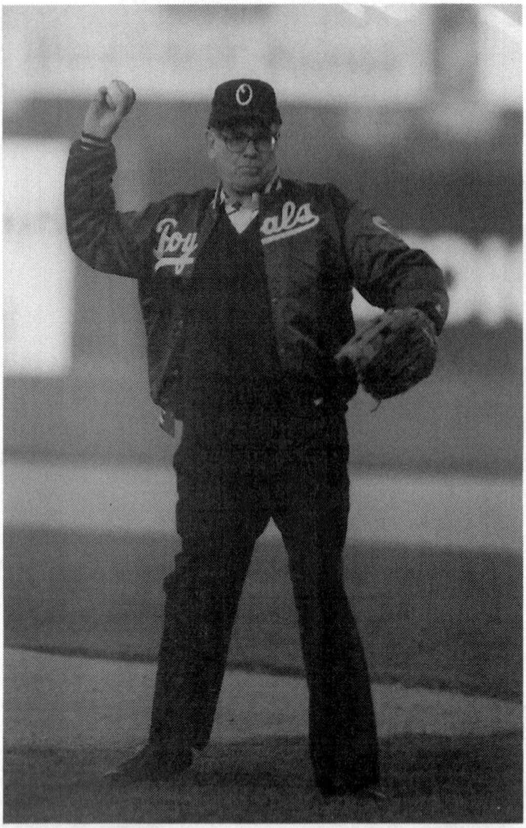

Buffett, co-owner of the Omaha Royals but no threat to Nolan Ryan, winds up for a pitch at Omaha's Rosenblatt Stadium at an Omaha Royals game. Right-hander Buffett called his pitch a "humiliating performance...I barely missed my foot."

(*Omaha World-Herald*)

(Photo by Nancy Line Jacobs)

Mrs. Susan Buffett; Buffett's grandson, Howie; Warren "The Whip" Buffett and Buffett's granddaughter, Megan, at Omaha Royals game in 1994. The insignia on Buffett's shirt is the closest thing Berkshire has to a logo.

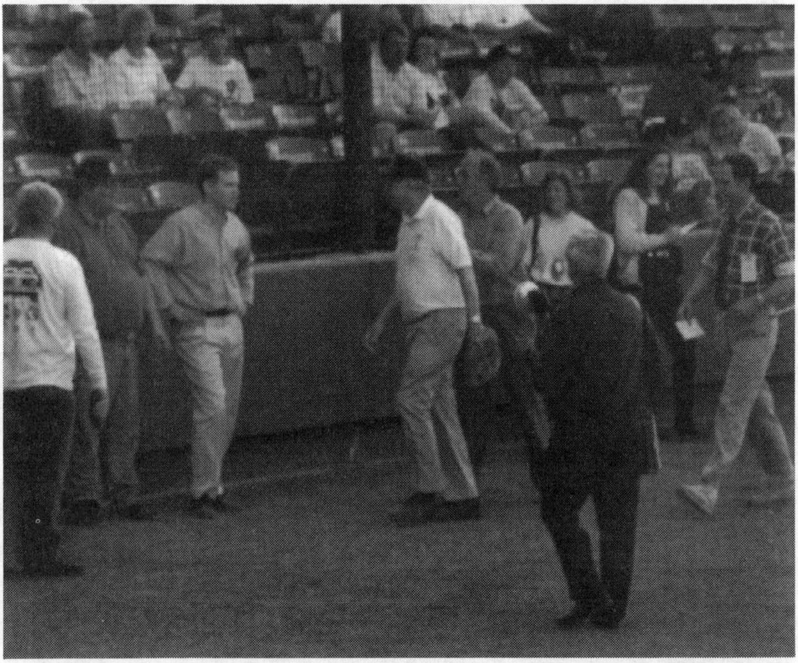

(Photo by Nancy Line Jacobs)

The Gloved One threw a strike at an Omaha Royals game in 1994. Buffett, and the cheering crowd, were surprised.

investors. For Buffett, this was a quick fix to save the local baseball team, not a long-term investment that would add to his billions. Yet Buffett remains one owner of the team.

The franchise, a farm team for the Kansas City Royals, might well have been lost had Buffett not stepped in with what was an act of good citizenship rather than the act of an opportunistic investor.

The hasty announcement was made in the office of Omaha Mayor P. J. Morgan, who said he was surprised to learn that Buffett hadn't visited the mayor's office before then. Buffett replied, "At a million and a quarter a pop, I can't afford it."

Once Buffett asked a lady, Betty Davis, on the elevator at Omaha's City-County Building, "Do you know what floor the mayor's office is on?"

"Third floor," she said.

Buffett thanked her and punched the button.

"I have a favor to ask you," Ms. Davis said. "Do you mind if I tell people I told Warren Buffett where to get off?"

"Not at all," Buffett said, adding, "People are always telling me where to get off." (Robert McMorris, *Omaha World-Herald*, November 25, 1992)

Buffett invited shareholders in 1994 to come to an Omaha Royals game where he planned to throw out the first pitch. He assured folks he would better his "humiliating performance" of last year when "I barely missed my foot."

Buffett walked to the mound, shook off the catcher's sign, wound up and threw a strike! The crowd cheered. The most surprised person was Buffett. The announcer declared the pitch a strike by Warren "The Whip" Buffett, but said it was timed at only eight miles per hour adding, "You'd better keep your day job."

In the 1994 Annual Report, Buffett said, "Opening the game that night, I had my stuff and threw a strike that the scoreboard reported at eight miles per hour. What many fans missed was that I shook off the catcher's call for my fast ball and instead delivered my change-up. This year it will be all smoke."

In 1996 his pitch hit failed to reach the plate. Buffett passed it off as "a premature sinker."

109

What's Berkshire Really Worth?

"Run naked through the money."

So-o-o, what's Berkshire really worth?

Well, that's a tricky one because Berkshire isn't the easiest company in the world to pigeonhole with a pricetag.

Here's how Beemer, the clown/magician who entertained at the 4th birthday party of Buffett's granddaughter, might do it, to be magically simple: Step 1. Calculate Berkshire's average investee P/E ratio. Let's call it 20. Step 2. Multiply 20 by the average of the last two years' look-through earnings of $487.50 per share. Poof! Berkshire's stock price should have been $9,750 at yearend 1991 when it was selling at $9,050.

Jumping forward to the end of 1993, the calculation would be to take the average of the 1992 look-through earnings of $604 million and 1993's $856 million. The average is $730 million. Divide that by the 1,156,243 shares outstanding and you get $631 times 20 for a closing 1993 stock price of $12,625.

(Photo by Nancy Line Jacobs)

Buffett before Berkshire's annual meeting in 1994. What is this brain worth? Inquiring investors want to know.

But Beemer says that is the Bear Market calculation, in honor of Ben Graham, who liked to be very conservative.

Even Beemer says you can take current look-through earnings of $856 million and you get almost $15,000. And if you increase look-through earnings for the first four months of 1994 at annual meeting time, you get about $16,000.

Since Buffett has said the yearend price ($16,325) was "not irrational," Beemer thinks Buffett is in the ballpark.

But Beemer has now developed a simpler method, the Beemer II Method, so Buffett won't have to make but one calculation: Take the look-through earnings per share ($740 in 1993) and multiply by the growth rate of Berkshire's book value since present management took over (23%) and the worth of Berkshire at yearend is $17,020!

The calculation for 1994 comes out to about $21,400 when Berkshire was trading at $20,400.

Buffett didn't give look-through earnings in the 1995 annual report because there were so many major year end changes at Berkshire, but promised them for 1996. He did say he and Munger wouldn't consider buying Berkshire at $36,000. The stock took a big hit, dropping $2,150 the day that news got out in March, 1996.

Shareholders and Wall Streeters often take stabs at Berkshire's intrinsic worth, and always the question is posed to Buffett at annual meetings (after all, father should know best). But usually he sidesteps the valuation question by explaining that he doesn't want to "spoil the fun" for shareholders who want to figure it out themselves.

Buyers and sellers generally have put a pretty fair value price on Berkshire stock. Buffett has said that he wants Berkshire to trade near its intrinsic value, or real business value, rather than at some inflated or depressed level.

And he adds that reasonable businessmen might value Berkshire

10% higher or lower than its intrinsic worth, that he and Munger might differ by 10% about Berkshire's intrinsic value.

It's doubtful that even Buffett carries around in his head a precise figure for Berkshire's worth, although everyone would like to know his 10% range. Sometimes Buffett takes this tack: "Well, add it all up and then subtract something because I'm running it."

Anyone can see you should tally it up and add something for Buffett's brain.

Occasionally Buffett offers little nudges when the price gets out of whack. After the stock soared to more than $3,000 a share following the excitement over Berkshire's stake in Cap Cities in 1986, he indicated the stock price was too high.

And there were signs he thought Berkshire's stock price too high in late 1989 when it soared to $8,900. That's when he issued zero coupon convertible bonds tied to Berkshire's stock price. Because buyers of Berkshire's convertibles had a right to convert into Berkshire stock and because Buffett does not easily issue new stock, the issuance at that time was probably a sign that he believed Berkshire to be overvalued.

He was right. For about the next two and a half years Berkshire stock, apparently overpriced, went absolutely nowhere.

Buffett said of a *Barron's* piece, February 12, 1990, which set forth the proposition that Berkshire's price was too high, that he did not necessarily disagree with the conclusion, just with some of the calculations employed to reach that conclusion. Besides telling shareholders, Buffett also told *USA Today* that the *Barron's* piece mistakenly undervalued some of Berkshire's holdings. "There's a mathematical error in their numbers," he said. "The figures are wrong."

Berkshire was then off its $8,900 high, trading at about $7,900 a share at the time, and the story had sent the stock down $700 in a single day. The writer, Thomas N. Cochran, concluded that Berkshire was worth only about $4,695 a share and that the $7,900 share price was a 68% premium to Berkshire's real worth, its intrinsic value. Berkshire shareholders and others fired off letters to *Barron's,* which published a few.

One letter, from Berkshire shareholder Dr. Wallace Gaye, said: "Poor Thomas N. Cochran. He apparently wouldn't be able to tell the difference in value between a lump of coal and a diamond because they share a similar structure."

One problem with the *Barron's* story was that it assigned the common stock market value to Berkshire's preferred stock holdings as if the preferred could decrease in value like common stocks. It was true that the stock prices of three of the four preferred stock investments were down sharply. But Buffett explained to shareholders that Berkshire didn't own the common stock of these companies that had taken a beating.

Berkshire owned the *preferred* stock, which had always continued to earn dividends of about 9%, tax-advantaged at that. There's little chance that the preferred could drop in value like the common because the preferred stocks can be redeemed for the original face value—short of bankruptcy—roughly the same amount Buffett paid.

So there was no loss—although later USAir did so poorly that Buffett wrote down that investment on the balance sheet.

And with conversion privileges these investments offer, not to mention the long periods they have to reach their strike price and become more profitable, Berkshire is sitting on nice investments not available to the general public. The only way to own them is through Berkshire.

As Ronald Reagan might say to Thomas Cochran, "There you go again!" Cochran came back with a story in *Barron's,* April 18, 1994, that Berkshire was worth $9,401 a share when it was trading at $16,100.

In a weak market, with the Fed raising the fed funds rate another quarter of a point that day, Berkshire could have been crushed, but was down only $295. It may have been Berkshire's finest performance by shareholders.

Letters again were fired off to *Barron's,* most centering on lack of mention of the insurance business. Michael J. Davey, of Sunnyvale, California, wondered why there was no mention of the valuable insurance business when each of the four largest reinsurers in the world buys coverage from Berkshire.

Daniel A. Ogden, president of Dock Street Asset Management in Stamford, Connecticut, wrote, "You may be right that Warren Buffett doesn't deserve a premium to book value, but if that's true, there are very few stocks worth owning. I'll do what I did in 1990 when you came to the same conclusion—hold on to Berkshire and worry more about the other stuff in my portfolio."

Michael Rhodes, a lawyer in Kansas City, told his Berkshire friends he thought most investors "might like the idea of having the world's best investor working for them with $2 of assets for every $1 of equity, particularly when the liabilities are mostly interest-free (deferred taxes and insurance float)."

In the 1993 annual report, Buffett told a story that included the Li'l Abner cartoon temptress Appassionata Van Climax, so one shareholder thought of writing: "Mr. Cochran, If you're right, you must be a pretty rich guy by now. Maybe we could meet for a drink. Signed: Appassionata Van Climax."

Cochran made no mention of $1.85 billion in cash, only half mention of more than $2 billion in fixed-income securities, no mention of Berkshire's valuable insurance businesses and left out about $2 billion in calculating Berkshire's stock portfolio.

Buffett was asked about the Cochran story at the Berkshire annual meeting in 1994: "I hope he hasn't been shorting the stock," Buffett said. "It's not the way I'd calculate it...apparently he forgot we were in the insurance business." Then Buffett launched into a dissertation about not making stock market decisions based on what others say, only on what you understand about the business.

Understanding the worth of the rest of Berkshire is a challenge. "The hardest value to figure by far is the worth of our insurance business," said Buffett at the 1991 annual meeting. "That doesn't mean it isn't valuable. It just means that it's hard to assess—although it might have a bigger effect on the valuation of Berkshire than See's Candy or *World Book*." Talk about understatement.

He added, "How the insurance table in our annual report (1990) develops over the next 20 years will be a major factor in what the intrinsic value of Berkshire is today...The source of intrinsic value of the insurance business is the ability to generate funds at a low cost. That's what creates value...If you can figure out how that table will look in the next 20 years, you'll have a good handle on our future. We think there is significant potential in it. In terms of dollars, we think that it's bigger than that of our other directly owned businesses."

In the first *Barron's* article, Cochran assigned a P/E of just 12 to Berkshire's operating businesses at a time when the market P/E was 14. (In the second story he said Berkshire's operating businesses were worth $2 billion, probably off by a factor of 2 or 3). Ask Buffett if he'll sell See's, the *Buffalo News* or *World Book* for 12 times earnings and see how long he stays on the phone.

Cochran used an old earnings figure in the first story but had it been the latest, Berkshire's earnings would have already plowed ahead. If you're talking about Berkshire from its latest report, you're probably millions of dollars behind the times.

For one thing, you'd be looking backwards at smaller numbers because Buffett reports as late as possible, about 45 days after the quarter has ended. You're even farther behind if you're citing figures from the annual report that comes out in late March and reflects financial conditions as of the prior December 31.

Also, at the time of Cochran's stories, the market was declining, so Berkshire's tab for deferred capital gains taxes should have been lower than the figure Cochran used.

And are deferred capital gains taxes really a 100% liability as Cochran implied? If Buffett sold everything, he would have to pay Uncle Sam a very large tax bill. No question.

But Buffett tells us he's not selling everything today. In fact, he may hold some investments *FOREVER*. Also, the deferred tax liability is non-interest-bearing and has no redemption date. If it were a bond, it might be sold for 20 cents on the dollar.

In 1993, Bill Ruane, head of Sequoia Fund, made a point about Berkshire's worth and the tax question. "Take its current book value which at the end of the year was $7,850. And that's after a reserve for taxes of about $2,200 or $2,300. If you add that back—and I'm not saying that you should add it back fully—but the prospects of those taxes being paid in the near future are low. So that money's really working for you even though it's not shown in the book value."

He said Berkshire was selling for a below market price-to-book ratio, adding that many of Berkshire's assets are undervalued on the balance sheet.

With Berkshire, he said, you're getting the "finest security analyst in the world."

Cochran made no mention of Berkshire's substantial "look-through" earnings. You can think of look-through earnings as intrinsic earnings that include important, unrecorded earnings not included in Berkshire's income statement. These invisible, unrecorded earnings are in a sense Berkshire's proportionate ownership of the retained operating earnings of Berkshire's major investees, but under generally accepted accounting principles they are not always counted in Berkshire's earnings per share. Coke, for example, earns almost $3 billion a year and Berkshire owns 8% of Coke, but generally accepted accounting rules keep Berkshire from including its share of Coke's income on its income statement.

Berkshire's "look-through" earnings are presumably reflected in the stock prices of the corporations in which Berkshire invests, and hence are included on Berkshire's balance sheet, even if they are not on Berkshire's income statement.

But Berkshire's value cannot be measured by numbers alone. Witness the large stock holdings. There is an extra kicker in Berkshire's commanding stock positions. Some suggest attaching a 20% premium for the huge stock positions. Many of Berkshire's stock positions are so large they are prized for their semi-controlling nature. Such huge positions have a disadvantage of being less liquid than a small position, but overall there's an advantage because their size offers more control as to the outcome. Witness GEICO.

Berkshire's convertible preferred stock positions are a factor. There is extra value resulting from their size and fat dividends. These stocks are redeemable at par, and the conversion privileges are potentially worth millions upon millions of dollars. The future compounding of the dividends of Berkshire's investees could be enormous.

There are other beauties at Berkshire. Consider how Buffett has structured the debt. He's paying 6.5% on all of his debt. He has very little debt compared to equity and is paying very little on his borrowings.

"His debt is triple A rated. There are not many companies in the country that can say that," notes one Berkshire shareholder. Berkshire is one of about 14 AAA-rated companies in the U.S.

Also consider what Buffett is paying for other people's money. At year-end 1990 Berkshire had a float from its insurance operations of about $1.6 billion. It was more than $2 billion by late 1991. Buffett notes the cost of those funds to Berkshire in 1990 was 1.63%; in 1991, 6.31%, perhaps a bit higher when other tax considerations are included. The cost of funds in 1992 was 4.76% and less than zero in 1993, 1994 and 1995.

The insurance operations have given Berkshire, in effect, interest-free loans over the years.

"If the float is $1.6 billion, and he's paying 2% for the money, then there's a built-in 6% profit and if you put a multiple of 10 on that, then the insurance business is worth $1 billion—and that's based on a 1990 figure and doesn't account for possible growth. A billion and a quarter for the insurance business would be a conservative figure," a Berkshire shareholder said in the summer of 1991.

Berkshire's float, with the buyout of GEICO is about $7 billion!

Get this: Buffett himself paid $2.3 billion for slightly less then half of GEICO and then wrote in the 1995 annual report that GEICO doubles Berkshire's growing insurance business. Isn't the worth of Berkshire's insurance businesses running hard at **A COOL $10 BILLION**?

And because of the huge capital of the insurance businesses, Berkshire enjoys the capacity to write business at any time propitious to Berkshire. "There is a hidden potential to write huge business in the future."

"And the fact that the insurance business has grown over the years—the fact that he can get to this position is indicative of the strength of the insurance business," said a Berkshire shareholder.

In any case then, what is Berkshire really worth? Adding the worth of the stocks and bonds is easy enough, even fun. Figure that the Coke investment is worth more than $8 billion. We won't consider whether the ocean of Coke stock would sell at an even greater premium were it sold as a block to a rich megalomaniac. Or to OPEC.

With respect to Berkshire's operating businesses, you should be able to put 20 times earnings on them to estimate their worth.

Berkshire's group of businesses apparently has among the highest return on equity of any group of businesses. That's a high return on equity with practically no debt. So let's loosen up a little and put a healthy P/E on things.

In 1993, *The Schott Letter*, written by Dr. John Schott figured Berkshire was worth $20,150 a share, and in 1994 it said it was worth more than $21,000. At the annual meeting in 1995, when Berkshire was trading at $21,600, Buffett said the stock price relative to its intrinsic value, "offers as much value, or more, than the majority of stocks I see."

(Photo by LaVerne Ramsey)

Dr. John Schott

Floyd Jones, a principal of First Washington Corp., calculates Berkshire's worth basically by using a comparison to GEICO, which traded at about 2.60 times book value over the years. "GEICO has an outstanding record, but then so does Berkshire," he says.

On April 30, 1996, Jones calculated Berkshire's intrinsic worth at $36,000 compared to a stock price of $33,5000, a 9% discount. Others calculated Berkshire's worth in the high $20,000 to mid $30,000 range.

What about taxes? Buffett is a keen reader of the tax code. Insurance operations get tax breaks. The dividends on the preferred stock investments are largely tax exempt. (Buffett's investment in low-income housing is another tax break.)

Many of Buffett's investments, such as stocks purchased by Berkshire's non-insurance subsidiaries, are carried at cost. Many businesses he purchased a long time ago are also carried at historical cost. Is See's, bought in 1972 for $25 million, worth more than that today? Of course. Is the Buffalo News worth the $33 million Buffett paid for it in 1977? Better to estimate $600 million, although large taxes would be owed if the newspaper were sold. But then Buffett isn't likely to sell See's or the *Buffalo News*. He's going to be buried with See's candies, Cokes and a copy of the *Buffalo News* carrying an obituary saying that he still owns the paper.

You can also be sure that Buffett's accounting is as conservative as it comes.

"And there are no hidden liabilities," says one Berkshire shareholder. "So many companies have large pension and health liabilities but Berkshire's pension plan is overfunded."

Berkshire has more than its share of diversity: stocks, bonds, cash, banks, tanks, newspapers, television and radio stations, razor blades, soft drinks, hard drinks, uniforms, candy, brokerage and financial services, oil, paper, steel, jewelry, furniture, encyclopedias, air compressors, vacuum cleaners, automotive compounds and so on. Even cutlery and spray guns.

And Berkshire has flexibility in a number of forms. With Buffett owning almost half of Berkshire's stock, decision-making can be almost instantaneous. Buffett can be on the spot with cash in hand, as when he bought Scott & Fetzer while other bidders were left calculating in the wings.

He has no limits on geography or industry as some other money managers have. He can buy in Malibu or Manchester and never leave his office. He can decide quickly that Berkshire would gain from more media or soft drink properties, or a shoe or food company, should something attractive be offered at the right price.

Isn't there extra value because Berkshire's managers pay themselves so little and Buffett and Munger serve on the boards of some of the investees? Their talent and time, for a tiny shareholder fee, is most valuable. Witness Salomon.

And Munger as a money manager did outperform the S&P 500 by a factor of about four over a period of about a dozen years, ringing up a 19.8% average annual return from 1962-1975 for his own partnership while the S&P 500 gained only 5.2% annually. For that, let's assign some value. How much, no one knows, but wouldn't you rather have made 19.8% than 5.2% on your money?

There are some technical things that add to Berkshire's worth—Berkshire's corporate structure enabling the insurance vehicle to make investments brings Berkshire some tax breaks. Also, Buffett operates with such size and efficiency that it's difficult to imagine that even his commissions, say, on a billion dollars worth of Coke aren't lower than any other fund manager's per share.

It's Buffett's "financial engineering" that really gives Berkshire an extra edge, says a report by Dominick & Dominick's *The Value Group* (April 8, 1991). The report says Buffett's record as a stock picker and a runner of businesses has been very good. The report figures that Buffett manages about a 20% return on his stock picking, and his businesses give him about a 21% return: so how has he managed an almost 24% annual return on equity?

> Low-cost borrowing is the primary advantage of a public company whose primary operating unit is an insurance company. Since insurance companies are nothing more than a good excuse to assemble a pool of investable assets, many successful investors own an insurance company...
>
> Berkshire Hathaway's second source of long-term no-cost leverage is the U.S. Treasury. Berkshire Hathaway has always used tax laws to its advantage. The most important source of borrowing from Uncle Sam at no cost is a long-term holding period...Combining long-term holding periods, with effective use of corporate exclusions for dividends, has permitted Berkshire to generate investment income and capital gains which were taxed at the dividend exclusion rate. Tax law has always permitted an intercorporate dividend exclusion. Currently this exclusion taxes only 20% of a dividend received by one corporation from another. Therefore the effective tax rate of a dividend is approximately 6%. Also, were a shareholder to tender stock back to a company retaining the same percentage of a company after the tender, the sale of the security is taxed as if it were a dividend. This means a corporation can sell a significant piece of a holding and have the gain taxed at 6%, not 29%. Time and again Berkshire Hathaway has used this quirk in tax law to lighten significant positions.
>
> The most obvious examples of this technique were:

1983—GEICO
1984—GEICO
1984—General Foods
1985—General Foods
1985—Washington Post"
[1993—Capital Cities]

The Value Group report stresses the advantages of stock buybacks. "Not only did it buy back its own stock in both 1964 and 1965, improving its returns, most of its important long term holdings have been companies that buy back their own stock."

Buffett has gained other "financial engineering" leverage through "tax arbitrage." The after-tax cost of the zero note borrowing is 3.5%; assume Buffett invests that money in a 9.25% investment in Champion International, 80% tax excluded, giving him an after-tax return of about 8.75%. "This gives Berkshire a 250% after-tax return on its money and an "option" to purchase Champion International Corp. at a fixed price for another eight years."

There's more:

> The last bit of financial engineering employed by Berkshire Hathaway is its consistent reduction of capital employed to run a business. Almost immediately after assuming control of Berkshire Hathaway, the company reduced its inventory, property, plant and equipment employed in running the business. It was this cash from the reduction of invested capital that produced the first pool of reinvestable cash...when Berkshire Hathaway acquired Kirby, the first move Berkshire made was to reduce its invested capital, thereby reducing the purchase price and raising the returns.

Whatever the advantages, if you could find someone who could bring you a 25% or 30% annual return for years to come, would that not be close to a priceless find? Even 20% or 15% would be a bonanza.

Berkshire might one day sell for $200,000 a share. If you are young enough, you might one day see it reach the $1 million-a-share mark.

Buffett cannot deliver anywhere near the average increase of 25% in stock price that he did in earlier years, but Berkshire should continue to outperform the market over the long term.

Berkshire is a world-beater investment vehicle. And there is a sort of X factor with Berkshire—some proprietary things that Buffett hasn't explained to shareholders. He has said, "There's not much of that sort of stuff." But there is some and it is unlikely that the worth of it is zero.

And there could be some future synergy. There appears to be very little now at Berkshire—a Coke machine and See's Candies cart at the Nebraska Furniture, some Berkshire insurance sold to See's. But what about selling insurance someday to every Berkshire investee, to Coke, Gillette, General Dynamics? Who knows?

Does it really make much difference what Berkshire is worth now if it can keep outperforming 90% of the world?

Would it have made much difference whether it was slightly undervalued or overvalued in 1965 when it traded at $12 a share? Wouldn't it have been nice to buy Berkshire at $20 or $200 or $2,000 or $20,000 a share, whether it was a bargain that day or not?

Finally, there is one other value. Buffett is running this operation, not Saddam Hussein. But Glenn Greenberg says there's one negative about Buffett—he will not be there one day. A key to Berkshire's worth is, "Warren Buffett's brain—whether it's alive or dead and he flies around a lot."

But Buffett alive is valuable far beyond his stock-picking and managerial abilities, although those traits may already be built into the stock price. But with access to such business leaders as Tom Murphy, Laurence Tisch, and Katharine Graham, can't something valuable suddenly materialize? Those sorts of people and Buffett are likely to come up with good ideas.

Buffett's elite circle of friends, in fact, retreats every two years to locations such as Lyford Cay in the Bahamas; Williamsburg, Virginia; the Queen Elizabeth II; Santa Fe, New Mexico; and Victoria, British Columbia.

The group (originally called the "Hilton Head Group" because it once met there) that Buffett calls the "Graham Group" and others call the "Buffett Group," began in 1968 with 13 people and now has 60, including Mrs. Graham, Murphy, Tisch, Keough, Gates, and Jack Byrne.

Buffett is friends with such business leaders as Walter Annenberg, and, in fact, advised him to go ahead with the $3 billion sale of his Triangle Publications, which included *TV Guide*, to Rupert Murdoch. Nancy Reagan is another friend. Mrs. Reagan once sent her son, Ron, to Buffett for a little career counseling.

Some of the country's best and brightest business folks run attractive ideas by Buffett. He can take the best one or two every year.

It's a plus that Buffett is on the boards of some of the companies in which Berkshire has investments. He can have some say over how their cash flows are invested, possibly bringing greater value to those companies. On the other hand, companies he invests in may have artificially higher P/Es because of his halo effect.

Finally, Berkshire's sterling reputation has value. Even in the precautionary prospectus for the Class B stock offering, its reputation (as opposed to unit trusts) is explained: "Though the point is impossible to quantify, Berkshire believes that its reputation has added significantly to the Company's intrinsic value over the years. Berkshire believes that its reputation, if it remains unimpaired, will produce substantial gains in the future as well."

If Buffett can keep working his magic at anything approaching his past rate of return, Berkshire will continue to make its way. The true value of Berkshire is in its future cash flows, adjusted for inflation.

If Berkshire could maintain a return of 23% on book annually, (Buffett says he can't do it), then by the Rule of 72, (72 divided by 23 is about 3), you'd double your money about every three years.

"Berkshire's not a company. It's an adding machine," says Berkshire shareholder George Eyraud of Birmingham.

When the Florida lottery was at a fever pitch in 1990 because the payoff was more than $100 million, ABC's *World News Tonight* was on the story.

You know how those features go—lots of folks in line giving brief interviews about what dreams might come true for the lucky winner.

Fleeting fame came to a heavyset, middle-aged man when a reporter stuck a mike in his face and asked what he'd do if he won $100 million; the fellow shrugged and replied before Peter Jennings and all the world: "Run naked through the money, I don't know."

The Schott Letter

December 1 1995

One view of Berkshire's intrinsic value is offered by Dr. John Schott of Harvard Medical School:

Stock Spotlight

Berkshire Hathaway*
(31,000; BRK; NYSE)

Berkshire Hathaway* is the holding company headed by world-famous super-investor Warren Buffett. It is the best long-term investment we know. This is our fourth Spotlight article on Berkshire in the last four years. The first was on 4/1/91 and the last preceding one was on 5/1/94. Because of Berkshire's significant price run-up in the last twelve months, we thought it timely to review our evaluation of the Company.

For newcomers to TSL, here is a brief background on Berkshire. Berkshire Hathaway was a struggling, nearly bankrupt Massachusetts textile company when Warren Buffett acquired control of it in 1969. Buffett had been trained in investing by the legendary Ben Graham. Prior to acquiring Berkshire he had run a highly successful investment partnership.

Following Graham's value investing principles, Buffett has proven to be a genius at spotting undervalued assets, inspired managers, and so-called franchise stocks.

Buffett and his side-kick, Berkshire Vice Chairman Charlie Munger, conceptualize Berkshire as a holding

Stock Spotlight: Berkshire Hathaway*
(Continued from page 1)

company with four major divisions - the insurance group; finance businesses; diverse manufacturing, publishing, and retailing businesses; and a portfolio of equity investments. While this conceptualization helps understand the Company, it should not be misconstrued to represent the way Berkshire actually functions. "World Headquarters", which is how Buffett has dubbed Berkshire's Omaha-based corporate offices, contains only eleven employees including Warren himself. Almost all of Berkshire's subsidiaries enjoy remarkable operational autonomy. Buffett's genius is in his financial leadership and organization. There is considerable functional overlap in the Buffett-Munger conceptualization. The equity investments are frequently done through the insurance portfolio and Buffett is the absolute arbiter of all investment judgments.

"Because of Berkshire's complexity and ... Buffett's penchant for privacy, there has always been divergence among the investment community as to how to best evaluate Berkshire Hathaway. ... We have employed four methods ... and now we will repeat that exercise for an updated evaluation."

Because of Berkshire's complexity and because of Buffett's penchant for privacy, there has always been divergence among the investment community as to how to best evaluate Berkshire Hathaway. In the past, we have employed four methods to evaluate Berkshire's private sale value and now we will repeat that exercise for an updated evaluation. These four methods are: 1) Traditional book value, 2) The use of traditional P/E methodology, 3) A P/E approach combining EPS with "look through" earnings, and 4) The method of evaluating each business sector.

Method One - Traditional Book Value

Warren Buffett has stated repeatedly that growth in book value is a corporate goal of BRK and a very good way to value the Company. Historically Berkshire book value has grown at 23.3% compounded per annum. Last year Company book value grew 13.9% from $8,854 to $10,083; but we estimate that the Geico acquisition will add approximately $750 to that figure, i.e. $10,833.

Would this be a fair private market value of Berkshire? No, it is far too conservative a figure clearly understating many assets and not giving fair value to the investment portfolio. It is really not possible to judge what premium a theoretical acquirer would pay.

However, there is one important thing to note. Historically Berkshire has tended to trade at approximately 2.4 x book. That would give a $26,000 figure, indicating Berkshire is currently somewhat overvalued.

Method Two - Traditional P/E

Berkshire's 1994 EPS were $495. We have no '95 estimates but the 9 month figure of '95 $344 vs. '94 $399 is probably misleading. With the Geico acquisition, BRK could come in somewhere between $525 and $600 per share. If we arbitrarily assign a P/E of 22, we get a fair market sale price of $10,890 based on '94 EPS or $13,200 based on estimated '95 EPS. Of course, this greatly underestimates Berkshire's real value since it completely ignores the considerable value of the Company's investment portfolio. to take this into better account, we must either utilize the earning from equity investments (Method Three) or add in its actual value (as in Method Four).

Berkshire Hathaway Value
P/E combining "look-through" EPS

BRK* operating '94 EPS	$606
(+) look through earnings	555
Adjusted EPS	$1161
(-) Tax estimate	71
Total EPS	$1090
Fair market value: 22 x $1090	$23,980

Method Three - P/E combining "look-through" EPS

Our third method attempts to correct the flaw in method two by

(Please turn to page 5)

*Berkshire Hathaway**
Business Sector Contributions to Share Value

Table A

Berkshire Hathaway* Common Stock Investments (11/22/95)

Shares (in millions)	*Company*	*Price*	*Market ($B)*	*Value/BRK* Shares*
27.8M	American Express	43	$1.95B	$865
20	Capital Cities/ABC	123 3/4	2.475	1,793
100	Coca - Cola	75	7.500	5,484
12.7	Fed. Home Loan Mtg.	75	0.952	690
6.8	Gannett	60 3/8	0.410	297
8.7	General Dynamics	60 1/4	0.524	379
36	Gillette	52 5/8	1.896	1,374
38.3	Guiness	7 1/8	0.272	197
19.7	PNC Bank	29 1/4	0.546	417
1.7	Washington Post	298	0.507	367
6.8	Wells Fargo	211 3/4	1.440	1,043
----	Other	----	1.240	848
			Value per BRK* share	$13,754

Table B

Berkshire Hathaway* Fixed Income Securities

	Estimated Market Value ($M) (4/1/95)
U.S. Treasuries & obligations of U.S. government corporations & agencies	$716
Obligations of states, municipalities & political subdivisions	6
Corporate bonds	
Redeemable pfd. stocks	4
Mortgage backed securities	
Total value	$1820
Value per BRK * share	$

Table C

Berkshire Hathaway* Wholly-owned Subsidiaries (4/1/95)

Company	*Business*	*After-Tax Earnings (in $M)*	*Multiple*	*Value*
Shoe group (H.H. Brown, Lowell, & Dexter)	shoes	$55.8M	18	$1,004.4M
Buffalo News	newspapers	31.7	20	634
Commercial & consumer finance	finance	14.6	14	204.4
Fechheimer	uniforms	7.1	18	127.8
Kirby	vacuum cleaners	27.7	18	498.6
Nebraska Furniture Mart	retail furniture	8.6	20	172
Scott Fetzer	home cleaning systems	24.9	20	498
See's Candies	candy	28.2	22	620.4
World Book	encyclopedias	17.3	18	311.4
Other	many different	36.4	18	655.2
	Total After-Tax Earnings	$252.3M	Total Value	$4,611.2M
			Value per BRK * share	$3,520

Table D

Berkshire Hathaway*
Insurance Group "Worth" ($M
(not including Geico)
(4/1/95)
(adjusted - see discussion)

'94 net earnings	$639.2
EPS	$463.2
Average P/E for similar companies	13
Value per BRK* share	$6021

Stock Spotlight ....
(continued from page 3)

utilizing the concept of "look through" earnings. We infer from comments Buffett has made that this would be his preferred method. To arrive at this, in the table on page 3 we have added to BRK's stated net EPS the retained operating earnings of BRK's major investments less the estimated corporate tax due if the earnings had, in fact, been distributed.

Given that this calculation is based on '94 earnings, we believe at least 15% must be added to give a closer approximation of market value. That gives a final estimate of $27,577 a share.

*Berkshire Hathaway**

Business Sector Contributions to BRK* Share Value

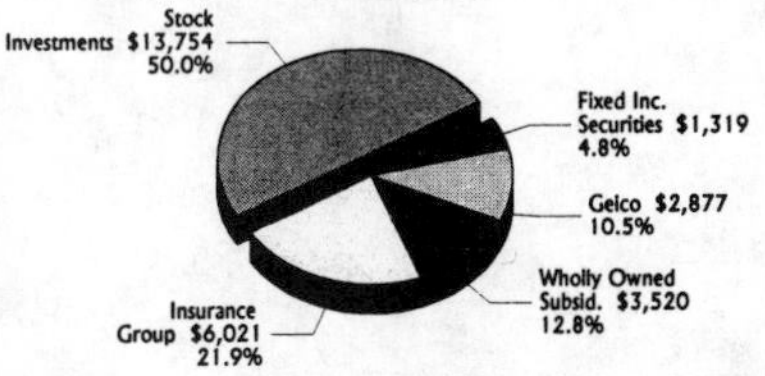

Method Four - Evaluating Each Business Sector

Method Four employs the following formula:

Berkshire's real worth = $(A + B + C_1 ... C_{10} + D + E) - F$, in which ...

* A = Berkshire's equity portfolio of publicly traded stocks. (see table A)
* B = Berkshire's fixed income portfolio. (see table B)
* $C = C_1 ... C_{10}$ in which $C_1 ... C_{10}$ are the values of Berkshire's nine largest wholly-owned subsidiaries (excluding Geico) calculated by using an inferred P/E multiple based on comparisons with similar publicly traded companies and in which C_{10} = a composite of Berkshire's 22 smallest subsidiaries assigning an arbitrary P/E of 18. (see table C)
* D = value of Berkshire's insurance group (without Geico) based on 13 times earnings. (see table D)
* E = the value of Geico.
* F = Berkshire's capital gains tax liability.

We believe this is the best approach to evaluating BRK, but also acknowledge it as far from perfect. Geico is treated independently because its recent acquisition gives a fair market value. Next year it probably will be included in the insurance division. Because we cannot get detailed information about Berkshire's insurance divisions, we believe we understate the value of the insurance companies ($6021 per BRK share) especially since Buffett/Munger have often indicated these are the most significant part of Berkshire. On the other hand, critics have said we are overstating the value of the wholly-owned subsidiaries by assigning P/E s that are too high. We readily accept this criticism but still think the methodology is a good one and that our distortion is P/Es may balance on both the high and low sides. Here are the figures:

* $W = (A + B + C_1 ... C_{10} + D + E) - F$
* W = ($13,754 + 1319 + 3520 + 6021 + 2877) - 1670
* W = $27,491 - 1670
* W = $25,821

Discussion

The results of Method Three ($27,577) and Method Four ($25,821) are even closer than they seem because #3 uses more '95 estimates than #4 employs. In any case, it is our opinion that Berkshire Hathaway is now about 20% overvalued. This is the first time since mid-1989 that we thought BRK was overvalued. Generally our estimates have shown it to be undervalued. Of course, it must be said that none of these methods assigns a dollar value to Warren Buffet's services.

What action should an investor take with regard to this overvaluation? Probably none. This is a long-term investment and should be bought as such. Buffett has often said, "If you can't tolerate a 50% drop in Berkshire's price, you probably shouldn't own it." Better than anyone, he understands market fluctuations and he knows one day Berkshire will have a major market setback. It has happened before and almost certainly will happen again. Obviously one could wait for that day to buy but experience has taught us that fear is the dominant emotion in bear markets and almost always prevents individual investors from buying after major market drops.

A case could be made for employing a stop-loss in BRK now that it is overvalued. This might make sense in tax advantaged accounts like IRAs and pension accounts. Most taxable accounts that hold Berkshire have substantial capital gains. It would be unwise to sell hoping that BRK would drop enough to compensate for the capital gains tax incurred. Our recommendation is to hold and indeed for anyone who does not own Berkshire to buy it. Its overvaluation would have to be for greater before we would recommend a sale.

(With permission of Dr. John Schott)

110

What's a Share of Berkshire Really, Really Worth?

An Abe Lincoln signature

If you ever tire of Buffett and Munger saying they won't reveal their exact idea of Berkshire's worth, here's a way to get an even more precise estimate than they can offer.

The formula:

Establish the worth of this note signed by Abe Lincoln when he was the 16th President of the United States, and there you have it:

"Sec. of the Treasury, please see this lady, (wife of a wounded soldier) who seeks employment. April 25, 1863. A. Lincoln."

Over time the price of the note and a Berkshire share have been almost precisely the same, according to Tim Burton, of Milwaukee, Wisconsin, citing Steven M. Berez's *Profiles in History.*

The following page lists the data:

	Lincoln's signature	Berkshire share
1982	$1,000	$965
1986	$3,000	$2,925
1992	$9,500	$9,275
1993	$12,000	$11,750
1995	$25,000-$30,000	$32,100
Early 1996	$29,500-$33,000	$33,000

With runaway inflation, however, Lincoln's signature and perhaps a BMW would beat the pants off Berkshire.

On June 15, 1993, someone called Burton to sell him a Lincoln signature for $15,700. Berkshire closed that day at $15,825. "I almost dropped the phone," Burton said.

What Berkshire shareholders really want to witness is the stock trading at the recent price of an Abe Lincoln letter and signature: $420,000.

Just to keep Berkshire shareholders a little on edge, Sotheby's has sold in recent times a document signed by Lincoln appointing an assistant paymaster in the Navy for just $3,850, but then, too, a page from Lincoln's 1858 handwritten "House Divided" speech commanded $1.5 million.

111

A Berkshire Shareholder's Thoughts Should Buffett Be Mortal

God forbid—what happens to Berkshire Hathaway when Warren Buffett dies?

One can surely expect a terrible one-day or more decline in the price of the stock. But then what? The decline would not be because of the prospect of a huge block of stock for sale from the estate, but rather because of the absence of this phenomenal manager.

Let's explore that more deeply. Warren Buffett has put together a company that owns many gems. A gem by definition is rare because it is valuable and long lived and relatively unaffected by other forces. Imagine if this were a fund of diamonds and a great genius with all his knowledge and expertise had accumulated these diamonds for the fund. When he died, the diamonds would still retain their gem quality; it's just that the fund no longer would have this genius to buy more great gems. So the future would depend on the growth in value of the existing gems.

So it is with Berkshire Hathaway. Will the sales of Coke or Gillette drop when Warren Buffett dies? No! (Except for a few Cherry Cokes.) It's just that there will be no new gem-quality companies added to the portfolio. Some of the companies owned by Berkshire Hathaway will go on just as before, while others may suffer slightly at the loss of Warren Buffett. The main areas to suffer will be the lack of growth from the insurance assets and the float, and the future allocation of assets.

If we are to believe what we are told, Charlie Munger is extremely competent and can offset the loss of Warren Buffett to some extent. Let's assume that Warren Buffett would have achieved his objective of 15% growth per year, and that without him, Charlie Munger manages to do 7%. That 8% difference is huge, as 8% on $10 billion is $800,000,000 per year, but it is not the end of the world.

The important thing to keep in mind is that with an intrinsic value today [August 10, 1991] of about $9,300, (price=$8,850) the gem already exists, so it's from this base that the growth starts declining.

A projection of intrinsic value can be made using different assumptions about the death of Buffett and/or Munger. Unless both should meet untimely deaths in the very near-term future, Berkshire shareholders should fare well.

As long as the market is not paying a premium for the growth potential of Warren Buffett management, the price should not decline sharply in the absence of this management. Only in the case of a premium for growth, should there be a substantial decline. Recently, however, the company has sold at below its intrinsic value. So the market is already valuing Berkshire Hathaway as if Warren Buffett were no longer here.

In conclusion, as long as Berkshire is selling at or below intrinsic value when Warren dies, there should not be a permanent loss of capital for the shareholders; there will undoubtedly be a short term adverse reaction, which may be limited when one considers the potential of the company with its existing portfolio.

There may also be some action taken upon his death that would have a positive effect on the stock price, such as a dividend, a buyback of stock, or a stock split (100 to 1).

Also on the positive side, consider the upside of Berkshire if Warren Buffett should have the business lifespan of an Armand Hammer.

—A longtime Berkshire shareholder
who wishes to remain anonymous.

112

Washington and Lee University gets 1,000 Shares of Berkshire

"That's what Warren Buffett did for me."

Ernie Williams, Class of '38 at Washington and Lee University in Lexington, Virginia, long has been a benefactor of the school he and three generations of his family love. But with Williams's recent gift to the school, he outdid himself when he and his wife, Marjorie, handed over 1,000 shares of Berkshire to W&L for professorships and scholarships. The gift was the second largest in W&L history.

"I was certainly surprised at the amount of capital gains he had in the Berkshire stock," said David R. Long, director of planned giving at W&L.

"I had known for some time he had a large position in the stock and was thinking about giving some of it to W&L...All along Ernie had wanted it to be anonymous but we convinced him to make an announcement to help with publicity in the fundraising campaign. He's very emotional when it comes to helping W&L."

So how did Williams come by 1,000 shares of Berkshire stock?

"I read a story in the October, 1977, issue of *Fortune* magazine by Warren Buffett," Williams recalled. "The logic of it overwhelmed me. I must have read it three, seven or ten times." Soon Williams bought a few Berkshire shares at about $80 each. Then he headed for Berkshire's annual meeting in April, 1978, and met Buffett. "I had about 150 shares and I really went out to see if I should buy more.

"There were 17 people at the meeting held in the National Indemnity headquarters building. Buffett was sitting one chair from me and never left and never said a word. There was a clock there on the wall behind Ken Chace who conducted the meeting. The meeting started exactly at 10 a.m. and it was over in exactly 10 minutes and he left.

"I got him out in the hall and said I'd flown all the way out and would he talk to me. We talked. I doubt it was more than 15 minutes. Mainly he told me that short-term there would be some problems at the *Buffalo News* but that things might work out well there in the long run. That was before the other paper—*The Courier*—folded."

Williams said there wasn't anything specific that Buffett said that made him realize Buffett was special. Still something about Buffett struck him so much that Williams immediately called his office to buy more Berkshire stock.

Williams, the former president of the old Mason & Lee brokerage house in Lynchburg, Virginia, called his office and put in an order to buy Berkshire shares, saying: "I want you to clean up the market for Berkshire."

When his office called back to say they had filled his order, he said, "Now I want you to go out and buy more Berkshire."

"I then flew on to Chicago in a snowstorm that day and I got there about 2:30 and I called my office and said I wanted to buy more Berkshire. I was told it was trading at a higher price. I said I want you to go out and buy," he said.

At the time the stock was trading without any fanfare in the pink sheets.

In those transactions that day of the Berkshire meeting, Williams picked up about 150 shares at an average cost of about $152 a share.

From that day forth until 1983 when Berkshire was trading at more than $1,300 a share, Williams continued to buy. In the end, Williams held a large number of Berkshire shares and became a multi-millionaire.

All of Williams's family members are wealthy, and W&L is a major beneficiary of his farsighted investment in Berkshire.

"That's what Warren Buffett did for me," he said.

Over the years, he followed Buffett into certain Berkshire investments such as GEICO.

For many years, Williams lived at Hilton Head, South Carolina, on Laughing Gull Road. Buffett and Williams occasionally were in touch. "He joked with me about my address," said Williams who now divides his time between Village of Golf, Florida, near Delray Beach, and Cashiers, North Carolina.

Williams relates another Buffett story of buying his first shares through his friend, Archie MacAllaster. MacAllaster is chairman of MacAllaster Pitfield, a firm specializing in over-the-counter securities, mainly bank and insurance issues.

Williams says that MacAllaster, who is often interviewed by *Barron's* magazine, was well regarded for his knowledge of insurance stocks, and that MacAllaster once met Buffett and talked about insurance stocks.

Williams said, "MacAllaster came away from a luncheon thinking he didn't know a thing about insurance company stocks compared to Buffett. He said Buffett knew more about insurance stocks than anyone he'd ever met."

That's right, says MacAllaster, who notes he was a market-maker in Berkshire stock at a time when Williams was putting in buy orders for Berkshire. "I was a little nervous about holding Berkshire."

As for Buffett, Berkshire shareholder MacAllaster said, "I talked to him (Buffett) way back. He knew all about insurance and financial stocks. He is one smart financial person. He understood insurance stocks in Nebraska and he understood them nationwide...He understood balance sheets."

The real hero of the story, Williams says, was Fitz Fitzgerald, MacAllaster's trader. "He didn't want to inventory any Berkshire. And he would call me and say, 'Look, I hate to see Berkshire break 300. I've got 300 shares you can have at that price.' And he did that every time he would take stock in. He didn't mean to be so good to me...I always bought it on the offered side. Good Old Fitz."

At the dedication of the Ernest Williams II School of Commerce, Economics and Politics at W&L in 1995, J. Alfred Broaddus, of W&L's Class of '61 and president of the Federal Reserve Bank of Richmond, praised Williams for his purchase of property on Hilton Head Island, S.C. in the 1950s and Berkshire stock in the 1970s.

"The audience knows these things, Ernie, and consequently and undoubtedly they would much rather have you up here giving them business advice and investment tips than some guy from the Fed," Broaddus said. (*The Washington and Lee Alumni Magazine*, Fall, 1995)

113

"Sir, What If You Die?"

"The exact location of my body shouldn't matter." The denouement; the gift to all humanity

"Sir, what if you die?"

This touchy question gets posed to Buffett almost every year, although usually more subtly. How would you like it if you were asked in public every year about walking into a Mack truck?

"Here comes the 'if I get hit by a truck question,' " Buffett has said under his breath.

Bob Sullivan, who runs R.M. Sullivan Trucking Co. in Springfield, Massachusetts, jokes that he takes exception to the "hit by a truck question."

"I run a trucking company and I've instructed our drivers to be careful not to hit [Buffett and Munger] because they have Berkshire and Wesco in their pension plan."

Buffett wrote Sullivan after the annual meeting in 1995: "Thanks for your note and the bunnies you sent. They were a big hit with the little kids at home and also the big kids here in the office.....P.S. No more mention of 'trucks!' "

It's a near certainty that Buffett will not die by being hit by a truck. Tooth decay, maybe.

"All in all, we're prepared for 'the truck,' " Buffett wrote in the 1993 Annual Report after explaining his stock will not be sold at his death, but will go either to his wife or his foundation. And he said there are plans for strong management.

"After my death, all of my stock will go to my wife Susie should she survive me, or to a foundation if she dies before I do. In neither case will taxes and bequests require the sale of consequential amounts of stock," Buffett wrote in the 1993 Annual Report.

"Nothing will be forced by estate taxes. I owe that to people in case I step in an elevator shaft absent-mindedly," Buffett said at the Berkshire annual meeting in 1986.

Asked at the annual meeting in 1991 what would happen to Berkshire should he die, Buffett deadpanned, "Our businesses are run as if I am not there. So the exact location of my body shouldn't matter."

Buffett has assured shareholders that nothing will happen to his Berkshire stock. "Not a single share of my stock will be sold," he has said. Almost all his Berkshire stock is going to The Buffett Foundation.

"It's a marvelous society that lets me do what I do. I wouldn't be worth a damn in Bangladesh or Peru or some place. The fact that I have a lot of fun with it and can consume some of it, I think I should give it back to society. I see no reason why I should create some dynasty of wealth that can go around fanning themselves," he said on Adam Smith's *Money World* show in connection with Berkshire's annual meeting in 1990.

Here's how he puts things in the 1990 annual report: "I feel strongly that the fate of our businesses and their managers should not depend on my health which, it should be added, is excellent—and I have planned accordingly. Neither my estate plan nor that of my wife is designed to preserve the family fortune; instead, both are aimed at preserving the character of Berkshire and returning the fortune to society."

Precisely how all this will work has not been publicly spelled out. "The sequence of its disposition depends on the order of death. But ultimately, it will go back to society," Buffett said at the annual meeting in 1991. Nor has it been detailed what will happen to Buffett's substantial personal portfolio.

What has been communicated is that the Berkshire shareholders should not lie awake at night and worry that Berkshire is going back to $12 a share the day Buffett goes.

"I don't do the normal exercise and I don't eat a normal diet. But we do have someone in mind who would be our successor if Charlie and I were to die at once. And on my death, not a share of stock has to be sold. I have promised people that my affairs will not cause people any surprises," Buffett said at the annual meeting in 1988.

At the meeting in 1991 he said, "You have two questions as shareholders that you have to think about: Will the owners behave any different as owners? And will the managers behave any different as managers?" He made it clear the answer to both questions is no.

Munger said, "I think it's obvious that if Warren died tomorrow the prospects of the company would be somewhat reduced. Certainly the capital allocation process couldn't be made better under any foreseeable scenario. However, I do think a company like Berkshire would have a lot of time to find a successor. And you only need one." Buffett: "Maybe less."

Munger: "And I don't think that you should assume that the personality who put the whole thing together would be incapable of finding a successor."

Buffett:

> It's an easy company to run. And the capital allocation process may be self-defeating anyway over time. And there's nothing that says we can forever allocate the capital better than you.
>
> So as the years go by, it's not inconceivable that we could have a policy on dividends that would be dramatically different than the present one because we believed you could do a better job of allocating the capital than we could—partly because the sums would be so large. And Charlie says we're looking forward to that day.

Michael Assael, at the Borsheim's party in 1991, kidded Buffett that he'd had a dream that Buffett's granddaughter, Emily, would be running the company one day. "Buffett grinned, and if I recall correctly, he chuckled, 'That's about right.' " Assael said.

But even if Buffett were taking Emily's investment ideas now, his current investments will live on. People will go on drinking Coca-Cola and buying *World Books*.

Berkshire would probably hit some air pockets afterwards, and some suggest a huge drop, knocking out of the stock what many observers call "a Buffett premium."

Such fears are summarized by *Newsday's* Allan Sloan: "I'd sure hate to find buyers for large blocks of Berkshire stock if Buffett weren't there." Still, that might be a moment to buy.

At the annual meeting in 1987, Buffett made a remarkable comment after an explanation about how if he should go, then Munger would run things "and we have a provision beyond that." What he said next is that he had almost never given a stock tip in his life.

Then he gave one: "When I die, buy the stock."

He suggested the stock price might drop, making Berkshire a real buy. He repeated his standard remark that none of his stock will be sold.

At the annual meeting in 1986, Buffett said, "Charlie will be running it. No Berkshire holding will be sold. It will be kept intact. Capital Cities, Gillette and GEICO will continue. There will be no surprises for management."

He said that when he dies the stock price shouldn't change much, wisecracking, "I'll be disappointed if it goes up a lot," a reference to some stocks rising in relief when certain CEOs go. "No you won't," Munger quipped.

Buffett said of Munger, "He'll be flattered," by Berkshire rising in anticipation of Munger's reign.

Should Buffett go, Berkshire would be run by Munger who for years has allocated the capital with Buffett. Would things be as good as under Buffett, the true glue that keeps the disparate parts of Berkshire together? No. They would not. Buffett is an original, one of kind. Would they be bad? Not at all.

As Munger has put it, "Capital allocation would not be as good as under him. But it would not be bad, either."

Says one Berkshire shareholder, "One of the most significant questions about Berkshire is what will happen when Buffett dies."

Munger has said, "Berkshire's chairman may get older, but the assets aren't going anywhere. And the nature of the Berkshire game is that we do not have to replace armies to make it work well. We've run so lean over the years that over time we've only got two or three crucially important bodies to replace."

"We'll get somebody like Warren," Munger has said. There's the rub, of course.

Says one Berkshire shareholder, "Munger can do everything Buffett does except be funny at the annual meeting."

Beyond Munger, will Berkshire find some superb individual to run the company? Sure. But just who has long been a mystery.

In Berkshire's 1995 annual report Buffett indicated that person is GEICO's Lou Simpson, calling him a person who could handle Berkshire's investments were something to happen to him and Munger.

Buffett always means what he says and says what he means.

"When I die, buy the stock." What does that mean? No one knows for sure. But, with Buffett saying it, it means what it says.

One shareholder says, "He probably means that if Berkshire took a big dip upon his death, the stock would be undervalued and be a buy."

Buffett never makes idle comments, and his comment about buying the stock means something, but it's unclear just what.

Buffett's comment certainly seems to suggest some finale. Expect a surprise when his estate passes to The Buffett Foundation.

Berkshire shareholder Judith Goodnow Prus believes Berkshire's denouement to the Warren Buffett era will strike a theme of Buffett-as-teacher. Ever since Buffett taught investment courses, in his early days in Omaha, he has been a teacher of sorts. His occasional talks, his writings, his fielding of questions at annual meetings all show characteristics of a teacher.

Indeed Mrs. Prus thinks Buffett may have accepted the Salomon post in part because of his love of teaching. "It seems to me the reason he was so quick to accept the Salomon challenge...it was a made-to-order opportunity to teach some ethical as well as economic lessons. I think he seized the opportunity for this reason, not just to protect an investment...

"I think he is so intelligent and so rational and so realistic, that he must understand that he is in a unique position to teach and has a responsibility to do so...Perhaps it doesn't make any sense for him to teach in the usual sense, that is one teacher, with a few pupils, but perhaps some day soon, with the new methods of communication, he would be able to invest some limited amount of time and reach a lot of people at once.

"Anyway, perhaps the denouement will be one big lesson. I hope so," Mrs. Prus said.

Buffett's net worth of about $17 billion would make his foundation the largest charitable organization in the nation; the Ford Foundation is now the largest with assets of about $6 billion. Buffett's children are each to receive a relative pittance of roughly $5 million. (*Wall Street Journal*, November 8, 1991) When the day is done, Buffett is a giver, not a taker.

"The other significant question about Berkshire is to figure out how to recognize the next Warren Buffett," said a Berkshire shareholder, adding that he has often tried to convince others of the appeal of Berkshire with almost no results.

"I have seen so many people pass it up," said one Berkshire shareholder. "I would like for my children to be able to recognize the next Berkshire that comes along."

Of course, one answer is to recognize this one and not worry too much about searching out another one. It's the same proposition for those investors who try to figure out where Buffett is investing or how to copycat his investments.

The way to be sure you are doing what Buffett is doing when he is doing it is simply to be a Berkshire shareholder, that is just sit back and leave the driving, the investing, to him. Why try to second-guess Buffett? Why not just enjoy what he's doing?

Occasionally, there are rumors that Buffett is up for a government job or is under consideration to head the New York Stock Exchange, but he has sidestepped all that with the assurance, "I'll keep doing this as long as I live." (*Los Angeles Times*, Linda Grant, April 7, 1991)

"I think he's an American genius...He has a sterling reputation," said Kahn Brothers' Irving Kahn, who adds that his only bone to pick with Buffett is why, as he's gotten older, Buffett has continued to concentrate on amassing wealth rather than giving more consideration to what that wealth can do for society. Kahn said:

> After all, it's money he's made from other people. He didn't create the telephone or invent something...Sooner or later some of that money should go back to society. Warren Buffett looks good versus the other nefarious collectors of corporate shares. Yet his gains equal the losses of all who sold to him...Maybe after so many brilliant achievements, Warren Buffett will use his energy and brains for broader and deeper national problems.

We shall see whether Buffett has given full thought to how that money will be used.

Buffett may feel that the more wealth he can accumulate, the more he can help the world. And of course Buffett has offered a lot in human terms already, setting examples in human and financial behavior for all. And the Buffett/Berkshire story is unfinished.

Almost everyone's first question about Berkshire is what happens when Buffett passes on. The query persists though Buffett is most assuredly not on his deathbed. It may well be that Buffett plans on surprising people by doing what he's doing until a very late age.

Perhaps a good response to the "what if he dies" question is, "What if he lives?"

He seems to be a healthy, happy and energetic man, and he just may live beyond the next quarter's earnings statement.

And how might Berkshire do if Buffett lives a long life? "Berkshire will generate significant sums of investable capital and Buffett will deploy this money successfully. Unfortunately, we can't put a number on this success. There's every reason to think the investments will do better than average, but there's no telling how much better, or what average will be," says Steve Wallman, who heads Wallman Investment Counsel in Madison, Wisconsin.

"Most people looking at Berkshire seem to suffer from a lack of imagination. They don't have the vaguest idea of where Buffett is taking the company, so they conclude that Buffett doesn't know where he's going either."

Buffett himself has given every indication that he has a few more chapters in his book, more painting to do on his Berkshire canvas.

Beyond that, things are not spelled out. But it is assumed that Buffett has researched the matter thoroughly and will leave his wealth to society in the least disruptive way to Berkshire shareholders.

"His integrity seems to me to be involved in his plans for the ultimate future of the company, when he is not there. Everyone who knows him seems to feel comfortable about whatever plan he might have for the company; we all seem to feel that it will be right, honorable and good. We trust his goodness," Mrs. Prus said.

The better Berkshire does, the more the foundation can do to achieve its lofty aims. One Berkshire shareholder has said that Buffett is not so much about money as he is about love.

What Buffett has reaped from society will be entirely given back to it. Buffett has an admiration for those who take a little from society and give a lot back.

In a letter to the *Omaha World-Herald*, January 20, 1980, reprinted in part in the *The Kiewit Story*, Buffett eulogized Peter Kiewit, the former head of Peter Kiewit Sons', Inc.:

> Pete Kiewit was overwhelmingly a producer, not a consumer. Profits went to build the capacity of the organization, not to provide opulence for the owner. In essence, one who spends less than he earns is accumulating 'claim checks' for future use. My guess is that he left claim checks worth some $150 million at the time

> of his death.
>
> During his lifetime, he and his family probably personally redeemed something like 3% of the claim checks that he produced. Upon his death, he left another 5% or so to his family. The balance was left to his community through a foundation whose intent, I believe, is to utilize a significant portion of those claim checks—stored-up consumption, in reality—for the benefit of the people of the Midlands.
>
> The bricklayer of 1920 turned out to be an extraordinary endowment manager, indeed. And now, at his death, that estimated $150 million endowment has been turned over to a group of foundation trustees who are likely to achieve Kiewit-type results in maximizing the flow of benefits to society from those funds. Peter Kiewit could not have better served his community and his compatriots.

That last line could someday be a well-deserved epitaph for Buffett.

Munger sheds some light on this question in his 1990 letter to Wesco shareholders.

> This eccentric, who heads Berkshire Hathaway, Wesco's parent corporation, believes for some reason that accumulated wealth should *never* be spent on oneself or one's family, but instead should merely serve, before it is given to charity, as an example of a certain approach to life and as a didactic platform.
>
> These uses, plus use in building the platform higher, are considered the only honorable ones not only during life but also after death. Shareholders who continue in such peculiar company are hereby warned by our example in writing this section: some of the eccentricities of this fellow are contagious, at least if association is long continued.
>
> If Warren were a homespun philosopher running a small creamery, who'd pay attention to what he says? The money gives him the base to communicate his ideas. Berkshire is, in many ways, an exercise in didacticism. (*U.S. News & World Report*, June 20, 1994)

Herein is the permanent value that Buffett and Munger have so brilliantly created.

As for Berkshire, surely it will pass into competent hands and continue to flourish whether or not Buffett is running it.

And Buffett plans to keep running it for some time. Once at Harvard Business School he was asked when he planned to retire. "About five to ten years after I die," he replied.

And he told Columbia business students October 27, 1993:

> Berkshire would be pretty easy to run. It's in marvelous financial shape, has a great set of managers in the operating businesses.
>
> The person that ran it would have to do two things. They would have to basically keep the present managers motivated and happy doing what they're doing. And that basically means leaving them alone and judging them by the right standards.
>
> And then they'd have to allocate capital. They could partially solve the capital allocation by simply establishing a significant dividend policy for one thing.
>
> They'd have to get one good idea a year on capital allocation. And the managing would be very simple.

In any event, one should not wish Buffett to be in any hurry to leave. Rather, we should wish him immortality as he has wished it for his managers.

We should fully enjoy the presence of this genius while we can.

As John Buchan wrote in *Pilgrim's Way*, of Lawrence of Arabia: "If genius be, in Emerson's phrase, a 'stellar and undiminished something,' whose origin is a mystery and whose essence cannot be defined, then he was the only man of genius I have ever known."

114

The Buffett Foundation

"A fund that's not yet activated"

Buffett's wealth, the fruits of his lifetime of long-term investing, is slated to go to The Buffett Foundation and then back to society.

Buffett's foundation could easily wind up as the largest in the country. The largest foundations in the U.S., according to The Foundation Center using 1992 assets, are:

1. Ford Foundation...$5.47 billion
2. W.K. Kellogg Foundation...$5.45 billion
3. Pew Charitable Trusts...$3.3 billion
4. John D. and Catherine T. MacArthur Foundation...$2.9 billion
5. Lilly Endowment...$2.6 billion

Buffett calls his fortune, "a fund that's not yet activated." (*Omaha World-Herald*, October 4, 1993)

The thrust of The Buffett Foundation's giving currently is for planned parenthood, reducing the risk of nuclear war, and education.

"His big interest has always been the problem of world population growth. He thinks it's a danger to the world...that you can have it all but if you have overpopulation the world will struggle with problems like housing," says his sister, Doris Bryant.

With the exception of some grants made in Omaha, the focus of the foundation is largely family planning, both domestic and international.

The foundation, with assets in 1994 of more than $20 million, has no grant guidelines except for its college scholarship program and doesn't accept applications for grants.

Buffett has decided not to dictate from the grave how the foundation should operate, saying that high-grade people living after him will be better judges of how best to use the money for mankind.

Buffett has shied away from saying too much about the foundation, formed in 1964, but he has said that most of his money will go back to society and that the conduit for building a better world is the foundation.

The foundation is still quite small and waiting for Buffett's vast wealth to multiply into a force for the betterment of mankind.

The Buffett Foundation's assets are currently a hodgepodge of stocks. The Buffetts have made donations through Berkshire's charitable giving program. So far the foundation has been the recipient of millions of the Buffett's billions.

The Buffett Foundation assets of only $1.4 million in 1981 grew to $8.4 million in 1986, largely because of good return on investments and Buffett's own contributions through Berkshire's shareholder-designated contributions program.

The *Forbes* story about Buffett being the richest person in the country in October 1993, figured that the Buffett estate could be worth $100 billion in 20 years, dwarfing the legacies of Rockefeller, Ford and Carnegie, even adjusted for inflation.

Buffett, sometimes criticized for not giving away his money now, said, "I wouldn't want to transfer Berkshire Hathaway shares to anyone while I'm alive. If I owned a wide portfolio of securities I could give them away. But, I don't want to give up control of Berkshire Hathaway...I've got this fund that's not yet activated, and it is building at a rate greater than other endowments, like Harvard's. It's growing at 25% to 30%." According to Foundation Incorporated records, The Buffett Foundation on June 30, 1990, had assets of $15,210,316. In the 12 months ended that date, the foundation made contributions and paid grants totalling $1,417,895 to more than 80 entities. Operating and administrative expenses during this period totalled $131,382. The largest of the grants was $200,000, and the smallest was $280 to Rudyard Theatre. Average amounts fell in the $1,000 to $10,000 range.

If that doesn't tell a whole lot, it still serves as a tantalizing blueprint of future giving.

What is known about the foundation is that on the asset side its stockholdings show Warren Buffett to be a stock market junkie.

The foundation's Form 990-PF for the year ended June 30, 1990, shows about 200 stock positions ranging from 200 shares of Abbott Laboratories to 110 shares of Zenith National Insurance Co.

And there's everything in between from 200 shares of American Brands, 10 shares of Cap Cities, 75 shares of CBS, 600 of Coca-Cola, 200 Freddie Mac, 100 GE, 100 J&J, 100 Eli Lilly, 750 Loews, 200 Melville Corp., 150 Morgan Stanley Group, 800 Philip Morris, 100 Playboy Enterprises, 100 Ralston Purina, 100 Rockefeller Center Properties, 100 Salomon, 100 Sears Roebuck, 100 Tiffany, 100 Torchmark, 200 Wal-Mart Stores, 10 Washington Post Co., 100 Wells Fargo, and many others.

The recipients are equally eclectic; Form 990-PF report shows the following were among the recipients of the foundation's contributions and grants:

ACLU Reproductive Freedom Project—$15,000
Alan Guttmacher Institute—$100,000
Cancer Research Institute—$1,000
Caring for Children—$1,000
Girls, Inc. of Omaha—$20,000
International Projects Assistance Services—$200,000
Omaha Zoo Foundation—$9,500
Planned Parenthood of Mid-Iowa—$30,000
Planned Parenthood of New York City—$100,000
Salem Baptist Church—$5,000
Sex Information and Education Council of U.S.—$15,000
United Way of the Midlands—$122,411

Alice Buffett Outstanding Teacher Awards—$10,000 each to 15 recipients. Alice Buffett was Buffett's aunt who taught in Omaha for 35 years.

In fiscal 1991-92, the foundation gave 73% of its donations, totaling $2.2 million, to groups involved in limiting population. (*Omaha World-Herald*, July 24, 1992)

The largest recipients were the Center for Reproductive Law and Policy, New York, $500,000, and International Projects Assistance Services,

Carrboro, North Carolina, which trains doctors and health professionals and provides equipment for medical clinics in developing countries received $250,000.

A story in *The New York Times* December 3, 1995, gave an update about the Buffett Foundation. "On June 30, 1995, the Buffett Foundation had assets of $21.6 million, according to the latest tax returns. About $7 million of that was invested in a smorgasboard of 184 stocks, from Advo to Zenith National Insurance.

"But despite the variety, one stock, General Dynamics, dominated the foundation's equities, accounting for $5.63 million, or more than 80% of their total worth. Loews was the far-distant, second-largest holding, with a value of $90,750 as of June 30."

The other main holdings were 1,200 shares of Coca-Cola, 800 shares of Philip Morris, 375 shares of American International Group, 900 shares of Pepsico, 800 shares of Campbell Soup, 600 shares of Anheuser-Busch, 600 shares of Hershey Foods and 600 shares of Leucadia National.

The cost of three major holdings was $2.65 million and the worth on June 30, 1995, was $6.08 million.

The *Times* story said:

> Aficionados speculate that the foundation... may be [Buffett's] research vehicle, a means of keeping track of annual reports from companies he likes to follow.
>
> The nation's best known investor keeps only 32% of his foundation's money in stocks. Most of the money, 57%, is in Treasuries, with the balance in cash and other assets... Companies can deduct the full value of an appreciated stock without paying capital gains on the appreciation, up to 10% of their taxable income. For example, two years ago, at Mr. Buffett's election, Berkshire donated 110,485 shares of Torchmark, an insurance company, to the foundation. The stock cost Berkshire $2.1 million, but the company got to deduct from taxes $4.8 million, the shares' value at the time of the donation, and did not have to pay the 35% tax on the gain.
>
> The nonprofit foundation, which then sold the stock, paid just the 2% gains tax to which it is subject. To top it off, Mr. Buffett got to direct the flow of nearly 5 million philanthropic dollars at a cost to Berkshire-

of just $2.1 million.

Buffett often speaks of working with people he likes, admires and trusts, so it's not at all surprising that he has chosen people close to him as officers and directors of his foundation.

The officers of The Buffett Foundation:

Susan T. Buffett, president

Warren E. Buffett, vice president & treasurer

Gladys Kaiser, secretary

Allen Greenberg, Buffett's former son-in-law, executive director

The directors of the foundation: Buffett and his wife, their daughter, Susan, Carol J. Loomis and Thomas S. Murphy.

Also Buffett has the tiny Sherwood Foundation directed by his children and Astrid Menks. For the year ended July 30, 1993, it had assets of $584,000 and gave away about $370,000. (*New York Times*, December 3, 1995)

The foundation paid more than half the first-year costs for tests needed to bring the French abortion pill, RU-486, to the U.S. market, according to the *Omaha World-Herald.* (Cindy Connolly, April 21, 1996)

"The Buffett Foundation gave $2 million in 1994 to fund clinical trials for the pill, which is called mifepristone in the United States. The money went to Population Council, a nonprofit research group in New York that holds the U.S. patent rights to the pill," the story said.

"The $2 million the Buffett foundation gave for the clinical trials was in addition to more than $5 million it contributed in 1994 to various organizations that work to limit population growth."

The story also said that since 1988 the foundation has been primarily devoted to limiting population growth.

115

All-American Alabama Football Player Kermit Kendrick Tackles Buffett for an Autograph

One day I went to a bookstore and bought a couple of copies of my first book about Buffett and gave one to a friend. As we were talking, a stranger happened by, saw the book and—entirely unsolicited—said how wonderful the book was.

He said he had read every word and that we were really going to enjoy reading it.

When I told him I wrote the book, he couldn't believe it.

I was so taken with the compliment, as the fellow praised the book and said Buffett was his hero, that I gave him my copy.

He turned out to be Kermit Kendrick, an all-American defensive back for the University of Alabama football team in the late 1980s and a stockbroker with Merrill Lynch (he's now the assistant athletic director at Alabama).

I autographed the book and then he asked if there were any way to

(Courtesy of the University of Alabama)

Crimson Tide's Kermit Kendrick tackles Buffett for an autograph.

get Buffett's autograph. I told him I didn't think that was possible.

When I got back to the office, I felt troubled about it and called Kermit, saying, "You really want that book signed by Warren Buffett?" We met immediately, he returned the book to me, and I sent it to Buffett.

A few days later, even though I had sent a regular mail stamped return envelope, Buffett via Federal Express on Christmas Eve—in a random act of kindness—returned the book, autographed.

(Photo by Pat Kilpatrick)

Response from Alabama Coach Gene Stallings and Kermit Kendrick. Author is at left. Actual photo of God can be seen in upper left area even though it looks like Coach "Bear" Bryant.

My note to Kermit said, "Many thanks for your unsolicited compliment about the book. I really do appreciate it. I hope your finances wind up in *better* shape than Warren Buffett's. All the best and happy investing! Roll Tide!"

Buffett's note to him read, "Kermit, Best wishes for a great career in investments. And good luck to the Tide unless the Cornhuskers are the opponent."

Said Kendrick, "This is probably the most exciting day of my brokerage career.

"...Just one other thing. Is there any way to meet him?"

Kendrick finally met Buffett at the annual meeting in 1996. Kendrick got in touch with Alabama's former offense coach, Homer Smith, who wrote Buffett about Kendrick. Buffett wrote back to Smith sending Kendrick a ticket to the annual meeting.

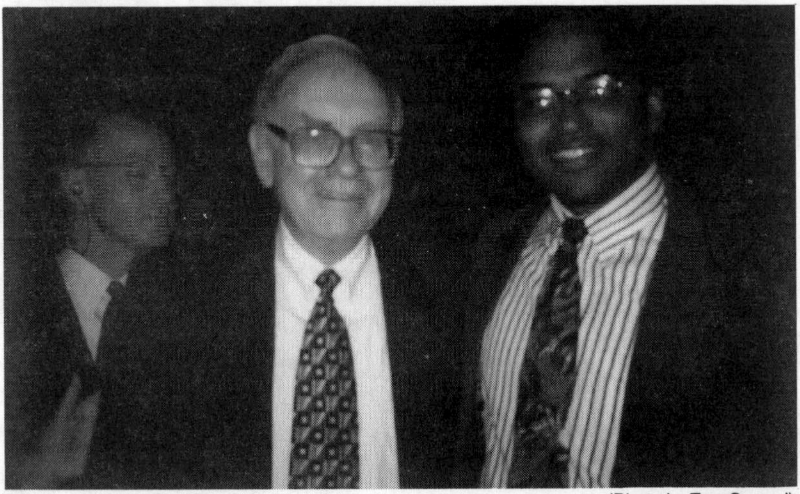

(Photo by Tom Conrad)

Buffett and Kendrick finally meet at Berkshire's annual meeting in 1996.

116

Warren Buffett Picks Up a Penny

"The beginning of the next billion."

This book has bandied about the B word—billion.

One day in the mid-1980s, Buffett got on the elevator at Kiewit Plaza in midtown Omaha. He was going to his office on the 14th floor.

On the floor of the elevator was a penny. None of the employees of Peter Kiewit Sons', the construction conglomerate, paid any attention. Buffett leaned over, reached down and picked up the penny.

To the Kiewit executives, stunned that he would bother with a penny, the fellow who would one day be the richest person in the world quipped, "The beginning of the next billion."

(Photo courtesy of Midlands Business Journal in Omaha)

Buffett Wannabe (as in I "wanna be" like Buffett) George Morgan, an Omaha stockbroker, explains what $1 billion is: "A man gave his wife $1 million to spend at the rate of $1,000 per day. In three years she returned for more. So he gave her $1 billion and she didn't come back for 3,000 years." Buffett could send his wife on a shopping spree for about 50,000 years.

(Photo by Nancy Line Jacobs)

Buffett picking up a penny at Omaha's Bookworm store November 4, 1994. Maybe the beginning of yet another billion.

117

"Something's happened, Doug. I've lost touch with the Warren Buffett in me."

118

The Wit of Warren Buffett

"Testing...testing... one million...two million...three million."

"I...prefer the iceberg approach toward investment disclosure."
(Buffett Partnership letter, July 22, 1966)

"These conditions will not cause me to attempt investment decisions outside my sphere of understanding (I don't go for the If you can't lick em, join 'em' philosophy—my own leaning is toward 'If you can't join 'em, lick 'em')." *(Buffett Partnership letter, January 25, 1967)*

"Our experience in workouts this year has been atrocious—during this period I have felt like the bird that inadvertently flew into the middle of a badminton game."
(Buffett Partnership letter in 1969)

"With value like that [Walt Disney at the time], I know I'm not going to get stuck with a Kentucky Fried Computer when it goes out of fashion." *(Forbes, November 1, 1969)*

"I, in fact, indirectly own some Ford convertibles (bonds, not cars)." *(Article by Buffett for the Wall Street Journal, August 15, 1977)*

"Our gain in net worth during the year was $613.6 million or 48.2%. It is fitting that the visit of Halley's Comet coincided with this percentage gain; neither will be seen again in my lifetime." *(1985 Annual Report)*

Buying bonds in inflationary times: "In runaway inflation, what you've bought is wallpaper." *(Fortune, April 25, 1985, and quoted in the Anagnos thesis in 1986)*

Here's Buffett's letter to Maria Anagnos after she sent him her thesis:

Berkshire Hathaway, Inc.
1440 Kiewit Plaza
Omaha, Nebraska 68131
Telephone (408) 346-1400

Warren E. Buffett, Chairman

July 3, 1986

Ms. Maria Anagnos,
300 East 62nd Street,
New York, New York 10021

Dear Maria:

Thanks for sending the thesis, which I enjoyed immensely. (Dale Carnegie once said that, next to "Would you like a drink?", a person's name is the most welcome sound in the English language.) I'm glad NYU gave you an "A"; so do I.

It probably is a good thing you finished your thesis when you did. A few more years of markets like this and we won't look so good—at least on a relative basis.

We're writing a portion of Continental Illinois's Director's and Officer's Liability Insurance this year, so be sure to keep everybody on their toes. And if you are out this way, stop by and bring me up to date.

Best wishes.

Sincerely,

Warren E. Buffett

WEB/gk

"When ideas fail, words come in handy." *(Buffett quoting Goethe)*

"The future isn't what it used to be." *(Buffett quoting Pogo)*

"All men's misfortunes spring from the single cause that they are unable to stay quietly in one room." *(Buffett quoting Pascal)*

"So convenient a thing it is to be a reasonable creature, since it enables one to find or make a reason for everything one has a mind to do." *(Buffett quoting Ben Franklin)*

"The term 'institutional investor' is becoming one of those self-contradictions called an oxymoron, comparable to 'jumbo shrimp,' 'Lady mud-wrestler' and 'inexpensive lawyer'." *(widely quoted)*

The hunt for acquisitions is like "bagging rare and fast-moving elephants." *(widely quoted)*

Establishing criteria for acquisition of companies is "a lot like selecting a wife. You can thoughtfully establish certain qualities you'd like her to have, and then all of a sudden, you meet someone and you do it." *(Annual Meeting in 1986)*

"You may quit having children if you keep having clunkers. But you just don't cast them out." *(Annual Meeting in 1986)*

On the advanced age of many Berkshire managers: "We find it's hard to teach a young dog old tricks. But we haven't had lots of problems with people who hit the ball out of the park year after year. Even though they're rich, they love what they do. And nothing ever happens to our managers. We offer them immortality." *(Annual Meeting in 1987)*

"If any of you would like to withdraw your proxy at this time, just raise your hand. As soon as we can get around to you, you will be ejected from the meeting." *(Annual Meeting in 1988)*

"If you want to be loved, it's clearly better to sell high-priced corn flakes than low-priced auto insurance." *(1988 Annual Report)*

Adam Smith: "Where do you get these aphorisms that you've gotten so well known for?"
Buffett: "Well, I don't know. They're about the limit of my intellectual capacities, so I have to work with one sentence."
(Adam Smith's "Money World" show, June 20, 1988)

Talking about excesses in the takeover field that year: "Toto, I have a feeling we're not in Kansas any more." Buffett quoting Dorothy from "The Wizard of Oz." *(1988 Annual Report)*

"After ending our corporate marriage to Hochschild Kohn, [a Baltimore department store Buffett bought for a bargain price] I had memories like those of the husband in the country song, 'My Wife Ran Away With My Best Friend and I Still Miss Him a Lot'." *(1989 Annual Report)*

On how he handles so many requests from people. "Well, I just use the Nancy Reagan policy. I just say no." *(Annual Meeting in 1989)*

"FSLIC has essentially allowed crooks and dopes to print money. Otherwise it's an unqualified success." *(Annual Meeting in 1989)*

"A takeover (of Coca-Cola) would be like Pearl Harbor."
(Fortune, April 10, 1989)

How Berkshire handles macroeconomic forecasts: Charlie (Munger) is our macroeconomics expert. Actually, I handle Omaha and Council Bluffs and Charlie handles the rest of the country." *(Annual Meeting in 1990)*

Munger's note: "Berkshire has not thrived in the past from making macroeconomic predictions. Therefore, we don't think a lot about it. We just try to do sound things and we figure economic trends will average out over the long run. We're agnostics on the economy." *(Annual Meeting in 1990)*

Value investing: "The fact that it's so simple makes people reluctant to teach it. If you've gone and gotten a Ph.D. and spent years learning how to do all kinds of tough things mathematically, to have to come back to this is—it's like studying for the priesthood and finding out that the Ten Commandments were all you needed."
(New York Times Magazine, L.J. Davis, April, 1990)

About making money: "I enjoy the process far more than the proceeds, though I have learned to live with those, also."
(Forbes, October 22, 1990)

In the midst of the 1990 stock market slump after Berkshire had fallen 36% from $8,675 to $5,500 and *Fortune* magazine estimated that Buffett had a paper loss so far for the year of $1.5 billion or $215,450 an hour: "I have not cut back from double hamburgers to single hamburgers."
(Fortune, November 5, 1990)

How about the corporate jet, he was asked. "That'll be the last thing to go." *(Fortune, November 5, 1990)*

His observation that if you could simply extrapolate the past into the future, the richest people all would be librarians. *(widely quoted)*

On once contemplating shorting a $1 stock, Buffett said he was told by a friend, "Isn't that like jumping off a pancake?"
(Annual Meeting in 1990)

"Wall Street is the only place that people ride to in a Rolls-Royce to get advice from those who take the subway."
(Los Angeles Times Magazine, April 7, 1991)

"Elephant bumpers,"—Buffett's term for bosses blinded by the limelight. "If they're bumping into elephants at industry meetings, they think they're elephants too." *(Fortune, April 22, 1991)*

"If you can eliminate the government as a 46% partner, the business will be far more valuable." *(widely quoted)*

Of preparation for the celebrity tennis match (February 9, 1992) in which Buffett teamed with Martina Navratilova to play Pam Shriver and former Dallas Cowboys quarterback Danny White: "I think that the majority of my training for this event is to learn how to say 'yours' in Czechoslovakian." *(Omaha World-Herald, January 21, 1992)*

"We believe that according the name "investor" to institutions that trade actively is like calling someone who repeatedly engages in one-night stands a romantic." *(1991 Annual Report)*

On longevity: "We take as our hero Methuselah." (Noah's ancestor is said to have lived 969 years.)
(Annual Meeting in 1992)

Once (September 2, 1992) Omaha stockbroker George Morgan walked up to Buffett, addressing him as "Mr. Buffett." "I know," said Buffett.

Acquisitions as frog-kissing: "I've observed that many acquisition-hungry managers were apparently mesmerized by their childhood reading of the story about the frog-kissing princess. Remembering her success, they pay dearly for the right to kiss corporate toads, expecting wondrous transfigurations...Initially, disappointing results deepen their desire to round up new toads. (Fanaticism, said philosopher Santayana, consists of redoubling your effort when you've forgotten your aim.)

"Ultimately, even the most optimistic manager must face reality. Standing knee-deep in unresponsive toads, he announces an enormous 'restructuring' charge. In this corporative equivalent of a Head Start program, the CEO receives the education but the stockholders pay the tuition.

"In my early days as a manager, I, too, dated a few toads. They were cheap dates—I've never been much of a sport—but my results matched those of acquirers who courted higher-price toads. I kissed and they croaked." *(1992 Annual Report)*

Tighter accounting: Managers thinking about accounting issues should never forget one of Abraham Lincoln's favorite riddles: "How many legs does a dog have if you call his tail a leg?" The answer: "Four, because calling a tail a leg does not make it a leg." (*1992 Annual Report*)

"We've long felt that the only value of forecasters is to make fortune-tellers look good." *(1992 Annual Report)*

"Our...conclusion that an increased capital base will act as an anchor seems incontestable. The only open question is whether we can drag the anchor along at some tolerable, though slowed, pace."
(1992 Annual Report)

Berkshire is one of the largest "super-cat" writers of insurance for catastrophes such as hurricanes and earthquakes: "Now you know why I suffer eyestrain: from watching the Weather Channel." *(1992 Annual Report)*

After introducing himself and Munger, he said he'd like to introduce the rest of Berkshire's board—"the entire three."
(Annual Meeting in 1993)

After adjourning the meeting in about five minutes, Buffett said, "You can see I don't get paid by the hour." *(Annual Meeting in 1993)*

"I'd like to introduce Berkshire's managers, except Mrs. B couldn't take time off from work for foolishness like a shareholders' meeting." *(Annual Meeting in 1993)*

"I was looking through the shareholder list recently and saw the name of someone not even born. I knew the mother was having a difficult pregnancy. I checked into it and found that the baby was our youngest shareholder. He was a shareholder two weeks before he was born. He's Riley Timothy Guerin (Rick Guerin's son)." At that moment a cartoon flashed on the screen of a baby saying, "What do you mean I have only two shares of Berky?" *(Annual Meeting in 1993)*

Buffett is known for advocating executive compensation based strictly on performance: "I've sat on 15 different boards and the only one in which I was invited on the compensation committee was at Salomon and we all know how that one turned out." *(Annual Meeting in 1993)*

To a question, after his explanation, Buffett asked Munger for his thoughts. Munger said, "I've got nothing to add." Quipped Buffett, "Sometimes he subtracts." Later at one of Munger's long pauses, Buffett said, "I feel a rebuttal coming on here." *(Annual Meeting in 1993)*

Munger launched into a long lesson about owning too many stocks, saying no one can follow 40 stocks in 30 different industries. "Can you?" he asked Buffett. "Not after that speech!" said Buffett. "You may only need one." *(Annual Meeting in 1993)*

Rick Berkshire, son of Robert Berkshire, asked if there were any plans to change Berkshire's name. "You don't have to worry about us changing anything at Berkshire," Buffett said. *(Annual Meeting in 1993)*

"How do you read an annual report?"..."Well, I start at the front and read to the back." *(Annual Meeting in 1993)*

Late in the meeting, Buffett launched into heavy criticism of business consultants, saying they were a form of intellectual prostitution. About that time a number of people began leaving the meeting. Said Buffett, "The consultants are now leaving the room." *(Annual Meeting in 1993)*

"In the early 1900s, a reporter was sent over from Europe to do a story on Andrew Carnegie. And he cabled back to his editors, 'I never realized that there was so much money in libraries.' That fellow might have had a career in writing investment reports." *(Annual Meeting in 1993)*

"Lights! Camera! Cash Flow! Capital Cities/ABC Chairman Thomas Murphy and investor Warren Buffett, whose Berkshire Hathaway owns about 20% of the network's stock, will appear on the August 27 episode of the ABC soap *All My Children*, returning after their cameos of two years ago. The network shells out $300 or so to each, about right considering their performances. When handed his check, Murphy said, "I'm going to frame this." Said Buffett: "I'm going to frame the stub."
(Fortune, September 6, 1993)

"All these little kids came up to me wanting my autograph (at a College World Series event where Buffett threw out the first pitch), so I wanted to look like Nolan Ryan"...Buffett describes bungling the pitch... "I looked up and saw these same kids erasing my signature."
(Interview by Sue Baggarly of WOWT-TV in Omaha, October 14, 1993)

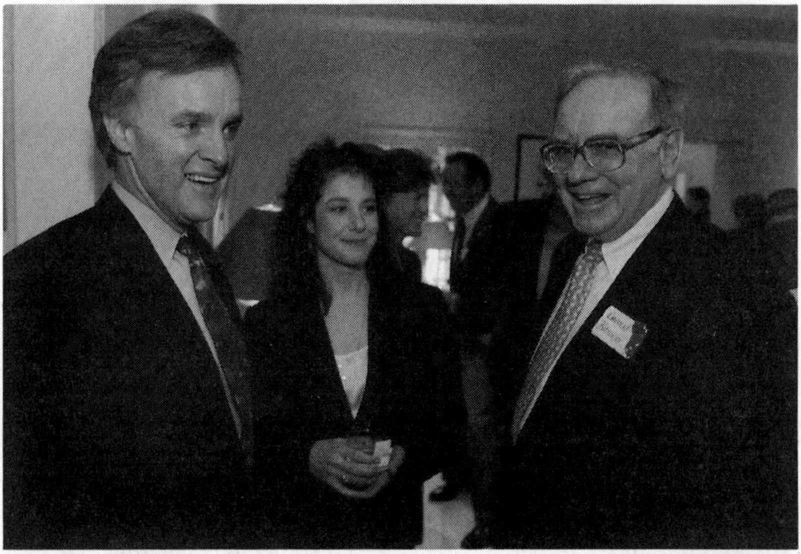

(Omaha World-Herald)

U.S. Senator Bob Kerrey, Debra Winger, Buffett.
"The real trick to this is having Debra (Winger) as a co-host. Otherwise, this room would be empty," Buffett said at a fundraiser for Kerrey that Buffett and Miss Winger co-hosted.

"My health is terrific. I just went for the first time in six or seven years for a general checkup. The doctor asked me about my diet and said, 'You're counting rather heavily on your genes, aren't you?'" *(Interview by Sue Baggarly, WOWT-TV in Omaha, October, 14, 1993)*

"Going short is betting on something that'll happen. If you go short for meaningful amounts, you can go broke. If something is selling for twice what it's worth, what's to stop it for selling for 10 times what it's worth? You'll be right eventually, but you may be explaining it to somebody in the poorhouse." *(Talk to Columbia business students, October 27, 1993)*

Buffett to Delta chairman Ronald Allen: "The airline industry is to the free-enterprise system what hell is to heaven."
(The Atlanta Journal/The Atlanta Constitution, July 23, 1994)

"I gave this advice one time at Harvard when somebody asked me, 'Who should I work for?' I said, 'Well, go work for somebody you admire. You're bound to get a good result.' A couple of weeks later, I received a call from the Dean, and he said, 'What did you tell that group? They've all decided to become self-employed!' " *(Talk to University of Nebraska students, October 10, 1994)*

Munger's fear of flying: "He's a guy who has a prayer session before he takes a bus." *(Omaha World-Herald, October, 1994)*

When he was 17, Buffett got $5 from *Barron's* for writing a piece about odd lot statistics. "Five dollars was the only money I ever made from using odd lot statistics." (*New York Society of Security Analysts, December 6, 1994)*

There was only about $12 million in capital at Graham-Newman when Buffett worked there. "That's a rounding error now at Magellan." *(New York Society of Security Analysts, December 6, 1994)*

"Ben (Graham) used to say he wanted to do three things every day—something foolish, something creative and something generous. He usually got the foolish done before breakfast. That was typical of Ben." (*New York Society of Security Analysts, December 6, 1994)*

Higher math talent is not really necessary to be an investor. "You've got to figure out the worth of the company and divide by the number of shares outstanding so it does require division." *(New York Society of Security Analysts, December 6, 1994)*

Commenting on the unprofitable airline industry, talking about when the Wright Brothers flew at Kitty Hawk: "If there had been a capitalist down there, the guy should have shot Wilbur." *(Fortune, April 3, 1995)*

"Charlie and I, at 71 and 64, respectively, now keep George Foreman's picture on our desks. You can make book that our scorn for a mandatory retirement age will grow stronger every year." *(1994 Annual Report)*

Of selling some Berkshire products like See's Candies and Dexter shoes at the Berkshire annual meeting: "Though we like to think of the meeting as a spiritual experience, we must remember that even the saintliest of religions includes the ritual of the collection plate." *(1994 Annual Report)*
(Note: Some Berkshire shareholders call Omaha, "The spiritual capital of the world.")

"Of course, what you really should be purchasing is a video tape of the 1995 Orange Bowl. Your Chairman views this classic nightly, switching to slow motion for the fourth quarter. Our cover color this year is a salute to Nebraska's football coach, Tom Osborne, and his Cornhuskers, the country's top college team. I urge you to wear Husker red to the annual meeting and promise you that at least 50% of your managerial duo will be in appropriate attire." *(1994 Annual Report)*

Munger: "Our chief contribution to the business we acquire is what we don't do."
Buffett: "He has spoken." *(Annual Meeting in 1995)*

Shareholder: "You've repeatedly said that you see many wonderful stock ideas, but can't invest because they're too small. Given the fact that many in the audience today have a lower dollar investment threshold..." Buffett: "In other words, do these stocks have names?" *(Annual Meeting in 1995)*

Buffett: "The government has a 35% interest - a profits interest - in the earnings of all corporations. So at a tax rate of 35%, they in effect own 35% of the stock of American business. And they own a significant share of Berkshire - we write them a check every year. We don't write you a check, but we write them a check. And we plow your earnings back to create more value for them." Munger: "Are you trying to cheer these people up?" *(Annual Meeting in 1995)*

"To paraphrase President Kennedy, a rising tide lifts all yachts." *(1995 Annual Report)*

"Soon after our purchase of the Salomon preferred in 1987, I wrote that I had 'no special insights regarding the direction or future profitability of investment banking.' Even the most charitable commentator would conclude that I have since proven my point." *(1995 Annual Report)*

"At Borsheim's we will also have the world's largest faceted diamond on display. Two years in the cutting, this inconspicuous bauble is 545 carats in size. Please inspect the stone and let it guide you in determining what size gem is appropriate for the one you love." *(1995 Annual Report)*

Reply to a suggestion that Buffett was getting as famous as the Pope or the President: "My first reaction is that maybe I should tell my barber that we should save the clippings and sell them." (*Annual Meeting in 1996*)

Munger told Buffett he had never actually seen him run formulas discounting future cash flows. "Well, some things you only do in private," Buffett replied. *(Annual Meeting in 1996)*

119

The Wisdom of Warren Buffett

"The fact that people will be full of greed, fear or folly is predictable. The sequence is not."

The joys of compounding: "One story stands out. This, of course, is the saga of trading acumen etched into history by the Manhattan Indians when they unloaded their island to that notorious spendthrift, Peter Minuit in 1626. My understanding is that they received $24 net. For this, Minuit received 22.3 square miles which works out to about 621,888,320 square feet. While on the basis of comparable sales, it is difficult to arrive at a precise appraisal, a $20 per square foot estimate seems reasonable given a current land value for the island of $12,433,766,400 ($12½ billion). To the novice, perhaps this sounds like a decent deal. However, the Indians have only had to achieve a 6½% return (the tribal mutual fund representative would have promised them this) to obtain the last laugh on Minuit. At 6½%, $24 becomes

$42,105,772,800 (42 billion) in 338 years, and if they just managed to squeeze out an extra half point to get to 7%, the present value becomes $205 billion." *(Buffett Partnership letter, January 1965)*

"The course of the stock market will largely determine...when we'll be right, but the accuracy of our analysis will determine whether we'll be right. In other words, we...concentrate on what should happen, not when it should happen...If we start deciding, based on our guesses or emotions, whether we will...participate in a business where we...have some long-run edge, we're in trouble. We will not sell our interests in businesses when they are attractively priced just because some astrologer thinks the quotations may go lower even though forecasts...will be right some of the time...The availability of a quotation for your business interests should always be an asset to be utilized if desired. If it gets silly enough in either direction, you take advantage of it. Its availability should never be turned into a liability whereby its periodic aberrations in turn form your judgments." *(Buffett Partnership letter, July, 1966)*

"All of our investments usually appear undervalued to me—otherwise we wouldn't own them." *(Buffett Partnership letter, July, 1966)*

"I am not in the business of predicting general stock market or business fluctuations. If you think I can do this, or think it is essential to an investment program, you should not be in the partnership." *(Buffett Partnership letter, July, 1966)*

"As Ben Graham said: 'In the long run, the market is a weighing machine—in the short run, a voting machine.' I have always found it easier to evaluate weights dictated by fundamentals than votes dictated by psychology." *(Buffett Partnership letter in 1969)*

"We ordinarily make no attempt to buy equities anticipating favorable short-term price behavior. In fact, if the business experience continues to satisfy us, we welcome lower prices as an opportunity to acquire even more of a good thing." *(1977 Annual Report)*

"When companies with outstanding businesses and comfortable financial positions find their shares selling far below intrinsic value in the marketplace, no alternative action can benefit shareholders as surely as repurchases." *(widely quoted)*

"(The) argument is made that there are just too many (investment) question marks about the near-term future; wouldn't it be better to wait until things clear up a bit? You know the prose: 'Maintain buying reserves until current uncertainties are resolved,' etc. Before reaching for that crutch, face up to two unpleasant facts: the future is never clear; you pay a very high price in the stock market for a cheery consensus. Uncertainty actually is the friend of the buyer of long-term values." *(Forbes, August 6, 1979)*

"We do not need more people gambling in non-essential instruments identified with the stock market in this country, nor brokers who encourage them to do so. What we need are investors and advisers who look at the long-term prospects for an enterprise and invest accordingly. We need intelligent commitment of investment capital, not leveraged market wagers. The propensity to operate in the intelligent, pro-social sector of capital markets is deterred, not enhanced, by an active and exciting casino operating in somewhat the same arena, utilizing somewhat similar language and serviced by the same work force." *(From letter Buffett wrote to John Dingell, chairman of the House subcommittee on oversight and investigations, in March, 1982, when Congress was considering whether to allow the Chicago Mercantile Exchange to trade futures contracts.)*

"Geometric progressions eventually forge their own anchors." *(1982 Annual Report)*

"I have seen no trend toward value investing in the 35 years I've practiced it. There seems to be some perverse human characteristic that likes to make easy things difficult." *(Talk to Columbia Business School in 1985)*

"The failure of business schools to study men like Teledyne's Henry Singleton is a crime. Instead they insist on holding up as a model executives cut from McKinsey & Company cookie cutters." *(Talk to Columbia Business School in 1985)*

"The fact that people will be full of greed, fear or folly is predictable. The sequence is not predictable." *(Channels magazine, told to Patricia Bauer, 1986)*

"Money, to some extent, sometimes lets you be in more interesting environments. But it can't change how many people love you or how healthy you are." *(Channels magazine, talk to Patricia Bauer, 1986)*

Business schools "reward complex behavior more than simple behavior; but simple behavior is more effective." *(Channels magazine, talk to Patricia Bauer, 1986)*

Arms control and population growth problems: "If we don't solve them, we don't have a world." *(Channels magazine, talk to Patricia Bauer, 1986)*

Patience: "You don't trade in houses, children and wives every year, so why trade companies around. I want to have fun with the companies, see them grow and develop. And also, I want to enjoy life. I can't understand the Carl Icahn's, Victor Posner's and Ted Turner's of the world. In the end all my money is going to charity. So it's crazy to live by being in uncomfortable situations, or being unpleasant towards others. What's the difference anyway, if the Buffett Foundation is worth "X" or "2X" at the end..." *(Anagnos thesis, 1986, quoting Buffett)*

"I do what I like to do. I don't spend five minutes a year doing what I don't like. And fortunately I have the luxury to do so, I don't care what anyone else does. I like people, and I like the people I associate with. I care about them and their businesses. And besides, I want to have fun!" *(Anagnos thesis, 1986, quoting Buffett)*

"We like to buy businesses, but we don't like to sell them."
(Annual Meeting in 1987)

"Anything that can't go on forever, will end."
(Annual Meeting in 1987, paraphrasing Herb Stein)

"I like the fact it's a big transaction. I can't be involved in 50 or 75 things. That's a Noah's Ark way of investing—you end up with a zoo that way. I like to put meaningful amounts of money in a few things.
(Wall Street Journal, September 30, 1987, shortly after Berkshire's $700 million investment in Salomon)

"It looks...impressive if it comes out of a computer. But it's frequently nonsense. The person who's making the decision is far more important." *(Outstanding Investor Digest, October 7, 1987)*

"I'm an analyst basically. I try to figure out what businesses are worth, then divide by the number of shares outstanding.
(Omaha World-Herald, October 18, 1987, quoting Money magazine)

"The market is there only as a reference point to see if anybody is offering to do anything foolish. When we invest in stocks, we invest in businesses. You simply have to behave according to what is rational rather than according to what is fashionable."
(Fortune, January 4, 1988)

"Our goal is to attract long-term owners who, at the time of purchase, have no timetable or price target for sale but plan instead to stay with us indefinitely." *(1988 Annual Report)*

"I want to be in businesses so good that even a dummy can make money." *(Fortune, April 11, 1988)*

"It's far better to buy a wonderful company at a fair price than a fair company at a wonderful price." *(widely quoted)*

On turnarounds: "The projections will be dazzling—the advocates will be sincere—but in the end, major additional investment in a terrible industry usually is about as rewarding as struggling in quicksand." *(widely quoted)*

"I don't know what it'll (the stock market) do tomorrow or next week or next year. But I do know that over a period of 10 to 20 years you'll have some very enthusiastic markets and some very depressed markets. The trick is to take advantage of the markets rather than letting them panic you into the wrong action." *(widely quoted)*

"It's just not necessary to do extraordinary things to produce extraordinary results." *(widely quoted)*

The importance of a franchise business: Adam Smith: "So it's the power of the franchise?" Buffett: "It's the power of the franchise." *(Adam Smith's "Money World" show, June 20, 1988)*

"The most important quality for an investor is temperament, not intellect. You don't need tons of IQ in this business. You don't have to be able to play three-dimensional chess or duplicate bridge. You need a temperament that neither derives great pleasure from being with the crowd or against the crowd. You know you're right, not because of the position of others, but because your facts and your reasoning are right." *(Adam Smith's "Money World" show, June 20, 1988)*

"Our outlook for inflation is always the same. We feel there's a big bias toward inflation—both in the U.S. and around the world...It's a world where prices are going to go up. It's just a question of how much. You could definitely have some explosive inflation at some point. Printing money is just too easy. I'd do it myself if I could get away with it." *(Annual Meeting in 1988)*

"We don't view precious metals and precious stones as great inflation hedges. But we don't bring anything to that game, so we don't play it." *(Annual Meeting in 1988)*

"It's hard enough to understand the peculiarities and complexities of the culture in which you've been raised, much less a variety of others. Anyway, most of our shareholders have to pay their bills in U.S. dollars." *(Annual Meeting in 1988)*

"We wouldn't care if the market closed for a year or two. It closes on Saturday and Sunday and we do just fine." *(Annual Meeting in 1988)*

"If principles are dated, they're not principles." *(Annual Meeting in 1988)*

On properly valuing a business: "To properly value a business, you should ideally take all the flows of money that will be distributed between now and judgment day and discount them at an appropriate discount rate. That's what valuing businesses is all about. Part of the equation is how confident you can be about those cash flows occurring. Some businesses are easier to predict than others. For example, water companies are generally easier to predict than building contractors. We try to look at businesses that are predictable." *(Annual Meeting in 1988)*

Something Buffett doesn't lose sleep over: "We're actually prohibited from buying other savings and loans. But that's not a prohibition that keeps us up at night." *(Annual Meeting in 1988)*

Money: "I think if you found an athlete that was doing well—and I'm not comparing myself—but a Ted Williams or an Arnold Palmer or something—after they have enough to eat, they're not doing it for the money. My guess is that if Ted Williams was getting the highest salary in baseball and he was hitting .220, he would be unhappy. And if he was getting the lowest salary in baseball and batting .400, he'd be very happy. That's the way I feel about this job. Money is a byproduct of doing something I like doing extremely well." *(Annual Meeting in 1988)*

"Anything can happen in stock markets and you ought to conduct your affairs so that if the most extraordinary events happen, that you're still around to play the next day." *(Buffett on Adam Smith's "Money World" show, June 20, 1988)*

"Great investment opportunities come around when excellent companies are surrounded by unusual circumstances that cause the stock to be misappraised." *(Fortune, December 19, 1988.)*

(IMPORTANT NOTE: Buffett steps into an elevator shaft July 4, 2034, leaving a billion trillion to The Buffett Foundation. Berkshire drops 23% in the first minute of trading to $99 billion a share. Munger steps up to the easel. Mrs. B is named vice chairman. Lou Simpson buys back stock and starts talks to buy China. Berkshire recovers to $107 billion as investors remember what Buffett said December 19, 1988.)

"Time is the friend of the wonderful business, the enemy of the mediocre." *(1989 Annual Report)*

"It's no sin to miss a great opportunity outside one's area of competence." *(1989 Annual Report)*

On why Berkshire borrowed $400 million and put the cash into Treasuries: "The best time to buy assets may be when it is hardest to raise money." *(Fortune, October 23, 1989)*

"I've often felt there might be more to be gained by studying business failures than business successes. It's customary in business schools to study business successes. But my partner, Charlie Munger, says all he wants is to know where he's going to die—so he won't ever go there." *(Talk to Emory Business College, November, 1989)*

"I'm not like a steel executive who can think only about how to invest in steel. I've got a bigger canvas, simply because I have spent my life looking at companies, starting with Abbott Labs and going through to Zenith." *(Fortune, January 29, 1990)*

"I think it's a saner existence here (Omaha). I used to feel when I worked back in New York that there were more stimuli just hitting me all the time, and if you've got the normal amount of adrenaline, you start responding to them. It may lead to crazy behavior after a while. It's much easier to think here." *(New York Times Magazine, L.J. Davis, April 2, 1990)*

"I love what I do. I'm involved in a kind of intellectually interesting game that isn't too tough to win, and Berkshire Hathaway is my canvas. I don't try to jump over seven-foot bars: I look around for one-foot bars that I can step over. I work with sensational people, and I do what I want in life. Why shouldn't I? If I'm not in a position to do what I want, who the hell is?" *(New York Times Magazine, L.J. Davis, April 2, 1990)*

"Any young person who doesn't take up bridge is making a big mistake." *(New York Times, May 20, 1990)*

"Stocks are simple. All you do is buy shares in a great business for less than the business is intrinsically worth, with management of the highest integrity and ability. Then you own those shares forever."
(Forbes, August 6, 1990)

Buffett's description of some of the ground rules for the Buffett Partnership. "I told them (limited partners), 'What I'll do is form a partnership where I'll manage the portfolio and have my money in there with you. I'll guarantee you a 6% return, and I get 20% of all profits after that. And I won't tell you what we own because that's distracting. All I want to do is hand in a scorecard when I come off the golf course. I don't want you following me around and watching me shank a three-iron on this hole and leave a putt short on the next one.' " *(1990 Investors Guide/Fortune)*

"A hyperactive stock market is the pickpocket of enterprise."
(widely quoted)

"You don't need to be a rocket scientist. Investing is not a game where the guy with the 160 IQ beats the guy with a 130 IQ. Rationality is essential." *(widely quoted)*

"In a sense Berkshire Hathaway is a canvas, and I get to paint anything I want on that canvas. And it's the process of painting that I really enjoy, not selling the painting." *(widely quoted)*

"You can't be smarter than your dumbest competitor. The trick is to have no competitors." *(widely quoted)*

"In the insurance business, there is no statute of limitations on stupidity." *(1990 Annual Report)*

"The most common cause of low prices is pessimism—sometimes pervasive, sometimes specific to a company or industry. We want to do business in such an environment, not because we like pessimism but because we like the prices it produces. It's optimism that is the enemy of the rational buyer. None of this means, however, that a business or stock is an intelligent purchase simply because it is unpopular; a contrarian approach is just as foolish as a follow-the-crowd strategy. What's required is thinking rather than polling." *(1990 Annual Report)*

"The most important thing to do when you find yourself in a hole is to stop digging." *(1990 Annual Report)*

"Someone's sitting in the shade today because someone planted a tree a long time ago." *(NewsInc., January, 1991)*

"Our stay-put behavior reflects our view that the stock market serves as a relocation center at which money is moved from the active to the patient." *(1991 Annual Report.)*

"The best CEOs love operating their companies and don't prefer going to Business Roundtable meetings or playing golf at Augusta National." *(Fortune, April 22, 1991)*

"To swim a fast 100 meters, it's better to swim with the tide than to work on your stroke." *(Annual Meeting in 1991)*

"There are a lot of profitable things you can do but you have to stick to what you can do. We can't find a way to knock out Mike Tyson." *(Annual Meeting in 1991)*

"We're not pure economic creatures...And that policy penalizes our results somewhat, but we prefer to operate that way in life. What's the sense of becoming rich if you're going to have a pattern of operation where you continually discard associations with people you like, admire and find interesting in order to earn a slightly bigger figure? We like big figures, but not to the exclusion of everything else." *(Annual Meeting in 1991)*

On the desire for big positions in the right business: "We own fewer stocks today at $7 billion than we did when our total portfolio was $20 million." *(Annual Meeting in 1991)*

No frills. "Whatever colors were on the corporate jet when we bought it are the ones that are on it today. There's no "WB" or "BH." And that's not likely to change." *(Annual Meeting in 1991)*

On not second-guessing the managers of his business: "If they need my help to manage the enterprise, we're probably both in trouble." *(Outstanding Investor Digest, May 24, 1991)*

"Easy access to funding tends to cause undisciplined decisions." *(Salomon conference with clients, September 13, 1991)*

On learning from mistakes: "I guess I had too much inclination originally to buy mediocre, or worse than mediocre, businesses at a very cheap price. That works OK, in the sense that you never lose money; but you never end up with a great business that way either. So that emphasis has shifted over the years. We don't want to buy the worst furniture store in town at the cheapest price; we want to buy the best one at a fair price." *(widely quoted)*

His biggest strength: "I'm rational. Plenty of people have higher IQs, and plenty of people work more hours, but I am rational about things. But you have to be able to control yourself; you can't let your emotions get in the way of your mind.

"In 1986, my biggest accomplishment was not doing anything stupid. There is not much to do; there is not much available right now. The trick is, when there is nothing to do, do nothing.

"I love what I do. All I want to do is do what I'm doing as long as I can. Every day I feel like tap dancing all through the day. I really do." *(widely quoted)*

Advice to graduating MBA students. "Go to work for whomever you admire the most. You'll be turned on; you'll feel like getting out of bed in the morning; and you'll learn a lot.

"That is what I did. I wanted to work for Ben Graham, but he didn't hire me immediately. I offered to go to work for him for nothing too, so it's even worse than it sounds. So I started trying to be useful to him in various ways. I did a number of studies I dreamt up. I tried to suggest ideas.

"If I were a student today, I would probably try to show the people where I worked what I could do. If I wanted to be starting quarterback on the Washington Redskins, I'd try to get them to watch me throw a few passes.

"As a corollary, I would never go to work for an operation that I had any negative feelings about." *(widely quoted)*

"Investment must be rational; if you don't understand it, don't do it." *(Forbes, October 19, 1992)*

Restaurants as investments: Not good, because a similar one can open up across the street. *(Business Week, Robert Stoval column, January 5, 1993)*

"Growth is always a component in the calculation of value, constituting a variable whose importance can range from negligible to enormous and whose impact can be negative as well as positive." *(1992 Annual Report)*

"What counts for most people in investing is not how much they know, but rather how realistically they define what they don't know. An investor needs to do very few things right as long as he or she avoids big mistakes." *(1992 Annual Report)*

"If options aren't a form of compensation, what are they? If compensation isn't an expense, what is it? And if expenses shouldn't go into the calculation of earnings, where in the world should they go?" *(1992 Annual Report)*

"Mrs. Blumkin recently sold her Mrs. B's Warehouse to the Mart and announced plans to operate her carpet business alongside a new store operated by the Mart.

"I am delighted that Mrs. B has again linked up with us. Her business story has no parallel and I have always been a fan of hers, whether she was a partner, or a competitor. But, believe me, partner is better." *(1992 Annual Report)*

"Overhead costs are under 1% of our reported operating earnings and less than ½ of 1% of our look-through earnings. We have no legal, personnel, public relations, investor relations, or strategic planning departments. In turn this means we don't need support personnel such as guards, drivers, messengers, etc." *(1992 Annual Report)*

Two kinds of information: "Those things you can know and those things important to know. Those things you can know that are important constitute an extremely small percentage of the total known." *(widely quoted)*

On investing: "Investing is not that complicated. You need to know accounting, the language of business. You should read *The Intelligent Investor*. You need the right mindset, the right temperament. You should be interested in the process and be in your circle of competence...Avoid overstimulation. Read Ben Graham and Phil Fisher, read annual reports and trade reports, but don't do equations with Greek letters in them." *(Annual Meeting in 1993)*

"I read annual reports of the company I'm looking at and I read the annual reports of the competitors...That's the main source material." *(Annual Meeting in 1993)*

Munger: "We like to keep things simple...so the chairman can sit around and read annual reports." *(Annual Meeting in 1993)*

Berkshire's price: "At no time has Berkshire's price been ridiculously out of line from intrinsic value. All along it's been reasonably priced." *(Annual Meeting in 1993)*

On selling off businesses: "We try not to sell the flowers to water the weeds." *(Annual Meeting in 1993, quoting Peter Lynch.)*

"If you advertise for an opera and a rock concert, you get a different audience...We try to attract the long-term shareholder. We don't want a lot of seat-changing. If you get the wrong shareholder, he'll leave you in six months...We're very unlikely to split the stock." *(Annual Meeting in 1993)*

On media reports of what he's buying: "Some are erroneous...We don't announce our acquisitions (unless legally required). Everyone in this room is a little richer because of that policy." *(Annual Meeting in 1993)*

"Daily newspapers are still good businesses, just not as good as before." *(Annual Meeting in 1993)*

On giving: "My feeling is you pick high-grade younger people to do it...I'm not going to give a tightly drawn document about it. You hope that they are a lot smarter above the ground than you are below ground. You should concentrate your shots in death as well as life." *(Annual Meeting in 1993)*

Inflation prospects: "It's basically just in remission." *(Annual Meeting in 1993)*

Restructurings—"That's a word for mistakes." *(Annual Meeting in 1993)*

The investment professional as a whole doesn't add value: "One factor people have not focused on enough is that obviously professional investment management in aggregate will deliver a poorer return than a simple indexed investment because of the frictional costs Charlie mentioned. Such a significant percentage of the $4 trillion equity market is managed by managers who are getting paid to do the job that their aggregate performance has to be a little less than average simply because of frictional costs.

"So therefore you have a profession where practitioners as a whole can add nothing to what you can do yourself. In fact, they subtract from it." *(Annual Meeting in 1993)*

"There's good money out of cigarettes which in turn kill people." *(Annual Meeting in 1993)*

Berkshire's future: "I see a lot of interesting things happening, but I haven't the faintest idea what they'll be." *(Nightly Business Review, April 26, 1993)*

On the wealthy paying a fair share under President Clinton's deficit reduction proposal: Buffett, who makes a $100,000 annual salary and $148,000 in director's fees, said, "If I make it into the top 1% (of taxpayers), I don't mind at all. It would be bad for America if we didn't do anything. We can't sit there and choose among 20 bills. I like the idea of more progressivity on the tax rates. I just wish it had been achieved more in spending cuts." *(USA Today, August 6, 1993)*

Where will you take your next vacation? "There's nothing to get away from." *(Forbes reporter Robert Lenzner's query of Buffett for an October 19, 1993, story)*

How's the 1993 stock market? "Common stocks look high and are high, but they are not as high as they look." *Forbes*, Buffett quoting Ben Graham's response before the 1955 Fulbright hearings in Washington, D.C. *(Forbes, October 19, 1993)*

Buffett as admirer of the British economist and investor John Maynard Keynes: "Keynes essentially said don't try and figure out what the market is doing. Figure out businesses you understand, and concentrate. Diversification is protection against ignorance, but if you don't feel ignorant, the need for it goes down drastically." *(Forbes, October 19, 1993)*

Summing up Ben Graham's teachings: "When proper temperament joins with proper intellectual framework, then you get rational behavior." *(Forbes, October 19, 1993)*

International portfolio: "I get $150 million earnings pass-through from international operations of Gillette and Coca-Cola. That's my international portfolio."*(Forbes, October 19, 1993)*

"I am a better investor because I am a businessman, and a better businessman because I am an investor." *(Forbes, October 19, 1993)*

"Children should be given enough to do what they want to do, but not enough to be idle." *(WOWT-TV in Omaha, October 14, 1993)*

Advice for someone coming into the investment field: "If he were coming in with small sums of capital, I'd tell him to do exactly what I did 40-odd years ago, which is to learn about every company in the United States that has publicly traded securities and that bank of knowledge will do him or her terrific good over time."
Adam Smith: "But there's 27,000 public companies."
Buffett: "Well, start with the A's." *(Adam Smith's "Money World," October 21, 1993)*

"The smartest side to take in a bidding war is the losing side." *(Fortune, November 29, 1993, quoting Buffett's talk to Columbia business students October 27, 1993)*

Picking the right business for a long-term holding: "If you're going to have a Catholic marriage, you'd better do it right." *(Omaha World-Herald, October 28, 1993, quoting from the same talk)*

"I feel competent...in a very few cases. I think that Bill Gates is one of the best managers in the world, but I don't have the faintest idea of how to evaluate what the stream of coupons will look like on a bond called Microsoft. *(Omaha World-Herald, October 28, 1993, quoting from the same talk)*

"It may be a sensational stream of coupons, but I just don't know enough about it to evaluate that. But if I can't evaluate it...then I'm not investing. I'm betting on whether a stock will go up or down tomorrow or next week or next month...I put a heavy weight on certainty." *(Omaha World-Herald, October 28, 1993, quoting from the same talk)*

"Risk is not knowing what you're doing." *(Omaha World-Herald, October 28, 1993, quoting from the same talk)*

"I would think very hard about getting into a business with fundamentally good economics. I would think of buying from people I can trust. And I'd think about the price I'd pay. But I wouldn't think about price to the exclusion of the first two.
"And that essentially, is what we're trying to do at Berkshire. And if I did that, would I think about whether I could buy it cheaper on Monday rather than on Friday or would I think about the January effect or other nonsense?" *(Omaha World-Herald, October 28, 1993, quoting from the same talk)*

Communications investments: "I don't like businesses where the technology is changing fast. Basically, I don't think I'm a great one for seeing the future when the future looks way different than the present. Generally, anything that is subject to a lot of change and technology, I tend to be critical of rather than excited by." *(Omaha World-Herald, October 28, 1993, quoting from the same talk)*

On common sense and believing in yourself: "In the end, I always believe my eyes rather than anything else." *(Omaha World-Herald, October 28, 1993, quoting from the same talk)*

Taxes: "Speaking for our own shares, Charlie and I have absolutely no complaint about these taxes. We know we work in a market-based economy that rewards our efforts far more bountifully than it does the efforts of others whose output is of equal or greater benefit to society. Taxation should, and does, partially redress this inequity. But we still remain extraordinarily well-treated." *(1993 Annual Report)*

"Diversification is a hedge against ignorance." *(widely quoted)*

Diversification: "The strategy we've adopted precludes our following standard diversification dogma. Many pundits would therefore say the strategy must be riskier than that employed by more conventional investors. We disagree. We believe that a policy of portfolio concentration may well decrease risk if it raises, as it should, both the intensity with which an investor thinks about a business and the comfort level he must feel with its economic characteristics before buying into it. In stating this opinion, we define risk, using dictionary terms, as 'the possibility of loss or injury.'

"Academics, however, like to define investment 'risk' differently, averring that it is the relative volatility of a stock or a portfolio of stocks—that is, their volatility as compared to that of a large universe of stocks. Employing databases and statistical skills, these academics compute with precision the 'beta' of a stock—its relative volatility in the past—and then build arcane investment and capital allocation theories around this calculation. In their hunger for a single statistic to measure risk, however, they forget a fundamental principle: It is better to be approximately right than precisely wrong." *(1993 Annual Report)*

"The pleasant but vacuous director need never worry about job security." *(1993 Annual Report)*

"There's no use running if you're on the wrong road." *(1993 Annual Report)*

"We know who the best baseball players are; why not know who the best teachers are?" (*Interview with Tom Brokaw of NBC News, April 12, 1994*)

"You can't get rich with a weathervane." (*Annual Meeting in 1994*)

"We'd rather multiply by three than pi." *(Annual Meeting in 1994)*

"Charlie and I never have an opinion about the market because it wouldn't be any good and it might interfere with the opinions we have that are good." *(Annual Meeting in 1994)*

"Virtually everything we've done has been by reading public reports and then maybe asking questions around and ascertaining trade positions and product strengths or something of that sort." *(Annual Meeting in 1994)*

Coca-Cola! "Coke in 1890 or thereabouts--the whole company--sold for $2,000. Its market value today is $50—odd billion. Somebody could have said to the fellow who was buying it in 1890, 'We're going to have a couple of great World Wars. There'll be a panic in 1907. All of these things are going to happen. Wouldn't it be better to wait?' We can't afford that mistake." (*Annual Meeting in 1994*)

"Nothing that I know about that product or its distribution system, its finances or anything that hundreds of thousands or millions of people don't know, too. They just don't do anything about it." *(Annual Meeting in 1994)*

"So the important thing that we do as managers generally is find the .400 hitters and then not tell them how to swing...And the second thing we do is allocate capital. Aside from that, we play bridge. That's Berkshire." *(Annual Meeting in 1994)*

"There's a huge difference between the business that grows and requires lots of capital to do so and the business that grows and doesn't require capital." *(Annual Meeting in 1994)*

"We don't have any meetings of any kind at Berkshire, but we'd never have an asset allocation meeting." *(Annual Meeting in 1994)*

Thinking for yourself: "You have to think for yourself. It always amazes me how high-IQ people mindlessly imitate. I never get good ideas talking to other people." (*U.S. News & World Report, June 20, 1994*)

A good business: "Look for the durability of the franchise. The most important thing to me is figuring out how big a moat there is around the business. What I love, of course, is a big castle and a big moat with piranhas and crocodiles." *(U.S. News & World Report, June 20, 1994)*

"Compound interest is a little bit like rolling a snowball down a hill. You can start with a small snowball and if it rolls down a hill long enough (and my hill is now 53 years long - that's when I bought my first stock), and the snow is mildly sticky, you'll have a real snowball at the end." *(Talk to University of Nebraska students, October 10, 1994)*

"I spend an inordinate amount of time reading. I probably read at least six hours a day, maybe more. I spend an hour or two on the telephone, and the rest of the time I think. We have no meetings at Berkshire. I hate meetings." *(Omaha World-Herald, October 11, 1994)*

"I'm sort of a Republican on the production side, and I'm sort of a Democrat on the distribution side." (*Associated Press, October, 16, 1994)*

"All these people who think that food stamps are debilitating and lead to a cycle of poverty, they're the same ones who go out and want to leave a ton of money to their kids." (*Associated Press, October 16, 1994)*

"All we want is to be in businesses that we understand, run by people whom we like, and priced attractively relative to their future prospects." *(Fortune, October 31, 1994)*

"We don't know and we don't think about when something will happen. We think about what will happen." *(Fortune, October 31, 1994)*

"You're lucky in life if you pick the right heroes. Ben was mine." *(New York Society of Security Analysts, December 6, 1994)*

About Ben Graham being generous with his ideas: Quoting Oscar Hammerstein, "A bell's not a bell until you ring it. A song is not a song until you sing it.. And love in the heart isn't put there to stay. Love isn't love 'til you give it away." *(New York Society of Security Analysts, December 6, 1994)*

"The professional in almost any field achieves a result which is significantly above what the layman in aggregate achieves. It's not true in money management." *(New York Society of Security Analysts, December 6, 1994)*

The basic ideas of investing are to look at stocks as businesses, use market fluctuations to your advantage and seek a margin of safety. "That's what Ben Graham taught us...A hundred years from now they will still be the cornerstones of investing." *(New York Society of Security Analysts, December 6, 1994)*

"We just try to buy businesses with good to superb underlying economics, run by honest and able people and buy them at sensible prices. That's all I'm trying to do. When I see a seven-footer, I think, 'Is the guy coordinated, can I keep him in school and all those things. "And then some guy comes up to me and says, 'I'm 5-6, but you ought to see me handle the ball.'" Says Buffett: "I'm not interested." *(New York Society of Security Analysts, December 6, 1994)*

On being named pitchman for economic development in Nebraska: "Easiest job I ever had." *(Omaha World-Herald, January 11, 1995)*

"The best time to sell a stock is never." *(USA Today, February 17, 1995)*

"When you find a really good business run by first-class people, chances are a price that looks high isn't high." *(London Independent, February 19, 1995)*

"I'd be a bum on the street with a tin cup if the market were efficient." *(Fortune, April 3, 1995)*

"Thirty years ago, no one could have foreseen the huge expansion of the Vietnam War, wage and price controls, two oil shocks, the resignation of a president, the dissolution of the Soviet Union, a one-day drop in the Dow of 508 points, or treasury bill yields fluctuating between 2.8% and 17.4%. *(1994 Annual Report)*

"Fear is the foe of the faddist, but the friend of the fundamentalist." *(1994 Annual Report)*

"It's far better to own a significant portion of the Hope diamond than 100% of a rhinestone." *(1994 Annual Report)*

Quoting Wayne Gretzky, "Go to where the puck is going to be, not where it is." *(1994 Annual Report)*

"We try to price, rather than time, purchases. In our view, it's folly to forego buying shares in an outstanding business whose long-term future is predictable, because of short-term worries about an economy or a stock market that we know to be unpredictable. Why scrap an informed decision because of an uninformed guess?" *(1994 Annual Report)*

"You don't have to make money back the same way you lost it." *(Annual Meeting in 1995)*

"We believe in managers knowing money costs money." *(Annual Meeting in 1995)*

"A stock doesn't know who owns it. You may have all of these feelings and emotions as the stock goes up or down, but the stock doesn't give a damn." *(Annual Meeting in 1995)*

"We try to find businesses with wide and long moats around them protecting a castle with an honest lord of the castle...all moats are subject to attack in a capitalistic society." *(Annual Meeting in 1995)*

"There are certain kinds of businesses where you have to be smart once and the kind where you have to stay smart every day to defend it. Retailing is one of them. If you find a retailing concept that catches on, you have to defend it every day." *(Annual Meeting in 1995)*

Advice to managers: "Think like an owner and give us the bad news early." *(Annual Meeting in 1995)*

"Projections do more harm than good." *(Annual Meeting in 1995)*

First thing Buffett thinks about when buying a business: "Can I understand it?" *(Annual Meeting in 1995)*

"If the accounting confuses you, don't do it." *(Annual Meeting in 1995)*

"I look for what's permanent, and what is not." *(Annual Meeting in 1995)*

Coca-Cola: "It's not a bad measuring stick against buying the things. I don't have any plans to buy more right now, but I wouldn't rule it out. And when I consider buying another business, I'll say, 'Why would I rather have this than Coca-Cola?' " *(Annual Meeting in 1995)*

Selling a familar stock is "like dumping your wife when she gets old." *(Business Week, August 21, 1995)*

On waiting until the last minute to decide whether to take stock, cash or a combination in connection with the Disney/Cap Cities merger: "I never swing at a ball while it's still in the pitcher's glove." (*Fortune, March 4, 1996)*

"In the early years, we needed only good ideas, but now we need good *big* ideas." *(1995 Annual Report)*

A man with an ailing horse: "Visiting the vet, he said: ' Can you help me? Sometimes my horse walks just fine and sometimes he limps.' The vet's reply was pointed: 'No problem—when he's walking fine, sell him.' In the world of acquisitions, that horse would be sold as Secretariat." *(1995 Annual Report)*

"We do have a few advantages, perhaps the greatest being that we *don't* have a strategic plan." *(1995 Annual Report)*

"We avoid the attitude of the alumnus whose message to the football coach is, 'I'm 100% with you—win or tie.'"*(1995 Annual Report)*

A question folks at Berkshire always try to ask: "And then what?" *(Annual Meeting in 1996)*

"If you find three wonderful businesses in your life, you'll get very rich." *(Annual Meeting in 1996)*

"We like businesses which are fundamental, simple and where the rate of change is not very fast." *(Annual Meeting in 1996)*

"We do not view Berkshire shareholders as faceless members of an ever-shifting crowd, but rather as co-venturers who have entrusted their funds to us for what may well turn out to be the remainder of their lives." *(Berkshire's "Owner's Manual," June, 1996)*

Please Speak English

Mutually understood

Buffett decodes fund prospectus

The Securities and Exchange Commission wants mutual funds to write their prospectuses in plain English *(story, 1B)* To show mutual fund lawyers how to do it, SEC Chairman Arthur Levitt asked Warren Buffett, the legendary investor and CEO of Berkshire Hathaway, to rewrite a typical mutual fund prospectus paragraph. Here is the paragraph — and Buffett's version.

By Marcy Nighswander, AP

BUFFETT: His rewrite was just half as long.

LEVITT: SEC chairman sets an example.

The original:

Maturity and Duration Management

Maturity and duration management decisions are made in the context of an intermediate maturity orientation. The maturity structure of the portfolio is adjusted in the anticipation of cyclical interest rate changes. Such adjustments are not made in an effort to capture short-term, day-to-day movements in the market, but instead are implemented in anticipation of longer term, secular shifts in the levels of interest rates (i.e. shifts transcending and/or not inherent to the business cycle). Adjustments made to shorten portfolio maturity and duration are made to limit capital losses during periods when interest rates are expected to rise. Conversely, adjustments made to lengthen maturation for the portfolio's maturity and duration strategy lies in analysis of the U.S. and global economies, focusing on levels of real interest rates, monetary and fiscal policy actions, and cyclical indicators.

Buffett's version:

Maturity and Duration Management

We will try to profit by correctly predicting future interest rates. When we have no strong opinion, we will generally hold intermediate-term bonds. But when we expect a major and sustained increase in rates, we will concentrate on short-term issues. And, conversely, if we expect a major shift to lower rates, we will buy long bonds. We will focus on the big picture and won't make moves based on short-term considerations.

(*USA Today*, October 14, 1994)

120

Lunch with Warren Buffett

"I'll have a Coke." ... "Attaboy!"

After *Warren Buffett: The Good Guy of Wall Street*, (my first Buffett book) came out in 1992, I received a short letter from him saying, in part, "You've treated me better than I deserve but as Charlie and I have repeatedly said, 'Who the hell wants only what they deserve?' "

Later I went to Omaha for some book-signings; at the first one at Village Bookstore, Buffett's daughter Susan came by and I autographed a copy for her daughter, Emily.

When I returned to the Red Lion hotel I was surprised to find a message from Susan. I returned her call and she said she had talked with her father and that he'd be glad to see me the next day.

"He's there all day. Just go up anytime," she said.

In the morning (October 2, 1992), I called Gladys Kaiser who said lunch would be a good time to come. My wife Pat and I parked in the

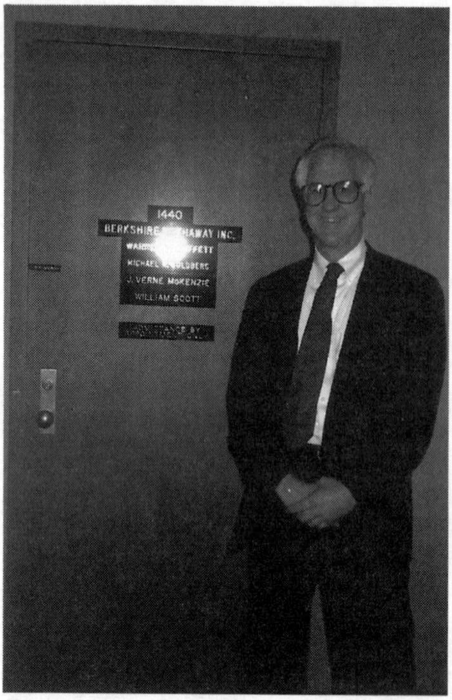

(Photo by Pat Kilpatrick)

The locked doorway into Berkshire headquarters. The author has arrived for a meeting with Buffett. At lunch author asks for a Coke and Buffett says, "Attaboy!"

Kiewit Plaza parking deck, talked to the guard who called Mrs. Kaiser, and we were told to take the elevator to the 14th floor to 1440.

We were buzzed through the security system and met the receptionist, who was answering calls. There was at least one request for a Berkshire annual report, a request that is transferred to a tape recording. We were told Mr. Buffett was on the phone but would be with us soon.

Pat and I sat and looked about at the tiny headquarters. We sat under a sign that had the symbol BRK on it and items such as the *Buffalo News*; to our left at the entranceway was a small sign: "A fool and his money are soon invited everywhere."

Debbie Bosanek came out and introduced herself and then Gladys Kaiser. Marc Hamburg, Berkshire's treasurer happened by. And in less than five minutes—about the time it takes him to conduct the annual meeting—Buffett, dressed in a purple tie and dark conservative suit came ambling down the hallway, saying, "Hi, Andy. Hi, Pat."

"Have you given them a tour?" he asked Mrs. Kaiser, realizing he was stuck with a quick tour.

He gave a several-minute tour, walking down a narrow hallway pointing to old front pages of the *Wall Street Journal*: "This was the high in 1927 and the low in 1932 in the Depression. We have them because they cost just a dollar." He showed us the document for the original Buffett Partnership.

Mrs. Kaiser pointed out the "library"—just a few books—and Buffett pointed out the "conference room"—two chairs and a small table.

He showed us an old-time Coke machine and his supply of Cokes.

The pale green-walled headquarters was a short line of offices, several groupings of filing cabinets and not much else. Headquarters, smaller and more cramped than advertised, reminded me of the narrow corridors of a Navy destroyer.

Buffett showed us some old leather-bound ledgers of the Berkshire and Hathaway textile firms, trying to find the signature of early shareholder Hetty Green, known for her wealth and uninviting personality. He couldn't find it.

The tour was suddenly over and we were following him out and down the elevator two floors to the Kiewit Plaza Club dining room.

I asked, "Where are the hamburgers and potato chips?" and he replied, "Oh, we have those, too."

So what would everyone have? He ordered a bacon, lettuce and tomato sandwich, a salad and iced tea. When I started by ordering a Coke, he said, "Attaboy!"

He looked fine, was energetic, talked fast, and was walking with an ever-so-slight limp. He was pale and looked as though he had been in a library all his life, never a minute in the sun. Still, he gave the impression of tremendous energy, genuine interest in everything about life, dominating conversations with stories and jokes.

"I saw your father's byline on the presidential series. In fact, I stopped the VCR to look at it...I watched it on a VCR so I could stop and not miss anything because the phone rings."

I asked him about his early purchase of Washington Post Co. stock. He said he'd gotten to know Katharine Graham, knew of the business from his paperboy days, had watched the stock go public in 1971 and then watched it decline.

"I knew The *Post* was going to outdo The *Star*, not necessarily that the *Star* would fold." He explained he bought his Post Co. stock quickly over a several-month period.

He also told a story about how Peter Kiewit once saved the *Omaha World-Herald* from the clutches of the Newhouse chain, which was after it. "Kiewit bought it over a weekend," Buffett said.

He asked all about the book—the editing, publishing and finances of it. He thought it was very difficult to keep track of things in the publishing world, that one of his sons was in the music business and knew that it was difficult to keep exact tabs on sales.

He was aware that a book about himself by Roger Lowenstein was coming out.

He still plans his own book, but maybe not right away, saying he thought he ought not to write two books, just one, and that there was still a lot left to do yet. "Of course, you don't want to wait until you're 98, or something."

He added, "Frankly, I haven't kept that many notes," to which Mrs. Kaiser said, "He has it all up here," pointing to her head.

Buffett repeated his joke about wanting Carol Loomis to do most of the work on the book.

I asked Buffett if I were to see the list of Berkshire shareholders, would there be more high-profile names than I had listed in the book. "You had a pretty good list, but, yes, there would be a lot of names you'd recognize." He gave only one vague hint. "There's a movie star who has been buying lately."

He told us a story about Paul Newman, with no suggestion Paul Newman was the movie star doing the buying.

Years back, he said, he once sat at a dinner with Paul Newman, and Senator Charles Percy's wife was between them. "She never looked at me the whole time. I could have been an empty seat." I asked Buffett if he had a chance to talk to Paul Newman, and he said he did a little. "But I practically had to knock her over to talk to him."

Later Buffett said he thought a book ought to be done about Don Keough, Coke's president. "There have been a lot of books done about Coca-Cola, but not about him."

He said that over the past weekend he had been to Seattle to see the Washington-Nebraska football game and had been with a group that included Bill Gates. "He read a book during the game," Buffett said.

"I met him through Meg Greenfield (editorial page editor of the *Washington Post*). About a year and half ago, she asked me to check on the affordability of her building a house," he said. But Buffett said he already knew the answer. "When you ask if you can afford it, you can. Otherwise you don't ask."

Buffett also said, "I'm for people doing what they want to with their money."

Buffett said Gates's late mother, Mary, was a Berkshire shareholder.

Toward the end of lunch he asked about my career change, and I told him I was studying for the Series 7 exam to be a stockbroker, and he related his Series 7 experience: "When I took over Salomon there was a requirement, as an officer of a securities firm, that I take the Series 7. But I kept delaying it until I left because I was afraid I wouldn't pass it."

Also, he said, because Salomon trades commodities and has foreign

(Photo by Michael O'Brien)

Buffett in his office at "The Pleasure Palace." "We read. That's about it," says Buffett.

businesses there were many rules requiring his fingerprints. "They took 12 sets of my fingerprints."

After lunch we all went back up the elevator (I did not see him check for pennies on the floor) two flights to Berkshire headquarters. The elevator did not magically open when he came up. We had to wait a minute.

I thought things were coming to an end without seeing his office, but then he motioned us to come on back at the same moment I said I'd love (read kill) to see his office.

We walked in and I pointed to the two black phones behind his desk, and I asked if that was the "bank" of phones where he placed orders. Yes, he said.

His office featured his rather small desk with another phone, and two small couches. He showed us a framed photo on the wall (his cameo appearance on ABC's soap opera *All My Children*), and with pride pointed to a notice of payment of $10 for his wardrobe fee. "My daughter says that's about what it's worth."

There was a photo of his father and there was an old ticker tape, but really very few things in the way of mementos.

Lining a shelf near his desk were some books, including a row of census books.

We thanked him for his hospitality and he walked us to the hallway, waved nonchalantly, and said for me to stay in touch about the progress of the book.

The little more than one-hour trip to the mountaintop was over.

121

A $10,000 Stock

"I've made more money with my rear end than with my head."

Berkshire's stock price began its first assault on $10,000 a share during the week of July 27, 1992. Actually on that day it didn't make any progress because it didn't even trade, but by the end of the week it rose to $9,525.

Then on August 3, it rose $25 to $9,550, an all-time high, and on August 4 it jumped $55 to $9,605.

It had been a heck of a run for all Berkshire shareholders, particularly for Malcolm Chace, remember, with a cost basis of 25 cents on his Berkshire stock.

On November 10, trading at $9,400, the stock closed up $50 on just 20 shares. The next day Berkshire roared up $225 to close at $9,675 and the following day it added another $150, closing at $9,825.

Over the weekend, Berkshire announced that third-quarter earnings dropped 60% because of insurance claims associated with Hurricane

Andrew.

But in the midst of a market down 27 points on November 16, Berkshire hit $10,000 on a trade at 11:35 a.m., closing at $10,200 on a volume of 210 shares, the last trade coming on a buy order from the Omaha brokerage firm of Kirkpatrick, Pettis where one person said: "Nobody's ever paid $10,200 for it." Replied a trader: "You just did!"

Suddenly Berkshire was a $10,000 stock! It was the highest any equity had ever traded on the New York Stock Exchange.

And that fouled up stock quotes everywhere. Some quote machines didn't record that Berkshire was over $10,000. The Bloomberg service, for example, said the stock closed at $9,950. Other services carried the bid and asked at $9,900 by $9,950. Others carried quotes from $200 to $950.

One broker called a Berkshire shareholder saying: "Did Berkshire split or what?"

Some of the lower quotes were recorded in the accounts of some Berkshire shareholders, really gumming up the works.

My account showed a negative net worth of $178,295, and a broker explained that a purchase of Berkshire shares that day went unrecorded for a time because, "It had to have special handling to accommodate the five digits." The Big Board had to give Berkshire stock quotes by means of an old-fashioned electronic messaging system to financial news services as technicians worked to accommodate the five-digit number.

LaVerne Ramsey, a stockbroker with Prudential Securities in Birmingham, Alabama, sent the following memo to Berkshire shareholders: "There is good news and bad news. The good news is that Berkshire went over $10,000...The bad news is that the 'broker book' system, along with many other financial services, has been unable to handle a five-digit stock price. Therefore the unrealized gain figure is way off because the system drops a digit. Our operations people are working on the problem.

"In the meantime, here is the incorrect copy for the month of November, 1992. It can be a souvenir of the historic milestone for Berkshire Hathaway."

The *Wall Street Journal*, reaching Buffett, got this comment: "What tickles my fancy is when the intrinsic value improves. I focus on what's happening on the playing field, not what's on the scoreboard."

The *Omaha World-Herald* got an even better quote when it asked about a stock price of $10,000 based on long-term holdings: Buffett, apparently enjoying things more than he was letting on, said: "I've made more money with my rear end than my head."

"It proves what Woody Allen said is true: '90% of life is just showing up.'"

Morgan thinks Berkshire shareholders should show up for life for at least another 15 years because if Buffett can manage an annual 20% net worth growth, the stock may be trading at $200,000 a share.

As Berkshire fans were celebrating $10,000, the stock bolted to $11,000, on a rumor that Buffett was a heavy buyer of AT&T stock.

On November 24, 1992, on 180 shares the stock rocketed $550—its highest one-day rise at that time—to close at $10,700. But many brokerage firm quote machines listed Berkshire as down $38 for the day.

The next day the stock jumped another $250, settling in for Thanksgiving at $10,950. Many quote services gave up on the business of $10,000 and listed Berkshire as closing at $950.

Charles Schwab & Co. wrote to its Berkshire shareholders: "You are probably already aware of the difficulty financial institutions such as Schwab have had in reporting transactions involving Berkshire Hathaway Inc. since the price of its stock rose above $10,000 per share. In particular, your Schwab statements, confirmations, and other forms of account information are unable to reflect a price-per-share above $9,999.00.

"In order for our systems to correctly calculate your account, summary balances, your statements, trade confirmations, and other account and trade information will report one (1) share of BRK as 10 'fractional shares,' each with a price of one-tenth (1/10) of the actual value of one share of BRK.

"For example, if you own or trade two shares of BRK when the price-per-share is $15,000, the quantity, or the number of shares, will be shown as 20 (2 x 10 fractional shares) and the latest price will appear as $1,500 (1/10 of $15,000). Total amount on confirmations and market value on statements will be shown as $30,000, the correct total for 2 shares..."

Berkshire shareholders were calling it the New Math.

122

A $15,000 Stock

He could buy 159,000 Cadillacs or 421 million jumbo pizzas. Five Cherry Cokes a day for 12 million years.

Berkshire's stock price first pierced $15,000 a share on May 24, 1993, then closed at $14,950. The following day it closed at $15,000, and despite falling off $200 the next morning in a weak market, Berkshire still rallied to close at $15,000.

At a price of $15,100, Jim Rasmussen wrote in the *Omaha World-Herald*, May 27, 1993, Buffett's stake was worth $7.16 billion. "That's enough money to buy 159,111 Cadillac Seville Touring Sedans at $45,000 apiece. Also it could buy 421.4 million Godfather's Jumbo Combo pizzas at $16.99 each—or 1,255 pizzas for every resident in the city of Omaha."

Or as *Fortune* pointed out in its June 28, 1993, issue: "With his $6.4

billion, superinvestor Warren Buffett, CEO of Berkshire Hathaway, could afford to guzzle his usual five Cherry Cokes a day for the next 12,058,407 years." Now he can drink them for about the next 35 million years.

"I was just joking with a colleague [about the time the stock was $14,000], that the stock was going to $15,000. We laughed. It was just a joke," said Dr. Robert Ford, head of Ford Headache Clinic in Birmingham, Alabama. Ford, a Berkshire shareholder, recalls the first time he met Buffett in the lobby of a hotel in Omaha before the annual meeting in 1991.

"I had made up my mind I wanted to meet the man who owned that much Coca-Cola stock...I saw him, and my wife, Kay, was saying not to bother him, but I spoke to him and told him I had owned 10 stocks but now I owned just three stocks—Coke, Berkshire and Glaxo. He said, 'That's a pretty good portfolio.'"

"I told him he was doing a lot better for shareholders than the Donald Trumps of the world and he said, "You'll be better off with me."

Then Buffett, always on the move, was gone.

The stock's price was leading the record keepers into an assortment of errors that ranged in many reports from $5,000 to zero.

Yes, Berkshire was zero, according to a chart offered by the Bloomberg news service.

123

A $20,000 stock 20/20 Are we seeing double again? A $38,000 stock

Seven years to the day after October 19, 1987, when Berkshire and everything else was crashing, Berkshire traded for a brief time at $20,000 a share.

The stock slipped back, but rallied on October 28, 1994, rising $550 to close at $20,450.

Berkshire—ten tons of gold—was a $20,000 stock.

In early 1996 Berkshire's stock price hit a high of $38,000 before falling back.

124

"A Do-It-Yourself Stock Split"

"We're giving shareholders a do-it yourself split, if they care to," Buffett said in a rare conference call with reporters.

Buffett came up with an unusual split not because he wanted to split the stock, but because he was ticked at unit investment trusts. The unit trusts were trying to piggyback Berkshire's success and exploit his reputation, selling units—with high commissions and management fees—of Berkshire and Berkshire related stocks for $1,000 units.

In offering a Class B share worth 1/30th of the original, now Class A shares (symbol BRKA), Buffett not only undercut the business of unit trusts, he also provided more flexibility to those trying to get Berkshire into their IRAs or giving up to $10,000 a year tax-free to children.

Buffett could have simply split the stock but said that might have led to a "slightly more speculative bunch," and he did not want a new shareholder base that might be "uninformed or have unrealistic expectations."

Buffett said Class B shareholders would not be allowed to participate in Berkshire's charitable giving program. In 1995 Berkshire shareholders could designate $13 a share to charity, but that would amount to 43 cents a share for a Class B shareholder. "It would be crazy to make 43-cent designations," Buffett said.

However, "unlike the indirect investments offered by the trusts, shares of Class B Common Stock entitle holders to the attributes of Berkshire shares, such as the power to vote on matters put to Berkshire shareholders, the right to receive Berkshire's annual report and other communications to shareholders, and the right to attend meetings of Berkshire's shareholders. (Prospectus for the Class B offering)

The stock offering was Berkshire's first except there was once a zero-coupon bond convertible into stock. Knowing there would be heavy demand for the issue, Buffett joked that there would be "less of a road show" associated with the Class B offering than most other offerings. "We've never felt any need to have a public offering," he said. "We're not trying to attract the most people, only the people attracted to us."

Buffett ended the conference call saying, "I look forward to reading your stories tomorrow."

Originally Berkshire planned to issue 100,000 shares, but sensing heavy interest it raised the offering to 250,000 shares, then to 350,000 shares and finally to 450,000 shares. So Berkshire raised at least half a billion dollars.

Under the symbol BRKB, the Class B shares started trading May 9, 1996 at $1,110, closing up $50 to $1,1160.

Buffett tolad Barron's (May 13, 1996): "I am more than pleased [with the offering]. We had some unconvential objectives in the offering, and when those were explained to Salomon, They figured out ways they thought would best achieve those objectives. I think maybe they got just exactly the kind of investor we want. We wanted people who are going to be with us for an indefinate future, and to design an offering in this kind of market, with a hot IPO market as a backdrop, that suceeds in getting these kinds of investors is a great credit to Salomon."

Berkshire's Class B shares are the second highest trading stock on the New York Stock Exchange after the Class A shares. The shares of The Washington Post Co. are the third highest.

A group of shareholders at dinner the night before Berkshire's annual meeting in 1996—obviously in a good mood—agreed that Berkshie might hit $40,000 in 1997. A fellow at the bar getting a drift of the conversation said: "Yeah, that's for the Class B share!"

Here's Berkshire's explanation of why a Baby Berkshire stock was created:

BERKSHIRE HATHAWAY INC.
NEWS RELEASE

FOR IMMEDIATE RELEASE FEBRUARY 13, 1996

Berkshire Hathaway Inc. announced today that its Board of Directors has approved a plan to create a new class of stock, to be called Class B Common Stock, and to simultaneously designate its existing common stock as Class A Common Stock.

The Company's shareholders will be asked to approve this plan at Berkshire Hathaway's annual meeting, scheduled for May 6th.

Each share of the proposed Class B stock will have the rights of 1/30th of a Class A share, with these exceptions: First, a Class B share will have 1/200th of the vote of a Class A share (rather than 1/30th of the vote). Second, the Class B shares will not be eligible to participate in Berkshire's shareholder-designated charitable contributions program.

As part of this recapitalization program, each share of Berkshire Hathaway's Class A common stock will become convertible, at the holder's option and at any time, into 30 shares of Class B stock. (The conversion privilege will not extend in the opposite direction. That is, holders of Class B shares will not be able to convert them into Class A shares).

To the extent that Class A shareholders choose to convert into Class B shares, a supply of Class B shares will become available for trading. However, for the purpose of creating an initial supply of the Class B shares, Berkshire Hathaway will itself make a public offering for cash of at least $100 million of new Class B shares. The offering will be made only by means of a prospectus. Since the shares issued will be economically equivalent to only 1/30th of a Class A share, a $100 million offering would have the effect under current market conditions of increasing Berkshire's total shares outstanding by less than 3/10ths of 1 percent.

The Company expects to make its offering of Class B shares and to carry out the other provisions of the recapitalization plan as quickly as possible after its annual meeting. As part of the process, the Company will apply to list the Class B shares on the New York Stock Exchange. Berkshire's existing common stock is traded on that exchange and closed at $31,900 on February 12, 1996.

Warren E. Buffett, Chairman of Berkshire Hathaway, explained the Company's proposed recapitalization as its reluctant response to certain largely-unpublicized moves that have been made by parties unaffiliated with Berkshire, eager to profit from the fact that Berkshire has chosen not to split its stock. These parties, in registration statements filed with the Securities & Exchange Commission, have indicated their intention to create unit investment trusts that would sell for relatively small amounts — say $1,000 — and that would purport to be miniature Berkshires or that would otherwise make an effort to associate themselves with Berkshire's reputation.

Said Mr. Buffett: "We have believed it in Berkshire's interest not to split its stock. However, it is clear to me that the promoters of these trusts will aggressively market them and will cause small

Berkshire Hathaway Inc.
News Release — February 13, 1996
Page 2

investors to incur costs — sales commissions, management fees, and tax levies — that will do them damage. Beyond that, holders of these trusts would not be on the list to receive Berkshire's shareholder communications and could not attend its annual meeting."

"We have no interest," said Mr. Buffett, "in enticing investors, large or small, to buy Berkshire stock. But given the prospect of these unit investment trusts, we believe it is better that we ourselves create a direct, low-cost way for small investors to invest in Berkshire. By issuing this new Class B stock, which can be expected to sell at about 1/30th of the price of the Class A stock, we'll do that."

Mr. Buffett said that the market will ultimately determine what the Class B stock sells for. "It is our wish, though," he said, "to forestall any speculative excesses in the market for Berkshire stock. We have some ability to ward these off by increasing the size of the Class B offering above $100 million, and we will do that if it seems wise. Though Berkshire has no need today for additional equity capital, management does not believe that the Company's stock is undervalued. Therefore, current shareholders will not suffer any diminution in per-share intrinsic value, no matter how many Class B shares the Company decides it is necessary to sell."

Mr. Buffett noted that the recapitalization plan will impose certain costs on Berkshire, including those that arise from the mechanics of handling a somewhat increased number of shareholders. The Company nevertheless believes that the right reaction to the promoters of these trusts is to provide a product so superior to what they have to offer that their products become unmerchandisable.

Mr. Buffett added that some existing Berkshire Hathaway shareholders wishing to give annual gifts of $10,000 — the size of gift that the tax laws permit to be tax-free — have found it inconvenient that Berkshire's stock sells at a price well above that. Should these shareholders choose to do so, said Mr. Buffett, they will be able to convert shares of their Class A stock into Class B shares and use these for gifts.

Mr. Buffett said that otherwise he believes it will be in the interests of existing Berkshire shareholders to retain their Class A shares, since these will have full voting rights and access to Berkshire's charitable contributions program.

It is Mr. Buffett's intention (leaving aside times when he himself might want to make small gifts) to hold Class A shares only, and he recommends that course of action to other shareholders. At present, Mr. Buffett owns approximately 40% of Berkshire's outstanding shares. In connection with the recapitalization, he and his wife, Susan T. Buffett, have agreed that, if their combined voting interest increases above 49.9%, they will vote their shares above that percentage in the same proportion as other shareholders vote.

Berkshire Hathaway and its subsidiaries engage in a number of diverse business activities among which the most important is the property and casualty insurance business conducted on both a direct and reinsurance basis. Common stock of the company is listed on the New York Stock Exchange, trading symbol BRK.

125

The Richest Person in the World

In the spring of 1993, Buffett became one of the richest people in America as Berkshire's rising stock price carried Buffett's worth above that of his closest rival, Microsoft's Bill Gates.

By that summer, Buffett's net worth exceeded $8 billion. For a man who inherited nothing, the achievement spoke volumes.

In its June 28, 1993 issue, *Fortune* (with photos of billionaires the Sultan of Brunei, Queen Elizabeth II, Ross Perot, Buffett and Bill Gates on the cover) ranked Buffett as the thirteenth-richest person in the world and the third-richest American, with $6.4 billion, behind Metromedia's John Kluge with $8.8 billion, and Gates with $6.7 billion.

Then the *Forbes* July 5, 1993, issue listed Gates as worth $7.4 billion, Buffett $6.6 billion and Kluge, $5.5 billion.

On September 4, 1993, the *Washington Post* reported that Buffett appeared to be the richest person in the U.S.

And the *Forbes* issue of October 18, 1993, said Buffett was indeed the richest person in the country with a net worth of $8.3 billion, topping Bill Gates at $6.3 billion, John Kluge at $6.2 billion and Sumner Redstone at $5.6 billion.

Forbes' five-page story about America's richest person carried photos of Buffett at an Omaha Royals game at Omaha's Rosenblatt Stadium. Buffett wore a bright red, short-sleeve shirt saying "Nebraska." He was eating Cracker Jack and drinking a Coke.

There he was—the richest person in the country, largely because of his stock-picking and long-term holding abilities.

The news led to a flurry of headlines such as, "The Sage of Omaha deposes Dollar Bill" and "Gates gets Buffetted."

In an interview, Buffett told *Forbes*, "I have in life all I want right here [Omaha]. I tap dance in here [his office] and work with nothing but people I like. I don't have to work with people I don't like."

Forbes said that when Buffett dies he probably will have "set the stage for the biggest charitable foundation ever, one that easily, as suggested earlier, will dwarf the legacies of Rockefeller, Ford and Carnegie. Over the past 23 years, Buffett's investments have compounded his wealth at an average annual rate of 29%. He probably can't keep that up. But give him 15%. If he lives another 20 years and does 15%, the Buffett Foundation will have well over $100 billion. If, as is quite possible, he lives a good deal longer...well, you get the picture."

Omaha World-Herald columnist Robert McMorris wrote at the time that he enjoyed claiming Buffett, who lived a mile away, as a neighbor. "Some day somebody will say to me, 'You're from Omaha? Isn't that where Warren Buffett lives?'

"And I'll say, "Oh, sure, I know Warren. He's practically a neighbor of mine.

"I may even allow that I've discussed investment strategy with him.

"That's more or less true. I once asked him what advice he gives investors who ask for tips on the stock market.

"He said he tells them: 'Buy low, sell high.'"

Later in the story McMorris wrote, "He doesn't have a computer in his office or home. No calculator, for that matter.

"Such toys are unnecessary, he told me, because his line of work is 'not that complicated.'

"For years, though, he had a dart board in his outer office that he claimed was his stock selector.

"He said he has since lost faith in it. 'It doesn't work any more, so

I'm going to give it to Bill Gates.' "

"I'll let him have the dart board so we can keep him in second place," Buffett said.

126

So long John Jacob Astor, Andrew Carnegie, John D. Rockefeller

Buffett is working on becoming the richest person ever in America, in real terms.

John Jacob Astor and Andrew Carnegie, among the richest of their time, were worth several hundred million dollars. Even if those fortunes were inflation-adjusted for today's values, Buffett would still be richer by far.

In its 1992 Richest 400 edition, *Forbes* said that John D. Rockefeller, the richest man of his day, would have a fortune of slightly more than $10 billion in today's dollars.

Buffett and Gates have now far surpassed that figure.

127

"Call him Secretary of Money."
—Andy Rooney

Commentator/humorist Andy Rooney at the end of CBS's "60 Minutes," October 31, 1993, said: "The other day I was looking at *Forbes* magazine in the CBS library. It cost $5, so I didn't buy it. I just looked at it.

This is the issue with the 400 richest people in America. *Forbes* says Warren Buffett is the richest: he has $8 billion. *Forbes* also says Warren Buffett's a nice guy. I'd be a nice guy, too, if I had $8 billion.

My boss, Larry Tisch, head of CBS, is one of the poorest of the 400 richest. He only has $1.3 billion. No wonder he's grumpy.

This list gives me an idea, though. The biggest problem we have in this country is the budget deficit. Make a special cabinet position for Warren Buffett; call him Secretary of Money. He'd control all government spending.

The national debt is $4 trillion. Now any company run that way would go out of business. You can bet Warren Buffett wouldn't run the country that way.

Here's the deal, Warren. The government spent $1,496,000,000,000 last year. It collected $1,241,000,000,000 in taxes. You can see there's a gap there, a deficit of $255 billion.

If you could run this country more like one of your companies, cut the waste and the stealing and spend only, say, $1,141,000,000,000, we wouldn't have a deficit. One trillion two hundred and forty-one billion dollars—what we take in, in taxes—minus only $1,141,000,000,000—what you'd spend—that would leave us a surplus of $100 billion.

We'll use half of that to start paying off the national debt. And we know we have to make this worth your while, so you'd get to keep half of that, $50 billion for yourself, Warren. Still a good deal for us.

We'd raise money the way your companies do, by putting the United States on the stock exchange. Any American would be able to buy stock, actually own a piece of this country. If we had trouble with some small country like Haiti or Somalia, we wouldn't send troops. We'd do what one of your corporations does: buy out the country and take it over. The United States would be out of trouble, and we'd erect a new memorial alongside the Washington Monument...

Rooney's show closed with footage of the Washington Monument with a dollar-sign monument superimposed.

128

"Is it okay with you if he shows up at your book signings?"

In late October, 1994, I sent a copy of my second book to Buffett via Federal Express's 10:30 a.m. delivery.

In about an hour, no more than an hour and a half, I got a call from Buffett's assistant, Debbie Bosanek.

"He's read your book. He likes your book....would it be okay with you if he shows up at your book signings?" she asked of three signings I had scheduled in Omaha.

I flew to Omaha, but arrived just in the nick of time for the first at the Bookworm store because my plane was delayed an hour in Atlanta. "Oh, USAir?" Buffett said.

Just outside the store, I ran into Gladys Kaiser and stopped to talk, not realizing anyone was in the book store. When I walked in, I saw the store was full of people.

"We're sold out," store owner Beth Black said, explaining people had either bought the book there or had phoned in orders.

Before going to Omaha, I had two book signings in Birmingham and had sold 25 and 71 books.

At the Bookworm, more than 100 were sold before Buffett showed up.

After signing books, Buffett and I signed book plates to go in more books that would be shipped to the store.

Buffett set the tone for the afternoon by handing me a photo of himself dressed in a Nebraska football uniform with a big number 1 on the jersey. And he gave me a photo for Kermit Kendrick.

Later he tossed a penny on the floor and asked if I wanted a photo of him picking it up.

Gladys Kaiser was one of the first people to get Buffett's autograph. "And keep on brushing" he wrote in reference to the joke she and I had started about how often she brushes her teeth.

Later a woman said she hoped her son would grow up to be like him. "Well, tell him not to eat quite so much," Buffett replied.

Then he was asked to hold a baby girl for a photo and the baby cried. Then someone asked Buffett to give her his wallet and when he started to, the girl howled. "Well, she behaves better than most women who've asked for my wallet."

Later in the afternoon we did a signing at Village Books where again the store immediately sold out. Again, Buffett had a quip for many and after a "Thank you" would say, "My pleasure."

When people started asking him to sign dollar bills, he said, "Can I keep half?"

For four hours that day he signed books. He seemed to enjoy it, but confessed at the end, "Well, it's gotten a little out of hand," as he stayed until 6:30 p.m. so everyone who came got his autograph. He said he had signed so many books, his autograph was becoming "devalued."

But even at the bookstore, you could get a glimpse of a mind still trying to learn. He asked the owners how much theft they had, what they did about it and later asked, "How well is *The Bell Curve* selling?"

Toward the end of the day, I really got to talk to him and asked him what the markets had done that day. He told me the stock market had been off about 40 points and that the long bond had sold off sharply.

I asked him how Berkshire fared. "I don't know. I didn't ask."

Because he doesn't have a computer, I asked how he keeps abreast of the market. He said, "I pick up the phone and call Salomon and they tell me about the market or some stock I'm interested in."

He talked about his reading and said he had 50 books at home he needed to get to. "I'm getting behind," he said.

The next day he showed up at Waldenbooks to cheers. He was citing the statistics of the first quarter of the Nebraska-Kansas football game.

One lady asked for a picture and Buffett said, "Well, the backside's better."

Not knowing Buffett was going to show, I had only sent 700 books to Omaha by our self-publishing unit. The books were delivered to the stores by a friend, Don Pippen of Southern Publishers Group, just in time.

Defying any of Ben Graham's formulas Buffett managed to sell 1,000 of the 700 books, including nameplates for future books.

That man can sell books.

After I told Michael Assael that, he wrote: "You'd make even Ben Graham's eyes pop out with your new book statistics: Selling 1,000 of 700 books! Ben might call that, 'selling your books short against their box.' "

About a month later I tried to get a book signing in New York, but was turned down by every book store there I could think of. "We don't do signings for self-published books; we don't buy books from you; we're too busy," were some of the objections.

Thanks to Pippen, who made calls from a phone booth in Florence, Alabama, I wound up with a signing in the lobby of the Millenium Hilton.

When I told Debbie Bosanek I had a signing there, she said, "The Millenium Hilton? That's where he's staying."

The morning of one the signings I walked through the lobby and saw a man reading the *New York Times*. He looked like Buffett. He was Buffett. I sat and talked with him several minutes. Later he went to speak to a Ben Graham commemorative luncheon sponsored by the New York Society of Security Analysts.

Afterwards he dropped by my signing, but I didn't have much business and he stayed only a short time. He signed a few books, changed a $100 bill at the counter and was gone.

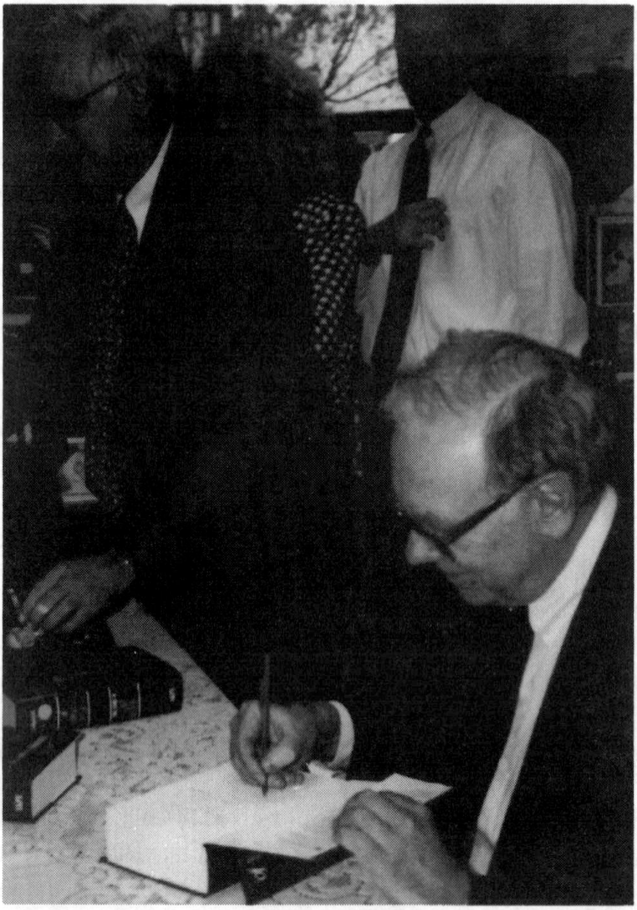

(Photo by Nancy Line Jacobs)

Buffett at a book signing at Village Books in Omaha November 4, 1994. The man can sell books.

129

A letter to shareholders. The Boston Tea Party...

BERKSHIRE HATHAWAY INC.
1440 KIEWIT PLAZA
OMAHA, NEBRASKA 68131
TELEPHONE (402) 346-1400

Dear Shareholder:

Normally, I write to you just once a year, a schedule that is a blessing for both of us. There are several items of interest this year, however, that make a brief interim letter appropriate.

First, I think you will enjoy the enclosed speech, recently given by Charlie Munger, your Vice Chairman, to MBA students at the University of Southern California. *Outstanding Investor Digest* attended the lecture and has graciously allowed us to reproduce their report. The final two-thirds of Charlie's talk deals with the business and investment strategies of Berkshire, articulated in his usual cogent manner.

Second, we have excellent news on the acquisition front. During the first half, Berkshire merged with two family-owned businesses possessing both outstanding economics and outstanding managements: Helzberg's, a chain of 150 jewelry stores operating in 26 states and R. C. Willey, the dominant retailer of home furnishings in Utah. Berkshire issued 15,762 shares in acquiring 100% of both companies, and I'm looking forward to telling you much more about them in the 1995 Annual Report.

Combined, the companies will have about $600 million in revenues this year, up from about $100 million in 1985. Though the jewelry and home furnishings industries are characterized by mediocre profitability, Helzberg's and R. C. Willey have been exceptions. And the managements that made them exceptional will continue unfettered: Charlie and I will limit our participation to applause.

Finally, I want to further explain the reason for the authorization of preferred stock that I wrote about in the 1994 Annual Report. It's clear that I didn't do a very good job the first time around: At the Annual Meeting, over 1% of our shares voted against authorization of the preferred, the closest thing we have had to the Boston Tea Party at Berkshire.

The key word is "authorization." Berkshire has to issue nothing: The preferred shares will be issued only if your management and directors believe we are obtaining appropriate value in return.

You may worry, if you wish, that Charlie and I will do something dumb in making acquisitions. That's always a risk. But the preferred in no way increases that risk, since we can also do something dumb when acquiring with cash or Berkshire common.

The preferred is simply an additional form of currency that we can use in a purchase. If a seller desires a preferred stock, *and if the cost to us is equivalent to what we would alternatively pay in cash or common stock*, we will use it. We can't be disadvantaged by such an option, and we may benefit if preferred of the same market value as common or cash enhances the appeal of a transaction to a seller.

Warren E. Buffett
Chairman of the Board

August 15, 1995

130

A Pearl of Wisdom from the Sequoia Fund

Buffett's close friend, Bill Ruane, chairman of the Sequoia Fund, wrote the following to Sequoia's shareholders in his report for the second quarter of 1995.

He had been discussing the craze surrounding the initial public offering of Netscape Communications, a company which allows customers to access the Internet:

> Lest you think that we are going the way of Neanderthals however, we think you should know that your Chairman, out of sheer curiosity resulting from all the media hype, asked a young technophile to lead him into the Internet one day last year. In search of something familiar, he further asked if there was an Internet

> "room" or "bulletin board" (our terminology may not be quite accurate here) designated for items relating to Berkshire Hathaway. Believe it or not, there is! And a gratuitous remark on this "bulletin board" read, I think Warren Buffett is highly overrated and Berkshire is a short, any comments? The stock was then about $18,000 per share (today's price: $24,850), permitting your Chairman to depart the Internet with the comfortable thought that technological sophistication does not necessarily equate to investment acumen.

It must be added, of course, that a comparison of the 1995 performances of Netscape and Berkshire stock prices is not a happy one for Berkshire shareholders.

Berkshire's performance was terrific. Netscape's was off the charts.

131

THE RECORD

"The best is yet to come."

Here's Berkshire's record for annual per-share increase in book value over the years, compared to the S&P 500 Index, which includes dividends.

Berkshire shareholder Ed Prendeville says, "The record is spectacular, and if you adjust some way for the low risks Buffett has taken, his record probably stands alone."

Relative results, in percentage terms, are shown in the third row. Has Guinness thought about this one? (Losses are in parentheses)

	Berkshire	S&P	Relative results
1965	23.8	10.0	13.8
1966	20.3	(11.7)	32.0
1967	11.0	30.9	(19.9)
1968	19.0	11.0	8.0

1969	16.2	(8.4)	24.6
1970	12.0	3.9	8.1
1971	16.4	14.6	1.8
1972	21.7	18.9	2.8
1973	4.7	(14.8)	19.5
1974	5.5	(26.4)	31.9
1975	21.9	37.2	(15.3)
1976	59.3	23.6	35.7
1977	31.9	(7.4)	39.3
1978	24.0	6.4	17.6
1979	35.7	18.2	17.5
1980	19.3	32.3	(13.0)
1981	31.4	(5.0)	36.4
1982	40.0	21.4	18.6
1983	32.3	22.4	9.9
1984	13.6	6.1	7.5
1985	48.2	31.6	16.6
1986	26.1	18.6	7.5
1987	19.5	5.1	14.4
1988	20.1	16.6	3.5
1989	44.4	31.7	12.7
1990	7.4	(3.1)	10.5
1991	39.6	30.5	9.1
1992	20.3	7.6	12.7
1993	14.3	10.1	4.2
1994	13.9	1.3	12.6
1995	43.1	37.6	5.5

Shortly before an Omaha Royals game the weekend prior to Berkshire's annual meeting in 1994, *Toronto Star* reporter Jade Hemeon talked briefly with Buffett about Berkshire. "It's a painting in progress. The best is yet to come," he told her.

132

Berkshire's Stock Tables—Traveling North by Northeast

1965	High Low
First Quarter	16; 12
Second Quarter	21; 16
Third Quarter	19; 17
Fourth Quarter	22; 18

1966	
First Quarter	27; 20
Second Quarter	27; 21
Third Quarter	23; 18
Fourth Quarter	18; 17

1967	High Low
First Quarter	20; 17
Second Quarter	19; 17
Third Quarter	21; 18
Fourth Quarter	21; 19

1968	
First Quarter	24; 20
Second Quarter	31; 23
Third Quarter	33; 26
Fourth Quarter	39; 32

1969	High Low
First Quarter	40; 34
Second Quarter	45; 35
Third Quarter	39; 31
Fourth Quarter	44; 34
1970	
First Quarter	47; 40
Second Quarter	47; 32
Third Quarter	43; 35
Fourth Quarter	43; 39
1971	
First Quarter	51; 40
Second Quarter	55; 48
Third Quarter	53; 51 *
Fourth Quarter	74; 70 *
1972	
First Quarter	76; 73 *
Second Quarter	78; 78 *
Third Quarter	84; 80 *
Fourth Quarter	80; 80 *
1973	
First Quarter	93; 80
Second Quarter	87; 85
Third Quarter	88; 83
Fourth Quarter	87; 71
1974	
First Quarter	76; 72
Second Quarter	76; 64
Third Quarter	64; 49
Fourth Quarter	49; 40

1975	High Low
First Quarter	51; 38
Second Quarter	51; 45
Third Quarter	60; 41
Fourth Quarter	43; 38
1976	
First Quarter	56; 38
Second Quarter	60; 55
Third Quarter	73; 61
Fourth Quarter	95; 66
1977	
First Quarter	97; 85
Second Quarter	100; 95
Third Quarter	107; 100
Fourth Quarter	139; 107
1978	
First Quarter	142; 134
Second Quarter	180; 142
Third Quarter	180; 165
Fourth Quarter	189; 152
1979	
First Quarter	185; 154
Second Quarter	215; 185
Third Quarter	350; 215
Fourth Quarter	335; 240
1980	
First Quarter	360; 260
Second Quarter	340; 250
Third Quarter	415; 305
Fourth Quarter	490; 385

1981	High Low
First Quarter	505; 425
Second Quarter	525; 485
Third Quarter	520; 460
Fourth Quarter	590; 460
1982	
First Quarter	560; 465
Second Quarter	520; 470
Third Quarter	550; 430
Fourth Quarter	775; 540
1983	
First Quarter	965; 775
Second Quarter	985; 890
Third Quarter	1,245; 905
Fourth Quarter	1,385; 1,240
1984	
First Quarter	1,360; 1,240
Second Quarter	1,345; 1,220
Third Quarter	1,305; 1,230
Fourth Quarter	1,305; 1,265
1985	
First Quarter	1,930; 1,275
Second Quarter	2,160; 1,725
Third Quarter	2,235; 2,005
Fourth Quarter	2,730; 2,075
1986	
First Quarter	3,250; 2,220
Second Quarter	3,160; 2,640
Third Quarter	3,100; 2,525
Fourth Quarter	2,925; 2,620

1987	High Low
First Quarter	3,630; 2,800
Second Quarter	3,530; 3,330
Third Quarter	4,220; 3,420
Fourth Quarter	4,270; 2,550
1988	
First Quarter	3,500; 3,000
Second Quarter	4,150; 3,400
Third Quarter	5,000; 4,040
Fourth Quarter	5,050; 4,600
1989	
First Quarter	5,025; 4,625
Second Quarter	7,000; 4,950
Third Quarter	8,750; 6,600
Fourth Quarter	8,900; 7,950
1990	
First Quarter	8,725; 6,675
Second Quarter	7,675; 6,600
Third Quarter	7,325; 5,500
Fourth Quarter	6,900; 5,500
1991	
First Quarter	8,275; 6,550
Second Quarter	8,750; 7,760
Third Quarter	9,000; 8,325
Fourth Quarter	9,125; 8,150
(Year-end 1991:	9,050)
1992	
First Quarter	9,000; 8,575
Second Quarter	9,300; 8,850
Third Quarter	9,950; 9,050
Fourth Quarter	11,750; 9,150
(Year-end 1992:	11,750)

1993

	High Low
First Quarter	13,200; 11,350
Second Quarter	16,200; 11,800
Third Quarter	17,800; 15,100
Fourth Quarter	17,800; 16,200
(Year-end 1993:	16,325)

1994

First Quarter	16,900; 15,150
Second Quarter	16,700; 15,400
ThirdQuarter	19,750; 16,425
Fourth Quarter	20,800; 19,200
(Year-end 1994:	20,400)

1995

	High Low
First Quarter	25,200; 20,250
Second Quarter	24,450; 21,500
Third Quarter	30,600; 23,400
Fourth Quarter	33,400; 28,850
(Year-end 1995:	32,100)

1996

First Quarter	38,000; 29,800

**** These figures were provided by the National Quotation Bureau but they only show the price on the last day of the quarter at a time when Berkshire was not listed in the National Association of Securities Dealers Automated Quotation (NASDAQ) system. Instead Berkshire was listed in the "pink sheets" because it was not a marginable security. The National Quotation Bureau has only end-of-the-month listings from that time.***

133

Summing Up, Final Quiz

"What's the combined IQ of Warren Buffett and Charles Munger?"

Berkshire shareholder Bill Scargle says he's wondered all along how smart Buffett and Munger really are.

"I've often asked myself what's the combined IQ of Warren Buffett and Charles Munger?

"I've finally decided what the answer is. It's the stock price of Berkshire."

So if you had asked, for example, what's the combined IQ of the two men in late 1995, then the answer was more than 30,000.

134

"My God, he was old."

The NBC affiliate in Omaha, WOWT-TV, Channel 6, on October 14, 1993, aired an interview with Buffett.

Reporter Sue Baggarly had asked him how others could be successful investors, and he had quipped that living a long life was one ingredient because of the effect of compounding money over time.

At the end of the half-hour session she asked, "How would you like to be remembered?" and Buffett shot back, "Well, I'd like for the minister to say, 'My God, he was old.'"

135

"He rests...He has traveled."

—James Joyce

"Maybe just once." An exalted journey.

There are three seminal works in literature using Homer's Odysseus as hero.

There is the original, Homer's *Odyssey,* the story of a hero who longs to return home to restore order in Ithaca after the Trojan War.

In our century, the two most comprehensive works based on Homer's work are *The Odyssey: A Modern Sequel* by a Greek poet and novelist, Nikos Kazantzakis, and *Ulysses* by the Irish novelist, James Joyce.

Each work portrays a hero—facing travels, adventures, and setbacks—who somehow prevails.

Odysseus was trying to return home; the Kazantzakis hero is a self-propelled, centrifugal soul trying to abandon his home and seek a bold new life beyond; and Joyce's Leopold Bloom was trying to survive the day in a small, imperfect, real world of work and home in Dublin, Ireland, and yet he too establishes everyday, yet bold victories.

Homer's Odysseus and Joyce's Leopold Bloom are centripetal heroes; throughout their travels and adventures, they seek to arrive safely at home. Kazantzakis's Odysseus rejects his home and hunts new worlds to conquer in search of freedom.

Each hero, in whatever setting, provides hope that although humankind faces a hostile world, one can master it and even extend man's boundaries.

And when the day is done, there is no higher salute than Joyce's toward Leopold Bloom: "He rests...He has traveled."

Buffett, who has hunkered down in his modest home and office in Omaha most of his life, and yet has also seen the bright lights of the world, has chalked up extraordinarily vast achievements, and riches, all of which he will generously hand back to our society.

He has lived in some ways an ordinary existence in Omaha, leaving at times to score brilliant achievements. His life is analogous to a life suggested by a cartoon on James Joyce's refrigerator:

1. Call bank.
2. Dry cleaner.
3. Forge in the smithy of my soul the uncreated conscience of my race.
4. Call Mom.

Wallman Investment Counsel's Steve Wallman says:

> In some respects, there never will be another Warren Buffett for the same reason there will never be another Babe Ruth. They're both far larger than the sum of their total skills and records. They're heroes in the true sense of the word. People may break Ruth's records, and Buffett's, too, but it will be generations before a player, or investor, captures the public's imagination the way Ruth and Buffett have.
>
> Babe Ruth was the first great home run hitter. I think Buffett is much the same—the first great stock market investor.
>
> Even if someone rivals Buffett's talents, he'll have trouble with the longevity issue. Ted Williams may have been the best hitter who ever lived (certainly the best old hitter), but his career was interrupted by military service twice. Very few investors will have the personality to keep playing the game as long as Buffett has. Even fewer will break into the big leagues at 25.

In the same vein, two Berkshire shareholders once engaged in the following conversation about Buffett:

Shareholder 1: "He's the kind of investor who comes along just once in a generation."

Shareholder 2. "Yeah, he's an original."

Shareholder 1. "Maybe, it's more than just once in a generation."

Shareholder 2. "Yeah, maybe just once."

A great student and teacher, Buffett has taught us that honesty and traditional values can prevail.

Buffett has made us think, has made us laugh and has amply enriched the world, creating great permanent value in many ways.

By any measure for heroes, Warren Buffett has made a transcending journey, indeed an exalted odyssey. He is the Odysseus for our time.

(Photo by Michael O'Brien)

Warren Buffett atop Kiewit Plaza and the world, looking out over his beloved Omaha. Buffett says he can think more clearly about the stock in front of him in Omaha than he can on Wall Street.

136

Orbiting bodies Synergy World Peace

Back in the Coca-Cola chapter, we found that Buffett and Coke are planning a CokeWorld on the Moon, a Disney-like concept which, if successful, could be exported to orbiting bodies.

Scientists still are sorting out photographic documentation, but they believe they see McDonald's Golden Arches peering from many of the orbiting bodies. Some experts say American Express is planning to issue a card for interplanetary travel. A California investor, thought to be Charlie Munger, thinks Wells Fargo's mutual funds now are being sold on Mars. The funds happen to own chunks of Gillette stock because the Sensor is selling well to men on Mars and particularly well to women on Venus.

Some say the one person who has the key to unlock all this synergy is a bespectacled fellow from Omaha.

It all has something to do with the American flag, an international flag. International icon. Buffett. Munger. Odysseus. Berkshire. Coca-Cola. McDonald's. The Olympics. Permanent Valve. Permanent Value. Do your homework. Eat your beans. Avoid dragons. Have fun. Press on. Follow your bliss. Leave it to Society. World Peace.

A

B

C

D

E

F

G

H

I

J

K

L

M

S

T

X

Y

Z

1

2

5

6